WAGNER'S *RING*

WAGNER'S *RING*

A fresh look at the dramatic and musical structure

CHARLES ELLIS

www.wagnersring.com

First published in Great Britain as a softback original in 2022

Copyright © Charles Ellis

The moral right of this author has been asserted.

All rights reserved.

No part of this publication may be reproduced, stored in a retrieval system, or transmitted, in any form or by any means, without the prior permission in writing of the publisher, nor be otherwise circulated in any form of binding or cover other than that in which it is published and without a similar condition including this condition being imposed on the subsequent purchaser.

Published by UK Book Publishing

www.ukbookpublishing.com

ISBN: 978-1-915338-04-4

This study is dedicated to three people

- to my wife, Connie Ellis, for her unfailing support over untold months

- to the memory of the late John Millar, from whom I learnt much since we first met at Bayreuth in 1963

- to Alwyn Mellor, whose first appearance as Brünnhilde in 2010 was the spur that set in motion the writing of this book

I would like to thank Peter Copley and David Stannard for the advice they have offered me over recent years. But if a reader should find something that is thought to be misleading or inaccurate, then the flaw lies with me.

I am also indebted to Professor Stephen Harrison of Corpus Christi College, Oxford and Sarah Wood, who have both checked over my analysis of ancient Greek drama.

A special thanks to Heidi Hankinson for her translation of *Sigurd der Schlangendtödter*. Her efforts find fruit in Appendix E, the only available commentary on Fouqué's dramatic poem in English.

CONTENTS

Part 1 – Evolution and Direction

1	Introduction and purpose	1
2	Wagner's conception of drama	5
3	The structure of plays and operas	22

Part 2 – Plot and Character

4	Building blocks	43
5	The hero Siegfried	64
6	Brünnhilde, the trophy bride	93
7	Hagen and the Gibichungs	103
8	*Siegfrieds Tod*	109
9	*Der junge Siegfried*	121
10	How Odin became Wotan	132
11	The invention of Alberich	146
12	Wotan's cosmos	158
13	Brünnhilde's transcendence	170
14	Wotan's journey	189
15	Questions about the *Ring*	202

Part 3 – Musical and dramatic structure

16	*Stabreim*, *Leitmotiven* and the 'symphonic' Wagner	221
17	The *Ring* motifs	237
18	*Das Rheingold*	265
19	*Die Walküre*	300
20	*Siegfried*	337
21	*Götterdämmerung*	380

Appendices

A	*The Nibelungen Myth as a sketch for a drama*	425
B	*Das Nibelungenlied* – a précis	434
C	*The Volsung Saga* – an extended précis	437
D	A chronology from 1843 to 1856	448
E	*Sigurd der Schlangentödter* – extended précis and analysis	456
F	Five books on the sources for the *Ring*	472
G	Bibliography	475

Two indexes: one on themes and people, one on chapter structure — 478

Vocal scores

Those by Peters, Schotts and Schirmer are virtually identical and are widely available.

A note on English versions of the *Ring* poem

A large number of musical examples are imbedded from chapter 16 onwards. Several include a singer's vocal line. To aid comprehension, an English translation is also offered where sensible words can be made to fit the musical line. Some are adaptations from old and venerable sources, some from newer and others are by myself. Where no words can be made to fit any English translation, a version is included in the main text. Frequently, I use that by John Deathridge because it concentrates on accuracy of tone and meaning without attention to the musical line. If the English cannot be made to fit, then at least it will be the more precise as to meaning.

Internal references

Within the text references are made, of the form (p.xx), to other passages within the text. These citations are to amplify and, if required, clarify what is currently being read. They can be ignored if so wished.

PART ONE

Evolution and direction

Introduction - Purpose and Structure

To my knowledge, this study is the first to explore in detail how the *Ring* may have developed *as a drama* in Wagner's mind. Discussion cannot avoid reference to those political, social and philosophical issues that ceaselessly worked away in his capacious brain, but these are to take second place.

The approach is to look at this many-faceted creation as a piece designed *for the theatre* on the premise that Wagner was as much a man of the theatre as he was a composer. From this it follows that everything that found its way into the four operas did so because he thought it would work on stage. This has the corollary that nothing that might fail in performance would be included in the plot, regardless of any extra-dramatic issue then turning in his mind. Extra-dramatic overtones there may be but they would *have* to fit into a vivid stage presentation.

The incessant exposure to all things theatrical in his infancy, so vividly expressed in his autobiography *My Life*, brought this upon him. There we can read of his father Friedrich (who spent far too much time with actresses, in the opinion of his wife), of his step father – the fulltime playwright/actor/producer Ludwig Geyer – and of his elder brother Albert, and elder sisters Rosalie, Luisa and Klara, who all went on the stage as actors or singers. His first creation – at the age of 14 – was an enormous play *Leubald und Adelaide*. (RW/ML, 3-13)

Wagner always had as much concern for dramatic as he had for musical failings in the performance of his works. This is well documented during the preparation for the first *Ring* performances in 1876 but it is of greater relevance to cite something nearer to the time when the work was conceived. So appalled was he at the acting and stage deportment of Josef Tichatschek – who had a superb voice – in the first performance of *Tannhäuser* in 1845, that he felt it necessary to cut a key passage in Act I for the time being, and also to elaborate on this in an essay *On the performance of Tannhäuser*, published in 1853. (RW/PW3,179) He is unsparing in his criticism of Tichatschek, who was a personal friend: 'The first singer of Tannhäuser - although eminently gifted as a singer – was unable to grasp anything other than that it was an 'opera'. He could not understand that [the deleted passage] demanded more of him as an actor than it did as a singer.' He goes on to 'pray' that every future singer of the role will understand that his delivery of the passage in question will not succeed until,

> he knows himself to be the master of the dramatic as well as the musical situation . . . The cry "Ach! Erbarm' dich mein", demands so piercing an accent that he will not get through as will a better trained singer. No – the highest awareness of the drama must bring forth such

energy of grief and desperation, that the notes seem to break from the very bottom of a heart that is burdened by terrible suffering. (RW/PW3, 181)

Wagner also insists that 'the singer who is not able to speak his role – as in a play – with the appropriate expression and feeling, will neither be able to sing or portray the role properly'.

So if the needs of the drama are to be at the fore, what about the impact of such social, political, historical and philosophical issues that we know concerned the composer? These are not disregarded but have to find their place in a theatrical context. Greatest weight in such secondary considerations is given to the philosophy of Arthur Schopenhauer, both because of Wagner's insistence on its force and also because it does contribute to an understanding of a number of complicated questions. The finished work makes more sense if we take seriously Wagner's assertion that reading *The World as Will and Representation* in 1854 made retrospective sense of the already completed *Ring* poem. This perspective, therefore, can be seen as an aid. Such is not always the case when a theory or philosophy has formed the basis of an analysis. In those cases, a ground theme surfaces with precise explanations of this or that person or incident. As a result, the drama has an interpretation forced upon it and I give one example. Robert Donington's *Wagner's 'Ring' and its Symbols* (1963) uses Jungian depth psychology as the analytical tool. This leads him to write of Siegmund, that 'incest . . . can lead to . . . entanglement in escapist infantile fantasies' (RD/WR, 139) and that, when he seizes the sword in Act I of *Die Walküre*, he is renouncing such escapist fantasies. Well, that may be so, for Wagner's conception is so protean that it is capable of many interpretations. Nevertheless, a director cannot *show* Siegmund pulling Sieglinde into his arms in such a way that a spectator thinks: 'Ah, yes! He is obviously renouncing an infantile escapist fantasy here!' The observation, therefore, does not help us understand what we see on stage: it is background to something that is not obvious.

The present enquiry proceeds by constructing how the story emerged from the sources and by tracing major themes from inception through to completion. The conclusion that emerges is that the line of the drama is fundamentally consistent from start to finish. This proposition runs counter to much past opinion, which maintains that Wagner's view of his work changed over the critical creative years between 1848 - when he wrote *The Nibelungen Myth, as a sketch for a drama* - and 1856 – when he made a revision to the closing scene in *Götterdämmerung*. A common view is that Wagner moved from optimism in 1848 to pessimism in 1856, and this study attempts to counter that opinion.

A cardinal principle is to assume that Wagner knew what he wanted to do and also knew how to achieve his intention. Humphrey Kitto, a professor of classics at Bristol University in the 1950s and 1960s, wrote as follows in *Form and Meaning in Drama:*

> If the interpretation [a critic advances] implies that the play is imperfectly designed, then either the dramatist has not done his job very well, or the critic has failed in his . . . If the dramatist had something to say, and if he was a competent artist, the presumption is that

he has said it, and that we, by looking at the form which he created, can find out what it is. (HK/FMD,v)

Michael Buckley takes this up in an article in 2004, emphasising that we should look carefully at what seems eccentric or implausible. If great artists allow 'apparent blemishes, it is sensible to assume that they do so for good reason and that they accept the implausibility or the inconsistency because it achieves something important'. (MB/FM,81) This is the correct attitude to adopt with Wagner who took endless pains to shape every aspect of his operas. We shall find that many critics do believe they sometimes knew better than did the composer.

Major works of art such as the *Ring* defy the allocation of a defined meaning. Themes can be found, of course, and here we can include the natures of freedom, the natural world and heroism, and the conflict between love and power. In January 1854 Wagner wrote thus to his friend August Röckel: 'I believe it was a true instinct that lead me to guard against an excessive eagerness to make things plain, for I have learned to feel that to make one's intentions too obvious risks impairing a proper understanding . . . In drama . . . it is a question of making an impression not by parading one's opinions but by setting forth what is instinctive.' (SS/SL, 308) This statement has been much put to use. The ambiguity within it, for example, has been used to support the presence of coded pointers to an anti-Semitic sub-text. I take it at face value to mean what it says; Shakespeare would have agreed had he been asked.

Nevertheless, it is possible to achieve a view of what would have been in Wagner's mind. This study is an exploration of how different mechanisms of dramatic and musical construction are made to work together. The forms and procedures Wagner uses to combine plot, text and music are there for us to examine. From these 'facts', and in accordance with Kitto's maxim, dramatic intentions do emerge. If a reader achieves a better vision of how the plot comes together in such a natural manner and how the music supports the plot, the book will have had some success.

Structure

Part 1 - This chapter and the two that follow consider broad issues of approach that were particular to Wagner, plus the principles of dramatic direction and structure.

Part 2 – This comprises twelve chapters, and digs into how Wagner used the medieval sources to formulate his poems and to shape his characters by choosing and/or avoiding particular characteristics and events.

Part 3 – Six chapters form almost half the content of the book. First there is an examination of the musical developments associated with the *Ring,* and this is followed by two listings of motifs designed to assist the telling of the drama. The analysis concludes with four chapters - one to each opera - that explore how and why the music and the structure of the poem combine to make drama.

Appendices – These provide complex interconnections with every element in the *Ring* and are integral to full comprehension.
- The full text of *The Nibelungen Myth* (A), as written by the composer in 1848.
- Summary of *Das Nibelungenied* (B).
- Detailed analysis of the *Volsung Saga* (C), with extensive verbatim dialogue where appropriate.
- The chronology from 1843 through 1856 (D) gives background to the events and attitudes which touched upon Wagner's life and work.
- A full elaboration of Fouqué's *Sigurd der Schlangentödter* (E), with long stretches of verbatim dialogue. The action runs parallel to that within the six Acts of *Siegfied* and *Götterdämmerung*. Such analysis is otherwise unavailable.

Indexes   This is a complicated book in which to track themes and content. The four chapters on the operas cannot bear repeated reference to the main characters. A full-out traditional index of the first 16 chapters would likely overburdenthe material.

However, those same chapters do have a narrstive line running through it, so there is an additional selective index, in page order. This may help to carry the reader through from one chapter and into the next.

Describing musical drama

This enquiry frequently makes reference to Shakespeare for the purpose of comparison or analysis. Very many books study the great poet and many of those go into fine detail about meaning and interpretation of the texts. However complex an issue in question may be, discussion is helped because, in one way or another, the subject matter is about words. The object is to make clear why and how the words work upon our sensibilities as they do.

This study tries to do something similar to an object that is not in words. An opera has words but, distinct from the works of Shakespeare, these are just the scaffolding for the drama. All books about music drama, therefore, suffer from the need to inform the reader about the meaning of something that must resist the straitjacket of wordy description. From the first page onwards this study is a preparation for the musical and dramatic analysis in the chapters on the four separate operas. In accordance with the previous caution, therefore, that analysis must fall short. The best that can be hoped is that the musical side is presented in such a manner that it carries the reader forward to a useful degree.

◊ ◊ ◊ ◊ ◊

2

WAGNER'S CONCEPTION OF DRAMA

A common approach in *Ring* analysis is to start with a discussion of the sources. Here we go back further and examine the dramatic background within which Wagner worked. What can we with some certainty presume to have been the dramatic principles and goals he had in mind when he started and then continued the work? In sequence this chapter will set down or explore the following:

- Wagner's two guiding principles with respect to drama
- His views on myth and mythology
- What he thought about playwrights
- The impact of Schopenhauer
- Showing and telling

Two guiding principles

The chronology in Appendix D refers to the publication of three relevant essays on dramatic and musical theory in the years 1849 to 1852: *Art and Revolution, Opera and Drama* and *A communication to my friends*. Passages from these offer an introduction to his thinking during the critical creative burst on the text of *Siegfrieds Tod*.

In the *Communication* Wagner reflects back on the theories set out in the two earlier works. His summing up is that the artwork of the future

> could only be the drama; further, that this drama could only find its proper attitude toward life when, in its every moment it should be completely present with that life, in its remotest relations so bound to it and issuing from it, in its specification of time and place and circumstance so characteristic of it, that in order to understand it there should be no need of the reflecting intellect but only of the direct feeling that seizes the emotions. (RW/PW1,278)

The idea that an audience should be able to absorb this revelation without conscious effort found fuller expression in *Opera and Drama*.

> Faced with a dramatic artwork, nothing should remain for the synthesising intellect to search for. Everything seen within it should be so convincing that our feeling about it is set at rest, for in this setting . . . resides the repose which brings us an instinctive understanding of life. In the drama . . . an action can be explained only when it is completely vindicated by the feeling. In the drama we must become *knowers* through *feeling*. (RW/PW2, 209)

The other guiding principle about good drama found within the *Communication* is that it must be 'completely present with [that] life'. 'Truth to Life' does not simply mean 'being alive'; it relates to an oft repeated reference to the 'purely human'. This concept of humanity is constant, central and critical in his work. For Wagner, a human being becomes truly alive in direct proportion to the degree that he or she is able to shake off the constraints imposed on us all over the centuries by social pressure, which he often calls 'fashion', by the State and by organised religion. The coercive activities of these three societal behemoths take upon themselves the right to prescribe how we live in both thought and deed. This finds expression in *Art and Revolution*:

> Man will never be that which he can and should be until his life is a true mirror of Nature, a conscious pursuit of the only real Necessity, the *inner natural necessity,* and is no longer held in subjugation to an *outer* artificial . . . arbitrary power. At that point Man will become a living man; whereas until now he carries on a mere existence, dictated by the maxims of this or that Religion, Nationality or State. (RW/PW1,71)

Wagner writes frequently about nature and in many contexts. The best way to think of it is that this 'purely human', natural, beneficent, at-ease-with-ourselves state is everything that is opposite to the condition forced upon us by authority and fashion.

In past times, according to the composer, and before the imposition of such 'arbitrary power', drama had been different. He held up folk song, created by ordinary people as a communal activity, as the ideal. Such folk song developed within the folk *play* in such a way that there was a built in connection between the words of the play and the music: words and melody evolved together and were designed to complement each other. The first operas only emerged around 1600 by development from dramatic cantatas and both forms focussed on the aria, which developed from folk song. The gentry who encouraged these operas had no knowledge of the artistic unity of the folk play. They liked the tune alone and the prime purpose of these cantatas and operas was to provide vehicles for vocal dexterity on the part of the singers: the virtuoso singer dominated from the start. Wagner draws comparison between the folk play in which the audience can find something akin to the natural beauty of real flowers and these 'cantatas' where is found the exotic silk and perfume of artificial flowers. To add diversity to the entertainment, dance was incorporated as a separate entity and the format of opera was completed by recitative, derived from the stultifyingly dry recitation to be found in the chants of the Christian church service. [A]

[A] See RW/PW2, pp.18-26, for the full text, of which this paragraph is a summary. This view is famously wrong. In the 1590s The Florentine *Camerata* were hoping to recreate Greek tragedy with the introduction of a new style of recitative that closely matched the emotion in the words. The first true opera, Jacopo Peri's *Dafne* (1596), was the artistic template upon which Monteverdi wrote the magnificent *Orfeo* in 1607. Wagner would have known this but, since he was constructing a targeted polemic, he altered matters to pursue his argument.

Into this gloom of failure came Gluck (and Spontini and Cherubini, who carried on where Gluck left off) and then Mozart. But their efforts in the years 1765 to 1815 were swept away by Rossini, seen as a master of triviality, whose style ruled a large part of the European operatic scene for 45 years. By and large, therefore, the first third of *Opera and Drama*, dealing with music, is structured to demonstrate the dramatic failings of opera composers: for only 50 years within the 250 years of operatic development was there an attempt to produce worthwhile drama. Wagner's summary of the present state was cogent: *Opera is supposed to be a drama with the music conveying the force of the story but now, in the year 1851, it is not like that. Now the plot is just there to provide hangers from which pretty arias, duets and quartets can be suspended.* (Adapted from RW/PW2,17) In short, the music drama of the future, as envisaged by Wagner, would have no connection with the operas currently being produced in European houses.

So opera seems a lost cause and the verdict, in Part 2, on current spoken theatre is scarcely better. Serious drama is at one remove from any immediate representation, in that the audience is asked to use its imagination, to *reflect upon* what it sees, in order to understand the stage action. The cramping grip of established critics and scholars has intervened, so that . . .

> . . . the drama is seen as nothing but a branch of literature, alongside the novel and didactic poetry; only with the difference that instead of being merely read, it is to be learnt by heart by several persons, declaimed, accompanied by gesture and lit up by the footlights. (RW/PW2,121)

This problem with theatre can be seen as a variant on that for the opera: current plays and their presentation are constricted and rigid in a similar way to the placing of opera inside a straitjacket of forms.

The discussion continues by comparing Shakespeare with Racine and Schiller, relating all plays either to the novel on one hand or to the precepts of Aristotle in his *Poetics* on the other. Important in his thesis are the problems inherent in the historical play:

> The poet who tries to adapt historical subjects for the stage, but who is careless [and necessarily so, for there is no other way] with historical accuracy and thereby distorts the facts of history in order to make the play work in accord with his own judgement, can create neither history nor drama. (RW/PW2,144)

This is the link to the value of myth – as opposed to history - which Wagner needed. For he had rejected what he called 'bourgeois' drama (the 'well-made play') and courtly drama (Racine) but had until recently still been contemplating historical subjects (p.454) alongside the huge theme of Siegfried. Accordingly, the last 32 pages of Part 2 in *Opera and Drama* are devoted to myth and mythology – thereby casting history aside - and to the forms of verse which the new poet must use in order to respond satisfactorily to the dramatic needs of a story from mythology.

Myth and mythology in the 'new' drama

Nowhere does Wagner say that this or that feature in the *Ring* is derived from any particular aspect of mythology. He does make clear, however, that every aspect of background and plot line stems from an ancient myth, namely from the medieval Germanic and Nordic sagas and Part 2 examines these. This section will confine itself to the influence of Greek myths as presented in the ancient Greek tragedies but will start with the theory of myth that Wagner developed in pursuit of his own dramatic goals.

<u>Wagner's theory of myth and its function in his dramas</u>

The theory of mythology with respect to Wagner's 'new' drama derived from the work of Ludwig Feuerbach, with whose philosophy he was much taken in the 1840s. His most influential book was *Der Wesen des Christentums* (The Essence of Christianity, 1841), in which he sought to undermine completely the basis of all religions. The thesis is simple: the human wish for and belief in *any* God is a reflection of mankind's expectation and image of his own perfection. Thus God did not create Man in his image (as in the Old Testament) but Man created God in Man's own image. We instinctively know what it is to lead the good life and idealise what such a being might be like.

Wagner used this thesis to argue that primitive man derived a first cause - the religious theory by which the natural world might be explained – from natural phenomena. Thus: 'God and gods are the first creations of men's poetic force: in them man represents to himself the essence of natural phenomena as derived from a cause'. (RW/PW2,154) The natural world is the start of all mythologies. From the observations of nature developed the idea of gods and heroes who explained these observations. Such a process would clearly apply to Wotan and the other gods. Wagner also directs the notion to Siegfried:

> We are now able to look with some clarity at the germ from which [the Siegfried saga] derives, thereby also learning about the essence of myths in general. We see here natural phenomena such as day and night, the rising and setting sun, condensed by the human imagination into personal agents who are to be revered or feared by virtue of their deeds. We can also understand the subsequent transformation of these man-created gods into human heroes who are supposed to have lived at some time. (RW/PW2,161)

The implications of Feuerbach's thought and Wagner's interpretation of it are crucial for an understanding of the *Ring*. On p.450 is a summary of the projected *Achilleus* drama, in which the immortal Thetis accepts that mankind, as personified by Achilles, is greater than the gods. Accordingly, there is a *necessity* that such a one as Siegfried will overcome such a one as Wotan, and that a thing is necessary implies that it is logical and not contingent: ie not resulting from chance.

<u>The eclipse of historical drama</u>

In *My Life* Wagner tries to present the evolution of the *Ring* as an ordered progression but this cannot have been the case. He had drafted a scenario for a drama about

Friedrich Barbarossa in 1846; he returned to and worked on it in October 1848, at the same time as he was writing *The Nibelungen Myth*. But he could not disentangle the envisaged play from the welter of history which surrounded the protagonist. Looking back in the *Communication* (1852), he wrote that he

> ...was driven to the primal source of old home saga [and] drove step by step into the deepest regions of antiquity where ... in the utmost reaches of old time, I was to light upon the fair young form of Man ... My studies bore me through the legends of the Middle Ages [ie the medieval *Nibelungenlied*] right down to their foundation in the old Germanic myths [ie the Nordic sagas]. I managed to see through the many layers of legendary lore with which the original vision had become encrusted and what I there saw was no longer the figure of conventional history . . . but the real naked Man – the true human being. (Taken from RW/PW1,357/8)

In constructing *Siegfrieds Tod*, Wagner intended to create his own myth about Siegfried and Brünnhilde. At that early stage, the initial story of Siegfried taking over and saving the degenerate gods was an allegory for the 'new man' taking over and saving the corrupt state. How he constructs this and then expands the result into the *Ring* is the subject of Part 2 of this study.

The Greek connection

As an immediate follow-on from Wagner's own version of his discovery of 'the true human being' as set down in the *Communication*, we read the following:

> I also turned once again to the soil of Greek antiquity which similarly pointed me to myth wherein the social structures of humanity were drawn in the same simple, plastic and distinct lines as those for the human being I had earlier recognized. The splendid ideal of Siegfried had long attracted me and it enthralled my every thought when I came to see it in its purest human shape, set free from its later legendary trappings. Now at last I recognized the possibility of making him the hero of a drama. (Taken from RW/PW1,358-359)

Always interested in the Greeks, in 1847 Wagner read for the first time and was entranced by *The Oresteia* of Aeschylus.

> I could see the *Oresteia* with my mind's eye, as if actually being performed and its impact on me was indescribable. There was nothing to equal the exalted emotion evoked in me by *Agamemnon*; and to the close of the *Eumenides* I remained in a state of transport from which I have never really returned in order to become fully reconciled with modern literature. My ideas about the significance of drama, and especially of the theatre itself, were decisively moulded by these impressions. (RW/ML,342)

It is remarkable that the political impact of the *Oresteia* was correctly perceived by Wagner, somewhat against the views of contemporary scholarship. The trilogy is a paradigm of drama which explained the current society to the people who comprised it. 'With Aeschylus one feels one is confronted with a forest of oaks and anyone who did not share the general belief in it would simply have been thrown out.' (CW/D1, 20/12/79) Indeed, the very idea for Wagner's eventual mammoth cycle may well have been germinating in his subconscious from the seed planted by his admiration of the antique trilogy. This was the hope that a future German audience for the *Ring* might perceive something of current history in the drama similar to the experience of the Athenians as they watched the *Oresteia*. A vivid presentation of this is to be found in the Birmingham Art Gallery - a painting, dating from 1884, by Sir William Blake Richmond: *An audience in Athens during a performance of* Agamemnon *by Aeschylus*. This audience is seen face on, from the perspective of the actors; the posture and expression of each person portrays the utmost tension and conviction that what was on view was directly relevant to the present life of the city.

This link to the very first master dramatist, and only to him, is self-aggrandisement. He writes as follows in *Art and Revolution*.

> His loftiest work of . . . art is the *Oresteia* with which he stands alike opposed as poet to the younger Sophocles and as statesman to the revolutionary Pericles. The rise of Sophocles, like that of Pericles, was fully in the spirit of the changing attitudes of society; the relegation of Aeschylus was the first downward step from the height of Grecian tragedy, the first beginning of the dissolution of the Athenian community. (RW/PW1,52)

That statement is based on no evidence at all; the Greeks did not disregard the often bitter political commentary that lurked in the plays of Euripides, for example. Wagner is asserting the debateable proposition that after *The Oresteia* everything was on the slide. The reason for this decline was social: 'With the . . . downfall of tragedy, art became less and less the expression of the public conscience. The drama separated into its component parts: rhetoric, sculpture, painting and music forsook the ranks in which they had moved in unison before.' This sad state of affairs has continued over the intervening 2300 years and the 'one true art has not been born again . . . for the reason that it cannot be reborn but must be born anew. Only the great revolution of mankind . . . can win for us this artwork . . . in the new beauty of a nobler universalism.' (RW/PW1, 52/53)

The cat is out of the bag, for this lauding of the *Oresteia* at the expense of Sophocles (Euripides is almost completely ignored) can be perceived as an integral part of the polemic contained in the three Zurich essays. Wagner was sincere in his admiration of Aeschylus but this can colour how we read other comments. In the *Diaries* Cosima records his observation that the *Oresteia* 'fits in with my work . . . [and is] . . . the most perfect thing in every way: religious, philosophic, poetic, artistic.' (CW/D2, 24/6/80) This affirms a connection between himself and Aeschylus: the two of them alone over the centuries have offered *gesamptkunstwerk* (total work of art) to the public.

This suspicion is strengthened by the paucity of information about Wagner's response to the actual plays *as drama*. There is no discussion of the dramatic techniques of the two Greek tragedians. The citing of Sophocles in *Opera and Drama* is solely to do with the *type of person* Wagner thought should feature in life-enhancing drama. The 15 pages of analysis of *Oedipus the King* and *Antigone* are devoted to social morality and societal stress. Wagner concentrates on the conflict between the natural instinct of the individual against the arbitrary power and mores of the State. Laius, the father of Oedipus, and Creon, the uncle of Antigone, put the State before Love. Oedipus and his daughter Antigone put Love before the State; Oedipus does no conscious wrong in wedding his mother Jocasta; Antigone's love brings humanity to the fore and defeats the corrupting power first engendered by Laius. These pages are a stage in Wagner's polemic against all types of coercive power: 'The virtue in any society derives from the virtues of the human individual; the State is built upon the vices inherent in any society'. (RW/PW2,193)

Nevertheless, Geoffrey Skelton may well be right to suggest that some plot lines may have their origins in plays by Sophocles. 'One can hardly doubt that Oedipus's encounter with his unrecognized father Laius suggested Siegfried's meeting with his unrecognized grandfather Wotan in the third act of *Siegfried,* nor that the incest which led to the downfall of Oedipus and Jocasta was in Wagner's mind as he dealt with Siegmund and Sieglinde in *Die Walküre.*' (GS/WTP,52) Skelton later identifies Brünnhilde with Antigone, both in their devotion to their respective fathers and in their actions 'when left to their own devices.'

This closeness to Greek drama has been accepted for many years. The most conspicuous advocacy has been by Michael Ewans in *Wagner and Aeschylus* (Cambridge University Press, 1982). The book seeks to twin the *Ring,* and its four consecutive parts, with the *Oresteia,* comprised of three linked plays. Many insights and valid comparisons lie within the book, which is a notably coherent and at times illuminating study of the great work. If a reader should find it lacks conviction, it will likely be because *any* specific approach that tries to encompass and explain the *Ring* entirely must court trouble. The book is still available in paperback.

The nature of the 'action' that resulted from using myth

Wagner was nevertheless more aware than most of the practical dramatic strengths within Greek drama, notably with regard to the concision and concentration we see in the finest Greek tragedies. For these instinctively chime with Wagner's dramatic instincts. He noted that the plots were uncluttered and moved inexorably to a single, clear and powerful 'action': 'The content of an action is the idea that lies behind it; if the idea is wide-reaching and draws upon man's whole nature in a particular aspect, it will ordain an action that is decisive, one and indivisible'. (RW/PW2,150)

This however is a quality possessed by all great drama. Greek plays are short by modern standards, lasting from between 75 and 90 minutes. Thus the whole of *The Oresteia* (comprising about 3800 lines) lasts about four hours which is the length of an uncut performance of *Hamlet* (3700 lines). In 2014 the text of the *Ring* was performed as a play in London; each of the four 'acts' lasted about one hour – making four hours in all. Making allowance for the short lines used by Wagner, the equivalent number of words also makes about 4000 lines. How many 'clear and powerful' actions are there, then, in each work? Michael Ewans posits one for each of the Acts/Scenes in *The Ring*. Deryck Cooke proposes just six for *The Oresteia; Hamlet* can also be seen to have six.

To get this small number, sub plots have been excluded: many in *The Ring* (eg Mime/Alberich; Fafner/Fasolt); the interaction and role of the gods in *The Oresteia;* the critical relationship between Hamlet and Ophelia in Shakespeare.

The *Ring,* as per Ewans, has thirteen 'actions'. (For concision, the operas are denoted by R - *Das Rheingold,* W - *Die Walküre,* S - *Siegfried* and G – *Götterdämmerung.*) Alberich takes the gold (R1); Wotan resolves to take the gold (R2); Wotan and Loge capture Alberich (R3); the gods take possession of Valhalla (R4); Siegmund and Sieglinde unite in love (W1); Wotan kills Siegmund (W2); Wotan renounces Brünnhilde vhto Siegfried (W3); Siegfried forges Nothung (S1); Siegfried learns that he can win Brünnhilde (S2); Siegfried and Brünnhilde abandon themselves to love (S3); 'Gunther' overpowers Brünnhilde (G1); Brünnhilde, Gunther and Hagen resolve to murder Siegfried (G2); Brünnhilde renounces the ring and sacrifices herself (G3).

The Oresteia has six 'actions'. Cooke splits each of the plays into two parts, since they have no Acts (AG=*Agamemnon*; LB = *Libation Bearers*; EU= *Eumenides*). Agamemnon arrives home from the Trojan War (AG1); his wife Clytemnestra murders him (AG2); Orestes, Agamemnon's son by Clytemnestra, arrives home from exile (LB1); he kills Clytemnestra and her new husband Aegisthus (LB2); Orestes, hounded by the furies, takes refuge in the Athenian temple of Apollo (EU1); he is tried and acquitted of guilt by means of a new dispensation of justice (EU2).

Hamlet is divided into the Acts as published in the First Folio and within them are six 'actions': Hamlet meets the ghost of his father and learns how he was murdered (1); he is aroused from his depression by meeting the acting company (2); he exposes the guilt of Claudius (3); he kills Polonius (4); he escapes from and eludes the plots of Claudius to kill him (5); he kills Claudius (6).

That the *Ring* has more is not surprising, given that it takes 15 hours on stage with the music. What we can see, however, is that there is nothing special about its manner of dramatic construction. The plays of the despised Racine are very spare in incident as are many of Verdi's operas – let the reader cast his mind over the story line of *La Traviata.*

Wagner and the theatre

Those operatic composers whom Wagner thought significant will be discussed in the next chapter. This chapter confines itself to dramatists. For Wagner significant figures (additional to Aeschylus and Sophocles) are Shakespeare, Racine, Goethe and Schiller. Of these, Goethe and Racine are quickly dismissed as dramatists. Racine is described in such a way that he will be easily discarded, for he is presented as the opposite pole to Shakespeare. Because all classical French *tragedie* was alleged to follow (and misunderstand) the principles of Aristotle's *Poetics,* Racine's plays are trapped in the straitjacket of conformity. Goethe was seen by Wagner as the greatest German poet and also as a quasi-philosophical guru but never as easy or natural when he came to write plays; he was afflicted with the pervading disease infecting German drama in the late 18th century and 'wrote literary-dramas for dumb reading . . . or else . . . instinctively turned . . . toward the reflective type of drama.'

Shakespeare

Pages could be filled with quotations from what Wagner wrote and said about Shakespeare, and they convey nothing short of idolatry. This is on record throughout his life, from 1840 until the 1880s. The focus is almost always on truth - truth to life. The presence and reality of the characters, and the immediacy of the dramatic conflict are the supreme qualities in the plays. Looking more closely, we see that the truthfulness he seeks entails the removal of fixed formats. Conformity to such conventions (eg. Racine), deadened and destroyed all it touched. The other main characteristic is that Shakespeare does not reveal himself in the plays: he is opaque. The first two examples touch upon this and the second two are concerned with the absence of form.

> How utterly inexplicable Shakespeare is! The way he allows the death of Falstaff to be related by a boy, who then dies a heroic death. And how the ground is prepared, as it were, for the subsequent shallowness of the King, as revealed in the French wooing – all of it unspoken, but it is there. Nowhere else can one get to know the world as one can through him . . . (CW/D2, 23/8/81)

> His dramas seem to be so direct a transcript of the world, that the artist's intervention in their portrayal . . . is absolutely untraceable, and certainly not demonstrable by criticism. (RW/PW5,107)

> What makes Shakespeare at once so incomparable and so inexplicable is this: those Forms which bond the plays of the great Calderon himself to prim conventionality, and made them strictly artist's works, he saturated with such life that they seemed dissolved away by nature. No longer do we think we see fictitious men, but real live men before us. (RW/PW5,108/9)

> Nothing could be more felicitous [in *Hamlet*] than this diversion of attention from the expected apparition, allowing it to make its impact suddenly; as always with Shakespeare, the height of artistry coincides with the waywardness of real life. (CW/D2,11/8/77)

All these aspects of Shakespeare relate to Truth. These and other examples are culled from the Diaries, recorded late in life, so it is comforting to be able to refer to a letter dating from 1847, as the idea of *Siegfrieds Tod* was ripening in his mind.

> I wish to create men of flesh and blood and bones; I wish my characters to walk and move about freely and truthfully. (SS/SL,133)

Schiller and the history play

Schiller is the only playwright other than Shakespeare whose active characteristics (the *how* as opposed to the *what*) are discussed. This is partly due to the vitality of his dramatic imagination and partly to the preponderance of historical subjects. For Wagner was always doubtful about the value of history as a topic for operas and plays, but nevertheless chewed away at the subject throughout his life. [B]

Wagner finds fault in Schiller as a writer of historical plays but he never doubts his power as a dramatist: 'other than Shakespeare, Schiller is the greatest'. (CW/D2, 3/3/79)

> The scene between the two queens [in *Maria Stuarda*] . . . how fine it is that the wide ranging and apparently entirely political play builds to this one scene which expresses the whole meaning.
> King Philip's soliloquy (*Don Carlos*) is Shakespearean and Carlos's excitement when he thinks the queen has sent for him quite unique . . . [Posa] is so *slim* and free. (CW/D2, 17/2/81, 2/1/82)

Nevertheless, Schiller does not succeed in his aims overall, for he deliberately selected only that material which lends itself to a predetermined intention, thereby adapting history to his own formula. Wagner's prose in *Opera and Drama* is at its clearest as he explains his objection to this approach. Of Shakespeare's historical plays (the touchstone) he says:

> Shakespeare translated the dry but honest chronicles into the living drama. This chronicle outlined with exact fidelity, and step by step, the march of historical events and the deeds of those engaged therein . . . [he] necessarily had to untangle the underlying motives from the group of facts and imprint these on the flesh and blood of their transactors. For the rest, the historic scaffolding stayed entirely undisturbed. (RW/PW2,143)

Such is clearly not the case in Schiller's *Wallenstein*, his finest play according to Wagner, because 'it contained the most life.' Max Piccolomini is one of the three pivotal characters and it is on his personal crises that the play pivots; but Max is a complete invention by the author, in contrast to the others who were real people.

Wagner could not accept Schiller's imposition of a moral or philosophical agenda on history in order to create a drama. Such an agenda followed from the now oftmentioned interposition of rational thought between the action presented on stage and the *emotional* response of the 'purely human' faculty within the audience – ie from the heart to the heart directly and without room for a moment of thought.

Acting, Mime and Gesture

Wagner was a spectacularly gifted actor. Evidently, nothing could surpass the emotional impact of Wagner simply reading the text of the *Ring* to a small group in a private room of a Zurich hotel. He was always aware of the potential power of physical presence and gesture. In the *Communication* he wrote *à propos* of *Tannhäuser*: 'I require the actor to be in the forefront and the singer to be only an aid to the actor.' (RW/PW1,337)

[B] The indexes to Cosima's Diaries have numbers of entries as follows. Aeschylus: total 38, *Oresteia* 17. Schiller: total 248, history plays 43. Shakespeare: total 378, history plays 86.

Heinrich Porges was commissioned to make a record of the stage rehearsals of the 1876 Bayreuth performances (*Wagner rehearsing* The Ring). He gives vivid testimony. Concerning Wagner's style of direction: 'Yet all the extraordinary things Wagner did at the rehearsals created the impression of having been improvised . . . as though . . . everything occurred to him in a flash.' (HP/WR,4) Concerning Shakespeare:

> The principles governing style of dramatic presentation were essentially in accord with Shakespeare's. All the directions that he gave pertaining to the action – to the gestures, the positioning, the articulation of the sung words – were governed by what he himself has described as the basic principles of Shakespeare's drama, namely mimic-dramatic naturalness. (HP/WR,3)

The Elizabethan apron stage was perceived as a major contribution to this power. 'You can tell that characters were being viewed from all sides because they are so detailed, in contrast to Greek tragedy. The emphasis was always on the necessity for natural speed and behaviour, without histrionics or exaggeration of gesture. In *Actors and Singers* (1872) he affirms that this necessity was brought about by '. . . the *one* fact that Shakespeare's actors played upon a stage surrounded by spectators on all sides . . . where performers moved before them in all directions with the full reality of common life.' Actors had to be good when in '. . . such immediate proximity' to the audience. (RW/PW5,191)

Wagner and the theatre - a summary

Wagner wrote discursively and sometimes obscurely on drama, both musical and spoken. Nevertheless, he had a simple attitude, free of theory and of preconceptions. He wanted the audience to believe in the people seen on stage. Characters must be real and respond to circumstances in real time, must 'walk and move about fully and truthfully. . . men of flesh and blood and bones'. From this premise two conclusions follow. The first is the necessity for a believable, straightforward plot, for if the situation is fantastical or difficult to follow then the characters will lack credibility. Such is particularly true with the subject matter of the *Ring,* with its array of gods, dwarfs, primordial forces, animals and a panoply of myths. Plot feasibility will govern Wagner as he chooses from options to be found in the sources.

The second consequence is that Wagner did not want the characters to be perceived as allegorical or symbolic and neither did he want them to have an additional dimension hovering over them. He lauded Shakespeare's 'ability to depict everything as it is, without explanation or solution' and contrasted this with Schiller. Wagner's prose is often very knotty and hard to unravel but it can be worth the effort. The following quotation from *Opera and Drama* uses only Wagner's words but with a multitude of subsidiary clauses and expansions removed. He is commenting on the motives of and background to the kings and princes in Schiller's historical plays. The verbosity that has been removed is due, as is often the case, to the importance of the matter he wished to explain. He uses Schiller as an example but his target is now the general state of *quality* drama (ie not that purveyed by the likes of Kotzebue) in 19th century Germany. Note that the abstract is written from the viewpoint of the contemporary playwright. Such writers

> ... of the newer historical romance seek to portray the spirit of an entire historical period as issuing from one historic individual. To arrange the mass of historical facts for easy survey we [ie those who write plays] regard prominent personalities as embodying the spirit of the age. The sometimes opaque manner in which these rulers acted allows us so far to misunderstand the spirit of history that we explain their capricious actions by higher, inscrutable influences. These 'makers' of history seem will-less tools in the hands of an extra-human power. Led by this view the expounders of history [ie Schiller] justified the arbitrary actions of its ruling personages by reference to 'ideas' which mirrored the consciousness of a governing world spirit. (Abstracted from RW/PW2,173)

The message is a distrust of any interposition of a philosophical prism between what happened in history and what is conveyed in the text, with the purpose of giving a particular slant upon the event.

A similar prism can relate to myth. Wagner writes much on this subject (fully 10% of *Opera and Drama*) and on its implied degree of penetration into all his works and into *The Ring* in particular. But almost everything that he writes also qualifies how the audience should properly respond to the myth-derived characters presented on stage. For most people, a mythic character has overtones of the imaginary - 'a unicorn is a mythical beast'. Of more significance, where this is not so, the common response is to invest them with an aura of remoteness, of being different from us common folk. We think of King Arthur, Achilles. Everything Wagner writes about drama should guard us against the notion that he saw his characters like that. He surely wanted the audience to see them as much as possible as he envisaged the Elizabethans saw Shakespeare's characters. In the *Diaries* he contrasts Shakespeare, where the characters were seen from all sides, 'in the round', with Greek tragedy where 'the figures are like silhouettes'. (CW/D1, 3/8/72) Note also that he bracketed together the medieval artisan Hans Sachs and the heroic Siegfried: both 'will be regarded as real people.' (CW/D2, 16/12/78)

Schopenhauer

This study eschews in principle those influences that lie outside the theatrical but consideration of Schopenhauer is mandatory. From the moment when Wagner 'discovered' the philosopher his thinking became part of the fabric of the composer's creative and intellectual life. Consequently, his philosophy found a secure home in the completed *Ring* poems.

When Wagner first read *The World as Will and Representation* in 1854, his mind was fertile ground waiting for the right seed. His interest in philosophy was genuine and long-standing. Reflecting on the revelatory experience of reading the philosopher, in his autobiography he writes: 'I had repeatedly experienced an inner impulse to come to some understanding of the meaning of philosophy. Several conversations with Lehrs in Paris in my earlier years had awakened this desire in my heart.' (RW/ML,509) He had tried but failed to get to grips, save with Feuerbach. That fourteen years passed between this reported interest and his awareness of Schopenhauer is not surprising. *The World as Will and Representation,* the masterpiece that Wagner read first, fell still-born from the press when published in 1818 - 'very nearly unsold, unreviewed and unread'. For 35 years he was ignored until 1853, when a positive article appeared in the British *Westminster Review* (then edited by George Eliot), which was immediately translated into German.

The impact on Wagner

The effect on Wagner was gigantic and it remained so all his life. A major reason for this is similarity of outlook. Bryan Magee [c] puts it thus:

> When reading Schopenhauer, I sometimes get the feeling that this is the sort of philosophy Wagner might have written if his gifts had been that of a great philosopher . . . In areas of the greatest significance for his art, such as depth psychology, sex, and beliefs about the nature of art in general and of music in particular, Schopenhauer had already arrived at many of the same insights as Wagner by a different route . . . Having studied both men and their work over a number of years I have acquired a sense of something almost inaccessibly deep-lying that they have in common and that cannot be put into words. (BM/WP,128/184)

Schopenhauer' prose is celebrated as amongst the best in the German language. His work also draws every major field of enquiry under the umbrella of his system; Wagner clapped hold of this and never let go. *The World as Will and Representation* alone, and leaving aside his other essays, examines - often in detail - the following: time, space, biological diversity, inorganic matter, harmony in music, human misery, sex, law and the state, religion, ethics, farce, poetry, architecture, rhetoric, psychology, psychiatry, physics, geology, physiology, race, cosmology, animal instinct, the nature of genius, child development, lunacy, natural beauty, the relationship between the arts, Greek tragedy, history, death, birth, evolution, heredity. Nothing evades his attention and this similarity of attitude with Wagner is crucial, who writes thus in *My Life:*

> In the tranquillity of my house [in Zurich] I became acquainted with a book, the study of which was to assume vast importance for me. This was Arthur Schopenhauer's *The World as Will and Representation.* Herwegh [Georg Herwegh, a poet also in political exile in Switzerland] told me about this book . . . I felt myself immediately attracted to it and began studying it at once . . . [but] . . . I was alarmed . . . by the moral principles with which he caps the work, for here the annihilation of the will and complete self-abnegation are represented as the only true means of redemption from the constricting bonds of individuality in its dealings with the world . . . [but] Herwegh made me reflect further . . . This insight into the essential nothingness of the world of appearances, he contended, lies at the root of all

---

[c] The two books by Bryan Magee, to be found in the Bibliography, must be the foundation on which any discussion of such influence is based.

tragedy . . . I looked at my Nibelung poems and recognized . . . that the very things I now found so unpalatable in the theory were already long familiar to me in my own poetic conception. Only now did I understand my own Wotan . . . and, greatly shaken, I went on to a closer study of Schopenhauer's book. (RW/ML,508-510)

On 16 December 1854, in a letter to Liszt, lies Wagner's first reference: 'I have now become exclusively preoccupied with a man who . . . has entered my lonely life . . . It is Arthur Schopenhauer, the greatest philosopher since Kant.' (SS/SL,323) Few critics have questioned his assertion. Ernest Newman wrote that the intellectual influence 'was the most powerful thing of the kind that his mind had ever known.' (EN/LRW2,431). Thomas Mann wrote: 'None of his earlier intellectual encounters - such as that with Feuerbach - can compare with it in personal or historical significance: for it meant supreme consolation, the highest self-confirmation and intellectual deliverance.' (TM/PCW,121)

A summary of Schopenhauer's philosophy

The fundamental issue from which the others emerge is the nature of reality and how this correlates to what each of us experiences through our five senses. This vast issue is exemplified in the title of Schopenhauer's masterpiece: the world (and indeed the universe) is on the one hand the experience we each have of it and, on the other hand and at the same time, the will or the energy to exist that all matter possesses, regardless of ourselves, and which we do not and cannot experience.

The nature of reality is a problem as old as philosophy itself, starting with Plato. In modern times Immanuel Kant (1724-1804) elaborated probably the most significant theoretical advance; Schopenhauer, in turn, saw his work as a development from that of Kant. The critical distinction made by Kant was between the *phenomenon* of an object - what we see, smell, touch, feel - and the *noumenon* - that aspect of an object that lies, as it were, hidden behind the phenomenon. Any phenomenon is actually located in the brain of the person (or animal) who perceives it and is there because an *extension* of the brain, namely the particular nerves which supply that perception are designed to *interpret* it so that we can know how to respond.

Two points may be useful here. The first is that a new-born baby does not comprehend what is seen, because to do so requires that the baby understands the context in which to place any phenomenon; it needs to be able to relate it to something else. Schopenhauer puts it like this:

> What the eye, the ear, or the hand experience is not perception; it is mere data. Only by the passing of the understanding from the effect to the cause does the world stand out as perception extended in space, varying in respect of form, persisting through all time as regards matter. For the understanding unites space and time in the representation of matter. (AS/WWR1,12)

The second is that an *optical* nerve from eye to brain would be of no use if it were connected to the ear. The nerve which carries the phenomenon from eye or hand acts as an interface between object and brain. All we can ever know comes from what our nerves tell the brain; accordingly, a person born blind can have no idea of colour or visual space.

We know, therefore, that things exist but it is impossible to move beyond the phenomena that represents them (hence *representation* in Schopenhauer's title). This impossibility is one of logic, for we cannot even conceive of what an object might be other than by means of some perception or other.

These are difficult matters and counter-intuitive. The answer to the question 'Why cannot things be just as I see them?' is that we ourselves are also part of the noumenon and what we experience *of ourselves* in ourselves are all phenomena. In the same way, the eye cannot see itself, so what it sees on our behalf cannot be the totality. Once this distinction is grasped, the attention of everyone (including Wagner, who did take it in) must pass to what Schopenhauer had to say about what the other aspect - that which we cannot physically experience - might be.

Kant said that the noumenon - sometimes described as the 'thing-in-itself' - is simply a completely unknowable object, 'hidden' in some way behind or beyond the phenomena of the object (sometimes described as 'sense data') as picked up by our five senses. We might conceive this as many individual noumana. Schopenhauer was not satisfied with this. He proposes that there are not innumerable noumena but rather just one single entity - the noumenon. The world and universe are one object, and that object is not in space or time. Only phenomena, the things as we observe them, are in space or time. Because that is so, one thing can *cause* something to happen to another thing: I brush against a vase at the edge of a table and cause it to fall. *Change*, the effect one object can have on another, only occurs in the world we see, since for there to be a change of any sort, it must happen in time. But if time is removed there can be no causality. The noumenon remains unchanged - a single entity which includes everything that exists, but which is impossible for us to apprehend.

But what *is* the *noumenon?* Schopenhauer struggles to find an adequate word to describe it, but comes up with *Will*. This is, but only in part, the *will to exist*, to strive, to maintain itself against all odds. This will, this drive or energy to exist - the kernel reality of the indivisible *noumenon* - is also the core attribute of each and every constituent part of it - be that part living or not. It cannot be defined.

> This question can *never* be answered, because, as I have said, being known, of itself, contradicts being-in-itself, and everything that is known is as such only phenomenon. But the possibility of this question shows that the thing-in-itself, which we know most immediately as the will, may have, entirely outside all possible phenomenon, determinations, qualities, and modes of existence which for us are absolutely unknowable and incomprehensible, and which then remain as the inner nature of the thing-in-itself. (AS/WWR2,197/8)

How the philosophy engages with the *Ring*
Keep in mind that Wagner had completed the entire poem for the four operas and composed the music for *Das Rheingold* and the first Act of *Die Walküre* before he read

even one word written by Schopenhauer. During his first read through he was, at the same time, composing the music for Acts II and III. No changes to the poems of any of the operas were ever made as a result of what he read. When we talk of influence, therefore, we are really referring to a *confirmation* in Wagner's mind of the coherence and solidity of his conception. What he had elaborated in its totality two years previously was a true vessel for the vision of humanity and the world as held by the philosopher. Wagner never spelled out those aspects of the story that he himself now understood better as a result of Schopenhauer's thought. In subsequent chapters we will have cause to examine five issues which were endorsed by Schopenhauer's philosophy.

1. How his view of the world and human life confirmed Wagner's own.
2. How Schopenhauer's view of the noumenon - the 'thing-in-itself' - adjusted Wagner's perception of death.
3. The role of the sexual impulse in human and animal life.
4. Wotan and his desire for power.
5. How Schopenhauer's view of music chimed with the composer's developing technique of composition. Consequently, the one change that is decipherable is that in musical style which followed. But a word of caution: the ripening of compositional technique was under way before Schopenhauer came on the scene.

The most we can say is that the philosophy was a confirmation of Wagner's conception of human life and an endorsement of the musical growth which was already under way.

To show or to tell

Finally, a small but important pendant to this broad chapter on dramatic style and principle. Early in the 20th century, as film was establishing itself as an art form, a prime benchmark was established, namely that the effective way of presenting a story was to *show* the audience what was happening rather than to *tell* them. Images, without words, will convey the essentials needed to understand what is going on. This power is in the hands of a film maker rather than the author of a play. Although not articulated during the 19th century, the principle can also apply to opera. As images without words create powerful film drama, so can the orchestra give meaningful substance to visible action. That Wagner might have been naturally aware is indicated by his view that Goethe 'wrote literary drama for dumb reading' (p.13). A corollary is that the audience picked up the plot by *listening* and *seeing* and not being *told*.

Two examples from film and three from opera will clarify. The 1991 film *Thelma and Louise*, starring Geena Davis, Susan Sarandon and Brad Pitt has the two examples. Thelma (Davis) is a sexually frustrated woman who makes a bid for freedom in the car of her friend Louise (Sarandon) and they give a lift to a drifter (Pitt). Nothing is said but the audience knows that the drifter will end up in Thelma's bed. At the end of the film the two women are trapped by the police. The only freedom now available is to drive forward into the canyon that yawns ahead through the one place without a blocking police car. They sit, they look at each other, they hold hands - and Louise accelerates at full throttle. No words needed.

Three occasions now from opera. At the end of Act III of Mozart's *Figaro* there is a courtly fandango that accompanies the betrothal of Susannah and Figaro. The music is insidious, erotic and speaks of intrigue, and over it the final trap is laid for Count Almaviva. We see activity but understand that more is happening than is expressed in words or any action. The opening of Act III of Puccini's *La Bohème* portrays an icy morning at dawn. Ordinary life proceeds as people greet each other at the customs post. Into this chilly, mundane world comes the ailing Mimi as she seeks sympathy and comfort from her friend Marcello. Without a word being said or sung, the audience senses the hostility of the everyday world to this forlorn figure. In Act I of *Tannhäuser* the protagonist breaks free from the over-heated Venusburg. He is greeted by the sound of a shepherd boy, both singing and playing his pipe, and the radiant freshness of a May morning. On all these occasions the story is not told to the audience but shown to it, by setting and by the music.

In *Opera and Drama* Wagner refers to the orchestra performing the same role as commentator on the action as did the chorus in antique Greek drama. We can easily forget that this has happened in all opera since 1596 when the first acknowledged music drama was performed. It is the function of most passages of orchestral music, as heard in every opera, to *show* us what is happening – for the orchestra cannot speak. *Leitmotiven* – the foundation of the *Ring* music – may be revolutionary but it is also a progression.

◊ ◊ ◊ ◊ ◊ ◊

3

The structure of plays and operas

Two structures underpin and give life to stories, be they written for the stage or read as novels. They are closely related but one is best viewed as the engine that moulds the detail within the narrative and the other as the shaper of structure on the large scale. Both are instinctive and have always existed. This chapter deals with both types. That concerned with detail is considered first as it is the more fundamental, and connects to the very movement of life, upon which all stories and drama depend. The second and longer part, concerning large-scale dramatic structure, explores how it shapes (or fails to shape) opera. The chapter concludes with a broad analysis of the *Ring's* structure.

THE TWO BASIC STRUCTURES

The dialectic within drama

The notion and nature of the dialectic is credited to Georg Hegel (1770-1831), the predominant German philosopher in the 1830s and 1840s. Wagner studied his works. The case for Hegel as a meaningful philosophic contributor to the content of the *Ring* is hard to maintain (p.66) but he should find a place in any broad study of the drama on account of the great advance in philosophic thought that is always associated with his name. This is the dialectic, the awareness that history, personal life and all drama consists of sequential states of opposition and resolution. This process imbues matters on the largest scale and on the smallest. A thesis (call it *A*) is proposed; matters may proceed well enough but *A* has a negative aspect and in due course an antithesis (call it *not A*) is placed in opposition; in due course a synthesis (some compromise between *A* and *not A*) is agreed upon. We can call this synthesis *B*. Matters do not stop there, however, for in due course a further antithesis to *B* is proposed (call it *not B*) and the cycle continues. We sense a merging of past, present and future, which can be summarised under the statement 'being is continuous becoming'. Such ceaseless movement, pushing onwards to the next critical point, 'continuous becoming', is at the heart of all drama, and the *Ring* is sometimes a paradigm case of such dialectic.

Wagner was certainly interested in Hegel but we are not to imagine that he associated the dialectic with him. This procedure was never actually explained in this fashion. All that we can know is that the notion was in the air. An example from Hegel's *The Phenomenology of Spirit* gives us the essence of the dialectic:

> The bud disappears when the blossom breaks through, and we might say that the former is refuted by the latter; in the same way when the fruit comes, the blossom may be explained

to be a false form of the plant's existence, for the fruit appears as its true nature in place of the blossom. The ceaseless activity of their own inherent nature makes these stages moments of an organic unity, where they not merely do not contradict one another, but where one is as necessary as the other; and constitutes thereby the life of the whole. (GH/PS,2)

The dialectic as the universal basis of drama

There is, of course, nothing peculiarly Wagnerian about this for the dialectic process permeates dramatic structure from the smallest unit of dialogue and up through each sustained stretch of dialogue between two people, to extended scenes and whole Acts. How it works in a play can be illustrated by considering the first scene of *Hamlet*. The operation within the smallest span within any play is shown with the opening lines in this scene. This can be broken down into four groups of three lines, each group being a dialectic progression. Each group has a purpose and, that purpose achieved, the narrative can move on to the next group.

Dialectic 1 - to set the atmosphere on the battlements at night	
Bernado: Who's there?	*Thesis*: a challenge is made in the dark and in apprehension.
Francisco: Nay, answer me. Stand and unfold yourself.	*Antithesis*: the challenge is not only accepted but made more direct and personal. The alarm level is raised.
Bernado: Long live the king!	*Synthesis*: the incipient crisis is resolved. The reply is either a password or an accepted form of greeting in such circumstances.
Dialectic 2 - the story moves forward to the next stage - to set the scene	
Francisco: Bernado?	*Thesis*: Am I right to relax?
Bernado: He.	*Antithesis*: Yes, you are.
Francisco: You come most carefully upon your hour.	*Synthesis*: The people are established - but we are told that the time of day matters.
Dialectic 3 - Further to establish the circumstance of the meeting	
Bernado: 'Tis now struck twelve; get thee to bed, Francisco.	*Thesis*: Midnight is universally seen as unsettling within stories.
Francisco: For this relief much thanks; 'tis bitter cold, and I am sick at heart.	*Antithesis*: The tension is raised even further: the weather is cold and this is subtly linked to current hard times.
Bernado: Have you had quiet guard?	*Synthesis*: But there is no problem at the moment.
Francisco: Not a mouse stirring.	
Dialectic 4 - New arrivals and the end of this, and the opening of the next, mini-scene	
Bernado: Well, good night. If you do meet Horatio and Marcellus, the rivals of my watch, bid them make haste.	*Thesis*: The plot starts to open. The last four words increase anxiety.
(Enter Horatio and Marcellus)	*Antithesis*: The anticipation of two new people
Francisco: I think I hear them - - Stand ho! Who is there?	*before* they arrive moves the plot forward in quick time.
Horatio (and Marcellus): Friends to this ground / And liegemen to the Dane.	*Synthesis*: These new characters proclaim the end of the first mini-scene and the opening of the second.

These four groups of three lines form one larger group. Francisco's last reply forms a close to the whole exchange of linked dialectics. This opening mini-scene establishes atmosphere, who the people are, time and weather. Small in scope as is each exchange, a key point is that each synthesis launches the audience into the dialectic that follows. The very minuteness of the information passed means in this case that the drama is small and low key. Even so, the narrative flows and builds dramatic tension.

Act 1, Scene 1 of *Hamlet*, on the battlements of Elsinore, is made up of seven such mini-scenes. The first - as analysed above - is shorter than the others but all progress the plot in a similar manner. Examination of the text will show that each mini-scene has a dialectic process behind it and that each also leads into the next. We will soon see how this operates over the entire play, be it in five or three Acts.

Real time drama

In a play, drama is in real time - dialogue in action, as it were. In opera this is by no means always the case. Often an aria is designed to make time stand still: we are invited to relish the emotion as it expands outside of time. What we have learned to call *dramma per musica* - drama by means of music - jumps that hurdle. The art of Mozart, Donizetti, Verdi, Mussorgsky, Britten and Puccini often presents people who sing their thoughts in real time in the same way that an actor speaks his thoughts.

But no composer does this better than Wagner, and this practice is particularly well exemplified in the *Ring*. His characters *always* sing in real time and this means that they *think* in real time: they sing their thoughts as they arise. In *Hamlet* each little exchange of conversation is generally an exercise in dialectic. Similarly, sometimes in the *Ring* each exchange between two characters can be seen as such an exercise and the dialectic progression can be continuous. It demontrates the 'ceaseless activity' of life wherein action is opposed to counteraction, thereby forcing a progression of 'continuous becoming'. Dramatic *necessity* informs the actions of each character as it develops within Wagner's imagination. The action of these characters, as moulded, is shown as real time thought in various progressions of musical development.

Freytag and Campbell

The universal template for effective dramatic construction that we are about to examine has also always existed. Both good and great practitioners have adopted it by instinct from Homer in about 700BC up until 1863. Thereafter a writer might also (for the instinct must still be there) have been guided by *theory* of dramatic construction, for in that year the German novelist and playwright Gustav Freytag published a monumental *Technique of the Drama*. Here can be found the detailed structure of Freytag's Pyramid which, for many years now, has formed part of all courses on creative writing.

Another seminal book in this field is *The Hero with a thousand faces* (1949) by Joseph Campbell, an American mythologist. This includes a narrative of the journey which is followed by all heroes and this journey runs a parallel course to the paradigm of story structure described by Freytag. So by considering both we are able to link story structure directly to theories of heroism.

<u>The Freytag Pyramid and the Campbell journey</u>
To start with Freytag: his Pyramid looks like this when applied to a tragedy:

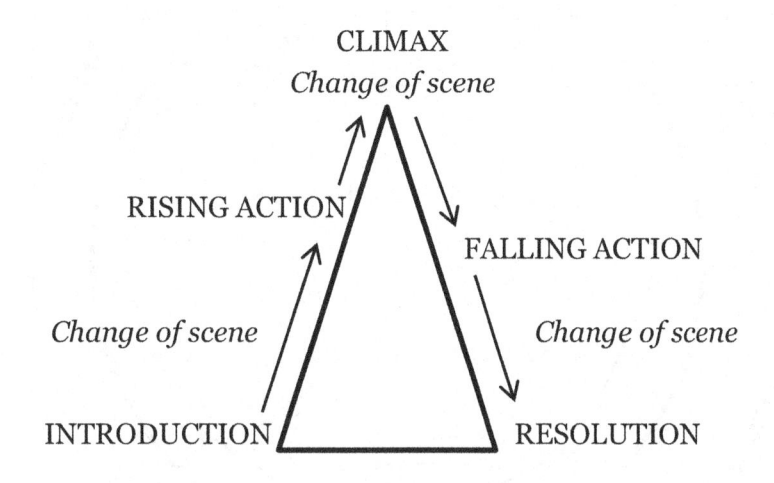

```
                    CLIMAX
                Change of scene
                      ▲
                    ╱ ╲
            RISING ╱   ╲
            ACTION    ╲  FALLING ACTION
                  ╱     ╲
   Change of scene        Change of scene
              ╱             ╲
      INTRODUCTION         RESOLUTION
```

Drama, and indeed all stories, can be broken down into five stages. Freytag specifies at least three changes of scene which we might take to mean four Acts. In the INTRODUCTION or Exposition, the play sets before us a critical or dangerous situation that prompts the protagonist or hero to solve a problem or overcome a difficulty. In the RISING ACTION he grapples with complications and obstacles that stand in his way and – at the CLIMAX – achieves the goal he strives for. Thereafter, in the FALLING ACTION, he meets with more serious reversals of fortune which lead to the RESOLUTION, which may be triumph or disaster. The staging of this structure is to be within three changes of scene – after the INTRODUCTION and CLIMAX and before the RESOLUTION. (GF/TD,115)

Wagner read many of the works of Freytag (and also met him more than once in Dresden) but since the comprehensive analysis was not published until 1863, there could have been no influence. Indeed, it would be as preposterous to make any such suggestion as it would be to think that Sophocles, Shakespeare or Racine created their dramatic miracles in accordance with any type of theory at all. All that theoreticians can do is to codify and give a logic to what has been seen to work on stage: what the dramatists have done is to apply the logic inherent in story-telling to the task of condensing a story into a drama.

Joseph Campbell's title - *The hero with a thousand faces* – tells us much. He argues that, whoever the hero may be and wherever he is called to action, the stories are all basically the same - being retold endlessly in infinite variations. This aspect explains our fascination with heroism, for it corresponds to a universal psychological need. He identifies key elements in a vast array of adventure tales from all cultures and creates from them a 'monomyth'. For our present purpose, the notable feature is that this monomyth has the same overall pattern of story structure seen by Freytag. Campbell expresses this in a diagrammatic circle, as opposed to a triangle.

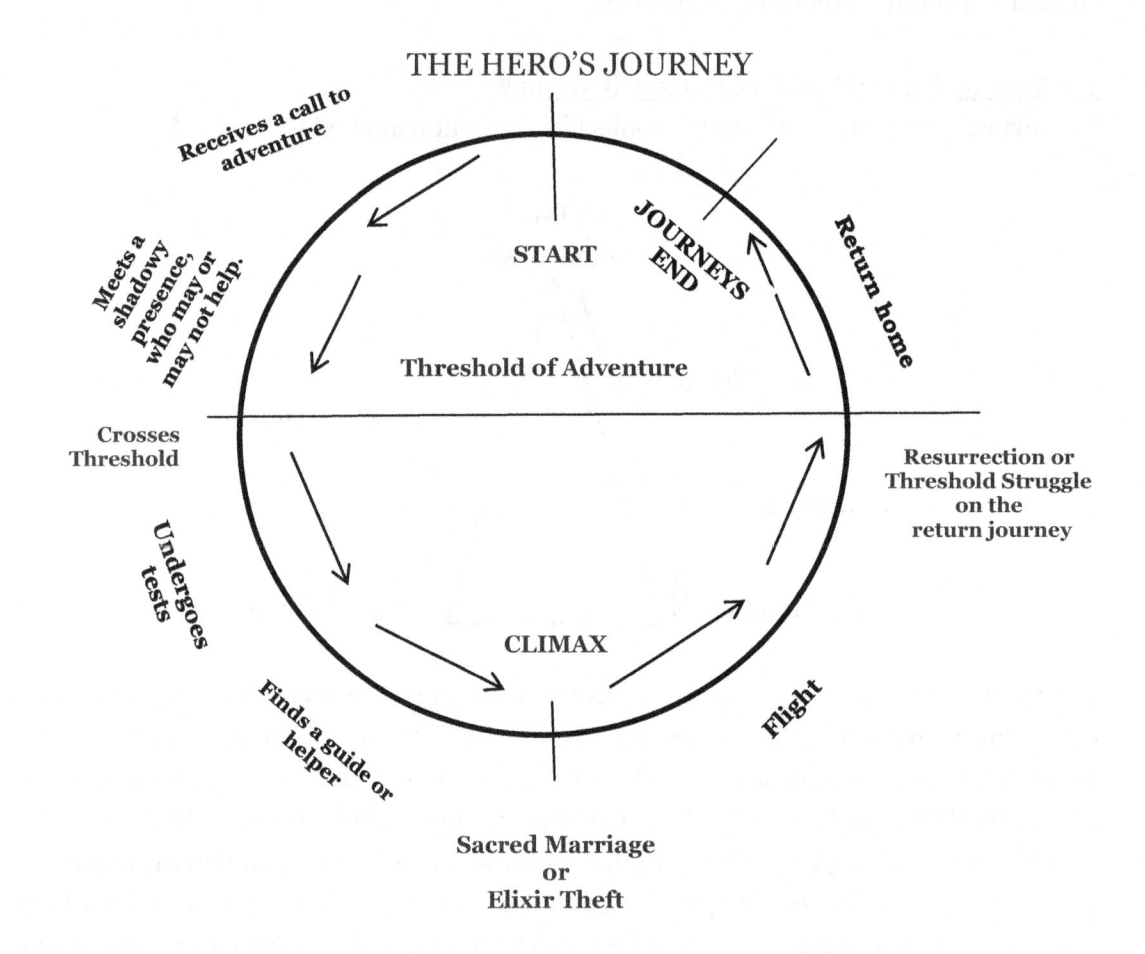

THE HERO'S JOURNEY

Receives a call to adventure

Meets a shadowy presence, who may or may not help.

START

JOURNEYS END

Return home

Threshold of Adventure

Crosses Threshold

Resurrection or Threshold Struggle on the return journey

Undergoes tests

CLIMAX

Finds a guide or helper

Flight

Sacred Marriage or Elixir Theft

Four story structures

We are going to examine and compare Freytag with Campbell, and also include two more structures, making four in all. The third is the analysis by John Yorke of the journey, away from and back to 'home', taken by every protagonist in a story. [A] The fourth an example of the archetypal fairy story.

The archetypal story chosen is *Jack and the Beanstalk*. Jack is the son of a widow so poor that she is forced to sell their only cow. On the way to market Jack sells the cow to a man for five magic beans. Jack's mother, furious at this waste of their last asset, throws the beans out of the window. Next morning they see a huge beanstalk rising up into the clouds. Jack climbs it to find himself in a kingdom in the sky ruled by a violent

---

[A] I am indebted to John Yorke for the conspectus on story structure within *Into the Woods: a five act journey into story*. (Particular Books, an imprint of Penguin Books, 2012) Mr Yorke's compelling treatment extends into detailed analysis of structure down to that behind each single exchange of action or dialogue. Most examples are from film and television drama.

giant who would eat him if he were captured. The giant has a hen that lays golden eggs. The giant can smell Jack but cannot find where he is hidden – actually under the giant's bed, where he stays all night whilst the giant sleeps. In the morning, Jack creeps out, picks up the hen, runs to the top of the beanstalk and starts to climb down. The giant has woken up, chases after him to the beanstalk and climbs down in pursuit. But Jack has a good start, gets to the bottom, fetches an axe and chops at the beanstalk. It breaks, the giant falls to his death and Jack and his mother live on – happy and rich due to the golden eggs laid by the hen.

Now we can put Freytag, Campbell, Yorke and Jack into a table and see how they compare.

Act	Freytag	Campbell	Yorke's 'journey'	Giant-killer Jack
1	Exposition – identification of a problem by the hero.	The call to adventure. Hero is called or lured away from the common round of his life.	The hero (or protagonist) and/or his community is threatened or has a problem.	Jack and his mother are poor and have lost their last asset – the cow.
2	Complications – the hero is obstructed but not stopped in his journey.	Hero defeats or conciliates a power that stands in his way.	He leaves his familiar world to go on a journey into an unfamiliar world. He overcomes obstacles.	Jack struggles up the beanstalk.
3	The hero reaches the climax – the conflict is at its highest point and the hero is at a crossroads.	Hero enters an alien kingdom, undergoes a supreme ordeal and gains his reward/elixir.	He enters a dangerous place where he finds and takes what he needs – perhaps with great struggle.	Jack finds himself in an alien kingdom and struggles to survive.
4	The conflict at the climax rouses greater opposition and obstacles.	The hero is pursued by foes as he flees with his reward/elixir.	He starts the journey home and copes with the consequences of taking what he needs.	Jack steals the hen which lays the golden eggs and is pursued by the giant.
5	Catastrophe or victory. The conflict is decided and the problem identified in Act 1 is resolved one way or another.	The hero returns with the elixir, to the benefit of all in his community.	He overcomes these trials, and arrives back at home. The problem/threat (personal or for the community) is solved/removed.	Jack climbs down, the giant is killed and he and his mother live happily ever after.

The similarity of structure between the four columns provides a universal template for stories. Since the subject here is drama, the table organises this template into five acts. In common sense, no such structure can be rigid; this is a matter of art and not science. The opening 'act' in particular can vary, sometimes having its own prelude which sets out for the audience the background situation before the principal character appears. The hero's action starts when he comes face to face with this situation. A good example of this is in *Hamlet*. The long opening scene is that between Horatio *et alia* and the ghost of Hamlet's father on the battlements. This tells us there is a problem and only in the second scene do we meet Hamlet himself. Another variation can be in the number of 'acts' or actions. Sometimes there are six as opposed to five. Nevertheless, the notion of an arc which curves up from an action at the beginning to reach a climax and then falls back to the ending is always clear.

Now is also the time to consider the modern three Act play. For innumerable centuries plays were broken into five sections, such as would now be regarded as Acts: all Greek tragedies, the plays of Shakespeare, Schiller and Racine amongst the classics; those of Victor Hugo, Eugene Scribe in the 19th century, plus many of those by Ibsen and George Bernard Shaw. A prime reason for the change from five to three may have been to accommodate the comfort of the audience. As both theatres and the seats in them became more comfortable, and when better toilet facilities were laid on, it was acknowledged that to have four breaks in a play was really more than spectators wanted or needed. Practical men of the theatre also realised - regardless of Freytag (should they have read him) - that within this structure lies the three-stage dialectic. The initial problem in any story (the Thesis) leads in short order to the need by the protagonist to do something about it, which becomes the substance of Act 1. The problem being engaged, the fulcrum round which the plot turns (the Antithesis) is the subject of Act 2 and the curtain falls with the audience waiting to know the outcome. So Act 3 follows Freytag's *falling action* which culminates in a resolution (the Synthesis).

In fact, as readers will find, in the examination of the drama in detail later in this book, the natural structure of a very large number of the Scenes within an Act is that they be in three parts.

The mechanisms that drive a drama

Within the five (or three) stage structure lie what one might call 'mechanisms' - those things that give energy and meaning to a story. There are many ways of looking at these but the main issues can be covered by consideration, with one or two examples, of the following:
- *The mid-point of the story* - the central plank, the fulcrum of story.
- *The protagonist and the antagonist* and the nature of the opposition between them.
- *The quest* to find a safer place or a new way of looking at things.
- *The journey* travelled by the protagonist.
- The *rise and fall* of a character and *role reversal* between characters in a story.
- The *final crisis*.
- *Resolution and reward*.

<u>The mid-point</u>
Freytag's and Campbell's theories of story structure achieved little initial support for they are at first glance at odds with what we see on stage or read in novels. The climactic

moments seem to come at or very near the end but reflection shows that this is not the case.
- In *Hamlet*, the turning point on which the plot hinges is the proof of Claudius's guilt, which is manifest in his reaction to the play-within-the-play. This occurs in Act III, at or very near the midpoint.
- In Schiller's *Maria Stuarda*, the climax at the mid-point (also in Act III) is clear for all to see: a confrontation between the queens of Scotland and England ends in a resounding personal triumph for Mary – a triumph which leads to her death.

The mid-point is when each of the protagonists acts in such a way that there is no going back. A great crisis occurs or a truth is revealed.

Protagonist and antagonist
The protagonist is the hero (which term includes 'heroine') who has to win through in his adventure. The antagonist can be a person or a situation.
- In *Maria Stuarda,* Mary of Scotland is directly opposed by Elizabeth of England.
- In *La Traviata*, Violetta's antagonist is the wider society outside Paris, of which Germont Père is a manifestation.

The 'quest' for a safer place
Many stories require the hero to find something and to bring it safely back home. In opera there is the clear example in *Fidelio* where Leonora finds Florestan and brings him back to life and to home.

In many cases, however, the truth sought and found is subjective – the drama is between two warring personality traits within the hero, and this leads to the discovery of a new truth, a fresh perception of self that changes the character for ever. Almost all these revelations occur at the mid-point in the play or opera; each is the climactic moment toward which the story has been moving and is the engine that drives everything else.
- In the middle of Schiller's *Wallenstein*, Max Piccolomini finds that his devotion to General Wallenstein is greater than that to his father and he breaks away. Max and indeed everything in the play is changed from that point.
- After Macbeth has murdered Banquo and is contemplating the slaughter of Macduff's wife and children (the foulest crime he commits), he says: 'I am in blood stepped in so far that, should I wade no more, returning were as tedious as go o'er.' He now knows what sort of man he truly is. (Macbeth may be a bad man, but he is also heroic.)

The journey
Both Campbell and Yorke lay emphasis on the journey undertaken by a protagonist. The generality now is that the journey be spiritual or intellectual. This journey is toward a personal completion and harmony, a balancing of contradictory elements to find a

wholeness. Most such 'journeys' can also be seen as moving from darkness to light - or vice versa – from light to darkness. Those from the dark into the light can be either tragic or comic/romantic.

- The tragic journey from darkness into light is from a situation of turmoil to one of clarity: the protagonist has certainty and serenity at the end of the story. Examples are: Bellini's Norma, Racine's Iphigénie, Mary Stuart, Hamlet, Verdi's Violetta.
- Joyful or comic journeys from the dark to the light are made by: Beethoven's Leonora, the entire cast of Mozart's *Figaro,* Viola in *Twelfth Night,* Georges in Boieldieu's *La Dame Blanche,* Poppea and Nero in Monteverdi's *L'incoronazione di Poppea.* The *Oresteia* of Aeschylus, as a whole and over its three parts, demonstrates this movement on a very large scale.
- The journeys from light to darkness are from 'home' to a dark place where there is no return: Othello, Macbeth and Racine's Berenice.

Rise and fall
Many dramas trace the rise and fall of the protagonist. *Rienzi* and *Macbeth* come to mind. Other's trace the rise of one character contrasted with the fall of another.

- Schiller's *Maria Stuarda* gives us everything. Mary of Scotland fails and dies but, in the process, rises from tribulation to transfiguration. At the same time Elizabeth of England falls from authority to a deserted desolation, even as her rival dies.
- *Richard II* sees Richard falling from power to death, exactly counterbalanced by Bolingbroke's rise from exile to power. The irony is that Richard is at peace before he dies whereas Bolingbroke ends with everlasting remorse and guilt.

The final crisis
Toward the end of every story, play or opera (in our scheme at the end of Act 4 or beginning of Act 5) there is a final crisis. This has greater power where the crisis erupts in the protagonist's heart and mind, when the quest involves an exploration of his other self. Then the drama is about whether the new self or the old self wins and which side of the character goes forward into the final conflict.

- In *Henry V* the battle is to be Agincourt and the prospect of victory is dim. Henry has been preparing for this conflict all his life, as he has turned from the dissipation of his youth to the serious business of kingship. The audience see his personal crisis acted out during the night before the battle – 'a little touch of Harry in the night'. He meets and melds with his soldiers and finally expresses a full understanding of his duties: 'Upon the King! . . . The King must bear all.'

Reward and resolution
The final crisis decided one way or another, the drama moves to its resolution and the characters receive the reward. Picking up the last example, the reward is just. Henry

wins the battle and also wins the girl in one of the most charming courtships ever put on stage.

The operatic dimension

An operatic story follows this same dramatic rhythm but has one particular quirk: if it is to work as drama, the emotional pull of the story *must* be told by the music. If this does not happen or if it happens but at the wrong moment, then the music is out of kilter with the story. Readers who are familiar with Verdi's fine *Ernani* may recognize such a moment at the end of Act 3 in the mighty ensemble 'A Carlo Quinto...' This tribute to the newly elected Emperor Charles V is the musical high point in the score but the opera is not about Charles V, nor about his nobility which brings forth the tribute. Magnificent as it may be, the music exalts that which is only a side issue in the drama of the doomed love between Ernani and Elvira.

Relative to that example from Verdi, it is also instructive to survey characteristic operas by some of the composers Wagner thought of note or influence. To analyse these against the criteria established by Freytag, Campbell and Yorke is not difficult. We can examine the dramaturgic attributes of each opera and look, in the first instance, for musical climaxes that correspond to dramatic climaxes. If there are turning points round which the drama hinges, then the music should rise in intensity to support them. Does this happen or does the lure and power of music push the weight of the drama away from key moments?

The results are to be found in the table that follows. The third column is Wagner's judgement as to whether the composer should be deplored or applauded for his contribution, the fourth indicates whether the opera is well structured in accordance with the criteria of Freytag *et alia* and the last indicates whether the two judgements as to quality concur or not.

Composer	Opera	Wagner's view: good/bad	The opera: good or bad dramatic characteristics	Concordance: Wagner and the criteria
Rossini	Guillaume Tell	bad	bad	yes
Meyerbeer	Les Huguenots	bad	bad	yes
Gluck	Iphigénie en Tauride	good	good	yes
Spontini	La Vestale	good	good	yes
Cherubini	Medée	good	good	yes
Mozart	Le Nozze di Figaro	good	good	yes
Beethoven	Fidelio	bad	good	no
Weber	Euryanthe	bad	bad	yes
Berlioz	Benvenuto Cellini	bad	bad	yes
Bellini	Norma	good	good	yes
Auber	La muette di Portici	good	good	yes
Boieldieu	La Dame Blanche	good	good	yes
Halevy	La Juive	good	good	yes

That twelve out of the thirteen operas have quality judgements that concur is less surprising than the reasons Wagner offers for approving or disapproving of each work. These always relate first to dramatic structure rather than to the music. All the operas he liked do offer first class drama. His dismissal of *Fidelio* is instructive. The kernel of his 'thumbs down' verdict is found in *A pilgrimage to Beethoven*, a short story he wrote in 1840. Wagner puts the following words into the composer's mouth: 'If I were to write an opera after my own heart, everyone would run away from it; for it would have none of your arias, duets, trios and all the stuff they patch up operas with today.' (PW7, 40/41) *Fidelio* too much followed the old rigid operatic formulas.

THE STRUCTURES WITHIN THE *RING* DRAMA

We can now apply in some detail the mechanisms inherent in the theories of Freytag, Campbell and Yorke - firstly to *The Ring* as a whole and then to its constituent parts.

The cardinal point is that what follows is derived simply from the text in accordance with the universal structure of stories. In principle, I use current commonly accepted, uncontroversial views of the cycle. An important aspect is to search for the character who goes on a moral or psychological journey and the requirement is to look for a coming together of discord or conflict within that character's mind and heart. In this and in all other plot matters dependant on the said mechanisms, prime evidence that we are on the right track is an increase of power in the music at key moments.

Readers can be assured that this analysis was completed many, many months before Part 2 was drafted and the detailed discussion of the operas in Chapters 18-21 was undertaken. It has remained unchanged; the result, therefore, is *sui generis*: it is based solely on underlying dramatic structures and the music which can be judged - from first perception - to articulate those structures.

The *Ring* as a whole

To say that the *Ring* is about Wotan is surely to diminish it, even though he is the protagonist. All of us know that there is far more to it than that but, nevertheless, the cycle does trace his journey.

The journey is in six stages - from the moment when Wotan endangers the world he controls, through to its collapse. The table which follows shows that the journey is personal during which he discovers who he is. He starts by establishing and supporting Law, then realises that Law is not enough. So he makes changes but Law still controls. Then events, which result from his actions but over which he has no control, show him what he *needs* (compassion and resignation) as opposed to what he thinks he *wants* (unlimited power to do good). Thus he seems to be both protagonist and antagonist.

THE STRUCTURE OF PLAYS AND OPERAS

Wotan holds on and, once he is clear about things, he understands that to succeed he will need help from the two existential extremes of his cosmos: mankind, the newest, and Erda, the most ancient of primordial spirits. This is consonant with Campbell's thesis, but the template to follow is that of Freytag. Wotan as protagonist is endorsed by the nature of the musical highlights, all of which follow from the god's actions.

Freytag	**Wagner**	**Musical highlights**
1 The problem	Wotan has created order out of primordial chaos but this order is governed by laws that rely on force. These laws push Wotan beyond safety; at the beginning he is between a rock and a hard place. (R2) [B]	
2 Start of journey	He starts his journey, perhaps with Erda as his 'guide and helper' (p.26) at the end of R4: he involves himself in the struggle by fathering children. Siegmund and Sieglinde are to do what he cannot do; Brünnhilde is to protect his empire and act on his behalf. (W1).	The love between Siegmund and Sieglinde (W1)
3 The climactic critical moment	The opposition of old laws stops his success and the unexpected reactions to events by his three children force him to re-evaluate and thus irrevocably change his views and actions (W2 and W3). Up till now Wotan thought he needed power but Brünnhilde changes his mind.	Wotan's farewell to Brünnhilde (W3)
4 The struggle to hold on	Things go as he hopes but doubts and fear of failure rise up: he needs the opposition (and therefore help) of Erda and Siegfried to fulfil his goals (S3.1).	The confrontation with Erda (Prelude and opening S3.1)
5 Crisis	Wotan accepts that change is inevitable and cannot be controlled, but is fearful that his plans may fail in the persons of Siegfried and Brünnhilde. (G1, G2, G3.1). It is not possible for him to order the world in the way he had first envisaged.	Siegfried's Funeral Music (G3.1)
6 Resolution	Brünnhilde, the personification of his inherent nobility of intent, rises to the challenge and prevents catastrophe. (G3.2)	The final Immolation

---

[B] From this point forward, references to each opera will often be abbreviated. *Das Rheingold* by an R and each of the scenes by numbers. Thus the scene in Nibelheim will be R3. Act 2 of *Die Walküre* will be W2. *Siegfried* has two scenes in Act 3 and these will be indicated by S3.1 and S3.2. *Götterdämmerung* has three scenes in Act 1 which will be indicated by G1.1, G1.2 and G1.3.

The first thing to note is that the summary of the story by itself - shorn of detail - presents an outcome that is essentially neutral. The story is neither triumphant nor tragic.

Four of the musical highlights have Wotan at the heart. The Farewell is his moment of truth which lies at the centre of his story. The confrontation with Erda shows the critical point as he is forced to accept the total loss of power. The Funeral Music is not just about Siegfried and his parents but is also a picture of Wotan's vision and his perhaps now shattered hopes. It relates back to each of the previous three operas (the Sword motif's first appearance triumphantly supports Wotan in R4) and also embraces music of the fourth opera. As such – despite its popular description – its dimension is larger than an elegy for Siegfried. The Immolation shows that vision victorious as the Valhalla motive, which is also a symbol of Wotan's majesty, rises in splendour. The love between Siegmund and Sieglinde is not directly about either Siegfried or Wotan but is an emblem of the new world brought about by the god's change in direction. Without their love for each other, there would have been no hope.

The five musical peaks spell out that Wotan's will is the engine behind the plot and the position of each in the plot in part explains why the *Ring* sounds and feels so coherent as a drama even if the detail of meaning may remain cloudy.

Das Rheingold

At first sight Alberich is the obvious protagonist: his grasp at the Rhine Gold sets the action of the opera going. This is followed by success: he forges the Ring from the Gold and enslaves his fellow Nibelungs, which include his brother. This forces Wotan to act and this happens in the middle of the opera, thereby driving the story through to its conclusion. Such a structure has an additional appeal as it traces Alberich's rise and fall.

So that first impression misleads. As soon as the Gold is stolen in R1 the emphasis switches to Wotan and how he responds to the news of Alberich's power. A notable feature of the dwarf is that he undergoes one change in his life and sticks to it. The sexual teasing by the Rhinedaughters causes that change: he will agree to forego the capacity to love and to replace it by a lust for power. Thereafter Alberich does not develop and interest switches to Wotan who does develop and change within this opera.

Thus Wotan is revealed as the protagonist and Alberich the antagonist, and the god's goal is to achieve total power in a direct struggle with Alberich. Wotan's opening situation is that he seeks power but is not willing to pay the price. Alberich's choice of gold as an alternative means to power both enables and forces Wotan to act. The crucial mid-point from which there is no turning back is not Alberich's capture. It is Wotan's earlier realisation that he must descend to Nibelheim and - in an act outside any possible law - capture and master the dwarf. Wotan gains the Ring by ignoble trickery. He then quickly faces the crisis, for he will not give it up. This is a bad moment for Wotan but also, and more importantly, for the world and the form of order he has established upon it. This last fact summons the oldest primordial law and wisdom in the form of Erda. The battle Wotan now has is with himself (Is he truly Licht-Alberich or a pale imitation of Schwarz-Alberich?) and he chooses law instead of the *certainty* of power. The resolution and reward after this battle is that Wotan maintains his power and his integrity but that this power is circumscribed and therefore his world is still threatened.

Wagner has a complicated story to tell and the template we require has six 'acts' rather than the standard five. Alberich taking the gold in R1 makes clear why Wotan has to make his fateful journey. This plot mirrors the journey as described by Yorke, and the musical highlights match the story highlights.

	Yorke	**Wagner**	**Musical highlights**
1	A prelude which sets forth the problem which the hero (Wotan) must solve.	Alberich sets himself up in opposition to Wotan (R1)	
2	The hero and his country are threatened.	Wotan has the power of Valhalla but cannot pay for it as he enters his new home. (R2)	
3	He leaves his familiar and customary world and starts his journey of self-discovery.	He engages in low trickery as suggested by Loge. (R2)	Everyone is seduced by Loge's sly manipulation.
4	Hero enters a dangerous place and takes the elixir that he needs. The mid-point climax.	(a) He descends into Nibelheim. (b) He captures Alberich, steals the gold. (R3)	The fearful power of the descent to Nibelheim. [C]
5	The journey home is obstructed by the consequences of taking the elixir.	Wotan puts the whole enterprise in jeopardy because of his need for power. (R4)	(a) The music of the curse. (b) Mounting tension and awareness of a new dimension as Erda arrives.
6	The hero overcomes these obstructions, arrives home and solves the problem that sent him on the journey.	Wotan listens to Erda, overcomes his lust for power at all costs and mounts to Valhalla, his new home. (R4)	The majesty of Wotan's final peroration and the blatant euphoria of the entry into Valhalla.

[C] A hero's journey 'into the woods' represents departure into an alien and dangerous place (think of Little Red Riding Hood) but this crossing of a threshold into an unfamiliar world is also often symbolised as going down into a deep cave (e.g. Orpheus descending in order to rescue Eurydice in Gluck's opera).

This structure does not remove the dramatic sub plot of the rise and fall of Alberich and the spectator may also be aware of the spatial movement within the scenes. Nothing takes place on the plain, undramatic earth. The action moves from below water to mountain top, then down even lower to the depths of the earth, a return to the mountain and then the final journey to the highest possible peak of all – Valhalla. These two factors appeal to the *feeling*, rather than the *reflective intellect* of the audience – patterns of rise and fall that find a deep response.

Die Walküre

If the protagonist here is Brünnhilde, then her antagonist must be Wotan. Her journey is from thoughtless childhood to compassionate understanding. The catalyst for her growth is the love between Siegmund and Sieglinde which is why W1 is part of Brünnhilde's story and why – as in *Das Rheingold* - the opera is in six rather than five 'acts'. The self-contained W1 love scene between Siegmund and Sieglinde is the prelude to Brünnhilde's journey. Without it we do not experience the emotional weight of the forces working on her: duty versus instinct. W1 establishes the nature of compassionate love and the audience must see this so that it understands the Valkyr's actions at the crucial turning point when the impact of the Wälsungs' love changes her for ever. [D]

The plot template that most corresponds to her journey is that of Freytag and is set out in the table below. The musical highlights match the critical dramatic turning points.

	Freytag	**Wagner**	**Musical highlights**
1	Prelude to Brünnhilde's conflict	Wagner sets forth in the strongest dramatic terms the nature of compassionate love. (W1)	The entirety of W1
2	Exposition – identification of a problem by the hero.	Brünnhilde understands fully the problems of Wotan. However, she is disturbed by what she learns of the history of the Volsungs. (W2)	The short scene after Wotan leaves (p.172)

[D] Deryck Cooke in *I saw the world end* argues that this moment of Siegmund's defiance is the hinge around which the action of the entire *Ring* turns, being the first assertion that love matters before all else. This study is to suggest otherwise, namely that the key moment in the cycle as a whole is when Wotan sees that he must relinquish power, in response to Brünnhilde's eloquence. From that moment there is no turning back for Wotan as, in this particular opera, there is none for Brünnhilde. Cooke's view of the central turning point has its own logic for he proposes that the *Ring* is a conflict between love and power to the exclusion of other issues, and this is the first moment that love comes first.

3	Complications – the hero is obstructed but not stopped in his journey.	Her foreboding concerning the Wälsungs is confirmed by awareness of the nature of the love between Siegmund and Sieglinde. (W2)	The *Todesverklärung*
4	The hero reaches the climax – the conflict is at its highest point and the hero is at a crossroads.	Brünnhilde is then overwhelmed by Siegmund's choice of love over glory in Valhalla, and disobeys Wotan. (W2)	Siegmund's defiance
5	The conflict at the climax rouses greater opposition and obstacles.	Things go badly wrong with Siegmund's death, Wotan's rage at her disobedience and his sentence upon her. (W3)	
6	Catastrophe or victory. The conflict is decided and the problem identified in Act 1 is resolved one way or another.	Brünnhilde is prostrate but she holds on to her new spiritual awareness. This crisis arouses her *understanding* of what she had previously felt and she wins the emotional battle with her antagonist Wotan. (W3)	Brünnhilde's pleading [E]

Siegfried

The structure of this opera is dramatically perfect on many levels.

- The hero's journey is from childhood to manhood, such as was Brünnhilde's in the previous opera.
- As hero, he has three opponents, each of which he defeats: first Fafner (as dragon), then Mime and finally Wotan. The defeat of each antagonist is symbolic of the satisfaction of three needs: an imperishable triumph as an initiation into heroism, freedom and an identity. To kill Fafner the dragon is the archetypal mark of heroic valour; killing Mime frees him from his past and the encounter with Wotan goes some way in the establishment of who he is. Each of the three victories can also be seen as a symbolic triumph by mankind over the three other life forces in the cosmos: the giants, the dwarfs and the gods. All have been corrupted by gold, as represented by the Ring. The forging of Nothung is the necessary preliminary to all three and, by its nature and originality, could also be considered as an heroic achievement in itself.
- The mid-point of no return follows the killing of Fafner when the revelations of the woodbird give him knowledge that changes him forever.
- The crisis point is the confrontation with Wotan (who would be a figure of awe and dread even when jolly) and the contest he must win is to brave the vast and engulfing fire - we know the fire is an illusion but Siegfried does not. These tests overcome, he gets his reward - namely Brünnhilde.

[E] The great closing scene is about Wotan and not his daughter and is therefore an aspect of the *Ring* as a whole.

THE STRUCTURE OF PLAYS AND OPERAS

- The spatial trajectory matches this progress: from inside a cave, and out into a forest (the classic place of danger), then up to the mountain pass and finally to the top of the mountain – an archetypal journey from darkness to light.

If the story were told in the conventional manner, the musical highlight would accompany Siegfried's victory over Fafner for that is the great heroic feat in the legend. That it does not is for two reasons. The first is that Wagner is more interested in Siegfried's coming struggle with Wotan and his winning of Brünnhilde; this is discussed in Part 2. The second is to do with Wagner's musical style (p.359). Otherwise the match of music to action is exact: The Forging Song to his emerging manhood; the Forest Murmurs to his emotional need as he searches for an identity; and the braving of the fire to his heroism. The love duet shows his ardent but tender desire as he comes to maturity. The table sets out the sequence. Campbell's structure is the most appropriate. Each stage (1-5) in the left hand column is followed by the Act in which the event happens. S3.1 corresponds to Act III, Scene 1.

	Campbell's 'journey'	Heroic journey	Physical Journey	Emotional Journey	Musical Highlight
1 S1	Receives a call to adventure	Forges Nothung	In a dark cave	Realises his need for freedom	Forging Song
2 S2	Trial 1 mastered	Kills Fafner	In the forest	Seeks identity	Forest Murmurs
3 S2	The midpoint Woodbird acts as guide Trial 2 mastered	Kills Mime		Finds freedom from his past	
4 S3.1	Trial 3 mastered	Defeats Wotan Passes through fire	At a mountain pass	Finds identity (1)	Braves the protecting fire
5 S3.2	Supreme reward - wins sacred bride	Reaches full manhood	On the mountain top	Finds identity (2)	Love duet

Compared to Wotan and even Brünnhilde - as we shall see - Siegfried's journey is multi-faceted. Aspects of Campbell, of the archetypal 'ordeal' and of the journeys both from darkness to light and from cave to mountain-top are inextricably bound together. On stage, the plot may seem straightforward but the mythic hinterland is complex. It shows how an archetypal hero achieves everything he needs: heroic status, freedom, an identity and the reward of a glorious woman.

But we can note that his journey ends at the halfway point in the Campbell circle (p.26) and this has implications for the following opera.

Götterdämmerung

The structure of this final opera is very different from that which precedes it. On the surface, both Siegfried and Brünnhilde are the heroic protagonists, and Hagen the antagonist. Certainly, the final victory is won by the actions of the two lovers. But all Siegfried's material achievements occurred in the previous opera and here he is largely passive and responsive to others: to Brünnhilde in G1.1 and G2 and to Hagen in G1.2 and G3.1. For him there can be no greater peak than that seen and heard at the end of *Siegfried*, for there he was 'home' and in no danger and under no threat. All that he – and indeed any man – would ever need was the love offered by his sacred bride. It is the valkyr who has the critical journey – a journey of the spirit and not the body, from partial to full knowledge. This is a process of self-awareness, from a desire for personal fulfilment to an awareness of the wider destiny envisaged for her by Wotan. At the beginning of the opera she thought she wanted love (symbolised by the Ring) but her journey showed this was not so.

The prologue shows both protagonists as innocent, unworldly and self-absorbed. They know they are special but think it is simply their love that makes them so. Siegfried's journey from their joint 'home' is necessary only because he is an action hero, and it is Brünnhilde who sends him off. The start of this journey is archetypal as both text and music declare: the woman sends the man on further adventures to the splendour of the Rhine Journey music. But the journey is shown as doomed, changing from joyous energy to gloomy enervation, as Siegfried moves into a world of extreme deceit. Siegfried is unreflectingly impulsive and ignorant, and this leads to his betrayal of Brünnhilde.

However, in retaining the Ring as her own possession Brünnhilde has also allowed herself to be misled and corrupted by the compulsive demands of love. The mid-point crisis for her and within the opera, when it is clear that all will inevitably come crashing down, is her realisation that she has been betrayed by Siegfried. Her worst moment is the crisis where all goes seriously wrong, when she agrees to the murder of Siegfried. So at the end of G2 the whole enterprise, as defined by Wotan, is endangered and universal total catastrophe is possible. Below is a representation of Brünnhilde's spiritual journey:

	Freytag	**Action**	**Journey**
1	Exposition – identification of a problem by the hero.	Brünnhilde urges Siegfried to fulfil the destiny she believes he has. (G1.1)	She believes that everything resolves around love, inspired by that between Siegmund and Sieglinde.
2	Complications – the hero is obstructed but not stopped in his journey.	Waltraute speaks unwelcome truths to Brünnhilde. (G1.3)	She evades the truth about the situation.
		She is betrayed. (G1.3)	She does not know what to think.

3	The hero reaches the climax – the conflict is at its highest point and the hero is at a crossroads.	She discovers the truth about her betrayal – a 'partial' truth. (G2)	She believes that love, truth and faith are lost.
4	The conflict at the climax rouses greater opposition and obstacles.	She learns the full truth from the Rhinedaughters.	There is a struggle between her character in W3 and that in G2. Wisdom wins the day.
5	Catastrophe or victory. The conflict is decided, and the problem identified in Act 1 is resolved.	She absolves and is absolved. (G3.2)	She realises that love is not enough and accepts her destiny in full.

Now there is a major oddity in this structure: we do not see the turning point when Brünnhilde comes to understand the purpose of it all, recalling once again the long history recounted to her in W2. This happens off-stage in stage 4, before G3.2, and we see the result in the Immolation. She learns the truth from the Rhinedaughters. And what is this truth? In part, of course, it is the information and moral message poured out to her by Wotan in W2 and by Waltraute in G1.3. There are also the perhaps uncomfortable truths she has learned about herself and Siegfried. We see none of this, and why is this so? Why did Wagner, *from the very beginning,* place such a hole in his narrative? The first words written down - *The Nibelungen Myth, as a sketch for a drama* - has the last scene of the cycle in outline as it is to be finally staged but the vast preponderance of detail is concentrated on what became the Immolation. Appendix A sets down these, his first thoughts, and they did not change. The complexity in the plot - as added later - had no evident effect upon Wagner. Did he disregard this possible encounter with the Rhinedaughters simply because he knew that the work had to end with some sort of musical and dramatic revelation and he realised that two such revelatory passages would not work? That an earlier burst of musical eloquence must weaken the impact of the final Immolation?

No audience would have this 'missing' scene in mind - it would be more likely aware of a mystery. If so, is it sufficient to call up again the words in the 1854 letter to Röckel? 'I believe it was a true instinct that lead me to guard against an excessive eagerness to make things plain' (p.3). [F] This has not always been taken at face value but perceived as Wagner wriggling himself off the hook about the meaning of the *Ring*, for Röckel had questioned him about the ending. However, Wagner's comments about Shakespeare's opacity (p.13) support the view that he meant what he said in his letter.

[F] This is from the first of two letters that Wagner wrote to August Röckel, with whom he worked in Dresden. These contain a large portion of his written explanations on the *Ring* and passages from them will be frequently quoted. This first was sent on 26 January 1854 and the second on 23 August 1856. Hereafter, as the analysis develops, they will be referred to frequently and will be called 'the 1854 Röckel letter' and 'the 1856 Röckel letter'.

Is it sufficient to say that some aspects of human life defy explanation and that even Shakespeare does not pretend otherwise? Consider Iago's motivation in *Othello*. His assertion that he believes the moor tried to seduce his own wife Emilia is made to the gullible Rodrigo, who had to be told *something*. This carries no conviction: his motivation is as obscure at the end as it was at the beginning. The extensive critical discussion about this has not led to questions about Shakespeare's competence. Is there a difference between Shakespeare and Wagner at this point?

The Aristotelian Unities

Reference to Aeschylus is not required to appreciate the concision within the overall plot. Wagner could well have had the classic unity of time in mind. Aristotle's examination of Greek tragedy in the *Poetics* revealed that the action of the plays took place over a period of 24 hours and this was proposed as an ideal.

- The action of *Das Rheingold* is in two parts. The first scene in the Rhine is really a prologue to the drama, which starts in Scene 2 and - put simply - is a struggle between Wotan and Alberich. From Scene 2, when Wotan awakens and sees Valhalla to Scene 4, when the gods climb toward it, the time frame is one day (Wotan: 'From morn until evening / in toil and anguish [Valhalla] wasn't happily won.')
- In *Die Walküre* Siegmund arrives at Hunding's dwelling in the evening, flees and mates with Sieglinde in the night. Brünnhilde fails to save him during the day and she is put to sleep by Wotan as night falls - a clear 24 hours.
- *Siegfried* seems to start in the afternoon (he has returned from the woods) and he arrives at Fafnir's lair on the following morning. He thrusts Wotan aside to awaken Brünnhilde in dawning daylight. This would suggest a total of 48 hours.
- *Götterdämmerung* was not conceived as part of a cycle in its first manifestation as *Siegfrieds Tod*, and the plot is complex. The first scene with the Norns - that which Devrient persuaded Wagner to add for the sake of clarity (p.452) - is designed by the composer as a prologue. Commentators have suggested that this prologue from the primordial Norns (presenting the cosmic overtones to the drama) through to the concluding orchestral depiction of Siegfried on his journey down the Rhine to the Gibichung court, represents a telescoping of time. And thus the period that Siegfried and Brünnhilde are together as happy lovers is far longer than one night. Whether or not that be the case, the timescale is not the same from the moment that Siegfried meets Gunther. Thereafter, Wagner specifies two nights - the first when Siegfried leads the defeated Brünnhilde back into her cave and the second as Gutrune waits in anxiety for Siegfried to return. Thus the story must take no less than three days.

The *Ring* has driving force. Temporal gaps are there – long between *Das Rheingold* and *Die Walküre,* and between *Die Walküre* and *Siegfried;* short between *Siegfried* and

Götterdämmerung. Nevertheless, leaving aside Alberich's theft of the gold and the Norns' scene, the total stage action of the four operas lasts about seven days.

The remarkable 'stretch' of the *Ring*

There will be recurrent reference to Campbell and Freytag when we consider how Wagner used his sources. There are, however, notable insights by other 20th century writers that seem presaged in *The Ring*.

The Canadian literary critic Northrop Frye, writing in 1957, argues that all literature derives from myth and ties different types of literature to the myth of the hero. He ties the myth of the hero's life cycle to other cycles – that of the seasons (derived from Sir James Frazer), the sun's daily cycle (from Friedrich Müller) and the cycle of dreaming and waking (from Jung). So we get the following template:

Type of story	Season	Day cycle	Dreaming / Waking	Hero's Life	Wotan /*The Ring*
Romance	Spring	Sunrise	Awakening	Birth	*Das Rheingold*
Comedy	Summer	Midday	Consciousness	Triumph	*Die Walküre*
Satire	Autumn	Sunset	Day dreaming	Isolation	*Siegfried*
Tragedy	Winter	Night	Sleep	Defeat	*Götterdämmerung*

This is an extraordinary construction but it is not difficult to see the sequence paralleled in Wotan's progress through *The Ring*. His rise as a god in *Das Rheingold*, his triumph at the end of *Die Walküre,* his isolation in *Siegfried* and his defeat/death in *Götterdämmerung*. (Augmented from Northrop Frye: *Anatomy of Criticism*, Princeton University Press, 1957.)

◊ ◊ ◊ ◊ ◊ ◊

PART TWO

Plot and character

4

Building Blocks

The final shot of the film *Shakespeare in Love* is of the heroine walking from the sea and across a wide deserted beach. She is the woman loved by the young Shakespeare, forcibly parted from him by class, and now shipwrecked. This catastrophe, the film tells us, is the inspiration that removes his 'writer's block' on a half-formed story and launches Shakespeare into the completion of *Twelfth Night*. This notion is the purist fiction. The two plays juxtaposed – *Romeo and Juliet* and *Twelfth Night* – were probably written some eleven years apart, and Shakespeare was a mature 36 years old and not an impetuous youth when he wrote the latter play. Nevertheless, the frequent scenes which show Shakespeare in the proverbial garret, struggling to find inspiration so that he can meet the deadline for his next play, neither jar nor seem implausible. This creative process is supported if we think of him as the prodigiously productive actor/director/playwright.

These scenes of inspiration in the garret, however, could not be further from the truth. That Shakespeare derived his history plays from Holinshed's Chronicles and a couple of other contemporary sources is well known. But these sources pale in comparison to those for *Twelfth Night*. Plausible sources for this one play number eleven: Plautus from antiquity, four 16th century Italian plays and stories and six English plays and poems. Scattered amongst these, in various combination, we find: confusion caused by twins, the page who falls in love with her master, the steward tricked into thinking he is loved by his mistress, shipwreck, the girl disguised as a boy, the lady of the house who loves and marries her steward, the names Aguecheek, Malvolio, Fabian, Viola, Orsino, Olivia and Cesario (the alias adopted by Viola in disguise). Two of the sources: *Gl'Ingannati* – an Italian play written by a collective of Siennese writers in 1531 – and *Apolonius and Sila* – a story written by Barnabe Riche in 1581 are held to be the main sources but all eleven can plausibly be called upon for some detail or other.

The moral of this story is not difficult to discern: in the *Ring* Wagner did what Shakespeare had done – and in much the same fashion. Where Wagner, for example, telescoped and adapted genealogies in order to craft the crucial union of Siegmund and Sieglinde, so did Shakespeare distort existing plot lines to bring about the final joyous union between Viola and Orsino, and Olivia and Sebastian. For in the sources the 'Olivia' character is first blackmailed by the 'Viola' character and then locked by her father in the bedroom with the 'Sebastian' character. This brings about the inevitable consummation and, therefore, the obligatory marriage. Shakespeare was not a writer of impulse but of premeditation who, in the words of Morton Luce, 'combined a marvellous spontaneity with an equally marvellous discipline of thought and command of material.' Concerning all great literatures of the world, he goes on to write:

> The higher creative genius has displayed itself by its power of transmuting the crude metal of popular fable or story into the fine gold of drama and epic . . . [and] . . . this power of transmuting was possessed by Shakespeare in a far greater degree than by any other literary alchemist. (Morton Luce, The works of Shakespeare, Methuen 1906)

These words also remind us that Shakespeare and other great classical and renaissance dramatists rarely invented their own plots. Aeschylus is reputed to have said his works were 'slices taken from the banquet of Homer'. Racine's plots were from the bible or from antiquity. Shakespeare, in mining Holinshed for his history plays, was acting in similar fashion, as was Wagner with *Rienzi, Tristan und Isolde* and the *Ring*. In all cases, the dramatist took a tale and tailored it to tell his own peculiar story. It was generally a process of omitting that which did not fit with the overall story plan. As a master dramatist, Wagner 'combined a marvellous spontaneity with an equally marvellous discipline of thought and command of material'.

This section of the book will try to set out how and why this is so and how the choices made in culling and mining sources were made inevitable by the nature of the drama being created. The study, as a whole, will investigate the activity of Wagner the craftsman rather than of Wagner the imponderable genius. There may be nothing miraculous in the process but there is nevertheless the mystery of artistic creation when it reaches the highest level. One is reminded of the riposte to a parent who remarked on a modern piece of abstract art that 'his eight-year-old son could have painted it': "Ah, but he didn't, did he?"

# # # # # #

Before we move on, an illustration can be used both to show the similarity between these two dramatists and also to distinguish the manner in which this study is to work. Of Shakespeare, Morton Luce wrote 'I must here repeat my conviction that Shakespeare was indebted to no *one* of the authorities I have mentioned but that he derived material or suggestion (it may have been a mere word) from most of them, if not from all.' (Morton Luce, *The works of Shakespeare*, Methuen 1906) Wagner did the same. In this study, however, unless the end product can be used to trace something of his creative path, I am not primarily concerned with the detailed derivation of the text. Readers should nevertheless be aware of Wagner the magpie.

On the left hand side below are Mime's lines as he describes to Wotan and Loge how the life of the Nibelungs changed once Alberich forged the Ring. On the right are the words of another dwarf Eugel from a play by Ernst Raupach (Hamburg, 1834) - *Der Nibelunghort*.

<u>Mime</u>	<u>Eugel</u>
Carefree smiths,	Our delight was always
we used to fashion	to fetch whatever shone

trinkets for our womenfolk,	and fashion from it
delightful gems and	skilful objects . . .
delicate Nibelung toys . . .	We were obliged to serve [and]
Now the criminal makes us	in forced labour do, what once
crawl into crannies,	we did of our free inclination . . .
ever toiling	day and night, increase the
for him alone.	hoard for him.

Wagner knew of the Raupach play and dismissed it as prosaic but the echoes of Eugel can be seen in Mime. There is no influence: Wagner is simply using in an appropriate manner something he had found. Eugel's words were apt and the echo we find with Mime demonstrates the mundane manner in which art is created by the gift of genius. Of further interest is how subtly selective is the choice of used material. Raupach's tyrant is not another dwarf, let alone Eugel's brother. He is a giant, named Kuperan. Wagner had giants in his plot mix, but deftly chose text that was useful and ignored the context.

The cast of Wagner's imagination

We can also briefly glance at how the composer's imagination worked. In 1853 he arranged a private printing, 50 in number, of the completed *Ring* poem. A copy was sent to his friend August Röckel; having read it he asked Wagner the question: 'Why, since the Rhinegold has been returned to the Rhine, do the Gods have to perish?' Wagner's reply was evasive. A good performance would provide the answer, which would not be one of logic. 'The Gods' downfall is not the result of points in a contract which can, of course, be interpreted and twisted and turned at will . . . no, the necessity for this downfall arises from our innermost feelings'. The necessity is felt in the emotions, for 'when Wotan finally gives expression to this sense of necessity, he is merely repeating what we ourselves already deem to be necessary.' (SS/SL, 309) This evasion has been used to support the view that he was not clear in his own mind about the matter. This alleged uncertainty will be considered later on; for the moment the object is to line up the observation with how Wagner's mind worked.

He was an inveterate synthesiser of ideas. In his writings he would seek to unify, to find links between disparate things in order to propound a theory. There is also his desire to include peripheral events or people in order to cement connections: the original idea that Wotan should be seen swimming with the Rhinedaughters, the notion that he should enter Hunding's house in Act I of *Die Walküre,* and that of the visitation by Parsifal to the tormented Tristan in Act III. The mental process whereby he came to these far-fetched situations is evidence of a mode of reasoning which we all have but which Wagner employed almost to excess. In rationalising a situation, we frequently use two established methods of logic: induction or deduction. With the former we proceed from a number of mutually supportive facts toward a conclusion - eg: the sun has always risen and therefore it will rise today. The deductive process is to move from an agreed premise to an inevitable logical consequence – eg: 'Because we all agree that murder is wicked, it follows that a murderer should be punished'. The most common form of day-to-day reasoning, however, is neither of these; a third legitimate form of argument often predominates. This resembles the advocacy we see in a court of law. In the course of building a case, a barrister selects a number of facts which may be different but which nevertheless support a particular way of looking at a situation. These are presented to the jury which is asked to look at the similarity between one thing and another, to compare or contrast one fact with another. And a case is seen to emerge when all these observations, comparisons and contrasts are put alongside each other. The facts which support the case are like the legs of a chair that support the seat rather than links in a continuous chain: the legs are independent but together they support the argument. The barrister contrives to make connections between facts and events that can be of a quite different nature. This is neither deductive nor inductive but is not without a form of logic. [A]

Wagner's method of reasoning was almost always in this mode. He was not a methodical thinker, however, and followed the procedure to extremes with sometimes bewildering results. Here are three examples; the first is general, and the second and third relate to the present discussion. The first example is from *Opera and Drama*. Here Wagner is talking about the development and increased complexity over the years of modulation from key to key. His method of argument is to juxtapose two separate sequences of cause and effect, and to mix them together as in this table. [B]

Thematic sequence A		**Thematic sequence B**	
In early years, the tonic key of a piece of music was fixed and unchanging.	→	This mirrors the control within a primitive tribe that its leaders impose on its members.	→
Men in the tribe thrust this control aside in order to find the desired sexual partner outside the tribe.	→	This created alliances between the tribes concerned.	→
In music this emergence of alliances is mirrored in the emergence of modulation.	→	Christianity removed the emphasis on tribes by bringing all of them into the one Christian fold.	→
In music, this is mirrored in the merging of the modulations from each different musical tradition.	→	Hence the vast expansion of modulation in modern music.	

We can see that two quite different issues are being brought together, one illustrating the other, rather as in a New Testament parable. The logic is that a reader who accepts

---

[A] See p.157, *Philosophy and Psycho-analysis* by John Wisdom. (Basil Blackwell, 1953)

[B] The detail of this can be found in RW/PW2, 287-8

the drift of the sociological example may be inclined to accept Wagner's theory about modulation, even though the first is obviously not a proof of the second.

The second example is from *Die Wibelungen,* that curious trawl through myth, history, religion and revolution which Wagner wrote whilst also writing the *Nibelungen Myth as a sketch for a drama* and *Siegfrieds Tod* in 1848. In one long paragraph Wagner manages to make links between the following: Augustus and the early Roman emperors, the later Roman emperors who were not Italian, degenerate pacific Roman citizens, Christianity, the emperor as priest, the Pope as supreme priest, Charlemagne, the earliest kingdom in Europe, Troy and King Priam. The result is an equivalence between Charlemagne and Priam. c

The third example connects to the Theban plays of Sophocles. Wagner has made a reasonable case that lessons good for all time derive from myth, namely that the personal catastrophes of Oedipus and Antigone bring about the ruin of the State, in the person of Oedipus's brother Creon (p.11). He then takes the argument further:

> Today we only need faithfully to expound the myth of Oedipus according to its innermost essence and we will discover an intelligible picture of the whole history of mankind, from the beginning of Society to the inevitable downfall of the State. (PW2,191)

This extreme proposition has been brought about by Wagner's chronic need to link everything together, but it also reminds us that the idea of personal virtue trumping coercive law is central to the polemical framework that informs *Opera and Drama*. He may not have been a systematic thinker but he was anything but superficial, and this social belief is the basis of the case against Wotan that emerges in the *Ring*.

Regardless of whether Wagner's advocacy convinces, the result is a highly romantic way of looking at the world. It wants to embrace every aspect of life and pull them into a unity. If 18th century rationalism sought to explain by breaking things down, 19th century romanticism sought to unify by finding commonality. This romanticism influenced not only Wagner but also the majority of scholars and interpreters of the legends and myths from which Wagner constructed the *Ring*.

> Romanticism was in its heyday in seats of learning as well as literary salons, and the belief in the intrinsic Oneness of the saga triumphed over the obstacles of the material. It was an age when inner necessity was widely recognized as the all-compelling argument. One common feature and a little ingenuity could suffice to find the most diverse persons and events identical. (EM/WN,5/6)

---

c This may make us smile today but our knowingness should not be directed at Wagner alone. For such has been the grip of the Trojan War on all cultures throughout the ages that historical links to Troy were universal. Wagner would have read in *The Prose Edda* that Odin was descended, through 20 generations, from King Priam. Virgil has Rome founded by Aeneas. Nearer home, Geoffrey of Monmouth maintained in 1136 that the Welsh were fugitives from Troy and, since the Tudors were Welsh, it was therefore in order for Thomas Hughes to greet Elizabeth at Grays Inn in 1588 as 'that sweet remain of Priam's state: that hope of springing Troy'.

Elisabeth Magee, in *Richard Wagner and the Nibelungs,* quickly offers us a fine example. Germanic legends seem chronically confused as to which set of people the name 'Nibelung' referred. Wagner himself, in *Die Wibelungen,* speaks of them as whichever German tribe owned the Nibelung treasure. The Burgundian kingdom was known to have three brothers as princes and *Song of the horny-skinned Sigurd* features three dwarf brothers. A connection was made between the two sets of brothers such that even the celebrated scholar Karl Lachmann, who was not considered over-romantic, could write: 'We . . . observe that where the northern saga first establishes the treasure in the power of the dwarfs, the South German saga, not without confusion, makes the first lords of the treasure into Nibelungs also, along with Gunnar and his entourage . . . One can therefore hardly doubt any longer that the former and the latter are the same race.' (See EM/WN,78)

Wagner would have found such scholarly proclivities natural, congenial and correct. He was an expert in finding 'one common feature' which, with his own ingenuity 'could suffice to find the most diverse persons and events identical'. Westernhagen, in a survey of the library Wagner had to abandon in Dresden as he fled into exile, cites a letter to a friend where Wagner writes: 'What happens to me is that I seldom actually read what's in front of me, but rather what I read into it.' (Quoted in EM/WN,13)

The scholars, from whom Wagner drew not only the translated texts but also the critical sub-text, saw *Das Nibelungenlied* as a reflection and reworking of the mythic sagas. The murder of Sigurd occurs half way through the book. The second half tells of the destruction of the Burgundian kingdom, including its royal family, and its enemies *as a direct result of that murder.* In the romantic view, this apocalyptic crash of Burgundy and its foes is a reflection of the catastrophe of the Nordic gods and the cosmos they superintend, as depicted in the sagas. Wagner would have been at home here. Someone who could link the personal fate of Oedipus with the fall of the state, would have had no difficulty in finding a connection between the fall of Burgundy and that of the gods.

That demise of the gods had the name *Ragnarök* and there are repeated references to it in the *Prose Edda* and *Sturleson's Edda.* The old Norse term can best be translated as 'doom of the gods' (not difficult to see how Wagner hit on his title). The gods know and accept that it will happen – theirs is no state of immortality. The process is of long duration with a prelude of three years when there is almost eternal darkness - frost, storms and famine in an eternal winter with no sunlight. This leads to civil war – brother killing brother and tribal rule collapsing – until there is universal depravity. This chaos reaches beyond humanity: first to the gods, giants and dwarfs who battle for suzerainty over the earth and then to even older cosmic powers and beasts who wrestle for control of the sun itself. These rival powers confront each other in a series of battles of indescribable ferocity and prodigious slaughter: the gods, giants, monstrous dragons and vaguely imagined primordial forces destroy each other. The last spasms cause the stars to disappear and the seas to rise and engulf the land.

As described, many will think that the conjunction by scholars with the collapse of a legendary German kingdom as overstretched, to say the least. But Wagner's long held concern for the nature of the German state would have found them acceptable.

Further on we shall see that the 'problem' of the *Ring* is seen by some as stemming from the coupling together of Siegfried's death and the downfall of the gods – a coupling invented by Wagner and one which he could never articulate to everyone's satisfaction. This must be put alongside that other coupling, namely the similar cast of mind which inhabited the heads of Wagner and the influential scholar Friedrich von der Hagen, who produced no fewer than four editions of *Das Nibelungenlied,* and whose romantic views on the 'oneness of things' were known to the composer.

In 1962 a German critic Hermann Schneider summarised succinctly this concatenation of Wagner's attitude with those of the romantic scholars:

> But it can be demonstrated that . . . Siegfried's life and death, the lament [over that death], and the peril of the Nibelungs [for which read 'Burgundians'] . . . are none other than the life and death of Baldur the God and the annihilation of all the gods in *Götterdämmerung*. (Quoted in EN/WN,204)

The upshot of all this is that the composer's inability to answer Röckel's question directly does not invalidate the answer that he does give. The need for the gods to be destroyed was one of romantic imagination and not of logic. Readers can bear this in mind, along with Wagner's 'marvellous spontaneity . . . discipline of thought and command of material' as we follow his creative journey.

The sources for the *Ring*

As is to be expected, the sources for *The Ring* were wider than those for *Twelfth Night*. In 1992 Elizabeth Magee identified every possible avenue of information and if multiple editions are discounted the total comes to 22. Some comfort, however, can be found: the vast majority of material used and adapted resides in seven primary sources.

Consideration of these seven primary sources are sufficient to map and relate the dramatic structure to the sources, to tease out the reasons for putting a particular incident or a particular character 'on stage' in the manner chosen by Wagner. The sources concerned are *Das Nibelungenlied, Thidriks Saga, Das lied vom Hürnen Seyfried* (Song of the horny-skinned Sigurd), *The Poetic Edda, The Prose Edda, The Volsung Saga* and Jacob Grimm's *Teutonic Mythology*. The roots of the first three lie in German legend and history about Sigurd, Brynhild and the court of Burgundy, and there is no mention of Wotan or the gods. The second three are Nordic myths where Odin, Frigg and Loki (Wotan, Fricka and Loge) and also the mythic Sigurd, Sigmund and Brynhild are found. That German and Nordic sources have influenced and interpenetrated each other finds confirmation in the last source, Grimm's *Teutonic Mythology*. This relates both cultures to the earlier myths of Greece and Rome. [D]

In addition to the above, Wagner almost certainly used one secondary source in the early creative stages: *Sigurd der Schlangentödter*, (Sigurd the Dragonslayer) a pseudo-drama by Friedrich de la Motte Fouqué. [E] This was published in 1808 and is based on the *Volsung Saga*.

A note on names to be used for the principals. Simplicity is required, for in the Germanic and Nordic sources each are variously named and each translator into English will use what is thought most appropriate and recognisable to the reader. This book will use Siegfried, Brünnhilde, Wotan etc only when it is discussing Wagner's operas or written works. When the person is mentioned in one of the sources, s/he will be referred to as Sigurd, Brynhild, Odin etc, regardless of what might be the name given by the translator or commentator.

# # # # # #

Das Nibelungenlied, written anonymously in 1200AD or thereabout, has been described as the unofficial national epic of mid 19th century Germany. It is one of the two sources written in the form of a continuous narrative with a beginning, middle and end, and in it is to be found the story of Sigurd arriving at King Gunnar's court on the Rhine, his dealings with Gunnar's sister and with Brynhild, and his murder at the hands of Hagen. (A summary of the story is to be found as Appendix B). [F]

Song of the horny-skinned Sigurd is also of German origin; written in the 16th century, the story told is crude and fantastical but it gives a different perspective on Alberich and the Tarnhelm, on the giants and on how Sigurd killed the dragon.

Thidriks Saga of Bern is a half-way house between the Germanic and Nordic sources. The narrative is similar to the *Nibelungenlied* with regard to the long period during which Sigurd served Gunnar at his court prior to marrying Gudrun and also to the manner of his death. Despite a clumsy construction and *non sequiturs* which detract from its artistic value, the narrative does effectively blend those courtly events with the separate story of Sigurd and Brynhild. That story is based on Nordic sources but is humanised and simplified. Here also we can read a version of Sigurd's conception, birth,

---

[D] The editions of each of the sources used are listed in the Bibliography.

[E] EM/WN, particularly pp 44-46

[F] Abbreviations will frequently be used hereafter, as follows:

NL for Das Nibelungenlied	*TS* for Thidriks Saga
HS for Song of the Horny skinned Seyfrid	*PE* for The Poetic Edda
DM for Grimm's Deutsche Mythologie	*VS* for Volsung Saga
SS for Sigurd der Schlangentödter	*SE* for Sturluson's Prose Edda

upbringing and early history that differs radically from that described in all other major sources and we will later discuss the significance of why this version was not used. Thidrik is identical with the Dietrich who features in *Das Nibelungenlied*. Both names refer to the historical Theodoric, first king of the Ostrogoth realm founded in Italy in 493AD, shortly after the collapse of the Western Roman Empire, with Ravenna as its capital. Despite the pronounced German element, the work was written in Norse in the 13th century.

The preponderance of material in the *Ring* is taken from the three Nordic sources. Here is found all incident and background to the gods, the giants and the nature (as opposed to the actions) of the dwarfs. We also find almost all of the critical events and background to the crucial relationships between Sigurd and Brynhild, and Sigmund and Siglinde/Signy.

The Poetic Edda derives from a manuscript written in about 1300 containing 29 poems, to which a further six poems were added soon after. These poems are by different anonymous authors and were brought together by an unknown editor. Before this effort at compilation they would have been versions individually familiar to the literate aristocracy and that some date back to the 10th century. The 35 poems are grouped into two sections: Lays of the Gods (14 poems) and Lays of the Heroes (21 poems). Of these, Wagner used six concerning the gods and eleven concerning the heroes.

The Prose Edda was written in about 1220 by Snorri Sturluson (1179-1241), a powerful aristocratic politician in Iceland. Sturluson's purpose was to provide a guide and primer to Nordic poetic literature and a systematic account of Norse mythology. The content covers the same ground as *The Poetic Edda*, from which it frequently quotes verses. There are, however, unique additions and amendments from material that is now otherwise lost and may not have been known to the editor of the *Poetic Edda*. The coverage and fate of the gods is in great and complex detail; that for Sigmund, Sigurd and Brynhild is terse and matter of fact.

The Volsung Saga was written by an unknown author sometime in the 13th century and is the only source for the origins of the Volsung tribe, the Sigmund and Siglinde content, and the myth of the sword in the tree. There is full coverage of Sigurd's life from birth to death and his relationship with Brynhild. Much of *Die Walküre*, *Siegfried* and *Götterdämmerung* are derived from this one source. The author uses the same material as in the *Poetic* and *Prose* eddas but, by contrast to those two works, he constructs a continuous narrative wherever possible. This runs from the genealogy of the Volsung tribe down to the birth of Sigmund and on to the death of Sigurd followed by those of his three children: a tribal history from its beginning to its end. As this is such an important source, a detailed summary is to be found in Appendix C.

Teutonic Mythology (1835) by Jacob Grimm is a massive, four-volume, groundbreaking investigation of both Germanic and Nordic cultures as it relates them to the earlier myths of Greece and Rome. References to Wotan, Loki, Sigurd, the Valkyrs and Norns were used by Wagner to round out and clarify his story where needed. [G]

Wagner's response to the sources and how he used them

One aspect, always to be borne in mind throughout the study, is that Wagner always adheres as closely as possible to the primary sources and does not falsify them except for good dramatic reasons. Time and time again, Deryck Cooke (whose torso of a book covers the matter like none before or since) reiterates this quality.

- Sometimes it is on the largest scale: 'In the sagas, the downfall of the gods is clearly represented as the inevitable retribution brought by fate on the dubious dealings in their quest for domination.' (DC/WE,86)
- Sometimes it relates to structure: 'The main outline of the first two acts of *Siegfried*, as well as the name Mime and the whole mysterious atmosphere - the lonely forge in the forest - he took from *Thydriks Saga*.' (DW/WE,106)
- Sometimes it is the manner by which Wagner combines elements from different sources: 'Exactly what original single story these various versions stem from is impossible to say but in Act 2 of *Siegfried* Wagner ingeniously reconciles all five elements in his own individual way: Siegfried wins the treasure by killing the dragon, who is also a giant, while the two dwarfs, Alberich, the Lord of the Nibelungs and Mime quarrel as to which of them eventually reclaim it.' (DW/WE,122)
- Sometimes it is to show how a somewhat obscure reference binds together various complex matters: 'Luckily Jacob Grimm stepped in . . . thus enabling Wagner to make the *Ring* a homogeneous German whole.' (DW/WE,129)
- Even on those occasions when Wagner virtually invents matters, he 'was clever enough to have it both ways: if he made water the original home of the *gold*, adopting Scandinavian tradition, he made the earth the original home of the *treasure,* following the German one - since in Scene 3 of *Das Rheingold*, the treasure which the Nibelungs make for Alberich is fashioned from gold found in the earth.' (DW/WE,136) All the above was fashioned 'out of the faintest hints in the mythology.'

From the sources Wagner took what he needed for his drama but also kept as true to the original as he could. In this he resembles Shakespeare in his history plays as he mines Robert Holinshed and the other chronicles he used for *Henry IV*.

[G] Readers may be interested in five studies which together contain a vast amount of detail. Two of them, *Richard Wagner and the Nibelungs* (1992) by Elizabeth Magee, and *I saw the world end* (1978) by Deryck Cooke have been mentioned before. The three others are *The Legends of the Wagner Operas* (1896) by Jessie Weston, *The Kingdom on the Rhine* (1982) by Nancy Benvenga and *Wagner and the Volsugs* (2000) by Ārni Björnsson. No study of the text can avoid reference to these authors; Appendix F offers some detail of the approach of each.

When good drama and history happened to coincide, he would give a faithful enough account of history as his informants had recorded it; when history proved recalcitrant to dramatization, he would ignore it or remould it to serve his purpose. As a result, the play combines details perfectly true with others wholly imaginary . . . Shakespeare remembers that Bolingbroke landed at Ravensburgh, swore an oath at Doncaster and met Hotspur at Berkeley Castle [but] when he makes the king older than he really was and Hotspur younger it is not out of ignorance but out of a sense of what will make his play more effective.' (M A Staeber, *The Complete Pelican Shakespeare Histories*, p.242)

This fidelity to sources wherever possible will be referred to often in the following pages: where Wagner abides by this precept and, importantly, where he does not.

Wagner's journey starts

This section of the book addresses how the drama may have developed but no precise chronology is proposed: it is an attempt to construct some sense of how the story shaped itself in the composer's mind. There will have been a given and accepted dramatic scene or moment where a problem generates a question as to how Wagner could have resolved it and moved forward. How this works will become clear as the story goes along. Readers will appreciate that the process was not linear: the problem may be 'parked' and only solved after a period of conscious and/or unconscious reflection.

On the trail of a Siegfried drama, Wagner was drawn into the mass of the listed sources. His journey seems to have started in 1843 and we can assume, from statements and hints in his writings, that Grimm's *Teutonic Mythology* and *Das Nibelungenlied* were the first to be studied. Alongside the 'strange enchantment' induced by Grimm as described in *My Life*, he also recorded that 'the inordinate wealth of its content' resulted in 'a confusing construction which at first sight appeared to me as a huge rocky crevice choked with underbrush. Nothing in it was complete nor was there anything resembling an architectural (for which read 'dramatic') line and I often felt tempted to abandon the seemingly hopeless effort to make something systematic out of it'. (RW/ML,260) Moreover, if 'the splendid type of Siegfried had long attracted' him (RW/PW1,358), he would indeed have found *Das Nibelungenlied* an eccentric representation. Siegfried is the great hero but his main function is to be the catalyst that brings about the destruction of Burgundy. As the brief summary in Appendix B makes clear, *NL* is a story about Gudrun, whose life is turned upside down by the murder of Sigurd. This occurs toward the middle of the story, after which she is steadily overcome by a fearsome lust for vengeance as she engages in a struggle to mutual death with Hagen - Gunnar and everyone else being drawn to catastrophe in her wake.

That Wagner's imagination was first engaged by Siegfried, as first encountered in *Das Nibelungenlied*, is the starting point of this study. Although Wagner could not see a coherent drama about the man, four critical features of the story were noted and carried forward.

Firstly, that the murder of Sigurd has cataclysmic repercussions and is the event around which the entire plot turns.

Secondly, that it is presented as a foul murder of an innocent man which taints and eventually destroys the Burgundian court.

Thirdly, that Sigurd and Brynhild are of a different order to the other characters: they are linked together by style of character and their superhuman strength. This is clearly indicated when they first meet, when she thinks that it is Sigurd who has come for her and he has to disabuse her by pointing out Gunnar as the destined suitor.

Fourthly – and linked to the above - that there is something fishy about the portrayed relationship between the two of them. As the summary indicates, the *Nibelungenlied* is ambiguous here. The critical scene is that in which Sigurd overpowers Brynhild in her marital bed, but the lead up to this is also odd, starting at the wedding banquet.

> The King (Gunnar) and the maiden Brynhild now took their seats and when the latter saw Gudrun at Sigurd's side – never had she suffered such torment – she began to weep so that the hot tears fell down her radiant cheeks . . . 'I have every cause to weep . . . It wounds me to the heart to see your sister sitting beside a liegeman and, if she is degraded in this fashion, I shall never cease to lament it'. (AH/NL,86) . . . [*and, when Gunnar makes his first sexual advances in their bed*] . . . 'Sir, you must give up the thing you have set your hopes on, for it will not come to pass. Take good note of this: I intend to stay a maiden till I have learned the truth about Sigurd'. (AH/NL,88)

When Gunnar persists, the amazonian Brynhild trusses him up and hangs him from a nail in the wall. On the following night, therefore, Gunnar calls on Sigurd to help. Sigurd agrees and promises that he will 'not make free' with the woman. He and Gunnar change places in the dark; he gets into the bed and wrestles Brynhild into submission. Then we read:

> Sigurd left the maiden lying there . . . and, without the noble queen noticing it, he drew a golden ring from her finger and then took her girdle . . . I know not whether it was his pride which made him do it. (AH/NL, 93)

Arthur Hatto (translator and editor of the *Nibelungenlied*) suggests that this is an obvious code: both ring and girdle have a symbolism which tells us that Sigurd *did* deflower Brynhild. The anonymous poet's coy evasion of why he acted as he did is the broadest of hints to his courtly, troubadour-influenced audience.

Taking Wagner at his word, therefore, that *NL* was his starting point, we *can* say that study of any of the Nordic sources – as he puzzled what to do with the story – would immediately have provided him with the stuff he needed in order to disentangle the matter. Nordic and Germanic legend and myth penetrated and influenced each other between the 9th to the 13th centuries, and in the Nordic canon it is manifest that Sigurd did encounter Brynhild more than once and at the first meeting, prior to that when he won her for Gunnar, they did pledge to love and marry each other. So his second encounter, resulting in Brynhild as the wife of Gunnar, provides a focus for explosive drama. Indeed, it is hard to find a situation with greater melodramatic potential.

At a stroke Wagner could dispense with the whole of the *NL* plot up to the moment when Gudrun reveals the fateful ring to Brynhild. The hocus-pocus of Sigurd's athletic contest with Brynhild and the near farcical trussing up of Gunnar on the wedding night were gone and a true plot of betrayed love which required mortal vengeance could be put in its place. This increase in scope gives context to Wagner's own description of the process, whereby he came to see Siegfried in his 'purest human shape, set free from all later wrappings [as in *NL*]. Now for the first time also did I recognize the possibility of making him the hero of a drama'. (RW/PW1,358)

A drama takes shape

The three Nordic sources cover much of the same ground in the relationship between Sigurd and Brynhild. Of the three, however, by dint of its coherence and continuity of plot, the *Volsung Saga* is the best source to use. Every detail suggests it was written after the *Poetic Edda* and *Sturluson's Edda,* and the unknown author also had access to other sources which were needed to round out his tale. [H] Because it is very nearly a continuous narrative, a summary of the whole - up to the deaths of Sigurd and Brynhild - is given in Appendix C. Key passages, such as touch directly on the *Ring,* are there quoted in full and are clearly indicated.

The following are the salient points with regard to Sigurd and Brynhild as they are seen in the Nordic sources.

- He was told of her existence by a wood bird.
- She was asleep on a mountain and surrounded by a fire.
- She greeted him as the expected person who would breach the fire and awaken her.
- She taught him her wisdom.
- They pledged mutual love and he departed for the Burgundian court.
- There he stays for about three years. Gudrun's mother Grimhilde gives him a drugged drink so that he forgets Brynhild and marries Gudrun.

[H] Elizabeth Magee maintains that Wagner could not have read the *Volsung Saga* prior to completing the *Myth*: it was not in his library when he left Dresden, there is no record of him borrowing it from the Dresden public library and he asked a friend to look out a copy as late as November 1852, when the poems of all four operas were virtually complete. Her thesis is that all the information needed came from Fouqué's *Sigurd der Schlangentödter*. Björnsson disagrees with Magee regarding *VS*, believing that the saga is so deeply embedded that it must have been known early on, but agrees that the composer must also have known the Fouqué treatment. Either way, the *VS* material would have been there for him. (See EM/WN,44-46; AB/WV,126)

- Grimhilde suggests to Gunnar that he marry Brynhild.
- Gunnar cannot get through the fire so Sigurd changes shapes with him and, in friendship, substitutes himself.
- Brynhild reluctantly agrees to marry 'Gunnar'.
- Sigurd, as 'Gunnar', takes from her the ring of Andvari (for whom read Alberich) and gives her another in exchange.
- After the wedding, Gudrun and Brynhild quarrel and Gudrun shows her Andvari's ring to prove that it was Sigurd and not Gunnar who went through the fire to win her. (At this point the plot of the *Nibelungenlied* relating to the murder of Sigurd takes over from that of the sagas.)
- After Sigurd's murder, Brynhild kills herself and orders a pyre to be made large enough for both bodies to be burnt together.

This was just the sort of thing Wagner could use and adapt to his purpose.

Great attention was paid in Chapter 3 to the various dynamics in structure that have been used over the centuries and how these shape the drama in the *Ring* as a whole and in each of its constituent parts. One tenet is the existence of a five-part structure and how this is manifest in many great dramatists: Shakespeare, Racine, Aeschylus. Readers can now examine an imaginary drama about Siegfried and Brünnhilde, as might have been perceived by one such as Wagner.

Given the above plot lines, it is surely not difficult to see how the composer, with his power of 'transmuting the crude metal of popular fable . . . into the fine gold of drama' grasped at a basic Siegfried story. There are of course other major issues with regard to the two protagonists which are not touched upon, the principal one being their background and upbringing. However, on the main crux of a drama *about these two people*, matters are clear and a structure can be perceived, which can be put into the five Act Freytag format as follows.

Act 1	Sigurd hears of Brynhild from the birds and sets off.
Set up [From *VS*]	Sigurd and Brynhild meet and pledge their love.
Act 2	Sigurd arrives at Gunnar's court, imbibes the draft of
Rising action	forgetfulness and falls in love with Gudrun.
[From *VS*]	Gunnar bargains with Sigurd over Brynhild.
	Sigurd and Gunnar swear blood brotherhood.
Act 3	Sigurd leaves with Gunnar. Magic power is used for them to
Mid-point truth	change shape and deceive Brynhild.
[From *VS* and *NL*]	Sigurd takes the ring from her.
	Sigurd and Gunnar resume their own shapes.
Act 4	On arrival at court, Brynhild sees that the ring taken from her is
Falling action	not on Gunnar's hand and understands she is betrayed by Sigurd.
[From *NL*]	

	She incites Gunnar and Hagen to kill Sigurd and reveals his weak point where a weapon can pierce.
Act 5	Sigurd is murdered.
Catastrophe	Brynhild kills herself.
[From *VS* and *NL*]	They are cremated together on the same pyre.

It would invite derision to suggest that Wagner saw it like this and simply decided to dispense with Act 1 as structured above, but it is not preposterous to propose that aspects may have occurred to him as he sought for a viable drama. As it is, the *Myth* (the first sketch for *Siegfrieds Tod*) starts as the hero arrives at Gunther's court. That was what he first envisaged and it required the advice of Eduard Devrient to get him past this point and see the need for the prologue.

Using the *Nibelungenlied* and the story of the lovers as main source we can see the outline of a story of two isolated people, filled with a triumphant, heroic love, which they pledge with a ring. (Neither in the *NL* nor in the sagas is the ring as special as it becomes in Wagner's hand.) This love is corrupted when it comes into contact with a degenerate civilization. They were true lovers, however, and Brynhild, in mounting the pyre to join him in a Viking funeral, would perhaps save her lover in something of the same fashion as did Senta. Together they cast off the corrupt world and rise to a Valhalla of some sort. This sexual coupling, as seen by Wagner, is a necessary part of being a complete person and Wagner would have needed this for such a totemic pair. It would have been a simple scenario without the epic, world-embracing dimension personified by the Norns, the Valkyrs, the 'water nymphs' and Alberich, and without significant reference to Wotan or narrative of past history. As such, this would not do for Wagner. Furthermore, he would likely now have his sights on a bigger canvas. Nevertheless, this putative *Siegfrieds Tod* is a viable drama.

Some choices made

Ignoring the prehistory, therefore, we can have a clear view of the input from each of the main sources into this proto-plot. We will also see why some matters were not included. That we who now contemplate the result could not ourselves have put it together is to be expected but we can with hindsight see how the choices were made. We will take each of the actions in that putative drama in the order it appears.

Sigurd learning about Brynhild from a wood bird is found in the three Nordic sagas and *TS*. The ability to understand birdsong is a sign in mythology of acquired wisdom; for Wagner it is both the best device for moving the plot along and also a symbol of Sigurd's distinction. For Odin has two ravens who gather news for him and, in one of the subsidiary sources read by Wagner, a Danish king Dag was similarly helped by a sparrow until the bird died and the king foundered.

Sigurd meeting with Brynhild presents us with the first choice that had to be made. As the reader can readily ascertain, Brynhild is portrayed in different ways in the *VS*. On the one hand as a princess who has a sister, a father *and* foster father, and a brother-in-law - one who *seemingly* preferred fighting to sewing but who is encountered making tapestry. On the other hand, she is a disobedient servant of Odin who was put to sleep as a punishment and deprived of her valkyr-like role. That there are two incompatible descriptions is probably because there were two separate stories, the first pertaining to an aristocrat so distinguished that she was 'engaged' as a valkyr, which then morphed into that of the semi-divine valkyr. The latter has been put to sleep on a mountain by Odin for disobedience. She is surrounded by 'flickering flames'. All the Nordic sources specify that Gunnar, as the betrayal of Brynhild is underway, fails to get through the fire and that is why Sigurd - in an act of friendly support - changes shape with him and helps him out. Given that, Wagner had no choice but to choose the heroic splendour of Sigurd passing through that fire at their first meeting. No consideration of the 'domestic' option was possible: it was not dramatic nor did it tie in with the rest of the story.

Sigurd and the memory drug is mentioned in two sources: *PE* and *VS*. (*SE* is so cursory that nothing can be made of it.) *TS* has no suggestion of memory loss: Sigurd simply helps Gunnar to his bride as part of his service to the king: the message to his former lover is that she is now being offered to his friend who is a great king to whom obligation is due. If Sigurd is not to appear either casual or venal as in *TS*, the drugged drink is a necessary plot device. In both sources where it is mentioned, the drug is administered by Gudrun's mother. The explicit suggestion in *PE* is that Sigurd was tricked and no commentator on the sources (as opposed to the *Ring*) has suggested that the drug is a coded way of saying that Sigurd simply betrayed Brynhild.

The problem Wagner then faced with the drug was that of dramatic pace. For the essence of *Siegfrieds Tod* is speed and violence. All primary sources move at a leisurely pace and events are spread over a long period. In all pertinent primary sources Sigurd spends considerable time at the court of Gunnar before the drug is administered by Gudrun's mother Grimhild, and its purpose is *not* to make Sigurd fall instantly in love with Gudrun but to make him forget Brynhild, so that he is then enabled to fall in love with the very beautiful sister of his kingly lord and blood brother. [1] This process of

---

[1] Newman and Shaw are to be cited as those who question the structure of the *Ring* but Jessie Weston in her *Legends of the Wagner Drama* makes a more fundamental objection. This is that the original legends of Sigurd, which were the starting points of both the Nordic and Germanic sources, have such deep roots that the events leading up to his death could have been made the subject of the whole tetralogy, disregarding any connection to the gods. Well, perhaps, but that would have been a drama about the fall of Burgundy and not about Sigurd's death. Nevertheless, one can see two operas being devoted to another sort of story in which Sigurd is shown as the warrior/diplomat/counsellor *par excellence* who is then betrayed. Then would the elaborate

assimilation is particularly emphasised in *TS* where Sigurd carries out many warlike and diplomatic feats on behalf of Gunnar and *also* of Gunnar's traditional enemy Thidrik (Theodoric), the central person in the story. After a crisis has been resolved to the satisfaction of both Gunnar and Thidrik, we read:

> Then King Theodoric and his warriors made the journey [to Worms, Gunnar's capital] with King Gunnar, Hagen and Sigurd. There the young Lord Sigurd married Gudrun, the sister of Gunnar and Hagen, who brought with her a dowry comprising half the wealth of the kingdom. The wedding celebrations lasted for five days.

None of this would do for Wagner – all too slow and complex. Nowhere in the sagas is there a 'love at first sight' drug – it is far too romantic a notion. The most famous example, which Wagner must have known, is in *A midsummer night's dream:* 'What thou seest when thou dost wake/Do it for thy true love take.' And another example lay nearer to home. For the first time specific reference can now be made to Fouqué's *Sigurd der Schlangentödter*. In this drama, securely based on the *Volsung Saga*, Sigurd is presented with the drugged drink by Gudrun's mother Grimhilde soon after arriving at court. His memory of recent events fades before our eyes; when all has receded, Gudrun is brought before him and instant infatuation overwhelms him (p.464). Some such dramatic device was imperative. In Shakespeare and now in Fouqué it drives the plot forward at breakneck speed. Instead of about three years, we see Sigurd make his fatal matrimonial blunder in a page of text. Wagner seized hold of this dramaturgic device. One further step was needed to tighten the plot, namely to dispense with the mother Grimhilde, whose only critical function in the sagas is to administer the fateful drink.

One can argue that the slower process is more feasible. Most recently, Roger Scruton says: 'This is clearly another of those transitions in which a long process is presented as taking place in a moment. The inevitable corruption of Siegfried by a world in which resentment and lust for power have made love negligible and is here presented as a symbol'. (RS/RT,125) The problem is that this is not how one sees it on stage and, at the same time, it ignores the universal understanding of compulsive sexual infatuation – the *coup de foudre* which overwhelms reason.

Gunnar's wish to marry Brynhild is the spring within the primary sources which sets the machinery of destruction into motion. The roots of this would have been a dynastic marriage in some long distant past and this survives in the sources where Brynhild is either an aristocrat of wealth and beauty or a queen with her own court. She is also renowned for wisdom, witness Gudrun's visit to her in *VS* 26/27. Grimhilde, Gunnar's mother in the Nordic sources, proposes the union in order to increase the prestige of

---

scenarios set forth in the sagas have been germane. Ms Weston does not suggest that Wagner should have followed this course. Her regret is that the *Ring* does not do justice to the complexities of the mighty range of fables on which it was based. (See Appendix F)

Burgundy, and this is the same reason that she wanted Sigurd to marry her daughter: her family would be allied to the two most celebrated people currently around. Note, however, that it does not need her presence on stage to put this reason forward; there is always Hagen.

An oath of blood brotherhood between Sigurd and Gunnar is critical for Wagner's plot. Breaking the oath is a necessary condition for his murder: such an oath is in the *Myth*: 'they drink to blood brotherhood and swear oaths.' Oaths are sworn in the sources but they are only of friendship and loyalty. That would have done but perhaps Wagner took advantage of Grimm who in *DM* refers to ceremonies involving mixing of blood - a practice endorsed by one contemporary scholar familiar to the composer. So the oath is now the strongest that it is possible to have - full blood brotherhood (see EM/WN,96/7). There is one more choice to make. Only in *NL* is this oath sworn before Sigurd marries Gudrun; he commits himself to help Gunnar win Brynhild because of his own wish to marry Gudrun: 'I love her as my own life and soul, and I shall serve you gladly to [this] end, that she shall marry me.' In all three of the Nordic sources, the oath takes place after Sigurd has sojourned in Burgundy for some time and after he has married Gudrun; the ceremony is the final cementing of the family relationship. This would not do for Wagner, who would need to place it earlier in order to drive forward the plot. Hence, the *NL* option is chosen.

Sigurd takes on the shape of Gunnar in the Nordic sagas to win Brynhild and this magic power is provided by Grimhilde. By this means Sigurd, in the guise of Gunnar, passes for the second time through the 'flickering flame'. This is the climax of the conspiracy that started with the drug of forgetfulness. All are of a piece – something evil is happening. This action requires the other two to complete the conspiracy.

Sigurd taking the ring from Brynhild in the guise of Gunnar is the centre of the Sigurd/Brynhild story - the point of no return. It happens in all five relevant primary sources and clearly speaks of a betrayal. But all sources present it as something rather formal for, although Brynhild is deeply disturbed by another man seemingly coming through the fire for her (p.95), she accepts it at face value and is prepared to live with it. The two Germanic versions, however, see her betrayed in a worse manner. In *NL*, she is tricked by Sigurd 'standing in' for Gunnar in the athletic contest, which obliges her to agree that Gunnar shall be her husband. However, before she will *accept* him and consummate the marriage, he must first overwhelm her physically and subdue her in bed. Gunnar cannot do this so a second, outrageous deceit follows. Under cover of darkness, as inferred in *Das Nibelungenlied*, Sigurd slips into her bed, wrestles her into submission and has sex with her. After which he swaps place again with Gunnar. This last outrage also happens in *TS*, and this time the transaction is explicit. Wagner now has to choose the Nordic or Germanic versions and he would choose the former in principle because the latter would be shabby and disgusting.

Brynhild sees the ring on the hand of Gudrun and this is always the manner in every source by which she realises the truth of her betrayal. Deeper sexual humiliation cannot easily be imagined nor can the magnitude of this moment in the drama be overstated. This has nothing whatsoever to do with the Ring either as a symbol of power or as curse-laden; its significance is that when Brynhild turns against him, Sigurd is done for. But it is clear that Wagner could not use the material as given. The movements of the fateful ring in this postulated 'domestic' drama are as follows: given by Sigurd as a pledge of love; taken back from her (by Sigurd in disguise) after she accepts 'Gunnar' as her new husband; given by Sigurd to his wife Gudrun, presumably as a new additional token of his love for her; finally flaunted by Gudrun before Brynhild's face. In the sagas the purpose of the action is to bring on the quarrel and for Gudrun to be the major figure. But for it to work on stage, the audience would have to see Siegfried give it to Gutrune in a small scene that adds nothing to the drama. So there is not stage time for Wagner to show how the ring ended up with her. The saga story would be feasible but far too cumbersome and with too much emphasis on Gudrun/Gutrune. Wagner always strained to use the sources truthfully but this defeated him and so the ring stayed on Siegfried's own finger.

Brynhild's incitement of Gunnar and Hagen to kill Sigurd, as described in the primary sources, is seemingly because she is driven mad by the revelation of her betrayal. *Volsung Saga* has her take to her bed, howl persistently with the door open, refuse to talk to anyone other than once with Sigurd and what she then says shows a disturbed mind. In no sense, however, are her actions in driving on her two co-conspirators thought unreasonable; by and large the facts are stated and left at that. She is always shown as relentless and the leader in the plot.

The murder of Sigurd is presented in two versions. In the Germanic sources he is killed by Hagen, speared through his back, where he is vulnerable, while he bends down to drink from a fresh stream. In the Nordic sources he is stabbed in bed by Gunnar's younger brother Guttorn; he carries it out so that Gunnar does not break his oath of brotherhood – an unthinkable crime in Viking countries. Before dying, Sigurd kills Guttorn by throwing his sword at him. This is weak drama. That it persists through into *VS* is probably because an ineradicable tradition had been passed down orally by the travelling bards – perhaps an ancient story of a family conspiring to murder an interloper. Moreover, Sigurd is in bed with Gudrun when he is killed. Wagner would not have given this a moment's consideration. The forest murder is clearly more dramatic with Hagen as a ready-made killer, even if his motivation in *NL* and *TS* is different.

Brynhild mortally stabs herself and this does not surprise, for her *raison d'etre* was destroyed with the revelation of the great betrayal. In the Germanic sources this does not happen: she simply disappears from the story, which becomes a death struggle between Gudrun and Hagen. But this can now be understood for her role is really to be the means by which the final turmoil of the Burgundian court is set in train.

The joint cremation of the two lovers is ordained by Brynhild after she has stabbed herself and is dying. They shall share the same funeral pyre. *PE* is the basic Nordic source and has her demand also that the sword Gram lie between them, as it did once before. Her will is obeyed without demur. This is an acknowledgement in the sagas of her heroism and virtue and was what Wagner would have wanted.

Wagner's originality

The initial purpose was a drama about Siegfried and the main lines of a viable Siegfried story could have been established by Wagner as soon as he got to grips with the Nordic sources. The *Volsung Saga* is the critical text for it disregards the actions of the gods, saving Odin's sporadic contact with the Volsung tribe. The work is short and direct and the translation used for this discussion runs to only 75 pages. The story sketched out on p.56 has powerful potential: the melodramatic outlines *of the action* chime with that in the *Myth* and in the poem of *Siegfrieds Tod*.

Examination of this proto-plot enables us to see the ingredients available for use and to see that there was likely to have been no particular difficulty in assembling it. Wagner tried to keep as close as possible to the myths in the hope of penetrating the *zeitgeist* of the German people in the same way that he imagined Aeschylus did with his own audience. What we have here is a distillation of the most stage-worthy elements in the sources, and what is used lies at the heart of the story about Sigurd and Brynhild.

All the building blocks are before us. These are four. Firstly - the sources; secondly - Wagner's wish to be truthful to them; thirdly - the manner in which his imagination would have worked upon them; fourthly - the looming presence of the gods, waiting to enter the story, and encapsulated in the narrative of their dissolution in *Ragnarök*.

The originality of Wagner's final conception is matched only by that at its inception, in the *Myth* and its immediate sequel *Siegfrieds Tod*. Wagner goes against the grain of everything similar that had gone before. The next chapter, for example, reveals a portrait of Siegfried that is distinct from the Sigurd elaborated in the six primary sources. These distinctions are subtle and never violate the intentions of the various anonymous writers. Nevertheless, Wagner's Siegfried is coherently shaped and his life has a trajectory and focus quite different from the original Sigurd.

I hope the extent and range of this originality will be clear as the chapters unfold. At some point a reader may be tempted to look through Appendix E, a synopsis and analysis of *Sigurd der Schlangentödter*, with detail on its background and its interaction with the *Ring*. Three matters at very least suggest that Wagner was well aware of Fouqué's dramatic poem: the structure of *Siegfried* and *Götterdämmerung*, the role of the Norns and the impact of Gutrune upon Siegfried. As much significance should also be accorded to where Wagner's treatment differs from that of Fouqué. Comparison shows how differently from all other artists Wagner saw the story and character of his hero. Until Elizabeth Magee made clear the almost certain contact between the creations of the two artists, almost the only reference to Fouqué by commentators was the possible influence on *Lohengrin* of his novella *Undine*. This link is made *via* ETA Hoffman's opera based on the novella and Heinrich Marschner's opera *Hans Heiling*. In comparison, *Sigurd der Schlangentödter* has been ignored and the appendix is the only available commentary upon it in English.

Wagner nowhere mentions Fouqué's work, probably due to his well-known reluctance to acknowledge influence from other than the greatest, such as Beethoven or Shakespeare, in whose august company he felt entitled to place himself. He must have read the work. It was a narrative that had jostled alongside the *Nibelungenlied* for 40 years and also concentrated upon Sigurd's rise and fall. Fouqué was both celebrated and a friend of his beloved and learned Uncle Adolph with whom he stayed in his youth, so it is even possible that he saw a copy as a boy.

◇ ◇ ◇ ◇ ◇ ◇

5

The hero Siegfried

This study is to raise the profile of Siegfried. The *Ring* story moves from a critical moment in Wotan's rule over his cosmos, through a period of about 50 years, at which point the god and his work are both destroyed. This destruction is brought about suddenly over a period as short as seven days, which culminates in the death of Siegfried. His death is the necessary and sufficient condition for the destruction. The detailed analysis starts (and will end), therefore, with this enigmatic man.

The full implications of the *Ring* cannot be grasped without first understanding how Wagner perceived and what he intended by Siegfried at the start of his work, and how these perceptions developed over the years until the text was completed in 1853. Siegfried is more complex by far than is Wotan and is the person most difficult to come to grips with.

Discussion of the plot so far has been hypothetical since no one can know whether the scenario proposed in the previous chapter was actually part of Wagner's creative process. Move beyond the hypothetical, however, and there is the *Myth* - which allows examination of what Wagner certainly did have in mind. Any examination, therefore, will also embrace the proto-plot sketched out in the previous chapter.

The mythic hero

Wagner particularly wanted to write a drama about a hero. After *Lohengrin* was out of the way, Friedrich Barbarossa, Achilles, Jesus and Wieland tussled with Siegfried for his attention (p.454). The one thing they all have in common, including Jesus in the extensive sketch made, is that the prime quality of each was heroism. But what does it mean to be heroic? Nowadays we want role models but that is certainly not the function of a mythic hero and Siegfried is not that sort of man. Wagner sought the archetype of a hero who would be good for all time, and not a role model.

Theories of such an archetype have emerged since Wagner created Siegfried, starting with Johann von Hahn (1876) and Otto Rank (1909), and they construct a picture different from modern expectations and thus more akin to the character and exploits of Siegfried. The most comprehensive treatment, taking account of von Hahn and Rank, is that of Lord Raglan in his book *The Hero* (1936). Below are the defining acts and characteristics from a total of 22 which apply to Siegfried in three developmental stages of the *Ring*.

Stage		Raglan	Proto-plot	Myth	Ring
Birth and upbringing	1	Mother is a princess	∧	1	
	2	Reputed to be son of a god	|	½	½
	3	Father is a king	N/A	1	
	4	Father related to mother	|	1	1
	5	Unusual conception	|	1	1
	6	Death is planned, usually by father or maternal grandfather	|	½	½
	7	Spirited away	|		½
	8	Reared by foster parents in a far country	|	1	1
	9	No details of childhood	∨	½	½
Adventures & victory	10	Goes to future kingdom	1	1	1
	11	Is victor over king or dragon	1	1	1
	12	Becomes king	1		
	13	Marries a princess	1	1	1
Period of success	14	Reigns for a time and prescribes laws	N/A	N/A	N/A
Decline	15	Loses favour with gods or his subjects	1	1	1
	16	Meets with mysterious death	1	1	1
	17	His body is not buried	1	1	1
			7	12½	11

Note: ½ = approximation.
2: Siegfried is the grandson of Wotan.
6: His death is planned by Regin in the sources.
7: He is saved by Sieglinde.
For the record, the items omitted from the list occur in the birth and decline stages and are: his mother is a royal virgin; he is driven from throne and city; death occurs at the top of a hill; his children – if any – do not succeed him; he has one or more holy sepulchres in his memory.

Apart from the remarkable manner in which Siegfried fulfils so many of the 22 criteria, what is noticeable is that the characteristics are attributes or actions and not moral qualities. Over half the attributes apply to parentage and youth, both out of personal control. The result conveys a mysterious and tumultuous history before maturity: the sense that 'herohood is predestined and not attained'. (JC/HTF, 274) A strange birth and obscure childhood is a *necessary* condition for epic heroism. In the second half of life, with maturity reached, action by the hero is needed as well as attributes. These actions also seem pre-ordained and ritualistic, for they also appear to be *necessary* conditions. When combined with those of the first half of life, we have the *necessary and sufficient* conditions to be designated a hero. These are the accreditations of heroism and the achievements are so common that we can indeed say that they are 'mythic' in two senses. The first is the universality of the attributes; the second is that they do not correspond to heroism as portrayed in our daily newspapers.

In the second half of life courage and character are required to perform the ordained feats. The purpose is to serve and benefit the community to a profound degree – to work for the common good - but in many cases it is the *result* of these acts of heroic ritual, and not the motivation, that counts. [A]

A note about Hegel's view of heroes and heroism.

At this point the question 'What about Hegel?' can arise. He certainly had much to say about heroism and we know that Wagner was reading *The philosophy of history* during 1848. Hegel's thesis was that history followed the thrust of what he called the World Spirit, and that historical progress required decisive action by an heroic individual. The aims of 'great historical man . . . involve those large issues which are the will of World Spirit. They may be called heroes in as much as they have derived their purposes and their vocation, not from the calm, regular cause of things sanctioned by the existing order but from a concealed fount . . . They are men who appear to draw the impulse of their lives from themselves. Such individuals had no consciousness of the general idea they were unfolding . . . on the contrary, they were practical, political men who had an insight into the requirements of the time - *what was ripe for development.*'

Hegel's paradigmatic heroes were Julius Caesar, Napoleon and Alexander the Great - political or military men who create or topple states. Claims can and have been made that Siegfried represents such a person - at least in the first draft of the *Myth* and *Siegfrieds Tod*. The claim is questionable. Siegfried - as we shall see - certainly 'drew the impulse' of his life from himself and 'had no consciousness of the general idea' that was to unfold. But it is hard to make connection between either the motivations of Siegfried and of Napoleon or Julius Caesar, or between their actions.

If Wagner took note of Hegel's wider philosophy, it is only as a background support to the thrust of his story as a whole and cannot be seen to shape the content of the drama

---

[A] This sense of ritual is also conveyed by Jacob Grimm in his *Deutsche Mythologie*. Of his genealogy and heroic qualities, he writes: 'Such a flood of splendour falls on Sigfrid in the [*PE*] poems *that we need not stick at trifles*; his whole nature has evident traces of the superhuman: brought up an elf Regin, beloved by a valkyr Brynhild, instructed in his destiny by the wise man Grippir [as in VS chapter 16]. He wears the helmet of invisibility, is vulnerable only on one spot of his body, as Achilles was in the heel, and he achieves the rich hoard of the Nibelungs.' (Grimm, 371) The early italicised comment [added by the author] that 'we need not stick at trifles' makes clear that Grimm is describing the *attributes*, the symbols and signs that Siegfried is a hero. There is not much morality or moral courage to it.

in any detail. It is easy to raise a possible connection without actually linking it to the drama. Moreover, when a connection between the philosophy and a particular moment in the drama *is* made, this can go no further than to assert that it *might* have been in the composer's mind. The connection is made *after the event* and does not illuminate the stage action. The same outcome can be traced within the general behaviour of human beings under stress. [B]

On occasion, a writer has gone further. Sandra Corse in *Wagner and the New Consciousness* (Rutherford, 1990) presents the *Ring* in terms of Hegelian thought. Like the better-known *Wagner's* Ring *and it symbols,* in which Robert Donington puts forward a Jungian view, Corse has to push the story into a straitjacket for her theory to work. In neither case can one call the effort mistaken but for many people the effort to absorb such a specific colouring will be an acquired taste.

Siegfried in the proto-drama

To return to Raglan's list. This can be divided into four stages, as seen in the table:
- A problematic birth and upbringing
- A series of successful adventures which culminate in triumph which (under item 10) can include finding distinguished service abroad with a local king
- A period of success following the triumph
- A decline – often brought about by betrayal or desertion – and death

The first of these is not included in the proto-drama: Siegfried's birth and upbringing are consequent on the lives of Siegmund and Sieglinde and will be discussed separately. We can also discount the third - the period of success. Sigurd nobly and effectively serves Gunnar and the Burgundian court as detailed in the *Nibelungenlied* and *Volsung Saga* summaries within the Appendices, and in *Thidriks Saga*. In the *NL* he lives several years as an impressive king in his own right before his fatal return to Burgundy. But this spread of years was of no use in a staged drama: in proto-plot and the *Ring* Siegfried moves in quick time from triumph to disaster.

The point of raising these matters now and in the context of the proto-drama is that the most crucial interpretative issues about Siegfried have nothing whatsoever to do with Wotan. In this proto-plot for *Siegfrieds Tod* we are considering a story about Sigurd as seen in the sources. The proto-plot is my fiction but this fiction is validated by Wagner's subsequent treatment of the sources in terms of the prototype of a mythic hero. In consequence, readers will note that no less than half of this chapter examines Siegfried as *imagined* in the proto-drama, and half as *seen* in the *Myth* and *Siegfrieds Tod*. Wotan is left entirely out of the count in this first part of the examination.

[B] See RS/RT, 22.

In our proto-drama, Siegfried fulfils three of the required tasks: Fafner is the slain dragon (and this feat occurs in all six of the primary sources), Brünnhilde is the princess to be won and the service to the foreign king is the help he gives to Gunther. He needs, therefore, to do no more to qualify as a mythic hero: he fits into the template that has emerged over the centuries and which defines epic heroism.

Killing a dragon has always been a primary function of heroes. Dragons are seen as agents of darkness and destruction: hence the Archangel Michael overcoming the serpent which is seen as Satan in the Book of Revelations. The non-Christian myth can be perceived in three different ways. When seen as the symbolic victory of order over chaos it is a struggle for sovereignty with the expectation that order will be restored. When seen as a victory of birth over death it is a symbol of fertility; those stories which feature a knight slaying the dragon in order to rescue a woman (eg St George) probably relate to that origin. The myths which present the story as the struggle between stagnation (in Winter) and growth (in the Spring) symbolise the annual cycle of the seasons.

That Wagner chose the last option as the background meaning is implied within *Die Wibelungen*, the essay written in early 1849 and therefore undergoing gestation at the same time as the *Myth* was shaping itself. In considering the 'oldest meaning' of the Nibelung Hoard myth we 'recognise Siegfried as God of Light or Sun God.' (RW/PW7, 263) Mankind identified creation with 'Light, the Day, the Sun . . . the breaking of day out of night . . . appeared to him as the victory of light over darkness.' (RW/PW7, 274) 'Light vanquished Darkness when Siegfried slew the Nibelung-dragon . . . we recognise the splendour of the earth - when seen in the dawn sunlight - as our possession to enjoy, when night and its gloomy dragon wings have finally been routed.' (RW/PW7, 276)

The text of *Die Wibelungen* must be taken seriously. It is obscure and a reader gets the distinct impression that Wagner was grasping at matters which were, in the final resort, not firm or concrete enough to be grasped at all. Nevertheless, within it he reveals his vision of mythic links between Siegfried, sun god, treasure, triumph followed by disaster and death. He felt these matters to be deep in the racial psyche of the people, and an audience presented with some form of dramatic realisation would comprehend the mythic subtext instinctively and without need for reflection, the mental process he so much denigrated.

Betrayal and catastrophe
Notwithstanding any such background, Raglan tells us that whatever the practical achievements such a hero has behind him, they are undermined and come to an end in due course: his people tire of him or he commits some involuntary crime or he is deserted by a protecting god. However worthy, he is sacrificed. Dragon slaying is again the link. In the Nordic sagas this is portrayed as part of Regin's plot against his brother and therefore not epic. Wagner absorbs this mundane motive into a deeper context. As Siegfried symbolises the sun god defeating the dragon of night in *Die Wibelungen*, so

must the cycle continue: as day yields to night and summer to winter, so must the sun god succumb to the forces of darkness – perhaps in order to be reborn in the spring as in the creation myth of Tammuz amongst others. [C]

A hero such as Siegfried must die. He is heroic because he is akin to the sun god. The sun *alone* can kill the darkness because of what it is rather than what it does; conversely, as the sun must go down so must Siegfried. Killing the dragon and winning the princess were seemingly the necessary and sufficient conditions to be a mythic hero; digging down through the ages to primal times tells Wagner that the former achievement is also a sufficient condition for his slaughter. Moreover, the association of Siegfried with the struggle between stagnation and growth carries with it the notion of rebirth in due time.

If Wagner's imagination embraced the idea that death waited in ambush, then this is germane to his view of Siegfried without any regard to a story line about Wotan and/or Alberich.

Underlying Wagner's view of Siegfried, therefore, is the fact that he must die as a sacrifice and this death is seen to have its origins in the death of the sun in winter, killed by the darkness. No such connection can be made to Sigurd in the sagas: Wagner is treating his Siegfried in a different way. But the cause of his death in a drama must be both believable on stage and must also be surrounded by a powerful message of misjudgement. Otherwise, there is a 'blankness', a sameness, in the ubiquitous action of killing the dragon and pain thereafter because of it.

The paragraphs above are an extrapolation, a derivation of Wagner's thoughts in *Die Wibelungen*, and have no connection at all with the Nordic or Germanic sources. When the sources are engaged, Wagner homed in on the single most important fact about Sigurd in the myths. This is that he was murdered, and the reason for the slaughter had nothing to do with being a symbol for the sun god and was also of far greater import than the killing of the dragon.

Siegfried in the *Myth*

Wagner's creative work from 1846 through 1848 coincided with increasing disaffection with his conducting job at the Dresden Opera (p.449) which then mutated into revolutionary fervour as he was caught up in Europe-wide political unrest. Whatever had

---

[C] Tammuz was a Sumerian fertility god and is recorded before 2000BC. In the Autumn he was killed by demons of the underworld but rose again in the Spring and married Annana - a goddess of fertility.

been the first impulse that focussed his mind on heroism, by now this had changed into a zeal to raze the existing order. This informs the *Myth* and *Siegfrieds Tod*. [D]

Self-evidently Wagner wrote the *Myth* only after he had read the seven main sources. The wide canvas in which Siegfried's story is set rose clearly before him and it is remarkable that so much of the plot of the final *Ring* lies in the first 35% of the *Myth*, prior to the detailed sketch for what became *Siegfrieds Tod*.

The nub and pith of the Sigurd story

The previous chapter demonstrates that the centre of the Sigurd/Brynhild story is the moment when he takes 'Andvari's ring' from her. In all five main primary sources (which here excludes *Song of the horny-skinned Sigurd*) he betrays her. He uses subterfuge or disguise and woos her on behalf of Gunnar. It is for this he is murdered. The errors are serious.

- In all five sources, except for *NL*, Sigurd had previously won her for himself.
- In four of the five he uses some form of deceit second time around: *NL* has him stand in as an athlete for Gunnar, wearing a cloak of invisibility, in order to win her; the three Nordic sources employ the ruse of changing shape so that he is disguised. (In *TS* there is no trick or disguise for Sigurd simply says he has sworn to approach her because Gunnar is a mighty king.)
- In all five sources he has sex with Brynhild before Gunnar does. In the three Nordic sources this occurs at the time of the earlier wooing: the *VS* has her bearing a daughter Aslaug as a result. It is worse in both *TS* and *NL* (by implication) when Sigurd deflowers Brynhild by slipping into her marital bed in the dark, and substituting himself for Gunnar, who had been trussed up upon attempting her himself.

There has to be a palliative for such behaviour and two are on offer. Firstly, in the Nordic sources, Sigurd is tricked into drinking a drugged drink and he loses memory of Brynhild. This is not presented as symbolic but as a true excuse – 'tricked by another' (HB/PE, 349). Secondly, in many cases, oaths akin to 'blood brotherhood' bind him to Gunnar and these would put powerful obligations on him, for Gunnar is a king and Sigurd is not. Nevertheless, as in most folk literature, it is the deed that counts and not the qualifications, and therefore guilt attaches to him. The betrayal of Brynhild is the central fact of Sigurd's story and he can be seen to bring about his own death.

This is the essence lifted from the mythic Sigurd in order to fashion Siegfried.

The Nibelung Hoard

This finds its first mention, is described as 'immense' and provides a further premonition of Siegfried's inevitable and fatal destiny. The connection is once again to *Die*

[D] Wagner's views were recorded by the singer/actor Eduard Devrient with whom he met frequently in 1848. The diary entry for 1/6/48 reads: 'Post-prandial visit from Kapellmeister Wagner; we again argued over politics in quite a barbarous way. He wants to destroy in order to rebuild, I want to transform what already exists in order to create a new world'. (SS/RW, 59)

Wibelungen where ownership of 'treasure' brings death in its wake. There are legends in the various primary sources about the Nibelung's Hoard but their origins lie in the ancient Germanic myth associated with the Fall. In Jessie Weston's words:

> The ethical idea of which the legend is an expression is undoubtedly that of the evil influence of gold which according to old German myth was operative alike on gods and men. The golden age, the time of the innocence of the gods, was before they knew gold, before the creation of the dwarf race, which wrought precious metal out of the earth, and thus brought the lust of gold and the passions of greed and avarice into the world. (JW/LWD, 57)

Wagner takes these notions and hardens them in *Die Wibelungen* so that the Hoard is the symbol of worldly power. The struggle between Day (good) and Night (bad) becomes a struggle for power and therefore the victor in any contest becomes the owner of the Hoard.

> When Light vanquished Darkness, when Siegfried slew the Nibelungen-dragon, he further won as victor's spoils the Nibelungen Hoard it guarded. But the possession of this Hoard . . . . . is also the reason for his death, for the dragon's heir now plots to win it back. (RW/PW7, 276)

Wagner is explicit about this in the *Myth*, where a penumbra of lust for treasure and power surrounds Siegfried's death. He is slain by Hagen who wants the Ring because it is the symbol of and route to worldly power. This aspect is mentioned in passing in *NL*, *PE* and *VS*: Hagen tells Gunther that if Siegfried were dead Gunther would be richer and more powerful. The connection between ownership of the Hoard and death is less potent than the struggle between Light and Dark but it is legitimate to see a link between Alberich, the original owner of the Hoard, and Hagen as his 'heir'. In *Die Wibelungen* Wagner imagines the heir of the slaughtered dragon to be Siegfried's enemy but it has greater force if that enemy is heir to Alberich who amassed the Hoard in the first place – as in the *Myth*.

The forging of the sword

Siegfried forging the sword himself is a significant change from all the Nordic sources, in which Regin is the smith. At this early stage in plot development and when Wagner was still thinking of just one opera the change is in the *nature* if not the stage actions of Siegfried. The *Myth* reads:

> Mime brings up Siegfried, and teaches him how to smith and forge. He brings him the two pieces of the broken sword, from which, under Mime's directions, Siegfried forges the sword Balmung.

It may not be much but this adjustment to the sources is a small indication of Siegfried's independence. For it is discernible from both the *NL* and the sagas as condensed into the *VS* that Sigurd is essentially passive throughout the *NL* and largely so in the eddas. In *NL* he may be active in helping the Burgundian royal family but this activity is merely a form of payment: he helps so that he can win Gudrun as his wife. None of the prodigious feats within the story (as opposed to the prehistory as narrated by Hagen) are of his own volition: all are responding to the wishes of Gunnar and Hagen. Sigurd's actions which made him heroic all occurred before the start of the story. *TS* shows him as an initiator on many occasions but noticeably not so in the brusque handing over of Brynhild to his social superior Gunnar. In the primary Nordic sources, the *only* independent action, taken against the advice of others, is his decision to kill the murderers of his father. Otherwise, he follows the advice of his mentor Regin when he kills the dragon and the advice of the wood bird when he seeks out Brynhild.

Wagner would not or could not remove this trait: would not because that would falsify the myth or could not because the references within the sources cannot be disentangled. But he needed to make his hero active, perhaps to ease him from the straitjacket of the hero myth. The forging of the sword is only the first such material change in the action that Wagner is to make, thereby distinguishing Siegfried from the mythic Sigurd.

The latter part of the outline for *Siegfrieds Tod*
It is notable how the brief and sketchy outline of Siegfried's rise to maturity and triumph follows the plot line that matters, namely the slaying of the dragon and the wooing of Brünnhilde. From the moment when he tastes the dragon's blood, through to the winning of Brünnhilde, the *Myth* sketch relates the essentials of the final design of S2 and S3.2. The outline is spare in the extreme and omits much that Wagner would have read in the Nordic sources, homing in on the simple fact that Siegfried learns of Brünnhilde, travels to where she is, penetrates the flames, and wakes and wins her.

The assault on Brünnhilde
The speed and thrust required for stage action entailed the removal of Gunther's mother as the giver of the drug of forgetfulness. For the same reason, the power of the drug – to switch Siegfried's affections from Brünnhilde to Gutrune – had to be instantaneous

Then there is the probable input from Fouqué's *Sigurd der Schlangentödter*. Appendix E shows in detail how Fouqué's dramatic poem may have shaped the two final operas in the cycle. In 1808, Fouqué cut through the complexities of Sigurd's involvement with Gudrun by introducing the drug which obliterates Brynhild from his memory (p.464). Once done, instant desire for Gudrun floods through him when he sees her for the first time. Wagner would have seized on this immediately, had he read it; he would have seen the potential for swift, graphic stage action.

Another way of looking at it, however, is that the intention was not to portray the drug as a trick but as a symbol of the corruption of Siegfried, which has occurred over a longer period. (The sources have Sigurd staying for a long time at Gunnar's court.) This view of the scene in the completed *Götterdämmerung* is taken by several writers, the most recent being the late Roger Scruton. The effect on Siegfried of the drugged drink is an example of a 'transition in which a long process is presented as though it takes place in a moment. The inevitable corruption of Siegfried in which resentment and the lust for power have made love negotiable is here represented as a symbol.' (RS/RT, 125)

He groups this event with others, such as the opening scene for the lovers in G1.1, when it can have been possible for Siegfried and Brünnhilde to spend some time together in the mountain top refuge before Siegfried left for his adventures, and the transition represented by the interlude of the journey to the Rhine. The first of these is as the two lovers make their first appearance on stage in a new opera, which leads to the second, being the orchestral interlude *Siegfried's Rhine Journey*. But whereas the position of these two scenes can persuade toward this interpretation, the collapse of Siegfried at the sight of Gutrune does not: the action is integrated into a believable drama about a *coup de foudre* that is uncomfortable to see. Wagner does not want us to reflect on what it might represent.

A variation on this theory is put forward by Derek Hughes. Until Siegfried arrives at the Gibichung court all his actions have been driven by 'primordial need'. He pursues his own innate desires (a matter that is comprehensively covered later in the chapter) which is to culminate in the winning of Brünnhilde. The Gibichung society, however, lives according to social conventions, so 'the drinking of the potion in *Götterdämmerung* signifies the boundary at which the restrictive artifice of society obliterates primal need'. (DH/C&S,196) Entering society changes Siegfried at a stroke. Wagner's scorn of custom makes this idea feasible. In consequence, it is not some general moral corruption within Siegfried (who to this extent is without fault) but is symptomatic of an inevitable degradation within our species. It is thus similar to Wotan needing his primal spear wherewith to govern the world, and the roots of both lie in Adam and Eve eating the apple from the tree of the knowledge of good and evil. Moreover, since neither Siegfried nor Wotan nor Adam and Eve could move forward without their respective actions, this perception becomes the foundation of all commentaries that see the *Ring* as pessimistic at its core. [E] Once again, however, theory does not match stage action.

To return to the narrative. The means by which Brünnhilde is deceived is, of course, the Tarnhelm and we can ask why the text specifically says that the idea of using it came from Siegfried with the added comment that 'Siegfried for the first and only time exerts his power as ruler of the Nibelungs.' He uses this power with enthusiasm, first by turning himself into a clone of Gunther and then by the instantaneous transportation from the mountain back to the palace. The results are described in brutal fashion. The *only* use of the immense potential which follows from victory over the powers of darkness is to transform himself into the shape of another man in order violently to subdue a woman he has never seen (as it would have seemed to him at that point), tear the wedding ring from her hand and force her into the cave.

It is difficult to make much of a case for Siegfried in this matter. The drug is portrayed as a trick, and its power to remove the memory of and love for one woman with passion for another can be necessary for dramatic pace. But the drug once taken, a straight reading of the text puts Siegfried in a bad light. He it is who thinks that this new

---

[E] This major issue will be taken forward in Chapter 15.

power can best be put to a very dubious use and he seems to carry out a disgusting stratagem with relish. One can see this as a third example of Wagner adapting the sources to establish a less passive view of Siegfried. It certainly does that and this is fine as long as it is not seen as too 'pseudo-analytical', viewing it like a Shakespeare text.

Siegfried denies taking the Ring from Brünnhilde

Requirement of staging also made it necessary to dispense with the scene in the sources when Brynhild sees that Gudrun has the Ring. That being so, the obvious and credible alternative was for her to see it on Siegfried's hand. The decision was taken early and shows careful thought: for the first time, Wagner sketches in the dialogue:

> Brünnhilde: So was it Siegfried who took the ring from her?
>
> Siegfried: I did not take it from any woman - my right arm won it for me from the giant/dragon; through it am I the lord of the Nibelungs, and to no one will I give over that power.

Now Siegfried could be lying, deliberately evading the thrust of the question and choosing to answer the different question of how he first came by the Ring. The problem with that is that it is shabby: whatever faults he may have, this is something he would not do. The implication, therefore, is that Wagner chose to afflict Siegfried with selective amnesia: the only matter forgotten is *everything* to do with the wooing and winning of Brünnhilde. This solution is simple, direct and successful: when an audience now hears this denial as amended for the final text, there is no feeling of unreality. Here is the first major example of Wagner diverging from his sources; in the urgency of stage action he presents the audience with a vivid, believable situation. Moreover, those three lines of text in the *Myth* bespeak the lack of guile which underpins Siegfried as Wagner saw him.

The composer is at pains to keep in the forefront of his mind the fatality attached to ownership of the Nibelung Hoard: 'through [the Ring] I am the Lord of the Nibelungs, and to no one will I give over that power'.

Siegfried's encounter with the Rhinedaughters

We have examined the reasons why Wagner chose the forest as the scene of Siegfried's murder and this location also provides a fourth chance to sketch in his early intention to rehabilitate the hero, to rescue him from anonymity and absence of 'character'. The solution is masterly. Siegfried has to die and has to know it for the sake of the drama. A hero, furthermore, should learn about such an ordained death from someone in a different plane of existence. [F]

Wagner's solution is to adapt an episode from the latter part of *NL*, after Sigurd's death (an episode which is also found in *TS*). Hagen and Gunnar are on their way to Hungary in response to Gudrun's invitation. Hagen travels ahead along the river Danube on reconnaissance and comes upon two water sprites bathing in the water. He

---

[F] Shakespeare has the ghost of Clarence haunting Richard III on the eve of Bosworth Field with: 'Tomorrow in the battle think on me! / And fall thy edgeless sword: despair and die!'

takes up their clothes from the bank and they offer to trade: the clothes for a prophecy on the outcome of the expedition. The answer they give is that the invitation extended by Gudrun is malicious, and will end in the destruction of the Burgundian Kingdom. Wagner improves this by removing all the negotiating paraphernalia and replacing it with a stark choice: Siegfried will die unless he throws the Ring into the Rhine.

The evidence that Wagner laid weight on this episode is – as the reader can see - the eruption into the narrative of the most sustained passage of draft dialogue in the *Myth* (p.431). The purpose is clear: to demonstrate his independence from all external forces. The dialogue, moreover, is preceded by the only explanatory, bracketed comment in the text. 'He is guiltless but he takes upon himself the guilt of the gods and atones for their sins by means of his defiance and independence.' Perhaps Wagner sensed from the start that he might get himself into something of a fix with the story about his hero as portrayed in the *Myth*.

The return of Siegfried's memory

Soon after the scene with the Rhinedaughters there is another that sympathetically rounds out Siegfried's character. No antidote to the drug is needed for him to recall Brünnhilde: 'his memory rises clearly now; how he surmounted the fire enshrouded rock and wakened' her. With these few words, a true poignancy touches the sketch for the only time - a weak echo of the moving scene of remorse given verbatim in *VS* 31:

> 'You surpass all men, yet no woman has become more loathsome to you than I'
>
> 'Something else is closer to the truth. I love you more than myself, although I was the object of the deceit that cannot now be changed. Always when my mind was my own it pained me that you were not my wife . . . I could not remember your name . . . I did not recognize you until you were married. And that is my deepest sorrow.'

In October 1848 it would seem that Wagner's instinct was to embrace the poignancy within these passages. Some may think it unfortunate that he was unable to hold on to the scene which shows a reflective side to Siegfried's character that contrasts with the prevailing 'action man' persona. The *Myth* shows a struggle between the brutality of the lead up to and manner of the assault, and the inherent tenderness deliberately inserted by the unknown *VS* author - for nowhere else is it mentioned. The Siegfried seen at the end differs from that seen at the beginning. A dramatist as resourceful as Wagner could have contrived a reconciliation between the two but he did not do so when he came to elaborate the sketch into *Siegfrieds Tod*. Moreover, to keep faith with the new brutality, Wagner had to introduce Hagen with his antidote. In no source is there a need for an antidote. Wagner ignores the hint that his memory returned by some sort of natural reaction. Why this is so will be explained on p.77.

Siegfried's dead hand rises against Hagen

Back in Gunther's palace, after the murder, it is in the *Myth* that the scene is introduced in which the hand of Siegfried's corpse rises against Hagen in defence of the Ring. This incident and its implications are of cardinal consequence.

The rationale for such an episode of fantastical hocus-pocus is not realistic or believable – as Wagner would naturally have wished it to be - but lies near the very roots of the developing story. For the sake of dramatic thrust he had made the inevitable choice that Brünnhilde must see the Ring on Siegfried's hand where, therefore, it had to stay. How could he continue to convey something special in Siegfried's heroic nature and how was he to stop Hagen, who had just killed Gunther, from taking the Ring?

Wagner must have thought long and hard over this problem: we can presume he did not like the credibility gap but could find no better solution than what we now see and which never changed. This is the sort of matter which an intelligent spectator can ponder upon and the reader is invited to come up with a better solution, noting that to date no one has done so. An indication of deep thinking by Wagner is that neither any of the sources nor any mythology has precedent for the raised dead hand. He must have seen some link to the incident in *NL* when Sigurd's wounds bleed as Hagen approaches his corpse. Now this is no more feasible than the arm rising up but because it is reactive rather than aggressive it grates less against reality. Perhaps it is due to this that the omen has retained a grisly romantic currency in peoples of Germanic origin, including the English. ᴳ Wagner chose not to use it and we can see the problems of keeping to the primary sources. Powerfully dramatic as it is, the time taken to register the incident slows the action for it entails that horror must be expressed in words and not *shown*. Given both that delay and Hagen's determination, it is doubtful that this would have stopped him from grabbing the Ring. Hence the device is conjured up by Wagner.

What then lies behind Wagner's invention of an incident so extreme? Hitherto within the *Myth* the Ring has been just an artefact that pushes the plot along. It has actually *done* nothing. Alberich does curse the Ring in *Myth-RG4* but no consequences follow from it for, at that stage, the giants have so little interest in it that they give it to the anonymous dragon along with the rest of the treasure. Thereafter it does not enter the narrative, until Brünnhilde sees it on Siegfried's hand. It is not until *Myth-G3.2* when Hagen claims it and Siegfried's dead hand rises up that something 'happens' to the Ring.

A number of possibilities rise to mind. Did Wagner sense the strangeness attaching to the heroic life, namely that it is not so much what the hero does but more what he is? Is the rising hand an indication that he is guiltless in the sense that he won the Ring in fair fight and was never interested in its alleged powers? Has Siegfried's murder – something *done* to him - atoned for the sins of the gods, so that – for that reason also -

---

ᴳ Note Lady Anne, speaking to Richard, Duke of Gloucester (soon to be Richard III), who has murdered her husband, Prince Edward, heir to King Henry VI, in Shakespeare's *Rich-ard III*:

> O, gentlemen, see, see! dead Henry's wounds / Open their congeal'd mouths and bleed afresh. / Blush, blush, thou lump of foul deformity; /For 'tis thy presence that exhales this blood / From cold and empty veins, where no blood swells; /Thy deed, inhuman and unnatural, /Provokes this deluge most unnatural.

the Ring thereby belongs to him as of right? Maybe it is not the dead Siegfried raising his arm but the Ring itself raising the arm to assert this?

Whatever the answer, the fact is that the Ring does not affect Siegfried as it does all other characters. The repulse of Hagen says that he is free of the curse laid upon it and in this he is different from all others.

Siegfried in *Siegfrieds Tod*

The poem was written in about a month at high speed at the same time as Wagner was also pondering upon *Friedrich Barbarossa*. Thirty-six of the forty-nine pages in the translation are identical as makes no difference to those in *Götterdämmerung*.

The oath of blood brotherhood

The sources needed to be tweaked in order to turn the routine medieval business of swearing friendship and loyalty into the drastic action that might have found a place in the proto-plot (p.60). Now, in the few weeks between the completion of the *Myth* and that of *Siegfrieds Tod*, there was generated a most violent stage action - the leeching of the blood of each brother-to-be in a goblet which is then drunk by them both. This is nowhere to be found in any source Wagner read and, indeed, the exact like is not to be found elsewhere. Mightily melodramatic, it sets the tone for the entire opera until Brünnhilde enters for the Immolation. It is an invention that creates a violent atmosphere of great tumult and also (in the final complete work) underlines the vile nature of Brünnhilde's later betrayal.

Siegfried's memory loss

Hagen makes very clear the nature of the loss, which is specifically to make a man forget all the women he has previously loved. On drinking the drug, Siegfried immediately and totally forgets everything. Gunther describes Brünnhilde as in *Götterdämmerung*, except that she is in a hall (see *VS 21/22* for reference to ramparts) instead of on a rock.

> On mountain high her seat, / A fire burns round the hall
> But he who through the fire breaks / will Brünnhilde's wooer be.

But there is none of that process of memory slipping away that we are to sense as Siegfried echoes the sentences in puzzlement in G1.2. Siegfried's response is immediate: I can do it for you so let's go and then Gudrun can be my wife. The big change from the *Myth* is that there now has to be an antidote administered by Hagen before Siegfried can remember Brünnhilde. Thus is lost the poignancy of powerful memories rising to the surface. Despite Wagner's wish to round out Siegfried's character, as seen in the *Myth*, he here abandons the best avenue that leads to such enrichment as he expands from the draft into the poem. He would not have done this lightly and the reason must be that he wished to reinforce those attributes which distinguish him from Sigurd; he has no time for Sigurd's diplomatic and social skills. I refer again to Sigurd as seen in *Sigurd der Schlangentödter*.

The assault on Brünnhilde

If the *Myth* presents Siegfried's attack on Brünnhilde in stark terms, these are exacerbated in *Siegfrieds Tod*. Siegfried it is who proposes the Tarnhelm as the means to the deceit; Wagner did not have to make it so for it could have been Hagen that reminded him. At the climax of the whole bad business, Siegfried has such phrases as 'You fly from me like a cowering dog which fears punishment . . . Men have been scared to court you for fear of ruin but I will now show the world how cowed you will be – spinning and weaving in my house.' The squeezing of the complex tale into a staged drama would of course make it terse at this point. Whereas the Nordic sources (see *VS 28 & 29*) are leisurely and even courtly over what is, in fact, a black transaction, condensation for the stage makes it quick and violent. Nevertheless, language such as Wagner gives to Siegfried is *designedly* repellent, particularly in the mouth of a potential husband. Wagner penetrated into the unpleasant core of the legend and did not flinch from its message. With reference to the distinction between showing and telling on p.20, it is clear that Wagner *shows* this distasteful matter to us. It is difficult to envisage this text retained should he have continued with this opera on its own. It disgusts, disconcerts and diverts sympathy from his hero. As we shall see, he is either unable or unwilling entirely to resolve this matter.

He also keeps to the sources in respect of the 'wedding'. These vary with regard to how long 'Gunnar' was with the conquered valkyr on the mountain or in her hall but all state unequivocally that the sword Gram lay between them and that there was no sex.

An interim summary

The text of the *Ring* was shaped over two separate periods, the first of which culminated in the *Siegfrieds Tod* poem in November 1848. For the two years thereafter from early 1849 to early 1851, Wagner was involved in revolution and was exiled, and his creative energy went largely into his major theoretical prose works. This is an appropriate point to take stock.

In his attempt to craft a Siegfried drama, Wagner penetrated to the heart of mythic heroism. It matters not whether this was conscious or unconscious but rather that, in advance of later theoretical analysis, he carved out from Germanic and Nordic primary sources something near to an heroic paradigm. He is a man doubly fated to die. If the story of Sigurd dying at the hands of the Gibich family of Burgundy is a legend, then the correspondence found by Wagner between Siegfried and the Sun God is something of greater weight: it is the creation of a new myth. The story which emerges doubly entails this death, first as residue of a fertility rite and second as possessor of the fabulous Hoard, cut down by someone whose father brought about its existence.

Siegfried might also be seen as triply fated, as being also 'marked for death' in the Nordic sources and, by implication in the Germanic, by his betrayal of Brünnhilde into the arms of Gunther. Wagner overtly adopts the notion – explicit in *PE* and endorsed by *SE* and *VS* – that Siegfried was tricked into forgetting Brünnhilde. This will not do. Accident or calamity to a character brought about by a trick played on him or her goes well in farce and can work in comedy when the trick exposes a perceived weakness in the character – witness Malvolio falling for the forged letter in *Twelfth Night* or any occasion when someone is persuaded to act out of character. But if the consequences are serious, then what seems to be a trick is a means to reveal something new. Othello falls unthinkingly for Iago's lies because of a complex twist in his personality, not previously sensed by the audience or the grandees of Venice or probably by Iago himself. Once stirred into life, however, the flaw emerges like a monster from its cave. This shocks the spectator who nevertheless instantly recognises it. No such obvious recognition comes to the reader when he reads Siegfried's brutal words addressed to the terrified Brünnhilde in *Siegfrieds Tod*. The personality loaded by Wagner on Siegfried does not accord with this behaviour and the reader is adrift, except for realising that Wagner intends to present Siegfried's actions as meriting punishment.

Wagner leaves us with a puzzle and we must accept that there can be no clear answer to the behaviour which follows from the drug of selective amnesia. The sources portray these effects in a bad light and Wagner, with no attempt to explain, wants to do the same. We can ask, however, whether he has absorbed and is transmitting something of Aristotle's thoughts on drama. He knew *The Poetics* and would well have understood the following with respect to the plot of a tragic play.

> Decent people must not be shown passing from good fortune to misfortune (for that is not fearful or pitiful but disgusting) . . . nor again should an utterly evil man fall from good fortune into misfortune (for although a plot of that kind would be humane, it could not induce pity of fear – pity is induced by undeserved misfortune, and fear by the misfortunes of normal people, so that this situation will be neither pitiful or fearful). So we are left with the man between these two extremes: that is to say, the kind of man who is neither distinguished for excellence and virtue, nor comes to grief on account of baseness and vice, but on account of some error – a man of great reputation and prosperity like Oedipus . . . So to be well formed a fable [must have] change from good fortune to misfortune; the cause must not be vice but a great error. (LP/AP, 33)

Somehow or other, Siegfried does make 'a great error' in handing Brünnhilde over to Gunther and he pays for it with his life. Perhaps the Nordic poets, who knew nothing of Aristotle, instinctively made this error the cause of the fall of their great hero - and Wagner took this up. For his Siegfried, as developed in *Siegfrieds Tod,* is not 'distinguished for excellence and virtue'. In his morals he is decidedly an ordinary man fated to die, firstly because of what he *is* (ie one with the attributes of a hero, which do not include wisdom) and secondly because he *makes an error.*

Wagner - as was his custom - kept faith with the sources but sensed that the cause of Siegfried's downfall could not be explicit. Hence his anxious comment in the *Myth* (which can almost be seen as an *aide memoire* to himself) that Siegfried 'is guiltless but he takes upon himself the guilt of the gods and atones for their sins by means of his defiance and independence'. Hence the Ring rising up on the dead hand to assert Siegfried's 'marked out' nature as a hero who owns it but is immune from its curse, as opposed to the muddled actions of an ordinary man.

The Poetics of Aristotle was the first survey of drama to emerge and remains the starting point for any discussion of the concept of tragedy or tragic theatre. But although the epitome of a tragic action for Aristotle was to be found in *Oedipus the King*, the Greek word *tragōdia* is best translated as 'goat song', for reasons that are not clear. What is clear is that the ancient word did not have the meaning it now has. Aristotle and his contemporaries thought of all the earliest plays as serious rather than tragic. The notion of comic plays was a development some few decades later. *Lohengrin* can probably be cast as a tragedy but perhaps not the *Ring* or *Tristan und Isolde* - as we shall see in due course. But all include situations that are painfully serious and in some way partake of the tragic – as we see here. [H]

Der junge Siegfried

The first direct statement about this 'prelude' to *Siegfrieds Tod* is in a letter to his Dresden friend Theodor Uhlig dated 10 May 1851. 'Next month I shall do the text for *Junge Siegfried*, for which I am now collecting my thoughts.' The prose draft and the envisaged poem were finished in June as anticipated. Scene structure, exits and entrances are those in the final *Siegfried*.

Siegfried's story follows the *Myth* outline in large part but with one omission. Left out is the expedition Siegfried undertakes to revenge himself on his father's killer. [I] Wagner had already hinted in the *Myth* that he would dispense with this side show, for he clearly indicates that it is Wotan who brings about Siegmund's death. As far as Siegfried is concerned, the only plot addition to that summary is his encounter with Wotan in JS3.1.

[H] Scholars are undecided whether or not Shakespeare would have been introduced to the *Poetics* at his grammar school in Stratford, or took note of them afterwards. Nevertheless, read between the lines from *Hamlet* which follow and see how the sensibility induced by the Renaissance transformed the notion of a *great error* into the more drastic *tragic flaw*, which became the touchstone of the tragic ethos.

> So, oft it chances in particular men, /That for some vicious mole of nature in them, /As, in their birth wherein they are not guilty, /Since nature cannot choose his origin /... Carrying, I say, the stamp of one defect, / Being nature's livery, or fortune's star, /Their virtues else be they as pure as grace, / As infinite as man may undergo /Shall in the general censure take corruption /From that particular fault.

[I] Much space is devoted to this, particularly in *PE*, presumably because the traditional honour of the Volsung tribe required it, entailing fleets to be mustered and sailed, and battles to be fought.

Shaping Siegfried's character

Here, in this poem, Wagner continues to shape the hero he wants and to do so he now must adjust the sources in order to create someone of greater force. This is achieved with good effect in three ways: the re-forging of Nothung, the demonstration of a powerful affinity with nature and the fight with Fafner the dragon. The *Myth* outline made a start with Siegfried as the forger of his own sword but whereas then Mime taught him how to do it, here in the poem Siegfried teaches himself as by instinct, taking over after Mime admits he is not up to the job. Wagner enlarges this episode into a step-by-step manual on how to use a file, fill a mould, rouse the forge fire and so on, right down to the triumphant use of the finished sword. The acquisition of the sword is turned into the major event in Siegfried's youth — a symbolic rite of passage into adulthood. This culmination of the first Act in the opera is final proof, if it were needed, that Siegfried is intelligent. But there is no exaggeration: Siegfried's forging does not move beyond the knowledge he would have derived by careful observation of Mime. This intelligence is evident from the time he first comes on stage.

The next new development of character comes to fruition in JS2, although a little of it is seen in the previous act, namely the moulding of him as a child of nature. Conversing with birds may be a sign of distinction which Siegfried shares with Wotan but communing with the life of the forest is different. This is a romantic renaissance concept alien to 13th century Nordic life and the sources offer no such emotional hinterland. But Wagner hits the spot exactly and it is difficult to think of any major dramatic character more likely to understand birdsong, excepting perhaps such a one as Ariel in *The Tempest*.

This episode is the prelude to the fight with Fafner and here again Wagner departs almost completely from the sources (see VS18) in which Sigurd kills Fafnir to fulfil a promise made to Regin (a good point) but not in a fair fight (a bad point). He succeeds by dint of a wheeze cooked up by Regin and Odin, and Wagner would want none of that. For all that the staged fight is often ludicrous or fudged or such that the spectator might want to put hand over eyes, it is intended to be one on one and to the death. That is necessary for heroic progress and it may be that Siegfried's absence of motive has the same root: it is just a rite of passage.

Siegfried's fearlessness

So far so good but we now come to a major development that can be seen as a mistake, namely Siegfried's lack of fear. The key matter is that the idea does not work in the drama, further examination of which will be found in Chapter 20. The starting point now is in *Sturleson's Edda,* where there is no mention of fearlessness at all. His summary of the business refers to the fire (there is no suggestion that Odin ordained it) as 'the flickering flame' and reports Brynhild as making 'a vow to wed only that man who dared to ride 'the flickering flame.' (SE,102) This is amplified in the *Poetic Edda* with Brünnhilde's assertion, as she awakens from the sleep induced by Odin, that she had vowed to 'marry no one who knew fear'. It may be, as suggested by Cooke (DC/WE,47), that Wagner seized hold of this because of his desire to keep close to the sources. But these references are the sum total. The only other achievement for which Sigurd might have been famed (and he was so lauded in *Das Nibelungenlied*) would have been the killing of the dragon even though this was achieved by trickery, as described above. Neither is the breaching of the firewall the same as seen in the *Ring*. When Sigurd first approaches Brynhild the text reads 'Ahead of him on the mountain he saw a great light, as if a fire was burning and the brightness reached up to the heavens.' (VS, 67) That is all: he then simply walks through the castle ramparts to find Brynhild. At the second visit, when he helps Gunnar, it is not Sigurd who goes through the flames but his horse who jumps over them. Gunnar's horse had shied away; Sigurd's horse Grani would not budge with Gunnar on his back; so Sigurd changes shape with Gunnar (See VS #29) and Grani then jumps as required. *Volsung Saga* quotes two verses (obviously seen as important) from a presumably lost poem that is not included in *The Poetic Edda*. The second verse reads 'the flames expired / before the prince, / the fire fell back / before the fame-hungry one'. (VS, 81)

The concept of fearlessness in the work of the Nordic skalds may be little more than a device to move the plot forward. But it was probably more than that for the composer. To have a complete lack of fear is so remarkable a feature that it might be seen to stand as a sufficient condition to be worthy of Brünnhilde, Wagner's paragon of womanhood. To be clear, however, total fearlessness is not a human characteristic at all: only an insane person has no fear. In normal life and parlance to be fearless means to be aware of extreme danger and then to overcome the inevitable dread. But for some obscure (and unnecessary, as Chapter 20 will reveal) reason it was so important to Wagner that Siegfried should be so unaware of fear that his actions were not enough: there had to be a sub-text, namely the well-known fable of the boy who knew no fear.

In his letter to Uhlig announcing his programme for the opera, Wagner also wrote: 'Have I not written to you concerning a non-serious subject? It was the one about the lad who leaves home to learn about fear and who is so stupid that he never learns what it is. Imagine my shock when I suddenly discovered that the lad in question is none other than young Siegfried.' (SS/SL,223) In fact, what transpires is a fiction invented by Wagner. The original is not as he reports to Uhlig. Fear is there identified with shuddering, and the lad tries to find something that will make him shudder. Neither sleeping under gallows with seven corpses above him nor a sojourn in a haunted house do the trick. Only when a bucket of cold water full of eels is thrown over him whilst asleep, does he shudder; this is not surprising and has nothing to do with fear. It is a rather silly story in fact, but Wagner was clearly much taken with it and initially, in *Der junge Siegfried,* he devoted a substantial chunk of the text to this wish to learn about fear. JS1 starts exactly as does S1 but Siegfried does not rush off, to leave Mime to get on and re-forge his father's sword; he allows the dwarf to try to teach him about fear.

Mime's real motive was not laudable so he hides it and just says that he is following the wishes of Siegfried's dead mother.

Doch hör', ich hab's	Now hear me, I have
was du hören must!	something you must hear!
Du willst aus dem wald	You want to leave the wood
fort in die welt?	and go out into the world?
Hör', was deine mutter	Hear then, what your mother
Mime vertraut!	confided to Mime!
Mime, sprach sie,	Mime, she said,
kluger mann!	clever man!
Wenn einst mein kind erwächst,	When at last my child is grown
hüte den kühnen im wald!	hide the bold boy in the wood!
Die welt ist tückisch und falsch,	The world is deceitful and false,
dem thör'gen stellt sie fallen.	and guiles the foolish to disaster.
Nur wer das fürchten gelernt,	Only he who has learnt about fear
mag dort sich leidlich behüten	may fairly defend himself there.

The whole scene is well crafted, as Mime tries to explain fear. He fails and Siegfried exits, saying that he will leave home when the sword is ready and learn about fear himself. In this first draft there is now another soliloquy from the dwarf before the Wanderer arrives in which he explains that he fostered the lad from birth so that he will be able to kill Fafner, thereby providing access to his treasure. To ensure this enterprise he has deliberately nurtured courage and fearlessness. And this strategy suddenly rebounds; at this critical moment they now impel him to leave before Mime can bring a properly armed Siegfried face to face with the dragon. He puts this question to himself: 'How to keep him now in my cave so that he will serve my ends?' He now sees the solution: to tell him anew about the necessity to 'learn' fear and that the best way to do that is stay until he can be brought face to face with this immense dragon. Newman explores this in fine and precise detail (EN/LRW2, 330-39).

This episode of promisingly logical plot development was discarded because the scene is too long and laboured. *Siegfried* is not to have this early exposition of the need for the hero to learn fear nor the clear reasoning behind it as explained by the dwarf. In the event, Wagner predicates that his Siegfried learns something about fear when he sees Brünnhilde but, for all the emphasis loaded on this moment, it is in large part a theatrical device that allows the more mature man to emerge.

Coverage of this issue has been extensive because Wagner made such a meal of it - to little purpose as readers will find in due course.

Siegfried and Wotan
Der junge Siegfried does tell us that Brünnhilde is Wotan's daughter and we know that Wotan's spear shattered Siegmund's sword. Neither of these, however, impinge on the confrontation with Wotan. This is very different in tone from the final version, for

Wotan does not bar Siegfried and his spear is not broken – this is a story about Siegfried and not about Wotan. A benefit is that Siegfried's character is rounded once again. Also the story connects back to and can take in a further matter, namely the sporadic contacts in the Nordic sources between Sigurd and Odin – which are all engineered by the latter.

Other than the issue of parentage, in JS3.1 there is none of the Wotan/Brünnhilde back-history which informs S3. So the text of the Siegfried/Wotan scene lacks the mounting tension which culminates in the sword smashing the spear. Instead there is a rather benign exchange. The scene is as in S3.1 up to the point when Siegfried retails the death of Mime at his hands. Then Siegfried explains the purpose of his journey; Wotan tells him that if he goes through the fire then he, Wotan, will lose his power. So what? says Siegfried. Wotan: the fire surrounds her so only he without fear can get through. Siegfried asks whether Wotan can teach him fear (for Fafner never managed it) and if he cannot then he should get out of his way. Wotan: See there the fire upon the heights; 'Ein Lichtmeer umlauchtet dein haupt' (carried through into S3). On you go then – and there you will perhaps learn fear.

The other function of this confrontation, which becomes a crucial turning point in the drama, is that it offers a faint trace of Odin's interest in and desire to meet Sigurd, such as we see in the *Poetic Edda* and *Volsung Saga*. Odin sires the Volsung race (VS#1), hovers over it and intervenes six times in the guise of an old man who wears a cloak and that floppy hat seen worn so often by the Wanderer in modern productions. Odin engages powerfully with Sigurd and this aspect obviously impressed Wagner. Successively, Odin:

- enters Volsung's hall and thrusts the sword into the Branstock tree at Signy's wedding (VS#3);
- bears away the corpse of Sinfjiotli, Sigmund's son, (p.139) along the river (and perhaps takes it to Valhalla?) (VS#10);
- interposes his spear so that Sigmund's sword breaks upon it and he is killed (VS#12);
- helps Sigurd choose Grani, a horse descended from his own horse Sleipnir (VS#13);
- saves Sigurd's fleet in the storm as he journeys to avenge his father (VS#17);
- tells Sigurd how better to ambush Fafnir (VS#18).

Sigmund and Sigurd are the only two mortals in whom Odin shows any real interest. His involvement with Brynhild is limited to the decision to punish her for disobedience; he otherwise ignores her. With regard to the Volsung men, therefore, one can agree that there is no *direct* connection between Sigurd and the downfall of the gods but not that Odin and Sigurd are detached from each other. Wagner seizes hold of this opportunity to create his own myth about this relationship by moving beyond the sources to make a direct link between Siegfried's death and the downfall of Wotan.

Wagner was not alone in doing so, for there is also William Morris's view of the story. In 1876 Morris published his poem *The story of Sigurd the Volsung,* based on the

Volsung Saga. ᴊ Morris was acquainted with Wagner's theories and may have met Cosima, but the impact of his work would have been minimal for Morris's attitude toward the composer was one of derision and contempt.

In the poem Odin meets with the Volsungs, as detailed above, but Morris adds one that is not in the saga. At the end it is Odin who places the totemic sword between the bodies of Sigurd and Brynhild: he is thus seen as guiding and embracing the lives of the two heroes from the start to the end of their journeys. Morris also sees the death of Sigurd as related to the eventual decay and collapse of the gods. The last lines of his poem are:

> Ye have heard of the Cloudy People, and the dimming of the day,
> And the latter world's confusion, and Sigurd gone away.

Siegfried, the sun god

Die Wibelungen reveals the sub text of Siegfried's heroic attributes - the god of light who defeats the dragon of darkness and gains thereby the 'hoard'. In *Der junge Siegfried* are three episodes when this sub text breaks to the surface: in Brünnhilde's greeting to Siegfried after he has awakened her, in Siegfried's confrontation with Wotan and in the question and answer episode between Wotan and Mime.

Upon waking up, Brünnhilde first words, with clear imagery of dawn, are 'Hail to you, sun! Hail to you Light! Hail to you light-bringing day!' Further on in their scene together, she addresses Siegfried as 'waker of life', as 'hoard of the world, life of the earth' and as 'light-bringing youth'. These most obvious of references are in the forefront of Wagner's mind, 30 months after writing *Die Wibelungen*. ᴋ

The two other references concern Wotan's missing eye, which he mentions to both Siegfried in JS3.1 and to Mime in JS1. When Siegfried notices - and none too politely - that the god has an eye missing, Wotan replies:

> With the eye which, as my second self, is missing
> you yourself can glimpse the one that's left for me to see with.

This can be paraphrased as: 'The light by which you see my one eye is both the eye of the sun and also the eye that I have lost, for that became the sun.' Wotan put it pretty

---

ᴊ This was republished by Longmans Green in 1922, in a revised addition and with some passages rendered into prose by Winifred Turner and Helen Scott. This edition is now available as print on demand or as an ebook.

ᴋ This first greeting is an echo of the following lines in the sagas, as the newly awakened Brynhild greets Sigurd *(HB/PE, 389)*:

> Hail day! Hail the sons of day! Hail night and her daughter now!
> Look on us here with loving eyes! Grant us the victory we await!

In the edda, however, this is no indication that Sigurd is to be seen as a sun god. Such connotations are foreign to Nordic mythology. Wagner probably just thought they worked well.

well like that to Mime in JS1: 'Only one eye shines in [my] head, because in the heavens the other shines as the sun'. Wagner asserted that he did not want his audience to reflect on what was seen and heard on stage. If so, the reason that this obscure and complex text remains may be that such allusions acted to reinforce in his mind the power of myth and thus aid his inspiration. He cannot have expected the audience to work it out. The reference to Wotan's eye in the scene with Mime was dropped when *Der junge Siegfried* was changed to become *Siegfried*.

This is not clear in the text but it was to be expressed by the music as written over 20 years later. In his great essay *The sorrows and grandeur of Richard Wagner*, Thomas Mann writes:

> The overpowering accents of the music that accompanies Siegfried's funeral cortège no longer tell of the woodland boy who set out to learn the meaning of fear; they speak to our emotions of what is *really* passing away behind the lowering veils of mist: it is the sun hero himself who lies on the bier, slain by the pallid forces of darkness. (TM/PCW, 100)

Siegfried and *Götterdämmerung*

After so much development it comes as little surprise that Siegfried's character does not change much. Each small additional change, however, is crafted to elevate him above the sources from which he is derived and this in spite of the widening of the story canvas and the movement of Wotan toward the centre of the plot.

Two changes come to mind. Firstly, our awareness of Siegfried's courage is further enhanced in his encounter with Wotan, who now opposes the approach to his fire-encircled daughter. How would he fare before this majestic presence whose mere glance would certainly wither the will of any normal person? We should remember that, as far as we know, he has met no person other than Mime, whom he understandably finds disgusting. But Siegfried confronts Wotan with nonchalance and charm, and then brushes him aside by his own will (for the spear and the sword can be seen as symbols of the will of those who carry them). This is another twist upon the several mythic encounters between Sigurd and Odin. None of those have confrontation: Odin is just quietly taking care of the man, and it is sometimes not clear whether the man knows the identity of his helper.

The Siegfried we see in *Götterdämmerung* is as developed in *Siegfrieds Tod* but with one major change, namely the way he treats Brünnhilde in the Act 1 assault. In ST1.2 his words were many and largely vile but now they are few and constrained, if still stiffly unpleasant: he announces himself as 'a hero who will tame you, if you resist my might.' This indicates, once again, the difficulty Wagner had in conveying the cause of Siegfried's 'crash to ruin', to use the words of Newman. He is doing something bad and this is an essential part of his history as set down in the sources. A critical question arises: Where lies the fault if it is his fate so to act?

Siegfried and Balder

The death of the Wagnerian hero and that of the shiningly beautiful god serve, in two different contexts, as preludes to the destruction of the world and also of the gods who rule it. This has understandably prompted commentators to seek other links.

Who and what was Balder and why was his death a prelude to *Ragnarök*? [L] He was the son of Odin and Frigg: beautiful and good, such that light shone from him. Although beloved by all, he had bad dreams about his death, so his mother put all matter (fire, water, stone, metals, trees, diseases, animals, birds and poisons) under oath to do him no harm. To honour Balder and their avowed love for him, the gods would playfully throw stones and branches at him but nothing strikes and causes harm. The half god Loki was jealous and approached Balder's mother disguised as a woman and extracted from her the information that there was one plant – the mistletoe - so small and young that it never could present any danger so therefore she had not placed it under the oath. Loki accordingly cut a branch from the plant and approached Balder's half-brother Hoth - who was blind and could not therefore join in the game – and offered to help him in his aim. Hoth agreed, the small branch was thrown and pierced Balder who fell dead. Grief was universal but, despite all intercessions to the higher powers, the death could not be reversed and Balder was cremated, along with his wife who could not live without him. With that, everything significant is said. He actually does nothing at all in *PE* and *SE*, and would have no hold on the imagination of later generations if it were not for his nature and the manner of his death.

Two after-stories tell us why Balder's death was linked to the destruction of the cosmic order. Firstly, Loki had always disrupted and muddied the lives of the gods, and the death of Balder was the final straw. He was pursued and captured and tied to a rock until the end of time. As the final great battle and apocalyptic storms intensified, Loki broke free and fought against the gods, dying in a one to one duel with Heimdall, the watchman for Valhalla.

Secondly and crucially, the earth survives that catastrophe, as does a resurrected Balder who was not associated with the violence of the old regime. Together with Hoth, the innocent who killed him, a new union is formed as a symbol for a new age of peace.

> The sun turns black, the earth sinks into the sea.
> The hot stars down from heaven are whirled.
> Fierce grows the steam and the life-devouring flame
> Till fire leaps high about heaven itself.
>
> * * * * *
>
> [The ground rises from the sea] . . .
> In wondrous beauty once again
> Shall the golden tables stand mid the grass,

[L] The summary of Balder's life and death that follows is condensed from p.48 of *Sturluson's Edda*. That one page is the only source upon which our knowledge is based.

> Which the gods had owned in the days of old.
> Then fields unsowed bear ripened fruit,
> All ills grow better, and Balder comes back:
> Balder and Hoth dwell again in Valhalla. (HB/PE, 25)

Balder was not notable amongst the gods because of what he did but because of what he was, namely an ideal of peaceful goodness and beauty. The gods revered him for those qualities which each of them conspicuously lacked.

There is no hint in Germanic or Nordic primary sources that the anticipated cosmic collapse is linked to the earthly collapse of the Burgundian kingdom. In particular, the resurgence of wholesome life and justice after *Ragnarök*, under the eye of the resurrected god, has no counterpart in *Das Nibelungenlied* or *Thidriks Saga*. The collapse of Burgundy as there narrated has its historical counterpart in the great defeat of 437AD. Thereafter the land was governed by client kings who owed allegiance to a Roman overlord or to the Frankish king for another 100 years until the kingdom was absorbed into that of the Franks and vanished.

Nevertheless, this did not prevent the romantically inclined 19th century scholars from seizing on the discernible connections and nor did it deter Wagner (p.48). Incontrovertible evidence lies in the prose sketch and the poem of *Der junge Siegfried* Act III. Wotan is explaining to Erda the background of the doom awaiting the gods. The sketch has 'The gods have been concerned about their end since Balder sank, the loveliest of the gods; until then the world was at peace . . .' (EM/WN, 132). Within weeks this reference was watered down: Balder's name was replaced by 'der erfreuende' - the joyful one. This reference was itself deleted in the revisions for *Siegfried*. The Balder of myth would simply get in the way of the drama: everything relevant about the god is subsumed in the heroic man.

Siegfried's murder is the prelude to a change in the existing cosmic order in exactly the same way as is Balder's murder. No consensus exists as to why Loki wanted Balder to die. Nevertheless, that he was not part of the destroyed pantheon does separate him from all the other gods. If some form of regeneration of the world was an inherent part of the Nordic mythology, Balder was fated to die early so that he would be free of the universal fate and rise again. The Immolation music at the end of *Götterdämmerung* is effulgent to a degree that has few parallels: it speaks to us of regeneration and this does link Balder's role in *Ragnarök* to Wagner's vision. As Balder was different from the other gods, so is Siegfried different from all others who comes into contact with the Ring, including Brünnhilde.

What is unique about Siegfried?

Wagner wanted to make his hero stand out from the generality by enhancing the character which he saw in the legendary Sigurd. Two particular matters come to mind when we view the totality of his creation: the broad scope of the character portrayal and Siegfried's own view of his past and present.

THE HERO SIEGFRIED

A particular feature of Siegfried which distinguishes him from all other men portrayed by Wagner is that all the salient features of his life are open to the spectator. We follow him from childhood through maturity to death. When he bounds on to the stage for the first time he is as a child, waiting to experience the events that will push him into adulthood. He is dissatisfied and senses there is something amiss; he is full of an as yet inchoate yearning; he has an instinctive empathy with nature for he is himself 'natural' man. Critically, he has never been shown genuine love. He is like a blank page on which his understanding of unknown things is yet to be written.

Then we see him grow into an adult and he does so by pursuing rites of passage. ᴹ To forge his own sword, to kill a dragon with it, to learn the language of birds, to avenge a father, to brave fire and to win a 'sleeping beauty' bride – all these are symbolic of coming to heroic maturity. He reaches the peak of fulfilment in the arms of Brünnhilde. This pitch of joy cannot be sustained and he then fails. His life is telescoped into a few big events but these are so wide in scope that its whole gamut is presented to the audience: from spiritual birth and sexual glory, through failure and betrayal, to a final vindication in death.

That first aspect of Siegfried's portrayal is, however, of far less importance than is his psychological make-up, the preeminent aspect being his perception of time – of his past and his present. Wagner's men are much dogged by their past lives. We only have to think of the Dutchman, Tannhäuser, Wotan, Siegmund and Tristan. Siegfried, by contrast lives in the here and now. He never looks forward; the only concern he has with the past is his parentage and, on inspection, that is really about the search for his identity. Barry Emslie puts this well: Siegfried is 'wholly liberated from notions of duty, destiny and despair, which otherwise play a big role in lives of other major characters.' (BE/WCL,75)

This indifference to his past is a defining character trait for it penetrates his whole personality. We all now know that what happens when we are very, very young moulds our personalities and attitudes to an extraordinary extent. Not so, however, with Siegfried. The strangeness of his infancy had certainly lodged itself in the back of his mind: how odd it was to have Mime as a father and to have no mother. He may have sensed that there was something wrong but he puts up with it. Any problem with a parent can cause powerful neuroses. But he just seemed to live with that unresolved issue, until the time came when he needed answers in order to find his identity. One can assume that Mime, whatever his motives, knew how to simulate affection. Siegfried is aware of these efforts and is therefore puzzled as to why he has always disliked the dwarf so intensely. Looked at in the whole, it is difficult to see any neurosis in his approach to life caused by his infancy. This total freedom from his past is contrary to most known psychology.

ᴹ These portrayals of a complete person are not uncommon in fiction – think of those epic family sagas – but are rare in drama. Prince Hal in Shakespeare's plays is the only case that might be thought to approach it - moving from irresponsible youth at the beginning of *Henry IV* to political maturity and power at the end of *Henry V*.

What is Siegfried's 'flaw'?

The essence is that he is entirely his own self and is influenced only by what his spirit accepts, without hang ups. Single-mindedly, he *seeks for what he needs* and ignores those things and people he does not need. So he tolerates/ignores Mime for all his conscious life, he brushes Wotan aside and cannot be bothered to listen to him, and he takes Fafner as he finds him. In the 1854 letter to Röckel, Wagner wrote the following:

> In Siegfried I have tried to depict what I understand to be the most perfect human being, whose highest consciousness expresses itself in the fact that all consciousness manifests itself solely in the most immediate vitality and action: the enormous significance I attach to this consciousness [which]... *can almost never be stated in words*. (SS/SL, 309)

The key phrases here are 'the most immediate vitality and action' and Wagner's italicised 'can almost never be stated in words'. The first translation into English (in 1897 by Eleanor Sellar, 90 years before that of Stewart Spencer above) reads 'in present life and action'. The second phrase from Sellar reads 'which can scarcely ever find adequate expression in words'. (ES/RWAR,102) It seems clear that the first paragraph on this page accurately describes what Wagner ascribes in this letter as the defining characteristic of 'a perfect human being'? Furthermore, if something cannot be expressed in words the implication can be that it may be possible to express it by the addition of stage action, by music or by the interaction with other people.

If this absence of inhibition and response to the primacy of 'present life and action' do define Siegfried, then these are also the seeds of his collapse on arrival at Gunther's court. With the exception of Mime, Siegfried accepted everyone at face value - Fafner, the Woodbird and Wotan. Wooing and winning the only desired woman is the prime wish in a man's life. What could go wrong? And so he also takes Gunther and Hagen at face value. We need neuroses and some inhibition to equip us for the dangerous real world. In *Götterdämmerung* he goes forth blithely from the security of Brünnhilde's love into the world of preternatural deceit engendered by Hagen. Nobody, regardless of circumstances, will survive without a proper attention to what may be harmful. There is no evidence that Siegfried does and when he gets the whole picture from the Rhinedaughters in G3.1 he has no means of focussing upon what matters. The proposition in this study is that Siegfried makes 'a great error'. This error or flaw in drama has been identified with the Greek *hubris,* so often associated with ancient tragedy. This is usually translated as *pride* but can also be translated as *over-confidence* - certainly an apt epithet for Siegfried. The two operas which conclude the *Ring* are a serious drama (the word 'tragedy' can be side-stepped) about the rise and fall of Siegfried. This drama is self-contained but it also nests within a wider drama with Wotan at its centre.

Uneasiness creeps in, however, at so simple an answer. The narratives in all the primary sources do imply that Siegfried 'comes to grief on account of baseness and vice', as described by Aristotle. He wins a woman's love and then hands her over to another. Wagner adopts this entirely, along with the ambiguity introduced by the potion of forgetfulness. He follows the main line within the primary sources and leaves us guessing.

Siegfried's death and the common good

The matter is complex. Error and deceit are present, however ambiguously they are displayed, but Siegfried is also fated to die because he was conceived by Wagner as inhabiting the pantheon of totemic sacrificial victims. Initially the Siegfried drama was to be an allegory about the replacement of bad government by good. It may have eventually changed into something which Deryck Cooke described as metaphysical - where a whole world order needed putting to right - but that is simply a change in detail and not in dramatic purpose. The key point is that all the spheres into which Wagner thinks of placing Siegfried are chronically damaged and that Wotan is explicitly associated with this damage. Throughout the ages sacrificial death has been seen as a remedy or palliative in such circumstances. It matters not whether the damaged world - as caused partly or totally by Wotan - was political or existential or whatever commentators like to propose: Wagner conceived the sacrifice of Siegfried as the remedy. The worlds of Wotan and of Siegfried wait for each other.

This brings the issue back to Odin and Sigurd. Why did the poets, the skalds, emphasise the interest the supreme Nordic god had in the preeminent - and indeed the only - human hero in the Eddic poems? [N] Odin is not a 'fatherly' figure in the sagas, as we shall see, and that he is a distant ancestor of Volsung would not of itself imply any *affectionate* interest in the hero - Odin was not that sort of being. But so powerful is this association, as desired by Odin, that William Morris *invents* the story of the god placing the sword between the bodies of Sigurd and Brynhild on the pyre. Might it be that the ancient poets also sensed some link between a historical collapse (which as it happened was in Burgundy) and the story encompassed by the final doom which settled on the gods in *Ragnarök?* The romantic 19th century scholars did make such a connection. In *Das Nibelungenlied* the murder of Sigurd brings on the historical catastrophe. The scholars saw this as a retelling of the collapse of the gods' world, and it is likely that Wagner saw it like this. Maybe both he and the 19th century scholars made a correct judgement.

Some commentators who elevate the importance of Wotan at the expense of Siegfried assert that the magnificence of the Funeral Music is beyond our expectations of

---

[N] The main contender is, of course, Sigmund. But as he dies he proclaims that his son will be the greatest of heroes. Sigmund's main function in the sagas is to be Sigurd's father. There is also Helgi, Sigurd's half-brother. But he is really a dry run for Sigurd - one who appears, shines brightly and then who disappears. One matter is significant, namely that Helgi specifically meets and marries a valkyr, but nevertheless the *Volsung Saga* gives him short shrift (p.439).

Siegfried, who has been revealed in many ways as a somewhat ordinary chap. They might take issue with Thomas Mann's assessment (p.86) and propose that the music is really a pessimistic commentary on Wotan's failed hopes. The issue would be resolved if we see the fate of one integral with the fate of the other.

From Sigurd to Siegfried

Following the proposed development of Siegfried's persona, as set out in this chapter, these are the peculiar characteristics of Wagner's portrayal which are different from the mythic Sigurd.

1. His death is ordained as a necessary sacrifice.
2. He forges Nothung with his own knowledge and skill, independent of Mime.
3. He takes the dubious initiative of suggesting the Tarnhelm as a means to deceive Brünnhilde.
4. He learns about his ordained death from the other-worldly Rhinedaughters.
5. He is shown as independent in all things that matter.
6. The raised fist of his corpse in defiance of Hagen lifts him above other heroes.
7. He is denied the gift of self-awareness with regard to his role in the deceit of Brünnhilde, such as is given to Sigurd.
8. As a result, his behaviour toward her is significantly worse than that of Sigurd toward Brynhild.
9. He communes with nature in a manner alien to Sigurd, whose capacity is limited to the understanding of birdsong.
10. He kills Fafner in fair fight.
11. He braves the fire surrounding Brünnhilde in person and does not rely on his horse to jump over it.
12. He confronts and defies Wotan.
13. His death and its consequences reflect those of the shining god Balder.
14. He lives in the present and without neuroses of his past. (The obverse of 7 above.)
15. His inability to fear brings about his death.

◊ ◊ ◊ ◊ ◊ ◊

6

Brünnhilde, the 'trophy' bride

This chapter is a continuation of the story of the two lovers as might first have been envisaged by Wagner. In the last chapter I proposed that the key aspects of Siegfried's character and history were conceived before Wotan moved to the centre of the story, and that the persona so developed was uniquely Wagner's own. What was the situation with Brünnhilde?

Brynhild in the proto-plot

The speculative proto-plot centres around Sigurd so not surprisingly the first choices made that affect Brynhild are not about her but about her lover. He surmounts the wall of fire to find and win her on the mountain, rather than visit her in her ancestral home. Then he violently wrests Andvari's ring from her on his second visit to the mountain. The ring is not thrust into her face by Gudrun but she sees it on Sigurd's hand.

Only in the last stages are choices made that shape her character. She chooses to die rather than live on after Sigurd's death and then ordains a joint cremation. These actions emanate directly from Nordic texts, where they make explicit that Brynhild was the destined mate for Sigurd. In no source does she match Gudrun in importance. She has only two functions: to be first the love of the hero and then to bring about his death. Her implacable desire for vengeance is evident in all the sources and can also be examined without reference to the wider struggle between Wotan and Alberich.

Wagner gives us no early clue as to how he saw Brünnhilde; his only observations about her came when all the main outlines were settled. So the place to start is the gross betrayal she suffered - the compelling action that drives the basic story of these two lovers - and widen this to the reality behind her mythology.

<u>Ritualised marriage</u>
All the sources symbolically show the first encounter and subsequent union between Brynhild and Sigurd in an exalted manner; all present Sigurd's successful wooing in human terms and as the winning of a remarkable woman by a carefully vetted suitor. We need to see her as the high-born aristocrat as described in VS 25. It is this myth of the winning in marriage of a high-born woman that provides a clear entry point into the story as developed by Wagner. One Brunechild is a likely and relevant historical source. In a tumultuous life in 6th century Austrasia – a large territory covering what is now Belgium, northern France and Germany as far across as Cologne – she first married one

King Sigibert, was widowed twice and died, according to legend, when two horses to which she was tied tore her apart. Brunechild was a formidable and successful administrator, and opponent when required, during the long period when she reigned as regent for a son still in his minority. Celebrated in her time for beauty and prowess, she would be a good candidate for any legend.

The Germanic *NL* and *TS* present Brynhild as human and with nothing of the supernatural, although she is of abnormal strength in the former. As a queen in *NL* and as the wealthy owner of a famous stud farm, a breeder of pedigree horses in *TS*, she would be a prominent marital catch. Wagner insisted that the *Nibelungenlied* was inadequate as a source for his drama, but even so the starting point for his Brünnhilde can be extracted from within it. The queen of Iceland, as seen within it, placed obstacles before any suitor for her hand. Firstly, he must be seen publicly to best her in an athletic contest in order for her to accept him as prospective husband; secondly, and in private, he must manage to subdue her physically as a prelude to sex. These are variations on the legendary marriage rite attaching to a sought after woman. They are there to deter and defeat unworthy suitors: who marries the queen, princess or heiress is of the highest import. Operatically, Walther in *Die Meistersinger* and Calaf in *Turandot* are other examples - and of course there is he who awakens the Sleeping Beauty.

For Queen Brynhild of Iceland, the arrival of Gunnar and Sigurd is obviously the decisive and defining moment in her life. To be wooed and won is to change her life in every respect for she cedes the rule of her kingdom to her new husband, and is to leave for a strange land. This proud and celebrated lady is always honest and direct. Although very angry after being tricked and losing the athletic contest with 'Gunnar' she controls herself and says 'Come forward to me my kinsmen and vassals. You must do homage to King Gunnar . . . . Then clasping him by the hand [she] gave him express authority to rule over her country.' The relationship between Sigurd and Brynhild may be ambiguous but the above text is not: Brynhild certainly thought Gunnar had won her.

The nature and history of Brynhild in the Nordic tradition is more complex but the identical marital theme surrounds her: to be the destined mate and then the implacable instigator of Sigurd's death. Her almost princely status must be there if she is to attract the eye of Grimhild as a prospective husband for her son Gunnar, King of Burgundy. Her human persona - no more than a wealthy daughter of a prosperous family - does not at first sight proclaim such a lineage. So this may be the reason that the writers of these ancient poems squeezed princedom in by making her the sister of Attila the Hun. This connection may be strained but does open options for those poets. Brynhild as sibling to the great Attila elevates her to the social level of Gunnar. To modern minds Attila is the marauder from Asia but he had a precise significance in the 11th century view of the world where he features as a major player in the changing political system in southern Europe. Consequently, he appears as the second husband of Sigurd's widow Gudrun in all five primary sources. The narrative in these legends binds Attila into a complicated plot and he is accordingly integral to the legends about the fall of Burgundy.

This social status gives focus to how Sigurd wins Brynhild. For the task of breaching the fire that surrounds the sleeping virgin (like the impenetrable briar thicket surrounding the palace in *The Sleeping Beauty*) must obviously be regarded in the same light as those in *NL* – this is a woman of high lineage who must be protected from poor suitors. The *Volsung Saga* describes the situation thus: 'Ahead on the mountain [Sigurd] saw a great light, as if a fire were burning and the brightness reached up to the heavens. And when he came to it, there stood before him a rampart of shields with a banner above it.' (VS#21/22) Such a be-flagged castle rampart, with shields of the defending warriors on display, has been a deterrent against possible attack since time immemorial and the practice is recorded in the time of the Pharaohs. *Thidriks Saga* may have an inconsistent narrative but a defining quality is to avoid anything out of the ordinary. The same protective theme is there but, instead of fire, guards stand in Sigurd's way. He duly kills them, thereby relating directly to the rampart of shields.

A consequence of the above ritualistic right to claim the bride can be discerned when he visits her family estate, as summarised in VS#24/25. In the *Nibelungenlied* Brynhild was a queen with unquestioned power to do what she wanted. The Nordic sources present her as a sought after woman who is nevertheless not her own mistress. VS#25 shows her returning to the family home, which is the house of Heimer, her foster father. Sigurd had arrived previously to enormous acclaim as the slayer of the dragon. His suit for the hand of Brynhild would therefore have been much welcomed. So the two scenes of courtship run in parallel to those in the *Nibelungenlied* where the queen is bested in the contest and then in the bedroom.

All five main primary sources have no hesitation in presenting her behaviour as irreproachable. Everything she does is correct up to the point when the moral and physical violence done to her is made clear. She can be charged with one questionable action in the *Nibelungenlied,* namely to persuade Gunnar to invite Sigurd and Gudrun back to Gunnar's court. This, however, is an additional obscurity, perhaps deliberate, to add to the 'hidden' marriage that impregnates the relationship of Brynhild to Sigurd. But no such doubt pertains to the narrative in *Volsung Saga*: she is straight and surrounded by those who are bent in one way or another. Although severely disturbed when 'Gunnar' comes through the fire she accepts the unexpected with dignity.

The enormity of the metaphorical, symbolic rape of Brynhild is clear. Furthermore, the extremity of the assault - as shown in the primary sources - gives context to the vengeance she seeks: in all versions, Gunnar is shown as a weak creature, whereas Sigurd is of the same ilk as Brynhild. If someone has to suffer it must be he.

Brünnhilde in the *Myth*

Note, therefore, the manner in the primary sources whereby Wagner's shamefully wronged Brünnhilde takes the lead in the conspiracy to kill Siegfried – and similarly in the *Myth*. But Wagner dramatically alters the plot. The Nordic sources are unanimous that Sigurd does not touch Brynhild sexually when he overcomes her in Gunnar's form and Brynhild never opposes this view. Wagner similarly honours Siegfried's behaviour but now Brünnhilde falsely accuses him of sleeping with her.

> She proclaims to Gunther that he has been fooled by Siegfried: "Not to you - to *this* man am I married – he it is to whom I gave myself."
>
> Siegfried charges her with shamelessness: Faithful had he been to his blood-brotherhood and his sword lay between Brünnhilde and himself. He calls on her to say that this was so.
>
> Deliberately, and thinking only of his ruin, she refuses to support him . . . Brünnhilde accuses him of lying: he has broken all the oaths he swore to her and Gunther, and now he forswears himself.

There is no ambiguity here, no suggestion that Brünnhilde's mind has slipped back to their first ecstatic union. No stratagem is too extreme for this scorned woman. The *Myth* lays this on: 'Brünnhilde's desire for revenge is sharpened by her jealousy of Gutrune.' Wagner establishes a note of equal violence with both lovers: the brutality of Siegfried after he breaks through the fire as 'Gunther' is matched by the thirst for vengeance at all costs by Brünnhilde. This momentous change is there from the very start.

The remaining references to the sagas within the *Myth* are straightforward. Wagner settled with greater ease on how he saw the heroine than he did the hero. She is a valkyr and a 'virgin goddess', duly protected by fire (*Myth* -W2/W3). The primary job of a valkyr was as in the *Ring*, namely to choose which of two men fighting each other was to die. All those who died in battle ascended to Valhalla and were to fight for the gods in the eventual cosmic battle. They also acted as 'wish maidens' who served the wine in Valhalla as the warriors dined. Brynhild was one amongst a total of nine. [A]

A valkyr would serve Odin but the Nordic sources are devoid of suggestion that Odin had much contact with or interest in any of them. The poems in *PE* have much interaction between the different gods but not with those who are their servants. There is one exception, of course, to this gulf and indifference, namely the punishment that Odin places on Brynhild, and this exception is significant for its purpose must surely be to link her fate to that of Sigurd. Her very first mention in the sagas is the disobedience that brings on Odin's punishment and she is mentioned no more after this short episode until Sigurd awakens her. The cause of her punishment is similar to Brünnhilde's protection of Siegmund but the circumstance has no context at all. Odin wants the victory in a fight to go to one combatant and Brynhild chooses to protect the other; there is no point in giving their names because they have no background and neither of them appear anywhere again in the sagas.

[A] Two others are mentioned by name: Sigrun and Salva. They are interchangeable and each muddles into a sexual and/or protective relationship with Helgi - son of Sigmund - Sigurd's half-brother. But these relationships have nothing of the clarity of that between Brynhild and Sigurd. See VS#9 for more detail. Other than Brünnhilde, the names of the valkyrs in the *Ring* are made up by the composer.

There is one last minor point to record with regard to Wagner's Brünnhilde. An echo of the woman Brynhild we meet in *Das Nibelungenlied* and *Thidriks Saga* remains in <u>Background to Götterdämmerung</u> within the *Myth*: 'on losing her virginity to [Siegfried] she also lost all her superhuman strength.' The Nordic valkyrs do not have great strength in the sagas and they are not warriors - as Brynhild, Queen of Iceland, would have been.

Brünnhilde in *Der junge Siegfried* and *Siegfrieds Tod*

This first chapter of the two devoted to Brünnhilde is restricted to her relationship with Siegfried and that with Wotan is left till later on. Thereby we consider her now as a woman in the grip of a powerful love affair; in due course she will be seen as a semi-divine immortal. At this stage, therefore, I include that part of the final scene of *Der junge Siegfried* that is not a narration of past events, namely the final love duet with Siegfried. (As will be seen, before the love scene Brünnhilde tells Siegfried of her previous history. This part was dropped from *Siegfried,* leaving just the love text, as set to music.) It is appropriate to include this duet within this discussion; in November 1848, the closing words of *Siegfrieds Tod* indicate some sort of continuing life for the two lovers in partnership with Wotan. But - as we shall shortly see - within three months Wagner saw that the dying away of the gods was the necessary end of his drama. This demise is featured and welcomed in the final pages of the first *JS* duet, as quoted overleaf.

This last episode of *Der junge Siegfried* is the first of the seven in which she appears from *Siegfried* Act III through to the end of *Götterdämmerung*. Three episodes are not with Siegfried: those with the valkyrs (ST1.1), with Hagen and Gunther in which Siegfried's death is determined (ST2) and the concluding Immolation scene (ST3.2). Those touch upon the wider themes, and the texts are much changed in *Götterdämmerung*. By contrast, the texts of the four episodes with Siegfried remained essentially unchanged when work on the poems was completed in 1856. These are the aforesaid closing duet in JS3.2, the opening duet in ST1.1, that in ST1.3 where Siegfried/Gunther assaults Brünnhilde, and the mighty ensemble scene of confrontation in ST2. Hence it is that the love between the two, for all its hyperbole, was from beginning to end that of a man and a woman in self-absorbed sexual fervour.

<u>The love of Brünnhilde and Siegfried in *Der Junge Siegfried*</u>
The love scene between Brünnhilde and Siegfried last some 30 minutes and comprises several phases. Joyous recognition is succeeded by turmoil as sexual desire grows in both, with urgent insistence in the man meeting anxiety and resistance in the woman, until this resistance turns into a rapturous abandonment of mind and body to an insistent and tender lover. Now the opening phases of recognition are not dissimilar to love scenes in other operas but the nature of the surrender to sexual desire is quite different. These are the closing words that Wagner composed for Brünnhilde in that first draft in 1851.

> Pass away, radiant world of Valhalla! / May your proud fortress crumble to dust!
> Farewell, resplendent pomp of the gods! / May your eternal race end in happiness!
> Tear asunder, you Norns, the rope of the runes! / Twilight of the gods, let darkness arise!
> I'm instantly lit by Siegfried's star; / for me he's for ever,
> my proper heir, eternally mine, one and all: / radiant love, laughing death!

Those of Siegfried speak of Brünnhilde only, for only she is of any interest to him. The words of both lovers are carried forward unchanged into the final *Siegfried*, as are those with which they first greet each other. They bear no resemblance to anything in the sources, and nor, one might say, to any other operatic love duet. It is the music that matters, of course, and that eventually written 18 years later certainly vaults and soars in marvellous excitement. In performance the singers always - and rightly - appear appropriately joyous but one surely has to say that the musical joy bears no relation to the words. These are either apocalyptic or self-centred.

The love of Brünnhilde and Siegfried in *Siegfrieds Tod Act 1*

This second scene is cut from the same cloth as the first, and now speaks of love triumphant. The episode is not in the *Myth* but was quickly added after Wagner read the prose draft to Eduard Devrient (p.452). He advised that to start the stage action in Gunther's palace, as in the *Myth*, was too sudden and spectators would not know what was going on.

The *Siegfrieds Tod* poem was written 2½ years earlier but no changes whatsoever were made in consequence of the 1851 *Der junge Siegfried* text. Once again, the tone of both is established by Wagner alone, has little in common with the sources from which they derive, and is deliberate and made with purpose.

The scene is used to bring the Ring itself back into an ongoing plot; it does not yet have the cosmic overtones that come later but is already the artefact that is to bring destruction. Crucially and uniquely Wagner also introduces a particular sort of betrothal that is to be symbolised by the Ring; he hands it over in words never to be changed.

> Siegfried
> Let me give you this ring / in return for your runes.
> It retains the virtue of my deeds, / all that I ever accomplished.
> I laid waste a savage dragon, / who guarded it grimly and long:
> preserve its power well, / as a solemn pledge of my faith!
> Brünnhilde
> If you want to love me, / think only of yourself,
> think of your deeds: / think of the savage fire,
> through which you passed without fear / as its flames encircled the rock.
> Siegfried
> Am I now to take action / through your virtue alone?
> You'll choose my battles, / my triumphs will be yours:
> on the back of your horse, / protected by your shield, -
> I feel I'm Siegfried no more, / I'm only Brünnhilde's arm.

I have described it as love, but the words convey just triumph itself and the love becomes an adjunct rather than a cause. The scene turns exclusively around Siegfried's imminent departure and the mutual support they will give each other whilst parted. Memories of Siegfried's prodigious feats, of recent love-making, of sworn vows, of wisdom given and received are to surround the 'new deeds' that are further to embellish his name.

This is nothing less than a call to arms, and a love that is surely not destined to give comfort. (In contrast here are Boito's words, to be sung by another great warrior - Verdi's Otello - as a day of violent weather and stressful action sinks to a silent starlight night: 'Now in the dark night all is stilled. My pounding heart is lulled and calmed in this embrace. Let war thunder and the world be engulfed if, after boundless wrath, comes this boundless love.') Brünnhilde and Siegfried have spent little time together; this is against nature. [B] It can be argued that the exigencies of staged drama push this natural order aside but Wagner was both a knowing and accomplished dramatist and we should therefore assume (cf. Kitto's principle) that he deliberately chose this eccentricity to convey the strangeness of the love affair. If the conclusion of the first was apocalyptic in tone, this second is of triumph on an Olympian scale. The heroic couple hail each other as though they are godlike. Triumphant energy is a feature of powerful sex, as in evidence here.

Brünnhilde opens the finale of the love scene before Siegfried leaves for his 'adventures'. This music has decided erotic overtones.

The tone of violence and triumphalism about their love in the text is seen in none of the Nordic sources. There the love exchanges between Brynhild and Sigurd are courtly and accompanied by a gloomy foreknowledge that matters could go awry. Foreboding and prophecy imbue all the love exchanges. In VS#25 Sigurd is importunate at the second meeting - that which occurs at the family home.

> The best day for us would be when we can enjoy each other... If we do not live together, the grief will be harder to endure than a sharp weapon.
> [To which Brynhild replies]
> It is not fated that we should live together... I am a shield maiden... I must review the troops of warriors and you will marry Gudrun, the daughter of Gibich.

Such foreknowledge and wisdom apply to Sigurd as well: he knows from his youth what will happen. In VS#16 Sigurd's uncle Grippir foretells his fate. No detail is given but Wagner could have referred to the poem *Grippispo* in *PE*. All is there prophesied to Sigurd, from triumph through his betrayal of Brynhild to death at the hand of Gudrun's

---

[B] Productions of the cycle which portray the lovers in domesticity in G1.1 do not work.

brothers. On hearing this, Sigurd says 'Now fare thee well! Our fates we shun not and well has Grippir answered my wish.' [C] There are also his dying words to Gudrun in VS#32/33: 'And now it has come to pass as has long been foretold. I refused to believe it but no one can withstand his fate.'

Concordance with *Sigurd der Schlangentödter* is there but with separate view points. In any dramatization two scenes between the lovers are imperative: one to meet and one to part. In his second scene, Fouqué may have given Wagner a prompt for Siegfried's abrupt departure when Brynhild says: 'Forth from my bed, into the world beyond, your brave heart will drive you, in search of new adventures' (EM/WN,90). By implication however - for Fouqué is writing a dramatic poem and not a stage drama - the lovers have spent some time together. Moreover, the note of foreboding in the sagas is even more pronounced here, and the trajectory of the story is very gloomy. Sigurd's ebullience is clouded almost to obscurity by Brynhild's apprehensions (p.462).

All this is powerful stuff, will have registered as such with Wagner, and in due course we must establish why he chose not to take any aspect of it into his work. With both Siegfried and Brünnhilde this omission has a long reach into the plot.

Brünnhilde imparts her wisdom to Siegfried

Whereas in the *Nibelungenlied* Brynhild's distinction above others was her athletic prowess (preposterous, in truth), it is her prophetic powers that lifts her to eminence in the Norse texts. In VS#26/27 Gudrun visits and ask for her help, and Brynhild foresees that Sigurd will leave her and marry Gudrun, and that the marriage will founder and bring destruction in its wake. After she stabs herself in VS#33 and before she dies, Brynhild foretells the universal death to the house of Burgundy and the fall of the kingdom itself.

Great weight is also laid on Brynhild passing her wisdom on to Sigurd. Indeed, the writer of *Volsung Saga* placed what we now would see as disproportionate emphasis on the runes passed by Brynhild to Sigurd. He quotes 28 verses, being the equivalent of 190 lines, and thereby passes on *in full* the detail of the runes and advice ('redes') as given in *Poetic Edda*. No other incident or conversation in the entire history of the Volsung tribe is accorded with anywhere like that number of verses. The runes are charms (eg: how to help a mother protect her child) and therefore a form of magic; they are not spelled out. The advice in the 'redes', however, is about how to behave, and is sensible and to the point.

In *Der junge Siegfried* Brünnhilde had welcomed the departure of her wisdom when faced with the onslaught of sexual desire and the palest reflection of that departed lore is found at the beginning in ST1.1 (and subsequently in G1.1) when, during the love scene, Brünnhilde passes her wisdom to Siegfried.

[C] Forward knowledge of one's fate is not given to ordinary folk and the likelihood is that both the author of the source poem and the compiler of *VS* are conveying to their readers that this is part of what it means to be a hero.

Devoid of wisdom, / yet brimming with need:
do not despise / the poor creature
rich in love, / yet freed of her power,
who just wants to give, / but can give no more.

We can surmise two reasons for such short-changing. The first is the undramatic nature of a very long recital; not only do the runes fit oddly into any modern interpretation but even Brynhild as the 'counsellor' to Gudrun is too unfocussed to make dramatic material. The second - to be examined when appropriate - is that her wisdom is to be conveyed by the music she sings and which surrounds her. The third may be the most important, namely that Wagner wanted to reduce the impact of her wisdom, in the same way that he 'simplified' the love between Brünnhilde and Siegfried. The conclusion to be drawn is that Wagner decided early on how the two lovers should react to each other and these decisions stood firm from first to last.

The confrontation over the Ring

The actions and character of Siegfried were established early, adapted from the Sigurd of the sources. The same applies to Brünnhilde. The central action of *Siegfrieds Tod* is her betrayal; Wagner got to grips with this most vividly in ST2 when Gunther leads in the captured Brünnhilde and so opens perhaps the mightiest scene of melodrama in all opera. This can be said, moreover, without reference to the music. Wagner here encapsulates and brings to culmination the kernel of deceit, betrayal and planned revenge that informs this part of the Nordic sources. In little over a month he fashions a text that differs totally from his other works. In no period, either earlier or later, did he write anything of such intuitive power. The German text crackles (though not in any translation!) with force and violence as Brünnhilde realises the truth:

Heil'ge Götter, Himmlische Lenker!	Sacred gods, arbiters of the skies!
Rauntet ihr dies in eurem Rat?	Is this what you muttered to yourself in council?
Lehrt ihr mich Leiden wie keiner sie Litt?	Teach her sorrows as none have suffered?
Schift ihr mir Schmach, wie nie sie geschmerzt?	Design her disgrace to give unimagined pain?
Ratet nun Rache, wie nie geras't!	Then tell me of vengeance, such as has never raged!

The dynamic of the whole plot was very clear in the composer's mind.

Summary

We cannot assume that Wagner analysed the betrayal of Brünnhilde, the trophy bride, as exemplified at the beginning of this chapter. Nevertheless, at this first creative stage, he shows Siegfried in a brutal light and the Brünnhilde of ST2 as vengeful in the extreme. He distorts the Brynhild of the sources, though not to the degree as he did with Sigurd. As with Senta, Elsa, Elisabeth and Sieglinde - he uses the woman rather than the man to give colour to the love between them. It is she who lifts their passion toward a self-regarding triumphalism. In no way does she resemble the semi-divine valkyr seen in *Die Walküre* but she would seem to match the historic Brunechild upon whom she may be based.

◇ ◇ ◇ ◇ ◇

7

Hagen and the Gibichungs

The three principals in the story of the doomed house of Burgundy - Gunnar, Gudrun and Hagen – find their places only as participants in Sigurd's death. Wagner came across them first in *Das Nibelungenlied* (Appendix B). He played down this encounter but the powerful drama inherent in some situations took root. Hagen cannot be disentangled from the Gibichungs and the lords Gunnar and Gudrun whom he serves. The hypothetical proto-plot in Chapter 4 ignores him because in all sources the key action is Sigurd's handing over of Brynhild to Gunnar - the action that brings about his death. The agent in the sagas is Grimhilde but, with her out of the plot, another option was needed. Hagen is always prominent as an antagonist to Sigurd in the *Nibelungenlied* so he was the obvious alternative. He became the major Gibichung player and, in Wagner's hands, one of the most impressive figures in all opera.

Hagen

The sources used

In the *Nibelungenlied* we read that Hagen was a mighty warrior with a forbidding presence, 'well-grown, broad-chested and long-legged. His hair was flecked with grey and his gaze was terrible. His carriage was majestic'. (AS/NL,216) Not a straightforward man, he is a formidable combination of the heroic and the sinister, with considerable common sense and political far-sightedness. This political sense has its dark side and this prompts actions with obscure but savage intent. Why is it Hagen who first proposes Sigurd's murder? 'His boast that he enjoyed my lady [Brynhild] shall cost him his life, or I shall die avenging it'. (AS/NL,117) No clear motive for this and other actions is offered but the reader can see, as did Wagner, that such ambiguity of character attaches to no other *NL* personage.

Alongside the above is a description in *Thydriks Saga*. As a boy . . .

> . . . Hagen was hard and strong and looked more like a troll than a human being . . . with a large, grim ash-pale face (TS#161) . . . [and as adult he] had black hair, a large nose, deeply falling eyebrows and a pale beard. His face was also pale and one eye was black. Large and powerful of build, he was grim . . . although clever and far-sighted he was always taciturn. (TS#174)

This captured Wagner's imagination. Hagen is the only person in the *Myth* to be physically described: 'sallow of complexion and saturnine and serious in behaviour; his features are prematurely hardened and he looks older than he is'. (Hagen is probably in his mid-twenties, though that is seldom perceived on stage.) He is 'cagey and careful with Gunther and Gutrune; in their turn they fear him but prize his foresight and experience. Gunther knows there is something remarkable about his father and that he is illegitimate: he calls him an Elf-son.' The most important fact about Hagen is that he is Alberich's son. 'As the hopes and wishes of the Gods depend on Siegfried, so Alberich sets his hope of gaining back the Ring on Hagen.' And so the following paragraphs in *Thydriks Saga* must have jumped off the page for Wagner:

> Aldrian was king of the Nibelungs.[A] One day when he was away, his wife drank too much and fell asleep in the garden. A man saw her whilst she slept and loved her. As the man left she awoke and thought she had been loved by her husband who had returned early. When the queen knew that she was pregnant the man came to her again.
>
> 'I am an elf and the child you carry is mine. When he grows up tell him about me but tell no one else. I think it will be a boy and that when he grows he will be strong but will also be troubled. If that happens and he does not know what to do, he can call on me for help.'
>
> The child came and was a boy whom the queen called Hagen; she said he was Aldrian's son . . . In due course, the queen bore three more sons – Gunnar, Gernholt and Gislher – and a daughter Gudrun. (TS#161)

We can now touch briefly upon Alberich who has not featured actively in the story since the *Das Rheingold* outline (p.34). It is a short jump from the elf in *TS* to a dwarf and the switch would have been encouraged by an episode from a minor source called *The Book of Heroes*. This episode recounts the story of one King Otnit whose mother has given him a ring containing a stone of power. Elberich is a dwarf lord who takes the ring from Otnit and shows him how to use it to disappear and then reappear. For the ring is his and it was he that gave it first to Otnit's mother. The climax of this particular encounter is the news that Elberich is Otnit's father for he had raped his mother the queen. Obviously the names Elberich and Alberich have one and the same root.

With help from these sources, Wagner transformed the formidable warrior of the *Nibelungenlied* into the black hero of the *Myth* and supplied him with a history and a motive. All this was completed before any mention of the most crucial issue within the *Ring*, namely the foreswearing of love.

- *Die Wibelungen* equates Siegfried with the sun god who kills the dragon of darkness and takes his fabulous treasure. The dragon has an heir who must kill Siegfried and take back the treasure.
- In the eddas, the treasure is the gold and the ring made from it, and is taken from the dwarf Andvari by Loki and Odin (VS#14).
- In the *Nibelungenlied* Sigurd acquires the treasure by conquest over the Nibelung princes; the custodian of this treasure is Alberich.
- Hagen is not related to Alberich in *NL* but is the prime mover in the murder of Sigurd amongst the Burgundian lords. He is also the most aware of the treasure's potential, gets hold of it after Sigurd's murder and then hides it by dumping it in

---

[A] Note once again the confusion between the Nibelungs and the Burgundians.

the Rhine. Critically, also, Hagen is the prime antagonist. He chooses to bring down Sigurd and does so by tricking Gudrun. After Sigurd is murdered he is singled out by his widow as her main foe, rather than her brother Gunnar.
- In *Thydriks Saga* the queen of Burgundy is seduced by an elf and gives birth to Hagen; she subsequently bears Gunnar and Gudrun.
- The dwarf lord Elberich in *The Book of Heroes* (see above).

There is nothing about Hagen in the Nordic sagas: no mention of him in the *Volsung Saga*. And whereas a distinction by name is made between the Sigurd of the sagas and Wagner's Siegfried, this does not happen with Hagen. There is a 'Hagen' figure in the *Prose Edda, Sturluson's Edda* and the *Volsung Saga*. Hogni is a younger brother of Gunnar. He offers wise advice but is often ignored. Thus although he goes along with the family decision to kill Sigurd, he counsels against it. 'Our swords should not cleave apart the oaths and vows we have sworn . . . we know no one on earth who is mightier . . . and while he lives, there is no higher kinship in the world'. (HB/PE,426) So although Hogni has some equivalence to Hagen, has an entirely different character and role. [B]

Hagen in the *Myth*

Wagner tells us more about Hagen than he does about anyone else. The scene with the Norns and the mutual pledging of the lovers, which eventually forms the Prologue to *Siegfrieds Tod* are not in the *Myth* and the first exchange in the action is Hagen telling Gunther of the glorious Brünnhilde. We read that he knew the formula for the drugged drink (and obviously for its antidote). In a few well-chosen words he cleverly supports Gunther as the man who had recently won the woman, implying that if Siegfried now has the Ring, he must have stolen it. He pricks and pushes Gunther into the plot to kill Siegfried by the promise of future riches.

All the above might well give the idea to someone who came to this text without preconceptions that the proposed opera is about Hagen and not Siegfried and Brünnhilde. If the opening scene were to be put together with the preceding 'background', it could be seen as a drama about Hagen's downfall, for his initiatives are always centre stage. He starts the plot going, manipulates the action, achieves his goal by destroying the relationship between Siegfried and Brünnhilde, and moves on toward success with the murder and the Ring within his reach.

In fact, one could go further. The structure of the story as first outlined can be seen as a tragedy about Hagen. He is a bastard son of unnatural parentage, of strange and ill-favoured appearance. Born into a privileged family, he makes his way to prominence within it because his cleverness – put at the disposal of the family - is valued. There

---

[B] Dr Benvenga identifies a historical character on whom the mythic Hagen could be based. The 7th century Khazar Empire lay by the Black Sea. The king (Khagan) was remote from his people and the running of the land was left to the deputy, entitled the Khagan Bek (ie The King's General). The 'Bek' part was dropped and we are left with the similarity of name.

suddenly arrives a man of splendour and fine address who possesses something that was his father's but was stolen from him long ago – a man who has everything he lacks. Roused out of subservience by rage at this injustice, he works successfully to destroy the interloper, take back what is rightfully his and rise to dominate his family. At the final moment, however, he is thrown down by forces he knows nothing about. A trick of fate destroys him.

This clarity and coherence as character and agent shapes *Siegfrieds Tod*. The spectator instinctively absorbs this whilst simultaneously the obscurity of Siegfried's character and actions linger uncomfortably in the mind. Hagen is Wagner's most effective villain by a long way: in the operatic repertory he is rivalled only by Pizarro and Iago. Perhaps it was the combination of Hagen's clear and precise villainy and Siegfried's loose and imprecise nature that had imprinted itself on Wagner's imagination by 1848 and perhaps this was the fundamental steer in direction that kept the *Ring* on the same track from beginning to end. The arrival of Wotan centre stage might push Hagen to one side but it was never going to upstage him.

Hagen in *Siegfrieds Tod*

This background is the reason that the *Myth* expanded effortlessly into the stage character seen in *Siegfrieds Tod*. Where the sketch is detailed in each of the three Acts, Hagen's presence flows into the poem. Moreover, the opening scene with Gunther and Gutrune, the central crisis in ST2 with Siegfried and Brünnhilde, the murder in ST3.1 and his defiance in ST3.2 are to be carried over word for word into *Götterdämmerung*. These scenes are unforgettable when clothed in music but the German words have power in their own right.

In sommerlich reifer Stärke	I'm witnessing the Gibich tribe
seh ich Gibichs Stamm,	in the summer of its maturity;
dich, Gunther, unbeweibt,	but you, Gunther, are unwed;
dich, Gutrune, ohne Mann.	you, Gutrune, have no husband.

****

Brünnhilde, kühne Frau,	Brünnhilde, dauntless woman!
kennst du genau den Ring?	Do you know this exact ring?
Ist's der, den du Gunther gabst	If it's the one you gave to Gunther,
so ist er sein,	it's his,
und Siegfried gewann ihn durch Trug,	and Siegfried cheated to win it –
den der Treulose büssen solst!	for that the swindler must pay a price!

The expansion brought in major new scenes in ST2. The sketch lacks both the pre-dawn dialogue with Alberich and the summoning of the vassals. Both are critical manoeuvres in the development and power of the final plot. The content of the pre-dawn scene with Alberich is completely different in *Siegfrieds Tod* from that in *Götterdämmerung*. The purpose is to give the audience the story of how and why Hagen is where he is. It summarily relates the pre-history as outlined in the *Myth*, from the grasping of the gold, through to Siegfried killing both the dragon and Mime, but excluding everything about how Siegfried was born. The extent is about 300 words: succinct but far too complex a narrative for an opera. It makes reference to the Ring of power, but without indication of why the power is there. In the prologue the Norns relate much the same content so Wagner cleverly presents the relevant pre-history from two contrasting points of view: one rancorously subjective and the other apprehensively objective. This might be thought the first step in widening the canvas of the proto-plot which is to culminate, four years later, with poems for four operas.

No glimpse of 'Hagen's Watch' – at the end of G1.2 – is seen in either the *Myth* or in *Siegfrieds Tod*. A version of it was written out early in 1849 but was not immediately developed, perhaps due to Wagner's growing revolutionary activities. Accordingly, the concept was not developed further for another 2½ years.

The summoning of the vassals and the build-up to the arrival of Gunther with Brünnhilde in tow is Wagner slipping back once more into Grand Opera mode. He was always a theatrical showman when such large scale splendour supported the drama. (For example, the second scene of *Lohengrin* Act II, from the dawn sunrise through the wedding procession to the cathedral was probably modelled on the similar scene in Halevy's admired Grand Opera *La Juive*.) The composition of the mighty choral ensemble lay 24 years in the future but a spectator of *Götterdämmerung* can envisage Hagen having enormous power at court. The dominance over almost everything is implicit but the only explicit role is as leader of the warrior vassals: they are under his control and cede authority to him. The audience know him to be traitorous in a manner far exceeding the *Nibelungenlied* use of that term. In a different story we could see him as triumphant in a coup, dispossessing the Gibichung royal family in a palace revolution. This aspect derives entirely from Wagner's imagination.

Hagen in *Götterdämmerung*

Wagner enhances Hagen's presence in *Götterdämmerung* over that in *Siegfrieds Tod* in two ways. Firstly, he now gives him a part in the Act II trio (previously designed as a duet) with Siegfried and Brünnhilde. He sings out of sync with the other two and this is unsettling in itself. Along with the emerged 'Watch' it shows Hagen as a man driven by lusts that are unknown to Siegfried and Gunther.

Secondly there is the change in the conversation between Hagen and his father at the opening of Act II. In *Siegfrieds Tod* Alberich exhorts his son: 'By craft and onslaught wrest back the Ring' and Hagen concludes the dialogue with: 'You shall have the Ring – you will again be free and the lord of the Nibelungs'. Contrast that with the final text as set to music. Alberich again presses his son to win back the Ring but this time the son responds: 'The Ring shall be Hagen's; leave me in peace.' Again: 'Swear to me, Hagen, my son!' which leads to the final terse: 'To myself I swear it; trust me and fear not!' Somewhat disconcerting for Alberich!

Along with the Norns in G1.1 and the scene between Waltraute and Brünnhilde in G1.3, this episode is used to bring to the fore the larger stage on which the drama is now played out. But in this case the additional effect is to throw all the emphasis on to the son and away from the father. For we do not need to be *told* anything about Hagen: the text, actions and music *show* us everything we need to know. He was so clear a personage to Wagner that this is succinctlyconveyed by what we see and hear

Gunther and Gutrune

In contrast to Hagen, the Gunther and Gutrune the spectator sees on stage are the Gunnar and Gudrun presented in the early pages of *Das Nibelungenlied*: the prince Gunnar is weak, despite appearances, and the princess Gudrun has high sexual allure. The emerging *Ring* characters are strongly drawn. The princess Gutrune is very beautiful, perhaps timid and certainly passive. Gunther is weak, shifty and lacks principle. The personalities of these two people suited Wagner's plot so he ignored the characteristics of those same people seen in the second part of the *Nibelungenlied*, which is not part of the *Ring* story and where the character and behaviour of each alters after Sigurd's death. (Gudrun morphs slowly from a grieving widow into a fearsome demon of vengeance, and Gunnar emerges as an intrepid warrior as his kingdom is threatened.)

In both Nordic and Germanic sagas, there are other brothers and also parents. Wagner has chosen that the father is named Gibich. In the sources he is called variously Dancwart (NL), Giuki (PE), Aldrian (TS). The kingdom they rule is called Burgundy (NL), Gjukungland (VS) and Niflungaland (TS). The capital, where the action of *Götterdämmerung* occurs, was Worms, still on the middle stretches of the Rhine. These names and the historical place have little impact on the *Ring*. Dr Benvenga lays stress on the historical roots of Hagen, and the Burgundian kingdom did collapse in the 5th century. But although Wagner may have had some of these facts to hand there is no reason to think that he shaped the dramatic structure and content of his plot according to any historical background.

◇ ◇ ◇ ◇ ◇ ◇

8

Siegfrieds Tod

George Bernard Shaw, in *The Perfect Wagnerite* (1896), claimed that the *Ring* is dramatically broken-backed. He saw the work as an allegory on current socio-political conflict. 'Really, of course, the dwarfs, giants and gods are dramatizations of the three main orders of men: to wit, the instinctive, predatory, lustful, greedy people; the patient, toiling, stupid, respectful, money-worshipping people; and the intellectual, moral, talented people who devise and administer States and Churches.' (GBS/PW,32) These three orders have failed and it needs a hero – namely Siegfried – to bring about the revolutionary change and 'make an end of dwarfs, giants and gods'. From *Das Rheingold* through to the Wotan/Siegfried encounter in *Siegfried*, Wagner carefullly sets forth – always in epic terms – the emergence of the hero from within the conflict between the 'three main orders' which contested for supremacy. Then the allegorical drama breaks down and, from the moment that Siegfried awakens Brünnhilde, the work descends from this high moral plane into the staple fare of operatic melodrama. There is then 'the loss of all simplicity and dignity, the impossibility of any credible scenic presentation of the incidents, and the extreme staginess of the conventions by which these impossibilities are got over.' (GBS/PW,94) Shaw was of the view that *Siegfrieds Tod* had a sound dramatic structure with a consistent logic. Thus, in writing of *Götterdämmerung* he says:

> Cut the conference of the Norns and the visit of Valtraute to Brynhild out of *Night Falls on the Gods* [sic] and the [original] drama remains coherent and complete without them. Retain them and the play becomes connected by conversational references with the three music dramas; but the connection establishes no philosophic coherence, no real identity between the operatic Brynhild of the Gibichung episode ... and the daughter of Wotan and the First Mother [Erda]. (GBS/PW,71)

Well, Yes and No. The 'NO' aspect has complexity. The scene structure is unchanged between *Siegfrieds Tod* and *Götterdämmerung*. The differences are in the text. The purpose of the Norns in ST1.1, of the Valkyrs in ST1.3 (instead of Waltraute in *Götterdämmerung*), and of Alberich in ST2 is to fill in the background. They relay to the audience the substance of the back story that the reader can now see in the first third of the *Myth* in Appendix A. By inference, for he is not writing an academic thesis, Shaw approves of that but decries references to the cosmic - what Cooke might think of as 'metaphysical'. For in the composed Götterd*ämmerung* it is to be the music of the Norns and Waltraute which takes the audience out of the present situation and back into Wotan's crumbling world. If all that is removed, what we are left with is certainly a powerful melodrama, but one wherein the actions of the two people who are to save matters would be for ever obscure. For without *Der junge Siegfried* and *Die Walküre* to round out Siegfried and Brünnhilde respectively, the former is something of an oaf and the latter a vengeful termagant.

Shaw's perspectives still have influence, 125 years later. In consequence, it is argued by those whose views take colour from him that Wagner either lost interest in Siegfried as Wotan moved toward the centre of the plot, or he lacked the energy and vision materially to change the style of the last opera, to give it the epic simplicity of *Siegfried*. Thus the first three operas have a clear and coherent dramatic thrust and purpose, which is then dissipated in the last. By implication, if Wagner had possessed the interest, energy or vision, he would have redrafted things to make everything more mythic and noble.

The road taken

The evidence, however, does not support Shaw and those who follow him. The plot Wagner put together in 1848 and the words in which he clothed it were constructed after much deliberation. He adopted whole-heartedly the sin (there is no other word for it) of Siegfried's betrayal of his wife as he hands her over to another man, and is careful not to exonerate him. Neither does Wagner exculpate his wife's behaviour after she realises the truth. She lies with intentional malice in order to rouse her weak husband to vengeance. By saying in public that Siegfried had slept with her on the mountain, she is asserting that he broke his oath of blood-brotherhood – a dishonour that Gunther cannot allow.

Conclusions about the two lovers within this chapter derive from the content of the *Myth* and the *Siegfrieds Tod* poem, with the addition of the closing section of the love duet in *Der junge Siegfried* (thereby excluding reference to the remainder of *Der junge Siegfried*). Such analysis is to be found in Chapter 5 on Siegfried, up to and including p.80, and in the whole of Chapter 6 on Brünnhilde. These sections make clear that the interpretations Wagner chose to adopt were not obligatory: whilst keeping to the central issue of betrayal by Siegfried and vengeance by Brünnhilde, there were other options he could have chosen. I have drawn attention to the hardening of Siegfried between the *Myth* and *Siegfrieds Tod*, particularly to do with the increased brutality with which he subdues the woman - a callousness not to be found in any of the primary sources. We can also find indications that he knew his portrait of Siegfried would present problems. In the *Myth*, his humanly touching memory of the subjugation of Brünnhilde was brusquely swept aside, even as it surfaced. At this early stage Wagner was taking pains to boost his hero's qualities above those accorded to Sigurd within the sagas (forging his own sword, his dead hand rising in defiance of Hagen) but here the composer diminishes his morality from that of the person seen in the sagas. Similarly, Brünnhilde is deprived of the wisdom and power of prophecy inherent in Brynhild the valkyr.

Look also at the depiction of the love Brünnhilde and Siegfried have for each other - as analysed in chapter 6 on the heroine. This relates to their depths of character, for there is a direct link between their love and the sagacity and insight they possess as human beings. The words of love they exchange are calls to arms and action, and not to peace and happiness. This is of profound significance for the whole subsequent project: if there be interpretative issues around the *Ring,* they stem from Brünnhilde and Siegfried. As will be seen in due course, Wotan is neither complicated in his derivation from Odin nor in his relationships with others. The problems which surround him and which emerge elsewhere in the study are clear and specific. He is very human and gets himself into a fix in a manner that is not difficult to grasp. This is not the case with these two lovers. The behaviour of both Sigurd and Brynhild in the Nordic sources is nuanced - with touching remorse, and complete foreknowledge of his triumph and doom in the man; with detailed and precise prescience of the betrayal she will suffer in the woman.

Wagner deliberately ignored these refinements and that this has not been recognised has influenced critical response. Those matters relating to the abandonment of wisdom by Brünnhilde can in fact be seen as of greater weight than those for Siegfried but that is not how it appears at first sight within the drama. Consequently, it is the man who is lambasted by commentators for the manner in which he betrays his wife, and questions are asked as to why Wagner found difficulty in explaining why and how he did so. The truth is that there remains a deliberate opacity in the dramaturgy. Everything concerning these two principal players follows from this. The love they have for each other lacks nuance and even humanity within the text. That does not entail falsity. All sources insist that the one is destined for the other. The nature of mythic masculine heroism and the legend of the unobtainable bride bring them together. Both have been pre-programmed, as it were. She is as one who fell asleep dreaming of a particularly admirable lover. He is like one who falls in love with a portrait - like Tamino in *The Magic Flute*. Only in this case it is an aural picture - the magical tones of the wood bird - rather than visual.

Once the mutual surprise and wonder with which they greet each other is over, sexual desire takes over and distorts everything else. They are quite different from all other Wagnerian lovers: we can read this in the roistering, apocalyptic words they sing as love is cemented in *Der junge Siegfried* and, after consummation in *Siegfrieds Tod*, as they hail each other as almost godlike. This is apparent in the words alone, regardless of the music in which they will eventually be clothed. Settling down to have children is not for them, whereas it is quite possible to think of other lovers doing so and these include Siegmund and Sieglinde, Walther and Eva, Lohengrin and Elsa, Tannhäuser and Elizabeth, and even Tristan and Isolde had they acknowledged their mutual attraction when she stood over him, sword in hand.

The consequent drama
These are flawed people. The Brünnhilde we see in *Der junge Siegfried* and *Siegfrieds Tod* is a cruder take on the womanly side of Brynhild as depicted in the Nordic sources.

As a mythic hero Siegfried was fated to die and Wagner prepares this with care; his self-centred overconfidence brought on his murder and this flaw was an inescapable part of his nature.

The resultant story is about Siegfried's error. Within the primary sources it is only the *Volsung Saga* that attempts to tell it in a rounded manner. By weakening the traditional features of the heroic, the anonymous author humanises him and, by ignoring this, Wagner acts to de-humanise him. This action is a counter to the many and clear efforts to present Siegfried as a real person. Consequently, Siegfried is surrounded with a mystery. The problem may stem from Wagner's attitude to his sources. They send conflicting messages that could be reconciled in a novel (as is attempted in *VS*) but not within the time/place confines of the stage. He keeps to the core of betrayal/vengeance because it is central to the sources, and this causes difficulty. A clue is to be found in Jessie Weston's *Legend of the Wagner Operas,* written as long ago as 1896. Here lies the most profound and respectful dissent from the *Ring's* structure. Ms Weston does, in fact, support the notion of continuity within the whole cycle.

> Regarded from some aspects, it may certainly be contended that the version given by the drama . . . does represent what was probably the original shape of the story more accurately than any *one* of the versions from whichWagner drew. (JW/LWD,148).

She concentrates on three sources: *Volsung Saga, Thidrik's Saga* and *Das Nibelungenlied,* and goes on to explain the difficulties Wagner had in shaping his narrative with the following:

> A tradition so colossal in its proportion, so *urweltich* in its origin, so extended in its ramifications and so obscure in its detail, could hardly be brought into any form which should represent swiftly and coherently the facts of the story, deal with the hidden meaning of its mysterious action, and do no injustice to the legend by the omission of much which is of importance. As a matter of fact, it would have needed not one Tertalogy alone, but two, if not three, to deal adequately with the source of the Hoard, the Life and Death of Siegfried, the vengeance on his murderers, and the final loss of the Treasure. (JW/LWD,149) [A]

To brush aside such 'hidden meaning' triggers uneasiness and perhaps did so to Wagner himself. *Siegfrieds Tod* was unfinished and unresolved - and unresolvable. It could perhaps have been turned into an effective opera but it would never have made a satisfactory stand-alone *drama*. This is not just due to the indigestible and undramatic mass of back narrative within it and the overly-didactic nature of the plot. Nothing could have addressed the peculiarity of Siegfried's behaviour. A relationship between Sieg-

---

[A] Almost all Deryck Cooke's comments about Weston in *I saw the world end* are derogatory and often based on the attitudes she displays about the incest between the twins. Indeed, he dismisses the significance of her as a woman brought up in the 19th century. In fact, within the smaller compass of her study when compared to Cooke's own, her summary of and choice within the main sources have an exemplary cogency and are of interest today. She understood what Wagner was after. (p.473)

fried and Wotan can be discerned in the *Ring*, as we shall see, but not in the single drama from which it emerged.

Nevertheless, in shaping the *Myth* Wagner did craft a man upon whom the larger edifice *could* be grafted. The first third is the vast and ill-defined moral background, and the remainder is a carefully considered outline of how Siegfried is enmeshed in deceit. The appearance of the *Siegfrieds Tod* poem within a month defies explanation. Nowhere in his correspondence does Wagner broach his espousal of *stabriem*, the alliterative verse wherein there is no rhyme but a reiteration of both consonants and vowel sounds. The composer would have obviously seen that the *Poetic Edda* used the form and he must have worked at it for some time. It leaps fully formed from the page. The content and style is unusual and differs totally from all his other works. In no other period did he write anything of such ferocity.

A new type of drama

The dramaturgy is also different and in marked contrast to that in *Lohengrin*. That opera is set forth in a series of tableaux, generally in a grand manner. The first Act is a drama played out by Elsa, Telramund, Lohengrin and Henry the Fowler (all the principals save Ortrud) before the assembled chorus who never leave the stage and strongly contribute to the musical fabric. The other two Acts are each in two parts: an intimate opening between two or three principals which then progresses to a tableau - again with the chorus prominent all the time. Contrast this with the eight discrete episodes in Act I of *Siegfrieds Tod*: the three Norns; Siegfried and Brünnhilde; Gunther, Hagen and Gutrune; Gunther, Hagen, Gutrune and Siegfried; Hagen alone; Brünnhilde alone; Brünnhilde and Waltraute; Brünnhilde and Siegfried. Act II has a central tableau but this is preceded and succeeded by episodes for principals alone. What starts in myth with *Siegfrieds Tod* ends close to Shakespeare in the complete cycle. This is something to which Porges refers in his record of the *Ring* rehearsals, where Wagner wished to combine 'the realistic style of Shakespeare with the idealistic style of antique tragedy; of bringing about an organic union between a highly stylised art, striving for a direct embodiment of the ideal, with an art rooted in fidelity to nature'. (HP/WR, 3/4) Shaw says of *Götterdämmerung* (for which read *Siegfrieds Tod* in this case) 'Not only the action, but most of the poetry, might conceivably belong to an Elizabethan drama.' (GBS/PW,94) Michael Ewans writes:

> *Götterdämmerung / [Siegfrieds Tod]* raises clear echoes of Elizabethan and Jacobean tragedy at many points . . . as Hagen develops his intrigues in a manner reminiscent of Iago. In addition . . . [in]. . .the final scene . . . vengeance is met with counter-vengeance, Gunther fights Hagen and is killed, and Gutrune collapses on his body, crying out in anguish against both Hagen and Brünnhilde. Much of this ending is in the spirit of Middleton and Webster. (ME/WA, 205)

Patrick Carnegy gave another comparative example in a talk to the Wagner Society in 2015: the 'dream' sequence between Hagen and Alberich, and that between Hamlet and his father's ghost. The former has 'Sei treu! Treu!' as his final words and the latter has the ghost departing with: 'Adieu. Remember me!'.

From the beginning, we see Wagner with a vision of a new kind of opera. The result – had amendments to make it a single viable opera been possible - would have been a melodrama of great force. Moreover, the *stabreim* style and metre is so different from *Lohengrin* that we cannot avoid the impression that he at least sensed a new musical form of some type. In 1844, Wagner wrote thus to a friend:

> I am attracted only by those subjects which reveal themselves to me not only as poetically but, at the same time, as musically significant. And so, even before I set about writing a single line of the text or drafting a scene, I am already thoroughly immersed in the musical aura of my new creation, I have the whole sound and all the characteristic motives in my head so that when the poem is finished and the scenes are arranged in their proper order the actual opera is already completed. (SS/SL,118)

In short, *Siegfrieds Tod* was the drama he wanted to create - a new start in every way. As the project grew, he made changes to the text but never varied from this conviction. The *Ring* includes a vast amount that is excluded from *Siegfrieds Tod* but virtually nothing changes in the relationship of Brünnhilde and Siegfried. From the beginning it was to be a drama of ritualised death to bring about a common good. This ritualistic aspect of a premeditated death is strongly drawn at the close. James Treadwell expresses this as follows:

> In the libretto of *Siegfrieds Tod*, unlike that of *Götterdämmerung,* there is a full on-stage rite of mourning and praise solemnising the hero and heroine's ascent to Valhalla. The perfected drama of the future, it appears, will stage a ritual death so that the audience can celebrate their own passage to utopia. (JT/IW,78)

It is a sacrificial expiation for otherwise irredeemable damage which weighs the world down. Treadwell could have gone further. ST3.1 as a whole is structured as a death ritual. The Rhinedaughters ritualistically foretell Siegfried's impending death (p.74). The Funeral Music is ritual from first to last. At the very close Brünnhilde mounts the flaming pyre in a self-immolation, much akin to a Hindu suttee.

If this surmise is correct, how could the composer ever have managed to adjust the text of *Götterdämmerung* as Shaw would have liked? The sacrificial ritual is paramount and, by its means, benefit is vouchsafed to the world.

The 'Immolation' texts

Universal joyous relief for that benefit, as received, is evident where one might expect it, namely in the closing 'Immolation' text. I say *Immolation text* but refer to all five versions with which Wagner experimented in the years 1848 to 1856. This chapter confines itself to just two versions: that in the original *Siegfrieds Tod* text of 1848, and that where a change is made to it within perhaps two months. The subsequent three are

SIEGFRIEDS TOD

all part of the finished poems for all four operas in the complete cycle, when the detailed plot was in place. These will be examined in Chapter 13, when many more elements of the story can be drawn in.

The original 1848 text

In 1848 the text for *Siegfrieds Tod* was shorter than that which replaced it in 1852. It can be broken down into 5 sections as indicated. The italicised text was taken forward unchanged into *Götterdämmerung*.

1 Eulogy for Siegfried links him to Wotan	*[Siegfried] was pure! Never were oaths more nobly sworn!* *False to his wife – true to his friend -* *from her who was faithful – she alone who was loyal -* *he sundered himself with his sword.* Have my thanks then, Hagen! As I told you and as I showed you, so have you acted and marked him out for Wotan, to whom with him I now go.
2 Sets the Scene	*Heavy logs heap up for me here in a pile at the edge of the Rhine;* *high and bright let the flames flare up* *and consume the noble limbs of the most exalted hero!* *Lead his stallion hither: let it follow the warrior with me:* *for my own body yearns to share in the hero's holiest honour -* *Do as Brünnhilde bids!*
3 Links the fate of the two lovers	You overweening hero, how you held me in thrall! All my wisdom I had to forgo, for all my knowledge I gave to you - what you took you did not use - in your bold defiance you trusted alone! Now that, appeased, you give it me freely, my knowledge returns once more and I read the runes of the ring. The Norn's ancient lore I can hear and understand all they say: the bravest of men's most mighty deed must now be blessed by my knowledge.
4 The curse is lifted as the gold returns to the Rhine	You Nibelungs, heed my words! Your thraldom now is ended: he who forged the ring and enthralled you restless spirits - he shall not regain it. But let him be free, like you. For I give this gold unto you, wise sisters of the watery deep! *Let the fire that now consumes me cleanse the ring of its curse:* *you will melt it down and safely guard* *the glistening gold of the Rhine that was stolen to your undoing!*
5 The result of the sacrifice	One alone shall rule: All-Father! Glorious god! Rejoice in the freest of heroes! Siegfried I bring to you now: grant him a loving greeting,

>   the bondsman of boundless might!
>   Rejoice Grane: soon we'll be free!

The texts of sections 4 and 5 are the first proclaimed moral goals of the Siegfried project, namely that those who have suffered will find release and that mankind (in the person of Siegfried) should save the gods who would continue to rule. Unequivocally, the new world will be a better place on both counts.

It must be this text to which Wagner refers in the 1856 letter to Röckel. He is clear as to his original purpose in the project, as he went through the process of fleshing out the *Myth* into the four completed poems in 1851. This is to show 'how a whole world of injustice arises from the first injustice, a whole world which is destroyed in order . . . to teach us to recognize injustice, root it out and establish a just world in its place.' (SS/SL,357) One world is destroyed in order that another and better one can rise.

The continued rule of 'All-father' (i.e. Section 5) is the only trace of the initial revolutionary spur to the work. The hint in the *Myth*, which makes its full appearance in *Siegfrieds Tod*, derives from Wagner's political views in the tumultuous, Europe-wide revolutionary fervour of 1848. In June of that year (four months before the *Myth* was written) Wagner, in his stirring speech to the Vaterslandverein, advocated the removal of the aristocracy and the establishment of a republic - but with the king at its head.

> You ask now: is all this to be accomplished with the aid of the king? I have said nothing that is incompatible with his being retained . . . If you admit it to be possible – or, as I do, to be more than possible – then the republic would be the right form of government, and we need only require that the king be the first and truest of all republicans . . . Let the republic be proclaimed, not by us but by the prince – the noblest, the worthiest king – and let him but say: I declare Saxony to be a "free state". The first law of this free state would ensure him his position. It would be: 'The highest executive power shall rest in the royal house of Wettin, and shall pass by law of primogeniture to his descendants.' (From HSW/W, p390/391)

Most would now agree that this was an odd idea but it was a political notion of a romantic stagey nature, the result of a short term political obsession: Wagner wanted political change and he was thinking of a stage work that would give expression to it.

The 'redemption in death' text

That the roots of this first conception were very shallow is shown by the speed of its rejection. It features in the *Myth*, is carried over verbatim into *Siegfrieds Tod* and then disappears. Probably within two months, namely by January 1849 Wagner crossed out section 5 completely and replaced it with:

> Blessed atonement I have seen for the holy, / sacredly ageless gods!
> Rejoice in the freest of heroes! / To the greeting of his brotherly gods,
> his bride is bringing him now! / Depart without power whom guilt now shuns.
> From your guilt has sprung / the blithest of heroes
> whose unwilled deed has expunged it: / you are spared the anxious struggle

to save your waning power: / fade away in bliss before the man's deed,
before the hero whom, alas, you created!
In the midst of your anxious fear / I proclaim to you blessed redemption in death!

This radical realignment of the closing text both obliterated the composer's short-winded, short-term interest in political recovery and established the real theme of the work as set out in the *Myth*. In that first sketch there are three places where Wagner points to this moral goal: the first is at R4; the second at the <u>Background to Walküre;</u> the third lies at the very end of the Sketch which covers ST3.2. We have, firstly, a prophecy from the Norns that the gods are doomed to destruction and secondly, an acceptance by the gods that, with the rearing of a heroic mankind, their power would pass away. The third statement is, perhaps, the most revealing: in Section 3 of the Immolation text, Brünnhilde's wisdom has returned now that Siegfried is dead: 'my knowledge returns once more and I read the runes of the ring. The Norn's ancient lore I can also hear and understand all they say'. This is that the gods are doomed to destruction. (Only one sentence in the *Myth* summarises the notion that 'All-father' shall continue to rule.) Clearly *any* notion of involvement by the gods also entailed consideration of their end. The Nordic sagas are impregnated with *Ragnorök* and Wagner absorbed this ethos: his perception that Siegfried's death was sacrificial melded with the fading from power of the gods.

The exact meaning of these new words announcing 'blessed atonement' is immaterial; what matters is that they add release for the gods to that granted to the Nibelungs and the humans gathered to watch the pyre which will consume the dead body of Siegfried and the live body of Brünnhilde. The joint sacrifice is to change the world for all. In Wagner's mind we can assume the message for his new audience would be that all levels of society would be better off – from the humblest labourer to those who ordered whatever system of government there might be.

This fundamental premise behind the drama lurked in the Immolation text from 1849 and the sentiments expressed are implicit in the changes made after the expansion from one to four operas and the poems of *Siegfried, Die Walküre* and *Das Rheingold* were completed.

The Norns and Wotan

The Norns, in the *Myth* and in *Siegfrieds Tod,* provide a concluding insight into the coherence within Wagner's creative process. Their function in the latter almost certainly derives from their appearance in Fouqué's *Sigurd der Schlangentödter*. However, in Wagner's drama they relate closely to Erda and as she rises to prominence as the mother of Brünnhilde, so does the role of the Norns diminish. They feature strongly in the *Myth* as the harbingers of doom to the gods but *Siegfrieds Tod* already reduces their role. They are now but narrators of events – rushing through the crucial episodes of the entire

Myth prehistory in 50 lines. No mention is made of their prophesy of the gods' doom - all they are noted for in the *Myth*.

They exist outside of time and do not die. There are three, as there are in the sources, and Grimm records that they '. . .spin for the hero the threads of his fate and stretched the golden cord in the midst of heaven.' (JG/DM,408) The Wala in *Poetic Edda* says of them:

> An ash I know, Yggdrasil its name,
> With water white is the great tree wet;
> Then come the dews that fall in the dales,
> Green by Urth's well does it ever grow.
> Thence come the maidens mighty in wisdom,
> Three from the dwelling down 'neath the tree;
> Urth is one named, Verthandi the next –
> On the wood they scored – and Skuld the third.
> Laws they made there, and life allotted
> To sons of men, and set their fates. (HB/PE,9)

Readers will recognize much in the above. Yggdrasil is the World Ash Tree. In due course Wagner will condense the above into the following in G1.1

> At the World Ash-tree once I wove
> When fair and green there grew from its branches
> Verdant and shady leaves.
> Those cooling shadows sheltered a spring;
> Wisdom's voice I heard in its waves;
> I sang my holy song.

Some characteristics Wagner ignored from the start as of no dramatic use, such as giving names to the Norns, but he did include different aspects of the Norns in the *Siegfrieds Tod* text. There they throw the rope to the compass points noted by Grimm ('one Norn tied an end of the thread eastward, another westward, a third fastened it northward') and they each speak in turn of what has been, is now and will be, as written in the sagas.

Left to last is a matter of real substance with regard to the creative process and this offers insight into how Wagner absorbed his sources right from the beginning. This is a fragment of text that is overlooked because it is not carried forward into *Götterdämmerung*. Almost their last words in *Siegfrieds Tod*, as they depart with the dawn and leave the stage to the lovers, are:

> *First Norn*: Wotan draws near my fountain.
> *Second Norn*: His eye fixes its sight on the well.
> *Third Norn*: Wise be his answer!

This exchange refers to the Well of Wisdom and is a conflation of two wells associated with Yggdrasil. One well nourishes the tree (as in the extract from *Poetic Edda* above) and the other (not quoted here) confers wisdom, at the price of an eye, which both Odin and Wotan paid - an unexpected glimpse of the primeval past. The answer required of him may well refer in some way to the request for wisdom. The words of the Norns show that Wagner had both aspects in mind, to the exclusion of all else concerning Wotan. Deryck Cooke argues persuasively that the 'first events' in the history of Wotan's world (as seen by Wagner and not the saga poets) are Wotan drinking from the well, paying for the wisdom he acquires with the loss of one eye and cutting the branch from the World Ash Tree, from which he makes his spear. There was no event or time before then - simply untouched nature, the Norns, Erda and the Rhinedaughters guarding the gold. After Wotan drank from the Well, conscious life began. (See DC/WE,248)

These lines are the more remarkable since they are the only reference the Norns make to the god in *Siegfrieds Tod*. When the drama required expansion, this background was to hand. To a contemporary reader of the 1848 poem these three lines would have made no sense whatsoever. In some way they seem akin to a personal note from Wagner to himself about the themes that can be found in the first part of the *Myth* and which were already developing within his imagination.

Two salutary perspectives

This study argues for a continuity of purpose from conception in 1848 through to the final text of 1856 and beyond. Such a view is at variance with much past opinion. Already within these pages several issues within the text cannot securely be resolved - and there will be more to come. These questions could not be answered or resolved by the Nordic skalds, nor by Wagner, nor by all the dozens of commentators on the *Ring* from the 1890s to the present day. This juncture, with many questions exposed to view, is a suitable moment to reflect on how difficult it is to establish an unambiguous narrative. I shall do so by offering two different ways of getting round issues concerning Brünnhilde and Siegfried. Each does so by cutting the Gordian Knot: both say that an issue cannot be solved so let us ignore it. (It is instructive at this point to bear Jessie Weston's observations on p.112 in mind.)

The first is to be found in the *Poetic Edda*. As we have seen, a problem with the valkyr in the *Ring* is to reconcile her first meeting with Siegfried as lovers with a later meeting when she is betrayed. One option in the *PE* runs so counter to all others that it disappears without trace after one fugitive mention. This is that Sigurd does not meet Brynhild at all before his long sojourn at Gunnar's court. Whilst he is there - and presumably already married to Gudrun - the two men lead an attack against Atli (Attila) and lay siege. Atli buys them off by offering his superlative sister Brynhild as a bride to Gunnar. She is reluctant but, having as yet seen neither man, agrees when she sees the splendid Sigurd and is told that he is Gunnar. She cannot have liked the truth when finally learned, but now there is no need for the ruse whereby the two men change shape.

The second variation is to be found in a redaction of the Nordic myths by Rosalind Kerven (*Viking myths and sagas*, Rosalind Kerven, Talking Stone, 2015). The first time Sigurd makes love to Brynhild in this retelling is when he breaks through the encircling fire in the shape of Gunnar. Until that moment neither have met, so Brynhild thinks herself to be awakened by her destined lover. However, Sigurd is in fact happily married to Gudrun and, as in the eddas, it is in friendship that he agrees to step in for Gunnar. Nevertheless, he and Brynhild engage in compulsive sexual intercourse. After marriage Brynhild's sexual response to her husband is never as on that first occasion, and Gudrun notices that Sigurd is distinctly less ardent toward her.

We see here two distortions which remove narrative problems. The *PE* variation tells us that Brynhild knew of the deceit played upon her from the very start and that Sigurd may well not have known anything about it. Ms Kerven's version leaves us to understand that Sigurd's sexual relationship with Gudrun was damaged by his 'adventure' with Brynhild, but also that this change was an unexpected consequence. Now readers may say that this last is a very modern take: the inadvertent result of a 'one-night stand'. Well, they may be right, but reflect that this sort of thing is sometimes put forward as an explanation for Siegfried's response to Gutrune.

The point is that neither the Nordic skald nor Ms Kerven had motive other than to construct order from a muddle, so that a coherent story emerged. Accordingly, they excised part of the histories of both Sigurd and Brynhild to make this happen. On the other hand, Wagner *required* that Siegfried should betray Brünnhilde in order to have a plot with dramatic traction and also, perhaps, to keep faith with the sources. Thereby he created puzzles for us all. And perhaps for himself. Nevertheless, it is not obvious that we are talking about 'confusion' in his mind. In such circumstances there is a temptation - as in much creative art - to say that the artist is struggling to *express* something and we look for what it is that s/he wants to express. It might be more useful to think that the artist - Wagner in this case - is struggling to *reach* something that is irretrievably obscure. The problem may be that the sources were themselves inconsistent, or because the answer could only inhere in a combination of character and situation which would be diminished by explanation, or because the drama left him no alternative.

Notwithstanding, an enigma is apparent from the beginning.

◊ ◊ ◊ ◊ ◊ ◊

9

Der junge Siegfried

The creation of the *Ring* poem can be seen as starting some time in 1847 and ending in 1856. The poem *Der junge Siegfried,* written in June 1851, lies at the mid-point of that period and can also be seen as the cusp of the creative journey - its central staging post. Before it lies the mental clambering through myths and legends, the extraction from them both of the plot for *Siegfrieds Tod* and a rich back story to support the drama. That first poem could not stand on its own and *Der junge Siegfried* is an attempt, that does not work, to spread and explain the back story within two operas. The story in the *Myth* is trying but failing to get out.

We can compare this with Michelangelo's four seemingly half-finished Prisoner (or Slave) Statues. Regardless of whether or not he left them unfinished on purpose to show humanity struggling to free itself, the statues are a vivid illustration of his express belief that 'every block of stone has a statue inside it and it is the task of the sculptor to set it free'. Wagner's block of stone was the legend of Sigurd which first found expression in the *Myth,* and it was the composition of the *Der junge Siegfried* poem that set his imagination free. Within the poem and in the original *Siegfrieds Tod* lie elements which hint at the full story struggling to emerge. It is as though the composer had laboured to the top of the hill and seen the road down on the other side, for the rest came in a rush: within 18 months from the poem's completion the text for the whole cycle was finished. Examination of the poem will reveal the yeast which produced the final creative surge.

The only difference in the action and structure between the earlier *Der junge Siegfried* draft and the final *Siegfried* poem is that Wotan does not try to bar Siegfried's progress with his spear. The scene structure of the two texts is identical, and the continuity between *Siegfried* and the two preceding operas is seamless. This first draft was written before Wagner determined on the need for *Das Rheingold* and *Die Walküre* and six months before he sketched their content. To make the story clear, therefore, the composer was obliged to include narrations and dialogues which supplied a potted history of all that went before, from the stealing of the gold, through Siegfried's parentage and birth, and concluding with an explanation of why Brünnhilde lay on the mountain in fire-surrounded sleep. The vehicles for the potted histories are the four conversations Wotan has first with Mime in Act 1, then with Alberich in Act 2 and finally with Erda and Siegfried in Act 3. In addition, there is one narrative that is to be cut completely: after Brünnhilde awakes and greets Siegfried she gives a long account of her personal history as a valkyr, concluding with her punishment at the hands of Wotan. *Die Walküre* rendered this redundant.

The style and form of the text is remarkable since it is so different from that of *Siegfrieds Tod*. Something like a fairy story (and so acknowledged by Wagner) is followed by something that can be likened to a family drama of greed, deceit and murder. *Der junge Siegfried* is the most mythic in form of all the four operas. There are the heroic aspects of the youth without fear, the forging of the conquering sword, the slaying of a dragon, understanding bird song, braving a fire and winning a 'sleeping beauty' bride. These very nearly alternate, in the telling of the story, with the four question and answer dialogues which make up the entirety of Wotan's contribution as he engages with each and every principal with whom he shares the stage. Such episodes occur frequently in the *Poetic Edda* and *Sturleson's Edda;* they are a central structural device in Nordic mythology. When combined with the archetypal acts of a hero, *Der junge Siegfried* is as close as is possible to the eddas in style and content – and in sharp contrast to *Siegfrieds Tod*.

Wotan and Siegfried

Wagner has given Siegfried definite, if ambiguous, characteristics in *Siegfrieds Tod*. This ambiguity is not seen in *Der junge Siegfried*. At the end of Chapter 5 is a list of the enhancements to character we can see in this opera, as crafted by the composer. Almost all are positive and in line with the requirements to be an archetypal hero. The narrative within the Nordic sources is the basis. With due name changes from mythic sources to *Ring,* Mime rears Siegfried with treacherous intent. The dwarf's plan is that Siegfried will kill Fafner and so win the Hoard and the Ring. Then Mime will kill Siegfried and help himself to the spoils. However, after the dragon is killed some of his blood touches Siegfried's tongue. As a result, he understands the language of birds and the woodbird tells him of Mime's intended treachery. Siegfried therefore kills the dwarf. The bird then tells him of Brünnhilde. Examination of the *Myth* shows that the above abbreviated plot is a digest of the *Siegfried* section.

The reader will also see that in the *Myth*, the composer's first written thoughts, there is no suggestion of any dramatic engagement by Wotan. So what is the significance of the plot as now developed? As seen in Chapter 5, the sagas do bring Odin and Sigurd together on several occasions. It may be, however, that Wagner did not see the purpose of this in his work until he sought to trace Siegfried's progress as a hero on stage. He uses Wotan's appearances to pace this heroic progress and, in fact, that is a key part of the god's function. The *Myth* tells us that Wotan knew the gods had to be destroyed and in *Der junge Siegfried* we get an idea of the intricate but still morally detached relationship that ties the god to the hero who must be sacrificed. Wagner had options in developing this plot. For example, at some point he could have cast Wotan in the role of Gripir (see VS#16), the relative who accurately foretells the life and fate that awaits Sigurd.

That Wagner did not take this option may have been due to the advent within the drama of the necessity that Siegfried must not be helped in any way. As Wotan says to Alberich 'Him whom I love I leave to his own devices; let him stand or fall, his own master is he: heroes alone can help me'.

Wotan as embryonic parent

The text is silent on a critical fact about the god, namely the parentage and early nurture of Siegmund and Sieglinde.

Caution is needed with regard to the relationship of Wotan to the Volsung twins as set down in this text. In answering Wotan's riddle question in the later *Siegfried* about which race of men does he most love, Mime says: 'The Volsungs / are the favoured race / which Wotan fathered / and fondly cherished.' These are the precise words as written in *Der junge Siegfried,* and carried forward into the final text and, with the sounds of *Die Walküre* in recent memory, a spectator will think of Wotan himself taking the name Wälse and being the father of the twins. But 'zeugte' also means to father a race rather than just individuals and this is what Wagner probably had in mind in the first draft. There was no need to change it, given the dual meaning. Brünnhilde makes the matter clear as she tells of her own history to Siegfried in the narration that was subsequently deleted.

Ein theures geschlecht	A treasured race
Zeugte sich Wotan:	was fathered by Wotan:
Die Wälsungen zog er sich auf.	he relied on the Volsungs.
Wie Allvater	How the father of all
die edlen liebte,	loved the noble ones
ich sinnende sah es wohl:	I saw very clearly:
schütz ich im streit	I protected the radiant race
mit dem schild die leuchtenden,	with my shield.
Siegmund hiess	One of Volsung's descendants was called
ein Wälsungenspross,	Siegmund.
Sieglinde hiess seine schwester:	His sister was called Sieglinde:
die maid ward Hunding vermält.	she was married to Hunding.
Nur zage söhne zeugten sie doch;	but she bore to him only weaklings.
tapfer sprossen darbte da	The brave one starved –
der weidliche Wälsungenstamm:	as true to the Volsung nature:
neid umgab ihn,	evil surrounded him,
hass und noth,	hate and struggle
fast erlosch sein strahlendes licht.	almost smothered his radiant light.
Da gesselte der schwester	Then Siegmund's own sister
sich Siegmund selbst,	joined him,
den liebended lachte die nacht:	and night laughed on the lovers:
den ächtesten Wälsung	so the outlawed Volsung
gewann da Sieglind.	won himself Sieglinde.

What we still have here is the Volsung history as laid out in *Volsung Saga #1* and is so summarised in the *Myth*. Wagner's mastery as a teller of stories is illustrated by comparing the family history in the sagas with what we are finally to get in the *Ring*. In the saga Odin is father to Sigi who is father to Rerir. It was Rerir's queen who had difficulty in conceiving. In consequence, Odin was persuaded by Frigg to send an apple of fertility to their grandson's wife. From this act was Volsung born. Volsung then fathered Sigmund and Siglind, from whom came Sigurd. So Odin was Sigurd's great-great-great-grandfather. Wagner telescopes this for his first outline by missing out Sigi and Rerir, and Wotan sends the apple to the wife of Volsung and thereby the twins Siegmund and Sieglinde are the result of his direct intervention. Within six months yet a further critical change was to be made: there is no apple of fertility and Wotan becomes the father of the twins rather than the grandfather. The condensation, then, is to be from great-great-great grandfather to father.

Erda

But what about Brünnhilde? The question takes us to Erda, a key character despite the short time she spends on stage. *Der junge Siegfried* is intended to tell us about Siegfried as a boy before he met Brünnhilde, and Erda has nothing at all to do with that. Wotan's discussion with her turns, as it does in *Siegfried*, round the inevitable downfall of the gods and his acceptance of it. In which case why Erda and not the Norns? They it were who foretold the gods' destruction in the *Myth*. Their last words as they leave the stage in *Siegfrieds Tod* are 'What we have spun bindeth the world.'

Wagner had the firmest grasp of the complex cosmic background that spawned *Siegfrieds Tod* and we have his letters to such as Liszt and Uhlig where he charts the expansion of the story. But these letters give no hint about the importance of Erda, nor that Brünnhilde is her daughter with Wotan as the father – that crucial invention and addition to the sagas. There is no mention of Erda's name in the *Myth:* she suddenly materialises out of nowhere.

She does so in a scene of contention and stress in opposition to Wotan and it is this which gives us the first reason why she supersedes the Norns. Neither *Siegfried* nor *Das Rheingold* nor *Die Walküre* attempt to match *Götterdämmerung* in melodramatic force but all three have confrontation between two people as the basic dramatic unit. The composer could not dramatise the background to the fall of the gods in a confrontation between one god and three obscurely characterised witch-like creatures.

The second reason is, of course, that he needed a mother for Brünnhilde. When, in JS3.1 Wotan asks Erda for advice, she in turn asks why he comes to her for an answer.

> A wishmaiden I bore to Wotan:
> heroes from battle he made her select for him.
> She is brave and clever as well:
> why do you waken me and not seek knowledge
> from Erda's and Wotan's child?

This comes as no surprise in the theatre, since the audience probably sat through *Die Walküre* two or three days earlier. But the words were written six months before *Die Walküre* was even sketched so the implications of her arrival on the scene are significant. Firstly, she irrevocably links Wotan to the Nordic cosmology – to the start of a significant development in the world and to the doom which awaits the gods. Secondly, as mother of Brünnhilde, Erda brings her daughter close to those cosmic matters. Thirdly, by fathering her, Wotan enters the story as a player. These three things are at the centre of the developing *Ring* and in Erda he finds the ideal agent to introduce them.

She is ideal because she is neutral and exists outside of time. She does not die, for she is of the earth. Wagner uses Erda as a catalyst, an agent that binds together the state of the cosmos, the leading person in that cosmos and the errant daughter of that leader. She can do this because she is not actually part of the drama but acts as a dramatic device. Of the three new dimensions Erda brings to the drama, only the cosmological, aspect is to be found in the primary sources. No one, let alone an 'Erda' figure, is indicated as Brynhild's mother and Odin is not her father. The inspiration is Wagner's: at some unknown date in the 30 months prior to May 1851, he felt the need to provide his plot with 'bottom'. The solution was the figure of Erda, with the dramatic threads leading from her to *Ragnarök,* and from there on to her godly consort and their child.

He found the needed powerful adversary for this scene in two *Poetic Edda* poems: *Voluspa* (The Wala's prophesy) and *Baldrs Drauma* (Balder's Dreams). *Wala* means 'wandering prophet' but in the ancient myths she has become an immortal figure. In Nordic mythology, the first beings were giants, from one of which, Ymir, the earth was born:

> Old was the age when Ymir lived; sea nor cool waves nor sand there were; Earth had not been, nor heaven above, but a yawning gap there was, with grass nowhere. (HB/PE,4)

Wagner chose from various possible interpretations to place the Wala as a contemporary of these 'giants of yore' when the 'tree with mighty roots' (that became Wagner's World Ash Tree) grew. Wotan acknowledges her as being of earlier origin than he and calls her 'urmutter' – a primeval mother with a deeper wisdom. At the end Erda is exhorted by Wotan to 'descend to ageless sleep' (JS3.1).

He found the mythic presence but not the name he wanted. At the centre of the *Ring* as it developed lies Wotan, but predominantly it is a story about people – creatures of the earth and not of the sky. Erda's name, relating to the German *erde* (earth), occurs in *Deutsches Mythologie*. Grimm also makes a connection between Volva, the name in *Poetic Edda*, to the Old High German Walewa or Wala (DW,227). Wotan addresses her by both names as he summons her in JS3.1: 'Erda! Erda! Eternal woman! Waken, awaken, you Wala, awaken!' In the two *Poetic Edda* poems in which a Wala figure appears, Odin rouses her from sleep, asks and learns about the future that awaits the gods. The first tells of the birth and make-up of the 'worlds' in which beings live, and ends with the description of *Ragnarök*. The second is related to it: the Wala tells Odin how Balder is to die. Both therefore are ominous and this is the role taken over straight from the sources into the *Ring*. The following could have been in his mind at the beginning of the JS3.1 scene:

> Then Odin rode to the eastern door. There, he knew well, was the wise woman's grave. Magic he spoke and mighty charms, till spell-bound she rose and in death she spoke. 'What is the

man, to me unknown, that has made me travel the troublous road? I was snowed with snow, and smitten with rain, and drenched with dew; long was I dead'. (HB/PE, 197)

In this episode he calls himself 'Wanderer' and the fraught exchanges include: 'Wanderer thou art not, as I thought before', to which Odin replies 'No wise woman art thou, no wisdom hast thou.' These find their place in *Der Junge Siegfried*, being characteristic of a mutual lack of tolerance between the two.

The Nordic Wala does not feature in many of the poems but the issues that surround her have a long reach, and Wagner mirrors this in the *Ring*. And as in the poems, everything about her is held together by visible ties; everything is shown to us and we need to be told nothing.

Mime

Wagner made big changes to Mime's history and background. From the beginning Mime was to be the brother of Alberich and not of Fafner, and a dwarf rather than a man. The relationship between Mime and Alberich is firmly limned in JS2. The mutual vituperative hatred between the brothers gives every appearance of having its roots in the violent scenes between them in *Das Rheingold* even though that text was set down many months later. The salient transactions between them are clear as is the disastrous loss of Alberich's hopes. [A]

The locations of JS1 and JS2 - lonely places away from all other people - were ideal: two caves deep inside a forest have strong mythic symbolism. He found what he wanted in *Thydriks Saga*. The plot has similarities to *Volsung Saga* and the other Nordic sources but with two appealing differences. Firstly, Sigurd's foster father is called Mime and he is a smith. Wagner needed to distance Siegfried from Regin and his background, and from the shabby, amoral tale of Loki killing Regin's other brother for no good reason, and then stealing the gold from the straightforward Andvari. That is not the sort of unity that ever appealed to the composer: there is no morality to it. Secondly, although Regin sees it as the beginning of *his* story, he is not a major player in the larger picture. Wagner needed a plot that had a beginning and the travails of Regin's family do not supply it. In fact, *Thydriks Saga* has a deeper myth behind it. Sigurd is found by

---

[A] This is in despite of one of the composer's most easily avoidable textual slip-ups. In the argumentative ding-dong, Mime says 'Where's the Ring now? It was wrested from you by giants, you coward'. This of course was *never* the case in any Wagner text, where it was always Wotan who purloined it and, in the *Myth*, gave it to the race of giants. Nevertheless, there is the error which sat there from first to last and was finally clothed in music.

This provides an opportunity to ponder matters that any publishing sub-editor would so easily have dealt with: in the beginning something inaccurate was written, with Wagner writing 'giants' instead of 'Wotan'. The likelihood is that he made the slip and never noticed it thereafter. This explanation has nothing to do with personal weariness. Once something inaccurate is written down, the writing eye passes over it: the words written are validated by the act of writing and the error remains hidden. Such errors are due to the lack of a sub-editor.

Mime as a baby abandoned at birth, and who was kept alive for three years on the milk of a hind who adopts it. This an appealing story with mythic tones but to include it would slow and clog the stage narrative. So it was dropped but the location in the woods stayed.

Wagner's take on the dragon-slaying (cf *Die Wibelungen*) had from the start rejected the notion that Siegfried might kill the dragon simply as part of a domestic quarrel, but he would want to keep the existing plot line of rival brothers. Perhaps it was at this stage that Alberich emerged as Mime's brother and as he who amassed the treasure, and thereby was merged with Andvari.

Alberich

We now come to the major player whose opposition to Wotan is the prime cause of the drama. And we can note that the vital issue concerning Alberich, namely the foreswearing of all love as the price to pay for the gold, is not mentioned. This action is not in the *Myth* and is not yet part of the plot in *Der junge Siegfried*. The point is not just that the text is silent on the matter (for neither is it mentioned in the later *Siegfried*) but rather that what *is* in the text hints at another - and anodyne - reason for Wotan and Alberich to be in opposition. As with all the dialogues in which Wotan is engaged, that with Alberich in JS2 is different from the final version. Newman gives an extended digest of their argument which he rightly calls 'a magnificent exchange' and which is cut completely from the revised *Siegfried*. [B] In it Alberich pours scorn on Wotan:

Wie gern hottest du einst	How gladly would you
das gold dem Rheine	Have looted for yourself
selbst geraubt,	the gold from the Rhine,
war dir die kunst	had you known
es zu schmieden bekannt:	the art of how to forge it:
doch täppisch warst du noch damals,	but you were inept at the time,
kindisch, der liste nicht kund!	childish and of no account!

There is no mention of any condition which must be fulfilled for using the gold: simply the statement that Wotan had no clue as to what to do but Alberich did. Furthermore, a potent symbol of the critical struggle is the bargain of Gold and Ring in exchange for Freya. Neither does this feature in the plot until the First Sketch of *Das Rheingold*, drafted between 3 and 11 November – five months later.

However, Alberich's lust for power and his renewed threats of what he will do if and when he regains the Ring are there within this first draft, and these are exactly as we eventually hear clothed in music:

> For once I grasp it again in my fist, / then, unlike the foolish giants,
> I'll use the power of the ring: / then tremble, eternal guardian of heroes!
> Valhalla's heights I'll storm with Hella's host: / then shall I rule the world!

[B]   See EN/WN, p448-450 for a cogent analysis of this scene, which Newman thinks more effective than that in the final *Siegfried*.

From first mention in the *Myth,* Alberich is unequivocally wicked, despite the admission that he had 'justice on his side'. He enslaves his fellow Nibelungs and 'sets out to gain dominion over the world and all it contains.' The envy and hatred the audience are to see emerge in *Das Rheingold,* and are to be the main focus of his eventual diatribe to Hagen in *Götterdämmerung,* are already evident in this draft.

The Giants

Wagner's Fasolt and Fafner are the last remnants of a vast Nordic mythology, virtually all of which was redundant to his purpose. I have mentioned Ymir, from whose giant body the world was made, and his function indicates much of the nature of the race. They represent massive primal forces and are often disruptive. Surt is a fire giant who rises against the gods in *Ragnarök* (p.48). Loki is actually a giant who fathers both the monstrous wolf Fenris - who is to eat the sun and engage in one-to-one combat with Odin in that final battle - and also Jormungard - the 'Midgard Serpent' which encircles all lands on the earth. None of this was of the least interest to Wagner. The final catastrophe in the *Ring* is brought on solely by Wotan's actions in the run-up to and during *Das Rheingold,* the consequences of which run through *Die Walküre* and *Siegfried.* The Wagnerian giants, and even the dwarfs, are actually onlookers in the matter.

Their only function in the *Ring,* lifted from the sagas, is that they built Valhalla. There is inevitably something inchoate in the plot's development. Fafner is named and identified as the last of the giants but what we are told about them is really just an expansion on the *Myth.* There Wagner describes them as 'primevally born' (as they are in the *Poetic Edda,* where they predate the gods) and 'strife' exists with the dwarfs, and the gods use it to forward the construction of Valhalla. The giants do not know how to use the Ring, hire a dragon to guard it and then the entire race 'fades away and ossifies into impotence.' In *Der junge Siegfried* this has not changed; Erda may have moved out of the shadows but the giants have not. The Wanderer and Fafner himself tell us of their status, the former in his answers to Mime's 'riddle' question and the latter in his dying words to Siegfried. Newman points out that in the Sketch for *JS* – written in May 1851 – the Wanderer tells Mime that the giants 'made war with the Nibelungs, coveting Alberich's Ring. They called the gods to their aid. For the gods they built a burg on the heights and asked for the Ring as wage. The gods took the Ring from the Nibelung.' (EN/LRW2,344) This is an augmented version of the *Myth.* But between sketch and poem there is a change. In the latter the giants are *not* at war with the Nibelungs before the story started. Wagner realised that this way to begin the drama was an irrelevance: if the giants and dwarfs are onlookers to the drama of Wotan, to emphasise a conflict between them shifts attention away from the god. Nevertheless, a trace of the theme identified by Newman remains in Fasolt's comment at the conclusion of Loge's narration: 'That gold I begrudge Alberich; / we've suffered much from the Niblung, and yet that angry dwarf / has always slipped through our hands.'

In the episode with Mime, in Act I of the *JS* poem, Wotan's narration is pure *Myth*. The giants . . .

> . . . as payment asked / for the golden ring:
> the gods wrested it from the Niblung, / and took hoard and helm as well.
> The giants gained everything / but around the treasure
> there circled strife: / he who possessed it
> was struck down in envy: / everyone wanted to hold it
> but none could keep it. / Then faded through its actions
> the whole race. / Now one only lives
> since the others fell: / Fafner the strongest giant
> as a worm guards the ring!

Fafner personalises the story when he tells his version of it to Siegfried. The race of giants is as a band of brothers who kill each other until Fafner kills the last of them. Fasolt finds no mention so obviously there is no reference to their particular quarrel. There is no fratricide and no mention of Freya. Fafner is just the last relic of the race which now falls to the 'flourishing hero'.

The plot stutters and it is easy to see why. Wagner had not yet formulated the great engine which drives it, namely the opening conflict between Wotan and Alberich – though he had hit upon the opposition of the names Licht Alberich and Schwarz Alberich. In this and in other elements in *Der junge Siegfried* (eg Erda and Wotan as the father of Brünnhilde) we catch a glimpse of the half-formed, still unshaped drama.

Style and characterisations

The new characters to arrive do so fully fledged. In the *Myth* and *Siegfrieds Tod* Alberich is really only there to fill Hagen in on the back narrative and thereby give him a history. But in *Die junge Siegfried* he is powerfully present – engaging Wotan in a long argument on the legitimacy of his actions. Mime is complete as a character and his behaviour in *Das Rheingold* is predicated in this text. The Alberich/Mime scene in JS2 is amongst the most revealing of both characters and will be carried verbatim into the final text. Alberich is also there outside Fafner's cave with his black cogitations at the start of JS2.

Wotan's presence and demeanour are clearly etched. Each of his scenes, with Mime, Alberich, Siegfried and Erda is unchanged in tone, though the actual conversations may differ in detail. He is majestic with Mime, thoughtful and combative with Alberich, involved with Siegfried and agitated with Erda.

Wagner asserted that before any text was written he had 'the whole sound and all the characteristic motives' in his head. The *stabriem* text written for Wotan with its repetition of consonants and vowels indicates something of the music that was eventually to clothe it: expansive and slow when he greets Mime:

Heil dir, weiser schmid!	Hail to you, wise smith!
Dem wegmüden gast	To a way-weary guest
gönne hold des hauses hird!	you'll not begrudge your house's hearth!

and harsh in confrontation with Erda:

DER JUNGE SIEGFRIED

Die Walküre, meinst du,	Do you mean the valkyrie,
Brünnhilde, die maid?	Brünnhilde, the maid?
Sie trotzte dem stürmbezinger,	She defied the master of storms
wo er am stärksten selbst ich bezwang.	when, with utmost effort he mastered himself.

The stage picture seems to be already in his mind.

The summer of 1851

Nevertheless, and despite the change of style and atmosphere between *Der junge Siegfried* and *Siegfrieds Tod,* nothing in the former concerning Siegfried and Brünnhilde contradicts the thrust of the latter. Indeed, the ritualistic, other-worldly structure of *Der junge Siegfried* - coming of age achievements by Siegfried (reminiscent of the fairy tale), the formalistic question and answer scenes for Wotan (his sole contribution) and the apocalyptic text for the lovers in the closing duet - can be seen to complement the death rituals of Siegfried in ST3. The governing factor remains the ambiguous portrayal of Siegfried.

The complete story as set down in the *Myth* lies very close to the surface now.

1. Many of the main themes of the bigger story into which the life of Siegfried is to fit are touched upon.
2. Erda is the only suitable mother for such as Brünnhilde. This is regardless of the facts that she is not mentioned anywhere in correspondence before she appears in *Der junge Siegfried* and that it will be a further six months before Erda is given the pivotal task of warning Wotan and thereby setting the story going at the end of *Das Rheingold*.
3. The Norns are already moving into the background even as the downfall of the gods is coming to the fore.
4. All the individuals introduced (the only main characters missing are Fricka and Loge) are strongly drawn with the exception of the giants. They are a race without personalities in the *Myth* and that is still the situation. Only Fafner is named and there is no hint of Fasolt.
5. Mime is completely drawn as a person, having been but a name in the *Myth*. We can clearly see why Wagner made the changes that turned him into a dwarf instead of a man, and a brother to Alberich rather than to Fafnir.
6. Alberich wants the power to which he thinks he is entitled but Wagner has not yet decided what price must be paid for this power.
7. Wotan is the father of Brünnhilde but is emotionally detached from her and therefore the *angst* in his encounter with Siegfried, that will drive him in the eventual version, is not present. He is also specifically portrayed as but a forebear and not the father of Siegmund and Sieglinde. Both his manner and behaviour are clearly drawn, but he remains remote. This weakness must have been clear to Wagner as he finished the poem.

DER JUNGE SIEGFRIED

# # # # # #

Nowadays we may look back on the development of the mighty work as a given and inevitable development. In the summer of 1851 it cannot have looked like that to the composer, and we can sense the agitated mental churning that was in process during the autumn and winter until all became clear. A high tide of invention found answers to the psychological motivations of Alberich and Wotan - unresolved in 6 and 7 above. When settled upon, these provided the two corner stones of the whole drama: the fearful price paid by Alberich for the power to forge the Ring and the advent of Wotan as the committed father of both Brünnhilde and the Volsung twins. It is this commitment that brings the god to the centre of the story.

Things moved rapidly. Wagner had a clearer idea of *Die Walküre* than he did of *Das Rheingold* in the autumn of 1851. The first sketch of the latter, written between 3 and 11 November is very short and lacks much of the content of the final text, but the first partial Prose Sketch of *Die Walküre,* written but a few days later, is precise. Early in 1852 Wagner jotted further thoughts about *Das Rheingold* and completed the final Sketch in April. The Prose Sketch for *Die Walküre* appeared between 17 and 26 May and this was turned immediately into the poem - completed on 1 July. Last came the poem for *Das Rheingold* which was completed on 3 November 1852. (See EN/WN, pp.459-461)

◇ ◇ ◇ ◇ ◇ ◇

How Odin became Wotan

Der junge Siegfried reveals little detail about Wotan. Most of his input in the dialogues with Mime, Alberich, Erda and Siegfried is retrospective narration. This chapter is to explore his actions and character in all three operas in which he appears. Firstly, there is the emergence of Wagner's Wotan from the Nordic sources: what the composer left out and the reasons for what he left in. Secondly, there is the full surfacing of Wotan as a father - the critical matter that brings him centre stage. This will bring discussion to the advent of compassionate love as a main focus of the whole drama.

From Odin to Wotan

The activities of Wotan dominate the pre-history to the stage action of *Siegfrieds Tod*, as set down in the *Myth*, and his presence was always near the forefront of the composer's imagination. In *Der junge Siegfried* his dramatic potential surges by making him the father of Brünnhilde. Two fundaments can be established. The first is that Wagner included only those aspects of the Nordic/Icelandic Odin that augmented the dramatic potential of his Wotan. The second point in the *Myth* is that Wagner portrayed Wotan as intrinsically noble, which is in contrast to how Odin is shown in those original sagas.

Odin

For modern readers (which term includes Wagner, the 19th century scholars who influenced him and ourselves in the 21st century) it is difficult to come to terms with Odin. This is because he has no discernible moral compass. He perpetually seeks for wisdom, and hands it out in proverbs and injunctions, but does not use what he learns to establish justice or respect for law in the cosmos under his jurisdiction. He supports and establishes royal dynasties amongst men but also protects outlaws. As a god of war, he does not uphold principles of honour in the same manner as does Thor, but uses his power to incite otherwise peaceful people to fight and kill each other. He is the acknowledged head of the 'Æsir' - the pantheon of male and female deities which orders the universe - but spends a large proportion of his time away from them and wandering around his cosmos to no good common purpose.

The name Odin derives from *Woðanaz,* in the earliest identified form of the Germanic language, and means 'master of ecstasy'. The areas of life in which he is concerned are warfare and death, wisdom and sorcery (which includes entering into altered states of consciousness, or shamanism), poetry and magic. The range is wide but Odin as the seeker after wisdom is prime. Extreme measures were endured. Odin wounded himself with his own spear and hung himself for nine days on Yggdrasil, without food or water or assistance from any source; the purpose was to possess the knowledge inherent in the runes carved by the Norns. The price to pay for drinking from the Well of Wisdom (Urth's Well) was the forfeiture of an eye. True to his name, all matters pursued by Odin include ecstasy - the battle frenzy of the berserk warrior in the case of warfare - and a defining quality emerges, namely the primal force that permeates all creation. This bursts forth in the life-altering actions of shamans, rebels, rulers, poets and warriors.

Odin's excessive energy extends to the sexual. In addition to Frigg, he was also married to Iordh and the Earth (hence, perhaps, Erda) whereby he is god of crops and the fertility of the land. In addition, he is said to have been married to Freya, to Saga, goddess of history, and to Rind, a human princess who only submitted to his advances under threat. He seduced one Gunnlod and stole the 'golden mead' of poetic inspiration from her. No detailed account of the rivalries between Frigg and Freya and Iordh and Rind and Gunnlodh remain, but it seems that much of Odin's time must be taken up by one or the other of these relationships.

Wonderful, indeed, but carrying a problem within a drama: because Odin has such multiple roles and manifests his energy everywhere, he is also unfocussed. How is one to portray someone who incites blood-lust in battle, involves himself in poetry and is prepared to hang himself to gain wisdom? The difficulty is demonstrated by attempts to portray on stage anyone with an extreme or psychotic personality. Stalin comes to mind: he was truly murderous but also had a fine tenor voice which he used sensitively, and wrote and appreciated poetry. The only way - and it has been done with success - is to give a clear illustration of his recognisably human traits but to place them on the surface of an underlying opaque personality. The result is that Stalin always plays the supporting role in a drama, which will have a central character whose task is to cope with and survive contact with such a monster.

Odin into Wotan

Thus Odin is a dramatic cipher: there is no part of him on to which a dramatist can hang a story. So Wagner picks just three aspects to portray Wotan: he is a seeker after wisdom (which encompasses a compulsion to roam the world), is inherently sexual and has a role as a war lord. Discarded are shamanism, altered states, poetry and any and every touch of the uncontrolled and the ecstatic.

The search for knowledge The closing words of the Norns in ST3.1 (p.118) demonstrate that Wagner was fully apprised of this aspect from the very beginning: in three lines he makes a link between Wotan's eye, the fountain or well of wisdom at the foot of the World Ash Tree, and wisdom itself. Wotan, like Odin, is to sacrifice an eye in order to gain wisdom. As the story expanded into the four operas the composer enriched this action: not only was it the first initiative the god is known to have taken but it also gave him the right to cut the branch from the tree from which he fashioned his totemic spear.

Wotan's visits to Mime and Erda in S1 and S3.1 respectively are also echoes of Odin's perpetual search for knowledge. Fourteen of the poems in the *Poetic Edda* concern the gods. In six of them Odin engages in question and answer debates, three centre on the present and future state of the universe as then understood, and in one the lives of Odin and his 'opponent' depend on who wins the contest. Think of Wotan in R4 and the relevant scenes in *Siegfried*. The two episodes with Erda and that with Mime are cosmological in one way or another; these three plus the episode with Siegfried in S3.1 are based around question and answer and in that with Mime the lives of both are on the line. Those with Erda also centre upon the fated end of the gods. This recalls Odin whose main concern was to learn about *Ragnarök*.

Wotan as a wanderer across his cosmos is frequently introduced. Fricka in her first exchange in R2 says that she supported the building of Valhalla because it was a way of binding him fast whenever he feels drawn away: 'a glorious dwelling, domestic bliss were meant to entice you to tarry and rest.' Waltraute in G1.3 tells Brünnhilde that after Wotan had put her to sleep, 'the father of the slain (*Walvater*) avoided Valhalla's valiant heroes: alone on his horse, without rest or repose, he roamed the world as the Wanderer.' Wotan presents himself to Mime thus: 'As Wanderer am I known to the world: already I've wandered widely and over the earth's broad back have oft-times wended my way.'

Promiscuous sexuality Wotan makes no attempt to refute Fricka's accusation in W2 of his repeated sexual infidelity: 'You've always played false with your true-hearted wife: where was the hollow, where the height where your lustful look didn't pry in seeking out ways of indulging your fondness for change and of tauntingly wounding my heart!' These words cannot be set aside but the modern spectator only sees this aspect in Wotan's siring of Siegmund, Sieglinde and Brünnhilde, and will probably think that he has reasonable cause given current difficulties. [A] Moreover, the infidelity is something we are told and not shown, and it is certainly not the casual, predatory sexuality often associated with men of power. It may serve, therefore, as a useful shorthand pointer to current marital discord rather than an aid to meaningful drama.

[A] A pause for thought, however, arises when we think of the slaughtered unnamed mother of the twins. It might well be that Wotan regarded her as 'collateral damage', necessary as part of a bigger plan from which he, of all people, would not shrink: not very nice! Moral he might be, but Wotan was not a kind person.

The inciter to battle   Waltraute's *Walvater* (Father of the Slain) is one of the titles which include *vater* to be found in the texts: *Siegvater* (Father of Victories), *Heervater* (Father of Armies), *Streitvater* (Father of Conflicts) - names lifted from Grimm's *Deutsche Mythologie*. Here we can indeed connect the Wagnerian and the Nordic god, for the many names reflect Odin's penchant for stirring people into battle frenzy. In W2, Wotan recalls the task he has given to Brünnhilde and the other Valkyrs: 'I bade you bring me heroes . . . you had to spur them on to onslaught and strife, honing their strength for hot-blooded battle, so that hosts of valiant warriors I'd gather in Valhalla's halls.' This is a direct echo of the sagas. Alberich's threat in RG3 to 'beware . . . when the Nibelung's hoard arises from silent depths to the light of day,' means that Wotan has need for warriors and also for the valkyrs to choose which will give best service. He is not arbitrarily shown as violent.

This third aspect of Odin, taken unchanged into Wagner's portrayal of Wotan helps us to understand the god's behaviour and attitude in *Das Rheingold* and also in the periods before the audience first sees him contemplating the newly completed Valhalla. Cooke brings to the fore a revealing exchange between Wotan and Fricka in W2. We do hear Wotan's words 'Unholy I regard the oath that binds those not in love' but not those with which he continues and Fricka's response.

Wotan: The woman's case weighs light with you
       if you consecrate the force
       with which Hunding married his wife.
Fricka: If brute force, obstinately savage,
       lays the world in ruins,
       who alone bears the guilt for the harm
       but the raging one, Wotan, you?
       The weak you never protected,
       you only stand for the strong;
       the anger of men with their harsh spirit,
       their murder and pillage, are your mighty work.

Cooke regrets that this was not set to music, probably for the reason that the action could not tolerate ever more complex argument. This is so but there may be a deeper explanation. These characteristics are laid against Wotan but they are not found in his actions, in anything that he actually *does* in the operas. On occasion the music portrays him as *Streitvater* – when, for example, in high rage he advances upon Brünnhilde and the valkyrs in W3. The audience gets the gist of the sort of man he is but that stops short of laying on his conscience mankind's liking for 'murder and pillage'. Wotan's desire for power brings problems in train (see below) but Fricka's words do not find echoes in his actions. The composer sought a god who would be 'true to life' in the manner of Shakespeare.

Wotan, rather than Odin

Those three characteristics are the only tangible personal connections between Wagner's creation and the mythic character on which he is based. The person we see on stage was forged in the composer's imagination. The following are either new aspects of character or far-reaching adaptations of those in the sagas.

The will to power   A corollary of his protean energy is that Odin sweeps all before him. This is just an inevitable consequence and is not willed, whereas Wotan's will to dominate is at the core of his personality. Wagner establishes the central conflict in the character, namely that between the seeker for wisdom in order to do the right thing and the ruler who desires to control everything - even by force. 'Everything' includes his own family and intimate circle, and this instinct by Licht Wotan is sadly similar to Alberich's domination of his brother. This is everywhere manifest and in contrast to somewhat strained insistence on Wotan as a war lord.

Deryck Cooke examines in detail the Wotan we see in *Das Rheingold* and *Die Walküre*. He is the archetype of the 'man in supreme power [who uses] . . . his conscious will to exploit his fellow man by establishing an authoritative state sustained by a rigid system of arbitrary laws' (DC/WE,248). Cooke is exemplary in his analysis of the means by which the god acquires and sustains his power.

The first was his willingness to sacrifice his eye in order to obtain wisdom. This enabled him to take the second step, namely to drink from the Well of Wisdom. This forfeiture and the consequent benefit is only fully explained (taking up the hints in *ST*) in G3.1 as part of the Norns recollection of past history. The drink then gave him the right to cut the branch from the World Ash from which to make his spear. Finally, by carving the 'prudent laws', which 'bind all elements', upon it, the spear becomes the means of recording the laws permanently.

That is something we are told for it cannot be shown. What the drama shows is the power of the spear to enforce those laws and that is why the name given to it in this study is *will-to-power*. Odin has a spear, Gungnir, but this is only used in battle. So the imperious force of Wotan's spear, which must be shown to the audience is not found in the sources but is devised by Wagner. There is no hint of this whatsoever in the *Myth*, only hints about the conflict of which it is to be part. There the outline is that a long-standing but stalemated, conflict between the three races of gods, giants and dwarfs has existed. This balance was destroyed by Alberich's theft of gold and by crafting the Ring. The giants turn to the gods for help against the Nibelungs. The gods also feel vulnerable to the dwarf and therefore ask the giants to build a fortress from which they can govern the world in security. When it is finished the giants demand the hoard in payment.

But although the spear is not mentioned in the *Myth*, Wotan's urge for power is: 'Wotan hands over the Hoard to the giants, but means to keep the Ring, which he will use to ensure his overall dominion . . . this power which enforces the existing peace is not legitimate for it was achieved by violence and cunning . . . the gods are compromised by their own moral failings. The power has been wrested from Alberich but this was not for any noble end. Therefore Alberich has justice on his side.' This passage, with obique implication, brings in its train a central plank in the whole drama. Wotan wants two things which conflict: to make the world a better place but to do it on his own terms and by any means. He uses the laws hewn into his spear, and the spear itself, to sustain his power and nothing suggests that the force inherent in the spear is anything other than coercive. Wotan is not interested in collaboration: as Fricka points out, he encourages strife within his world, provided he can control it.

The intent of the passage from the *Myth* is obvious: it is to register that the god has a critical flaw. The error that dogs Wotan from the beginning is the reckless use of Freia within a dangerous bargain. The god puts the personification of youth and love in hock to the pursuit of power, and we now understand that he does this *before* he is aware of Alberich's threatening power. This is a major invention on Wagner's part. Odin and Wotan are different. Scholars think that predilection to break oaths by the Norse gods - the broken oath with the giant who built the castle is simply the most prominent - is a failing that leads to *Ragnarök*. Wotan's flaw is different: it is his overwhelming desire for personal power in the *Ring* that leads him into his own particular quagmire. (See CL/NM pp.97,98)

Wotan the moralist   Despite the above and in contrast to the Nordic god, the the *Myth* shows Wotan to be highly principled. He understands that if he succeeds in his enterprise to raise mankind's 'strength so high that he may rid himself of the gods' protection . . . [then] their own power would pass away.' Benign intent is manifest: 'Wotan bargains with the giants to build a castle from whence the gods will be able to rule the world in peace and good order.' They show 'daring, moral enterprise . . . organise the world, bind all elements by prudent laws and devote themselves to careful nurture of the human race . . . moral awareness by all is [their] objective.' Cooke may describe him as the archetypal 'chieftain, king, emperor, dictator, president – primordial, historical and contemporary man-in-supreme-power' but he really does want to use his power for maximum benefit. His goal is the emancipation of Man from the laws that he, Wotan, has imposed and this freedom is to be total so that 'of his free will he can do what he sees for himself to be necessary.' This wish mirrors Wagner's socio-political belief that moral health requires that life be 'a conscious pursuit of the only real necessity . . . no longer held in subjugation to an outer . . . arbitrary power' (p.6). When this goal is achieved, the gods will disappear. Wagner made his famous observation in the 1856 letter to Röckel that 'Wodan (preferred name in the early stages) rises to the tragic heights of *willing* his own destruction' (SS/SL,307) but he could also at that time simply have made reference to the content of the 1848 *Myth*. This verdict on the character was made when he was but background, the force against which the hero Siegfried was eventually to pit his heroism - and it never changed.

Nevertheless, as the detailed exposition of *Das Rheingold* in Chapter 18 will show, the audience is not shown this as the plot first gets going. The motivations behind the god's first actions are little different from those of Alberich and it is only by having learnt about them from some acquaintance with the *Myth* that the audience is aware of Wotan's moral compass. Undoubtedly the first magnificent proclamation of the Sword motif (to be called *wotan's sword* in this study) has positive moral overtones but it is hard to discern them in Wotan's first fraught discussion with Fricka as the sun shines on the distant Valhalla. The plot of *Das Rheingold* was the last to be set down in detail and Wagner gives Wotan an upward moral slope to climb at its opening.

Wotan's desire for wisdom Neither can Wotan's desire to wander and to search for knowledge be seen in the same light as Odin's, which often seems to be erudition for its own sake. The Wanderer cares for others and not only for himself, witness his words to Mime in S1:

> Much I've fathomed, / much made out:
> matters of moment / I've made known to many I've saved
> from whatever irked them, / cares that gnawed at their hearts!

To Alberich in S2: 'I came to watch and not to act: who'd bar the Wanderer's way?' The music for the Wanderer supports this in contrast to that motif which signifies Wotan's *will-to-power*. The w*anderer* motif reflects his wish to learn and prepare himself for the hazard that Siegfried and Brünnhilde may not succeed.

The humanised god Wagner has taken the mythic Odin and humanised him. He is the supremely powerful ruler who wants to make his world a better place. This ambition has damaged him in a manner that is fully human. All trace of a god disappears in this description of his own behaviour to Brünnhilde in W2.

> When youthful love's delights had faded, / I longed in my heart for power:
> impelled by the rage of impulsive desires, / I won for myself the world.
> Unwittingly false I acted unfairly, / binding by treaties what boded ill:
> cunning Loge lured me on . . .

Previously in R2 Wagner expanded on how and when he employed Loge:

> Where freedom of mind is called for, / I ask for help from no man;
> but to turn to advantage an enemy's grudge / is a lesson that only cunning and craft can teach,
> of the kind that Loge slyly employs. / He who counselled me on the contract
> promised to ransom Freia: / on him I now rely.

We only see one 'unfair' action, namely the intent to trick Fasolt and Fafner, but the clear implication is that deceit was regularly used when useful.

Having submitted himself to Loge's wiles, however, and with the giants insisting on Freia as payment (lifted directly from Sturleson's Edda, p.35) there was no way out but to agree and then to look for an escape route. It is possible that Wagner had the *Oresteia* in mind. Professor Ewans, in *Wagner and Aeschylus,* draws a parallel between Wotan and Agamemnon, this being the pressure of 'necessity' upon each of them. Agamemnon commits an offence, grave in itself regardless of the loathing it arouses in his wife, by sacrificing his daughter Iphigenia. The fleet he commands is ready to sail for Troy but is becalmed, and only the death of his daughter will remove the impasse. In the play that bears his name the verdict of the chorus on this fearful choice is that 'he put on the harness of necessity'. The choice, as Ewans says, 'is at the same time both inevitable and freely taken.' (ME/WA,85) The parallel pressure on Wotan is clear. Faced with the real and dangerous threat represented by the Ring on the hand of Alberich, he has little choice but to take it from him. But again it *was* his choice, and freely taken.

The action that inaugurated Wotan's epochal power - the crafting of the Spear from the World Ash Tree - and that which inaugurated his downfall - the tearing away of the Ring from Alberich's hand - have this aura of necessity in common. They are strong examples of the lengths that a man will go when in obsessive pursuit of a goal, and they are on such a grand scale that they can be truly called mythic.

Wotan, the father

The keystone of the god's humanity is his role as parent. For the moment we shall consider him as father of Siegmund and Sieglinde, and how this reveals much about Wagner's use of the primary sources. The development within the plot of the two lovers is amongst the most radical manipulation of these sources.

The sagas relating to the Volsung twins have thirteen players in all, in a complex story. (Detail can be found in Appendix C, #1-13.) The god **Odin** sires a tribe that is particular to him. Three generations later **Volsung** is the king and he has amongst his children the twins **Sigmund** and his sister **Signy**. The latter is unhappily married to the malevolent **Siggeir**. This neighbouring king invites Volsung and Sigmund (and his other brothers) to his kingdom with the express purpose of slaughtering them all. Volsung is killed but Sigmund survives this battle and, with the help of his sister Signy, escapes from the subsequent death trap prepared by Siggeir. Hiding in the forest, Sigmund is again supported by his sister; she hates her husband and wants him dead. To engineer this, she magically disguises herself, visits and makes love to Sigmund in his hideaway, conceives and gives birth to **Sinfjiotli.** When the boy is old enough she sends him to his father in the forest and they live together as outlaws, marauding throughout the neighbourhood. In due course they attack Siggeir's palace but are captured. Signy once again arranges for their escape, and father and son burn down the hall, killing Siggeir. But Signy chooses to die in the flames rather than leave with them; she has fulfilled her life by killing her husband, who had treacherously slaughtered her father. Sigmund and Sinfjiotli move back to his kingdom and defend it against several enemies amongst whom is **Hunding.** Sigmund marries **Bjornhild** but Sinfjiotli seriously offends his step-mother who poisons him. Sigmund understandably rejects her and courts **Hjordis**, daughter of King **Eylemi**. She chooses the Volsung, comparatively old as he now is, in preference to the younger King **Lyngvi**. Accordingly, Lyngvi attacks the kingdom and kills Eylemi and Sigmund. Hjordis escapes however and, remarried to one King **Alf**, gives birth to **Sigurd** – conceived with Sigmund just before his death.

The totemic sword Gram (Wagner's Nothung) is woven into the tale. At Signy's wedding celebrations Odin enters the hall and thrusts the sword into the great central tree; only Sigmund can pull it out. When he and Sinfjiotli are captured by Siggeir, Signy steals Gram from her husband and smuggles it to the captives who use it to cut through the great stones which entomb them. In Sigmund's last battle Odin interposes his spear and Gram shatters upon it, following which Sigmund is killed. As dies he hands the shards to Hjordis: she must preserve them for their unborn son who will be a great hero.

The above cast of thirteen people patently cannot be contained in a drama. The pruning started with the elimination of Sigmund's first wife Bjornhild and the kings Eylemi and Alf; these are bit players even in the sagas, there to facilitate the actions of others. Then he removes Siggeir and Lyngvi, who both serve as victims of the vengeance of Sigmund and Sigurd respectively and merges them into Hunding - a named enemy king not involved directly with the family. This is a clever constructive character meld exactly matching similar examples in the Shakespeare history plays where the actions and roles of several lords are merged. By this means Wagner reduces six originals to one, namely Hunding. Eight saga characters are still standing. Signy and Hjordis are to be merged into one, who is given the name Sieglinde (that of Sigurd's mother in the *Nibelungenlied*), Sigurd and Sinfjiotli into the figure of Siegfried, and Odin and Volsung are merged to form Wotan in the guise of Wälse. Thus the original thirteen is reduced to five: Wälse, Siegmund (who is the only person not to be merged with another), Sieglinde, Hunding and Siegfried. If we include the conception of Siegfried after the curtain falls on Act 1, Wagner hangs the entire action of *Die Walküre* upon them.

This pruning occurred at a very early stage within the process of shaping the scenario for *Siegfrieds Tod*. The text of the *Myth* demonstrates that the composer had sorted everything within his mind with the exception of the merging of Volsung with Odin. Almost all of it, moreover, was not needed for the plot construction in the last two thirds of the *Myth* - the prose sketch for *Siegfrieds Tod*. The only reference in the poem is Hagen's explanation to Gunther in ST1:

> From Wotan sprang Wälse, / and from him a twin pair -
> Siegmund and Sieglinde: / they begat the truest of Wälsungs.
> His father's blood sister / gave birth to him in the forest.

This is as described in the *Myth*. The text makes sense when carried forward into *Götterdämmerung*, where we have seen it previously enacted, but is not relevant in *Siegfrieds Tod*. Siegfried as the hero who famously killed the dragon would have conveyed all the heroism needed.

From Volsung to Wotan

The actual nature of Sigmund's elevated lineage is expunged from Wagner's outward story but it surfaces in the central issue of why Wotan finally emerges as Siegmund's father. With hindsight Wagner must have seen that Wotan had to be the father of the twins; no written note or jotting is available until the Prose Sketch for *Die Walküre* of November 1851. The idea may have crystallized round the decision to designate Brünnhilde as his child. That particular relationship is of greater moment for the central action of the whole *Ring* but Wotan, as the forebear of *every one* of the humans who are to take over the story, enriches it beyond measure.

The lives of Siegmund and Sieglinde are fully and completely set forth in the personal story that each of them tells. Everything we need to know about them is clear and everything is original and from Wagner's pen. Siegmund, in particular, bears no resemblance to the Sigmund that the reader will find summarised in the *Volsung Saga*. Sieglinde has a life that resembles that of Signy (of Hjordis there is not a trace) in that she is unhappily married but that is all. Their lives are as they are because Wotan is their father and - as Fricka rightly says - he has plotted what has happened to each. To look for any clues within the saga lives of Sigmund and Signy is to look in vain: Siegmund and Sieglinde only became clear to Wagner when Wotan became the parent. We saw a half-way house in *Der junge Siegfried,* when Brünnhilde tells Siegfried about his parents (p.123). Sieglinde is married and has children but they are weaklings. Siegmund, however, is not married and is portrayed as perpetually hounded. The source is VS#8, where Sigmund spends considerable time as an outlaw. His companion is his son Sinfjiotli, born of his union with sister Signy. And we see here a compelling difference between *Die Wälkure* and the sagas: Signy disguises herself when she gives herself to Sigmund and passion between them is absent. Signy just wants vengeance.

Nevertheless, Sinfjiotli is the only person in the pure blood line, and Wagner would have wanted to hold on to this, thereby doing what he could to mirror the sagas without diluting the plot. Hence the merging of Siegfried and Sinfjiotli.

Wagner used every device possible to distinguish his sacrificial hero from all others. No better option can be conceived than to have Siegfried as 'the child of both son and daughter . . .' who are themselves not simply born of a hero, however great he may be, but of the mightiest lord of the world. Once this logic was perceived, the inevitability of Wotan as the forebear of every human who is to save him is obvious.[B] He is tied to the big story of the damaged world both morally and personally. He pushes himself wholeheartedly into the stressful and consuming world of parenthood, as he first fathers and then nurtures for many years two children by a human. Dear also as they are to him, he

---

[B] Productions of the *Ring* are not slow in bringing the love of Wotan for his children to the fore. The celebrated 1976 Bayreuth production by Patrice Chereau has Wotan lifting the dying Siegmund into his arms in W2. The 2013 Seattle production has the Wanderer longing in vain to make himself known to his grandson as he leaves for the woods in S1.

brings suffering upon them: he strengthens the daughter by allowing her to marry a man who – as her behaviour shows – has almost certainly beaten her, and accompanies the son for some good time as a hounded outlaw before he finally leaves him to his own devices.

Some writers in the 1870s thought that Wagner included incest gratuitously to shock, and some modern writers pick up on the undoubted love he had for his elder sister Rosalie. All tentatively imply that some such extreme motivation on the one hand or personal passion on the other lay vaguely behind both music and words of the lovers. The answer may be Yes to both. Wagner's views on incest can be found in his writings: his analysis of the Oedipus myth was published in *Opera and Drama* one year before the sketch for *Die Walküre*. The exoneration he offers is that the love between Oedipus and Jocasta was true, that they fell in love before the truth was known. From the union came the 'divine' Antigone, whose hold on truth brought down the state which had first been betrayed by treacherous Laius, the father of Oedipus. (See RW/PW2,181-186.) But Wagner must have been aware that a big majority of the Bayreuth spectators would have agreed with Fricka. They would have been shocked. If so what was Wagner's purpose in making the incest so explicit? The force of Wagner's invention moves it beyond existing myths about brother/sister incest. In the sagas the twins Freyja and Freyr were children of a brother and sister who are, in turn, accused of sleeping with each other. The Egyptian Isis and Osiris are brother and sister, *and* man and wife. The difference between all these and the conjunction of Siegmund and Sieglinde is the nature of their offspring: in modern terms half Siegfried's DNA is that of Wotan and both his parents are as strongly schooled in self-reliance as it is possible to imagine. No greater heroic lineage is possible. Siegfried is to be the supreme hero and his conception occurs within a sexual union of optimum personal and compassionate dedication; that they know the truth of their relationship before the sexual union does but increase their arousal.

If that were Wagner's view of the matter the corollary is that Siegmund would not be whole without such an experience. What, moreover, did Wotan expect? He warmly welcomes the love between his children in his argument with Fricka but it is obvious that he does not yet understand the force of their passion. Wotan has to learn about love from Brünnhilde; until that point it has to be an abstract matter. c

The power of love

At some point in the autumn of 1851, Wotan emerged as the immediate forebear of the four people who carry the story forward. We cannot know what prompted this critical development but it might well be that Alberich had something to do with it. In the first

---

c   Robert Donington's thesis in *Wagner's Ring and its Symbols* (RD/WR) - as mentioned on p.2 - may not be to the taste of everybody, but the opening of chapter VII *The Valkyrie* illuminates why the modern audience is not revolted by the action.

very brief outline for *Das Rheingold,* written between 3 and 11 November 1851, there is the first note about his drastic bargain: 'The gold gleams, "How can that be won?", "Whoever curses love." ' On 12 November Wagner writes to Theodor Uhlig. He describes how Alberich steals the gold after being spurned by the Rhinedaughters; it is a trinket 'but another power resides within it which can be coaxed from it only by the man who renounces love'. (SS/SL,233) These are the first references to Alberich's avowal, which is absent from the *Myth*. Once Wagner had hit upon this idea the polarity of Licht Alberich with Schwarz Alberich was obvious. Whereas Alberich abjures and means to destroy love Wotan, in fathering children, will be embracing love. There are many types of love, some of which fail when put to the test. What does not fail is the parental love which Wotan has for Siegmund, for Siegfried and - above all - for Brünnhilde. In fatherhood, Wotan commits himself to love in a similar way in which Alberich expels himself from it.

This change is revealed in Wotan's robust exchange with Fricka at the beginning of W2. In many of the preceding years he had nurtured the Volsung twins as they grew into adults. And, as Siegmund narrates, after the mother was killed and Sieglinde abducted, he spent some years as an outlaw with his father Wälse. For the first time, perhaps, Wotan would have seen and understood at least part of what compassionate, caring, social love entailed. His actions then would have been a far cry from those castigated by Fricka in the words (not set to music) she throws at him: 'the weak you never protected.'

This polarity of Licht Alberich and Schwarz Alberich is the issue that impacts with such force when we see the cycle on stage. Once grasped by Wagner and understood by the rest of us, it has an inevitability. We perceive the huge theme rise out of the *Myth* as if hewn in rock and present itself to our minds as the natural fulfilment of the elements from which the story derives. We perceive that the plot had to develop as it did as the composer strove to find moral and emotional motive and cause for the huge events leading up to *Götterdämmerung*.

Ernest Newman, in reflecting on the manner in which the story developed and Wotan moved to the centre of the cycle, suggested that Siegfried became 'merely a pawn in the tremendous game of Wotan's moral problem'. (EN/LRW2,349) Might it not be truer to say that Wotan himself became a pawn in that great game from the moment he fathered Brünnhilde? For, in truth, it is his children who thereafter control events and, by implication, control him. When Fricka points out that Siegmund is dependent on Wotan he is apparently stymied; we know what she means when she destroys Wotan's arguments about Siegmund in W2 with the words: 'in ihm treff' ich nur dich, den durch dich trotz er allein.' (In him I find only you, for you alone he defies us.) But although Fricka may be right in logic, she proves to be mistaken in the drama. Not only Siegfried, who is designedly entirely his own man, but also Siegmund, Sieglinde and Brünnhilde prove to be defiantly independent when it matters: Wotan has no power over them. (This is no more than the norm. However well children love their parents, parental love is greater and more consuming, and most parents are - in consequence - weak before their children.) Each of Wotan's descendants breaks free from him according to their individual needs and it is this emancipation that brings him salvation. At the end of *Das Rheingold* Wotan is in a bind. He knows he cannot do anything himself to rectify things. So he creates noble beings who sequentially are impelled, by the direct or indirect influence of sexual love, first to break free from his parental power and then to work to do what he himself cannot do.

The significance, therefore, of the change in the role of Wotan, from an imperial arbiter to the forebear of those who carry the story forward is that it is a dramatic necessity. No melding or manipulation of the sources has greater dramatic force than this inspiration whereby Wotan is pulled into both personal and epic conflict. It was the dramaturgy that drove Wagner and not a desire to bring Wotan to the fore at the expense of Siegfried: the god's dilemma is the source of the energy that drives the story. He is consciously active in seeking for a resolution, and to sire children whom he (mistakenly) believes he can control is as good an initiative as can be devised to further his ends. This is almost a matter of logic: for the *Ring* to have an ending that rings true, the defiance of Wotan's offspring, either implicitly like Siegfried, Siegmund and Sieglinde, or explicitly like Brünnhilde, must be seen to be both a necessary and sufficient condition. Nothing else will do. Even as Wotan was emerging as a character, as detailed earlier in this chapter, the lock between Wotan and Siegfried was being forged - one of the bonds between father and offspring that dominate the drama as a whole.

Another aspect of the *Ring* is revealed here: the need or, to put it more strongly, the *right* of the individual to break free of all coercion. Power may be necessary for order but, by definition, it must stand in the way of individual freedom. And if we are prompted to think of Wotan as tragic we can take into account the inevitable conflict between his need for power and the freedom fought for by his children.

The centrality of *Die Walküre*

The pivotal development in the *Ring* is the appearance of Wotan's three children. The preceding events in *Das Rheingold* and the action in the two later operas turn around the emergence of these three people. It is no accident that almost every spectator responds more vigorously to this opera than to any of the other three. Neither the taut, cogent drama of *Das Rheingold,* nor the ebullient energy of *Siegfried,* nor the concentrated musical mastery of *Götterdämmerung* can overtop the emotional power of the relationship of Wotan with his children, and the relationships between those children.

The prose draft of W1 and W2 were completed by the end of 1851 - six months after the poem for *Der junge Siegfried*. The text of these two Acts, which encompass the life of Siegmund in totality, frame the emotional heart of the entire drama. We have seen that Siegfried is a particular type of hero - one who is fated to die because of what he is rather than what he does. Siegmund's heroism is human and one we recognize: brave, uncompromised and uncompromising, kind and compassionate. His history as an outlaw suggests sufferings long-born and relentless. He is so described in *Der junge Siegfried:* 'evil surrounded him, hate and struggle almost smothered his radiant light.' Sieglinde is fully his match as a heroine who bears tribulation and waits patiently for deliverance.

The audience sees Siegmund and Sieglinde as exemplars of heroic humanity. This conception widened the story, increased its emotional temperature and provided Wotan with a personal focus. The love of Siegmund and Sieglinde is the bridge by which Brünnhilde crosses from divinity to humanity. It was glimpsed in *Der junge Siegfried* and burst forth to transform the whole story six months later.

◇ ◇ ◇ ◇ ◇ ◇

The invention of Alberich

The trajectory of the *Ring* story is set going by two drastic, bad actions. The dwarf Alberich seizes hold of the Gold in the Rhine in pursuit of power and the godly Licht Alberich, also in pursuit of power, places Freya - and therefore all the gods - in jeopardy. It is reasonable to surmise that Wotan's reckless negotiation with Fasolt and Fafner took place at about the same time that Alberich left Nibelheim and found himself at the bottom of the Rhine.

On stage what we see first is the aggressive action of the dwarf and this triggers a reaction from Wotan. The plots of *Die Walküre*, *Siegfried* and *Götterdämmerung* are consequent upon the actions and initiatives of the god at the end of the first opera, but everything starts with Alberich and what he does in *Das Rheingold*. Wagner's dramatic invention reaches an unsurpassed peak in all matters to do with Alberich, and this applies to the very beginning of the *Myth* when, as far as we can see, Alberich was not yet seen as an actual player in the staged drama. The opening sentences of the *Myth* are as follows:

> In the womb of night and death the Nibelung race was engendered. It lives in Nibelheim - a place of dark underground clefts and caverns. With restless energy they burrow through the bowels of the earth, like worms in a dead body; they heat, refine and forge metal. Alberich seized the pure and noble gold of the Rhine, wrested it from the water's depth, and with the most cunning art forged it into a ring which gave him absolute power over his whole race, the Nibelungs. So he became their lord, forced them to work from then on for him alone, and amassed the immeasurable Nibelung hoard.

Note the certainty of Wagner's narrative line. These opening sentences of the *Myth* are a prime example of how a work of fiction should begin. The opening words of the *Myth* have something of the same quality as those in two famous examples of this skill - by Jane Austen in *Pride and Prejudice* ('It is a truth universally acknowledged, that a single man in possession of a good fortune, must be in want of a wife.') and by Shakespeare in *Hamlet*. ('Who's there?' – 'Nay, answer me. Stand and unfold yourself.') Both pitch you straight into a story that is waiting to be told.

Of equal significance is that the most important events emerged newly minted from Wagner's imagination and without reference to the mythology. Much of the invention with regard to Alberich goes hand in hand with that for Wotan as father. His move toward compassionate love is the obverse to Alberich's actions, as played out in the opening scene.

The following table identifies each event and situation to do with Alberich at the opening of *Das Rheingold*. The top of the table covers background, the middle portion deals with the action that sets the story going and the last section covers the consequences of that action. Each has an index of the degree to which background or action is original with the composer. The index column shows '1' where strong reference is found in the sources, '½' with weak reference and '0' where there is no reference.

Stage event or situation	Whether in the sources	Index
BACKGROUND		
The setting of R1 is at the bottom of the Rhine, where the Rhine Gold is fixed.	There is nothing in the sources save some minor links between gold and water.	½
Nibelheim lies adjacent to the Rhine.	The underground realm where he lives is a construct by Wagner, in contrast to the gods who exist on the heights.	0
Alberich finds his way from his home to the bottom of the Rhine.	No mention of this in any source but Andvari, the dwarf from whom Loki took gold and ring, did sometimes take the form of a pike.	½
Alberich has a brother.	No dwarf resembling Alberich has a brother. Regin (ie Mime) does: Fafnir the dragon.	½
The Gold is guarded by the Rhinedaughters.	Nowhere in any source do water-sprites guard anything at all.	0
THE ACTION THAT STARTS THE STORY		
Alberich is sexually and romantically attracted to the Rhinedaughters; they entice him in turn but each rejects him.	Nothing whatsoever like this is in any of the six primary sources.	0
The Gold reveals itself in the water and is acclaimed as something very special.	There is no indication in any mythology that such an emblematic piece of gold might exist.	0
The Rhinedaughters tell Alberich that the Gold is of no value. However, it can be transformed into a Ring of immense power by the person who swears to renounce love.	No such oath is expressly required for any reason in any mythology; no source postulates that a ring with such power can be fashioned, with or without the oath.	0
Alberich accepts the condition, renounces love and wrests the Gold from its rock.	In no source, whether Germanic or not, is this to be found.	0
The Gold is 'pure' - namely an ideal. The person who acquires it by renouncing love can change it by compression - from a lump to a Ring.	No such quality inheres in any gold in any mythology, whether Teutonic or not.	0

Stage event or situation	Whether in the sources	Index
THE CONSEQUENCES OF THE ACTION		
The Ring fashioned by Alberich can divine where gold lies in rock and enslave all other members of the Nibelung dwarf tribe.	Andvari's ring has the power to divine where gold is but has no power to coerce.	½
The Ring imparts one other piece of crucial knowledge, namely how to craft the Tarnhelm. This is a cap that has three powers to aid the wearer: to make him invisible, to enable him to change shape and to transport him instantly from one place to another.	In *NL* Sigurd attains a cloak that both confers invisibility and can transport the wearer. However, the ability of the wearer to change shape is original to Wagner	½
Alberich becomes a tyrant.	No such tyranny is to be found in the sources.	0
The power of the Ring	Whatever it is, it does not convey power as promised.	0
Alberich places a curse on the Ring when it is taken from him by Wotan.	Andvari similarly curses his ring when Loki takes it.	1

Fifteen key factors or events are listed in the tables. The primary sources can claim a total of 3½ points out of 15. However, the five crucial actions in the middle section of the table - those to do with how the Gold can be taken and turned into the Ring of Power and why Alberich is prepared to accept the condition - have no connection whatsoever to the sagas.

So the opening action of the *Ring*, when Alberich vainly woos the Rhinedaughters, learns of the power inherent in the Gold, accepts the condition which releases the power, uses the power to enslave his tribe and thereby brings about the fateful confrontation with Wotan - all these were dreamt up in their entirety by Wagner. To achieve this, he not only had to envisage the *dramatis personae* but also place gold at the bottom of a river and powerfully present it as something that can easily be seen by the spectator as priceless. To a considerable extent, the incidents and characters in the second and fourth scenes of *Das Rheingold*, and the entirety of the three operas which follow derive from the six main primary sources. All this activity, however, follows on from the situation and actions of Alberich - almost all of which emerge from Wagner's imagination.

Deryck Cooke, from whose book much of this information is derived, was the first to adumbrate the superlative invention of plot which makes up the first scene of *Das Rheingold*. His book - as published - is work-in-progress. Its focus would have sharpened had he lived, and he is likely to have brought out clearly the feature that is common to all these inventions and others like it. This is that all followed from the needs of the drama. There is no manipulation of the sources - no 'compressions, fusions and alterations' (to use his words) - which will work better on stage.

The exploration of the fifteen themes will also be split into the same three sections as the table: those which establish the background, those which are the crucial actions which emerge from the background, and those which are consequent upon those actions.

The background set-up

The gold in the Rhine

After introducing the Nibelungs, the *Myth* describes what was to be the stage setting: the bottom of the river Rhine where is fixed a moderate sized lump of gold. We can ask two questions: Why is the gold in the water? and Why is that water the Rhine?

Water as the home for golden treasure is twice indicated in the sources (DC/WE,128): Andvari's golden hoard is in a cave under a waterfall (HB/PE,358), and gold is also called 'fire of water and rivers' because a sea god used the glitter of gold to illuminate a great banquet (SS/E,95). That, however, is not the real point within the drama. What matters is that the precious gold is made visible on stage, and that anything in water is accessible and vulnerable. This piece of gold is most precious, but it can easily be wrenched from its moorings if the necessary conditions are met. The gold is only of real value when it becomes the Ring and it is inconceivable to the Rhinedaughters that anyone would turn completely away from love. They are described as the 'guardians of the gold' but are not given any power, there being no need for power to be exerted.

The choice of the Rhine was obvious. The legendary Sigurd's climactic death occurred in historic Worms and good reason would be needed if the early life of Sigurd and those of his parents were to be located at a distance. Moreover, in all the sources except *Thydriks Saga,* the final resting place of the golden hoard is in the Rhine. In the *Poetic Edda* Gunnar and Hagen submerge it there, in the hope of raising it later, before they depart for the journey to Attila's palace which is to end in death. In the wider context of dramatic structure one can also see a reason, namely the symmetry of the gold leaving the Rhine at the start and returning to it at the end.

The Nibelungs and Nibelheim

'Nibelung' is the first use of a name in the *Myth*. The Nibelungs are dwarfs and the justification for their name is valid even if odd. In the *Nibelungenlied* the Burgundians are not called by their real name but are referred to as Nibelungs; this is because the tribe owned the treasure stolen by Sigurd from two Nibelung princes and their steward/treasurer - the dwarf Alberich. In short, the tribe who possessed the totemic Nibelung Hoard were called Nibelungs, and since in the *Ring* Alberich's tribe has the treasure, so is it to be called the Nibelung tribe. Wagner chooses that they be dwarfs, for the strict derivation of *alben* is elves. His depiction of them reflects how the eddas perceived dwarfs, who 'had been generated . . . in the earth like maggots in flesh. . .[and] . . . came into being in the flesh of Ymir.' (HB/PE,16) Grimm comes to Wagner's aid with: 'The dwarfs . . . are cunning smiths . . . their forges are placed in caves . . . and our German folk-tales everywhere speak of the dwarfs . . . slipping into cracks and crevices in the hills.'

In making them dwarfs, part of the reason may also be his notion of describing Wotan as Licht Alberich when he came to write *Der junge Siegfried*. In *Die Wibelungen*, written at about the same time as the *Myth,* Wagner wrote: 'In the religious myths of the Scandinavians, the term . . . Nebelheim (the home of mists) comes down to us as a designation of the subterranean region of the Schwarzalben (Night Spirits), as opposed to the heavenly dwelling of the Lichtalben – (Light Elves)'. (RW/PW7,275/6) But Alfheim in the primary sources, the place where the Light Elves (the gods) live, is only vaguely located as in the heights and Svartälfeheim, the home of the Black Elves, has no special location. Wagner ignores all this in the *Myth*. He uses words which relate to the darkness of underground caves to invent a specific land that is the opposite of that in which the gods live. His instinct for symmetry may well have played a part in this and it works well on stage. Moreover, since it is underground, direct access to the bottom of the Rhine is the more feasible.

Alberich and Mime

Alberich is seen by Wagner as the epitome of malevolence and the first naming of him in JS1 as *Schwarz Alberich* is intended to reinforce that aspect. It works for the audience since *schwarz* is contrasted with *licht* at that point, and the opposition of the essentially bad Alberich with the essentially good Wotan makes a clear and quickly understood distinction. Authority for this description is thin. *Schwarz* refers to the colour of the Nibelungs (the epithet can mean dark or dingy as well as black) and/or to where they live, but not to their morals. Grimm writes: 'Some have seen, in this antithesis of light and black elves, the same dualism that other mythologies set up between spirits good and bad, friendly and hostile, heavenly and hellish, between angels of light and darkness' (JG/DM,440), but he is clearly not convinced. The only two bad Nibelung dwarfs are Alberich and Mime, but Wagner skates over this and deftly manages to merge location with morals: the enlightened Wotan lives on the heights and the degenerate Alberich in the ground. (See DC/WE,194-197)

Alberich is an amalgam of four within the sources.

- Alberich is the ferocious dwarf in the *Nibelunglied* who serves the Nibelung princes as custodian of their treasure.
- Andvari, in the eddas, who is forced to yield up his store of gold and his ring to Loki, as in VS#14, is also a dwarf.

- The third is the unnamed dwarf in *Thydriks Saga* who fathers Hagen, the half-brother of Gunnar and Gudrun.
- The fourth is Elberich who also has a son by a queen who he is said to rape and who owns a ring which confers invisibility. (It may be that we see here a single trace of Elberich's ring. One can assume that he used his ring of invisibility to effect the rape of the queen (p.104). Wagner is reticent about this unnatural transaction between an ugly dwarf and a high aristocrat, and the use of a ring of invisibility would both enable the act of intercourse and also qualify as a rape. The only problem is that the assault must happen before Alberich lost the Ring.)

The fearsome dwarf, created by Wagner from traits within each of the above, straddles the *Myth,* and his fathering of Hagen extends the reach of that action to the final catastrophe. His character in JS2 may only come alive *to us* in the scenes with Mime and Wotan but one suspects his nature and underlying significance were clear to Wagner from an early stage.

Alberich's background is completed by his relationship with Mime. At some very early moment, Wagner had a clear vision of Mime as the foster father of Siegfried (by adopting the narrative in the sagas) but declined to have him as the brother of the dragon (as Regin was brother to Fafnir). The reason is simple: in the sagas the narrative line of Regin's relationship with Sigurd is clear but that with the dragon Fafnir is clumsy. Once that was settled, however, it is evident that a brother for Wagner's Mime is not essential. But there is a fundamental requirement *in the drama*, and that is for Alberich always to have a close relationship with *someone*. So, before Wagner even envisaged the poem of *Das Rheingold*, he chose to give him a brother - for which there is no authority in any source. It may have pleased the composer that to give Mime a brother also gave a nod to Regin's saga history but the invention owed nothing to that history. Put simply, any staging benefits by such a potent relationship.

<u>The Rhinedaughters</u>
No source includes anything at all about water sprites defending anything at all. [A] Nevertheless, the call to the stage they receive to open the cycle when it expands is not that surprising. They are there at the very end of ST3.2 to receive the Ring from Brünnhilde and take it down into the waters from which it was stolen, so there would be a logic to have them there at the beginning. The three are clearly drawn in ST3.1 and

---

[A] It took some time for Wagner to sort out these 'water sprites'. They appear strongly characterised and other worldly in *Der junge Siegfried* but a few months later, in the short sketch for *Das Rheingold* of November 1851, Wagner depicts them as the nieces of Fricka - and therefore existing in the same limited temporal framework as the goddess. Such a relationship then disappears when the sketch becomes a poem, in which Fricka says of them: 'Of the watery brood I'd rather not know; for many a man - to my grief - they have lewdly lured to their watery lair.' Clear connection is made to legends of mermaids, by their beauty, or the Lorelei, by their voices, luring sailors to a drowned death.

claim this earlier connection to the gold. Once there at the beginning, they fit neatly into the drama, supplying both information and setting Alberich on his fearsome course. The Rhinedaughters are primeval and seemingly children of nature. They say that their 'father' warned them about the nature of the gold they guard and the assumption must be that he is a nature god of the river.

The action that starts the story

Alberich and the Rhinedaughters
Momentous as is the encounter, which comprises the whole of R1, it can be simply described for it is as written down by Wagner and without reference to any source whatsoever, regardless of culture or ethnic origin.

The Rhinedaughters are first on the scene, three creatures of extreme beauty. Alberich is presumably prominent as a Nibelung but has no particular status amongst the tribe. He is enraptured by their unearthly allure, and their charm. Initially, there is a romantic aspect to this rapture but this quickly changes to aggression when they reject him: not all men would wish to rape a woman who first teased and then rejected them. As the Gold catches the light of the sun, the music proclaims the splendour of its purity and Alberich is once again entranced. But in the same way that he wanted one of the Rhinedaughters, so does he *immediately* want the Gold *if it were to be useful*. ('Is the gold only good for your diving games? Then it would serve me little.') And when he learns of the price to be paid, he is as prepared to rape it from its hallowed place as he was prepared to rape a Rhinedaughter. It is a simple and obvious symbolism.

This whole scenario, original to Wagner is itself the creation of a perfect myth, by which is meant that there can be no better illustration of a malign grasping at power.

The price paid to turn the Gold into the Ring
Wagner's first intuitive grasp of the nature of the ring of power was that absolute power requires something absolute in return. No other expansion of plot would have had the same force. Alberich abjures love and replaces it with lust - or by lust and money. If you cannot have meaningful compassionate love, you can turn to sex on its own - either forced by muscle or paid for with money. There *had* to be such a horror for the drama to have proper force. This price that Alberich is prepared to pay is to be found only within the myth that Wagner creates. Alberich thinks he is cursing love ('so *verflucht ich die Liebe!*') but of course every sentient spirit has to desire something. What Alberich does is to choose to love power and not people - and that includes his own brother. To expel all personal love from the heart is recognized as a terrible thing and anyone who does so crosses a threshold into a black place. As so often, once perceived, the drastic transaction is obvious, and Wagner presents it in stark simplicity.

THE INVENTION OF ALBERICH

Examination reveals something even more terrible. For Alberich believes (and we have no reason to think that he is mistaken) that the abjuration of love can be imposed on all who submit to him as he wields the power of the Ring. There are few more chilling words than those with which Alberich threatens Wotan in R3

> As love has been forsworn by me, / so all that lives
> shall also forswear it: / lured by gold,
> you'll lust after gold alone.

The view is commonly and understandably held that the music of *Das Rheingold* is a primer for the three operas that are to follow. But this is not everywhere the case and surely not at this moment in the drama. The music of the whole passage which surrounds and imbues these words fizzes with malevolent energy and brings home the frightfulness of Alberich's goal. What he envisages, as the gods succumb to his onslaught, is a bestiality. In the same passage he makes clear that sex remains on the menu, for he will rape any woman or goddess he chooses. But perhaps, rather than rape, it will be mutual depravity. Wagner had both a very strong sex drive and a gargantuan personality, and was accordingly highly attractive to women. [B] One can imagine that he was an attentive lover, that women responded reciprocally to his ardour and that, therefore, he would have observed sexual voracity in women as well as in men. Without love sexual intercourse would perhaps have degenerated into the rutting of animals – men and women alike caught in the joyless trap of lust from which *Tannhäuser* seeks to escape. Alberich's curse was to remove all meaningful relationships between men and women.

The Rhine Gold

In the *Myth* Alberich lays hands on 'the pure and noble gold of the Rhine'. In Teutonic mythology, gold is seen as pure until it is tampered with by gods and dwarfs (p.71). Wagner seizes hold of this: the *leitmotif* of the gold is entirely unsullied and this is complemented with the ecstatic cry of greeting 'Rheingold' by the Rhinedaughters. On stage it is usually shown as a substantial but not massive lump that can be wrenched away from rock without too much difficulty. The music suggests it is an incarnation of golden purity, an embodiment of the *idea* of gold.

The background and properties invested in the Gold are all invented by Wagner. There are three aspects to this invention.

(1) There exists no other example in any mythology of a piece of gold with the quality described.
(2) Such an object is surely outside of time and similar in this respect to the World Ash Tree.

[B] Let us not also overlook his physical appearance. He was of small stature but his face is of striking, individual beauty. In the painted by Lenbach in 1871, for example, the piercing blue gaze is compelling.

(3) This piece of gold has a particular and unearthly power exemplified by the unique manner whereby it becomes a ring. The lump of gold is forced (zwingt) into a circle - solid matter is compressed and crushed down to a far smaller mass. When Brünnhilde returns the Ring to the Rhine at the end she invites the Rhine-daughters to loosen or untie (löset) it so that the Gold reassumes its original form. In doing so we might assume that it survives the final cataclysm, in contrast to the World Ash Tree. (See DC/WE,207)

What is unarguable is that the Rhine Gold music implies goodness and is a symbol of hope.

The consequences of the action

The Ring

The gold and the ring are the same substance in different formats. The idea is most compelling. The Ring has a complexity of meaning and function which defy direct connection to anything in the sources. It has two remarkable and original features: firstly, the very notion of a ring which purportedly *endows* its owner with immeasurable power did not exist before Wagner and, secondly, the nature of that power is difficult to establish. Wagner uses the primary sources to flesh out detail of his Ring. Within them are five significant references to a ring.

- Two are in *NL* and *TS*, where a ring is taken from Brynhild by Sigurd and given to Gudrun.

- Two unconnected rings having some power to generate gold are found in the eddas. One belongs to Odin and 'every ninth night there would drip from it eight rings equal to it in weight' but with no indication as to why. The other is Andvari's ring, which does have the capacity to find gold which is taken from him by Loki. Andvari asks Loki in vain 'not to take it from him, saying that he could multiply wealth from the ring if he kept it.' (SS/E,100)

- The fifth reference is that of Elberich which confers invisibility on whoever wears it, and this power is transferred to the Tarnhelm.

The Ring taken from Brünnhilde by Siegfried is not given to Gutrune because that would slow the stage action (p.61) but the sight of it on his own finger in the *Ring* and on Gudrun's finger in the sagas have the same dramatic function: they jolt the action forward.

The Tarnhelm

In the *Myth* we read that the most important treasure within the hoard was the Tarnhelm – a work that Alberich forced his own brother Mime to forge. Thus equipped, Alberich 'strove for the mastery of the world and everything in it.' Taking everything about the Ring into consideration, it may seem odd that the Tarnhelm seems the more useful artefact of the two - a device of unprecedented versatility and one that anyone can use, independently of the Ring itself (except poor Mime!).

It has three powers: to render the wearer invisible, to transport the wearer on the instant from one place to another and to enable the wearer to adopt the form of anything he wants. Alberich uses it to make himself invisible and take the shape of serpent and toad; Fafnir uses it to take the form of a dragon; Siegfried uses it both to take the shape of Gunther and to transport himself back in advance of Gunther and Brünnhilde in G2.

Only the first two of these capabilities are found in one form or another in the sources. When Sigurd takes the treasure from Alberich in *Das Nibelungenlied,* he also takes a cloak which can both render him invisible and also transport him around. This he uses in the process of winning Brynhild for Gunnar. There is also a similar cloak in *Lied des Hurnen Sigurd* which he is given and which saves his life when he wears it. Grimm's *Deutsche Mythologie* states that elves have the power of making themselves invisible. Instead of a cloak, Wagner has Alberich design a helmet.

The last feature, the power to adopt the physical form of any other living thing, is unique to Wagner. In the sources, Sigurd does stand in for Gunnar on more than one occasion but this is either by becoming invisible which enables him to help without being seen to help or by means of magic spells, such as that applied by Grimhilde, Gunnar's mother, to swap Sigurd with Gunnar.

Alberich as a slave driver

With these powers Alberich subjugates the Nibelungs. A few things must have come first as a dramatic spur toward the project as a whole, and it would not be illogical to think it might have been slavery. From this would be borne the notion of the dwarf as a tyrant, for which there is no authority in the sources.

In the two years since the Spring of 1847 (p.449) Wagner's political views had radicalised, and his revolutionary fervour was high throughout 1848. They remained so into the Spring of 1849 - the time of the composer's first revolutionary essay *Art and Revolution* in which we read this direct reference to slavery:

> See there the mass of people who stream out of the factories, where they have made and fashioned fine clothing. They and their children, however, are naked frozen and hungry. The fruit of their labour belongs not to them but to the rich and mighty master who owns them and also the earth. See there those who troop at the end of the day from field and farmyard. They have tilled the earth ... and their labour has produced enough food for everyone. Yet they also are poor, naked, starving; for not to them ... belongs earth's blessings but rather to their master who owns them and the land they work on. (RW/PW8,235)

Alberich as a fearsome tyrant was a necessity, and mining for gold was the obvious work for such slaves. Wagner is sensibly down to earth in his depiction of modern slavery, as he saw it - workers in a garment factory or on the land - but digging for gold under extreme coercion is something of an archetype, and gold is to hand in the mythology.

The power of the Ring

The Ring does not work like a magic wand and there is an unanswered ambiguity about it. If the Ring did immediately give total power to its holder, all Alberich would have had to do is thrust it at Wotan in R4 as he does at the quailing Nibelungs in R3: Wotan would also quail and Alberich could take his spear from him. One power that certainly lies within it is that which lay in Andvari's ring, namely to divine the presence of gold in the earth. According to Alberich, everyone can be subjugated to the desire for wealth. Instead of love, 'lured by gold, you'll lust after gold alone.' R3 shows this acquisition of wealth in action, as Alberich first drives in his Nibelung slaves as they carry in the gold mined that day and then drives them out again. A force of compulsion contained in the Ring is heard in the music for the first time as they rush away to continue digging. The nature of this compulsion is hard to define. Wagner initiates this rush off stage by having Alberich kiss the Ring and then hold it out to the Nibelungs. This suggests a 'force field' which tortures body and mind.

The Ring does not seem to have any other power than in some way to force the Nibelungs to work and thereby make the dwarf lord rich. *Never* does it protect its wearer and, indeed, Alberich boasts to Loge that someone might steal it whilst he slept unless he used the Tarnhelm to make himself invisible. The Ring prevents neither Wotan from wrenching it from Alberich, nor Siegfried from Brünnhilde.

Is the Ring, therefore, a dramatic *construct*? Alberich and Mime want it for its power to make money; for everyone else it is something like a talisman for hope and for the future. Can we think of it as a tool for moving the plot onwards? The drama is about the spiritual development of the main protagonists. The crushing impact of the music may not, therefore, represent the power of the Ring itself but rather the gnawing, relentless grip of greed on those it has truly infected. Its very existence ensures that those people - Alberich, Mime, Hagen, and Wotan for a short time, will desire it to desperation.

Alberich's curse on the Ring

The issue is not helped by the curse placed on it by Alberich in R4. What actually is it? We see Fafner murder Fasolt and this is one of the two actual *crimes* it instigates. But even that is not clear cut. The murder results from a squabble over how the loot should be shared. The Ring only becomes part of the ransom because Fasolt gets a glimpse of Freia's eye and it is the only bit of the hoard not already handed over. Only when the spoils are being divided does Loge egg Fafner on by a whisper of the Ring's importance. Siegfried kills Fafner for no good reason and certainly not to get the Ring. Siegfried tears it from Brünnhilde only because she says it protects her – and then he forgets about it. (As he previously forgot that he gave it to her in the first place.) The only other crime caused by the Ring is Siegfried's murder.

Alberich states, as part of the curse, that *everyone* will desire it. Wotan, of course, wants it from the beginning and before it is cursed, and the results would have been appalling had he been able to keep it without sacrificing Freia. After the curse is laid, Gunther and Fafner want it *in a way* but not because of the power inherent in it. Fafner uses only the Tarnhelm and Gunther seemingly only comes to blows over it because it is the property of Gutrune, Siegfried's widow. After the curse is laid in RG4, only Mime, Alberich and Hagen really want it – and thereby become alien to all other creatures. This takes us back to Alberich's original curse on love, when he is simply *choosing* cash instead of compassion. By forging the Ring, Alberich is subjugating himself to its power – a form of self-enslavement - and its very creation puts him under a curse.

◇ ◇ ◇ ◇ ◇ ◇

12

Wotan's Cosmos

In previous chapters we have explored how Wagner's instinct for drama abstracted from the sources those key elements of personality and background needed to shape his characters. A survey of Wotan's world, and the people and races who inhabit it will complete that part of the picture.

Wotan in time and place

Michael Tanner coined the term 'the domestication' of Wagner, with particular relevance to the *Ring*. (MT/W,48) He deplores the recent instinct in directors to remove the heroic from staging and characterisation, and maintains that this leads to a loss of dignity, restraint and moral grandeur. Wotan can appear as a failing businessman, Siegfried as an unruly youth in a baseball cap and the whole show can become mean in scope. Nothing in the following pages is intended to support such a view of the work and nothing should be taken by readers as a hint that the story as a whole or in its parts is other than an epic moral tale.

However, the *Ring*, for all its ambition, is circumscribed by finite time, space and society. This must be so if the audience is to engage with it: the human mind cannot comprehend or engage with infinity. The scale is large, of course, but must remain within the compass of human life. The story the dwarf sets in train is not timeless but runs its course in a precise time frame: the entire action within the four operas takes place over a period of about 50 years. This assumes that three are allowed for Alberich to amass his hoard, a further three for Wotan to father Siegmund, Sieglinde and Brünnhilde, 25 for Siegmund - hardened by adversity - to find Sieglinde, and 19 years between the conception and murder of Siegfried. This is positively headlong, given the eons gone by since time began as Wotan tore the branch from the World Ash Tree.

This swift narrative is inherent in the Nordic sources. There are two poems in the *Poetic Edda* which bring *Ragnarök* to the fore. The first - *Voluspa* (*The Wise Woman's Prophecy*) - is that in which Odin engages the Wala in a cosmological debate about the beginning and end of things. This concludes with a discussion about the oncoming doom: the valkyrs are mentioned first - gathering warriors for the coming battle - and then Balder's death is introduced. The second poem, *Balder's Dream,* is also assumed to be with the same wise, eternal woman and is about the death of Balder. So this drastic death (p.87) was already in the past for both poems, and the coming catastrophe is evident in both. The Wala's last words in *Voluspa* are:

> Ride home, Odin - be ever proud. / For no one of men shall seek me now
> Till Loki wanders loose from his bonds / And to the last battle the destroyers come.

The very first expansion of the story - *Der junge Siegfried* - clearly places the gods' downfall as a current threat. The reference to Balder in the sketch to that poem may have been removed but the text still has: 'The gods have been anxious about their end since the bringer of gladness fell.' This urgency continues to echo with Loge in R4 ('They [the gods] are hurrying towards their end, though they think they will last forever.') and with the Norns in G1.1 who foretell the imminent downfall, by fire, of the 'immortal gods'. On Erda's warning in R4 that 'a day of darkness dawns for the gods', Wotan gets to work and the action is swift. In both eddas and the *Ring* we are clearly moving quickly toward the end of an era. And also, perhaps, toward the end of time in a particular and inevitably obscure sense.

If Wotan and the gods are finally destroyed, they must have had a beginning, but the Nordic myths are muddled on the subject. We see this most clearly in *Sturleson's Edda*. He vainly attempts to reconcile creation stories that run counter to each other. Sturleson was a Christian (Iceland had been Christian for two hundred years) and did not believe in Odin and his like. He 'interpreted them as kings of great power who came to be worshipped by ignorant people. He presents these kings as having migrated from Asia Minor . . . and as being descendants of King Priam of Troy, who migrated to Scandinavia in prehistoric times'. (SS/E,xiii; comment by Andrew Faulks, translator) This, however, does not preclude a story whereby Odin came into existence as son of 'a complete man' named Buri who was himself put together rather like the biblical Adam. The creation of Buri was broadly contemporaneous with the giant Ymir, from whom the earth was born and who was contemporary with the Wala. This Odin settled at Troy at a later date, having killed the creation giant Ymir [A] and himself created the first man (Ask) and woman (Embla) from whom all mankind descended.

Wagner wisely skirts around all this, with only the vaguest hints about the beginnings of things. In the *Myth* the giants are 'primevally born', and the gods 'nurture' the already existing 'human race' and 'bring up Man for this high destiny, to be the canceller of [the gods'] own guilt.' Later on, Wotan acknowledges Erda to be older than himself and that's about it. Cooke cogently reasons that Wotan's act of drinking from the Well of Wisdom indicates a beginning of time. But if so, it cannot be the beginning of Ymir's time, so let us call it the beginning of Wotan's time, as the conflagration at the end of G3 is the ending of his time. Let us think of him at that initial moment as a spirit who knows his time has come. This coming is drastic, for Wotan's first action is to tear

---

[A] Zeus similarly destroyed the Titans - an older generation of deities - in order to become the ruler who lived on Mount Olympus.

the branch that is to be his spear from the World Ash Tree, thereby wounding it. This wound saps life from the Tree and is therefore a symbol of decay. It is Wagner's invention, his way of replicating the affliction that destroys the mythic Yggdrasil. In the eddas, the roots of the Nordic 'world' tree are relentlessly gnawed away by a dragon. (At its foot there is also the well, previously referred to, whose waters impart wisdom.) As with the *Ring*, this devastation of a 'world' tree is seen as a portent of catastrophe: Yggdrasil dies as *Ragnarök* approaches and the dragon - its job done - rises to join the final battle, fighting against the gods.

It is a distortion to portray the action of the *Ring* as timeless: both the eddas and the *Ring* are moving forward toward the end of an era. With respect to Wagner's story, I suggest the audience gets the feeling that this era has lasted a very long (but not an *immeasurably* long) time. Neither Odin nor Wotan are gods 'of creation' outside of time. For the *Ring*, the crafting of the spear is the initial act that establishes an era that had a beginning, a middle and an end. Tolkein pulls the same trick in his concept of Middle Earth. The narrative of *The Lord of the Rings* is the final action of the immense corpus, which shows the victory of order over disorder. The many and various other tales, *The Silmarillion* being the best known, give details of the world before that concluding episode. Wagner's *Ring* is also about the conclusion of a past epoch. We know nothing at all about the time before Wotan drank from the well to find the wisdom he needed. We can assume a world of certain primal elements: of nature untrammelled in every respect, with the Rhine, the Gold in the Rhine, the Rhinedaughters, the Norns, Erda - and spirits such as the primitive Wotan. (Those in particular who see nature as a major theme should find this idea most ready of acceptance, and perceive any despoliation as an inevitable concomitant of the story.) There is no reason to deny the existence of men and other sentient beings before Wotan's formative action, nor deny that such beings might also interact with such as Erda and the Norns.

Not everybody sees it like this. Their thesis is based on the famous prelude to *Das Rheingold* - 136 bars in E flat without a single accidental. This is often described as representing life and movement emerging from nothingness - the 'beginning of things' in Newman's phrase. This view is supported by the letter from Wagner covering the despatch of the completed *Ring* poem to Liszt in February 1853: 'Mark well my new poem,' he writes 'it contains the world's beginning and its end!' (SS/SL,281) The music also bolsters this thesis with its aural impression that we are moving up from an inert river bed to the swift currents above. This impression of physical stillness to movement is undeniable and a spectator may well move beyond that to the existential - that we are moving from nothing to something, back to 'the world's beginning.'

Such a specific interpretation can be thought, however, to dilute rather than to intensify the drama. Wagner's comment to Röckel might be a clear, even flagrant example of 'an excessive eagerness to make things plain', thereby 'impairing a proper understanding' (p.3). To think of the prelude as a representation of the universal beginning of everything is surely too much, for it invites the audience to engage imaginatively with a concept that cannot be given a concrete reality. Once again we are being *told* something, by Wagner and sundry commentators, but not really *shown* it. The reader is reminded of the passage from *A communication to my friends* (p.5), that for the spectator 'there should be no need for the reflecting intellect but only of the direct feeling that seizes the emotions.' He did not like the interposition of rational thought between what was seen on stage and the emotional response to it. [B]

Another interpretation put forward about what Wagner intended is to think upon the earliest event of all that impacts on the plot, namely when Wotan crafted his Spear of Power from a branch of the World Ash Tree. That Wagner was aware of that matter from early on is evident in what the Norns say at the beginning of ST1.1 (p.118). But the temptation to bring this in as part of the drama has lead people to equate Wotan's drastic action, which wounds the tree to death, with Alberich's terrible clutch at the Gold in the Rhine: both can be interpreted as despoliations of nature. This wounding of the tree is an important event that has existential and societal impact but it is perverse to see it as inherently bad.

A better viewpoint than both of the above might be Roger Scruton's: the prelude 'is the musical equivalent of the "state of nature" which does not precede history but which lies beneath it, the unseen depth of an innocence forever lost, because never truly possessed' (RS/RT,245). Wagner undeniably laid great store on the importance of the natural world. The prelude can properly be seen as the first large scale demonstration of this; Porges records Wagner's view that 'no longer conscious of the music, we . . . become immersed in the primal feeling of all living things.' (HP/WR,8)

At a more basic level, for those who see the work more than once, it can simply herald the beginning of the world's mightiest drama. The gargantuan scope of the plot dwarfs in some way all available forms of structure and there *has* to be something like the growling E flat to set it going. The great journey is to take off from a still, silent moment. It is something of an invitation to settle down and wait.

Natural judgement is for the audience to take the start of the story to be where Alberich accosted the Rhinedaughters. To do otherwise *when in the theatre* is to reflect on what is seen, to *interpret*. If that is what people want to do, so be it, but it may not be responding to the drama in the manner which was closest to Wagner's heart.

And if, as argued here, there be a time - or epoch - before Wotan, it follows that there will be one that follows. This is specified in the primary Nordic sources and the Immolation cannot convincingly be seen as an announcement about the end of the world. It is certainly the end of the epoch ruled by Wotan, but the Rhine, the Gold within

---

[B] For Wagner, this was not just theory but also a matter of truth to humanity, as we can hear in *Siegfried* Act III. Brünnhilde is explaining to Siegfried why and how she has always loved him, and this is what she says: 'You I've always loved because only I could sense Wotan's idea: an idea which I was never to name, which I did not think but only felt . . . my love for you.' (JD/R,521)

it at the end and the Rhinedaughters continue. And as Erda is acknowledged by Wotan to be of a different immortal order than he, why should not she and her daughters the Norns also survive? [C]

The destruction at the end of the cycle is as in myth: fire and flood rise together to destroy Wotan's world. If that were extended beyond the Rhine, then that wider world will surely go down too. The extent of Wotan's power is imprecise. The music is imperial in every way - both literally and metaphorically. But, with rare exceptions, stagings of the cycle do not present Wotan as an all-powerful Emperor with immense reach. The audience does not mind because the music fills the gap. Regardless of whether the stage production is one that tries not to move far away from Wagner's vision of woods, forests and mountains in close proximity to the Rhine, or is one sited in a particular, distinct and conceptualized environment - such as where S2 is set in a defunct factory, for example - staging seldom presents far-reaching imperial power. The Nordic primary sources have a big creation myth and an immense destruction myth involving many galvanic forces and agencies, whereas Wotan's physical world has prescribed, implicit boundaries. From this it follows, for example, that grandiloquent representations of imperial power at the conclusion of *Das Rheingold* are generally just there to show the hollow *hubris* of the gods.

How Wotan's world is peopled

Dwarfs and giants
Wotan moves between the world of myth and the world of men. The scope of the world of myth is the subject of Mime's three questions to him, and Wotan's three answers correspond to the mythic beings: the dwarfs live underground, the giants 'on the earth's broad back' and the gods in the heights - Nibelheim, Riesenheim and Valhalla. These mirror the Nordic Swartalfheim (home of the black elves), Jutenheim for the giants and Asgarth for the gods. Wagner disregarded five locations and peoples: Vanaheim, where lived another godlike race called the Vanes; Alfheim, where lived the elves; Musspelheim, home of the fire-dwellers and their lord, the fire giant Surt; Nifelheim, home of the dead; and Nithafjoll where lived another race of dwarfs.

The roles of both dwarfs and giants in the drama have been examined in the chapter *Der junge Siegfried;* a brief look now at their background. Over forty dwarfs are listed

---

[C] It has been loosely argued that Alberich survives because every other principal but he is seen to be destroyed. This assumes that Wagner sought to construct a 'well-made-play' in which all the ends are tied up; this is not the case. The dramatic structure demonstrates that Alberich has lost the struggle: the Gold will not again be removed and without it he is lost. Shaw may well be correct when he states that Siegfried's function in the drama is to 'make an end of dwarfs, giants and gods'.

in the various primary sources and most are just names. They are not big players in the sagas and it is significant that only the stories of those used to construct the composite Alberich of the *Ring* have impact in those sources. That he enhanced the importance of the two dwarfs in his drama from that which he found in the primary sources is not surprising. He would want to be as realistic as possible as the 'races' in his tale crossed paths. So he would recall that dwarfism has always existed and that people of dwarf-like proportions do move among us. That Wagner chose to have them as malevolent is no indication of a stereotypical prejudice: except with regard to Jews he does not seem to have been that sort of a man. (In this study the issue of Wagner's anti-Semitism becomes sterile. Whatever the truth may be of its influence on the composer's work, it does not *of itself* resonate in the theatre with a modern audience.)

His adaptation of the sources with regard to the race of giants is the exact opposite and one of the reasons is that giants don't walk amongst us. To keep them realistic (critical for Wagner) they must have prescribed roles, detached from human life. So they are reduced in scope and power, and in number. The sagas present us with more than forty and no less that thirteen play very big roles in the mythic stories. From this race of immense power, forever in strife with the gods (whom they very likely pre-dated within the cosmos) they shrink to just two, whose characteristics bear no resemblance to any of the giants who people the mythologies.

Mankind

Tribes of men existed independently of Odin/Wotan. The tribes believed in these Nordic gods and perhaps Wagner had in mind the following from *Sturluson's Edda*: 'In whatever country the gods [on their way from Troy] stopped, there was then prosperity and good peace there, and everyone who had power saw that they were unlike other people they had seen in beauty and wisdom.' (SE/E,4) Brünnhilde and Gunther call on Wotan as the 'oath-bearing guardian of vows', and Hunding has called upon Fricka to aid him hunt down Siegmund.

The gods have mated with humankind (as did the Greek gods): in the *Myth* both the Volsungs and the Gibichungs have godly ancestors, though this idea is later dropped with regard to the latter tribe.

The minor gods and the roles they play in the operas

In the *Myth*, before the plot was fleshed out, the only god mentioned was Wotan. Thereafter, every choice that Wagner makes with respect to the gods who subsequently appear in his drama - Fricka (Nordic Frigg), Loge (Loki), Donner (Thor), Froh (Freyr) and Freia (Freyja) - has the purpose of articulating the one and only action we see Wotan complete, namely the building of Valhalla. At the same time, Wagner focusses the action and consequent morality upon Wotan, thereby removing responsibility from the secondary gods. These are best seen as foils for Wotan. This even applies to Fricka and Loge, whose characters are sharply drawn. [D]

Wagner makes a change from the mythology, in which Odin is the father of Thor (but not by Frigg), and that Freyr and Freyja (brother and sister) belong to the other different race of gods - Vanes rather than Æsir. Wagner keeps the same identity for Wotan and Loge but makes the other four gods brothers and sisters to each other. Thus Fricka describes Freya as her sister on occasion. We cannot be clear about Wotan's status and origin, and Loge presents quite a different persona from the four minor gods. But the other four are of the same generation and are likely therefore to be younger than Wotan. The dramatic thrust is not difficult to see: Wotan needs to be as free of close family ties as possible in order to give room for his powerful commitment to parenthood when it comes.

The five secondary gods were chosen from a much larger pantheon: estimates vary but it is reasonable to list eleven male Æsir and fourteen female Asynnur. It would be otiose to list all of the seven male and twelve female, who are necessarily left out. But we can record that Tyr (the great warrior god who gives his name to Tuesday) and Heimdall (the gatekeeper to Valhalla) are among the male gods, and Saga (the number two goddess after Frigg) is among the females who are dropped.

We can now look at what Wagner does with his sources. Those readers who wish to study closely what the composer includes and what he excludes should read Cooke, who covers this in great detail. My pages here are much indebted to him. The five included gods have each a different function in the narrative; each is a complement to the other and each one is there to add depth but also to focus the drama onto Wotan.

Fricka For dramatic energy the most necessary was Fricka. The confrontations between Wotan and his wife are used by Wagner to clarify the moral issues that surround three things. These are the building of Valhalla, the relationship of Siegmund and Sieglinde and the validity and substance of Wotan's entire strategy. The argument about the first occurs in R2, and that about the second two in W2. This second altercation has greater impact and pushes the drama towards a major crisis; it is in two parts: the first part

---

[D] Here I skirt, but I hope not too slyly, around comments by Fricka and Wotan. In R2 Fricka upbraids Wotan for trusting 'that cunning trickster', and Wotan acknowledges that he uses 'cunning and craft . . . of the kind Loge slyly employs . . . to turn advantage and enemy's grudge . . . He who counselled me on the contract [with the giants] promised to ransom Freia: on him I now rely.' In W2, Wotan tells Brünnhilde that 'unwittingly false, I acted unfairly, binding by treaties what boded ill: cunningly Loge lured me on.' Elizabeth Magee uses this to argue that the gods are corrupted by Loge: 'hopelessly enmeshed in . . . perplexity and guilt.' This last seems a bit excessive even though the argument has a logic. The point within the drama is that the initiatives are always presented as Wotan's, and the drama is weakened if we see Loge as anything more than a counsellor.

brings Fricka forward as the guardian of marriage and the second presents her as the person closest to Wotan and who therefore knows best how he thinks.

Fricka as the defender of the marriage vow is nowhere to be found in the three relevant primary sources. In truth, the Nordic Frigg is there accused of adultery by Loki - not only with Odin's brother but also with 'the gods and elves who are gathered here, each one as thy lover has lain.' (HB/PE,162) One reason that Wagner could not contemplate this is obvious: if she is to berate Wotan for his promiscuity, she must be the opposite. But there is a deeper reason, rooted in the needs of the drama. As we shall see in the discussion of Siegmund's death, Wagner *required* one such as Fricka to uphold the marriage vow. Regardless of the issue of incest, in the *Myth* Wotan brings Siegmund to ruin for the marital crime of adultery. For such as Hunding, Siegmund's actions would have been no laughing matter.

Whereas Wotan is recognisably related to Odin, Fricka is wholly Wagner's creation, with characteristics put together for a purpose. Her moral compass and goals are the opposite to those of Wotan. By using her as the engine through whom many of the problems facing the god are explored, the composer was able to contrast his essential nobility and wisdom with his wife's parochial attitudes. This does not belittle Wagner's invention but is an example of his craft as a dramatist. In Chapters 18 and 19 are details of Fricka's myopic societal morality. She has little interest in emotional bonds or in any picture wider than her own personal status, and disregards Wotan's longer vision. On stage and in her music, Fricka is fully rounded and not without dignity. She must be so if the audience is to engage with her as a personality and the manner by which it dovetails into and contrasts with that of Wotan.

Freia The evidence suggests that for the three years between November 1848 and November 1851 no notion existed that the nature and existence of love should be a bargaining chip in the drama. But with the words 'Whoever curses love', in the short sketch for *Das Rheingold,* the whole story changed. From that moment, despite the fact that she is totally passive, the one essential secondary immortal in the plot became the goddess Freia. Her role is to be the symbol and personification of love but the other capacity she has is the more crucial, namely the harvester of the golden apples which keep the gods young and vigorous. When the values and benefits which Freia represents are actually put to the test in R2, it is this loss of vigour rather than the loss of love that spurs Wotan into action. After the giants take her away, thereby bringing home the need to negotiate, Loge puts it to the gods thus:

> But you staked all on the youth-giving fruit, / as the giants knew full well.
> your very lives they've threatened: / now look to ways of saving yourselves.
> Without the apples, old and grey, / grizzled and grim,
> withered and scorned by the whole of the world, / the race of the gods will perish.

This is the culmination of the bridging mini-scene between the major episode of Loge's narration which sets forth the big problem that must be solved and the capture of Alberich that is seemingly to solve the problem. It is effective in the short term, jerks the plot forward and demonstrates mastery of large structure.

Wagner needed this device of the golden apples, for this goddess of love has not the powerful presence, for example, of the Greek Aphrodite, who caused regular havoc, nor even of the Nordic Freyja who was accused by Loki of sleeping with her brother Freyr. It would, therefore, have required much on-stage argument - either over-complicated or pointless - to make the point that to give away love is not a good idea. A foretaste of a prompt diminution of vitality was a quick and ready lesson for the gods to learn. The return of Freya is not a presage or indication that love was to be looked upon with renewed reverence. In the drama it is the passion of Siegmund and Sieglinde and its effect on Brünnhilde that changes the game.

So much for the dramatic narrative, but what about the weak impression made by Freia herself? Cooke suggests a number of reasons for this, amongst which is this lack of space which would give room for the goddess of love to bloom. Additionally, he points out that in the ethos of *Das Rheingold*, love 'does not exist' and the figurehead for it has shrunk into a 'weak, helpless, hunted figure'. [E] Wagner wanted this and expected his audience to recognize what he was after, namely that both Freia and Fricka have been deserted by Wotan. Additionally, he did not *want* the audience to have much awareness of sexual love at this point. For he must have known that in *Die Walküre* Act 1, there was waiting one of the most powerful outlines for a love story that exists in opera.

In the event, the brilliance of combining within one goddess the symbolism of the value of 'woman's love' (to use Loge's phrase) and the immediate loss of vigour works very well. Both aspects are put up as a pledge to be redeemed with the completion of Valhalla and, as both aspects involve Loki in the sagas rather than the Nordic Freyja - who has nothing to do with the building of any castle - they will be discussed in consideration of Loge, which follows.

Loge   Wagner's fire-god - he who is forced by Wotan to protect Brünnhilde and summoned in turn by her to transform the earthly fire she has ignited into the conflagration that will consume Valhalla - is amongst his most brilliant creations. He pops up in many different ways in the sagas as Loki, and Wagner takes and turns to his use many small and large traits and events. The Nordic Loki has input into the building of a great fortress which is to become Wagner's Valhalla. He shapes the qualities that inform Freia. His spirit governs Loge's attitude in the closing pages of *Das Rheingold*. (His trapping of Andvari has, as already seen, imbued the capture of Alberich.)

First, to his role as the god of fire. In fact, only in the *Ring* does Loki/Loge have any specific role - as this fire-god - and this is really Wagner's invention: Cooke identifies two fleeting references in *Deutsche Mythologie* and one in the *Poetic Edda*. But there

---

[E]   Cooke is surely too simplistic, even though we know what he means. Love may not exist but affection does, as shown by Fasolt toward Friea and, in the past, between Wotan and Fricka.

may be deeper influences: the first relates to the great Nordic fire giant Surt, and the second to Loki's very nature. Surt is a demonic force for destruction and a prime mover against Odin and the Æsir at the time of *Ragnarök*. As lord of the southern region Muspellheim he 'has a flaming sword and at the end of the world he will . . . wage war and defeat all the gods and burn the whole world with fire.' (SS/E,9-10) Loki, as previously described, broke free from the fetters in which the gods had placed him after he engineered the death of Balder and fought alongside Surt. They were joined by two of Loki's 'children' - the Midgard Serpent, who encircled the lands of men, and the great wolf Fenris.

> All fetters and bonds will snap and break. Then Fenriswolf will get free. Then the ocean will surge up on to the lands because the Midgard serpent will fly into a rage and make its way ashore . . . Fenriswolf will go with mouth agape . . . flames will burn from its eyes and nostrils. The Midgard serpent will spit so much poison that it will bespatter all the sky and sea . . . and it will be beside the wolf. (SS/E,53)

This information provides Loki's essential nature: he not only mated with a giantess who gave birth to the wolf who threatens the heavens and the great serpent who encircles the world of men, but he was also the son of a giant. In the Nordic sagas those who are in perennial strife with Odin are the giants (and never the dwarfs): another reason that Loki finally lines up alongside Surt.

These are the character traces on which Wagner bases his Loge. But the dramatic context is different, for Wotan's end is not Odin's: both may be preordained but whereas the Nordic Odin's catastrophe is impersonal and embroils the whole world, Wotan's cosmos is contained and governed by the actions of the god alone. The responsibility lies with him and his end is not nemesis but salvation via the good offices of Siegfried and Brünnhilde. Nevertheless, Wagner spells out Loge's animosity toward Wotan and the other gods. He delights in the prospect of their end as proclaimed by Erda and probably in the double-dealing that encourages Wotan to pledge Freia to the giants. His malevolent hostility and nihilism is expressed verbally at the end of *Das Rheingold* and musically in the descent to Nibelheim with Wotan at the beginning of R3. Elizabeth Magee argues that Loge is an evil genius who influences Wotan. This goes beyond the eddas, where Loki is detached from Odin, and also weakens the drama if it passes responsibility for the looming danger from Wotan to Loge. (See EN/WN,196-202) Wagner's tactic is to take the purgative quality of Surt's fire and invest it in Loge.

Loki impacts on Freia and on the building of Valhalla. In the sagas he is at the centre of both the story of the apples which rejuvenate and another about a trick that was pulled by the gods on a builder who contracted to build a fortress. To take the apples first. In the sagas they are the property of a goddess Idunn and not Freia. The story is that Loki was captured by a giant on account of his reckless behaviour and released on the condition that he would lure Idunn away from the gods' fortress. He did so and 'the Æsir . . . became grey and old', and very angry with Loki until he managed to return Idunn to them.

The fortress story is as follows. A builder offers to construct a fortress for the gods in three seasons, on condition that the goddess Freyja shall be his wife and that he shall also be given the sun and the moon. The gods use Loki as negotiator and he strikes the bargain: the builder will get what he wants if he completes the work in just one season. The builder uses his stallion - an animal of prodigious strength - to haul the stones up to the site of the fortress. Such is the progress that, with three days to go before the deadline date, the fortress was virtually completed. The gods round on Loki - he had failed them. So Loki turned himself into a mare, the stallion 'went frantic and tore apart his tackle and ran toward the mare'. This continued for three days, the fortress remained unfinished and the gods were saved by Loki's trick. Freyja remained with them. [F]

Cooke covers all this like no one before or since. He extends his enquiry into 'a comprehensive view of the nature of thought' and moves on to say that 'Loge, then, really functions as this elemental power of mind, which Wotan has been able to harness and use to only a limited degree, as intellect.' (DC/WE,170) It is not clear what Cooke means by this but the impulse may be the manner in which his various motifs crop up repeatedly throughout the *Ring*. They represent fire, cunning and what might be seen as mental energy, and it is not difficult to see which is which.

As Hagen is the *consigliere* to Gunther, so is Loge to Wotan, but with this difference: Wotan knew what he wanted and used Loge to achieve it, whereas Gunther did not and needed Hagen to guide him. The Norns in G1.1 have this to say about the looming destruction of the gods:

> The shattered spear's sharp-pointed splinters
> Wotan will one day bury deep in the fire-god's breast:
> a ravening fire will then flame forth
> which the god will hurl
> on the world ash's heaped up logs.

Wotan is in control to the end; his is the initiative to bring matters to a conclusion.

Donner   Derived by Wagner from the mighty Nordic/Germanic god Thor (Thursday, of course) Donner is reduced in function and weight so that he is simply unrecognizable. Thor was famous for his great hammer - there being stories both serious and comic in which it is involved. Thor was, in fact, the number two god in the pantheon and there are as many stories about him as there are about Odin. All that Wagner wants him for is the hammer, which he wields to effect at the end of R4 to summon the rainbow bridge; thereafter his motif occurs rarely - but once memorably - to accompany the fleeing Siegmund. Wagner presents Donner as being not too bright but he is a useful sounding board on the plot as he interposes his views - those of the normal guy somewhat out of his depth. And of course he helps out when needed within the action.

[F] The result was that Loki, in the form of a mare, gave birth to Sleipnir, 'the greatest of horses', and that used by Odin.

Froh The Nordic god Freyr (Friday in the calendar) was also major and, as with Donner, he is hugely diminished. In the mythology he is brother to Freyja but that distinction is nullified since Wagner makes him brother to Donner and Fricka also. Freyr is the god who controls rain and sunshine, hence Froh becomes the bringer of the rainbow. He is pallid in character but his music has a bright charm and is not as weak as some commentators have asserted. Like Donner, he is not too bright and one questions whether Wotan would have much consulted either of them about the construction of Valhalla, as is asserted by Fricka when she complains that she and Freia were left out of account. Like Donner, he is necessary on stage as a reactor to the big events moving around Wotan and also to facilitate something of the stage action.

Froh has one prop, namely the Rainbow Bridge. In the eddas, Bifrost is the rainbow bridge that links the earth to the abodes of the gods. Used daily, it has as guardian Heimdall, the gatekeeper to Valhalla - an important god ignored by Wagner. In the final battle of *Ragnarök,* tribes from Muspell storm the bridge which collapses.

# # # # # #

This chapter concludes the examination of what might be called the scaffolding of the drama. The object has been to identify those aspects of each main character or stage property, as displayed in the sources, which are made to cohere within the plot. This exercise reveals why Wagner adopts or rejects the implication of the source and how this decision binds the character or property to others within the whole.

The survey also serves to increase the wonder at Wagner's achievement. The portraits of Wotan's offspring derive largely from the *Volsung Saga* and since that source presents each in markedly human terms, the task of shaping swift and sustained drama was straightforward. With everyone else it is different. Taking colour from Cooke's analysis, the earlier chapter *The invention of Alberich* marvelled at the skill used to create a new story about gold being stolen - a story which is mythic in its penetration. To this achievement can be added the skill to fashion a focussed narrative from an indigestible mass of disparate, ill-connected stories which contain a prodigious variety of options. Choices made from this plethora govern the pictures we see of all the gods, of the Norns and Erda, and of Loge. Carolyne Larrington's elegant conspectus of Norse mythology in *The Norse Myths* (CL/NM) bewilders with the many complexities, the narrative dead ends and diversions that make up the histories of gods and giants. Wagner immersed himself in this stuff. He disregarded over 90%, and this and previous chapters together point to an unerring focus on to a concise and coherent narrative.

◇ ◇ ◇ ◇ ◇ ◇

13

Brünnhilde's transcendence

We should not doubt the glory that Brünnhilde is intended to represent. Joseph Campbell, in *The hero with a thousand faces,* portrays in a diagram the journey an archetypal hero such as Siegfried must take (p.26). The climax of the journey is a sacred marriage with a goddess who is described as The Lady of the House of Sleep. A hero moves through a succession of thirteen rooms, each of which contains a woman of ever increasing beauty asleep on a couch. The myth continues: 'But when he reached the thirteenth chamber and opened the door, the flash of gold took the sight from his eyes. He stood awhile till the sight came back, and then entered. In the great bright chamber was a golden couch, resting on wheels of gold.' And on the couch was The Lady of the House of Sleep. Campbell identifies her as Brynhild. He certainly knew about the *Ring* but there is no mention of Wagner and all references are to the Nordic Eddas. Here he is describing the goddess who is awoken and won by the hero – a constant feature of his journey into the wider world and his supreme reward. It is impossible to think of better words in which to paint such an ideal vision. We might also infer, from this description, the splendour which Wagner saw in his Siegfried – a man worthy of such a woman.

> She is the paragon of all paragons of beauty, the reply to all desire, the bliss-bestowing goal of every hero's earthly and unearthly quest. She is mother, sister, mistress, bride. Whatever in the world has lured, whatever has seemed to promise joy, has been premonitory of her existence – in the deep of sleep, if not in the forests of the world. For she is the incarnation of the promise of perfection; the soul's assurance that, at the conclusion of its exile in a world of organized inadequacies, the bliss that once was known will be known again; the comforting, the nourishing, the 'good' mother – young and beautiful – who was known to us, and even tasted, in the remotest past. (JC/HTF,92)

Wotan is the only character who either appears in or whose presence is felt in each of the four operas, and his is the cosmos explored in the *Ring*. For these reasons, the god is the main protagonist within the cycle as a whole, as set forth at the end of Chapter 3. But Campbell's glorification of 'The Lady of the House of Sleep' and the dominating presence of Brünnhilde in the action from W2 through to the end of *Götterdämmerung* (for she is the goal and purpose of Siegfried's quest in the intervening opera) suggest that she is the engine, the agent of deliverance. The main action of the drama is spread over the three operas in which she appears and in that sense she is the central character.

BRÜNNHILDE'S TRANSCENDENCE

The dramaturgic perfection of the journey

We can use Campbell's structural scheme to describe her journey; although he is concerned with mythic masculine heroism, his diagrammatic journey mirrors that of Freytag. Stories tell how the protagonist takes a dangerous journey away from home and then has to find his or her way back to safety. This final haven can be spiritual as well as physical or topographic. Many, perhaps most, of the great dramas have at their core a journey toward self-knowledge (p.29). The *Ring* is about many things but no staging of the drama can avoid showing the audience what each of the main characters learns about him or herself, and also about the world in which they live. Brünnhilde's journey is a journey from ignorance to knowledge. The table sets this out.

Freytag	Campbell	Brünnhilde's emotional journey	Brünnhilde's journey from ignorance to knowledge
1 Set up	The call to adventure; lured away from the common round.	She is pulled away from her steady life by Wotan's command to sacrifice Siegmund. (W2)	She learns that Wotan's commands are fundamentally flawed.
2 Rising action	A need to conciliate or defeat a power that stands in the way.	She overcomes Wotan's wrath after she disobeys him, and wins the right to protection by fire. (W3)	She realises that her personal salvation is the hope for a loving union such as she saw with the Volsung twins.
3 Mid-point	Entry into a dangerous place where a reward is gained.	She is put to sleep and awakened to new life and to sexual love by Siegfried. (S3.2)	She experiences a sexual fulfilment that obliterates all else from her mind.
4 Falling action	Attacked by foes as the journey continues.	Hagen conspires against her, and sexual love leads her on to the wrong course. (G1.3 & 2)	Sexual betrayal teaches her that the obverse of sexual ecstasy is an agony of hatred.
5 Victory	The necessary journey back home is achieved.	After the catharsis of Siegfried's murder, she regains the quality she had at the beginning of the journey. (G3.2)	Reflection on everything she has learned and experienced brings an understanding that only she can have.

Here again is evidence of Wagner's intuitive mastery of structure, this time spread over three operas. So natural is good dramatic composition to him that it encompasses but does not contradict the shorter journeys taken by her in *Die Walküre* and *Götterdämmerung* - in both of which she is also the protagonist. In the former opera she moves from ignorance to a full understanding of compassionate love. In the latter she starts with a new - and destructive - understanding about love, brought about by her discovery of sex, and ends with a comprehension of both types of love.

BRÜNNHILDE'S TRANSCENDENCE

The means by which Wagner achieves this is to deprive Brünnhilde of almost all the runic knowledge and prophetic powers with which Brynhild is invested in the *Volsung Saga* and the *Poetic Edda*. Such deliberate manipulations were made at the earliest stage so that the drama focused on the raw brutality of her betrayal and reciprocal vengeance (p.95/6). As the scope of the story subsequently widened, and the qualities of the valkyr were bolted on to those of the wronged woman, Wagner rectified this absence of wisdom by means of music. The first, magnificent passage whereby this is achieved is the short scene after Wotan furiously storms off at the end of their first scene together in W2: we then hear music which speaks of a comprehensive compassion like nothing before it in the *Ring*. If a first time spectator had not by then realized the remarkable nature of this woman, he or she would awaken to it now. The sense of aching

loss in the music surrounding the words 'Alas, my Wälsung! In deepest grief a faithful woman must faithlessly forsake thee' and that which follows convey a disinterested love never before felt by anyone in Wotan's cosmos. Wagner's music has the prodigious capacity to condense intense but complex emotions into the 14 bars in the orchestra, as illustrated above. (Note the elaborately detailed markings and expression given to the passage.) The spectator senses that the daughter is in receipt of an understanding that is denied to the father. The runic knowledge described in the sagas was useless for Brynhild there, and therefore cannot be used in a drama. So Wagner discards it and uses music to do the job. This is what Campbell describes as her 'call to adventure', where her stature is revealed (p.26).

This first time spectator, therefore, will not be surprised when Brünnhilde, at the end of *Götterdämmerung*, as she brings peace to Wotan, sings these words: 'All things I know . . . all is clear to me now.' When we put this with the observation (in the version not set to music) that she '. . . saw the world end', it brings home that her final contribution is the emotional knowledge and wisdom she has acquired. That gives us her victory in the concluding Stage 5. The musical passage above can be thought to stand for stage 1 of her journey and the words just quoted depict the end of it. So we have here

Stages 1 & 5, and because the dramatic structure is clear, it is not difficult to pinpoint the other three stages expounded by Freytag and Campbell.

To move forward into Stage 2, Rising Action, she absolutely *must* impress upon Wotan both what she has learnt and also that his agreement to Loge's protective fire is essential to her future. Stage 3 is the moment of no return, as she falls in love with Siegfried after he wakes her up. At this, the mid-point of the journey, Brünnhilde rejoices that her wisdom is fading away before mounting sexual desire: 'The wisdom of heaven flees from me, chased away by the joy of love!' This corresponds to the mid-point of Siegfried's journey which is his triumphant arousal of Brünnhilde from sleep to a joyously untrammelled sexual union. Stage 4 of the journey is the way back after the revelation experienced at the mid-point. Campbell's thesis can be paraphrased here by 'the heroine is pursued by foes as she flees with the elixir'. In this case the elixir is the transforming but one-sided view of love, and Hagen and Gunther are the foes. In G2, Brünnhilde is in a bad spiritual place. Finally, all comes good in G3.2.

There is yet another manipulation of the sources to consider, in addition to that concerning Brynhild's. As we have seen, in the sagas to which Campbell refers, Brynhild has two different personae: on the one hand as an aristocrat, celebrated for beauty and wisdom and on the other hand as a semi-divine, possibly immortal, servant to the gods and to Odin in particular. The *Volsung Saga* and Fouqué's *Sigurd der Schlangentödter* both try to combine the two. Fouqué is deft and more effective than the original: the two personae are made one by switching to and fro between them and by some adept papering over the joints. He contrives, and with some success, to merge the two into one. (See Appendices C and E for details.) Wagner also brings the two different stories together even more effectively than did Fouqué: Brünnhilde starts as a semi-divine valkyr but is transformed into a woman in one action. This benefits the drama in three ways: Firstly and most simply, it provides a clearly perceived narrative line - a before and after. Secondly, and of greater import, this narrative furnishes the plot with its most far-reaching and profound turning point, namely when the immortal valkyr becomes the mortal woman. Thirdly, only when she is a mortal woman does she discover the dangerous nature of sexual love.

Yet another enhancement to the dramatic structure follows. If being lowered for about nineteen years into a magic sleep by her father and then aroused from it by her lover are supreme moments in Brünnhilde's life, the impact on father and lover is equally profound. Putting his daughter to sleep is part of the key event in Wotan's life and waking her to love and a new life is supreme for Siegfried. In short, the two great events in the life of the valkyr correspond to the mid-points, the points of no return in the journeys of both Wotan and Siegfried. This coming together of events of mutual importance is despite the different dramatic span of the journeys taken: the plots of four operas for Wotan, three for Brünnhilde and two for Siegfried. From this it should follow that if her journey is from ignorance to knowledge, the implication must be that the same type of journey is pursued by Wotan and Siegfried, the two other positive forces within the whole story. The next chapter will examine whether this is so.

The journey from the beginning to the point of no return

At the beginning of Brünnhilde's story, the opening of W2, she knows almost nothing. She is physically mature but has the emotions of a teenager. The most important element in her life is the love for her father; she is aware of but has never seen her mother and is indifferent and unaffected by the evident dislike of her stepmother. She knows about sex but in a rather smutty way: Ortlinde in the opening of W3 advises the others to keep the mares away from the stallions! Like many young girls, she is much attached to her pony - Grane in this case. Her life is a game – jolly fun, riding Grane though the skies and bringing dead heroes to Valhalla. It is again the music that is to demonstrate this. The Ride of the Valkyrs shows the straightforward, energetic and thoughtless manner in which they all undertake what is a serious and perhaps complex task.

<u>Brünnhilde's call to action</u>
So, in *The Ring* we see a person who starts by knowing nothing and ends by knowing everything. It is very difficult indeed to think of any other drama which shows this. People learn about themselves but they always start with a good degree of self-knowledge. In novels it is easier to show such growth. In *War & Peace,* Natasha starts as an ebullient 13 year old and ends as a saddened but wiser 24 year old in the epilogue. But she is nevertheless always very self-aware – even at 13. When Brünnhilde first bounces on to the stage, she has no self-awareness at all – she is as a spoilt, privileged Daddy's girl. Then she is taught by Wotan (and she learns quickly, as she is daughter of Erda) that the world is not as she imagined. It is not a game and the issues involved are massive and dangerous. Such is brought home when she dares to say to Wotan that she will disobey the instruction to abandon Siegmund. She realises that never before has anything of like moment so affected him. The growth in comprehension as she mourns the betrayal of Siegmund that is to come is startling. She knows that her life will never be the same again.

<u>Brünnhilde attains domination over Wotan</u>
The valkyr's character had changed by the time Wotan left her in his rage and was an open door for the impact of Siegmund's passion. We can suppose that when Siegmund chooses personal love above all else this is the first occasion when such a choice is made in Wotan's cosmos. Cooke maintains this to be the crux of the entire *Ring* (Footnote, p.36). I disagree with respect to the structure of the drama but concur that it is the event of the greatest consequence in the *Ring* universe as devised by Wagner: Siegmund's

choice is part of the developing struggle between love and power. That Brünnhilde is bowled over by the revelation of matters hitherto unknown to her is obvious to every spectator. Not so obvious, perhaps, is the attitude of Wotan at this moment. He was clearly deeply affected by Siegmund's death and his rage at Brünnhilde is in part due to this, but the collapse of his will-to-power in the face of his daughter's advocacy of love is quick and it is total. This is why Wagner uses a transformation of the Spear motif (which will be called *will-to-power* in this study) to represent Brünnhilde's pleading on behalf of love. She recognizes the conflict between love and power as being near the centre of the drama, but does not as yet understand them.

This recognition awakens the power of prophecy within her. In the sagas, Brynhild is strongly possessed of the prophetic gift. Wagner critically and crucially withholds this from Brünnhilde (p.101) but introduces it here to enhance both the valkyr's growth and the dramatic narrative. The emotional force of the music, allied to this most far-reaching prophecy, conveys Brünnhilde's understanding of the big issue, and compensates for the necessary loss of runic knowledge. In this great scene with Wotan, she becomes a fully human young woman as she articulates the impact of Siegmund upon her. At this point, she leaves Wotan behind; he may kiss her *gottheit* away but she has already abandoned it, both emotionally and intellectually. She has realised that mankind, this time personified by Siegmund, has a willingness to sacrifice for the sake of others that the gods lack – and is thus of a higher moral order (p.450).

From immortality to mortality
Wagner breaks new ground once again, at this most crucial moment in Brünnhilde's life, and this is also a plot changer in the *Ring*. [A] To swap immortality for mortality does quite frequently occur in myth but not in the way it happens to Brünnhilde. The common myth is that an immortal *wants* to become mortal so that s/he can experience the joy of sexual love: this is the theme of the operas *Lohengrin, Rusalka* (Dvorak), *Undine* (Hoffman) and *Hans Heiling* (Marschner). There are also myths of goddesses falling in love with a mortal and, without losing immortality, bearing a son: Aeneas is the son of Venus and a mortal, Achilles is the son of a water sprite and a mortal.

The situation for Brünnhilde is different. Instinctively, as the beloved confidant of her father, she would not want to lose her immortal status and there is no other important example in literature and drama of such forced transformation. But then there comes the realisation of the significance of Siegfried to her personally. Not only, as she tells Wotan, will 'the holiest hero . . . arise from the race of the Volsungs' - he whom Wotan longs for - but that man will also be the only one worthy of her. She longs to feel the passion she saw between Siegmund and Sieglinde, for she realises this to be a greater spur to life than any other conceivable motivation or emotion. Wagner was well aware of this - 'she had renounced her divinity for the sake of love' (in the 1854

[A] Shaw saw the change at the moment when Siegfried woke Brünnhilde and thought it spelt the end of the epic drama he admired. He did not see that the change was dramatically necessary.

Röckel letter). From this follows the third original facet: the *nature* of the transformation from immortal to mortal is also unique in major literature and drama: she is not just awakened from a sleep but she is also *reborn*. The music tells us this as she comes alive in the bright sunlight. When the themes of the plot were first maturing in Wagner's mind, Siegfried was identified with the sun god and this strain remains as Brünnhilde affirms: 'Waker to life, conquering light!'. After this she then goes through a second rebirth as she is awakened into and is captured by a world of powerful sexuality; she encounters sex in ignorance of its full impact and consequently she is overwhelmed. Brünnhilde has witnessed Siegmund's turmoil and it filled her with awe - but that was second hand. First hand experience turns her life upside down.

She - and Siegfried in this respect - are still as children confronted with the miraculous excitement of new knowledge and experience. As adults we cannot think ourselves back into the time when we were very young children and everything was new and exciting. However, from the moment when Siegfried reaches the mountain top to the end of *Siegfried*, the music takes us as near to that emotion as we are likely to get – a long episode of unadulterated discovery as one new revelation is followed by another.
[B] Is it therefore surprising that their love is self-centred? Neither have known real pain or loss so they will have little idea of how to cope with a setback, and they have no knowledge of the world. Siegfried, to this point, has had nothing that has troubled him and has always succeeded (most significantly, in his mind, with the sexual conquest of Brünnhilde), and Brünnhilde has never failed in anything. She has second-hand knowledge of the epic struggle in which Wotan is engaged but knows nothing of the real world. Her only real problem has followed from her disobedience to Wotan but cajoling a father is not *that* difficult a problem for a much loved daughter.

Schopenhauer

If readers accept both the impact of the philosopher on the *Ring* and that Brünnhilde is the main agent for deliverance, it should not be a surprise that some key aspects of his thought should be applied first to her rather than to Wotan. There is his approach to sex and to death in particular. His views about sex illuminate her response to Siegfried and what he said about death will assist further examination of the Immolation texts, which were last looked at in connection with *Siegfrieds Tod* (p.114). In *Die Walküre* both plot and the music which surround her demonstrate a prodigious growth in understanding and moral awareness. She has become the wisest of people by virtue of her knowledge and compassion. She has a compassionate love for Siegmund and Sieglinde that is beyond the capability of her parents.

[B] If, in this and in other ways, Brünnhilde and Siegfried are as children, we can also reflect that compassion is not a characteristic of the young. This is another aspect of the one-dimensional nature of their love as previously described.

Knowledge of sexual love

This wisdom leaves her, however, as soon she is awakened into the totally new world of mortal mankind and is engulfed by sexual enchantment, the most compulsive emotion known to man. Brünnhilde had welcomed the ebb of wisdom before the flood of sexual desire in S3.2 and the consequence is seen in G1.1, where the text alone, regardless of the music, speaks of mutual self-glorification. Her love for Siegfried and his for her is flawed: the ecstatic sexual release at the end of S3.2 is akin to infatuation which, when extreme, drives out common sense in all whom it infects. Her fall from wisdom is seen in the Scene in G1.3 with Waltaute, for everything she is there told should reinforce what she was taught about the cosmic problems by Wotan in W2, the solution for which were that the Ring should indeed go back to the Rhinedaughters. Looked at objectively, her response contrasts badly with everything she did in *Die Walküre*.

Here now are what Wagner had to say about sex before he read Schopenhauer. First up, in the 1854 Röckel letter there this observation about Brünnhilde.

> From the moment Siegfried awakens her, she no longer has any knowledge save that of love. Now - the symbol of this love - after Siegfried has left her - is the *ring*: When Wodan (sic) [via Waltraute] demands it back from her, all she can think of is the reason for having left Wodan (when she acted out of love) and there is only one thing that she now knows, namely that she had renounced her divinity for the sake of love. But she knows that love is uniquely divine: Valhalla's splendour may fall in ruins, but she will not sacrifice [love] . . . But if you shudder at the thought that this woman should cling to this accursed ring as a symbol of love, you will feel exactly as I intended you to feel, and herein you will recognize the power of the Nibelung curse raised to its most terrible and tragic heights. (SS/SL,309)

Wagner seems to be stumbling, using many words to explain something that resists explanation. The last sentence appears to be an unexplained 'catch all': the power of the Nibelung's curse is dangerously near to being defined in part by something it is designed to explain. If so, it is circular and can be thought to have no meaning at all. This is not so, however, but the reason for this must await discussion until chapter 21 on *Götterdämmerung,* where a likely and profound truth that both relates to this obscurity and also cuts to the bone of the *Ring* itself can be appropriately revealed. (We must remember that Wagner was doing his utmost to convey something to his friend that would not come to fruition for a further 20 years.)

But two other observations about sex from the same letter are more specific and of different import.

> But the full reality of love is possible only between the sexes: only as *man* and *woman* can we *human beings* really love, whereas all other forms of love are mere derivatives of it, originating in it, related to it or an unnatural imitation of it. It is wrong to regard this love as only *one* manifestation of love in general, and to assume that other and higher forms must therefore exist *alongside* it. (SS/SL, 303)

> There is no doubt but that our love for a child or for a friend is merely a kind of makeshift solution, which is most clearly recognized as such by those who have found perfect happiness in sexual love. (SS/SL, 304)

Thus, before Schopenhauer came on the scene, Wagner thought that love for children, charitable love and compassion were all 'mere derivatives' which offer 'make-shift solutions' to a distinctly mystical idea of sexual love; all are an 'unnatural imitation' of it. Now we can consider some of the things Schopenhauer wrote about sex and, in doing so, bear in mind the similar cast of mind of composer and philosopher that Bryan Magee observes on p.17.

> The genitals are the real focus of the will . . . the life-preserving principle assuring to time endless life (AS/WWR1, 330)

> Sexual desire . . . is not only the strongest of desires, but is even specifically of a more powerful kind than all the others are. For it is the desire that constitutes even the very nature of man . . . It is so very much the chief thing, that no other pleasures make up for the deprivation of its satisfaction . . . It peeps up everywhere, in spite of all the veils over it . . . It is the daily thought and desire of the young and often of the old as well, the hourly thought of the unchaste, and the constantly recurring reverie of the chaste even against their will. (AS/WWR1, 512/3)

> Indeed, it may be said that man is concrete sexual impulse, for his origin is an act of copulation, and the desire of his desires is an act of copulation. (AS/WWR2, 514)

> The essential thing is not perhaps mutual affection but possession, in other words, physical enjoyment. The certainty of the former, therefore, cannot in any way console us for the want of the latter; on the contrary, in such a situation many a man has shot himself . . . and even greater is the number of those brought to the madhouse by the same passion. (AS/WWR2, 535) [c]

In no uncertain terms Schopenhauer stresses, as does Wagner, the difference between the universal animal impulse toward copulation and all other matters that drive human beings. For both men, the distinction between sex and affection or love is decisive. This can be thought in accord with the texts that depict the two lovers (pp.98/99) and the rampant energy of the music is redolent of an irresistible sex drive.

If Schopenhauer's view of sex has had any traction in discussion of Wagner, I suspect it to have been something like: 'Oh, all right then; Wagner had good logic on his side and we can accept his comments.' But as much as most of us recognize the potency of the identical views of both men, most will also think that copulation is not the be-all-and-end-all of love. It is essential for human survival but parental love and compassion are not 'mere derivatives'; they are also essential, this time for both survival and for salvation. Wotan experienced the first when he yielded to Brünnhilde's eloquence in *Die Walküre* Act III and she completely understood the nature of the second. The audience

---

[c] All the above is remarkably frank writing, dating from the first part of the 19th century. This is emphasised by one further observation, slipped in by the philosopher: 'No less in keeping with this quality is the fact that it is the great 'unspeakable', the public secret which must never be distinctively mentioned anywhere, but is always and everywhere understood to be the main thing.' (AS/WWR2, 570/1)

feels she already understands matters in a manner foreign to Wotan. The important point is that the music for all the above episodes is so emotionally powerful that it tells us that Wagner himself cannot have believed what he wrote to Röckel in 1854. The conclusion must also be that Schopenhauer misses the point. I shall briefly return to this later in the chapter.

The nature of death

We are on surer ground with Wagner's thoughts about the nature of death and perhaps extinction than we are with love. We know that they became very close to those of Schopenhauer, such that they penetrated and controlled the story of *Tristan und Isolde*. Scholars surmise that the first sketch for this may have dated from the autumn of 1854, at the very time when he first imbibed the philosopher's thoughts.

A human being as part of an undifferentiated totality (p.19) has a close affinity with Buddhism and Schopenhauer only realised this as he worked away at *The World as Will and Representation* and his other essays. These references in his work were, in turn, the stimulus for Wagner's abiding interest in the religion and its goal of attaining nirvana.

> We are told that [Nirvana] is permanent, static, imperishable, immoveable, ageless, deathless, unborn, and unbecome; that it is power, bliss and happiness, the secure refuge, the shelter and the place of unassailable security; that it is the real Truth and the supreme Reality; that it is the good, the supreme goal and the one and only consummation of our life – the eternal, hidden and incomprehensible Peace. (EC/B,40)

This description of the final peace will remind readers of the destination toward which Tristan and Isolde travel.

The journey is, of course, toward death. This death is the end: there is then nothing that resembles life as we know it, and therefore death nullifies the earlier Immolation in *Siegfrieds Tod*, in which Brünnhilde appears 'on horseback, helmeted and in the dazzling armour of a valkyr, leading Siegfried by the hand through the sky'. We do not know whether Wagner believed in life after death and the *Ring* is clearly pagan. Absorption in Schopenhauer may have clarified his attitude to death, and this is the sort of thing he read:

> If considerations ... awaken the conviction that there is something in us that death cannot destroy, this nevertheless happens by our being raised to a point of view from which birth is not the beginning of our existence. It follows from this knowledge that what is proved to be indestructible through death is not really the individual ... [who] ... exhibits himself as a mere difference of the species, and as such can be only finite. Accordingly, just as the individual has no recollection of his existence before birth, so can he have no recollection of his present existence after death. (AS/WWR2, 490)

> Since, in death, the knowing consciousness obviously perishes, either death [is] annihilation ... or we must resort to the assumption of a continuous existence ... My philosophy leads us out of this dilemma ... it puts man's inner nature not in consciousness but in the will - not united with consciousness but related to [it] - as something illuminated is related to light ... Now we can grasp the indestructability of the real kernel and true inner being that is

ours, in spite of extinction of consciousness in death and its corresponding non-existence before birth . . . The brain . . . is the product or phenomenon - a secondary thing - to the will, and it is the will alone that is imperishable. (AC/WWR1,199)

Death is a return to where each of us came from - the unknowable and unknowing, timeless and indivisible, noumenon. The phenomenon of our existence - what we perceive in space and time - may expire, but the noumenon - the elusive mass of indivisible matter of which each of us is part - continues. In the case of animals, Schopenhauer says 'that the arising and passing away do not concern the real essence of things, but . . . remains untouched by them, hence is imperishable, consequently that each and every thing that wills to exist continuously actually does exist continuously and without end. Accordingly, at every given point of time all species of animals . . . exist together completely'. (AC/WWR2, 479) Bryan Magee puts Schopenhauer's thought like this: 'in the ultimate ground of our being, we are, all of us, the same thing, or rather the same something, something that it is impossible for us to apprehend.' This 'something' is immaterial and outside of time but it has an unending *will to exist*. [D]

The Immolation

We have now come to the last phase in Brünnhilde's journey, where obstacles are overcome and triumph gained. This is where the knowledge she has acquired during her life will include Wagner's understanding of death.

She left the stage in turmoil and despair, with Siegfried's murder plotted and in train. We do not see her again until the final scene when she is completely transformed. Some vision has been granted her in the night, though its nature is not made clear. Wagner makes no effort to explain matters and there is a good reason for this. No practical way could be found to present such a transformation. Essentially, we have to guess as to the events which changed Brünnhilde and the point surely is that the change from the depth of despair to the ecstasy of triumph is so extreme that any 'spelled out' explanation, if it were not to be trivial, would necessarily be extensive and elaborate - a mighty episode. [E] Wagner would probably have been capable of doing justice to any such scene at any time after 1856. But it would detract from the Immolation: two immense, revelatory episodes would not be effective in such close proximity. The critical issue is how things will appear and sound on stage.

[D] This will-to-exist is an essential part of, but is not identical with, the *Will* that Schopenhauer identifies as the unseen part of the noumenon. This aspect will be tackled in the following chapter, on Wotan.

[E] One existing example of this is when Brünnhilde suddenly tells Sieglinde that she is bearing Siegfried in her womb. Her attitude changes in an instant from deepest despair to the highest exaltation, and even Wagner finds that difficult to bring off.

On the surface and according to all theory this is flawed dramatic construction. All we know is that she met with the Rhinedaughters in between G2 and G3.2; as they left Siegfried they told him that Brünnhilde will understand all the matters he is unable to grasp. Their knowledge may be very partial and there is no reason to think they would either have known about or been interested in the drug of forgetfulness, but they are primeval and perhaps have an intuitive knowledge to which Brünnhilde can connect.

We can of course list the issues she could have reflected upon as she walked by the Rhine, perhaps hearing and seeing the cortège that is bearing the dead Siegfried back.

- on the cosmic issues, as already known but reinforced by her talk with the Rhinedaughters;
- on what Wotan had told her about Hagen in *Die Walküre*, thereby reaching a full understanding of his treachery;
- on her own progress from ignorance, to a profound spiritual knowledge;
- on the seeming necessity for betrayal in order to cope with the messy reality of life - Siegmund by Wotan, Fricka by Wotan, Wotan by Brünnhilde, Brünnhilde by Wotan, Brünnhilde by Siegfried, Siegfried by Gunther, Gunther by Hagen;
- on the reality that only by cutting all ties to help from others, including herself, could Siegfried have lifted himself clear of Alberich's curse, for all such help might lead him back to Wotan. This must also include the crucial advice she gave to Hagen that he must strike Siegfried in the back if he was to kill him;
- finally – and surely decisive – on her own fatal abandonment of all wisdom under the compulsion of sexual desire.

And so she enters and tells all on stage that she understands 'everything.'

Nevertheless, Wagner was in doubt how to find the ending he needed. In the 1856 letter to Röckel Wagner says that the effort to find the right words to end the work was a 'torment'. The *Ring*, like other great dramas, is pregnant with meaning and meanings, but, like them, such meanings cannot be put into a precise form of words. 'Meaning' has to emerge in performance. But, in contrast to most dramas, Wagner and innumerable commentators have felt some need to summarise the vast edifice and attention always turns to the text of the Immolation. Chapter 8 has the suggestion that the two earlier *Siegfrieds Tod* versions expressed joy at the benefit received from the ritualised sacrifice of Siegfried.

This final version does not have the precision or simplicity of that first *Siegfrieds Tod* but the essence of the drama is not changed and the concluding celebration of the audience is not that different from that described by Treadwell: 'a ritual death so that the audience can celebrate their own passage to utopia'. Brünnhilde's pact/bond with Siegfried is not obvious in *Siegfrieds Tod* but by 1852 it is established that some form of universal love - much wider than the sexual passion the two lovers had experienced - prompts Brünnhilde to reach beyond Siegfried's mandatory and incognizant end, and to cap it with her own full comprehension ('Alles, alles weiss ich') as she chooses to die with him. So far, we have looked at the two versions which relate to *Siegfrieds Tod* and there are three remaining. Only one of these, however, is basic - that composed in 1852 on completion of the poems for all four operas, as an amendment to the original *Siegfrieds Tod*. For the new text, however, hope in the future continues to be the dominant theme in every version. Such steadiness of vision by the composer is a tenet of this study. The observable thematic consistency of the texts has been obscured because critical attention has been directed at the divergences between them - divergences which often take the form of moral homilies. Not one of these amendments or additions to the text that follows was used when the music was composed in 1874.

Despite this clear matter, these changes have been seen as evidence that Wagner's social and philosophical perspectives altered over the years 1852-1874 and he wanted his great work to reflect them. This study takes a different view. Within the sub-text, lie mythic themes that would seem both trite and pompous if put into words. Wagner sought for universality, for a work that joined everything together in the prevailing view of German romantic scholarship. However, his personal life was influenced by social revolution, by Buddhism and by the philosophies of Feuerbach and Schopenhauer, and he briefly thought he could convey something of the moral messages derived from such influences. The composer was seriously exercised by the matter. In the 1856 letter to Röckel he explains some of the reasons behind his change of mind over the years. He undoubtedly wanted to find words that would convey a conclusive moral statement but - like everyone since then - was unable to do so. The relevant portions of the letter form a useful counterpoint to the texts and will be referred to as appropriate. The inbuilt mystery of Siegfried's death enabled Wagner, as it has since enabled everyone else, to posit 'meanings' which rationalise it. By a strange and paradoxical inversion, this mystery gives the *Ring* an underlying coherence. I shall use the various texts of the Immolation to show a consistency that has often been denied.

Examination of the different versions can take in three viewpoints. Firstly, the degree and manner in which the texts convey the sentiment that all will be well. Secondly, the force and purpose of any changes or additions and how these fit into the underlying sentiment of joyous hope. Thirdly, the degree to which these changes suggest that Wagner was uncertain about what he was doing.

The 1852 text

This has amendments from the version of early 1849; the lines that were carried over from *Siegfrieds Tod* are shown in italics.

1	*Heavy logs heap up for me here in a pile at the edge of the Rhine;*
Sets the scene	*high and bright let the flames flare up*
	and consume the noble limbs of the most exalted hero!
	Lead his stallion hither: let it follow the warrior with me:
	for my own body yearns to share in the hero's holiest honour -
	Do as Brünnhilde bids!

BRÜNNHILDE'S TRANSCENDENCE

2
Eulogy for Siegfried

Purer than sunlight streams the light from his eyes:
the purest of men it was who betrayed me!
False to his wife – true to his friend -
from her who was faithful – she alone who was loyal -
he sundered himself with his sword.
Never were oaths more nobly sworn;
never were treaties kept more truly;
never did any man love more loyally;
and yet every oath, every treaty, the truest love -
no one betrayed as he did!

3
Address to Wotan. She has suffered and knows what must happen

Do you know why that was so?
Oh you, eternal guardians of oaths!
Direct your gaze on my burgeoning grief:
behold your eternal guilt!
Hear my lament, most mighty of gods!
By the bravest of deeds, which you dearly desired,
you doomed him who wrought it to suffer
the curse to which you in turn succumbed -
it was I whom the purest man had to betray,
that a woman might grow wise.
Do I now know what you need?
All things, all things, all things I know,
all is clear to me now!
I hear the rustle of your ravens' wings:
with anxiously longed-for tidings
I send the two of them home.
Rest now, rest now, you god!

4
Prepares to return the ring to the Rhine

My inheritance now I take as my own.
Accursed band! Fear-ridden ring!
I grasp your gold and give it away.
Wise sisters of the watery deep,
you daughters who swim in the Rhine,
I thank you now for your sound advice!
I give to you what you covet:
from my ashes take it as your own!
Let the fire that consumes me cleanse the ring of its curse:
in the floodwaters let it dissolve,
and safely guard the shining gold
that was stolen to your undoing.

5
Pronounces that the gods' time is over.

Fly home, you ravens!
Whisper to your lord what you heard here by the Rhine!
Make your way past Brünnhilde's rock:
tell Loge, who burns there, to hasten to Valhalla!
For the ending of the gods is dawning now:
thus do I hurl the torch into Valhalla's proud-standing stronghold.

BRÜNNHILDE'S TRANSCENDENCE

6	Grane, my horse, take this my greeting!
Greets	Do you know, my friend, where I am taking you now?
Siegfried in mutual	Lit by the fire, your lord lies there - Siegfried my blessed hero.
sacrifice.	You whinny with joy to follow your friend?
	Does the laughing fire lure you to him? -
	feel how the flames burn in my breast,
	effulgent fires seize hold of my heart:
	to clasp him to while held in my arms
	and in mightiest love be wedded to him!
	Heiayoho! Grane! Greet your master!
	Siegfried, Siegfried! See! In bliss your wife bids you welcome! [F]

Three things to point out. Firstly, this text remains a joyous affirmation that the task of redemption is accomplished and is in that sense the same as that for *Siegfrieds Tod*: the joint sacrifice will wash the world clean. Secondly, there is no indication whatsoever about Wagner's own notion of death or extinction and there *can* be none that relates to Schopenhauer because Wagner did not come across him for a further two years. Brünnhilde's hope is that she will vaguely be 'wedded' to Siegfried, but with no indication of what this might be. Wagner is almost waiting for Schopenhauer to point the way. Thirdly, Section 3 is new and not related to anything in previous Immolations. In it she first expands on her personal sorrow, and then acknowledges the responsibility laid upon her at the end of *Die Walküre* Act III. This is the main signal that it is her journey that is central to the emancipation from guilt offered to Wotan. As the footnote points out, this Section is the mid-point and, of course, the call to Wotan to find rest is and remains central to the Immolation.

The 'Feuerbach' ending

Almost immediately, however, Wagner deemed this purpose and 'meaning' inadequate. He surely was 'groping' when he came up with the following lines, addressed to the Gibichung people, and *added them* to the end of the existing section 5:

> You, blossoming life's enduring race: heed well what I tell you now!
> For when you've seen Siegfried and Brünnhilde consumed by the
>   kindling blaze;
> and when you've seen the Rhine's daughters return the ring to its depths,

---

[F] The narrative moves from a prelude which sets the scene (1) through evocations of the necessary roles that the lovers play in the process of salvation (2) and (3), the conclusion of which is the lifting of the curse (4). This leads to the climax, namely the teleological, moral purpose of the story (5), followed by the final act of sacrifice upon which all turns (6). It is the nearest thing in Wagner to the *scena* that is such a common feature of Italian opera.

If one applies the Freytag structure to the Scene as opposed to the Act, the mid-point is the end of section 3, when the gods are bid to rest. Note the strong structure when compared to the earlier version, where the eulogy precedes the set-up and there is no powerful mid-point.

> to the north then look through the night:
> when a sacred glow starts to gleam in the sky,
> then shall you know that you've witnessed Valhalla's end.
> ... Though I leave behind me a world without rulers,
> I now bequeath to that world my most sacred wisdom's hoard -
> Not wealth, not gold, nor godly pomp;
> not house, nor land, nor lordly splendour;
> not troubled treaties' treacherous bonds,
> not smooth-tongued custom's stern decree;
> blessed in joy and sorrow, love alone can be.

The last five lines are critical and this piece of text is commonly dignified as the 'Feuerbach' ending. That philosopher, however, might well have laughed at the simplistic sentiments, which are characteristic of the story-book of every romantic novel. Wagner himself dismissed it in the 1856 Röckel letter:

> But I also recall once having sought forcibly to assert my meaning – the only time I ever did so – in the tendentious closing words which Brünnhilde addresses to those around her, a speech in which she turns their attention away from the reprehensibility of ownership to the love which alone brings happiness; and yet I had (unfortunately!) never really sorted out in my own mind what I meant by this "love" which, in the course of the myth, we saw as something utterly and completely devastating. (SS/SL, 358)

This does but confirm, however, that if Wagner was groping for a moral in 1852, he was surely still groping in 1856. He was right to say that sexual love is not the answer: the myopic mutual obsession between Brünnhilde and Siegfried is flawed. We can assume that Brünnhilde's knowledge of love embraces three forms: her own destructive passion, the sublime consummation of Siegmund and Sieglinde, and the mutual need between father and daughter as made clear in the farewell scene between them that closes W3 (p.335). Accordingly, Wagner's downgrading of love is dubious and inclines toward the phoney. Furthermore, this takes account of and discounts the accord between Wagner and Schopenhauer as previously noted. If Wagner did not believe what he wrote to Röckel in 1854, he is now writing in August 1856, and we can bear in mind that between June 1854 and March 1856 Wagner had composed the music of *Die Walküre* - the opera, above all, in which the audience sees the triumph of what I have called 'social' love, in contrast to that generated by the sex drive. The context may help. Wagner was trying to explain difficult matters to his friend. He knew he had a problem with the complex and conflicting consequences of love and he could not bring himself to admit that the Feuerbach text was just nonsense. But he must have seen that it added nothing at all to the basic text that he had just completed.

The 'Schopenhauer' ending
In May 1856, Wagner had taken full cognizance of Buddhism as a religion related to the philosophy of Schopenhauer It was then that he sketched out *Die Sieger* (The Victors) about two lovers who are separated by caste. They accordingly sublimate their mutual

desire as the Buddha teaches (he is a character in the plot) and find peace together in nirvana. In 1864 Wagner was still expressing a hope to Ludwig that both composition and performance might be achieved by 1870 - evidence of an ever-present interest. In June he wrote to an acquaintance that he was to revise the ending of *Götterdämmerung* because

> it has become clear to me that the poem has travelled far beyond its original schematic tendency, as still retaining its [1852] ending; this is consequently a cramping and spoiling of the achieved result. (Quoted in EN/LRW2,356)

Perhaps in July or August, Wagner wrote what became known as the 'Schopenhauer' ending below, to replace the entire 'Feuerbach' ending.

> Were I no more to fare to Valhalla, do you know whither I fare?
> I depart from the home of desire;
> I flee forever and from the home of delusion;
> the open gates of eternal becoming I close behind me now:
> to the holiest chosen land, free from desire and delusion,
> the goal of the world's migration, redeemed from reincarnation
> the enlightened woman goes now.
> The blessed end of all things eternal, do you know how I attained it?
> Grieving love's profoundest suffering opened my eyes for me:
> I saw the world end.

This text reflects the content of Buddhist thought (p.179), and it is not difficult to understand its appearance at this particular time. *Die Sieger* centres round passion which must be renounced and thereby leads to a full redemption and acceptance into Buddha's congregation. The newly suggested *Ring* text can be seen as fitting neatly into such a drama; it would also be fine coming from the mouths of either Tristan or Isolde as they express that peculiar passion we are to see emerge in music within twelve months of leaving off the composition of *Siegfried*. But Brünnhilde would never have expressed such sentiments. Wagner always portrays her as of a positive disposition: an outgoing, responsive daughter to Wotan, defiantly decisive as she is 'turned' by Siegmund, assertive with Wotan as she pleads for her integrity, and magnificently vindictive as she plots with Gunther and Hagen after her betrayal. Negative, solipsistic withdrawal just does not and never would fit such a woman. Everything about the text is *untrue to life*. It is therefore no wonder that Wagner never set it to music.

In all events, when he wrote to Röckel in the 1856 letter, it is Schopenhauer and not Buddha that lie in and between the lines.

> Well, I scarcely noticed how, in working out this plan [the 1851 expansion from one to four operas], nay, basically even in its design, I was quite unconsciously following a quite different, and much more profound, intuition and that, instead of a single phase in the world's evolution, what I had glimpsed was the essence of the world itself in all its conceivable phases, and that I had thereby recognized its nothingness, with the result, of course – since I remained faithful to my intuitions rather than to my conceptions – that

what emerged was something totally different from what I had originally intended . . . it required a complete revolution in my rational outlook, such as was finally brought about by Schopenhauer, to reveal to me the cause of my difficulty and provide me with a truly fitting key-stone for my poem, which consists in an honest recognition of the true and profound nature of things, without the need to be in any way tendentious. (SS/SL, 357/8)

Similarities subsist between Buddhism and Schopenhauer but Nirvana is not the equivalent of the noumenon. Nirvana is something that must be attained by enlightenment in order to avoid reincarnation. To be reabsorbed into the noumenon is the lot of all after death. What we read in the letter refers to the noumenal. All creation may exist there but it is unknowable, and it is the place from which further life may arise. This is the nature of all things and is not negative in itself.

What is different about the 'Schopenhauer ending', however, is the reference to suffering, which occurs in no other version. Brünnhilde says that 'grieving love's profoundest suffering opened my eyes for me.' This reminds us that amongst all the principals it is Brünnhilde who has had by far the worst experience. This is so bad that in G2 Wotan himself was also execrated as a betrayer: she asks whether he intended to 'Teach her sorrows as none have suffered? Design her disgrace to give unimagined pain?' From *Siegfrieds Tod* onwards, Brünnhilde personifies betrayed humankind; in that first draft, in fact, the disgusting attitude of Siegfried as he wrests away the Ring makes Wagner's original take even worse than it eventually became.

Nevertheless, the words were not to be set to music. This last effort was never a realistic attempt to 'explain' the *Ring* at all. By rejecting it, Wagner returned to Schopenhauer's notion of death which probably reflected his own when he started the project in 1848. The thesis presented here is that Wagner's Siegfried project has both continuity and dramatic coherence from inception in the *Myth*, through *Siegfrieds Tod* and into the completed cycle. This continuity lies in the fated death of Siegfried and the grappling of this death to the fate of Wotan. This is never spelt out – we are not *told* about it – but it is shown to those 'who have eyes to see'.

Although not set to music, the words remain a legitimate handle in discussion as to whether the *Ring* is pessimistic, which will be examined in Chapter 15. In the meantime, one can think of the two 'philosophical' inserts as glosses – further attempts by the composer to express what cannot be expressed.

* * * * * *

What Wagner gives us in Brünnhilde is a person who has experienced the widest range of emotions and situations imaginable. These situations are to be found in the 1852 text. This is testimony to the composer's grip, the manner in which the plot seized hold of so many moral issues. As it happened, Schopenhauer gave context and a conceptual background to these same issues. Underlying everything is the notion that people can be governed by disruptive forces they do not understand and to think clearly when these forces are in play is nigh impossible. The impulse toward sexual satisfaction can be seen as a symbol of this destructive force.

◇ ◇ ◇ ◇ ◇

14

Wotan's Journey

The one journey examined so far has been that of Brünnhilde - the journey from ignorance to knowledge. Four others must be defined: those of Wotan and the three Volsungs - Sieglinde and Siegmund, and Siegfried. The journeys of Siegmund and Siegfried are tied to that of Wotan. Those of Siegfried and Wotan bear upon the entire *Ring* and, if both journeys concern knowledge gained, they must be different from that of Brünnhilde. Whereas she moves from knowing very little to knowing a great deal, such growth cannot be ascribed to either her father or her lover. I have also suggested that the stories of the god and the hero are destined to come together (p.91) and we must assess if and why this holds. (Discussion of Sieglinde, whose life and death are in part separated from those of Siegmund and Brünnhilde, will be deferred until the dramatic and musical analysis of *Die Walküre*.)

Ernest Newman's error

The greatest contribution to Wagner scholarship came from the pen of Ernest Newman. From *A study of Wagner* in 1899, via *Wagner* (1904) and *Wagner as Man and Artist* (1914), his work culminated in the four volume *Life of Richard Wagner* (1933-1947) and *Wagner Nights* (1949). To describe his work as indispensable is a big understatement. Nevertheless, the influence of his work can be and has been distorting. He had a precise, forensic mode of thought and could not tolerate what he saw as woolliness. Therefore, he can write:

> Whether the course of Wagner's thinking in [the *Ring*] can ever be made entirely clear is open to doubt: the more one studies the drama the more conscious does one become that the process by which it was built up over the years inevitably led to a certain confusion in Wagner's mind with regard to one or two elements in it. Perhaps the root cause of all his troubles was the impulse that came over him, presumably some time in 1851, to combine the Siegfried myth with that of the downfall of the Gods. The two have no connection in the ancient mythology. (EN/LRW2,358)

The judgement is succinct and unambiguous: Wagner was unable to cope with the story he had devised. Readers are now reminded of the precept of Humphrey Kitto (p.2): 'If the interpretation [a critic advances] implies that the play is imperfectly designed, then either the dramatist has not done his job very well, or the critic has failed in his . . . If the dramatist had something to say and if he was a competent artist, the presumption is that he has said it, and that we, by looking at the form which he created, can find what it is.'

In pursuit of clarity I have, in Chapter 4, surmised the existence of a 'proto-plot', constructed from the coming together of parts of *Das Nibelungenlied* and the *Volsung Saga*. Its purpose was to set forth how such a plot - without gods and dealing with human beings alone - might have developed in the composer's mind. I can make no claim that it did but I *can* say that had it concretely so formed itself, as described, without any supernatural involvement, then Newman's thesis would hold. Any dramatist would have a problem with the introduction of gods, giants and dwarfs into the scenario set down on pp.56/7. The germane issue, whether this be a fanciful fabrication on my part or not, is immaterial in one sense at least: in the first draft of the story, namely the *Myth,* Wotan is there from beginning to end even though he does not appear on stage. Moreover, in that original sketch the first culpable act was that of Wotan, who forces Alberich to ransom his life by handing over his gold and the Ring. Alberich is not there shown to be at fault in wresting the gold from the river bed. This emphasis changes as the plot was developed. The story of the final *Ring* starts with both Alberich and Wotan - at roughly the same moment – seeking power at any cost, within their own terms.

The *Myth* demonstrates that Newman's judgement can be questioned. This is made evident more than once. The three primary Nordic sagas insist on Odin's abiding interest in the Volsung tribe he has 'fathered' (p.84). This can be likened within the drama to the most telling piece of information in the *Myth*: that Hagen is Alberich's son. This ties the very beginning of the sketch - Alberich seizing the Gold - to the very end of the envisaged dramatic action - Hagen being pulled 'down also into the depths' by the Rhinedaughters. *Siegfrieds Tod* is a complete (if unwieldy) drama in its own right but nevertheless needed an expansive theme to match the whopping incident with which it culminates. The expansion chosen, namely to embrace Siegfried's world into Wotan's cosmos was the only satisfactory option.

He says as much to Röckel in the 1856 letter. His first idea in early gestation of the work was that the character of Siegfried 'could be used to show how a world of injustice might be replaced by a new, just world'. He continues: 'Well, I scarcely noticed how, in working out this plan [ie the *Myth*], nay, basically even in its design, I was unconsciously following a quite different, and much more profound, intuition, and that, instead of a single phase in the world's evolution [i.e. the redemption of a corrupt system by means of a ritual sacrifice] what I had glimpsed was the essence of the world itself in all its conceivable phases.' This sentence is generally used to support the thesis that Wagner was muddled but, as positioned here, it can be seen to support the opposite. He did not need to change his original plan - much detail and the entire kernel of the *Ring* is contained in the *Myth* and this furnishes the whole project with continuity and coherence. This inherent unity was inchoate in Wagner's mind and only started to take shape with the poem of *Der junge Siegfried*.

For Newman to have described the composer's crafting of plot as an 'impulse that came over him . . . to combine' the stories of Siegfried and Wotan is surely a misreading of the situation. We examine the form and structure of the drama, as advised by Kitto, and find them whole. Correctly portrayed, the link between Wotan and Siegfried is one of logic, particularly if 'logic' is as perceived by Wagner (p.144). This undermines Newman's assertion: if that is allowed to stand, then *any* attempt to claim coherence for Wagner's work must fail.

The history of Wotan's world

The examination of character in this study started with Siegfried, and that must now be matched by one on Wotan, the main protagonist in the *Ring*. Wagner lays the seeds of the end of Wotan's time in its very beginning. In answer to Mime's question about the gods in *Siegfried* Act I, Wotan makes clear that he knew the World Ash tree would start to wither once he had cut away the branch to be crafted into his spear. Moreover, he did not believe, and there is no evidence that the Norns or Erda thought, his action to be either arbitrary or venal. Without such action there cannot be progress. A sense of order was needed and that could not be established without some instrument of power, and only a being of high order could fashion such. Wagner gave the matter much thought and must surely have had Wotan in mind when, within a year of completing the *Myth*, he wrote the following in *The Artwork of the Future*:

> From the moment when Man perceived the difference between himself and Nature, and so began his own development as man by breaking loose from the unconsciousness of natural animal existence and passing over into conscious life - when he thereby confronted and opposed Nature and, from the unwelcome feeling of his dependence on her which then arose from that opposition, the faculty of Thought developed - from that moment Error began, as the first expression of consciousness. For Error is the mother of Knowledge, and the history of the birth of Knowledge out of Error is the history of the human race, from the myths of the earliest times down to the present day. (RW/PW1,70)

When applied to Wotan, we can assume his 'birth of knowledge' to be when he drank from the Well of Wisdom, the first moment in his recorded time. The 'error' that results is both primal and necessary, and includes within it some sort of ending. Balanced consideration of Wotan's motive is possible and once again the *Myth* and *Siegfrieds Tod* give clues. The *Myth* establishes Wotan's essential benevolence: the gods 'intend to rule the world in peace and order . . . [and] . . . bind all elements by prudent laws.' *Siegfrieds Tod* opens with the Norns hoping that Wotan will indeed be wise as he bends toward the Well of Wisdom, to drink from which being the necessary precursor to breaking his spear away from the World Ash Tree. There is no way in normal parlance that Wotan's action can be described as bad. He acts in the nature of all decent humanity - to move forward, to plan, to hope, to try. Wotan 'formed the dream of creating an order that would end the sway of the primitive as well as the stupor of the primordial, transforming the world into a far nobler and more admirable place, in which life could be lived more meaningfully and worthily.' (K&S/FE,71)

The essence of that spear was something like absolute power, provided it was exercised within the law. If 'Wotan resembles us to a tee' as he informed Röckel, and if power corrupts irrevocably, we can then observe Wagner tweaking his plot to make this clear. In the *Myth* Alberich is already on the war path and might therefore be seen as forcing Wotan's hand into the dubious bargain needed for Valhalla: Alberich is a bad guy with rising power and something must be done. Wotan performs three actions that govern the entire drama. He crafts a spear that can bear the universal runic laws upon it; he hazards the well-being of the gods in order to build Valhalla and he avoids the consequences of that gamble by stealing the Ring.

As the first of these activities, crafting the spear, was necessary, so was the third. Without the theft of Alberich's Gold, Tarnhelm and Ring, in order to ransom Freia, the gods would atrophy. But the second action, the gamble with Freia that threatened the future of all the gods, was *not necessary*. Wotan *chose* to build Valhalla and it was his determination to carry this through that pushed him to gamble with Freia. Thereafter, the only escape was for Wotan to break his own laws. In stealing from Alberich he reached beyond the outer limit of law and morality and thereby crippled himself. This self-inflicted wound - *hubris* in its purest sense - was waiting to happen. The doom of the gods was made inevitable. Stewart Spencer draws attention to the extended prose draft of *Das Rheingold* in which Erda expands on the inevitability of the gods' decline: 'All things that are - end. A day of darkness dawns for the gods. I counsel you: shun the Ring.' After these words we find the following, which were not set to music: 'It bodes no good that the gods are deceitful in their treaties; far worse is in store if you retain the ring; your end draws slowly nearer, yet it will overwhelm you with precipitate suddenness if you refuse to relinquish the ring.' (Stewart Spencer, p.365 in his translation of the *Ring,* Thames & Hudson 1993, where he quotes from Strobel, writing in 1930.)

Wotan realises this at the end of *Das Rheingold* and the start of his journey is an understanding of what was necessary. The action of stealing the Ring from Alberich was momentous and imposed the greatest stress upon him. So bad have things become that he realises - for the first time since his spear gave him power - that none of the older orders which have contested for supremacy can help. He alone sees the potential in mankind and so turns himself in that direction. His words to Fricka in W2, 'a hero is needed who, lacking godly protection, breaks loose from the laws of the gods' acknowledges this and sanctions something outside the remit of the power of his spear.

Fricka then unwittingly points out that he has not gone far enough. She does not, in fact, understand the situation, for her simple goal is to win the argument and thereby bend Wotan's will to her demand. Only Wotan sees the implication, namely that he requires someone or something that is both entirely outside the ambit of his power and also outside of his understanding. This we can assume has *never* happened before and the handling of which leaves Wotan completely at a loss. Hence the despair in his great narration in W2: 'Let all I raised / now fall in ruins! / My work I abandon; / one thing alone do I want: / the end - the end!' There is but one problem: the near impossibility of nullifying the curse upon the Ring. Not only is the action required to remove the curse beyond his reach but Fricka has unknowingly demonstrated that to do so requires an action by someone or something that Wotan can neither control nor indeed conceive. He has created a situation which seems to have no good outcome.

His desolation at this point is compounded by the two actions which follow. His impotence is underlined in one direction by the defection of Brünnhilde, his most trusted confidant - and it is clear that such a defection had never previously happened. This brings on the second consequence, namely that it is Wotan - at first hand - who brings death to his son. This is the person with whom he had shared perhaps years of companionship in the wilderness. To kill one's own son!

Hence the almost ungovernable rage launched at Brünnhilde when he runs her to ground. Perhaps the moment of lowest morale is in W3, when he compares his situation with that of his daughter as she responded to Siegmund's passionate heroism:

> Weren't you then enjoying blissful pleasure.
> Weren't you gaily extracting from the fountain of love
> the wanton frenzy of erotic feeling,
> while for me divine necessity mingled with corrosive bile?

The despair is personal rather than cosmic as the reality of loneliness strikes him. For he realises that his daughter has moved ahead of him and has experienced a type of spiritual joy that he has never had. The German text of the last line (impossible to match in translation) calls forth a descending vocal line of unsurpassed bitterness ('Als mir göttlicher Noth - nagende Galle gemischt'). The gloom is accentuated by the falling bass line in the orchestra and the whole diminishes from *pp* to almost dead silence. Wotan's moment of greatest danger is probably that conveyed in Siegfried's Funeral Music, when - on impotent tenterhooks in Valhalla - he looks upon his grandson murdered by a dominant Hagen in league with his own daughter. But at this moment in W3, alone with Brünnhilde, his spirit is at breaking point, brought there by awareness of personal failure regarding his murdered son Siegmund and his divergent daughter.

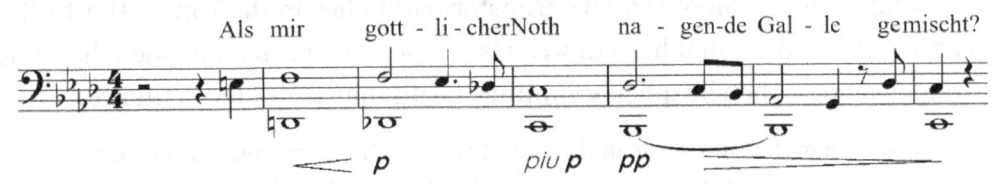

The closing scene between Wotan and Brünnhilde in Act III of *Die Walküre* is a miracle of drama. The bitter interjection cited above is the critical low point for the god, brought about by the truth he perceives as Brünnhilde puts the indubitable moral case for her behaviour in shielding Siegmund. The music in that short passage shows him shaken and with nowhere to go. Just before this he admits that 'consuming torment' had 'inspired the terrible wish to end my eternal grief in the ruins of my own world'. Thereafter, the text has but little argumentation within it. Wotan sets out broadly what will happen, seemingly ignoring or casting aside Brünnhilde's various interjections. But when her fate is pronounced - to be taken as a subservient wife by the man who awakens her - she jumps in with the solution of the protective 'magic fire'. With no confirmatory words whatsoever, all becomes clear to both of them: the only heroic hope of the world - Siegfried, Wotan's grandson - will be the one to claim her, the god's daughter. No explanation or detail of what will or might happen is subsequently given. No implications are tendered or discussed. Except for one thing: in his last sentence he understands and endorses the need for him to step aside: 'He who fears my spearpoint shall never pass through the fire!' It is a hope that Siegfried will reverse the smashing of Nothung by smashing the spear: an acknowledgement that only a person with both the personal history and peculiar characteristics as attached to Siegfried can break the curse on the Ring. This scene is the clearest example in the cycle where every facet shows rather than tells the audience what is happening: Wotan is handing over to Siegfried and Brünnhilde.

At the conclusion of Chapter 5, the background to the conjoined fates of the god and the hero was summarised. Wotan's last words - as above - are the link *within the drama* that is to shackle his fate to that of his grandson. They give voice to the understanding that Wotan gains though the agency of Brünnhilde's vision and her enhanced morality. The circle is complete. With that completion, Wotan's active history is at an end: Wagner describes him to Röckel as 'a departed spirit'. In *Siegfried* he is portrayed as keeping watch over his grandson. In this he takes up the role outlined by Campbell as an inactive 'fairy godfather'. But of course he is not detached: we first see the Wanderer in this role in *Der junge Siegfried* and even there his apparent passivity masks anxiety. This becomes explicit in the dialogues with Erda and Siegfried in *Siegfried* Act III.

A seeming elucidation of Wotan's transformation lies in the 1854 letter to Röckel. The lead-in tells us that what he is to write is important: 'For me my poem has only the following meaning.' Then he quickly continues with the oft-quoted sentence:

> We must learn to *die,* and to *die* in the fullest sense of the word; fear of the end is the source of all lovelessness, and this fear is generated only when love itself is already beginning to wane . . . Wodan (sic) rises to the tragic height of *willing* his own destruction. This is all we need to learn from the history of mankind: *to will what is necessary* and to bring it about ourselves. (SS/SL,307)

The words *fear of the end* must be taken to mean *fear of death* for, if not, any attempt to find meaning will take us into complex and fruitless discussion about we know not what. At the common sense level, it is hard to understand what Wagner means. Fear of death is *not* the source of all lovelessness, and inspection reveals that the whole statement about fear is circular. What comes first - the lack of love or the fear?

On the other hand, the business of Wotan willing his own death is clear-cut. We can all see that it is both true and crucial. (There is no need to read Schopenhauer before coming to this conclusion.) He is speaking about himself and about you and me - and not about Wotan alone. The cash value of the whole statement is that one cannot shrink from death if it is seen to be necessary. Wotan is magnificent at the end of *Die Walküre* as he bids farewell both to the person he most loves, to the principles and methods of his entire previous existence and accepts the demise that is to follow from these. His consolation is that Brünnhilde implicitly takes ownership of and responsibility for her father's problems: the burden of remedial action is lifted from Wotan's shoulders.

Wotan and Siegmund

There remains, however, something Wotan has to answer for outside the issues of Freia and the theft of the Ring. The conclusion of *Die Walküre* Act II, with the death of Siegmund, is the most unsettling moment in the entire cycle. Betrayal hangs in the air. The audience feels (as does Wotan himself) that Siegmund has been let down. Moreover, the audience can also perceive self-betrayal: the god has let himself down. If it believes - as it invariably does - that Brünnhilde is morally right, then the same cannot be said for Wotan. The audience may well feel sorrow and understanding for him but Wagner pushes it toward an unconditional rapport with his daughter's action on behalf of the steadfast Siegmund and the heroic Sieglinde. If *Die Walküre* is the emotional heart of the *Ring* this centrality has two aspects. Firstly, the audience sees in Siegmund the paradigm of defiant, uncompromisingly moral behaviour - unfailingly noble in the best tradition of human life. Wagner makes him as different a type of hero to Siegfried as is possible. Secondly, it is the story of the beginning, fulfilment and consequences of the love between Siegmund and Sieglinde and, as Siegmund differs from Siegfried, so is this love in direct contrast to that of Siegfried and Brünnhilde. Being human rather than heroic, it impacts with greater power on the audience. It conquers Brünnhilde who, in turn, uses it to dominate Wotan. For Wotan has failed and it is possible to ask why Wotan does not stick to his guns and support the enamoured twins when he is confronted by Fricka?

This failure hits home to the audience for, amongst other things, it is not too strong to see W1 and W2 as the tragedy of Siegmund. Again I leave it to the reader, if so inclined, to trace the detail of the beginning, middle and end of his story. But if it be possible to perceive the original *Siegfrieds Tod* as a tragedy about Hagen (p.105), then the poignant rise and fall of the most noble Siegmund, abandoned by his father, hits home with power. If we are talking about knowledge gained and if Siegmund had time to realise what was happening, he would die in black despair.

The inevitability of Siegmund's death

The tortuous progress to his demise is traceable through the three different arguments used by Fricka against Siegmund and Sieglinde. The first to be lined up is that they are adulterers. This was the only reason given in the *Myth* where, in truth and by its prominence, it sits very oddly. ('Wotan . . . sentenced him to death in expiation of the marital crime.') At the time of writing, the sin of adultery would not in principle be levelled by Wagner against any true lovers. The dramatic sketch *Jesus of Nazareth*, written just shortly after the *Myth*, has these words from Jesus:

> The commandment says: thou shalt not commit adultery! But I say unto you: you shall not marry without love . . . [and] in your wedding you sin against god; and the sin itself makes amends by working against the law, in that you break the marriage-vow . . . I preserve you from this sin, inasmuch as I give you the law of God, which says: you shall not marry without love! (RW/PW8,303)

There is much more like this in his writings at this time where the laws of marriage are identified with the laws of property. Surely, therefore, Wagner would not have written something in the *Myth* so at variance with his general tenor of thought without taking due care. The argument might best be seen as akin to a paper tiger - very easy to knock down. Fricka, in her role as the defender of marriage - a role manufactured for her by Wagner - asserts the crime Siegmund has committed and for which he must die. Wotan brushes this aside: 'Unholy I deem the vow that binds unloving hearts' - words, written three years after *Jesus of Nazareth*, that repeat the sentiments within it.

Fricka then switches to the incestuous nature of the union. Wotan won't have that either: the twins love each other and therefore there can be no sin (p.142). Wotan then argues that the heroic man he has sired is a necessity. He is to act independently of existing law and perform the deed that 'the god is forbidden to do.' He is now floored by Fricka's third argument: Siegmund is not independent but is supported by the invincible Nothung and by Brünnhilde's shield. Wotan's account of this defeat to Brünnhilde is that Siegmund must be his own man - and he is not. So the imperative which destroys Siegmund is not an immutable law; rather it is because Wotan can see no way to bypass the power structure upon which he has relied. And as he had created this structure, so is he now stymied by his own character and actions. Thereby he betrays both himself and his son.

This is the crux around which the *Ring* turns and once again it is a matter of logic. Power that is absolute can only be ceded if the cessation is also to be final and absolute. An offer of independence that is partial is in fact itself dependent upon the authority of the person who offers it. Thus the authority over Nothung given to Siegmund remains dependent on Wotan's say-so, as is clearly demonstrated by the ease with which the spear destroys it. The only way it could be otherwise is for Wotan to give up all power for all time. In the same way that the Ring cannot be reconstituted from the Gold once it has been returned to the Rhine so (one surely feels) will it be impossible for Wotan to craft another spear of power once he abandons that which he has. At this point he cannot contemplate such a step. For the overwhelming imperative within his nature remains the need to be in control of everyone and everything. Wagner disguises this critical feature and presents the dilemma as contingent when it is in fact a matter of logic. The stakes will only be level when he is prepared to put the entirety of his power, the symbol of this being his spear, into his confrontation with Siegfried.

Nevertheless, as the audience instinctively knows that Brünnhilde is right in her debate with Wotan, so it also instinctively turns away from Fricka in the debate with her husband. The self-regarding sentiments revealed in her closing aria-like sequence qualify sympathy. Moreover, Fricka's response to Wotan's speedy capitulation has nothing whatsoever to do with Nothung or Brünnhilde's shield. She regards the victory as a vindication of her personal honour: if Siegmund goes free he will 'heap shame on my head': Fricka - as the guardian of marriage - will be profaned.

The episode with Siegmund and its aftermath is a vivid demonstration that Wotan's antagonist in the *Ring* is his newer and wiser self, as implied on p.32. If so, his problem may be that the two parts of his character never do come together in reconciliation. He fights to the end. The spear is thrust across Siegfried's path to symbolise the clash between the old and the new order. The bigger crisis is earlier, however, namely with the death of Siegmund, where the spectator is obscurely aware that Wotan has lost his way and is far more affected by this failure than by the god's bad actions in R4.

Wotan, Schopenhauer's pessimism and the *Will* [A]

Wotan is thwarted as never before and has lost his way. To be thwarted in what we want is the experience of everyone and we can turn again to Schopenhauer for insight into how Wagner probably came to see this. So far we have seen how the philosopher's view of sex and death can be integrated into Brünnhilde's experience of life and attitude toward death. Wotan's fate directs attention toward Schopenhauer's more general view of life.

Wagner's disillusion
The initial notion in the *Myth* and *Siegfrieds Tod* that the sacrifice of Siegfried would save Wotan and the gods was quickly replaced by the expectation that they would fade away and find 'atonement' (p.116). In itself this did not cause Wagner to lose his revolutionary fervour. In 1849, leading up to and following the flight from Dresden to Switzerland, his most inflammatory political essays, *The Revolution* and *Art and Revolution* appeared. These were written well after the first change to the original Immolation text. But disillusion with politics soon afflicted him. In Zurich he became an observer rather

---

[A] It is useful to differentiate between definitions of the word. Except where the word is found in a quotation by Schopenhauer or Bryan Magee '*Will*' refers to the term as defined by the philosopher; 'will' refers to normal English parlance.

that activist and this detachment (living quietly, thinking and writing) persuaded him that politics was a lost cause. The rising in Dresden had been put down with decisive force. Some close friends were imprisoned and Wagner himself could not return to Germany without being arrested. The year 1848 had seen revolutions or unrest in favour of democratic reform in 50 countries across the world. All had been crushed within about a year. The blow to Wagner was severe and he experienced a period of depression.

We must remember that he was a revolutionary only because and on behalf of his art: his bad experiences in the latter part of the Dresden sojourn persuaded him that only a drastic change in the style of governance would produce conditions in which work such as his could flourish. The *Ring* needed a new type of audience - one emancipated from the thraldom of arbitrary custom and constraint. And so he went to the barricades to do his bit. Universal failure persuaded him during the years 1852-3 that politics was futile. 'Suddenly, because there was no hope of revolutionary political and social change, there was no hope for the future of art, and therefore no hope for the future of Richard Wagner.' (BM/WP,128)

Existential pessimism

In the circumstances, we cannot doubt that Wagner read *The World as Will and Representation* in 1854 with gloomy relish. If anyone seeks a voice to express crushing pessimism, let him turn to Schopenhauer! He uses his exceptional skill as a writer to express his revulsion from what he saw as the way the human and animal kingdoms work things out. His disgust amounts almost to horror and it is worth quoting him at some length. First, the animal kingdom.

> The futility and fruitlessness of the struggle of the whole phenomenon are more readily grasped in the simple and easily observable life of animals . . . We see only momentary gratification, fleeting pleasure conditioned by wants, much and long suffering, constant struggle all against all, everything a hunter and everything hunted, pressure, want, need, and anxiety, shrieking and howling; and this goes on for ever and ever, or until once again the crust of the planet breaks. (AS/WWR2, 354)

Then he turns to mankind.

> Here too life by no means presents itself as a gift to be enjoyed, but as a task, a drudgery, to be worked through. According to this we see, on a large scale as well as on a small, universal need, restless exertion, constant pressure, endless strife, forced activity, with extreme exertion of all bodily and mental powers . . . Seized by this, every living thing works with the utmost exertion of its strength for something that has no value. But on closer consideration, we shall find here also that it is rather a blind urge, an impulse wholly without ground and motive. (AS/WWR2, 357)

> This world of humanity is the kingdom of chance and error. They rule within it without mercy in great things as in small, and along with them folly and wickedness also wield the scourge. Hence it arises that . . . what is noble and wise very rarely makes its appearance, becomes effective or meets with a hearing, but the absurd and perverse in the realm of thought, the dull and tasteless in the sphere of art, and the wicked and fraudulent in the

sphere of action, really assert a supremacy that is disturbed only by brief interruptions. (AS/WWR1, 324)

Schopenhauer provides broad analysis and also precise detail.

> How man deals with man is seen, for example, in Negro slavery, the ultimate object of which is sugar and coffee. However, we need not go so far; to enter at the age of five a cotton-spinning or other factory, and from then on to sit there every day first ten, then twelve, and finally fourteen hours, and perform the same mechanical work, is to purchase dearly the pleasure of drawing breath. (AS/WWR2, 578)

This prefigures Wagner's thoughts on slavery (p.155) but for Schopenhauer the deeper malaise lies in the human condition itself.

> We painfully feel the loss of pleasure and enjoyments, as soon as they fail to appear; but when pains cease even after being present for a long time, their absence is not directly felt . . . For only pain and want can be felt positively; and therefore they proclaim themselves; well-being, on the contrary, is merely negative. (AS/WWR2,575)

The *Will*

We now come the core of Schopenhauer's philosophy: the existence and nature of the *Will*. At heart it is the *noumenon* itself - that unchanging, unknowable single entity that lies behind and beyond the *phenomena* we experience in our senses (p.19). He contrasts the *Will* (the noumenon) with the intellect.

> The *intellect* grows tired; the will is untiring. After continuous work with the head, we feel fatigue of the brain . . . all *knowing* is associated with effort and exertion, willing on the contrary, is our very nature, whose manifestations occur without any weariness and entirely of their own accord. (AS/WWR2, 211)

This dominance is not beneficial to humanity, for it has the appalling consequence that we are never satisfied.

> Every human life continues to flow on between willing and attainment. Of its nature the wish is pain; attainment quickly begets satiety . . . The wish, the need, appears again on the scene under a new form; if it does not, then dreariness, emptiness and boredom follow, the struggle against which is just as painful as is that against want. (AS/WWR1, 313)

> [The will] always strives, because striving is its sole nature, to which no attained goal can put an end. Such striving is therefore incapable of final satisfaction; it can be checked only by hindrance, but in itself goes on for ever . . . For all striving springs from want or deficiency, from dissatisfaction with one's own state or condition, and is therefore suffering so long as it is not satisfied. No satisfaction, however, is lasting; on the contrary, it is merely a starting-point of a fresh striving. (AS/WWR1, 308-9)

Bryan Magee sums up the implacable force of the *Will* (a.k.a the *noumenon)*:

> The will as such has nothing, I repeat nothing, to do with human agency or conscious experience of any kind. It has nothing to do with aims or goals, or desires, or wants or intentions. There is as much will in a Black Hole as in a human being. The will is in us only

because it is in everything. It constitutes us as it constitutes everything. But it is not directly accessible to our knowledge. (BM/S,444) B

Thus the *Will* has nothing whatsoever to do with the knowledge within the intellect. 'The will, considered purely in itself, is devoid of knowledge, and is only a blind, irresistible urge, as we see it appear in inorganic and vegetable nature, and in their laws, and in the vegetative part of our own life.' (AS/WWR1, 275) C

Denial of the will-to-live
So far so very bad! But Schopenhauer has to supply some form of escape, a way back into life. He does so by conjuring a sub-set of the *Will* - the will-to-live. 'Everything presses and pushes toward *existence*, if possible toward *organic existence*, i.e. *Life*'. (AS/WWR2, 350) From this he postulates a safety valve - the option to abrogate, deny or turn away from the will-to-live. He who perceives that dissatisfaction is guaranteed 'will understand the essential nullity and nothingness of his own life. This insight, if grasped really deep down, will liberate him from the thraldom to that will to live which the whole world of illusion is manifestation . . . he will achieve a condition in which he is unseduced by willing, undiverted by it, unconcerned, uncorrupted, in other words, simply independent of it.' (BM/S,221/2) Those who break free see the illusory nature of hopes and actions, and acquire a knowledge that 'becomes the *quieter* of all and every willing'.

> There arises in him a strong aversion to the inner nature whose expression is his own phenomenon, to the will to live . . . [and he] . . . renounces . . . this inner nature. He ceases to will anything, guards against attaching his will to anything, tries to establish firmly in himself the greatest indifference to all things. (AS/WWR1, 380)

This is the denial of the will-to-live and it is the aspect of Schopenhauer that Wagner could recognize and associate with Wotan. It surely forms the basis of his assertion in *My Life* that only after reading this philosophy did he 'understand my own Wotan' (pp.17/18). It is not fanciful to think that the great scene with Brünnhilde in *Die*

B   Magee regrets that the philosopher ever used the expression. In fact, his first intent was to use the word 'Kraft' (force) and to have some such word as that or 'energy' in mind can be a useful antidote. It removes the idea that the term is anthropomorphic: a piece of rock has the *Will*, the force, to continue to exist. The force that drives each person is not the desire that we might have for something. It is the hidden core that we cannot control.

C   An expression of the effects of the *Will* lies in the 'Wahn' monologue in *Die Meistersinger*, Act 3. Sachs laments the extent of the chaos that erupted the previous evening. This sent the citizens of Nuremberg into a frenzy, for no identifiable reason and he concludes with:
> Who will give it its name? / It is the old madness,
> without which nothing can happen, / nothing whatsoever!
> If it halts somewhere in its course / it is only to gain new strength in sleep:
> suddenly it awakens, / then see who can master it!

Walküre Act III represents just such an epiphany for Wotan. He may well have been ready for such a change. Wotan's despair in W2 after Fricka has bested him is monumental, a lament about the ceaseless bind of endeavour which has gripped and driven him onwards for countless years. The incessant striving had finally forced him into a situation where he had no power at all. He cries 'My work I abandon! There is one thing only that I want: the end! The end!' Aeons of labour have turned to dust.

But there is more. It will be argued in the *Siegfried* chapter that Wotan, as the Wanderer, still revels in the power contained in his spear (p.346) even though he is now ostensibly just an onlooker. This gives us a clue to his behaviour in his final confrontation with Siegfried, and to his demeanour after returning with his shattered spear as reported by Waltraute in *Götterdämmerung*. Schopenhauer has this to say:

> However, we must not imagine that, after the denial of the will-to-live has once appeared through knowledge that has become a quieter of the *will*, such denial no longer wavers of falters, and that we can rest on it as on an inherited property. On the contrary, it must always be achieved afresh by constant struggle. For as the body is the will itself . . . as phenomenon in the world of representation, that whole will-to-live exists potentially so long as the body lives, and is always striving to reach actuality and to burn afresh with all its intensity. (AS/WWR1, 391)

To the point in S3.1 when Siegfried smashes the spear, the plot has traced how the two aspects of Wotan's personality - what he thinks he wants and what he actually needs - have struggled with each other. He seems to reconcile the two at the end of W3 but this is illusory: they continue to struggle to the end. The driving *Will* sweeps aside his reason and forces on the final contest between the old and the new, namely the second encounter between spear and sword. Even then the *Will* is not dead and declares itself in the fear described by Waltraute to Brünnhilde in G1.3. There is no rational motivation, for these are manifestations of his inner being. At the end of *Die Walküre* Wotan may have intellectually understood and accepted that his time was limited, but his inner *Will* did not. The emotions of fear, jealousy and the headiness of power strove 'to reach actuality and to burn afresh with all [their] intensity.'

The destruction of his power at the hands of Siegfried brings upon him the change we hear about from Waltraute in *Götterdämmerung*. She sees it primarily as one of hopeless dejection.

# # # # # #

To be clear, and to resist looking for connections everywhere: some specific statements about the will that relate to Wotan do *not* also relate to Schopenhauer's *Will*. Examples are the observations in the 1854 Röckel letter that Wotan 'rises to the heights of *willing* his own destruction', that 'his will is broken' and that 'following his farewell to Brünnhilde [he] is no more than a departed spirit' (SS/SL,308) – all these are simply intended to *explain* the drama to his friend.

◇ ◇ ◇ ◇ ◇ ◇

15

Questions about the *Ring*

Now is the occasion, with detail about plot and character examined in previous chapters, to address those unresolved issues which will not go away and those which lurk just beneath the surface. There are five and to avoid fudge they are presented as questions. The answers proffered must not contradict the analysis of the drama and music to be found in Chapters 18 through 21.

1. What was Wagner's purpose in casting Siegfried and Brünnhilde as portrayed in the *Myth* and *Siegfrieds Tod* along different lines from the Sigurd and Brynhild depicted in the Nordic eddas? Once settled, these portrayals did not materially change as the cycle developed.
2. Is the *Ring* pessimistic? To be more specific, is the state of things better as Valhalla goes up in flames than it was whilst the stronghold was being built? Alongside this lies another question. If Wagner was a pessimist what was the nature of his pessimism?
3. To what degree and in what manner is the *Ring* a tragic drama?
4. What might be the nature of the Ring?
5. What is to be made of Siegfried in totality?

Siegfried and Brünnhilde in the beginning

The conclusion to Chapter 8 on *Siegfrieds Tod* refers to the lack of clarity about Siegfried and Brünnhilde because of complications in the sources. Limited further insight into the two lovers emerges during ensuing examination of *Der junge Siegfried,* but there is nothing decisive. The best reason for the relationship as seen in *Siegfrieds Tod* remains the need for Wagner to keep things simple for stage presentation: he sensed and perhaps reluctantly accepted the truth that found expression in Jessie Weston's cautionary comment: to alter the ancient myths would over-simplify the many strands within the story (p. 112).

He therefore cut his own Gordian knot, in the fashion of the edda's author and of Rosemary Kerven as described on p.119. This action exalted them above the level of normal humanity but at the same time dehumanised them. The on stage vitality they show is of iconic, mythic heroism - not that of day to day humanity. Not only does this question come first because it is the first to arise; it also leads into the second, which follows.

Is the *Ring* pessimistic?

It is suggested in the previous chapter that Wotan's anguish is a reflection of Schopenhauer's gloomy view of all sentient life. If this be accepted it is an easy step to extend this hypothesis to cover the entire *Ring*, and to suggest that people will always behave badly. This is not only an academic matter: Wieland Wagner is reported as saying that *Götterdämmerung* should really end in the desolation of Siegfried's Funeral Music. And from this, given Wagner's commitment to Schopenhauer, it can follow that the cycle is also saturated with such pessimism.

Wagner's unhappiness in 1854

As a preliminary, there follows the only examination of Wagner's life in this study outside the chronology of the 1840s in Appendix D. This explores in detail the year 1854 when Wagner was very unhappy indeed. On 7 October of that year he wrote a letter to Liszt that includes within it the only direct avowal, the only concrete statement of overwhelming pessimism that can be thought directly to reflect Schopenhauer's pessimism. Understandably this has been judged to tie up with both the *Ring* and with his attitude toward mankind and society. This is what he wrote:

> Let us look upon the world through the medium of contempt alone. It is worth nothing else; to found any hope on it would be deceiving our own hearts. It is bad, *bad, thoroughly bad:* only the heart of a *friend*, the tears of a woman, can dispel its curse. We do not respect the world. Its honour, its glory, or by whatever name its shams may be called, are nothing to us. It belongs to Alberich, to no one else. Let it perish! . . . I have a deadly hatred of all *appearance,* of all hope, for it is self-deception. But I will work; you shall have my scores; they will belong to us, to no one else. (FH/CWL2, 50) [A]

A complete hopelessness about everything is evident and the task is to unpack the four strands that force out these words so that we can understand all the pressures upon him in the latter part of 1854. These are despair that his works would ever be understood, shortage of cash, disillusion with friends, and the misery of his love for the unattainable Mathilde Wesendonck.

Despair about how his operas were received was prominent in the letter to Liszt from which the previous quotation was taken.

> Do not talk to me of my fame, my honours, my position, or whatever the name may be. I am positively certain that all my 'successes' are based on *bad*, very *bad* performances of my works, that they therefore rest on misunderstandings, and that my public reputation is not worth an empty nutshell. Let us give up all diplomatic contrivances, this dealing with means which we despise for ends which . . . can never be achieved, least of all by these means . . . I

[A] This translation by Francis Hüffer is used rather than that by Stewart Spencer, as it is only here that the complete letter is to be found in translation. The one significant difference is that Spencer uses the more violent *evil* rather than *bad*.

sometimes cannot understand your ironical enjoyment of life, which gets over your disgust at these people by making fun of them. Away with all this stuff, this glory, this nonsense! (FH/CWL2,48)

The prompt for this letter was the failure to secure what might well have been satisfactory (and profitable) performances of *Tannhäuser* and *Lohengrin* in Berlin. Note that the almost identical sentiments are transferred from the world in general to distaste for the current world of theatre. [B]

Severe shortage of money A good contract with the Berlin Opera would certainly have cheered him up for at this time he was in greater need of income than at almost any other period. His coffers were empty and he could not find people to give him a loan. The situation was extreme.

- On 31 May 1854 he reports to Hans von Bulow that he is now permanently bankrupt.
- Accordingly, he writes to Ernst Benedick Kietz, his long-term (and not rich) Paris friend of 15 years, and apologises for his inability to repay a personal debt.
- Relief came in early July when Liszt produced some money to keep Wagner going - but thereafter, nothing.
- He asks his brother-in-law Avenarius for 1000 thalers (two thirds of his annual salary when Kapellmeister in Dresden) for 'unpaid accounts': he has already tried Sulzer, Liszt and the publisher Brendel and now wonders whether Avenarius could approach the publisher Härtel; if successful, Wagner will give a formal 'note of hand' for the end of the year.
- Later in July, he tries Liszt again in the hope that he and Avenarius together might work on Härtel to advance a sum against future profits. He adds: 'No one can help me here [in Zurich]; I exhausted everything to secure my existence from last winter until now . . . In my great trouble I wrote to Brendel some time ago, asking him whether he could get me amongst my Leipzig 'admirers' 1000 thalers on a bill of four or five months' date. Answer: No.' (FH/CWL 2,41)
- Early in August he writes a long letter to his devoted friend Wilhelm Fischer, who was instrumental in the 1842 breakthrough production of *Rienzi*. In it he confesses that he has put off writing a letter for months because 'I ought to have sent you money for disbursements; but just now, in fact, since last winter, I have been so infamously hard up that I could not spare anything.' (JS/LDF,384)
- On 14 September, a comprehensive letter to his Swiss friend Jakob Sulzer lays out the problem of his debts. The suggested solution is that his friend should sound out the possibility of a contract for 10,000 francs immediately, and for 2,000 francs for a further two years. Such an arrangement would be against an anticipated income of 21,000 francs from German theatres who mount *Tannhäuser* and *Lohengrin*. The

---

[B] There is clarity of expression when his life is the subject matter as compared to some discussions of his artistic expectations.

letter concludes: 'Look at me! *I* can no longer help myself, since everything is so pressing, and since I cannot, in the immediate future, abandon myself to the random chance of agreeable surprises'. (SS/SL, 317/8) Sulzer talked to Wesendonck who provided 7,000 francs for the most immediately pressing debts. (One franc equalled 0.8 thalers, so 7,000 francs would have been over 4 times his Dresden salary.)

- But even Wagner baulked at the efforts of von Bulow in Weimar. He had been asking all and sundry for cash loans and, at about the same time as the letter to Sulzer, Wagner begs Hans only to try his hand with a real prospect! This undated letter would have been written very early in September 1854 for he reports to Hans that the composition score of Act 1 of *Die Walküre* was just completed; the composition had taken just over two months. I shall return to this as it marks a significant milestone.

- With that immense task over, Wagner turned once again to money and in a terse letter dated 16 September he asks Liszt to put his mind to organising some concerts in Belgium, for these would quickly earn him a much needed 10,000 francs.

Disillusion with friends and desolation in love were both compounded with a growing withdrawal from Zurich society. Alienation from friends also seems directly linked to their inability to supply him with funds. They either could not or would not - other than Liszt in July and Wesendonck in late September or early October. His expectation of 21,000 francs from German theatres was not unreasonable and good income did materialise in time. But his friends were now more than ever careful.

And if they were unable to help him in the manner *they* could, perhaps the realisation was dawning that Mathilde Wesendonck was also unable to love him in the manner/degree he needed. This finds no reference in the letters or autobiography, save perhaps for the strange reference to 'the tears of a woman' in the seminal letter to Liszt, which opens this section. No one can know the nature of their relationship, namely whether or not they consummated matters. That the two were powerfully drawn to each other is clear and although we cannot know the make-up of Mathilde's desire, we know that Wagner's would have included a strong sexual element toward a younger, nubile, sympathetic woman. This was now in full flood, witness the 'sixteen easily decipherable allusions' (CW/FR,67) to Mathilde in the composition sketch to Act 1 of *Die Walküre*. [c] Open union was impossible and the erotic force of the love music in this Act may well be testament to Wagner's passion.

Die Walküre and the withdrawal from society

So Wagner was broke, isolated, doubtful of the immediate prospects for his art and in love with an unattainable woman. In consequence of these cumulative blows, Wagner withdrew into himself in an unusual manner. The first reference in correspondence is

---

[c] The first of these, 'L. d. m., M?' (Leibst du mich, Mathilde?) occurs during the sketch of the orchestral passage during which Siegmund and Sieglinde await the entrance of Hunding.

to Fischer on 8 August 1854, in the same letter in which he confesses he has not the cash to repay the loan. He had not seen his friend for five years and unburdens himself thus:

> About myself, I have nothing to say to you. I live on the whole a life full of sorrows, however little it may seem so to many - for I have become silent respecting my inner life . . . work is the only thing dear to me. (JS/LDF,385)

In late September he wrote the following to Minna. She was away on a visit to Dresden and to see old friends in other German cities which lasted over two months.

> My life is moving on completely inwardly, you see; and with me that finds its fittest record in my works. I am purely a worker; if I don't or cannot work, I feel unwell, and my thoughts keep hankering after work again . . . Only now have I resumed the second act of *Walküre*; yesterday when I got your somewhat mistrustful letter, I was on the point of composing Fricka's entry; it wasn't at all a bad match. You consider, though, that I'm working all this out for no one but myself: it may turn out so, too - and yet I'd rather cease to live, than not be working at a thing like this. (WAE/LMW2,155)

These are home truths from husband to wife (the reference to Fricka is poignant by any standard) and the refrain is taken up again in the critical letter to Liszt: 'But I will work; you will have my scores, they will belong to us, to no one else.' The need to work is clear, even though it is tainted by somewhat childish self-dramatization, the 'club-of-two' stuff. Wagner was surely closer to the truth about himself in early September when calmly responding to Avenarius, his brother-in-law, who has declined to send him some cash.

> There'll always be a screw loose with me, you see: if I were thoroughly happy - I should need hardly any money at all; but like this, I keep oscillating between an often quite eccentric craving for the sweets of life and - a loathing of life itself; whilst as artist and man, on the other hand, I become more and more incapable of making the smallest concessions to the wage-paying world of today. (WAE/FL,211)

The letter to Liszt has an underlying theme of withdrawal and the four letters cited: to Fischer, Minna, Avenarius and Liszt represent the culmination of this process. Writing of the year 1854 in general, Newman says: 'Creative work and philosophical brooding were now his only refuge from the fast-increasing miseries of his life. He had grown out of touch with Zürich society . . . The intellectual and spiritual cleavage between Minna and himself was widening . . . [and] the one woman who could have brought him balm . . . was unattainable. The demand for his early works . . . was necessarily a diminishing quantity now. He was more deeply in debt than ever, with little prospect of any increase in his income.' (EN/LRW2,430).

The catalyst for this withdrawal is evidently the composition of Act I of *Die Walküre:* all four letters refer obsessively to his dedication to work. Wagner had long been aware of the revolutionary and original nature of the music he had commenced upon. Early in the composition of *Das Rheingold*, on or around 14 November 1854, he had written as follows to Liszt:

> My friend! I am in a state of wonderment! A new world stands revealed before me! The great scene in the Rhinegold [probably R1] is finished: I see before me riches such as I never dared suspect. I now consider my powers to be immeasurable: everything seethes within me and makes music. (SS/SL,295)

Now he was embarked on the composition of *Die Walküre* Act 1, the sketch of which was started on 28 June and finished on 1 September. A break of three weeks on an abortive conducting engagement meant that the bulk of composition occupied only about four weeks during August. By common universal judgement, the transformation of his artistic powers between *Das Rheingold* and *Die Walküre* has been seen as prodigious, as almost unmatched in music. Wagner saw this early on: 3 July sees him writing to Liszt: 'How curious these contrasts are - I mean, between the first love scene of *Valkyrie* and that of *Rhinegold*.' (FH/CWL2, 41) We can recall the words of Elgar with regard to the big tune that became *Land of Hope and Glory*: 'a tune that comes once in a lifetime... that will knock'em dead, knock'em flat!' On an immeasurably larger scale, Wagner knew the same of the music he had just written. Indeed, he acknowledged that he was most powerfully effected by the fates of Siegmund and Sieglinde when he was composing the music. [D]

So whilst he knew well that he was widening the emotional power of music as it had never been done before, he was broke, and in love with the wrong woman, and felt his art to be misunderstood and himself to be neglected. These, I venture to suggest, are Wagner's reasons for thinking the world 'belonged to Alberich'. They are personal matters affecting Richard Wagner and not because the symbolism of Alberich's malign power controlled the world of the *Ring* and also the world in which Wagner lived. Nevertheless, in bad straits as he was, the almost impossible vision of the *Ring* did not fade. Detachment, even disgust with the world persisted but these found no place in the resplendence which surrounds Siegmund and Sieglinde, and in the closing scene of W3 between Wotan and Brünnhilde which followed four months later.

The overall impact of *Die Walküre* cannot be over-estimated. The core story that slumbered in the *Myth* surfaced in *Der junge Siegfried* and burst into life six months later, transforming the emotional range of the *Ring* at a stroke. The composition period during August 1854 exponentially widened the romantic and emotional expressiveness of music. It should come as no surprise that Wagner's reaction on its completion, as he came down to earth to face all his problems, was a spell of deep depression.

Depression, however, is not the same as pessimism. Cosima's diaries portray Wagner as depressed from time to time but not as persistently pessimistic, and no

---

[D] During the three months August to October, the period spanning the critical correspondence, Wagner's life was uneventful and conducive to the alienation from the world evident in the letters. For a large part of it Minna was away. He sees the Wesendoncks from time to time but otherwise lives in seclusion, taking long country walks by himself. The composition sketch for W1, from the beginning of Siegmund's narration ('Friedmund darf ich nicht heissen') to the end was written during August, being completed on 1 September.

biography says that he was a pessimist by nature but speak of his ebullience and vitality. Pessimism is of two types. The first is to do with chance or fortune and predicts that if something can go wrong it will go wrong. The second is to do with human nature and predicts that if people can behave badly they will behave badly. It is worth recalling that Wagner was inclined to believe people when they sympathised with his lack of money, hence is fury if he should think they let him down. Verdi, in contrast, was suspicious by character and not inclined to offer the benefit of the doubt. This may be seen to influence his work.

So is the *Ring* pessimistic even if Wagner was not always so?
In broad terms and by different routes the cycle is portrayed as optimistic by Carl Dahlhaus (CD/WMD, 140), Owen Lee (OW/WR, 37/38), Michael Ewans (ME/WA, 55) and Robert Donington (RD/WR, 272). But of recent years, taking colour from a growth in pessimism about social issues as a whole, this view is not now universal: it may well be that Wagner did believe, under the baleful influence of the *Will,* that mankind could not but behave badly, particularly when up against it. In short that the world and humanity's place in it were bad, are bad and will continue to be bad (the second and more drastic type of pessimism), and that this is the final message of the work. I take this to be the 'cash value' criterion of those who claim the *Ring* to be fundamentally pessimistic.

The very title of an essay by Warren Darcy to be found in the 1993 compendium *Wagner's Ring,* edited by Barry Millington and Stewart Spencer, is *The world belongs to Alberich*. (This is a quotation from the opening letter to Liszt and the article ends with the bald statement that by the 1870s Wagner thought the world not worth the saving.) Darcy sets out this thesis at greater length in *Wagner's Das Rheingold* (OUP, 1993). He builds his argument on foundations laid by Shaw and Newman, but he also draws attention to similarities between *Götterdämmerung* and *Das Rheingold*. Both have a preliminary scene detached from the main action and each features three sisters - the Norns and the Rhinedaughters. Siegfried's departure from the Gibich palace (with Gunther) to get the Ring from Brünnhilde, reflects Wotan's departure from the foot of Valhalla (with Loge) to get the Ring from Alberich. Hagen and Gunther trick Siegfried, and Wotan and Loge trick Alberich. The Ring is brutally wrested by Siegfried from Brünnhilde, and this recreates the initial theft by Wotan from Alberich. Hagen's domination of the Gibich tribe is a reflection of Alberich's tyranny of the Nibelungs. Both operas have a fatal encounter toward the end between two brothers - Gunther and Hagen in G3.2, and Fasolt and Fafner in RG4. Brünnhilde and Erda both intervene to save the situation. The message of the *Ring*, therefore, is that nothing changes: as the gods, dwarfs and giants misbehaved so do the humans Siegfried, Brünnhilde, Gunther and Hagen. It is an endless cycle of rise and collapse: should a new era dawn, that will also end badly.

This readily matches *Siegfrieds Tod* as a stand-alone project, particularly in light of the removal from the poem - within two months of the first draft - of the godlike ascent of Siegfried and Brünnhilde, and the annulment of Wotan's continuing rule. Neither gods and godlike lovers continue to exist and the overall impression is of malevolence winning out over virtue. Early in 1849 the plot was inchoate and it is possible to imagine the composer agreeing with Warren Darcy that human activity toward each other matched that of the immortals as portrayed in the *Myth*. [E]

John Deathridge, writing 14 years later in 2007 would have been one of this party. His focus is on Siegfried, with Shaw the base of his argument.

> If our Nordic superman is the man of the future who leads us with phenomenal strength into a new age of light and social harmony, why is he doomed? The simple answer is that despite the brilliant visions of a future social utopia that flash past in *Siegfried* - not to mention the fake happy ending of *Götterdämmerung*, the almost Disney-like artificiality of which Shaw's icy gaze immediately recognized - Wagner intended the whole *Ring* project *from the start* (author's italics) as a profoundly pessimistic comment on the human condition'. (JD/WGE,66)

In the same year as Deathridge, Derek Hughes proposed a similar but more measured theory, namely that the drinking of the potion which leads to Siegfried's betrayal of Brünnhilde in *Götterdämmerung* does not indicate a personal corruption but is a symbol of a decline in human culture whereby the 'primordial need' of Siegfried is obliterated by the 'artifice of society' (p.73).

Byran Magee, writing in 2000, focusses on Wagner himself. He believes the cloud of pessimism that descends over the work in the years between 1848 (the year of *Siegfrieds Tod*) and 1856 (that with the so-called Schopenhauer ending to Brünnhilde's *Immolation*) to be caused by the absorption of the philosopher's apocalyptic view of life as a whole.

> He realised now that it was simply not the case, and never had been, that Society was getting better all the time: tyranny and the abuse of power were perennial, as were cruelty, selfishness, greed, stupidity, and the failure of compassion ... The belief that [these were] going to change radically to a new order of things in which love, happiness and self-fulfilment were the order of the day was just a pathetic illusion. (BM/WP,186).

Magee's emphasis on Schopenhauer and the quotations in the previous chapter make one pause. If prepared to say that the philosopher confirmed Wagner's takes on sex and death (as in Chapters 13 and 14) what reason can be found to hold back from a similar reaction here? Does what we hear as the music bear witness to the notion? Chapter 21 will detail how the manifest virtues of Brünnhilde and Siegfried dissipate when the action reaches the Gibichung court. There much of the music is infected by the malign tones of Alberich and Hagen.

[E] The shadow never completely goes away. In the 'Schopenhauer' ending to the Immolation, written in 1856, Brünnhilde is seen as a symbol of suffering humanity. This reflects the philosopher's perspective that life is never free of anguish. That it was not set to music does not alter the message: that people can do very bad things.

A similarity between discussions about anti-Semitism and about pessimism

The issue of possible infiltration of Wagner's notorious anti-Semitism into the *Ring* finds no place in this study. But, if that has no foothold, two opposing arguments in the dispute about it may with advantage be brought to bear on this issue of pessimism. The anti-Semitic debate was intensified by the publication in 1992 of *Wagner, Race and Relations* by Paul Lawrence Rose, followed in 1995 by *Richard Wagner and the anti-Semitic imagination* by Marc Wiener. The word 'imagination' in the second title gives the clue to the thrust of these two books: in order to make the case for the existence of the anti-Semitism, it is not necessary to find written intention nor to be able to find actual musical examples that are identifiably anti-Semitic.

> Both Wagner and his contemporaries perceived his works through associations - linking a given set of values and beliefs to specific bodily imagery - that may no longer be automatically evoked in performance today . . . As the cultural context in which the works are performed . . . undergoes transformation, so too do the associations that an opera-going public brings to a work. Ironically, however, such a shift in the horizon of expectations . . . has led to a widespread *disavowal* of precisely the racist . . . dimension . . . of his music dramas that would have been so obvious to a 19th century audience. Wagner never included the word *Jude* in his works for the stage because he didn't need to; the corporeal features [which include sound as well as sight] deemed obvious signs of the Jew in his culture would have made the anti-Semitic nature of his representations of purportedly Jewish characteristics self-evident in his time. (MW/W,13)

The author's intention is to bring these matters before the modern reader. And here is the rebuttal as put forward by Byran Magee. (No judgement is being made on the merits of the arguments of either man.)

> 'Some . . . authors can be endlessly resourceful in arguing that the apparent absence of something is itself a proof of its presence . . . Most audiences, including the Jews in those audiences, failed to perceive the connection we are now being told was self-evident . . . There is one basic form of argument that is used over and over again by writers of this sort . . . It is that x was already associated in people's minds with Jews, and therefore any public reference to x would automatically be taken as relating to Jews without anyone having to say so . . . There is a reason why such writers are persistently driven back on this form of argument and it is that usually they can find no such evidence . . . and the great thing about this particular form of argument is that it explains the absence of evidence.' (BM/WP, 377)

With variations, Magee's argument can be mounted against those who assert a pessimistic ground floor to the *Ring* and, ironically, this applies to Magee himself. Wagner was the most self-explanatory artist who seemed to expound upon everything. Nowhere does he indicate that the *Ring* is pessimistic, by which I mean that people must always behave badly toward each other. This is despite the fact that he *shows* that the compassion at the heart of *Die Walküre,* the energy and hope that invest *Siegfried,* fade and are coloured by the malice and deceit of Hagen and Gunther in *Götterdämmerung*, and an attempt will be made to give context to this in Chapter 21.

# # # # # #

So what rejoinders can be made to Darcy, Deathridge, Hughes and Magee?

To the view that nothing changes the answer might be a counter-question: 'What did you expect?' Nothing happens in the *Ring* action that guarantees good future behaviour. What we have on the positive side is a promise of new ways of life. Siegmund and Sieglinde open the prospect of joyous sexual fulfilment and compassionate commitment to something outside of self. The implication of this is understood by Brünnhilde. The hope aroused in her changes the direction of Wotan's life and the result of that is essentially neutral: he becomes a bystander in *Siegfried*.

Can one turn for an answer to a thesis in *Finding an Ending* by Philip Kitcher and Richard Schacht? In eight steps the question is pursued of 'whether and how human life may be endowed with significance'. Often a positive answer is presented as a possibility and then given added significance if the advance contributes 'to the possibility of . . . realisation in the lives of others' as well as in the individual. Sometimes a benefit can contribute to 'the transfiguration . . . of commonplace existence . . . [such that it is] . . . endowed with and enriched with such values.' Their conclusion is that 'This . . . can be done even in failure and defeat, if a transient and imperfect realisation of important values finds an ending that preserves and even enhances its significance, and so is vindicating in spite of all.' (K&S/FE, 61/62)

To espouse a pessimistic *Ring* requires belief that Wotan's project ends in 'failure and defeat' and *also* a denial that the drama discloses 'a transient and imperfect vindication of important values'. This belief is difficult to sustain. Wagner was optimistic in 1848 but does that also mean that he was a Panglossian fantasist who believed that all would 'be for the best in the best of all possible worlds'. The Immolation music does not tell us that all will be well in a new-born world, as might be the implication of the new, green and flourishing land that arises from the sea after *Ragnarök*, as portrayed in the sagas. Grief, loss, pain and wickedness cannot be eliminated: if people can be good they must also be allowed to be bad. The main action of the cycle embraces the initial creation and ultimate destruction of a mythically powerful agent of ruinous evil and the associated demise of Wotan and Alberich. The former introduced a fatal form of autocracy; the latter sought to subvert and replace this with extreme tyranny. Both autocracy and tyranny are brought low and it is reasonable to see that as a message of hope.

Finally, it may be salutary to close this matter with the acknowledged truth that the state of mind and/or temperament of an artist frequently has no impact on that artist's work. Beethoven's 5th Symphony is a clarion call for courage and of future hope. It was written in the despairing aftermath of a final rejection in 1808 by the beautiful Josephine Deym, who was probably the woman he most needed at that time, and his letters to whom were more passionate than to all his other prospective lovers. And no sooner was the ink dry on that work than the pen was dipped to finish the interrupted 6th (Pastoral) Symphony: 'concerned with peace, contentment, and God'. (JS/B, 461)

Tragedy, pessimism and the *Ring*

A consideration broader than the *Ring* follows from what Wagner wrote and said about Schopenhauer. It is possible to cast a pall of existential pessimism over the ten operas (the *Ring* being four) from *Der Fliegende Holländer* to *Parsifal*. This finds a focus in the recurring desire for oblivion - a complete cessation of existence distinct from death - being the expressed wish of the Dutchman, Tannhäuser, Wotan, Tristan and Isolde, Amfortas and Kundry. This desired fate can be seen as an absorption back into the *noumenon* (p.179) and can be interpreted as a tragedy about life itself, as applies to all of us. Accordingly, something further can be said about pessimism and tragedy and, by extension, to the *Ring* and Wotan.

<u>Classic tragedy</u>
Tragedy is an immense subject and hundreds of books address the scores of questions that can be asked. For simplicity I will set down the three main criteria which, over the years, have commonly been used for a plot to be labelled 'tragic'. The merit of this approach is that the criteria are so firmly established that they become impossible to dislodge. Other factors have emerged over the years, but often these become matters of opinion and thereby produce disagreement.

- The first principle is that defined by Aristotle: neither a bad man or woman can be tragic, for such a person would deserve the bad end that awaits (p.79). I cannot see that this proposition is to be gainsaid.
- The second principle dates back 2700 years to Homer's *Iliad* - 700 years or so before Aristotle's *Poetics*. This is that our lives are governed by forces that lie outside our knowledge and control. Demonic energy can pounce and cause a person fatally to damage both himself and those he loves. In the *Iliad* these powers are the Greek gods such as Zeus and Aphrodite, who frequently intervene and interfere in the Trojan War.

    Sometimes these forces are explicit in the text, as when Gloucester, in *King Lear,* says 'as flies . . . are we to the gods, they kill us for their sport'. What power implanted in Racine's Phèdre a soul-destroying sexual passion for her stepson? She herself says, in a moment of horrible perception: '[my love] is no longer just a hidden hunger in my blood, but Venus herself wholly fastened on her prey.' Thus she sees the goddess of love taking a direct and personal interest in her destruction. The upshot of this disruption is that there is always something mysterious that is never expressed; questions hover as the curtain falls.
- The third main plank of high tragedy is that the suffering inflicted on the victim is very often not commensurate with the either the evil done or the mistakes made. Despite awareness that it was Lear's abrogation of his duty to rule that sets chaos loose in the realm, no audience has difficulty in agreeing with him when he says 'I am a man more sinned against than sinning'. Not only the stage chorus but also the audience can weep as the self-blinded and now outcast Oedipus is lead off stage.

Classic tragedy can be summarised as play of catastrophe, mystery and pain. And crucially with no redemption in most cases. Compensation for past injustice or excessive pain are absent - the catastrophe is final. 'Beyond the tragic there lies no "happy ending" in some other dimension or place or time.' (GS/DT, 129) [F]

The emergence of 'near-tragedy'
Significantly, Sophocles died in 406BC, Shakespeare in 1616 and Racine in 1699. Accordingly, the criteria for classic tragedy are based on plays written before 1700. Due to many pressures dramatic presentation changed during the 18th century and the only play to appear that might be thought to measure up to the three classic principles was Schiller's *Maria Stuarda* (1800) in which the suffering of the protagonist transmutes into the highest grandeur as she dies. Of the many pressures, two are dominant. The first was a prolonged theoretical struggle amongst playwrights as to what made good theatre. (The Elizabethans would have thought this debate to be most singular.) The second was the rise of the middle class. The theatrical debate paralysed invention by offering a conflict of views and the growing middle class by and large just wanted to spend its money on being 'entertained'. Then at around the turn of the century emerged the phenomenon of Romanticism. Emphasis was on the individual, on intense emotion, and on intuition in preference to the rationalism of the 18th century. Authentic tragedy of the old school had to find a way through a thicket of muddled theoretical goals, the wish of the middle class for easy entertainment and the individualism inherent in Romanticism. (To Wagner's disgust as set forth in Chapter 2.) It did so by introducing the saving grace of remorse in the evil-doer's mind. By due penance the tragic figure is redeemed. This satisfied the emotional needs of the emerging middle class audience who now supplied the bulk of those who attended plays and the opera. But a problem has been introduced.

> Dramas of remorse cannot be ultimately tragic. The formula is one of 'near-tragedy'. Four acts of tragic violence and guilt are followed by a fifth of redemption and innocence regained. 'Near-tragedy' is precisely the compromise of an age which did not believe in the finality of evil. (GS/DT,133)

Hence the amazing success of Meyerbeer's *Robert le Diable* in 1831 and of Bellini's *Norma* in 1835. (In pairing these two operas, there is no suggestion of an equality. Bellini's opera is amongst the best in the output of all Italian composers whereas Meyerbeer produces an ill focussed drama with some clever music.)

19th century opera
Only one opera in this century can claim to be a tragedy in the classic mould, namely Verdi's *Otello*. Superbly adapted from Shakespeare, the audience is presented with the mystery of *Why him?*, the second mystery surrounding the motive of Iago, the immense

---

[F] A full elucidation of this subject is to be found in *The Death of Tragedy* by George Steiner, Faber & Faber, 1961.

and unjustified suffering and the bleak finality of the epilogue to the Moor's suicide - that cavernous growl of black despair as the curtain falls.

Almost all other operas from 1815 onwards are 'near-tragic' as they embrace redemption before or after death. Only in Italy do we find major operas with remorseless conclusions, such as Rossini (*Ermione*, 1817), Donizetti (*Roberto Devereux*, 1838). And of course Verdi: *Ernani, Rigoletto, Un Ballo in Maschera, Don Carlos*. Readers may recall this last, with the four main characters who remain alive (Philip II, Elizabeth de Valois, Don Carlos and Princess Eboli) maimed for life and without hope.

It may disappoint some readers to learn that *Lohengrin* is the only opera by Wagner that might be tragic in the classic sense - and this is provided one considers Elsa as the main character who goes on a journey. All the others have redemption at the core. In this Wagner was of his time. Generally - and in this study also - *Der Fliegende Holländer, Tannhäuser* and *Lohengrin* are designated as romantic operas to distinguish them from the *Ring* and those that came after. The distinction remains sound for the later works are indeed *dramma per musica* - the music makes the drama - and are no longer in the main tradition. But the *Ring* text speaks of redemption and for decades the motif that returns at the end of the Immolation was called *redemption through love* or somesuch. So the cycle is a 'near-tragedy' as described by Steiner.

Wotan

If the tetralogy as a whole is 'near tragedy', can any of the characters within it be called tragic? What about the main protagonist? We will keep to the three criteria described above. The benefit is that they are firmly established and that they are technical or structural and not moral.

With regard to the first criterion, Wotan cannot sensibly be described as a bad person. It verges on the perverse to equate his actions with those of Alberich, as Cooke seems dangerously near to doing. (See DC/WE,159.) Wagner asserts in the *Myth* that he is benign and this study finds this to be so. Parity between Wotan and Alberich does not work in principle and neither does it or can it have live dramatic force or function, and for two reasons. The first is that we are only *told* about one crucial aspect, namely the creating by Wotan of his spear by cutting a branch from the World Ash Tree. We are told this in *Götterdämmerung* after Wotan has left the stage for the last time. Cooke sees equivalence between this and the 'forging' by Alberich of the Ring, but to that point the audience has *seen* no gross misuse of its power such as Alberich brought to life. [G] The second and more potent reason, as will be explored in Chapter 20, is that the tone speaks not of wickedness but of majestic strength. This majesty alone destroys the case

---

[G] It is possible to make the case that Wotan is very like Alberich, but only if we ignore the fact that Wagner is writing a drama and not a social thesis. The drama mandates that Wotan is first seen in a bad light, so that we see the result of his actions, that Wotan himself also sees them and that we then trace his struggle to overcome the problem he has caused.

put by Simon Williams that 'the root cause of all evil [is] the striking of a limb off the world's ash tree'. (*Wagner and the romantic hero,* Yale University Press, 2004, p.74) That cannot be the situation if the drama is to have any meaning.

That said, Wotan's experience is miles away from fulfilling the second condition: that tragic lives are governed by forces outside of the protagonist's knowledge and control. There is one obdurate matter that is not of his own making: the cosmos he commands will soon come to an end, as spelled out by the Wala in the sagas. Erda (a.k.a. Wala) tells him so. But this cannot be brought into the orbit of the second principle: there is nothing to suggest that Odin/Wotan ever saw themselves as immortal. But both claimed to be the supreme arbiter and to a degree beyond that listed by Cooke. For in a world of kings or emperors or tycoons there are other kings, emperors and tycoons, and they would parley and negotiate amongst themselves. But Wotan is entirely supreme in his world. He is so powerful that no one in his universe (this excludes, Erda, the Norns and the Rhinedaughters) can act independently for very long without his say so. Anything and everything of consequence requires his support. Everything, save that this cannot apply to the return of the Ring (and the subsequent re-emergence of the Gold) to the Rhine. [H]

There is, however, something whereby Wotan differs from all other characters in drama. All his problems were self-inflicted. He made the rules and, having broken them, was unable to save himself. This circularity is surely tragic in a peculiar way that applies to Wotan alone - in *all* drama. We see displayed the ultimate case where a protagonist is up against another aspect of his own character. This conflict remains unresolved and perhaps Wagner sensed this aspect. At the rehearsals for the *Ring* in 1876, Porges records that Wotan's terrible cry in W2 at 'Endloser Grimm! Ewiger Gram!' (HP/WR,28) is set to the music of the greatest musical climax in the descent to Nibelheim. Wagner said that this represents the god as he 'rails against his compulsion to rule the world.' This compulsion never left him and it would seem that he never found an abiding sense of peace – and in that unique sense he is a tragic figure.

Wotan's offspring

So if Wotan may be tragic in this peculiar sense, what about the others? More general matters about Siegfried are discussed below. But he is clearly not tragic. For Siegfried's life is defined by heroic and not by tragic sacrifice. Whatever weak points can be found in the examination of his life, they are not such as point toward tragedy. He is also the one who suffers least and whose diminished suffering, when compared to Siegmund, is in accordance with the changes to his character made by Wagner himself.

The lives of Brünnhilde and Sieglinde are not tragic. Both are on dangerous and tumultuous journeys. Sieglinde's is from self-aware suffering through glorious release

---

[H] We can disregard the third criterion, that the suffering should be seen by the audience as being almost beyond contemplation. For it is impossible for any person to put himself through something he knows he would find unendurable.

to fulfilment. The audience may perceive the lonely nine months of Siegfried's gestation as tragic, but she does not if the last music she sings is anything to go by (p.329). Brünnhilde's situation was discussed in Chapter 13.

This leaves Siegmund. His life obviously bears features that invoke tragedy. After an extremely tough early life, a supernatural agency promises a release in the future, but then leaves him. Life becomes even worse - cursed in every sense. But then the promised release comes and with it an added bonus of the highest felicity. All seems set fair but, at the critical moment when there is the probability of a full life of freedom and love, he is brutally struck down. Nothing is as a result of his own actions: in essence he is betrayed and he is the only person who is tragic in the classic mould.

The Ring

Wagner is specific that when the Ring is reabsorbed into the Gold, the curse upon it will pass from the gods and from the whole world. Coercive power, whether through law or tyranny, will be a thing of the past. This can be unwarrantably utopian but the message certainly lies in all versions of the Immolation texts.

However, the Ring has been shown to have little power beyond its capacity to garner riches and enslave the Nibelungs in some unidentifiable fashion. This can lead to a notion that the Ring as a destructive force that undermines hope. We cannot know that Wagner thought like this, but the notion can arise unbidden that the Ring partakes of the energy that emanates from the *Will* within the *noumenon*. The drive it generates is destructive, in the same way that Schopenhauer sees as bad the results of the *Will* in people, namely the universal distress of mankind. It is not unreasonable, therefore, to think that the underlying 'meaning' of the *Ring* can be expressed by the notion that everything is at the mercy of the disruptive force of the *Will*, as perceived by the philosopher, and that this can drive out common sense. This places the Ring itself as a manifestation of a malign force that breaks to the surface as it is crafted by Alberich and gathers into itself every weakness that is found within each of the players in the drama, engendering desires that are essentially unachievable and lead to perpetual conflict. Is it therefore possible to redraw the central conflict as being between that malign force and any virtue that might oppose it? The participants in the conflicts die and return to the vast unknown. From that same, immutable and eternal unknown, new hope will arise.

If no Ring, or no similar future talisman with the potential to bring out the worse in people, there might be no such unavoidable conflict in the future. If so, that must give hope. Below the surface, the cycle is a romantic drama of salvation. The drama defies a tragic ending and also the harsh and logical necessity that mandates the collapse of Wotan's efforts to bring benefit to humanity. That is surely not utopian.

Siegfried

The detail discussion started with this man and also ends with him. Two questions about Siegfried plague those who examine the *Ring*. These are over and above that attached to the changes made between Sigurd and Siegfried as previously discussed. They are: What was Siegfried's error that brought about his murder? And: Why does it convince that this death is inevitable? Two more questions can be asked that relate to Schopenhauer's philosophy. They are: How does Siegfried fit into the philosopher's view of the world? And: Does his concept of the *Will* connect to Siegfried?

<u>Siegfried's fatal error</u>
Discussion so far has not advanced beyond the 'great error' assigned to him - and without explanation. This will not do for many. We want to understand what Wagner is trying to show us. The first thing to establish is that the betrayal of Brünnhilde that is to bring about Siegfried's death is not brought about by Alberich's curse on the Ring: that he is free from this is demonstrated by the rising of his dead hand against Hagen. Secondly, if the magic draft of forgetfulness is just a trick, this makes Siegfried innocent and therefore, at least in Aristotle's terms, his murder is unwarranted, and we know we are not meant to think this.

If the theory that the drinking of the potion represents a longer period of corruption is held not to work on stage the answer *must* be the *coup de foudre*: Siegfried's love for Brünnhilde is swept aside when he sees Gutrune and, from then on, he 'sees' only her. Hence the amnesia he has when face to face with his true wife in G2. This is unavoidably clunky as drama, almost certainly brought about by the force of the myth surrounding the event which Wagner would not or could not avoid. The wonder is that he made it work on stage and in Chapter 21 we may see how and why it does so.

Part of the reason that it works may be that Wagner had experienced such passion himself. The clearest evidence of all restraint being swept aside lies in his first letters to Minna, when he fell for her in 1836 – aged 23. They met when both worked in Magdeburg. The company they both worked for collapsed so they parted: Minna went to Königsberg and Wagner to Berlin. They corresponded, but irregularly on Minna's part, and this brought the following desperate response from the lovelorn composer:

> People say that love in its first stages is more glowing and ardent, but never during the two years we have been in love have I been in such a state of burning and consuming passion. No, you will never again be loved as I love you now, and I must be away from you for *a quarter of a year longer!!* . . . Why should god permit this blight on my life? What have I done? I can't go on, my misery is overwhelming me! (BC, 51)

At that time in his life, sexual love was an ideal for Wagner: all his correspondence shows he wanted her totally and could think of little else.

The necessity for Siegfried as he is portrayed

Wagner repeatedly demonstrates why Siegfried must be as seen and heard and the difficulty of him being otherwise.

Brünnhilde is the first port of call. As early as the eulogy over his body in the *Myth* she says that he relied on his own powers alone. Everything she might have gifted to him before he departed for the Gibich palace is either downplayed or goes for nought and it is obvious why. The valkyr received her gifts from Wotan and to hand them on to Siegfried in any way would mean he was not independent of the god. It was OK for him to love the woman but not to take advantage of those aspects of the valkyr that the woman retained. Brünnhilde was equipped to understand matters at her meeting with the Rhinedaughters in the night, and in a manner quite beyond Siegfried's comprehension - as is to be witnessed in G3.1.

Wotan himself understands why his downfall is and must be umbilically linked with shackles of iron to that of Siegfried. 'He who fears my spear-point shall never pass through the fire' - the closing words of *Die Walküre* - give this message. As will be seen in *Siegfried* Act II, Wotan is to stand aside and hand his fate over to his grandson. This be does in his declaration to Alberich that Siegfried must 'stand or fall' by his own powers alone. This is a matter of logic as well as dramatic necessity. In general terms, for the drama to ring true all Wotan's offspring must defy him (p.144). But specifically, logic mandates that only Siegfried can break Alberich's curse upon the Ring. Inadvertently, he is beholden only to the wood bird for assistance, and that by right of his own unique nature, of the purity invested in him – as we shall see - by Wagner's music (p.358/9). From no one else that he meets in his entire stage life does he take advice.

Wagner's comment to Röckel that the essence of Siegfried 'can almost never be stated in words' now makes sense. We need to identify him through his relationship with others, by his actions on stage and by the music that surrounds him. He and he alone is immune from Alberich's curse. He is not interested in the Ring for any dubious reason associated with its reputed power, and its 'sanctity' as a love token – as understood by Brünnhilde – was swept aside by the infatuation with Gutrune. We are both told and shown this in significant detail in his dialogue with the Rhinedaughters in the *Myth*. This comprehensive indifference to the Ring is only seen in this man.

That substantial catalogue argues for Siegfried's independence. Each dwindles in impact, however, when placed against the forging of Nothung. In the sources, Sigurd gets assistance and Wagner evades this: untutored, Siegfried fashions the instrument for freedom he needs and this gives him the authority over Wotan that all others lack (p.196). Nothung can accordingly destroy Wotan's spear. This is a matter of logic.

Siegfried seen through the lens of Schopenhauer

Consider this general observation from the philosopher: Final satisfaction of a wish . . .

> 'is only apparent; the wish fulfilled at once makes way for a new one; the former is a known delusion, the latter a delusion not as yet known. No obtained object of willing can give a

satisfaction that lasts and no longer declines; but it is always like the alms thrown to a beggar, which reprieves him today so that his misery may be prolonged until tomorrow.' (AS/WWR1, 196)

Nothing is further from the truth with Siegfried. He acts instinctively and very often without deliberation. Once he has come to a conclusion or clear perception, he proceeds immediately to what he wants to do, and acts entirely without inhibition. His wishes are concerned with the moment, with a disregard for both past and present (p.89). If he serves the community, he does so unwittingly. There can be nothing to add to this. All that can be done is to bring to mind the difference between Siegfried and all other men, to which we will return in Chapter 21.

Siegfried and Schopenhauer's *Will*

The suggested symbiosis of thought and attitude between Wagner and Schopenhauer and the *exceptionalism* of the hero as described above prompt the notion that Wagner's paradigm hero is an exemplar of the *Will* in action. Indubitably he is a puzzle and, since Wagner manipulated the sources to give us the picture we see, the puzzle is deliberate.

Schopenhauer insists that 'the will . . . is devoid of knowledge.' Now it is easy to argue that Siegfried learns nothing over the course of the two operas in which he features. He is not unaware of the colossal background before which his life unfolds - witness the conversations with Fafner, the wood bird, Wotan and the Rhinedaughters - but he does not probe and seems uninterested. If the absorbed philosophy boosted Wagner's confidence in the course already taken in the *Ring*, then the congruence of Siegfried as a stage character who embodies the *Will* and the concept of the *Will* as being void of knowledge gives context to the hero's disinterest. The best way to describe him is as existing 'outside' knowledge.

◇ ◇ ◇ ◇ ◇ ◇

PART THREE

Musical and dramatic structure

16

Stabriem, Leitmotiven and Wagner, the 'symphonist'

The ten years 1846 to 1856, between the composition of *Lohengrin* and that for *Siegfried* Acts I and II, witnessed remarkable development in Wagner's technique for and attitude toward composition, and the poems to be used. This chapter examines the theories behind *stabriem* and *leitmotiven* as set down in *Opera and Drama*, how the theories worked out in *Das Rheingold* and *Die Walküre* and how that for *leitmotiven* changed as Wagner matured.

Stabriem

Nothing is known for certain about the evolution in Wagner's mind of *stabriem* - the *modus operandi* in words upon which *Das Rheingold* is built – nor do we know when the determination upon the new style took firm root. Wagner came across *stabreim* in his exploration of the Nordic sources at any time from 1843 onwards and in his Dresden Library was found a translation from the old Norse of *Voluspa* (The Wise Woman's Prophecy) as made by one Ludwig Ettmuller and published in 1837. As it is, without prior notice, the poem of *Siegfrieds Tod* appeared in November 1848, two years after the conclusion of the creative composition sketch for *Lohengrin*. The decision to use this verse format did not by itself entail the introduction of *leitmotiven*. The new-style verse might posit the new-style music but it does not necessitate it (p.113).

Emergence
The second part of *Opera and Drama,* which discusses the current state of theatre, ends by giving detail about the text for the ideal new musical drama. The words were to come first and were likened to male semen which impregnates the female egg. Wagner suggests that this seed is equivalent to the understanding and hence to the intellect. If this idea is pursued, the female egg represents the other side of the personality, namely the creative. In short, the male intellect (poetry) impregnates the creative female spirit, the result of which is music that is joined organically to the words which brought it forth.

For all the excellence of *Lohengrin*, this unity is not present and much of the dramatic dialogue is both pedestrian and overwrought. The example overleaf (16.1) is taken from Act II Scene 2, when Telramund accuses Lohengrin of witchcraft. The music fully expresses the outrage and the accusation is grave. The English text cannot be sensibly matched to the music, but goes: 'Who is he who came to these shores drawn by a wild

STABRIEM, LEITMOTIVEN AND WAGNER THE 'SYMPHONIST'

16.1 Telramund accuses Lohengrin of witchcraft

swan? To call a man honest who is served by such magic creatures is folly!' In this opera, whenever such strong emotion exists, the expression is always the same: the entire episode from which this is extracted is of unremitting hysteria. The style works well in the duet between Ortrud and Telramund, where the duologue imposes variety and restraint. But, without that, it wearies the ear and loses impact. This may have made Wagner think it would not do and this revived existing recollections of *stabriem*.

16.2 Alberich is engulfed by lust for the Rhinedaughters in the opening scene of *Das Rheingold*.

Compare the *Lohengrin* example with a tense moment from *Das Rheingold* when Alberich prepares to seize one of the Rhinedaughters (16.2). On the surface there might not appear much difference, but the *Lohengrin* extract is surrounded by interjections in the same vein whereas *Das Rheingold* has every variation one can think of as to how the text can be melodically expressed. (To make a representative comparison the extract is free of motif accompaniment, as is *Lohengrin*.)

Poetic theory in 1851

Stabreim had been adopted for *Siegfrieds Tod,* and the switch to the new format came during the two years following *Lohengrin*. In *Opera and Drama*, yet another two years on, Wagner rationalised its inception and value. The first task was to establish that neither of the two types of current modern verse would do. The following is an abstract of pp 239-245 and pp 249-251.

> Modern verse is of two types. One is rhythmic and is exemplified by the pentameter; the other uses end rhyme. Neither is sympathetic to the demands of melody. Rhythmic verse wants to dictate the melodic emphasis and the latter can only break free by distorting the verse. End rhyme [as used in *Lohengrin*] has each line moving toward its last, rhyming syllable – a sort of long cumulative upstroke, preparatory to the downbeat of the rhyme. This also puts melody in a strait jacket... Neither rhythm nor rhyme assist the development of melody. Melody either emphasises the rhythm, which verse seeks to smooth over, or – if it does not do this – it obliterates the sense. A melody has its own logic and structure and this pays no heed to verse, however good that is. In practice, what the musician does is turn the verse into a prose that suits.

> *Stabriem*, in the hands of Wagner, is to solve matters. This is to be based on three principles: alliteration, condensation and free rhythm. Of these, condensation of lan-

guage is central. 'Accidental, petty and indefinite' references, adjectives, conjunctions and prepositions are to be removed wherever possible, so that the words that remain are pregnant with dramatic force. The free rhythm that follows the emphasis and weight of these words, as positioned by the writer, would allow maximum flexibility of accentuation. Finally, alliteration brings an unexpected bonus by juxtaposing words which may start with or include the same consonant but can have opposite meanings.

This is the theory as set down: the words were to generate the music. Melody (not recitative) that matched the emotion in the text would emerge organically, such that it would seem natural and inevitable. Jack Stein puts it like this:

> This union of word and tone is the very core of the synthesis propounded in *Opera and Drama*. When the precise quantitative relations between accented and unaccented syllables of the poetic verse is observed by the melodic line, the stronger rhythmic force of the music will strengthen the basic pattern of the verse, making possible the articulation of emotional subtleties otherwise impossible to record. For by means of the melodic line, the unaccented syllables as well as the secondary accents can be placed in a dynamic relationship and can sweep up to a climax or fall away from it, as the sense requires. (JS/RWSA,71)

If the words came first, they had to do their job. Wagner adapted *stabriem* to produce a text that was *inherently* rhythmic in accordance with the emotion to be expressed. The melody was to be governed by the rhythm of the verse, which in turn depended on the nature of the emotion expressed. 'The life-giving focus of dramatic expression is the verse-melody of the performer.' (RW/PW2,335) The purpose was to do more than produce heightened recitative: there was to be a complementary parity between the text and the music. The one needed the other.

Leitmotiven have nothing intrinsically to do with it. But if a pithy and pregnant piece of verse were directly to bring forth a memorable 'verse-melody' that conveyed the emotion behind the words, this would stick in the mind and the sentiment behind the melody would be recalled when it recurs. By and large, when we thrill to the vocal style, in whichever of the four operas we find it, we are responding, in Jack Stein's words, to 'the basic pattern of the verse, making possible the articulation of emotional subtleties otherwise impossible to record.'

The theory in practice

Wagner's attempt to achieve his prime melodic goal worked remarkably well. It is true that sometimes the resulting German is clunky, but it is still effective for most of the time. Examples must serve to illustrate and here are two. In R2 Fricka has contempt for the gods who egged on Wotan to put Freia into the scales as the price for Valhalla and here are her words and the verse melody. Nothing can equal the scorn of 'bösen' in bar

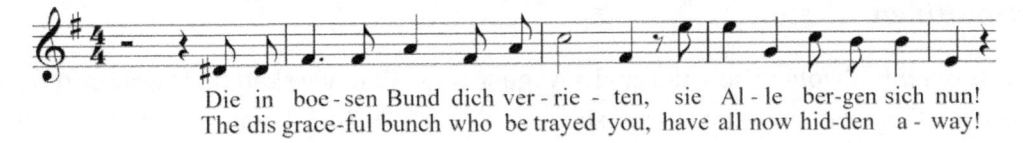

Die in boe-sen Bund dich ver-rie-ten, sie Al-le ber-gen sich nun!
The dis grace-ful bunch who be trayed you, have all now hid-den a-way!

16.3 Fricka's contempt for the male gods.

2 but the English 'betrayed' fits very well in the second bar. The falling fifth to the tonic E on the last note gives a splendid finality: the rising notes in the first phase produce a complex chord which reveals itself to be in E minor as it resolves into the thumping tonic.

The second example is from Siegmund's narration in W1, at the point when he returns home to find his mother dead, his sister gone and his home destroyed: the moment when his life took its first drastic step for the worse. Save for three bars toward

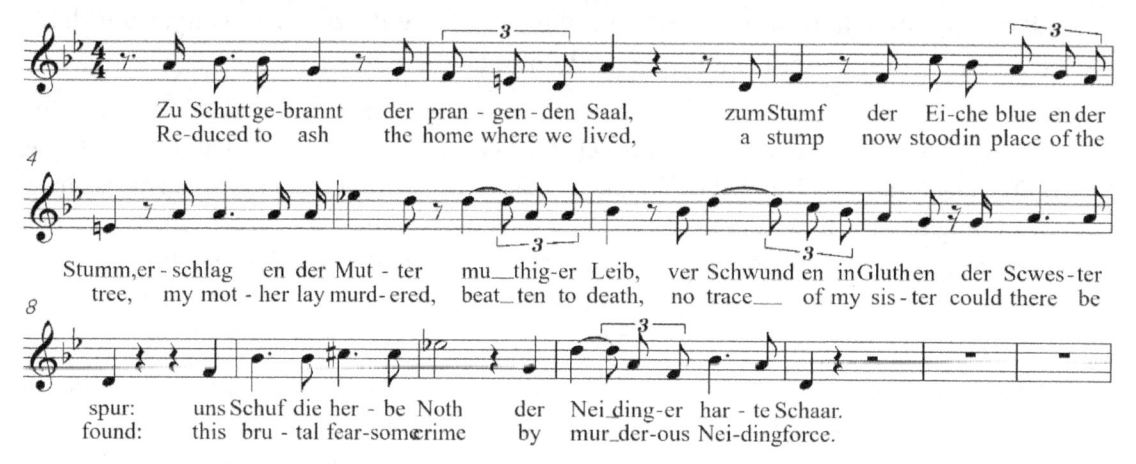

16.4 Siegmund's grief

the end, the vocal line is virtually without accompaniment. There is beauty, nevertheless: this is not recitative. The falling lines in bars 2, 3, 5, 6 give structure, the high *f* E♭ on 'Mütter' signals powerful grief and the last three bars turn the grief into rage. Verse and melody are as one. As Roger Scruton says: 'The extra-ordinary characters . . . are not *accompanied* by music: they are *realised* in music . . . because the words and music are inseparable. The audience hears the musical accents as though they were verbal accents: the music speaks, just as the words sing.' (RS/RT,147)

Confidence grew quickly as composition progressed. Wagner's control was remarkable from the beginning considering that the style was new. Very rarely is there plain recitative in *Das Rheingold* such as is found in *Lohengrin*. The words always shape the melodic line and frequently the match is perfect, as in the previous example. From the start the inherent rhythmic impulse of the words did produce melody. By and large this verse-melody takes little heed of *leitmotiven*; these are either absent or provide a memory-filled tapestry which the vocal line touches or joins for a fragment, but otherwise floats upon it.

Leitmotiven

Leitmotiven took longer to emerge. In August 1850 Wagner sketched some 150 bars of music for the opening of the Norns' scene in *Siegfrieds Tod*. Themes that were to find a home in the *Ring* are there but no hint of a *leitmotiv*: the style is as that for the more leisurely sections of *Lohengrin*. It is only with the publication of *Opera and Drama* that first acquaintance is made.

The creative impulse

Why and how did Wagner hit upon the use of the technique. It was obviously designed to facilitate the composition of the *Ring*; even if it did not logically follow from it, the enormous scope of the story would have pushed for some such musical evolution. A common observation is that each of Wagner's operas has a particular harmonic, melodic and instrumental texture. This is so even in the three earlier romantic operas: a passage from *Tannhäuser* would sit uneasily in the fabric of *Lohengrin*. The expansion of *Siegfrieds Tod* into two and then into four operas, all of which would partake of the same musical *tinta* (to use the word adopted by Verdi) required an additional attribute that over-arches everything if the operas were to hang together as a whole. The vast scale of the drama *required* some new musical system if it was to hang together, and hence the *leitmotiv*.

Modulation in theory and in practice

Opera and Drama introduced two methods by which the music would be shaped by the words, and seemingly pre-eminent was modulation. Wagner was very taken with the idea that the meanings behind words could influence harmony. He focussed in particular on words that started with the same syllable but had different or even opposite meanings. He obviously set large store by this at the time, for the only set of precise examples in his exposition of the new music are devoted to this issue. [A] The following is abstracted from *Opera and Drama,* pp.291-3.

> *Stabriem* can couple together words of opposite emotional expression such as *Lust* and *Leid, Wohl* and *Weh*. We see this in the following.
>
> | | |
> |---|---|
> | *Liebe giebt Lust zum Leben* | Love gives delight to living |
> | *Die Liebe bringt Lust und Leid* | Love brings delight and sorrow |
> | *doch in ihr Weh auch webt sie Wonnen* | but in the sorrow also comes pleasure |
>
> The first line has no change of emotion, so there is no key change, whereas the pair of lines which follow might have a change of key on *Leid* to convey the change of emotion and, at *Wonnen*, the reverse modulation back to the opening key. These modulations bind the two opposites *Lust* and *Leid* in a unique way in our consciousness, and similarly with *Weh* and *Wonnen*. Additionally, the music also relates *Wonnen* to the original *Liebe* and *Lust*. The poet indicates the generic emotional bonds which only the music is able fully to illustrate – harmony does what word play cannot do.

However, despite all such detail, Wagner did not follow matters through. Many examples of modulation exist, which exactly reflect some change of emotion, but they do

---

[A] The preamble to this excursus is also a prime example of Wagner's particular cast of mind and is to be found in detail on p.46.

not crowd upon each other in the manner implied above. This tells us that such matters were floating about in the composer's mind and also that they advanced no further.

Leitmotiven as a theory

In Wagner's letters we get little clue about when and how the technique cohered but unmistakeable allusions lie in *Opera and Drama* Part 3. This was written in between the completion of the *Siegfrieds Tod* poem (late 1848) and the expansion of that story by the drafting of *Der junge Siegfried* in June 1851. The first hint about the book comes in a letter to a friend dated 20 September 1850 and it was completed four months later - obviously written at white heat. Part 3 is chaotic, repetitious and opaque but a steady line of thought can be traced and we find there the core of what developed into the *leitmotif*. With *stabriem* as the new format, five elements can be isolated. This is the nearest we can get to the conception of *leitmotiven*.

1. Pithy words, pregnant with drama would generate a memorable melody in the voice - the prototype *leitmotif*. Such verse-melody would have a natural force that prompted natural vocal delivery, without sentimentality on the one hand and/or hysteria on the other.
2. Thereafter, when heard in the orchestra, the emotions behind the words would be revived in the mind of the listener. The melody is thus a 'motif of reminiscence' - a hint to remember a past emotion.
3. Another form of motif is of 'premonition' rather than of reminiscence. These first appear in the orchestra and convey 'foreboding'.
4. To reinforce the meaning of a motif of reminiscence, it should be sung again to slightly different words. The melody is thus more strongly associated with the thought behind the verse.
5. Both forms of motif can be used to sustain the dramatic pulse when the 'word tone' language of the actors is toned down into the language of everyday life. The purpose now is not to generate emotion but to move the plot forward.

Leitmotiven in practice

Of these only the first three find their way consistently into the composition of *Das Rheingold* and *Die Walküre* two years later. The notion that a motif first heard in the voice should quickly be heard again (#4) could not hold its place. Jack Stein points out that only once does this happen - and early in *Das Rheingold*. The *ring* motif was first introduced in a manner described by Derrick Cooke as 'embryonic'. Sung by *Wellgunde*, it is repeated by Alberich very soon afterwards. Fleet-footed and in $9/8$ time on first appearance, its full unsettling force is only obvious in Cooke's 'definitive' form, presented five times in the interlude between Scenes 4 and 5 - but now in a measured $4/4$. More drastic still is the non-appearance of #5, the use of the orchestra to sustain the emotional temperature when the voice is used for plot development. In Wagner's words: 'Wherever, for the purpose of defining the dramatic situation more clearly, the word-tone language of the actors . . . descends to the point where it resembles the language of everyday life . . . the orchestra compensates for this through its power of musically conveying a foreboding or a remembrance so that the awakened feeling remains in its uplifted mood' (RW/PW2, 345) The orchestra then withdraws into the background as soon as the actor takes up melodic verse again. There is not the slightest attempt to put this into practice.

The other major change as theory moves to practice is a switch from motifs introduced in the voice to those first heard in the orchestra - a switch from remembrance to foreboding. This started right at the beginning of composition. In *Das Rheingold* that called *life choice* (M6) in this study is first heard in the voice, as are *force of the gold* (M5) and *ring* (M7) but this is not so for *valhalla* (M8) or *will-to-power* (M12) - and not for *nature* (M1), the very first motif of all. Every list of motifs compiled is different but, of the 30 substantive motifs listed for *Das Rheingold* in the chapter that follows, 23 (or 76%) emerge from the orchestra; in *Die Walküre* 15 out of 20 (75%) do so. The percentage is greater in *Siegfried* and *Götterdämmerung*.

Little of this would have registered in the 1870s. The music when first heard was so unusual that guidance on how to listen to it came quickly. In 1878 Hans von Wolzogen produced the *Thematischer Leitfaden* (Thematic Guide). This ran to 125 pages and listed some 120 motifs. [B] The great work would have been a vast puzzle without that guide; of immense influence, most of Wolzogen's motifs remained current through the 20th century and many listings use the same names to describe many of them: Ernest Newman in 1937, Robert Donington in 1963, Deryck Cooke in 1967, J K Holman in 1996 and Roger Scruton in 2016. On embarking on a work of such magnitude and complexity, the temptation (even initial requirement in the case of Wolzogen) to name motifs and then to hang on to those names was and remains immeasurably strong. They come in from different angles and are of massively different rhythms and melodic contours and we think we can connect more easily on to the plot with named handles.

Deryck Cooke on the *Ring* motifs and the problems he found

The best person to use as a guide is Deryck Cooke. We can construct his intentions by bringing together material from four sources: two articles, currently to be found in *Vindications* (1982) and *The Wagner Companion* (1979), the book *I saw the world end* (1978) and an audio guide to the motifs. This last dates from 1967 when he was commissioned by Decca Records to devise a musical guide to the recently completed Solti recording of the *Ring*. This was published as vinyl LPs (now on two CDs) and introduced listeners to the *leitmotiven* and to some of Wagner's manipulations of them in 193 separate examples. Within these four sources he confronts all the different issues within an illuminating exegesis of the motifs. His authority has never been challenged. Bryan

---

[B] This study will use the word *motif* (singular) and *motifs* (plural).

Magee knew and understood Cooke very well and, introducing the book *Vindications*, he avers that '[Cooke] knew the scores better than anyone has ever known them, including Wagner himself . . . and he had a startling ability to perceive relationships between configurations of notes at widely different points in a work . . . His understanding of the music was unique and irrecoverable.' (DC/V,20)

Cooke's book is so full of insight, information, new ways of looking at things and meaningful research that everyone interested in the *Ring* will benefit from it. He was drafting his *provisional* copy, however, and who knows how his own final listing might have turned out. From the CD, different categories of motifs can be separated. When duplications are removed, there remain 179 motifs or combinations of motifs. These can be tentatively divided into three types. First there are 39 primary motifs, the bedrock of the remainder. Second come 45 which are clearly derived from one of the primary 39. Putting these together, we have a sub total of 84 musical motifs. The remaining 95, therefore, are derivations, with twists or distortions, of the 84 main motifs or key combinations of two or more. These can be seen, by those who care to spend the time, as examples which 'clarify the psychological implications' within a motif during 'its long and complex development.'

Four problems emerge from Cooke's work. These are (a) the contradictory or inconsistent meanings that have been attached to particular motifs, (b) the contradiction that exists between how Wagner thought drama should be absorbed and what he actually gives us in the *Ring,* (c) the confusion caused by an over-elaboration of motifs and (d) the immensity of any comprehensive analysis of the *Ring*.

(a) Contradictory or inconsistent meanings between motifs

This problem need not exist. Note the following clear statement in the introduction to the 1967 audio listing.

> Wagner's motives have, in reality, a fundamentally psychological significance, and his score is a continuous symphonic development of the stage action. In consequence, a comprehensive analysis of the *Ring* would be an enormous task. It would involve clarifying the psychological implications of all the motives, and tracing their significance throughout the whole of their long and complex development.

Given this principle, what is the reason that Cooke puzzles unnecessarily over why and how the same motif that accompanies Wellgunde's initial statement that only the abjuration of love will gain power over the Rhine Gold can also accompany Siegmund as he clasps the sword that will afford him the freedom to love the woman he wants, even though he knows it can bring about his death (p.2). The reason is obvious, given the quotation above: Alberich and Siegmund are each making a choice about how their lives will be lived.

My own listings in the chapter that follows attempt to follow the precepts established by Cooke, and the hope is that readers will have consistent guidance as to the function of each motif.

(b) Contradiction between principle and practice

Any such clarification does not manoeuvre us clear of this further contradiction. Wagner was very clear that thinking about the music as it was heard was a bad idea (p.5). Music itself is not drama and when analysed the intellectual process obtrudes on the emotions. This may not matter 'in the school room', but offers a dead hand in the theatre. Exposure to music contains within itself an education *about* music. After a while our sensibility absorbs the implication of a key changing from major to minor and it learns to anticipate with delight, for example, the miraculous ability of Schubert in this respect. The process of listening by-passes the intellect and teaches the emotion what these matters mean. But if something needs to be explained/described then the very act of description gets in the way. Thus the problem Wagner hands on to us is that the *Ring* needs explication despite his insistence that this should not be so.

(c) The over-elaboration of motifs

Cooke's ambition, had he lived must have been to promulgate a full exegesis of *leitmotiven* and how they developed through the cycle. This would have been a continuation of work that first saw the light in 1967. Cooke's list is not complete both by his own admission and also by the judgement of later writers. JK Holman lists 145, 33 of which are not included in Cooke's 179; Scruton, coming late to the task in 2016, finds 201 of which 60 are unique to his list. With just three commentators we have over 270. (Errors and omissions excepted: this cannot be an exact matter.) This study has 82 of which seven are unique, making a total of 275. Additionally, there are 59 listed examples in the next chapter of what I call *compositional* motifs. These are important. The prime motifs, impregnated with the memories of past appearances as they may be, are often glued together by a compositional motif. These hold together the musical fabric within a particular scene or mini-scene, driving the drama forward. Often they derive from a substantive motif and details are given in the following five chapters. [c]

Thus there are some 330 motifs which have been identified and which Wagner uses in little and in large. This need not surprise. Robert Rayner in his book on *Die Meistersinger* contrasts its simplicity with that of the *Ring*, which . . .

> can portray every vicissitude of the human soul - timidity and fearlessness; heroic endeavour and dogged labour; helpless despair and hopeful energy; blithe amorality and brooding regrets; the love of father and daughter, of brother and sister, of mother and unborn son; the inhibitions of virginity and the ecstasy of passion that overcomes those inhibitions; wrath, pride, rapture, hatred and grief. It can bring before us a crawling toad, a flashing sword, gathering clouds, rustling leaves, a flowing stream, a pattering rainstorm. It shows

---

[c] What, moreover, are we to make of the ubiquity of Loge's music? Where fire and cunning are within the plot, there is no problem; but frequently one of his six themes comes up when the situation and emotion is unrelated to either element. Often it seems to convey energy and excitement and when this is so the motif becomes compositional.

us what it feels like to ride through the clouds as a Valkyrie, to swim in the depths of the Rhine like a mermaid, to guard buried treasure like a dragon, to forge a sword for oneself, to tramp across a rainbow-bridge into the abode of the gods. (RR/WM,54)

(d) The gargantuan nature of the task

Cooke writes about the contrast of musical styles between *Tristan und Isolde* and *Die Meistersinger*. Of the two operas which were composed during the interregnum between Acts II and III of *Siegfried* he simply says that the former is about two lovers and the latter is 'a straightforward tale . . . woven around the historical figure of Hans Sachs'. He draws a distinction with the *Ring:*

> The original intention in creating the *Ring* (however much he may have expanded and modified this intention later) was to set forth the evils of modern civilization and adumbrate a possible amelioration of them . . . [the *Ring*] has at its core . . . a text that is almost as much a "play of ideas" as is a work by Ibsen or Shaw . . . yet the fact that this play of ideas has proved opaque to our intellects makes the tetralogy fall short of being a perfect work of art.' (DC/WE,12)

In fact, there is more to the issue than Cooke suggests. The *Ring* is a hybrid, by which is meant a mixture of music and drama. Although the musical methodology was almost forced into existence in order to do justice to the vast drama as it emerged, the whole was not conceived as a unity. The story, as encapsulated by Rayner, and as its development has been deployed in Part 2, has so many facets, and sources of such diversity that it *required* some sort of new musical structure. Cooke asserts that the text is like 'a play of ideas' but that it is also 'opaque'; this implies that the ideas do not cohere. Questions about Siegfried and Wotan's betrayal of Siegmund leave puzzles that no amount of poring over text and sources remove. The music succeeds but the ambiguity with which we learn to watch and listen is not resolved. Music cannot do that. This ambiguity is not the same as that experienced with *Hamlet*. People discuss his last words before he dies: 'the rest is silence'. The words resonate but the meaning is not clear. There is something unexplained as the curtain falls, and the audience finds that this is as it should be. With the *Ring* there seems is an ongoing attempt to explain: the moral issues are thrust forward but no conclusion can be reached.

The range of the story and its hybrid nature are intractable, which may explain how, nine years after the spoken introduction to the LPs, Cooke had got no further than the first half of the first part of his projected work. No evidence exists that his musical analysis moved beyond what we can hear in the two existing CDs. It may well have been that had Cooke lived on it would have taken a long time to complete the book as envisaged. [D] Moreover, it is likely that the result would have overwhelmed the reader.

[D] Cooke's immeasurably vast task can remind us of William Ashton Ellis's intention to translate and then to expand upon an existing biography of Wagner by Carl Glasenapp. Volume 1 appeared in 1900 and, with prodigious labour, five more large volumes appeared in the

No one has attempted it since. In the intervening 40 years, the only effort has been by Warren Darcy in his 1992 study of *Das Rheingold* and even in this, the simplest of the four operas, he makes little attempt to trace the psychological drama.

There are pitfalls for anyone who tries to use the music to explain matters that the poem cannot resolve. It is salutary to recall that Wagner was critical of composers when they used music to overcome weaknesses in the plot, such as Weber and Berlioz, in *Benvenuto Cellini*. (All we know about *Les troyens* is that he could not make head nor tail of the libretto. He admired his music extremely.) More importantly, the spectator/listener can be sent out on a wild goose chase. No one has pointed this out as amusingly and brutally than Sir Denis Forman, a businessman with a flair for the arts.[E] *The Good Wagner Opera Guide* was published in 2000 when he was 82. In it he writes:

> A motto can be as short as two notes or can be stretched out like chewing gum . . . A motto can change its colour in a trice. All mottos are related to other mottos, say the Mottologists, indeed all mottos can trace their family tree back to the great Mother Motto, the chord of E flat with which the piece begins. Here a sceptic will suggest that with enough changes of gear, [such as one sees in films as the face of Dr Jekyll is transformed into that of Mr Hyde] you can transfer Winston Churchill's face into that of the Madonna, but when it's all over they still look different people. *Pop goes the Weasel* can be turned into the Grand March in *Aida* in ten easy stages but that doesn't mean the tunes have any real relationship. (DF/GWG,132/33)

The convergence of Wagner's natural development as a musician with Schopenhauer's views on music

To absorb or to be able to act quickly upon Schopenhauer's theory of music was unlikely. So we can assume that it did not impact upon the composition of *Die Walküre* Act III, which was completed in December 1854, three months after starting to read *The World as Will and Representation*. However, since the composition of *Siegfried* Act I began in the summer of 1856 we can *assume* that changes in the mode of composition from that date are a consequence of, or are at least related to, what the philosopher had to say.

Schopenhauer on music

The main principle behind Schopenhauer's philosophy can be found on Chapter 2. This is that the world one can see, hear and touch - the world of phenomena - is not

---

following eight years. But this sixth volume took him only as far as January 1859. The remaining 24 years which was to see the completion of *Tristan and Isolde*, the composition of *Siegfried* Act III, *Götterdämmerung*, *Die Meistersingers* and *Parsifal*, the move to Triebschen with Cosima and the work at Bayreuth were not touched upon. The author drowned in the currents of information that swirled around the composer and never progressed further. He died in 1919.

[E] In the 1950s he was Chairman of Granada Television. He loved all opera and was Deputy Chairman of the Royal Opera House from 1983 to 1991; he died in 2013 at the age of 95.

objectively real. They are the observable manifestations of one single unobservable entity - the noumenon. This entity is also the 'place' from which every living thing has emerged and to which it returns after death (p.179/80).

The fourth major aspect relevant to the *Ring* is music, which is akin to, part of the noumenon. All arts other than music do indeed communicate something beyond the mere phenomena of sight and sound. A painting is often a revelatory representation of a visible thing. At a performance of *Hamlet,* the words, gestures and acting skills of the actors (all phenomena) represent particular interaction between people. Both may offer insights; for the picture it may be the nature of light, for *Hamlet* a deeper awareness of the complexity of human relationships. These insights lie behind the phenomena we take in and Schopenhauer saw this as a *mediation* between the phenomenon and the noumenon. The former may be thought to give us an indirect glimpse of the latter. Music, however, does not represent anything in the phenomenal world; it connects directly with the noumenon itself.

> Music, since it . . . is independent of the phenomenal world, positively ignores it, could, to a certain extent still exist if there were no world at all. (AS/WWR1, 262)

> Music . . . never expresses the phenomenon, but only the inner nature, the in-itself of every phenomenon, the will itself. Therefore music does not express this or that definite pleasure, this or that affliction, pain, sorrow, horror, gaiety, merriment, or peace of mind, but joy, pain, sorrow, horror, gaiety, merriment, peace of mind *themselves* . . . without the motives for them. (AS/WWR1, 261)

> Music expresses the metaphysical to everything physical in the world, the thing-in-itself to every phenomenon. Accordingly we could just as well call the world embodied music as embodied will. (AS/WWR1, 262)

Absorbing and agreeing with this would have put paid to any idea of parity between words and music. From now on the words were to be subservient to the music. Wagner produced two theoretical essay following the period when he read such as the above by Schopenhauer and it is in his long 1871 essay 'Beethoven' that the *volte face* finds concrete expression:

> Through the experience that a piece of music loses nothing of its character when even the most diverse texts are set to it, it becomes clear that the relation of music to poetry is a sheer illusion: for it transpires that when words are set to music, it is not the poetic thought which penetrates the mind . . . but at most the mood that thought aroused in the musician when it inspired him to music. A union of music and poetry must therefore constantly result in such a subordination of the latter that it is only surprising to see how our great German poets have again and again pondered and even tried for a union of the two arts. (RW/PW5, 104)

Nothing could be clearer: the theory within *Opera and Drama* is to be jettisoned. From *Siegfried,* the composition of which began in summer 1856, and through all the operas that followed up to and including *Parsifal,* the music progressively pushes into the foreground. This is perceived in the increasing number of long orchestral passages, in the manner in which the melody bends the verse to its will and in the heavier 'presence' of the orchestra throughout. In consequence, almost all new motifs are orchestral, and there is a big increase in the use of them. This not only in quantity but also in density; on many occasions they crowd in and overlap each other so that sometimes three motifs can occur simultaneously in the same bar.

Wagner did not shy away from Schopenhauer, as we can read in the first paragraph of the extract from another long 1860 essay - *Music of the Future* - the first theoretical expression of this break in style. For clarity I have assembled a summary of Wagner's argument culled from a modern translation. All the words are the composer's but there is some slight reordering. He starts with a reference to Beethoven (whom he saw, of course, as his musical forebear) and moves on (at the italicised 'rational thinking') to a passage that could have been written by Schopenhauer. This allusion to Beethoven is eleven years in advance of the essay *Beethoven* referred to above.

> The Beethoven symphony . . . has brought into the world something the like of which has never been known before in the art of any period or people . . . The listener is riveted by a purely musical expression of unprecedented length and inconceivably manifold nuances; with a power no other art can equal it stirs his inmost being. And this language is governed by an ordering principle of such freedom and daring that . . . *rational thinking*, governed by relations of cause and effect, appear to have no foothold on it whatsoever. Such a symphony, therefore, cannot but have the appearance of a revelation from another world. In truth, it does relate the phenomena of the world to each other in a way completely different from the normal laws of logic.
>
> In the drama as I conceive it the orchestra's relation to the stage action will . . . embody the harmony which alone makes possible the melody's specific expression; it will maintain the melody in a state of uninterrupted flow so that the motives will be able to work with the maximum effect upon the audience's feelings. To give you a final idea of this great melody which I visualise spanning the whole idea of a music drama . . . I cannot resist drawing your attention to the structure of a Beethoven first movement. *What we see is a dance – melody split into its tiniest fragments, each one of which – it may amount to no more than a couple of notes – is made interesting and significant by a pervasive rhythm or significant harmony. The fragments are continually being reassembled in different formations – coalescing in a logical succession* (author's italics) . . . And the outcome, never before achieved, of this procedure was the expansion of a melody, through the richly varied development of all the motives it contained, into a continuous large-scale piece, which in itself constituted a single, perfectly coherent melody. (*Music of the Future*, translated by Robert Jacobs. From pp 27,38,40 in *Three Wagner Essays*, Eulenberg Books, 1979)

Wagner as a 'symphonic' composer of operas?

It is a commonplace that Wagner's compositional technique became more 'symphonic' from Siegfried Act III inwards. The best way to look at this is to examine the italicised sentences in the previous quotation. The italicised words point to Wagner's technique of breaking substantive motives down into fragments and perhaps just using just one of these as cells from which sustained passages can be constructed. This approach also applies to the use of compositional motifs that can hold together an entire passage of music. The first movement of Beethoven's 5th Symphony is the classic and universally recognized example of this innovation: the vast bulk of the movement stems from the famous opening motto theme. The purpose here is not to compare the skill of Wagner in this respect to that of Beethoven but to alert the reader to instances, particularly in the last two operas, where the technique can be seen, and to the numerous passages in *Die Walküre* where compositional motifs (the 'tiniest fragments' as described in the essay) drive the structure. In the composition of *Siegfried* in 1856 Wagner revels in his skilfulness: small scale in the prelude to Act II where he speeds up one motif fourfold and turns it – just once – into a violent sequence.

We will return to this shortly but can establish now that when Wagner called Beethoven to his aid as an explanation of the *Ring* music he was not thinking of sonata form developed in the Viennese Classical Style, as brought to maturity by Haydn and also used by Beethoven. The *Siegfried Idyll* has a substantial design with aspects of sonata form but the pattern is nothing like the structures that are found in the *Ring*. Wagner made this explicit in an article in the *Bayreuther Blätter* (the house journal for the Festival Theatre) shortly after the first production.

> To be an artwork as music, the new form of dramatic music must possess the unity of the symphonic movement . . . This unity centres upon a web of themes, which contrast, complete, re-shape, divorce and intertwine with one another as in a symphonic movement; *yet here, the requirements of the dramatic action dictate the laws of separation and combination.* (Quoted in MB/TBLF,50 – italics added by author)

Mark Berry, in his book, says that Wagner's claim represents only a slight exaggeration.

Nevertheless, something has driven people to make extreme cases that place strictly musical forms at the heart of the mature dramas. Alfred Lorenz's overly detailed explorations are now widely disregarded. Sir Donald Tovey implied but never gave detail that the 'music drama consisted essentially in giving music the same time scale as that of the drama' (Tovey, *The form of music*, 131) and suggested that *Tristan und Isolde* was organised on the same principles as a Beethoven symphony. Joan Peyser wrote the following in 1971:

> The affinity between Wagner and Beethoven becomes clear. Despite the fact that Wagner wrote operas, his focus was centred on what was played by the orchestra - not what was sung on stage . . . His musical fabric is a complex one, held together by *leitmotifs* which not only identify particular characters and situations but unify purely musical texture in the way the thematic material unifies a symphony. (JP/NM, 72)

Neither of these two distinguished writers would contemplate a proposition that was untrue but, notwithstanding, the case is over-stretched. The answer may lie in the italicised portion of the previous abstract from *Beethoven*. The reassembling of fragments is what happens in all classical first movement development sections; this is what does happen from *Siegfried* Act III onwards. Wagner was not interested in form for its own sake. One place, for example, where you think it might be found is in Siegfried's Funeral Music. He would have been perfectly capable of constructing a sustained threnody, on a smaller scale but in the same vein as Beethoven and Elgar in their 3rd and 2nd symphonies respectively: witness the prelude to *Lohengrin*. But he needs to tell a story and stories do not fit into musical forms. So what we get is akin to a 'processional': motifs, punctuated with ever more vociferous renditions of the *death* compositional motif.

There are gradations in this. Carolyn Abbate points to passages in *Götterdämmerung* which contain, 'symphonic stretches in which the musical idea overwhelms the meaning of the text.' (CA/AO,105) Long passages of music hang together so marvellously and so freshly that we listen to that and barely notice the text to which it is set. The majesty of Wagner's conception absorbs whatever text is used. Thus comes true what the composer is to write in 1871: 'a piece of music loses nothing of its character when even the most diverse texts are set to it.'

For is not this matter already dead in the water? The relationship between words and music was seriously on the move in Wagner's conception of dramatic music before he read and absorbed Schopenhauer. Sections in *Die Walküre* Act I, to follow, reveal that 'the musical idea overwhelms the meaning of the text'. Such is Scene 7 (p.308), where compositional motifs indicative of Sieglinde's sexual arousal make superfluous the words she sings: we would not notice if they were a listing from a telephone directory. Bryan Magee writes thus of the close of Act III of the same opera.

> The whole scene is launched by an orchestral introduction . . . of a sonic magnificence unparalleled in the history of music up to that time. Nowhere . . . before has the orchestra, by itself, stormed the heavens and opened them up like this . . . From then on, for the rest of the opera, the orchestra pursues an impassioned course of its own alongside the voice, on one occasion taking up from the voice one of the most beautiful and sustained melodies of the *Ring*, one that will come back in purely orchestral form in a later opera to heart-stopping effect. (BM/WP,197)

The 'heart-stopping melody' referred to is the culmination, the goal of Wotan's farewell. Fifteen years later, Roger Scruton has this to say on this self-same episode.

> This massive statement [of the *brünnhilde's sleep* motif (p.245)] at once assumes enormous significance, as the motif is repeated, suitably stretched, at each inversion . . . so as to erect a great pillar of triadic harmony. We begin to hear the motif's potential. It can be expanded and compressed so as to accommodate different [series of chords] of the same harmony; it can be adapted . . . to form an accompanying figure, and a figure, moreover, capable of moving smoothly between keys. Above the motif, sounding softly on violas and cellos, Wotan now sings his farewell, which shifts back and forth between C major and E (minor and major) taking in neighbouring keys along the way . . . Wotan himself [is] reduced by

16.5 Wotan's farewell to Brünnhilde

Brünnhilde's purity to a subject in his own sovereign space, both of them outlined by the chromatic melody against the shifting tonal background, in which the destines of Siegfried and Brünnhilde are subtly and pre-consciously entwined. (RS/RT,165)

Carolyn Abbate writes: 'For Wagner, the symphonic was a continuous spinning-out of never-ceasing thematic webs' rather than 'a work that is densely interconnected, that evolves organically to its final moments, that is comprehensible as pure music.' (CA/AO,115) He wanted to use what we can call Beethoven's 'musical cell' device to construct episodes, each densely formed from a precise number of such cells, some long and some short. Typically, these last for periods between 15 and 100 bars and extend up to periods of four minutes. They depend upon the imponderable miracle that lies at the heart of the *Ring* motifs, namely the manner in which one motif is able to conjoin with almost any other. Of the motifs, of all types, as listed in the next chapter, only a handful defy such conjunction.

The chapters which then follow, one on each of the four operas, include examples of how this is done and trace the development of the techniques as the number of motifs increased alongside the growing complexity of the drama. A key aspect of this is the ability (due to the continual development of the technique) and the means (the growth in available material) to pile motifs, one onto another, in counterpoint and by conjunction. This will explore the changes in the nature of the drama, as commonly perceived by all who come to know the work, from comparative simplicity to overt complexity. These four chapters, one per opera, could be overwhelmed however, if every nuance of compositional skill were mentioned. It is in Act III of *Siegfried* that the style becomes fully established. Readers might, therefore, like to take an early glance at pp.375, 376, 377. Within these three pages are the technique described as 'molecular' growth. Fragments of motifs - cells, as described by Wagner on p.233 - burgeon to the degree that a listener may know the music is related to a motif but cannot consciously see how.

Beethoven's methodology is the engine that matters and this is in accord with Schopenhauer's view that music was not only the preeminent art form but was also different in kind and of profounder essence than all the other arts. We can perceive that the notion of a parity between words and music was losing its grip. Wagner may quickly have realised what we can now see, that words (save some by such as Shakespeare) have meanings too precise, that this precision circumscribes the emotional meanings attached to the music associated with them, and that the use of *leitmotiven,* the welter of compositional motifs which emerge from *Die Walküre* onwards, and his own prodigious growth as a composer - all provide the composer with means of expression hitherto undiscovered. Nevertheless, a word must be found to describe the musical style and it would surely be perverse not to label it *symphonic*? So that is how it will be in the following chapters.

◇ ◇ ◇ ◇ ◇

The *Ring* motifs

First, a point of style. All motifs are in italics and without an initial capital. This is to distinguish them within the text, whether they appear as the first word in a sentence or not, from the character/object to which they apply.

The music of any episode that concentrates on a particular aspect of the drama will employ motifs that relate to that aspect. Accordingly, the names given to each motif are designed to reflect their role and purpose in the drama. Thus what have commonly been called 'sword' and 'spear' are here called *wotan's sword* and *will-to-power*. The reason is simple: a sword is just a sword but *wotan's sword* suggests a beneficent goal which Nothung may help Wotan to gain; a spear is just a spear but *will-to-power* is an attribute of character held by both Wotan and Hagen. This last continues to assert itself throughout *Götterdämmerung*, when Wotan is no longer a player in the drama.

The names given to each motif are designed to reflect their role and purpose. The aim is to replace artefacts and precise situations by human goals or states of mind. This assists the pulling of each motif toward others that chime with it: often a Scene or episode will be filled with just two or three motifs that relate to each other dramatically or psychologically. There are additionally 59 compositional motifs which are designed and used by Wagner to cement shorter sections together. These tend to come and to go, often never to return. They function powerfully when they are used.

Many listings dispense with names for a large number of motifs and give only number. The purpose here is to aid comprehension of the drama as it goes along. Understanding the music is helped by the ability to follow the *leitmotiven* as they emerge and develop, and for this names are needed.

Accordingly, this chapter offers two separate listings. The first gives the motifs in the order they appear in the score and the second, which follows, reorders these alphabetically. *The former listing uses the Act and Scene divisions as designated by the composer and not those used in this study.*

With all such naming systems, however, there is no fool-proof method of making this uniform and each reader might think of better solutions! And let no one forget that the composer wanted people to *feel* the drama rather than *think about* it. But – alas – what else can we sometimes do!

THE *RING* MOTIFS

The motifs in order of appearance

Das Rheingold Scene 1

M1 *nature*

M2 *life energy*

M2A *river movement* (basic)

This is an expansion of *life energy* (M2) spread over the same four bars.

M3 *rhinedaughters*

CM1 *river movement* (1)

This is M2A, speeded up.

CM2 *clumsy alberich*

Only appears here and in *Siegfried* Act 2

CM3 *seductive allure*

M4 *rhinegold*

M5 *force of the gold*

As the action progresses we hear more baleful tones.

M6 *life choice*

Nur wer der Min - ne Macht ver - sagt, nur wer der Lie - be Lust ver - sagt
He who the lure of love for swears, he who re - jects all forms of love

CM4 *alberich's rage*

THE *RING* MOTIFS

CM5 *river movement (2)*

Das Rheingold Scene 2

M7 *ring*

M8 (A to D) *valhalla*

A   B

C   D

M9 *domestic life*

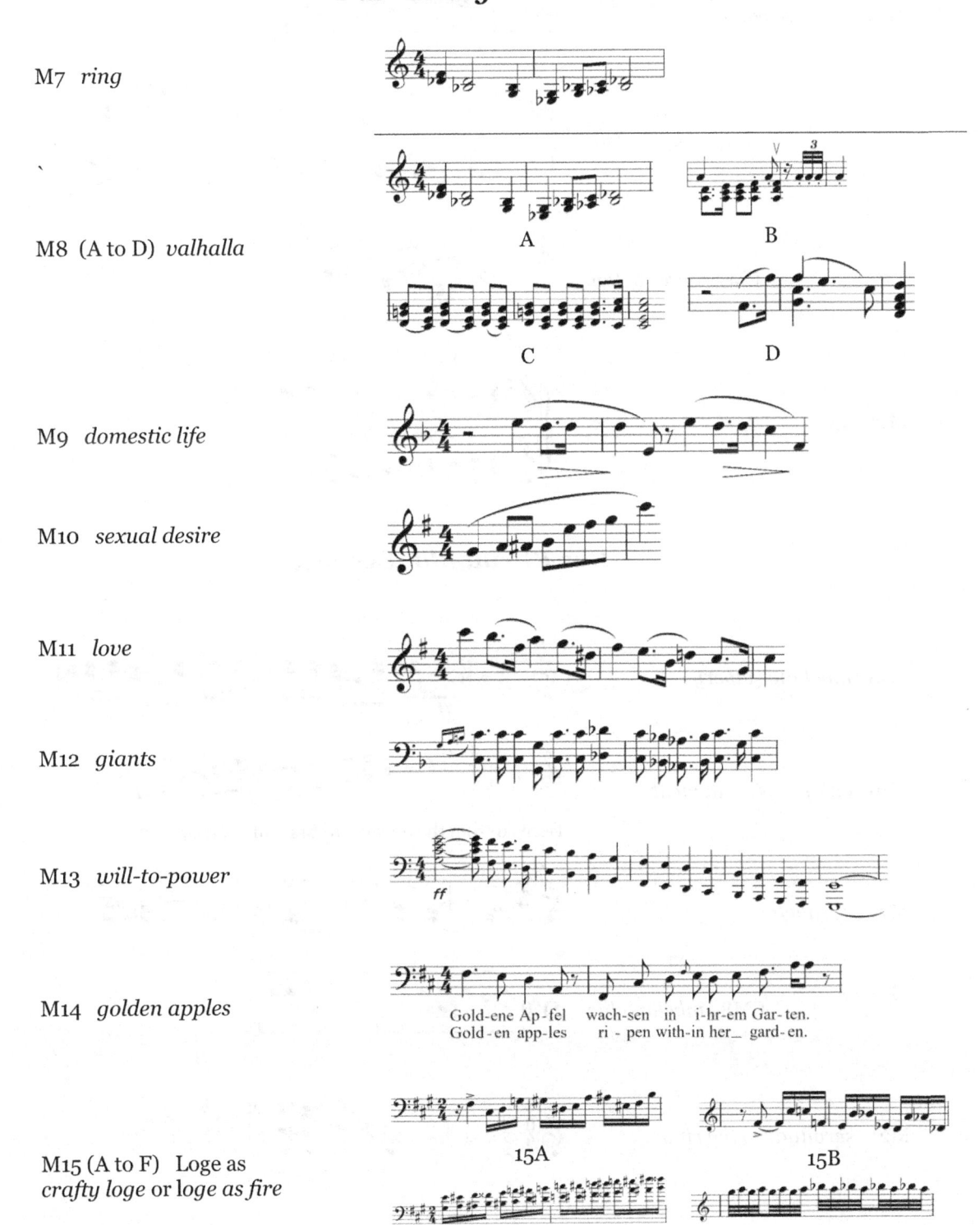

M10 *sexual desire*

M11 *love*

M12 *giants*

M13 *will-to-power*

M14 *golden apples*

Gold-ene Ap-fel   wach-sen in   i-hr-em Gar-ten.
Gold-en app-les   ri-pen with-in her gard-en.

M15 (A to F) Loge as *crafty loge* or *loge as fire*

15A   15B

THE *RING* MOTIFS

crafty loge or *loge as fire* — 15C, 15D

M16 *core life value* — 15E, 15F

CM6 *natural life*

CM7 *fierce action*

M17 *woe* (FRICKA: We-he! We-he!)

Das Rheingold Scene 3

M18 *nibelung slavery*

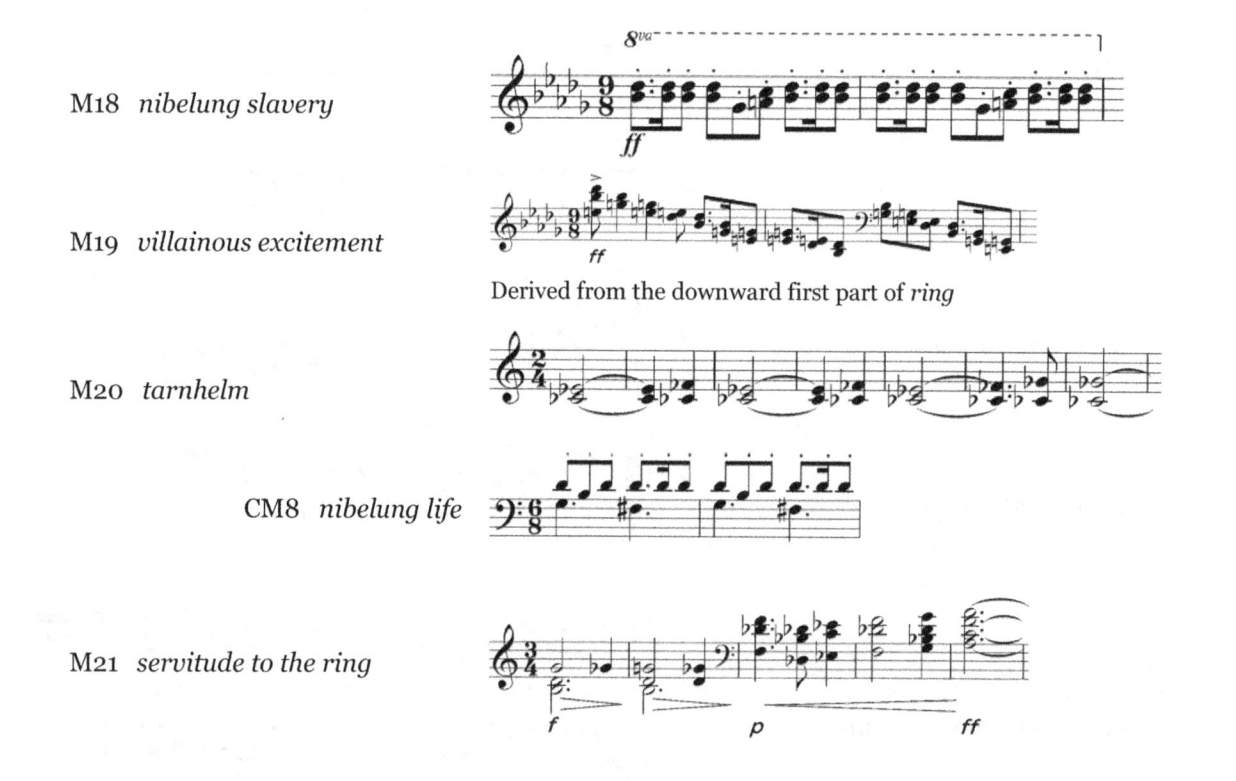

M19 *villainous excitement*

Derived from the downward first part of *ring*

M20 *tarnhelm*

CM8 *nibelung life*

M21 *servitude to the ring*

240

THE *RING* MOTIFS

M22 *hoard*

M23 *dragon*

Das Rheingold Scene 4

M24 *malice*

M25 *curse*

Wie durch Fluch er mir ge rieth, ver flucht sei die-ser Ring!
Since a curse gained it for me, a curse lies on this Ring!

M26 *erda*

M27 *downfall*

M28 *storm call*

M29 *rainbow*

M30 *wotan's sword*

CM9 *rhinedaughters' lament*

THE *RING* MOTIFS

Die Walküre Act I

M31 *siegmund*
M32 *sieglinde*

Siegmund, bars 1/2 & 3/4; answered by Sieglinde, bars 2 & 4

M33 *love's bond*

M34 *volsung empathy*

M35 *hunding*

M36 *fated volsungs*

CM10 *sieglinde comes alive*

CM11 *volsung battle cry*

CM12 *sieglinde's passion (1)* The first bar is the accompaniment – calm and steady – to the *Wintersturme* love song. The second is that which immediately follows, in which Sieglinde takes up the riff which is made urgent by the insertion of rests.

CM13 *sieglinde's passion (2)*

THE *RING* MOTIFS

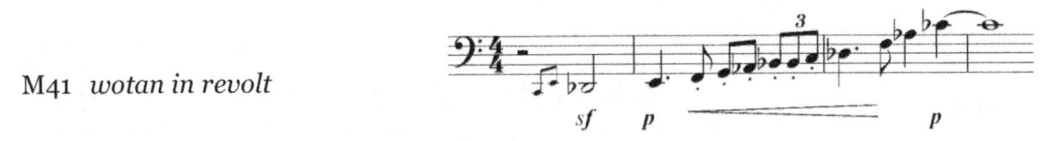

CM14 siegmund's passion

O sus-ses-te Won-ne!

CM15 naming of Siegmund

Die Walküre Act II

M37 valkyr

M38 war cry

Ho-jo-to-ho!

M39 conflict

M40 wotan's balked will

M41 wotan in revolt

CM16 despair

M42 wotan's struggle

CM17 brünnhilde pleads for siegmund

THE *RING* MOTIFS

M43 *wotan's rage*

CM18 *sieglinde's anguish*

M44 *destiny*

M45 *lament of death*

CM19 *siegmund's defiance*

CM20 *siegmund's scorn*

Die Walküre   Act III

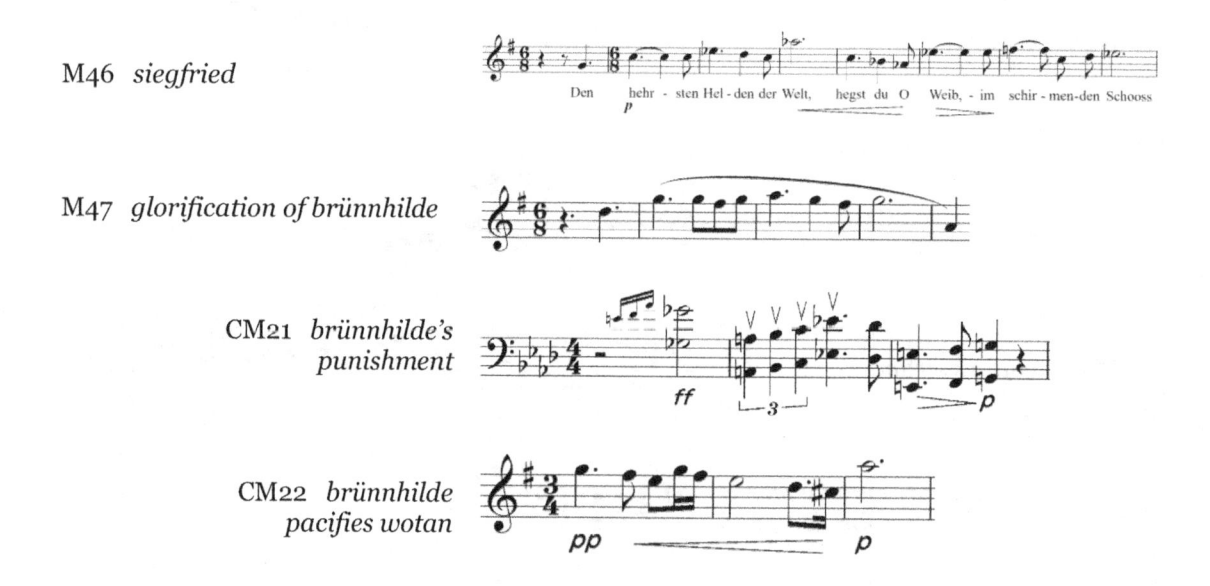

M46 *siegfried*

M47 *glorification of brünnhilde*

CM21 *brünnhilde's punishment*

CM22 *brünnhilde pacifies wotan*

THE *RING* MOTIFS

M48 *brünnhilde's purity*

War es so schmae-lich, was ich ver - brach, das mein Ver - brech-chen so schmae-lich du be - strafst?
Was it so shame - ful, that I have done, that such de - grad - ing an end should be my fate?

CM23 *brünnhilde pleads for herself (1)*

CM24 *brünnhilde pleads for herself (2)*

M49 *magic sleep*

M50 *brünnhilde's sleep*

Siegfried Act I

M51 *scheming*

M52 *horn call*

M53 *youthful energy*

CM25 *mime as nibelung*

M54 *longing for love*

M55 *siegfried's mission*

THE RING MOTIFS

M56 *wanderer*

M57 *clever mime*

CM26 *filing*
CM27 *bellows*

CM28 *cooling steel*

CM29 *mime and siegfried thinking*

CM30 *hammering*

Siegfried Act II

M58 *fafner as dragon*

M59 *wood bird*

CM31 *fafner's obsequy*

CM32 *wheedling mime (1)*

THE *RING* MOTIFS

CM33 *wheedling mime (2)*

CM34 *wheedling mime (3)*

CM35 *joyous agitation*

Siegfried Act III

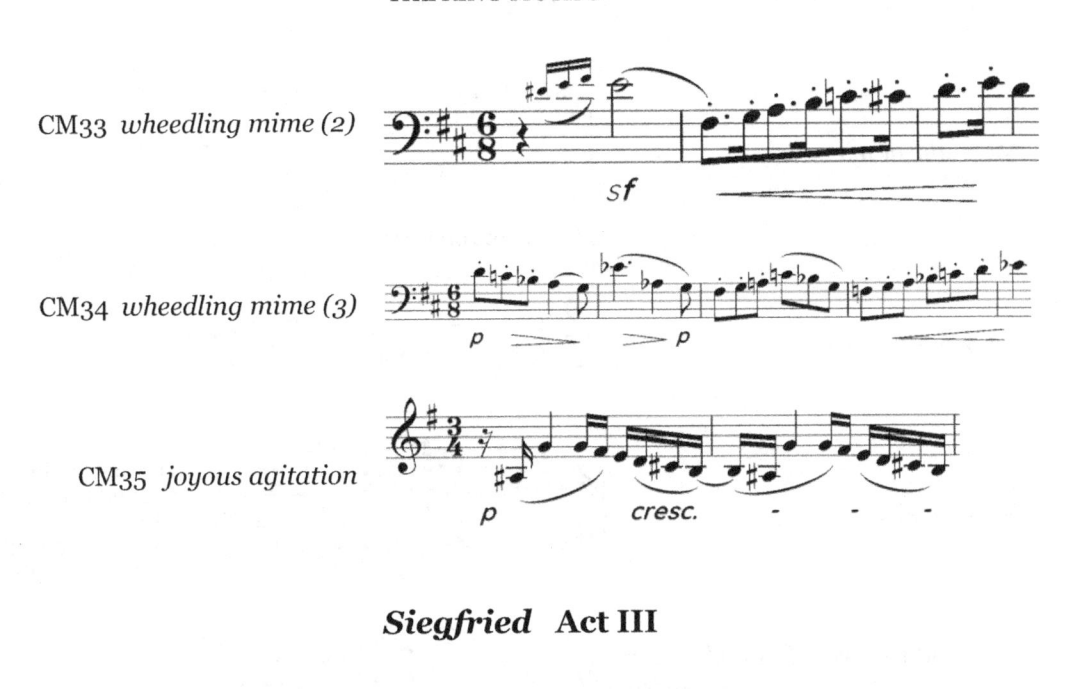

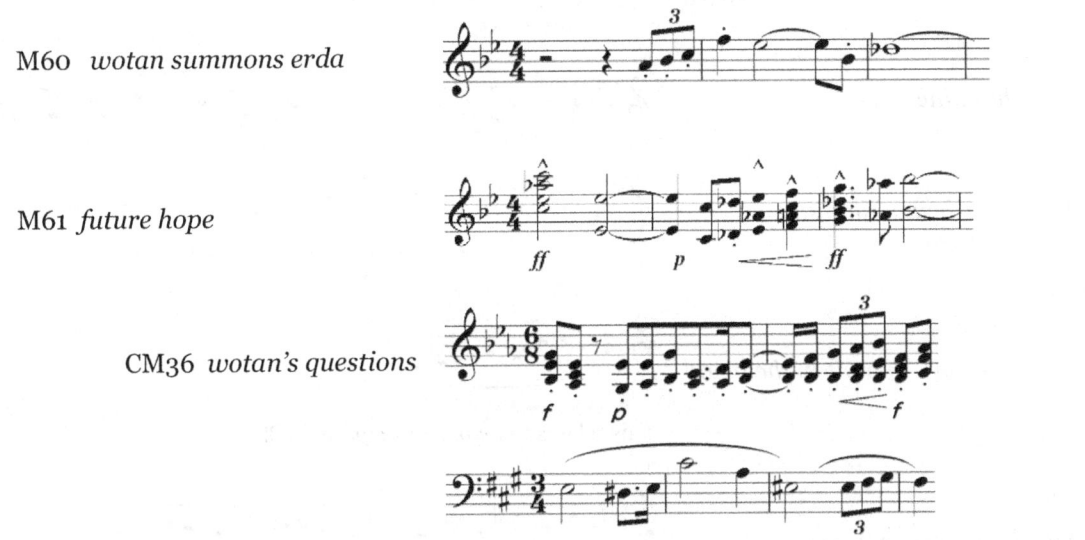

M60 *wotan summons erda*

M61 *future hope*

CM36 *wotan's questions*

CM37 *volsung bond (1)*

First appears in S1, when Siegfried wonders about his mother. Is prominent in S3.2 - Siegfried's Scene with Wotan - and in agitation when he first sees the woman Brünnhilde. Example 21.36 in the text is more extensive, thereby showing the triplet dominance.

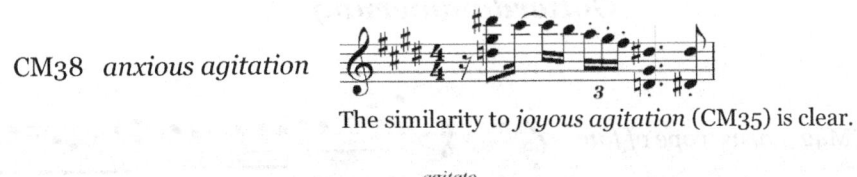

CM38 *anxious agitation*

The similarity to *joyous agitation* (CM35) is clear.

CM39 *volsung bond (2)*

THE *RING* MOTIFS

M62 *the dawn*

Motif in the orchestra

M63 *heroic love*

M64 *love's ecstasy*

The motif is in the treble clef and below, in the bass, is *siegfried*. This type of counter-point is to become more evident.

CM40 *brünnhilde's love for siegfried*

M65 *happiness*

M66 *how brünnhilde saw siegfried*

O Sieg — fried, Herr - lich - er Hort — der Welt!
O Sieg — fried, glor - ri-ous man, wealth of the world!

CM41 *tumult in the blood*

This relates to *joyous anticipation* (CM 35)

M67 *laughing at death*

This relates to *youthful energy* (M53)

Götterdämmerung Act 1

CM42 *norns' rope of fate*

M68 *world ash tree*

THE *RING* MOTIFS

M69 *power of the gods*

M70 *womanly brünnhilde*

M71 *manly Siegfried*

M72 *victorious love*

CM43 *siegfried's energy*

CM44 *treachery*

M73 *the gibich hagen*

M74 *gibichungs*

M75 *hagen*

CM45 *wholesome gutrune*

M76 *deception*

M77 *potion*

THE *RING* MOTIFS

M78 *friendship*

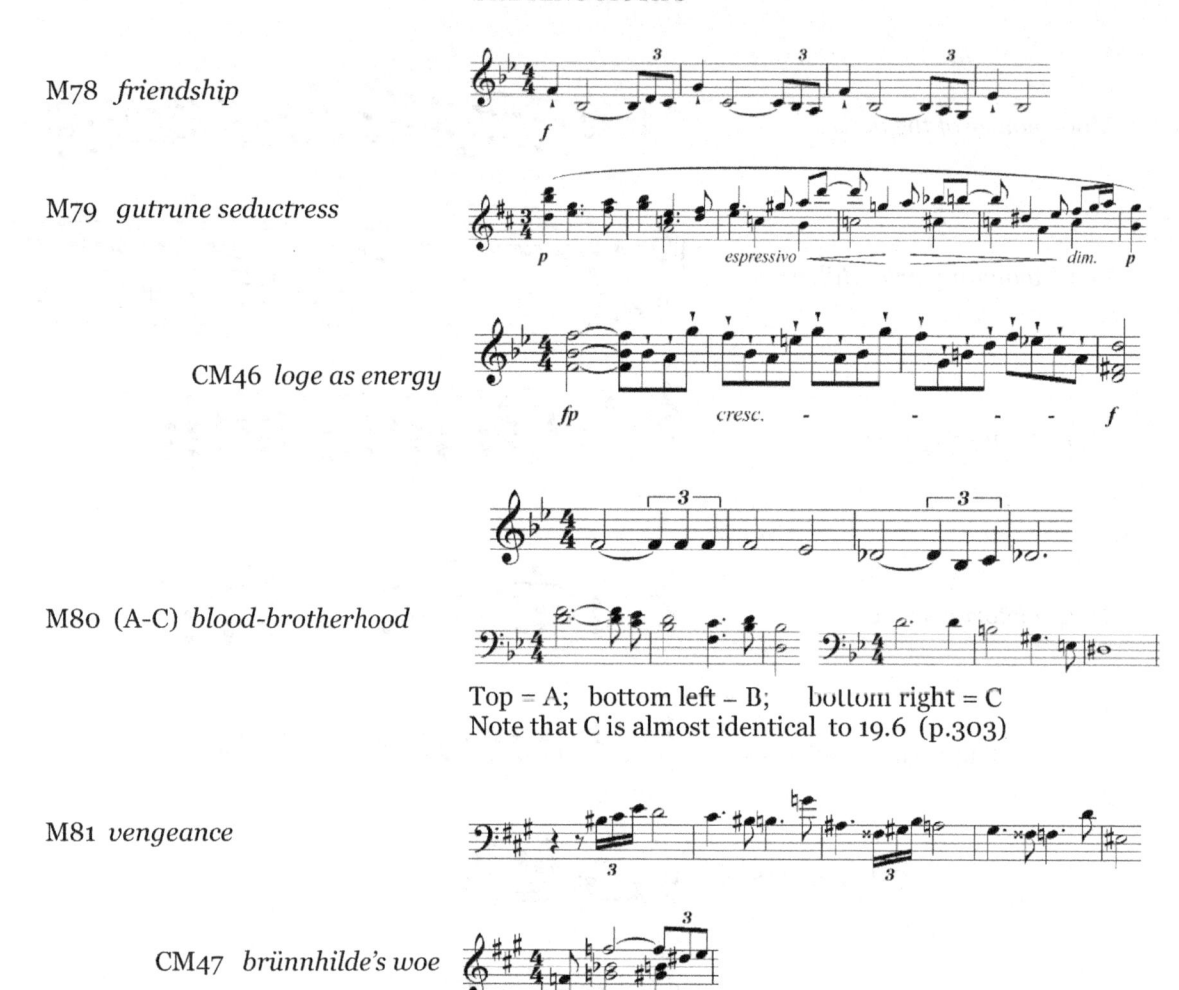

M79 *gutrune seductress*

CM46 *loge as energy*

M80 (A-C) *blood-brotherhood*

Top = A; bottom left = B; bottom right = C
Note that C is almost identical to 19.6 (p.303)

M81 *vengeance*

CM47 *brünnhilde's woe*

Götterdämmerung Act II

CM48 *siegfried & gutrune*

CM49 *siegfried's evasion*

Motif in the lower line; above is a reference to tarnhelm.

CM50 *vassals # 1*

THE *RING* MOTIFS

CM51 *vassals #2*

M82 *death oath*

CM52 *siegfried soothes gunther*

CM53 *brünnhilde's lament*

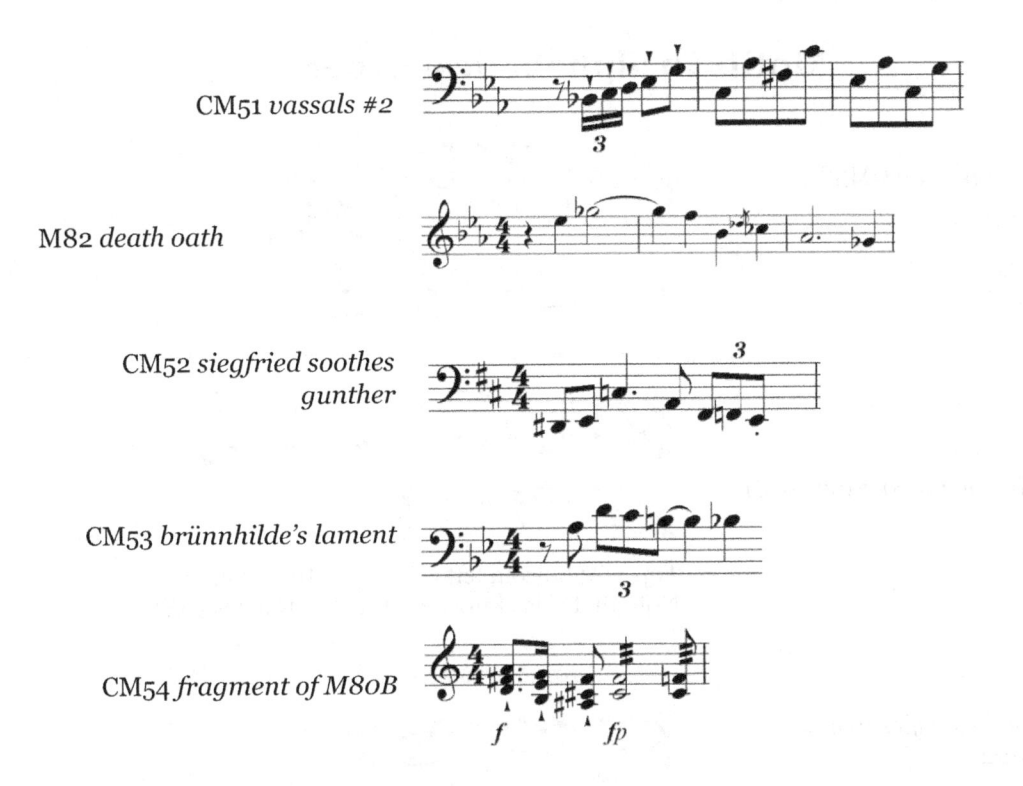

CM54 *fragment of M80B*

Götterdämmerung Act III

CM55 *mature rhinedaghters (1)*

CM56 *mature rhinedaughters (2)*

CM57 *siegfried's imp*

CM58 *death*

CM 59 *recollections of love*

THE *RING* MOTIFS

Motifs in alphabetical order

anxious agitation CM38

bellows CM27

blood-brotherhood M80 (A-C)

Top = A; bottom left = B   bottomright =
Note that C is almost identical to 19.6 (p.303)

brünnhilde pacifies wotan CM22

brünnhilde pleads for herself (1) CM23

brünnhilde pleads for herself (2) CM24

brünnhilde pleads for siegmund CM17

brünnhilde's lament CM53

brünnhilde's love for siegfried CM40

brünnhilde's punishment CM21

brünnhilde's purity M48

THE *RING* MOTIFS

brünnhilde's sleep M50

brünnhilde's woe CM47

clever mime M57

clumsy alberich CM2

conflict M39

cooling steel CM28

core life value M16

curse M25

> Wie durch Fluch er mir gerieth, verflucht sei dieser Ring!
> Since a curse gained it for me, a curse lies on this Ring!

death CM58

death oath M82

deception M76

despair CM16

253

THE *RING* MOTIFS

destiny M44

domestic life M9

downfall M27

dragon M23

erda M26

fafner as dragon M58

fafner's obsequy CM31

fated volsungs M36

fierce action CM7

filing CM26

force of the gold M5

fragment of M80B CM54

THE *RING* MOTIFS

friendship M78

future hope M61

giants M12

gibichungs M74

glorification of brünnhilde M47

golden apples M14

Gold-ene Ap-fel wach-sen in i-hr-em Gar-ten.
Gold-en app-les ri-pen with-in her gard-en.

gutrune seductress M79

hagen M75

hammering CM30

happiness M65

heroic love M63

hoard M22

horn call M52

THE *RING* MOTIFS

how brünnhilde saw siegfried
M66

O Sieg___ fried, Herr - lich - er Hort___ der Welt!
O Sieg___ fried, glor - i - ous man, wealth of the world!

hunding M35

joyous agitation CM38

lament of death M45

laughing at death M67

life choice M6

Nur wer der Min - ne Macht ver - sagt, nur wer der Lie - be Lust ver - sagt
He who the lure of love for swears, he who re - jects all forms of love

life energy M2

loge as fire
and
crafty loge
M15 (A to F)

15A   15B

15C   15D

15E   15F

loge as energy CM46

256

THE *RING* MOTIFS

longing for love M54

love M11

love's bond M33

love's ecstasy M64

magic sleep M49

malice M24

manly siegfried M71

mature rhinedaughters (1) CM55

mature rhinedaughters (2) CM56

mime and siegfried thinking CM29

THE *RING* MOTIFS

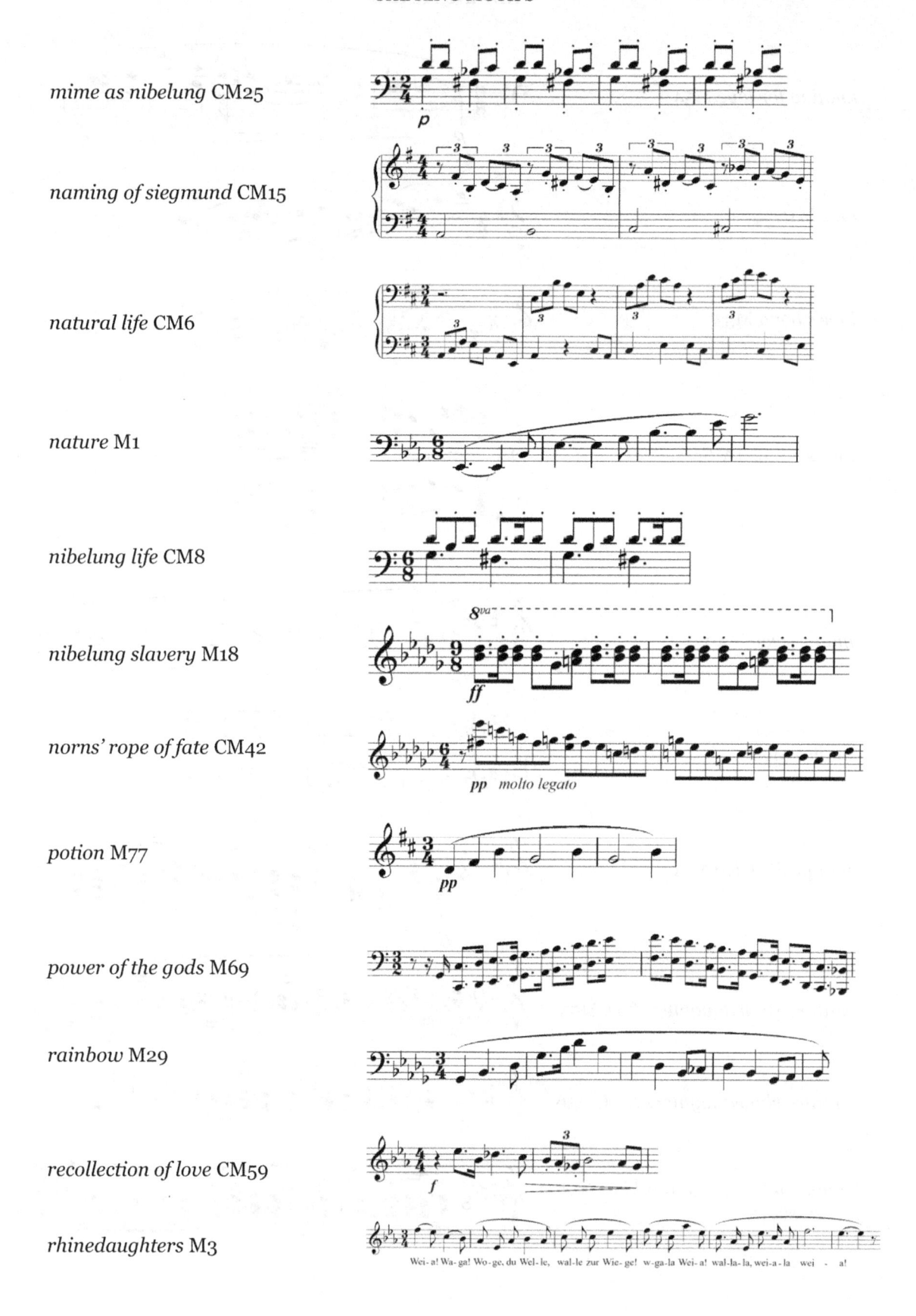

mime as nibelung CM25

naming of siegmund CM15

natural life CM6

nature M1

nibelung life CM8

nibelung slavery M18

norns' rope of fate CM42

potion M77

power of the gods M69

rainbow M29

recollection of love CM59

rhinedaughters M3

Wei- a! Wa- ga! Wo- ge, du Wel- le, wal- le zur Wie- ge! w-ga-la Wei- a! wal-la-la, wei-a-la wei - a!

THE *RING* MOTIFS

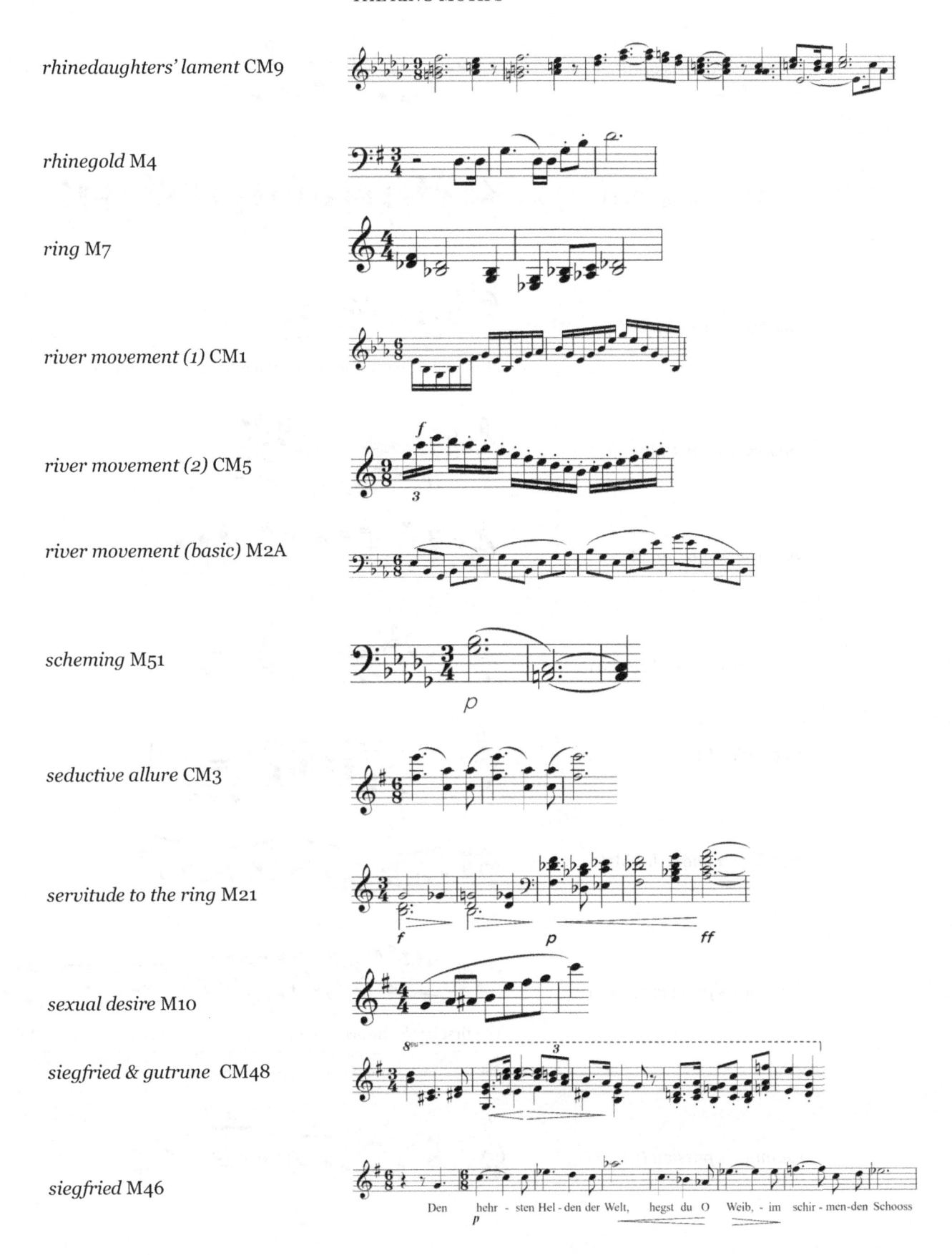

rhinedaughters' lament CM9

rhinegold M4

ring M7

river movement (1) CM1

river movement (2) CM5

river movement (basic) M2A

scheming M51

seductive allure CM3

servitude to the ring M21

sexual desire M10

siegfried & gutrune CM48

siegfried M46

Den hehr - sten Hel - den der Welt, hegst du O Weib, - im schir - men-den Schooss

THE *RING* MOTIFS

siegfried soothes gunther CM52

siegfried's energy CM43

dolce e stacatto

siegfried's evasion CM49

Motif in the lower line; above is a reference to *tarnhelm*

siegfried's imp CM57

siegfried's mission M55

sieglinde comes alive CM10

sieglinde M32

sieglinde's anguish CM18

sieglinde's passion (1) CM12

The first bar is the accompaniment – calm and steady – to the *Wintersturme* love song. The second is that which immediately follows; Sieglinde takes up the riff which is made urgent by the insertion of rests.

sieglinde's passion (2) CM13

THE *RING* MOTIFS

siegmund M31

siegmund's defiance CM19

siegmund's passion CM14

O sus-ses-te Won-ne!

siegmund's scorn CM20

storm call M28

tarnhelm M20

the dawn M62

Heil dir, Son-ne! Heil dir, Tag!

Motif in the orchestra

the gibich hagen M73

treachery CM44

tumult in the blood CM41

valhalla M8 (A to D)

A B

C D

261

THE *RING* MOTIFS

valkyr M37

vassals #1 CM50

vassals #2 CM51

vengeance M81

victorious love M72

villainous excitement M19

volsung battle cry CM11

volsung bond (1) CM37

volsung bond (2) CM39

volsung empathy M34

wanderer M56

THE *RING* MOTIFS

war cry M38

wheedling mime (1) CM32

wheedling mime (2) CM33

wheedling mime (3) CM34

wholesome gutrune CM45

will-to-power M13

woe M17

womanly brünnhilde M70

wood bird M59

world ash tree M68

THE *RING* MOTIFS

wotan in revolt M41

wotan summons erda M60

wotan's balked will M40

wotan's questions CM36

wotan's rage M43

wotan's struggle M42

wotan's sword M30

youthful energy M53

◇ ◇ ◇ ◇ ◇

18

Das Rheingold

Describing the music of the *Ring*

Any rounded verbal description of music is an impossibly uphill task, and for obvious reasons. The impact of a melody or a harmony can be attempted but the thing itself cannot be examined. The drama in the *Ring* is constructed by the close connection between words, melody and harmony, and the musical part cannot avoid being presented in terms of the *leitmotiven* Wagner employs.

Occasionally a statement about the harmony employed can find a place, but this deadens the mind if not sparingly used. The author is not a musician but, even if he were and possessed of the knowledge of the late Deryck Cooke, the emotional impact of the music would quickly be lost by too much such technical detail.

But the point cannot be too strongly made that the *Ring* music is not just a succession of motifs. The motifs are miraculous in that almost all of them can combine with any other to create an evolving musical tissue. The hope in this study is that the names of the motifs may impact to the degree that hearing the music will slowly establish the relationship each motif, be it substantive or compositional, has with the others around it – and that this will promote understanding of the musical and dramatic tissue. An added dimension is the several examples where it can be shown how the said relationships actually make the drama.

The structure of the analysis in this and the following chapters

By breaking down Wagner's large structures into smaller units the dramatic construction is more clearly revealed. It is easiest to call these units 'Scenes', noting that the word is used differently by Wagner. In *Das Rheingold* he indicates a new scene where there is a new setting, making four in all. In the other operas the entrance or exit of a major character prompts a new scene. Here, however, in this chapter and in the three that follow, a different approach is taken to both those configurations. A Scene is taken to start and to stop in step with the flow of the dramatic and/or musical narrative. This methodology will see if and how the principles of dramatic construction as set forth in Chapter 3 apply in these new Scenes and also how these smaller units give strength to the larger structure in which each lies - generally in the Acts of each drama.

# # # # # #

DAS RHEINGOLD

Das Rheingold consists of seventeen such dramatic units, as in this table. Wagner's division into four scenes is shown in the left hand column.

W1	1	Alberich comes upon the Rhinedaughters as they sport around.	90 bars	
	2	The Rhinedaughters entice and tease him sexually.	189 bars	603 bars in total
	3	When Alberich realises this he becomes sexually aggressive. All stops as the sun lights up the Rhine Gold. Alberich learns of the power inherent in the Gold and the price to be paid.	239 bars	Average per Scene = 151 bars
	4	He takes it in order to forge the Ring.	85 bars	
W2	5	Wotan and Fricka argue about the events that have led to the building of Valhalla.	234 bars	
	6	Fasolt and Fafner arrive to claim Freia, are fobbed off by Wotan, who waits for Loge. Donner and Froh enter and face up to the giants.	189 bars	1103 bars in total
	7	Loge comes at last, deliberately procrastinates and thereby causes agitation.	135 bars	
	8	Loge tells everyone about Alberich's actions which stirs up bad instincts all round. The giants leave, telling Wotan that they will exchange Freia for the Gold.	325 bars	Average per Scene = 184 bars
	9	Loge sees the problem: with Freia gone the gods will fade. They must give up the Gold in order to keep her with them.	107 bars	
	10	Wotan descends to Nibelheim with Loge.	103 bars	
W3	11	Alberich torments Mime and takes the Tarnhelm from him.	170 bars	929 bars in total
	12	Loge wheedles information out of Mime.	186 bars	
	13	Alberich returns and brutally makes clear to Wotan and Loge what he intends.	300 bars	Average per Scene = 232 bars
	14	Loge tricks Alberich. He and Wotan capture and take him up from Nibelheim.	273 bars	
W4	15	Wotan steals Ring, Tarnhelm and Gold from Alberich, who curses whoever should hold the Ring.	412 bars	1106 bars in total
	16	Wotan is persuaded by Erda to hand over Ring, Tarnhelm and Gold to Fasolt and Fafner. Fafner kills his brother and leaves.	365 bars	Average per Scene = 364 bars
	17	The gods enter Valhalla.	329 bars	

Total = 3741 bars

The drama as a whole

The number of bars in each 'Scene' is to indicate comparative proportion within the whole opera - as with *Das Rheingold* - or Act - as in the subsequent operas. This works pretty well in the large. Like all good operatic composers, Wagner changed tempo from slow to quick and back to slow to give variety of texture and emphasis, thereby keeping the plot on the move. Thus proportion with regard to bars does broadly keep pace with proportion as to stage time.

In this opera the bar comparisons immediately give information about the dynamic of the plot. Wagner's tableau at the bottom of the Rhine has four Scenes, the average length of each being 151 bars. The second tableau, on high ground below Valhalla, has six Scenes with an average of 185 bars. The four Scenes of the Nibelheim tableau average 232 bars, and the three Scenes in the last of Wagner's tableaux - back on the mountain again - average 364 bars each. Wagner's delineation of *Vorabend* tells us that this is 'the evening before' the actual drama; it sets the scene. The increase in the average duration of the Scenes over the four stages of the plot - from 151 bars to 189 to 226 to 364 - indicates the growing complexity of the drama. At the beginning the matter is simple: sexual frustration further warps the behaviour of an already warped person. Complexity slowly grows thereafter, one matter at a time, but the plot thickens in the three Scenes in which the giants are on stage. In Nibelheim the expanse of the drama grows to give room for exposition of the horror within Alberich's intentions and, in the final three Scenes (15-17), all strands of the story come together and the average length of each episode is almost twice as long as those that concerned the previous squabble between gods and giants.

Scenes 1-4 and 11-14 centre on Alberich; scenes 5-10 and 11-14 turn around Wotan and the gods. As described in Chapter 11 - *The invention of Alberich* - almost everything about him is manufactured by Wagner. The plot lines in the Scenes on the heights with the gods are a residue distilled from a large amount of material to be found in the eddas, and much that is relevant is to be found in Chapter 12 - *Wotan's Cosmos*. We will see if this impacts on Wagner's dramatic invention.

Briefly with regard to the overall structure. The four opening Scenes in the Rhine are obviously a prologue - a set up - for the whole, which is itself a prologue to the other three operas. The logical chronology is that Alberich grabs the Gold at about the same time that Wotan might have made the contract with Fasolt and Fafner for the construction of Valhalla: both dwarf and god seek increase in personal power at the expense of compassion. In Scene 5 - the argument between Wotan and Fricka - Wotan's position catches up with that of Alberich, so that Scene can also be seen as part of setting the original position for the whole drama. This starts in earnest, therefore, with the arrival of Fasolt and Fafner in Scene 6. From that moment the action moves rapidly towards Wotan's fateful decision to rescue Freia at all costs; one can assume that his willingness to use her as a bargaining chip was different in kind from previous *realpolitik* in which he had dabbled. However, with that decision made, Wotan now has to make good: the 'journey home' for him is that to Valhalla. The confrontation with Erda in Scene 16 is the crisis point where his better side wins out, and the way home is found.

Das Rheingold is distinct from the other operas by having no less than five orchestral episodes. In the above table, the famous prelude (137 bars) is excluded from Scene 1. Impressive as it may be - either as a means of setting the whole drama going, or as a graphic musical picture of river flow from deep down to the surface, or as a representation of either nature or creation (p.160), it does not connect with the action which follows, save for introducing the music that represents the flow of the Rhine. The core motifs which represent nature and the thrust behind it belong to the cycle as a whole. The other musical episodes do relate to the events that come before or after and are included in the analysis where the dramatic emphasis points.

# # # # # #

Scene 1: Alberich encounters the Rhinedaughters
[Schirmer: 5/3/1 to 12/1/5. Text from 'Weia, Waga!' to 'Lasst ihn ins kennen!']

18.1 *nature* **M1**
From this chord derives the rising shape of energy and such phenomena as the Rhinegold and the Rainbow Bridge.

Although the prelude does not relate dramatically to this Scene it contains two central motifs. Remarkably, the basic *nature* motif - from which so many others derive - makes only one additional appearance outside this prelude and then only surfaces again in *Götterdämmerung*. Westernhagen reveals that this seminal motif took some time to emerge. The opening interval of the first draft was not the fifth, as shown, but a third; the arpeggio started on C (rather than E♭) and proceeded upwards to E, G, C. Wagner's lift to the larger opening interval is 'the simplicity of genius' which transforms 'an ordinary sequence of notes [into] a living tonal shape'. (CvW/FR,58) By contrast to this rarity of appearance, *life energy* (M2) and the arpeggio *river movement (basic)* (M2A) with the rising chords spanning one rather than the two octaves of M1, spreads vigorously and in

life energy **M2**

18.2 *river movement (basic)* **M2A**
Each of the four bars fills out those in M2

various guises not only in this opera but in all four. It is here called *life energy* on account of the inherent rhythmic drive which is both part of nature and which is also much used when the going gets tough for an individual.

At the rise of the curtain Woglinde announces herself and her two sisters, Wellgunde and Flosshilde, with the *rhinedaughters* motif. The melody of this song (M3) stays in the mind although it is seldom heard. In this Scene we hear it (or part of it) four times; thereafter twice in Scene 2 and then not at all until the very end of *Götterdämmerung.*

This first Scene is very short, the point being that the story starts in the next and Wagner wants to get to that moment quickly. So the Rhinedaughters gaily disport in the water, Alberich climbs out of a cleft and wants to make acquaintance. The music is fluid when surrounding the water sprites and jerky as it mirrors Alberich's ungainly stumbles in the water. The first compositional sketch gives detailed movements for these sprites as Alberich stumbles after them; right from the start, stage action was in Wagner's mind as he composed. A motif representing flowing water - *river movement (1)* - comes to the fore. This first appeared in the prelude but was largely obscured by the growing welter of sound. It transmogrifies into many fleeting variations and steadily encroaches whenever the Rhinedaughters glide and swim. The motif only occurs in these Scenes in the Rhine - a compositional device that glues together many discrete and separate episodes. The notes are as in M2A, but at greater speed.

18.3 *rhinedaughters* **M3**
We are to hear the similar song of a cousin, as it were, as sung by the wood bird in Siegfried - a creature of the air alongside a creature of the water.

18.4 *river movement (1)* **CM1**
The notes are identical with the top stave of 18.2 but at twice the speed.

Scene 2: The Rhinedaughters sexually entice and tease Alberich
[Schirmer: 12/1/6 to 24/3/4. Text from 'Die neigt sich herab' to 'Nähet ihr nur Trug, ihr treuloses Nickergezücht.']

That there are three water sprites (the source, to be found in the *Nibelungenlied,* has just two) may be to match them with the three Norns but, of greater moment in the drama, they articulate the progression of seduction technique employed and the musical changes to illustrate them. The audience must feel for Alberich and this is a finely constructed Scene of simple structure. (Porges reports that their 'utterances must be infused with a naïve gaiety.' (HP/WR,9)) In sequence, Woglinde, Wellgunde and Flosshilde tempt Alberich. The technique of each grows more flagrant as does the length of each little episode: 40, 54 and 86 bars respectively. Prime motifs are few. The compositional *river movement* attends Woglinde and Wellgunde as they elude the dwarf. There are also two graphic motifs that Wagner subsequently finds he has little use for. The first, picked up by Cooke, illustrates Alberich's clumping and awkward gait (CM2) in an alien environment. The second -

18.5 *clumsy alberich* **CM2**
Used here and in Scene 11 only.

269

DAS RHEINGOLD

18.6 *seductive allure* **CM3**
Used with the Rhinedaughters only.

most evocative of overt sexual seduction - changes the tone of the music, announcing Wellgunde as she first descends toward the dwarf. Wagner's first pencil sketch of this passage, on two staves, actually emphasises this rocking motif (CM3) as it floats above the vocal line. This expression of sexual allure is only associated directly with the Rhinedaughters and once, indirectly, to Freia. Never could it apply to Sieglinde or to Brünnhilde. Gutrune, on the other hand, is ripe for such a portrayal as her physical beauty overwhelms Siegfried, and in due course we will see why this did not happen. A useful name is *seductive allure*.

With Flosshilde and the full arousal of Alberich the tone changes yet again. For 70 bars we hear a love duet that might well find a place in a French opera of the 1830s or 1840s. In his book *Wagner Androgyne* Nattiez specifies a passage from the love duet in Meyerbeer's *Les Huguenots* as a model.[A] The thesis is that Wagner was parodying what he saw as conventional and therefore meretricious love music. In particular, Flosshilde's music exaggerates the conventions so that they become caricature and therefore false. If Nattiez is correct, Wagner was having a double dig at Meyerbeer, for he is on record as admiring this duet: sly therefore to demean a good passage rather than a bad! But it is pretty music and certainly there is nothing else like it in the *Ring*.

Scene 3: The frustrated Alberich tries to take a Rhinedaughter forcefully but is pulled up short by the revelation of the Rhine Gold and all that it entails.
[Schirmer: 25/1/1 to 47/3/2. Text, at beginning and end: 'Wallala! la la lei!]
In much fiction, the starting point can be one particular image or scene in the author's mind from which all else follows. It is hard not to think that the appearance of the Gold in the sunlight would not have been the germ from which this Scene developed. Most myths are changed or adapted through the ages and Wagner, with his hand freed by his own invention, must have seen that he was also presenting a new myth. The certainty of grasp of this foundation to the whole drama enables the composer to cover big issues. This particular Scene is by far the longest episode at the bottom of the Rhine, on a large scale and commensurate with the moment when the music comes to grips with the story. Accordingly, this episode within the Scene can itself be broken down into five parts.

A   For the first time, the Rhinedaughters sing a full-throated trio as all three now taunt and entice Alberich.
B   In consequence, rape rather than love fires him and he furiously chases each of them to powerfully concise, purpose-filled sound.
C   The pursuit stops as the Gold comes into view and is greeted with a second concerted rapturous trio from the Rhinedaughters.
D   From them Alberich learns about the Gold and the powers that lie within it.

[A] *Wagner Androgyne*, 64-68. Princeton University Press 1983. Translated from the French by Stewart Spencer.

DAS RHEINGOLD

E   The Rhinedaughters continue to taunt the dwarf in a third ebullient trio.

There is symmetry in the above. A, C and E are dominated by vocal ensembles of great beauty; B and D are studies of Alberich, first as he is physically provoked and goaded, and later as he is verbally insulted even as he learns of the crucial power in the Gold. This cannot be by chance.

Episode C of this Scene contains the heart of the story as it is played out down in the Rhine. This runs from Alberich's cry 'Fing'eine diese Faust!' (This fist need only catch one!) to the conclusion of the Rhinedaughters' glorification of the Gold. The effect here is such that only musical drama can offer. Alberich's cry - picked out by Porges as 'a striking example of Wagner's power to pinpoint every emotional nuance' (HP/WR,9) - leads immediately to the stillness in which all (characters and audience alike) hold their breath in expectation of the revealed, magic Gold. As the sunlight touches the Gold the sound we hear is pure and noble. *rhinegold* (M4) can and will take a doleful turn but is never malevolent.

18.7 *rhinegold* M4
Built from the basic chord of G major. Indicative of that which is solid and of central value to the cosmos of Wotan.

Then comes another crucial motif. As the Rhinedaughters greet the sight, what is best described as *force of the gold* (M5) rings out in the voices of the three water sprites. So to describe music that is initially so joyous must seem odd. But this motif will in due course generate *servitude to the ring*, *woe* and, in *Götterdämmerung* – a motif that is best described as *treachery*. We see that *force of the gold* is one of the most protean motifs of all: Cooke's adage that motifs develop over the four evenings for psychological reasons must refer to the psychology of the situation as perceived by the personage most involved. A name such as *force of the gold* will be suitable for many such occasions as the drama develops. This passage, from the dwarf's enraged cry to the end of the of the joyous central trio occupies 57 bars bang in the middle of this Scene which starts and ends with similar trios.

18.8 *force of the gold* M5

There follows, in episode D, the fateful disclosure of the power within the Ring, as Wellgunde sings the provisional form of what is to develop into the definitive *ring* motif. It now pops up four times in quick succession whilst the Rhinedaughters give Alberich its background. Soon after this we hear Woglinde intoning the first draft of the motif (M6) that von Wolzogen called 'renunciation of love'. For the reasons given in Chapter 16, this is not helpful and *life choice* will be used in this study. Of the three motifs only *force of the gold* becomes part

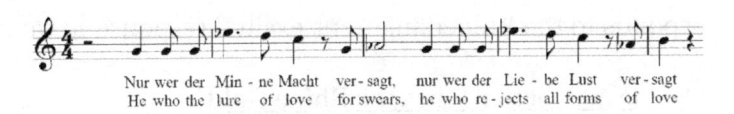

Nur wer der Min - ne Macht ver-sagt, nur wer der Lie - be Lust ver-sagt
He who the lure of love for swears, he who re - jects all forms of love

18.9 *life choice* M6
Almost always when this motif is heard (which is surprisingly seldom) the person at the centre of the action is making a life-defining choice.

271

of the musical fabric. *rhinegold* occurs five times in nineteen bars and then but once thereafter in this Scene. *life choice* features only once; no more is needed, so pregnant and memorable is this melody. Episode E follows with the third trio.

So what is the texture of this music over the 239 bars? The three separate trios present three different messages: the first is a concerted taunt at, and enticement of, Alberich; the second is joyfulness at the sight of the Rhine Gold and the third – after Alberich learns about the Gold - is a mixture of joyfulness and enticement. In all, 86 bars or just over one third of the Scene, feature these ensembles. The melodies for each are geared to the different messages but all have the same rhythmic and melodic profile which is a mixture of *rhinedaughters* and *force of the gold*. Thus these bars, although based on *force of the gold,* do in fact break free of the motif and stand as an affirmation of the purity that is now to be endangered.

The other large passage is the brilliantly effective representation of Alberich's vain pursuit, which extends over 40 bars. The beginning passage is a tightening of the dwarf's clumsy movement (CM2) into a short symphonic development and the closure returns to the jerky ungainly music from which the symphonic passage develops. We also hear a periodic compositional motif that represents *alberich's rage* (CM4) and a return of *seductive allure*. Additionally, there is one most powerful melody that expresses Alberich's striving (18.11). Such long tunes, as heard in *Lohengrin,* occasionally occur in this first opera and also in *Die Walküre*. Due to the growth of *leitmotiven* and Wagner's skill in using them, they then become increasingly rare, but are powerfully effective when the composer calls upon them.

18.10 *alberich's rage* **CM4** derived from rhinedaughters.

18.11 Alberich's effortful chase of the Rhinedaughters.

The bedrock compositional motif throughout is *river movement*. The music until now has been in ⁶/₈, saving the eighteen bars when Alberich first tries to reach Woglinde and where Wagner was at maximum pains to show his physical awkwardness. But when the Gold is about to be revealed, the composer shifts the time signature from ⁶/₈ to ⁹/₈, as shown here. The increasing fluidity of movement corresponds to the Rhinedaughters' excited response to their treasure. (See CM2 in 18.4)

18.12 *river movement (2)* **CM5**

Scene 4: Alberich takes the Rhine Gold
[Schirmer: 47/3/3 to 53/6/2. Text from 'Die Welt Erbe gewann'ich su eigen durch dich' to 'Hülfe, hülfe! Weh!]
This momentous event is over and done with quickly and that dynamic is more in tune with the terse Verdi than the expansive Wagner. That this is deliberate is probably

because the required expansion - Alberich spelling out what he intends - must wait for the upcoming scene with Wotan.

The *rhinegold* motif and the prototype *ring* motif accompany Alberich's cogitation and determination. When the deed is done *river movement (2)* takes over as Alberich disappears into the depths. For 34 bars this C minor postlude to the action conveys extreme loss as the swirls of water rise higher by three octaves and then sink down again.

Familiarity with this prologue at the bottom of the Rhine can dull us to Wagner's narrative achievement. The music extends for 600 bars and the action occupies about 25 minutes of stage time, but the journey taken is large - from unsullied innocence to malevolence and danger.

# # # # # #

It bears reflection that these opening Scenes in the Rhine (the action minus prelude and postlude) features no more than five motifs: *rhinedaughters, rhinegold, force of the gold, ring* and *life choice*. The last two are fleeting, for all the long-term importance they bear: *life choice* appears but once and *ring* (in the form Cooke describes as 'embryonic') seven times, and these two motifs occupy no more than 20 bars. The *action* lasts 571 bars. Of these, and disregarding what other music there might be in them, 188 feature the various compositional *river movement* motifs. This derives from the later stages of the prelude. As the current in the Rhine rises to the top, so does it increase the speed to 12 semiquavers to each $6/8$ bar and thus it accompanies the cavorting of the Rhine-daughters (CM1 in 18.4). In the run up to the appearance of the Rhine Gold the composer shifts the time signature from $6/8$ to $9/8$, and *river movement* increases in speed by 50%, to become a helter-skelter (CM5 in 18.12). The swiftly moving configurations change but the fundamental rising and falling within each bar does not. The three remaining motifs – *rhinedaughters, rhinegold, force of the gold* – occupy 58 bars between them and almost all are accompanied by a *river movement* motif. Thus, of the 571 bars, 45% depends for continuity upon these motifs. In this sense, the opening four Scenes in the cycle could be described as a 'symphonic poem', based on compositional motifs. This may not be what has been meant by commentators over the years but is does provide *Das Rheingold* with a musical sophistication that has not been readily perceived.

Moreover, *river movement (2)* – CM5 - comes magnificently into its own in the postlude, after Alberich takes the Rhine Gold and the swirling water rises over 14 bars to reach F above the stave before sinking to a low A in the bass stave. In that concluding passage it accompanies perhaps the most poignant rendering of *life choice* in the whole cycle. This tremendous passage of 31 bars is 'owned' by this one motif – one of the longest examples of such dominance in the cycle. It is the motif's 'swan song': it does not feature outside these first four Scenes.

Each Scene in the *Ring* has its particular structure, according to dramatic needs. We see that these first four Scenes may feature variations of *river movement* but do not rely on substantive *leitmotiven*. Chapter 16 also argued that *stabriem* was a greater driving force than *leitmotiven* in the early stages and here is a telling example. The emotions of the key passages in the interchanges between the dwarf and the water sprites are rendered meticulously into 'verse-melody', and we see that substantive motifs have little impact within the symphonic structure.

# # # # # #

Scene 5: Wotan and Fricka at cross-purposes
[Schirmer: 53/6/3 to 67/4/4. Text from 'Wotan, Gemahl! Erwache!' to 'Die im büsen Bund dich verriethen, sie alle bergen sich nun!']
Remove the particular cosmic circumstances surrounding these two people - as detailed in the text - and we have an archetypal conflict between a man, obsessed and ruled by his work, and his correspondingly neglected wife. He is seldom at home and spends his time travelling abroad or consulting with business colleagues. With these he makes the important decisions that affect everyone, not excluding his wife. She may well be a senior director or a partner in the business but still finds herself side-lined. She suspects her husband to be unfaithful. In putting the situation so I am not 'domesticating' Wagner, to use Michael Tanner's phrase. I am not reducing Wotan to the level of a business tycoon - the issues here could not be larger - but this first Scene is a true-to-life domestic argument - a prime example for Porges of the composer's 'principle of bringing fidelity to nature.' (HP/WR, 14)

The Scene sets Wotan's actions in a clear light and he is not flattered by what is to be seen. The argument has five stages:

A Wotan contemplates what he has just done and what he hopes from it.
B Fricka voices genuine fear about the implications of his action.
C Wotan knows he is on shaky ground and so he changes the subject.
D Fricka ignores this and brings Wotan down to earth.
E Finally Wotan comes clean about what he intends.

Examination of the text shows that without exception each stage follows in principle the dialectic as used to analyse the opening scene of *Hamlet* in Chapter 3. In stage A, Wotan has two speeches which act as a sandwich to one by Fricka. In stage B, the two speeches lie with Fricka, and so on alternately up to the end of stage E. (In stage D, Fricka's second speech is capped by that from Freia as she rushes on but both women are making the same point.) There is no killer blow, no mid-point, for the purpose is to clarify by means of a progression from one point to the next. Now we must see how music and words impact on the drama.

A *Wotan's hopes*   The latter third of the interlude which carries the spectator from river depth to mountain top is a musical prelude to the action in this Scene. It starts with the definitive *ring* motif (M7) as the stage direction specifies that the waves have changed into clouds. Five calm repetitions of *ring* reach a stasis of uncertain key before settling on the majestic D♭ major of *valhalla* (M8). The whole motif runs its course for 20 bars but within four bars the music switches back to *ring* - twice sounding as Wotan sings his opening words 'The happy hall of delight is guarded by door and gate.' *valhalla* then sweeps back in and, after a short interjection by Fricka, supports Wotan for 20 bars as he greets the castle in the morning light with a notable peroration. That is stage A in its entirety. Wotan's achievement and the hopes he has for it are clear.

18.13 *ring* M7

18.14 *valhalla* M8
This is the opening phrase only; the full motif is found in the complete listing.

Reference to the *ring* motif is appropriate at this point, even though it appeared earlier in a different form when the Rhinedaughters first mentioned it. The significance is that the definitive form, as above, appears in close proximity to that for *valhalla* and their similarity is made clear by the transition: for *valhalla* emerges from *ring*. The tone of *ring* in this transition is notably calm, more so than anywhere else in the cycle. But if we nevertheless perceive that motif to be ambivalent at best, what we seem to have at this point is nobility emerging out of corruption. This can suggest that deep down Wotan knows he is at fault but cannot acknowledge it: *valhalla* generally serves as a proxy for the god. What is to be made of this and also of another similar example that is to follow in *Die Walküre*? Brünnhilde there announces to Sieglinde, to the *siegfried* motif, that she is bearing a child. It is a commonplace that *siegfried* is similar to *curse,* and this suggests that the *ring/valhalla* duality and that for *curse/siegfried* must be thought of in the same fashion. In both cases, it is surely too simplistic to think this represents something good emerging from something bad. Rather than incipient corruption, might it not be a signal that nothing is wholly good? *ring/valhalla* relates to power; *curse/siegfried* is a polarity of opposites. The ambivalence of *force of the gold* (18.8) is another example seen earlier in this chapter, which proclaims that the Rhine Gold can bring on both the good and the bad.

B *Fricka is fearful*   These and Wotan's dismissal of them are expressed in a recitative that is melodic but still with a subdued vocal emphasis. Wagner wants much information conveyed quickly and clearly - 32 lines of text in 36 bars. The substance of Fricka's complaint is that Wotan does not take seriously the danger to Freia and has made all his plans in league with the other male gods without referring anything to her.

C *Wotan ignores all this*   Fricka speaks true, for Wotan changes the subject and returns the discussion to Valhalla, which Fricka also wanted built. When she says that her motive was to keep Wotan by her in their home and she did not imagine he would

DAS RHEINGOLD

build an actual fortress, Wotan puts her down. He has to work - 'wandering and change inspire my heart.' (There is a touch of Odin here and although the Frigg of the eddas does argue with Odin, it is never about this sort of thing.) When Fricka speaks of the delights of a calm life at home a gently, lilting

18.15 *domestic life* **M9**

motif *domestic life* (M9) enters and is repeated by her husband as he teases her. This motif is not plastic, the issue is tangential to the larger plot and its function here is to give a realistic humanity to Fricka – somewhat like a bourgeois matron - and to reinforce the domestic nature of the Scene. (Its function is to change in *Götterdämmerung*.)

D *Fricka is relentless* She brushes off Wotan's reminder that he was prepared to lose an eye in order to win her. That the situation is now close to home is made clear when Freia rushes in as she flees from Fasolt. For the first time, as she enters, there is heard the two motifs which she stands for: sexual desire and compassionate love. Shown separately here, the last note of *sexual desire* (M10) becomes the first note of *love* (M11). The full extension of *love* is only to come with the passion of Siegmund and Sieglinde: on this first appearance both are fast, barely accompanied and express agitation.

18.16 *sexual desire* **M10**   *love* **M11**

Cooke argues that Freia is a pallid creature and that her motif barely attaches to her, and that this is because love had no place in the world of *Das Rheingold* (see Cooke, 155-158). We will find, however, that Fasolt has a complex affection for Freia and also that Mime is to reflect on the contented life of the Nibelungs before Alberich forged the Ring. The salient point is that the onset of meaningful love needs to be carefully placed in the drama and Wagner had the *Die Walküre* poem before him where love is established. Cooke may also have been aiming in the wrong direction. The dramatic purpose of Freia is not to represent the force of love and sexual desire, but rather to serve as a device. She focusses the plot on to the crucial issue that will concern the audience: not the fate of the goddess but the consequences of Wotan's reckless gamble.

E *Wotan is forced to show his hand*   The arrival of Freia in the presence of his bitter wife brings out the truth. He is waiting for and dependent upon Loge (we hear a fragment of his music for the first time) and this infuriates Fricka for she sees him as the cardinal example of the male adviser she so deplores. Wotan admits that he sometimes needs Loge to bring policy to fruition. Freia finally screams in terror for her brothers Donner and Froh to a repeat of Freia's dual motif, but they do not turn up. Fricka's contempt for these two (her brothers also) is as clear as is her concern for Freia. The last phrase she sings: 'Die im bosen Bund dich verriethen, sie Alle bergen sich nun!'

(All who betrayed you in evil alliance have fled to save their skins) is fine, and came late in the creative process, for the first sketch was pedestrian. [B] Without dense motifs Wagner was now able to bring off such great individual moments.

Scene 6: Fasolt and Fafner arrive to claim Freia, are fobbed off by Wotan who waits for Loge. Donner and Froh enter and face up to the giants.
[Schirmer: 68/1/1 to 77/4/1. Text from 'Sanft schloss Schlaf dein Aug'; wir Beide bauten Schlummer's die Burg' to 'Begreif'ich dich noch, grausamer Mann?']
With the entrance of the giants all the gears in the plot engage with each other. The first thing that strikes is the certitude with which Wagner gives just enough character traits, background and musical characterisation to Fasolt and Fafner, such that a clear and concise line of plot is established. In the chapter on *Der junge Siegfried* is a summary of the somewhat vague choices concerning the giants that the composer then made from within the sources (p.128). Then came silence for ten months until the prose sketch, finished in April 1852, where there is concision and focus.

The previous Scene ended, as far as Wotan was concerned, with comments on and hopes consequent upon Loge's arrival. This Scene plays out the danger gathering around Wotan if Loge fails in his task. The drama unfolds in real time with tension increasing over three cycles. The first centres around Fasolt as he states why he and his brother have come and the indignation when Wotan questions the deal. The second continues in the same vein until Fafner intervenes and switches attention from Freia to the golden apples. The third and final cycle that follows is powerful: the conflict and mistrust evident in the music is extreme when Donner and Froh arrive and face up to the giants.

Motifs are now plentiful. New is *giants* (M12) as they first enter, and quickly to follow is *will-to-power* (M13). Those previously introduced are *sexual desire, love* and *valhalla*. With a few exceptions, however, these are not blended with each other on this occasion but serve as story sign-posts.

18.17 *giants* **M12**

18.18 *will-to-power* **M13**

The first cycle is Fasolt's. To *giants* and *valhalla* he records the history of why they are now here; when Wotan derisively denies the contract, the motif *will-to-power* (M13) comes twice fortissimo to convey the giant's dismay. The motif first crept in when Fricka expressed her fears in Scene 5 but when Wotan here quells the giant we hear the brutal compulsion inherent in the weapon as wielded by the god. Fasolt then launches a fine, richly accompanied melodic *arioso*.

The second cycle starts with Wotan's brutal derision of the giants as a race. This launches Fasolt into a passionate plea for something of grace, namely Freia, to come into his current graceless life. The musical halo comprises delicate renditions of *sexual*

[B] This phrase is used as a marker for Wagner's new vocal style in Chapter 16 (p.223).

DAS RHEINGOLD

desire and *love*. The whole is a short aria which brings in fragments of *valhalla*, *life choice* and *giants*. The whole passage is the musical highlight of the Scene and makes Wotan look shabby.

After Wotan's derision and Fasolt's yearning comes the third cycle, with Fafner's hard grasp on the reality which has been missed by the others: Freia also harvests the golden apples that keep the gods vigorous. With them the giants will thrive and without them the gods will fade. *golden apples* (M14) is everywhere in this passage. Fafner's tough message ends with a crescendo on a rising phrase and introduces the mounting anxiety which characterises the third cycle. Demands fly to and fro; Freia cries out in fear; Donner and Froh finally arrive and Froh holds his sister close whilst Donner raises his hammer against the giants. Wotan intervenes between the god and the giant by interposing his spear. Freia believes herself abandoned and Fricka is overcome with disgust.

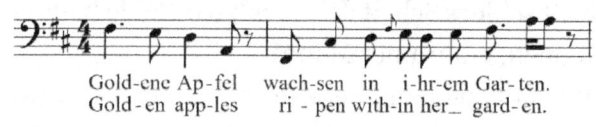

18.19 *golden apples* **M14**
This is another motif that very seldom combines with any other.

The contrast in structure between this Scene and that between Wotan and Fricka alone is notable. That prior Scene is akin to the whole of the preceding sequence in the Rhine: both set the story up. As there is a back story to tell, easily recognizable motifs were introduced to aid understanding. After the set up Scenes we have now been pitched into the ongoing drama and with what mastery! The device of holding the entrance of Loge back is doubly clever: it enables the drama to reach a boiling point very quickly and secondly the spectator has the distinct idea that Loge is deliberately late. He enters into a hot house atmosphere where all are at sixes and sevens.

# # # # # #

Earlier it was asked whether the level of invention differed between the Alberich Scenes (original to Wagner) and those concerning the gods and giants. This Scene shows that there is none. It can, in fact, be more difficult to sift and filter from the work of others than to start from scratch.

# # # # # #

Scene 7: Loge arrives and his procrastination increases the tension
[Schirmer: 77/4/2 to 84/4/4. Text from 'Endlich, Loge!' to 'Halte Stich! Wo schevieftest du hin und her?']
This short Scene acts to wind up the gods. Wotan's surly invitation allows Loge to give a resumé of the current situation: Fasolt and Fafner were contracted to build the fortress that would become the gods' new home and I, Loge, have not been idle - I have examined the work and found it good. This infuriates the gods: they know all this very well for that is the reason they have been hanging around for Loge to arrive. And this, of course, is his purpose. He then prods at the fury engendered in each of them (excepting poor

Freia). Under pressure from Wotan he agrees that he promised to look for a better offer for the giants than Freia afforded - but what if there were none? Fricka and Froh call him a liar; Donner threatens destruction. To all these Loge sneers: it's their own blunder but they blame me. Fasolt and Fafner lose patience and so, finally, does Wotan. Danger advances at accelerating pace and Loge's music dances.

Of the 135 bars in the Scene, 66 are of Loge's music and an additional 24 are when he is speaking. Every person on stage reacts to him. Loge's music is ubiquitous throughout the *Ring* and is difficult to characterise. There are six separate motifs but each can be used to portray fire or craftiness. One is illustrated here and all can be found on pp.239/40. To put the use to which each is put *loge as fire* or *crafty loge* will be indicated. In this Scene it is craftiness. The tie between Wagner's Wotan and Loge is not the same as that between Odin and Loki, where there is perpetual discord and the two are on opposite sides in the final *Ragnarök*. Even so, Wagner makes every effort to show Loge as inherently hostile, thereby reflecting that original animosity (p.167). The prevalence of his motifs at this point indicate that he is manipulating each and every one of the gods. In their turn they say - and the music supports the words - that they dislike and distrust him.

18.20 *loge* **M15A**

Wagner's cleverness is fourfold:
(a) He brings in just as much from the eddas as needed to link his narrative to those sources.
(b) Loge's hostility goes hand in hand with Alberich's to convey the concrete danger which surrounds Wotan's world.
(c) The result of his behaviour is to make everyone prone to take corruption so that what they really want is obscured. This is the core dramatic purpose of the Scene.
(d) His iconoclastic wish to bring things down has found a *modus operandum* that cannot but lead toward a catastrophe of some sort.

But none of the above is overt. Loge has neither family ties nor sympathy with the gods, and this is conveyed by his detached, flickering music.

Scene 8: Loge's tale about Alberich and the Gold adds greed to the anxiety felt by all. Finally, the giants leave with Freia.
[Schirmer: 84/4/4 to 101/3/3. Text from 'Immer ist Undank Loge's Lohn' to 'Rettet! helft!']
This long Scene is in three parts, of which Loge's narration is the first. He gives his listeners the precise amount of information required to plant a corrupting germ in the minds of his stage audience. This teases out questions from them in the second part and each answer causes growth of the germ in each mind in accord with the moral flaw that lies within each. Finally, in the third part, clear-eyed Fafner voices the issue that is in all minds: all want the Gold, and the giants are prepared to trade Freia for it.

The content and structure of this Scene is immaculate as is the support the music gives to the drama. In contrast to the seven preceding Scenes, this is filled with *leitmotiven*. They are presented clearly and have two functions: to help the telling of a complex story and, as an adjunct, to speed the telling and thereby guide the spectator.

Part 1: Loge's narration
This marks a quantum jump in Wagner's achievement as a composer. Previously the most potent narration would by general consent be Tannhäuser's in Act 3, who tells Wolfram the tale of his pilgrimage. The story occupies ten minutes of stage time; the music is expansive and melodramatic. His story is in three parts but the substance - all about Tannhäuser himself - is the same. It is a simple, self-contained story with a beginning, middle and end. What is heard now is very different. The scope is so wide that the reader may be surprised to learn that it takes only about five minutes of stage time - half that of Tannhäuser's, and is marvellously clear and concise. The narrative is also in three sections. First, Loge rehearses the enormous task he agreed to undertake: to find a substitute for Freia. Second, he advises that 'he asked everyone living in water, earth and sky' one question but could find 'none who will relinquish love and woman'. Third, and almost as an afterthought, he tells them of Alberich and his actions - news to everyone. He deliberately does not end the story but leaves the facts hanging in the air.

Section A – the task A plenitude of motifs lie in the narration as a whole in comparison to what has gone before. But not in this opening section, where Loge's task is set out in 21 bars but 17 of them are melodic recitative of striking resonance. Of the other four bars, one presents his craftiness and the conclusion is the first appearance of one of the central motifs in the entire cycle. Of recent years it has been called 'woman's worth' because those are Loge's word when first heard. However, JK Holman in his 'Companion on the *Ring*' indicates that it means far more than this. This study, therefore, will call it *core life value* (M16). The falling contour of this melody may well strike an immediate response; it closely resembles the second part of *life choice* as sung by Woglinde to Alberich in Scene 3. But here, with Loge's words 'women's worth and delight' sombrely matched by cor anglais and four horns, we know it is something important in its own right. Not only in itself but because it acts as the transition to the second section.

18.21 *core life value* **M16**

Section B – the need for love This takes off with a remarkable compositional motif. The contour is first heard as a counterpoint to *nature* that indicates the essentially benign consequences of following nature. The tone of *natural life* (CM6), however, is quite different, being sensuous first and wholesome second, and perfectly shaped to lead into

18.22 *natural life* **CM6**

sexual desire. For 36 bars this compositional motif bears the weight of hopeful love as it supports Loge's lyricism which takes in a second hearing of *core life value*. A big message is quickly imputed. The conclusion is that love for a woman is essential for a man, and *vice versa*. That lyricism concludes in an ecstatic rendition of *sexual desire*.

Section C – Alberich's choice   The music then drops abruptly to earth as Loge moves on to his third statement: love is essential for all save Alberich. Aided by clear, continuous motif development, he tells of the dwarf's drastic action. *rhinegold, force of the gold, rhinedaughters, ring* are deftly combined and culminate in a sombre *core life value* - ominously low as first heard but now on cello and double bass. The key is a doleful G# minor and this gloominess continues as *force of the gold,* with a shifting of two notes, takes its first step away from the initial G major of its first appearance into E minor (18.23).

18.23 First corruption of *force of the gold*

The Rhinedaughters are bewailing the loss of the Gold. This is an important moment in the musical narrative. In Chapter 11 the Gold in the Rhine is seen as a symbol of hope that is unsullied until tampered with; in the *Myth* Wagner describes it as 'pure and noble'. In Scenes 11 and 13 of this opera the joyous purity of that initial greeting is to be further altered so that it represents the polar opposite - servitude and numbing, forced oppression. This is part of a continuum, from joy to a corruption that stains all it touches and which finds first expression in this example. The gloom does not persist as the pure sound of *rhinegold* rings out twice to be followed by five bars of *river movement (2)*. Loge rounds off with a characteristic throw-away: the Rhinedaughters asked me to tell you this, Wotan, and I've done so! Then *loge's craftiness* descends quietly over two bars as he waits for a response.

Part 2: Corruption takes root

Temptation floats over the entirety of the second part. The straightforward giants do not hold back, in contrast to the scheming gods. Fasolt fears that Alberich will harm them if the Ring gives him power, so Fafner asks what is so special about the Gold and the Ring. [c] No motifs here for the question is neutral but Loge's response and Wotan's reaction - his tongue now loosened - are anything but neutral. These are mounted upon a combination of *force of the gold* and *ring* in a symphonic sequence of ten repetitions spread over 18 bars. As Wotan weakens the *ring* motif oscillates up and down. Fricka is the next to yield: the issue for her is how well the Gold would adorn a woman. Loge understands her hidden agenda and assures here that no husband would dare betray a wife whose jewellery were made of the Gold. This exchange signifies Fricka's myopia and lack of interest in any bigger picture. The object is to save Freia but the limitations

---

[c]   This is a trace of a discarded element of the plot as presented in the 1848 *Myth,* which hints at long standing conflict between giants and dwarfs (p.128).

of her vision take over (p.165). At this point we hear a second sign of corruption in something wholly pure. As Fricka hopes Wotan will now get the Gold, we hear *rhinegold* but the first interval is reduced by a semitone - from a pure to a diminished 4th.

Wotan is now hooked and pushes the discussion to the next stage. What does one have to do to wield the Ring's power? *ring* and *life choice* give the answer: to forswear love. Within the immediate agitation that follows we hear a motif of dotted triplets. This is a compositional motif that is repeatedly used to demonstrate energetic or *fierce action* (CM7). The rhythmic outline will be heard as accompaniment to the valkyrs' ride and as Siegfried forges his sword. In this its first hearing it leads

18.24 *fierce action* **CM7**
This, with rhythmic variations, is sporadically but widely used to accompany energetic activity.

straight into a fierce rendition of *core life value*. This sounds as Loge sings of Alberich's success in forging the Ring and demonstrates that a motif can be used to colour what is heard: Loge is not on the side of the gods.

In this case it also acts as a full stop in the music, which takes off in another revealing direction. Donner, whom Wagner presents as somewhat dim (p.168) gives voice to the sentiment as rendered by John Deathridge's translation (We'll all be under the dwarf's yoke, if the Ring's not prised away from him.) This he sings to the accompaniment in the bass of a fragment from *sexual desire*. Wotan is manifestly the boss and now he says

18.25 Wotan is influenced by Donner.
The fragment of *sexual desire* over which words are spoken lies in the lower stave.

firmly for the first time that he wants the Ring (Den Ring muss ich haben!). But he says so over the same fragment as introduced by Donner's thoughts. This is truly psychological, as Cooke describes it, for we see Wotan picking up on Donner's more primitive instinct. Additionally, it is the moment when Wotan submits himself to that power inherent within the Ring, as to be described by Alberich in his curse. This is therefore the moment when the god's baseness reaches its peak.

The next step is obviously how to get hold of it and Loge shocks them by proposing theft. With this clarification of the lengths to which the gods must go, Loge's work is done. His final call that he hopes the Rhinedaughters will get their Gold back via the gods is a brilliant flourish in D major to the accompaniment of *force the gold* and *river movement (2)*. He contributes no more to this Scene but stands back and watches the expansion of trouble he has caused.

Now all are drawn in and accept without a qualm that if they want the gold they must steal it. The music is now a continuous tapestry of motifs: *crafty loge, rhinegold, force of the gold* (to reflect the hope the Rhinedaughters have that the Gold will be returned to them), *river movement (2), rhinedaughters,* the compositional motif *seductive allure* and fragments of *sexual desire* (to represent the Freia part of the bargain). After his first blunt assertion, Fafner has kept silent and Wagner skilfully gives him the last word in this flowering of universal temptation from that early germ - the brutal advice to Fasolt that the Gold will be more useful to them than Freia. We have reached the conclusion of the second part of the Scene, the final notes of which are the tolling of the Rhinegold 'bell'. This is heard in the original key of D major but with a dissonant B♭ instead of B natural. This is one of the few places in the entire *Ring* when one gets such a tonic closure – and one that extends over five full bars. (See CvW/FR,39) Over this closure, and the musical rest which follows, lies the mist of corruption. Porges records Wagner's remark that 'for the first time the gods realise that another power exists beside their own, namely the power of gold.' (HP/WR,24)

Part 3: The giants give an ultimatum to Wotan
Then Fafner turns to Wotan and the Scene slips into its third part, which is short and sharp. He and his brother will forgo Freia in return for the Gold. When Wotan angrily refuses, the giants take Freia away: Wotan has until evening to get the Gold - and otherwise the goddess will stay with them. The tone of the recitative changes from essentially lyrical to rough, and the music steadily speeds up.

<u>Scene 9: Loge sees the problem. With Freia gone - she who tends the apples that keep them going - the gods will fade away.</u>
[Schirmer: 101/3/4 to 107/3/6. Text from 'Über Stock und Stein' to 'Erstirbt der Götter Stamm.']
Loge has said nothing for 94 bars but now steps forward as crisis mounts. In the 110 bars of this Scene no less than 102 are a monologue, as Loge turns the screw on the gods' discomfort. A question that cannot be answered one way or the other is whether he knew in advance that Wotan *had* to take the critical step of stealing the Ring, but one can assume at the least that Loge foresaw the extreme danger to the gods, let alone to Freia. Whatever the answer, there can be no doubt that he is enjoying himself.

As so often, the Scene is in three parts. Firstly, Loge describes the departure of the giants as they stride away with Freia. Secondly, he notices the growing physical weakness of Froh, Donner and Fricka, and finally of Wotan 'who seems already grown old'. Thirdly, he sees (or pretends to see) the fatality consequent on Freia's absence, namely that without the golden apples the gods are doomed. The whole is a tremendous narrative; nothing like it is to be found in *Lohengrin*. The force of the plot brings all issues into the light.

The opening, descriptive part is freely composed. The second part, as Loge contemplates the fading gods, introduces extraordinary sounds never before heard in the opera house. The fabric is of ghostly echoes of *sexual love* - as symbol for the misted out Freia – and of her *golden apples*. Additionally, we hear another dramatically relevant appearance of the transformation of the first notes of *force of the gold* into its obverse - which we can now call *woe* (M17). Fricka expresses the dismay that all feel as the loss of their vitality looms unless something is done. (Strictly speaking, it is Alberich who sings the relevant notes when he realises that the Rhinedaughters are fooling with him. But the pain behind the woe is *caused by* Alberich, so to describe his distress as the first source misses the point. The gods and mankind, and not Alberich, are to be the victims and it misleads to impute first cause to the Rhinedaughters.) The third part sees the veil over the sound withdrawn as Loge understands matters; the music is almost all *golden apples* with intervals of *loge's craftiness*.

18.26 *woe* M17

Scene 10: Wotan descends to Nibelheim with Loge
[Schirmer: 107/4/1 to 112/6/5. Text from 'Wotan, Gemahl' to 'O kehre bald zur bangenden Frau!']
Pertinent here is Wagner's view of social morality and societal stress that emerges from the extensive examination of Oedipus and Antigone in *Opera and Drama*. In particular, the courage of Antigone brings about the eclipse of the authority of the Theban state. Hence 'the virtue in any society derives from the virtues of the human individual; the state is built upon the vices inherent in any society' (p.11). Wotan can be used to symbolise a coercive state. For this Scene contains the crucial turning point in the opera, when Wotan undertakes to steal the Ring from Alberich. Within opera such a momentous action requires music to match its importance, and we hear this in the descent to Nibelheim. This may be dubbed an interlude but dramatically the descent represents the grave implications of Wotan's recent decisions and this aspect makes up 60% of the Scene. 'Decisions' is in the plural because the degradation of love is the main subject of this episode. Grave as is the decision to bring upon his head the guilt of stealing the Ring (as established and written down in the 1848 *Myth*) that pales when compared to his disregard of love.

DAS RHEINGOLD

The dialogue that precedes the descent has few motifs. This must be by design as is the one clearly noticeable motif heard within that dialogue, namely *force of the gold*. In the previous Scene this had born forth *woe* but here, as Loge pretends that the object of the descent might be to return everything to the Rhinedaughters, we hear *force of the gold* subtly harmonised to show the direct opposite (18.27). Motifs surge and compound in the descent, which starts with ten bars of *crafty loge*,

18.27 *force of the gold* corrupted.
It is the low A flat that supplies the dissonance at the opening of the first two bars that does the trick.

in a variation that we are never to hear again: descending semi-tones in the treble, matched in the bass first by rising semitones and then by four cavernous octave descents which end on the lowest E imaginable. Porges notes that as Wagner rehearses the actors 'a demonic force erupts revelling in its power to destroy the realm of freedom and love . . . the Loge motif rises to a gigantic power, imbued with a fury of destructive lust.' (Porges, 27) Thereafter all that represents joy and virtue are shown as in shock and besieged: *core value*, *rhinegold* and *love* - this last in a fast roiling down-ward spiral. The climax is a vastly slowed

18.28 *nibelung slavery* **M18**

down *love*, screamed out by the brass. High above this, *nibelung slavery* (M18) is heard clearly and violently (*ff*) for the first time as we pass from the domain of Wotan into that of Alberich. (This motif made a fleeting appearance in the previous Scene as Loge described to Fricka the efficacy of the Nibelung jewellery.)

Scene 11: Alberich torments Mime and takes the Tarnhelm from him
[Schirmer: 113/1/1 to 122/2/1. Text from 'Hehe! hieher, tückischer Zwerg' to 'Ho-ho! hört ihn, er naht: der Nibelungin Herr!']

In effect, this first Nibelheim Scene begins in the orchestra before the stage action, as it takes up the rhythm of the anvils at the latter end of the descent interlude: a fresh start in every way. We hear *nibelung slavery* and below it a slow, lumbering surge from the bass; as it climbs it gets louder

18.29 *villainous excitement* **M19**
A remarkable example of imagination: the opening downward sweep of *ring* speeds up to make something entirely new.

and when the score reads *ff* we hear two partial *ring* fragments and then a development, based on the *ring* chords which descends with great violence over four octaves. We are to hear this motif (M19) throughout the *Ring* at moments of *villainous excitement*. At

DAS RHEINGOLD

this moment Alberich is hoping to take possession of the Tarnhelm. This short Scene concentrates on this artefact and the music before and after its first appearance is largely free composition with few motifs, which also matches the rough and violent action and emotions. The music is graphically fierce and jerky to

18.30 *tarnhelm* **M20**

give context and contrast to the *tarnhelm* motif (M20). This eerie music - something so far unheard in the opera house - is of tremendous force. Note also that as it is here put to use, it slides almost imperceptibly into *woe*. Within the *Ring* there are three types of magic: those associated with Loge (i.e the 'magic' fire), those emanating from the Ring itself and those from the Tarnhelm. The extranormal functions of the first two ambiguously influence the whole cycle. But there is nothing ambiguous about the Tarnhelm. The music tells us that this artefact can in no way be used for good or wholesome purpose (p.154).

Alberich makes himself invisible by means of the Tarnhelm, gives Mime a beating and notice to the rest of the Nibelungs as to what is in store for them. He then rushes

18.31 The violent exit of Alberich
nibelung slavery in the treble, *woe* in the bass

off to music of vicious and extreme violence which ends with three bars of *woe*, alongside *nibelung slavery*. Twenty-two bars of music are constructed from two motifs, with much syncopation.

Scene 12: Loge wheedles information out of Mime
[Schirmer: 122/2/2 to 130/1/5. Text from 'Nibelheim hier' to Nehmt euch in Acht, Alberich naht!]
This Scene is all about Mime, as Loge deftly prompts him to reveal information. He asks three questions: 'What gave [Alberich] the power to bind you?'; 'And you were so idle that you were whipped?'; 'If you're clever, why did you fail?'. The first question elicits the genesis and characteristics of the Ring; the second brings forth the potential that lies in the Tarnhelm; the third tells the gods that Alberich can use it to vanish. The Scene (186 bars) lasts about five minutes and Mime sings for about 60% of the time. Wagner is meticulous in this narrative: every piece of information gleaned from Mime is to be instrumental in the ruin of Alberich. He takes his time. 69 lines of intensely informative narration fill these minutes of music. That these Scenes in Nibelheim are on average about 50% longer than those at the bottom of the Rhine is due to the accumulation of information that has to be passed to the listener.

The first of Mime's three responses sets forth what life was like for the Nibelungs before Alberich forged the Ring and this conveys a material element in Wotan's cosmos. Mime describes his past happier life when he and his follows 'forged for our women trinkets and jewels.' It is not uncommon to read that what one can call 'wholesome' love is absent from the world of *Das Rheingold*. Cooke, for example, says that 'Freia stands as the goddess of love in a world that has rejected love.' But here Mime touchingly recalls recent family happiness. The music does the job for us. The initial *nibelung slavery* motif (M17) has an edgy 9/8 time signature but when Mime describes his lost happiness we hear *nibelung life* (CM8) for the first time. This variation in 6/8 has an engaging lilt. But immediately the emerging flexibility of the *leitmotif* is demonstrated: as Mime describes life under Alberich, the motif drops from the D above the stave to the G at the bottom - an interval of a 12th - and above it we hear *woe*, increasing in volume from *p* to *f* and culminating in the second appearance of *villainous excitement*. It then astonishes that the lilting 6/8 becomes fierce by making every - as opposed to alternate - triplet dotted, as Mime concludes his descent from happiness to misery.

18.32 *nibelung life* **CM8**

As Mime answers Loge's second question, all is about the making of the Tarnhelm and Mime's forlorn hope that he would master the magic associated with it as devised by Alberich. *tarnhelm* and *ring* are the motifs, with snatches of *nibelung life*.

Having elicited the hitherto unknown importance of the Tarnhelm, the third question from Loge elicits from Mime the power that does lie within it. *tarnhelm* is ever present along with fierce variations of *ring* as the beating handed out by Alberich is described. The Scene ends with the approach of Alberich to the ominous, pounding of *nibelung life* in the low bass.

Scene 13: Alberich makes brutally clear to Wotan how he intends to use the powers he has acquired.
[Schirmer 130/2/1 to 143/4/4. Text from 'Sein harren wir hier' to 'Enststeigt des Nibelungen Hort aus stummer Tiefe zu Tag!]

Wotan took the decision in Scene 10 to purloin the Ring with some hesitation: this was to be larceny on a very grand scale. This episode with Alberich must have persuaded him that the decision was necessary. Its dramatic purpose is to reveal the dwarf to the audience in all his monstrosity. The *Myth* portrayed him as a victim and we can easily feel sympathy as he is cruelly enticed by the Rhinedaughters. But as the poem for the cycle was rounded out his demonic destructiveness established the full scope of the whole drama.

The Scene is in three parts as is that with Mime which preceded it but the dynamic is quite different and demonstrates Wagner's mastery of contrast. The first and third parts are solos by Alberich. In the first he demonstrates his power to enslave his fellow Nibelungs and in the third he sets forth his future plan to enslave the gods. In between he confronts Loge and Wotan with confidence. Loge may introduce himself but Alberich knows full well that it is Wotan who has come to visit. All is verbal sparring until Wotan brings on the second tirade by asking the crucial question which opens the floodgates of his crazed and terrible intent: 'What's the use of your wealth?' For there's nothing to buy in Nibelheim.

The first of Alberich's two tirades is opened by 18.33, and is built on yet a further corruption of *force of the gold*, as it takes the colour of *woe*. These blend in symphonic style over nineteen bars, which starts *p* and ends *ff*. This comes to an abrupt end when Alberich takes notices Wotan and Loge: twelve bars of *malice* are transformed to make a rhythmic riff of violent force in 6/8 time [18.34]. This rhythm returns as the Nibelungs make their terrified exit, driven by the power that lies within the Ring as wielded by Alberich's whip. The motif that brings on the panic is most powerful, and is also an obvious progression away from the C major joy and purity inherent in the Gold. This moves via the E minor 'corruption' (18.33) to this most powerful motif of menace. The name most suited is *servitude to the ring* (M21). The music rises to the first of the three big climaxes in this Scene.

18.33 This is the start of the passage over which Alberich vents his aggression toward the Nibelungs. It starts p but builds up to ff over 19 bars.

18.34 The psychological power of Alberich's whip, demonstrated by the relentless rhythm and the pulsing switch between piano and a following crescendo.

18.35 *servitude to the ring* **M21**
This is a more extreme version of 18.32.

We see here an illustration of how Wagner develops his motifs. He manipulates something that is initially joyous by clouding it with the semitone heard so clearly as sung by Fricka at the height of the gods' distress. It is by no means sure that Wagner foresaw how the first motifs that surfaced in *Das Rheingold* would develop. For good reason, therefore, he did not much approve of the precise schedule established by Wolzogen in 1878. All may be clean cut in the early Scenes of the cycle but perception is obscured with these motifs associated with the Rhine Gold. For purposes of the drama we only need to see that something pure has an obverse impurity. Motifs associated with woe and corruption are many and various in the *Ring*. The spectator will sense the connections between them and also see that the root of each lies in the Gold that lies at the bottom of the Rhine. The hope that is generated by the response to the Rhine Gold - as first expressed by the Rhinedaughters as the sunlight penetrates the water - quickly morphs into a musical symbol of slavery.

DAS RHEINGOLD

The middle part of the Scene, in which Wotan and Loge probe into Alberich's present situation is less intense. (It starts when the dwarf addresses the gods: 'Was wollt ihr hier?' The dominant motif is 14A - *clever loge* - as he teases and jokes grimly with Alberich. The music is quick-footed and - given the serious dramatic substance - has a casual easiness. One new motif - obviously to be called *hoard* (M22) - is introduced as the dwarf dismissively describes the gold piled up by the Nibelungs when they first entered: 'Das is für heut; ein kärglich Haufchen!' (That's just for today!) The arresting orchestration has bassoon and bass clarinet in the upper line with the melody; the lower, lead in line, has cellos and double basses. Immediately after this the tone changes when Wotan asks the key question which brings forth Alberich's vicious intent: the hoard can lift him to world dominion. The words are supported by *hoard* in tandem with *ring* and, as this is clearly spelled out, the music rises to its second big climax.

18.36 *hoard* **M22**

The third part of the Scene starts with Wotan asking how this will be accomplished. I have surmised that the germinal episode, the starting point which seized Wagner's imagination for the Rhine Scenes was the appearance of the Gold as it glittered in the sunlight. This current group of four Scenes in Nibelheim turns around Alberich's response to this question and I surmise again that this was the stage and sound picture that he first imagined most clearly. Note that it starts at bar 530 - just over half way through the total of 929 in Nibelheim. Each Act - or in this case - groups of Scenes in a play or opera has its revelatory moment and Alberich's tirade at this point brings home to Wotan a new and nasty reality of which he was previously unaware. The music ought to lift in power and it does so here, swelling up to one of the high points of the score.

The dwarf launches into an operatic *scena* in five parts, lasting 2½ minutes and spread over 97 bars (one third of the Scene). The form is A, A', B, C, D; the tempo is moderate and does not change. The two A sections are closely related in structure, comprising firstly a sneering take on *love*, then *sexual desire* and concluding with a staccato run up from the bass over two octaves and a shuddering slip back to the current home key. The substance of both is that the greed for gold will bring down the gods. But to A' Wagner adds the chilling words about sex which are the essence of his depravity (p.153). The composer's singularly brutal view of Alberich's sexuality can be compared to Puccini's Baron Scarpia but not to much else within opera. Wagner had not encountered Schopenhauer when he wrote both text and music for *Das Rheingold* but one can surmise also that when he did read it some nine months later he would have felt the justification as described by Thomas Mann on p.18. Section B is a sarcastic commentary on how the gods currently live in comfort - all to the sounds of *valhalla* which starts in its original key of D♭ major. Section C is very short - nine bars of virtually unaccompanied recitative. Wagner wants the utmost clarity as Alberich spells out the brutality inherent in his earlier expectations with regard to sex: 'Beware! Beware! - for when your menfolk yield to my power, your pretty women, who spurned my wooing, shall forcibly sate the lust of the dwarf, though love may no longer smile upon him.' The contrast with the other sections is startling. This reiteration leads straight into Section D, the *scena's* coda. The composition is tight: the section starts with the rising bass scale that occurs in the middle of A and A′, and goes on to specify how Alberich's army and the gold they have will rise from the deep and sweep all before them. A combination of *hoard* and *woe* rise to an enormous climax.

Scene 14: Loge tricks Alberich who is captured. Loge and Wotan take him up from Nibelheim
[Schirmer: 143/4/4 to 156/3/8. Text from 'Vergeh, frevelnder Gauch!' to 'Nun schnell hinauf: dort ist er unser!']
The previous Scene was expositional: it displayed the nature and extent of Alberich's threat - a threat to the entire world order. This Scene is all trickery and action as Loge flatters to deceive him, and prompts him to boastfulness. The power of the Ring to terrorise is already demonstrated; all that remains is to show what the Tarnhelm can do. Loge learnt the basics from Mime and Alberich now fills in the detail - he can both disappear and also take the form of any living creature.

Motifs are plentiful but simply presented. Thus when Loge flatters we hear the *clever loge*; *valhalla* when power is mentioned; the necessary enslavement of the Nibelungs brings on *nibelung life*. The previously perceived power of the Ring summons *ring*. When Alberich sneers at Loge's cleverness we hear *clever loge* and *tarnhelm* accompany his recital of its powers. The one new motif is *dragon* (M23) as Alberich goes through his first transformation. That Loge's terror is simulated is made clear by the *loge* motif. The Scene ends when Alberich is caught.

18.37 *dragon* **M23**

Here, at the end of Wagner's Scene 3, Westernhagen focusses on the advance in dramatic technique evident in the variety of vocal colour for each of the four characters: 'Each of the four male voices - two tenors and two basses - is treated in a quite different manner, one might say orchestrated: Wotan's *bel canto;* Alberich's declamatory delivery, often rhythmically unbridled and verging at one point on free recitative; Mime's wails, coloured by short, sobbing acciaccaturas; Loge's ironic hauteur - the whole possibilities of vocal expression was already fully envisaged.' (CvW/FR,43) He also confirms that all four Scenes in Nibelheim were 'written out in one continuous outpouring, in spite of the huge span of its action and . . . of its emotional compass.' (ibid,48)

DAS RHEINGOLD

<u>Scene 15: Wotan steals Ring, Tarnhelm and gold from Alberich who curses whosoever should hold the Ring</u>
[Schirmer: 156/4/1 to 178/4/8. Text from 'Da, Vetter, sitze du fest' to Gönn ihm die geifernde Lust!']

This Scene, of 412 bars is the longest in the opera and clarifies Wotan's fall from grace. The earlier and greater lapse, namely the trade with Freia, forces him to this immense larceny. That the theft of the Ring is necessary does not hide the badness of the action: Wotan's moral nadir. Wagner was clear about this defection in the *Myth:* despite his faults, Alberich has justice on his side.

For the first time, Wagner finds himself instinctively using a full Freytag mini-drama format in this Scene, with Alberich and Wotan as protagonist and antagonist. The subject is the destruction of Alberich. The three musical high points occur where the drama intensifies and are different in musical nature, thereby providing contrast and accumulative dramatic power.

Freytag	**Action**	**Musical highlight**
1 Set up	Alberich needs to free himself from a bad place.	
2 Rising action	The price is made clear: he must hand over his gold.	The gold surfaces from the depths.
3 Mid-point crisis	Alberich learns the worst: he must forfeit Tarnhelm and Ring also.	
4 Falling action	He argues his valid case powerfully but to no effect.	Altercation between Wotan and Alberich
5 Catastrophe	The Ring is torn from him and he curses those who will hold or try to use it.	The curse

Of the 412 bars no less than 258 belong to Alberich and his music and, as one should expect, the musical high points also belong to the dwarf. There are three.

The first is the mighty crescendo as the Nibelungs bring the gold up to the mountaintop. This is based on *nibelung slavery, woe* and *hoard*. The duration is 65 bars, virtually all of which feature *nibelung slavery*. Above this ostinato, rising repetitions of *hoard* come next and these finally switch into massive orchestral cries of *woe*. Everything sounds natural and inevitable: an early example of Wagner's instinctive ability to fashion themes that seem made for each other. The climax is heavier than the descent to Nibelheim because it results from one slow but immense *crescendo*.

The second is the altercation with Wotan after he learns that he must give up the Ring, the form of which tells us that he has the better of the argument. Wotan asserts that Alberich has no clear right to own it and the music is strong. But the dwarf's response is withering: You couldn't make the Ring because you would not pay the price.

291

In shame and distress, I carried out the curse-laden, fearful deed - and now you want the benefit. If I have sinned it was only against myself alone but, if you take advantage now, your sin will be against the whole of morality. The above is conveyed in 34 bars of magnificent invective, as good as almost anything in the cycle, but described by Wotan as mere 'chatter'. He has and can have no answer, so he attacks and violently wrenches the Ring from the dwarf's hand. The comparison between their vocal lines (18.38) shows how Wagner conveys the greater force of Alberich's case. Both passages use almost the same musical contour but that of Alberich has greater extent and wider, sharper intervals in the melodic line.

18.38 The music shows that Alberich betters Wotan in argument.
Wotan's phrase occurs 12 bars before that of Alberich (Schirmer, 170/171). Wagner seems conscious of the contrast: only the expression marks for Alberich are given in the score.

The third musical highlight is that which contains the curse upon the Ring that sets the drama going. Two major motifs are heard in the final section. The first is *malice* (M24) which accompanies Alberich's description of the grief that will attach to those who hold the Ring. The second is the *curse* (M25) on the Ring itself. Cooke points out in his 1967 audio guide that a composite chord made up of the first four descending chords of *ring* forms the harmonic base of *villainous excitement* (see 18.29), *malice* and *curse*, and *scheming* (to appear in *Siegfried*) - namely of much that is seen as malicious. In this Scene, *malice* is repeated no less than 18 times but *curse*, in its primal format, occurs only once. The captions give some idea of why and how each motif is memorable. In the case of *curse* (as seen in 18.40), however, there is an additional power. What is known as the *curse* motif is but the first part of a long passage that extends over 63 bars and 28 of these deploy, in Alberich's vocal line, a pattern of similar intervals in each of

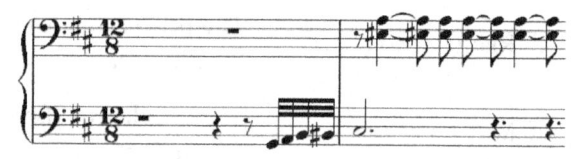

18.39 *malice* **M24**
This is one of the motifs the harmony of which relates to *ring*. But, that said, nothing else like it is to be found in music. The degree of originality is baffling. Where does it come from?

18.40 *curse* **M25**
The exposure of the melody over the unchanging low F# and the closing modulation into the key of A are reasons it sticks in the mind. The notes echo those of the rising conclusion of *ring*.

the five rising and four falling melodic lines, as seen below in 18.41. The listener is aware of the general impact of this repetition but will not pay much attention to the switching from major to minor third, with the seconds and fourths also thrown in for variety. There is similarity but no repetition. Given the impact on the music from this lone first appearance, one can but marvel at the composer's economy and the memorability of the motif itself.

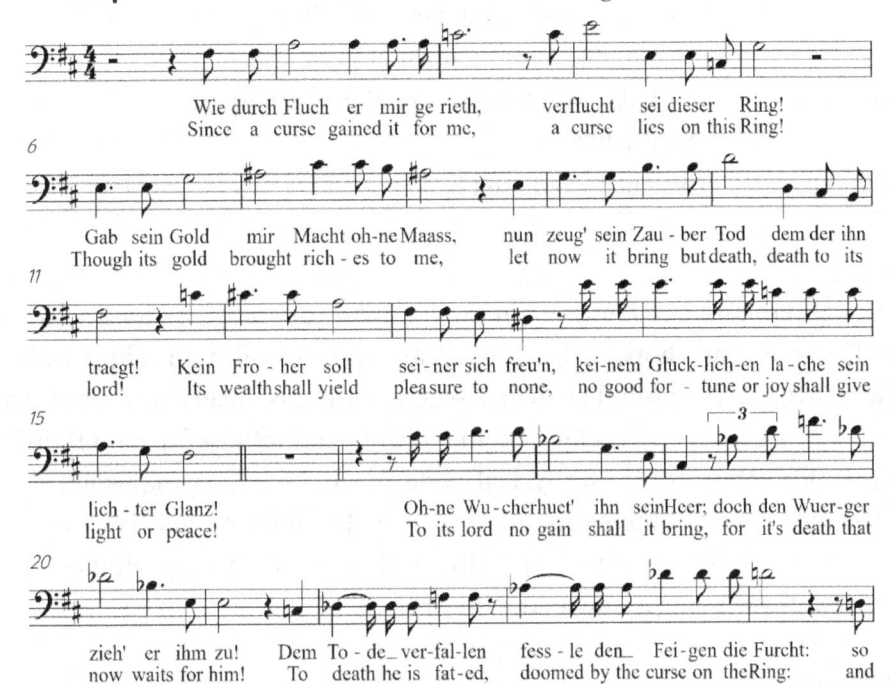

18.41 The intervals in Alberich's vocal line during the extended curse

[Musical notation with text:]
Wie durch Fluch er mir ge rieth, verflucht sei dieser Ring!
Since a curse gained it for me, a curse lies on this Ring!

Gab sein Gold mir Macht oh-ne Maass, nun zeug' sein Zau-ber Tod dem der ihn
Though its gold brought rich-es to me, let now it bring but death, death to its

traegt! Kein Fro-her soll sei-ner sich freu'n, kei-nem Gluck-lich-en la-che sein
lord! Its wealth shall yield pleasure to none, no good for-tune or joy shall give

lich-ter Glanz! Oh-ne Wu-cherhuet' ihn sein Heer; doch den Wuer-ger
light or peace! To its lord no gain shall it bring, for it's death that

zieh' er ihm zu! Dem To-de_ver-fal-len fess-le den_ Fei-gen die Furcht: so
now waits for him! To death he is fat-ed, doomed by the curse on the Ring: and

lang' er lebt sterb' er lech-zend da-hin, des Rin-ges Herr als der Rin-ges Knecht!
while he lives fear shall stalk all his days, the Ring's great lord, and the Ring's own slave!

- In these 28 bars readers will find five groups of rising intervals (basically a third) and a corresponding group of four, with falling intervals.
- Rising: bars 1, 6, 9, 21, 25. Falling: bars 11, 14, 17, 19.
- The falling intervals of a third variously and often represents coercion throughout the *Ring*, such as the domestic tyranny suffered by Sieglinde.
- The empty bar in stave 4 is different – a short passage, based almost entirely on *malice*. (Music obviously not shown.)

Scene 16: Wotan is persuaded by Erda to hand over the Ring and Gold to Fafner and Fasolt. Fafner kills his brother and leaves.

[Schirmer: 178/5/1 to 200/2/4. Text from 'Lauschtest du seinem Liebesgruss?' to 'An den reif rühr'st du nicht mehr!']

In the preceding Scene and in this lie Wotan's two actions that drive forward the drama: the purloining and then the relinquishment of the Ring. These Scenes are twice as long as those opening Scenes in the Rhine because the intentions and consequences of all preceding actions in the opera are gathered together. This Scene is more intense than the last because the after effects of the theft of the Ring are embraced. The structure is as follows and the meat of the action - and the climax of the opera - lie in the middle two episodes.

1	Set up	Joy at the return of Freia	58 bars
2	Rising action	The handover negotiations are prolonged by Wotan's refusal to hand over the Ring	189 bars
3	Wotan's crisis	Erda's intervention is the mid-point which concludes with Wotan's decision to relinquish it to the giants	137 bars
4	Conclusion	The murder of Fasolt by Fafner	28 bars

1 Set-up
This is brief and the music is entirely in the fresh air tones of C major and its dominant G major. There are also hopeful hints of a care-free sexuality in a hopefully care-free world. Twice over, in the prelude and also when Donner is observing the return of Freia, there occur three bars of the rocking theme of CM3 *seductive allure* - a motif that does not survive *Das Rheingold*. The lyrical style is obvious and four-square, to match perhaps the facile view of the situation as seen by the minor gods. The only motifs are *giants*, quietly muttered in calm expectation of the arrival and expected resolution, and *golden apples*, these being associated with Freia.

2 Rising action
Many motifs now, as the giants enter, as Freia stands whilst the gold is piled up to hide her, as the conflict between Donner and Fafner is eased by Wotan, as the Tarnhelm is needed to hide her hair, and Fasolt sees the gleam of her eye and the Ring is demanded from Wotan - who refuses to yield it despite the pleas of Fricka and Froh. This catalogue of action suggests speed and also simplicity. The motifs used are *giants, core life value, sexual desire, love, nibelung slavery, golden apples, tarnhelm, hoard, force of the gold, rhinegold, ring, woe*. Twelve in all, but the motifs are presented separately and are there to support the story played out on stage. The result is that the steadiness of motif occurrence and repetition progressively builds tension, slowly at first but with increasing speed as Wotan's resistance mounts until he declares 'den Reif geb ich nicht!'. This increasing momentum creates the dramatic climax, based on musical energy, and heralds the appearance of Erda (p.124). Porges tells of the impact in the 1876 rehearsals. 'Something completely new and unheard-of now takes place. That craving for power which has seized Wotan . . . awakens a superhuman power whose workings have hitherto been wrapped in mystery.' (HP/WR,37).

Wagner varies his technique to articulate the drama. Here there is no great surge of emotion or sudden reversal; rather it is a steady build of relevant motif after motif - clearly defined - over 181 bars. With the exception of Loge, the seven remaining characters on stage - Wotan, Fricka, Donner, Froh, Freia, Fafner and Fasolt - are at sixes and sevens (Wagner's direction is 'all stand confounded') and this is marvellously conveyed in the mounting musical tension. The episode lasts some eight minutes and this is needed to give it full weight.

3 Wotan's crisis

The contrast that follows the god's explosive denial could not be greater. The stage darkens and, as Erda rises from the ground, from the depths of the orchestra there slowly rises the *erda* motif (M26). This motif, obviously related to *life energy* but in a minor key, is in common 4/4 time in contrast to the initial 6/8. Hence the configuration of the arpeggio which soon accompanies it has eight notes per bar instead of six. But the intent is the same: *life energy* would naturally ally with the water of the Rhine. Erda's remit, however, is wider and the accompaniment to her motif finds a nearer cousin in the compositional motif *natural life*; affixed to the Wala, it might be thought to represent hope. Eight times it sounds before *malice* gives context to her message: that the gods are in great danger if Wotan keeps the Ring. Thereafter *woe* leads to two repetitions of *erda* before we hear *downfall* (M27), the celebrated inversion of the Wala's motif. Surrounded by this theme, Wotan learns the danger of keeping the Ring. As she disappears Wotan tries to detain her but is held back by the other gods and, with a final sounding of her motif, she is gone.

18.42 *erda* **M26**

18.43 *downfall* **M27**

Ragnarök is the threat to Wotan, as to Odin (p.48). Wotan seems to know this. Porges tells us that at his crisis point, the words 'Soll ich sorgen und fürchten, dich muss ich fassen, alles erfahren!' (If I am to live in disquiet and dread, I must catch you, learn everything!), that these words 'should be sung in a voice trembling with emotion... this is the only time in the *Das Rheingold* that Wotan completely loses that majestic self-control which he displays in all his other utterances.' (HP/WR, 38)

The episode to that point has lasted 5½ minutes and is followed by a very short coda: Donner bids the giants stay and Fricka pleads as Wotan stands motionless. His crisis point, in the Freytag format, is upon him and his wiser, second self emerges reluctantly into the light with one short brass fanfare: Wotan announces that the giants can have the Ring also. The episode ends with a powerful *core life value* and a jubilant celebration of *sexual desire* and *love*.

4 Conclusion

All is speed now, for the drama of Wotan's decision is over. Nevertheless, the musical construction of these 28 bars is deft. The first seven are a jointure of *giants* and *nibelung slavery*. The following seven are recitative. Then Loge responds to Fasolt's invitation to judge the competing claims of the two giants. It is this advice (maliciously provocative as ever), namely that only the Ring really matters, which brings on the first disaster. At that point the temperature rises and eleven bars of *malice* and *ring* lead to one of those violent *crescendi* that Wagner could summon almost out of nothing. The climax, as Fafner strikes Fasolt down, shocks the gods as it can still shock the audience. The hammer blows portray bludgeoning to perfection. Then Fafner leaves the stage.

Scene 17: The gods enter Valhalla
[Schirmer: 200/3/1 to the end. Text from 'Furchtbar find'ich des Fluchtes Kraft!' to 'Falsch und feig ist, was dort oben sich freut!']
To have an accurate overview of the conclusion of *Das Rheingold*, we must look with care at both text and music. The Scene extends over 329 bars and lasts between fourteen and fifteen minutes or about 10% of stage time. The composer has serious matter to convey and to deny that it is about some form of vindication of the gods is surely perverse. Wotan greets Valhalla with 'Thus I salute the stronghold, safe from fear and dismay' and he speaks truly. From the moment that the thunder clouds are summoned by Donner, the music is majestic and open, and the closing 181 bars are in D♭ major - that of Valhalla. The tone of Donner, Froh and Fricka matches the confidence conveyed by Wotan, and the audience can recall that these three gods were wisely instrumental in changing Wotan's mind. Few characters ride with such aplomb into so confirmed a tonic D♭ major as does Froh in the build up, as the clouds disperse, to the newly revealed Valhalla. This conclusion is not great music but it matches the stage action perfectly and need not be bombastic.

As it happens, the Scene is an extended dialectic. Thesis: fear and dismay at the murder. Antithesis: recovery of spirit with the revelation of Valhalla. Synthesis, as fear and hope are brought together when the gods enter the hoped for refuge.

Thesis: Wotan is deeply troubled by his near miss with disaster
This is introduced by two mighty iterations of *curse*. (Loge then interposes but, in this his last appearance, he merits separate treatment.) To *ring, erda, downfall* Wotan expresses his fear and need to meet again with the Wala. Fricka vainly tries to cheer him.

Antithesis: Donner counters this with hope for the future
He steps forward to make clear, despite inevitable foreboding, that everything is changed. As he summons the storm that is to bring forth the rainbow of hope, we hear one of the few motifs that clearly relate to *nature*, namely *storm call* (M28). The skies clear and the music moves from B♭ major to D♭ major, the majestic open tones of

18.44 *storm call* **M28**

which run to the opera's conclusion. Straightforward as this passage sounds, Wagner had to work hard to perfect it. Changes were made to Donner's vocal melody, then 'the whole conjuration of the storm was crossed out with a vigorous wavy line and a new version written out immediately after it'. (CvW/FR,60) This section concludes, of course, with the appearance of the rainbow. Along with Valhalla, the Ring and Nothung, this rainbow bridge Bifrost is one of the few artefacts within the eddas that is retained by Wagner. But its function is changed: in the sagas it is just part of the landscape but in the

18.45 *rainbow* **M29**

Ring we hear it as the symbol of hope, as first seen by Noah when the rain stopped. The *rainbow* motif (M29) is introduced by Froh and sounds finally as the gods march into the safety of Valhalla. But not to list it (as often happens since it is only heard in this Scene) is to overlook the clear relationship to *nature*. It may surprise readers to learn that *nature*, the motif from which much is derived, only appears in its primitive form in the preludes to *Das Rheingold* and *to* G3.1. Nevertheless, its bold intervals of 3rd, 4th and 5th are central to *wotan's sword*, *rhinegold* and *rainbow*. In this Scene *rainbow* is heard in sequence no less than seven times and hope is restored with its first appearance.

Synthesis: hope is brought in opposition to fear
Wotan's closing peroration and what follows both conclude the opera and act as a bridge to *Die Walküre*. Within its embrace lie hope in and fear for the future. Wotan seizes the hope but acknowledges it was not happily won; the expression of hope is accompanied by the continuations of *valhalla* (M8a and M8b), and fear by *ring*. The synthesis of hope and fear for Wotan is represented by the mighty entrance of what is universally known as the Sword motif. But Nothung has no meaning in itself - the motif signifies the emergence of a mission for Wotan, which is to protect his cosmos from the danger into which he has placed it. As a composite recollection of both the mission and the artefact, *wotan's sword* (M30) is the name in this study. Twice the motif sounds

18.46 *wotan's sword* **M30**
(The key signature is D♭ major but the motif sounds out in a triumphant C major.)

and leads into the processional entry into Valhalla, based upon *valhalla*, *wotan's sword* and, of course, *rainbow*.

The procession is interrupted by comments from Loge and the bewailing of the Rhinedaughters for the lost gold. These are both instructive but in different ways. Loge now reveals his open hostility to the gods. He thinks himself a cut above them - clearer in vision and without hypocrisy. His forebears are giants, the traditional enemies of the Nordic gods and his malevolence reminds the audience of future danger (p. 167). That

18.47 *rhinedaughters' lament* **CM9**

over, the march to safety continues but serious damage has been done. A Rhinedaughter was the first to sing in the opera and here the three of them together are to be the last to sing. This *lament* (CM9) for their lost gold is a plangent complaint directed at the gods. After this appearance, it is to lie dormant until it reappears as a reminder of a purer time whilst Siegfried makes his fateful journey to the Rhine in *Götterdämmerung*. In response, Loge tells them that they should be happy 'to bask' in the gods' new found splendour. This is undoubtedly a reflection of power-hungry Wotan. But the final grandiloquent march into Valhalla is introduced by the magnificent sound of *wotan's sword* at maximum volume. Vague as it might be in his mind, the god plans restitution and rescue. This is the sound the audience carries forward into *Die Walküre*.

Wotan's will-to-power is a major engine that drives the drama and he is never able to release himself from its grip. We see this lust at its most virulent when he decides to steal the Ring from Alberich; but in the Scene which precedes this one, under the influence of Erda, he steps back from the disaster inherent in the theft; in this Scene, the sounds of *wotan's mission* tell us something is to be done to rescue the world from the danger generated by the theft.

# # # # # #

A preliminary analysis of the *Ring* on p.32 posits that Wotan is both protagonist and antagonist: on the one hand is the power-hungry god who can be compared directly with Alberich and on the other is the benevolent autocrat, self-described as 'Licht-Alberich'. (p.129) From Scene 5 through Scene 15, his goal and the means to achieve it are little different from those of Alberich, and he comes close to being the mirror image of the dwarf as described by Cooke. (DK/WE,159.) The encounter with Erda changes everything and the scales fall from Wotan's eyes as Fafner murders Fasolt. The music shows us what is happening. Up to that point, the *Myth* may *tell* us that Wotan is benevolent but neither action nor music supports such a view. The structure of the drama and the music for Scenes 16 and 17 *show* us that he is transformed.

# # # # # #

Composition of the opera started on 1st November 1854 and was finished on the 14th January following. This new type of music flooded out in a torrent: evidence of pent-up creativity after the six years of silence, saving for the fragments from 1851. In this aspect,

Wagner aligns himself with all other great artists. The fact that his operatic output totals only a modest 32 hours of music would seem to distinguish him from such as Bach (of whom Newman has suggested that a copyist, working a normal working day, would require over 70 years just to make a fair copy of his compositions), Mozart and many others, who all produced a prodigious amount of work. In this company comes Shakespeare. In the year 1599, he finished, completed or started *Henry V, Julius Caesar, As You Like It* and *Hamlet*, and in addition largely organised the establishment and building of the Globe Theatre. Such compulsion to create is a feature of all great artists and in this Wagner is no different. His precocious productivity, however, did not result just in 'product' (to use a modern word) but in a mass of hidden, deep thought that drove him on toward as yet unknown lands, during the years 1848-1856.

◇ ◇ ◇ ◇ ◇ ◇

19

Die Walküre

ACT ONE

Wagner breaks this Act into three scenes (marked W): Siegmund and Sieglinde alone at the beginning, the scene with Hunding, including Siegmund's narration and Hunding's declaration of enmity and the love scene between Siegmund and Sieglinde which concludes the act (Column 1). The actual dramatic structure breaks down into nine Scenes. The number of bars for each indicates the proportionate length within the whole.

W1	1	Sieglinde finds and tends Siegmund	260 bars		Part 1
W2	2	Hunding arrives and takes command	95 bars	Rising action	668 bars
	3	Siegmund narrates his entire life	197 bars		
	4	Hunding declares his enmity to Siegmund	116 bars		
W3	5	Siegmund, alone, calls on Wälse to help	138 bars	Mid-point	
	6	Sieglinde and Siegmund perceive a bond	160 bars		Part 2
	7	The sexual passion between them grows	186 bars	Falling action	737 bars
	8	Sieglinde works out who they are	107 bars		
	9	Siegmund claims Nothung as his own	146 bars	Triumph	
				Total	1405 bars

This Act has always been amongst the most admired. One reason for this that has not been emphasised is its overall structure. The Act as a whole is in two parts. Scenes 1-4 establish all the dramatic ingredients. In Scene 5 Siegmund is alone and in a dark place and Scenes 6-9 see him move from darkness to light. It astonishes within Scene 5 that at bar 701, *exactly in the middle of the action,* Siegmund has just sung 'seiner Rache Pfand ich hier' (in pawn to his vengeance I rest here now). It is not possible to think of a more precise example of placing the moment of greatest danger, as per Freytag, right in the middle. So astonishing is it that it seems impossible for this to be simple coincidence. Structural symmetry as now understood was not studied in the 1850s so Wagner could not have any knowledge-based awareness. This matter is truly a mystery. Moreover, as the music moves forward into the second half of the Act, Siegmund immediately reflects on the hope that the sight of Sieglinde offers. The structural vitality of the whole permeates down into the structure of each of the nine Scenes.

Prelude

As with *Das Rheingold* but unlike *Siegfried* and *Götterdämmerung* the prelude of *Die Walküre* is not part of the stage action. With this opera it tells us what happened to Siegmund before the action starts. He is in flight to save his life, running through the forest and in a gathering storm. He thinks himself lost but the audience knows that the events stem from Wotan; the time has come to instigate the plan he has nurtured for some 25 years. So, by some magic means, he is guiding his son to the house of his twin sister. In this home Wotan has also planted Nothung, the sword that Siegmund will use to bring him the necessary victories. These will include the slaughter of the dragon of legendary ferocity and strength who has so far proved invincible and, in so doing, take beneficent possession of the Ring he now holds. To aid him in this is his sister; both have been schooled in hardship and are of a higher moral order than other men and women.

The prelude is simple: it vividly represents a man running very fast as he at last succeeds in escaping his pursuers. Wind, rain and thunder mount as the storm reaches its climax but, as the noise dies down after the climax, the audience realises that the man has never stopped running. The prelude is about Siegmund, even though the dire situation in which he finds himself was orchestrated by Wotan. The emphasis placed by some on the traces of *will-to-power* in the pounding repetition of Siegmund's desperate strides is misplaced if it diverts attention away from the Volsung onto his father: the trace is not obvious and at this point any thought of Wotan gets in the way of the drama. Other than that trace it is only *storm call* that reminds us of *Das Rheingold,* which announces the imminence of the approaching climax to the storm. We have clearly left the first opera behind.

Scene 1: Siegmund and Sieglinde
[Schirmer: from 5/4/4 to 15/5/6. Text: from 'Wes Herd dies aus sei, hier muss is rasten' to 'Wehwalt hiess ich mich selbst: Hunding will ich erwarten']
This very first encounter between the two lovers potently exemplifies the mastery of the whole, and perhaps more than any other Scene, for this is a mini-drama in five parts and 260 bars which exactly follows the pattern codified by Freytag.

1 *Set up* The principals are two people each of whom is lost and alone when they meet. (64 bars)
2 *Rising Action* Each senses that the other is emotionally and not just physically attracted. (82 bars)
3 *Mid-point* This experience is hitherto unknown to them. When Sieglinde brings the mead for them to share, they move into this unknown territory and each finds something that they know will change them forever. (41 bars)
4 *Falling Action* This knowledge is so powerful that they are not sure what to do with it. (42 bars)
5 *Resolution* They struggle with the issue but finally accept their mutual fate; they are no longer lost and alone. Their short journey is completed. (31 bars)

The Scene mirrors an awakening to a new life for these two outcasts; this drama lasts about 12 minutes and is constructed from four motifs. These are to occur over 50 times,

19.1 *siegmund* (**M 31**) appears first in the bass, and *sieglinde* (**M 32**) follows in the treble in the next bar.
They are shown here together as a paradigm example of a perfect musical match.

and occupy 101 bars or 40% of the score. The first of the four – *siegmund* (M31) – embodying man as an outlaw - combines with *sieglinde* (M32), a motif of intense femininity. This is a prime example of Wagner's capacity to meld disparate motifs so that they seem to be made for each other. The music repeats itself in sequence - a third higher in pitch, as seen in this example. Hope is there from the start.

When these motifs are fully established, *love* reappears and the motif finds its first secure home in the tetralogy. Its arrival is signalled by the heart-stopping chord with the low F below the hanging B♭ in bar 4. The orchestration is identical (even to the solo cello at the start) to that used by Verdi as the lead in to his greatest love music, between Desdemona and Otello - solo cello for three bars, then all the cellos as *love* enters. Wagner's method is not Verdi's, of course, and the composer then continues from the closing E♭ in 19.2 with four bars in which *love* is subtly amended. Note lengths are halved and semi-tones introduced. These intervals of languish and longing reappear frequently and are peculiarly attached to Siegmund and Sieglinde. An appropriate name is *love's bond* (M33).

19.2 The arrival of compulsive love into the world. *siegmund* in bar 1 leads to an echo of *sieglinde* in bar 2. This ends in the hanging B♭, and *love* (**M11**) enters in bar 4 where the low F accompanies it.

Finally, there emerges the fourth key motif, the first of two that encapsulates the ill-starred fortune of the lovers (M34 *volsung empathy*). This motif crops up subsequently many more times than others because it is open-ended: designed both for repetition and to be linked without effort to other motifs.

19.3 *love's bond* **M 33**
The opening E♭ is the last note in 19.2

And now for a crucial matter. For musical drama to work there must be conjunction between the dramatic and musical high points; we have also seen that the five-unit

19.4 *volsung empathy* **M34**
This combines instinctively with *sieglinde*.

dramatic structure is closely related to and possibly derived from the three-unit structure (p.28). There are three points in the 260 bars where the four motifs identified coalesce into quasi-symphonic commentaries within the orchestra. They start respectively at bar 82, bar 166 and bar 244 (roughly 1/3 and 2/3 through, and at the end of the Scene) and record the three moments that turn their lives around: the instantaneous physical and emotional attraction, the ritual drinking of mead that cements the attraction, and their acknowledgement of this as they wait for the arrival of Hunding. These three moments occur at the conclusions of stages 2, 4 and 5 respectively, and each tips the story forward into the episode that follows.

Scene 2: Hunding's arrival
[Schirmer: from 16/1/1 to 21/2/1.Text: 'Müd am Herd fan dich den Mann' to 'Gast, we du bist wüsst ich gern'.]

The motif that heralds his appearance is one of those comparatively few that is identified with one thing. The motif *hunding* (M35) occurs seven times, largely at the beginning and at the end of the Scene. The forbidding sound encompasses and cramps the middle section in which we hear poignant echoes of the previous music of the lovers. Simply and calmly Hunding dominates the stage.

19.5 *hunding* **M35**
This motif always stands alone; it never combines with any other.

His welcome is surly, and ominous when he feels the need to warn Siegmund, whose first words were protective of Sieglinde. No motif can now sensibly be apportioned to this music but musical contour and dramatic context matter. Sieglinde has previously said that both she and their house belonged to Hunding, and Siegmund is to flout Hunding's title to the woman. Siegfried is also to break the oath of blood-brotherhood with Gunther in *Götterdämmerung*. For both Hunding and Gunther these actions are anathema and they lead to the deaths of Siegmund and Siegfried respectively. The phrase in 19.6 is to be found as part of *curse* - illustrated in full on p.293. It casts its shadow forwards here, and also into *blood brotherhood* (p.252).

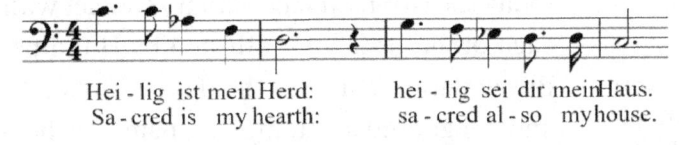

Hei - lig ist mein Herd: hei - lig sei dir mein Haus.
Sa - cred is my hearth: sa - cred al - so my house.

19.6 Premonition of *blood-brotherhood*
Danger to both Siegmund and Siegfried and musically rooted in Alberich's extended *curse*.

Scene 3: Siegmund's narration
[Schirmer: from 21/2/2 to 32/3/5. Text: from 'Friedmund darf ich nicht heisen' to 'Nun weisst du ... warum Friedmund nicht heisse']

This Scene does not have the same structure as Scene 1. That was a small drama in its own right; this is a sequence of facts that trace the fateful trail of Siegmund's life.

I assume Siegmund to be a tough warrior, about 25 years old, who has endured perhaps eight years of hardship after Wotan left him. The narration is the second longest scene in this Act and is in five parts.

A   The first describes his early childhood, up to the time when Wotan and he returned home to find the house destroyed, his mother dead and his sister gone. Siegmund's journey begins.

B   He is apprenticed to hardship, as he survives as an outlaw with Wotan, perhaps for two years. The music in this second part builds and accelerates into violence and then collapses as Siegmund finds himself abandoned by his father - the lowest point in his life.

C   The third period is that which I imagine to last about six years; he is a friendless outsider and shunned by both men and women. This takes the story forward into the present and it is the interjections from Hunding and Sieglinde which break the narration into two parts and thereby rushes the narrative forward into the immediate present.

D   This is the culmination of his struggle: the final, dangerous failure which is symptomatic of his whole life. He vainly attempts to prevent a woman being married against her will. He fights and loses.

E   There follows headlong flight and refuge in Hunding's house.

The first three parts of this narration are almost devoid of motifs, but such sparing use highlights how motifs influence the musical texture. *hunding* is undoubtedly a substantive motif and we hear vestigial mutterings in C through E. They seem brought into service as illustration of the general menace which surrounds Siegmund. Until today the two men have had no contact with each other, as is later attested by Hunding. But when we come to the day's events (D), and Siegmund's attempt to help the harassed woman, the relentless rhythm tells us that Hunding has something to do with it. In totality, 25 of the 197 bars in this Scene feature substantive motifs and 14 have *hunding* as what can be seen as threat in general. Thus the power of the Scene is not down to *leitmotiven* and there is nothing 'symphonic' about it: most of the Scene is powerful arioso. We can compare this with Loge's narration in R2 which is crammed with motifs and now have a clue as to why this latter is so spare with them.

19.7 This derivative of hunding is a very short term compositional reminder of perpetual threat. This is present in 14 bars.

For the narration works perfectly as it is: there is no lack of *musical* drama: well performed it is riveting to both hear and see. The reason is that it depends solely on Siegmund's own limited and constrained point of view. The end of this Scene is signalled by the entrance into the drama of two powerful pieces of music. The first is the

DIE WALKÜRE

[Musical notation with text: "Nun weisst du frag-en-de Frau wa-rum ich Fried-mund nicht heis-se"]

M36 *fated volsungs*

19.8 These fifteen bars comprise the conclusion of Siegmund's narration.

They encapsulate the melancholy story of the Volsungs. The first three is a repetition of *volsung sorrow* (M34) and lead into the wonderful tune wherein Siegmund describes the dire situation that now dogs his life.

In the last bars there enters *fated volsungs* M36.

This is another example when 15 bars sum up the entire situation.

unforgettable melody to which Siegmund sings 'Now you know, questioning wife, why my name cannot be Friedmund' and which is to return just one more time, appropriately enhanced in measure of its poignancy, in Siegfried's Funeral Music. The other is the appearance of the second motif associated with the twins - *fated volsungs* (M36). [A]

Scene 4: Hunding and Siegmund as foes
[Schirmer: from 32/3/6 to 34/4/6. Text from "Ich weiss ein wildes Geschlecht' to 'Mein Wort hörtest du: hüte dich wohl'.]
Action falls to almost zero during which only Hunding speaks. The Scene is like an interlude - still but menacing - between two periods of high tension. Thereby the Act is cut into the before and the after; these are roughly equal in length.

The three-part structure of this Scene is dramatically simple: Hunding's hostility, at start and at end, is contrasted with but is unable to dominate, the strange magic world in which Siegmund and Sieglinde find themselves. This other-worldly 'freeze-frame' ambience makes the scene difficult to stage. The music is also simple: all about Hunding at first and last, with the long orchestral passage in the middle belonging to the lovers. This is, indeed, the situation in which they find themselves.

[A] There is also a theme used by both Siegmund and Fricka to describe persecuted womanhood. Altogether, these are the two only occasions we hear this motif and it occurs seven times in total. It is a confusion to think of it as a motif at all but the temptation to do so has cause, for it makes a powerful impact. There are several such fragments that Wagner conceives but then can find no continuing use for.

Scene 5: Siegmund alone and resolute

[Schirmer: from 37/1/1 to 42/4/6. Text: 'Ein Schwert verhiess mir der Vater' to 'Tief in des Busens Berge glimmt nur noch lichtlose Glut.']

This short Scene is the centre of action in this Act and also stands out in the *Ring* as a whole because of its concentrated emotional force. The musical construction is a pure demonstration of 'verse melody' as set down in *Opera and Drama*. The listener is immediately aware of the unforced and almost inevitable match between word and tone and the Scene suggests anew that the impact of *leitmotiven* is secondary to that of verse melody in the *Ring* as a whole.

But there is more to this Scene than that. Firstly, it presents us with a classic Hegelian dialectic - thesis, antithesis, synthesis. The thesis is the bad situation in which Siegmund finds himself which forces from him the question: Where is the sword as promised by his father? This question is then answered (the antithesis) by the fire glinting on Nothung as it rests in the tree-trunk, which brings before him the memory of Sieglinde. The synthesis is the combination of resolve and peace that wells up within him: 'shadows of darkness [may] gather around me [but] deep in my breast there lingers on that last smouldering glow.' Secondly, the music (lyrically passionate to a degree) is almost devoid of motifs: only four soft *sword* references plus three muttered *hunding* echoes. Perhaps this is because Siegmund lives and feels simply as a persecuted man, quite independent of the big story in which he is part. This aloofness from cosmic matters, here and in the opening parts of the earlier narration, is deliberate on the composer's part and he is most skilful in bringing the big picture before us as the story arrives at this most critical day in the Volsung's life.

Scene 6: Siegmund and Sieglinde acknowledge their bond

[Schirmer: from 42/4/7 to 52/1/1. Text: from 'Schläfst du, Gast?' to 'Halt ich die Hehre umfangen, fühl ich ich des schlangendes Herz'.]

This Scene lasts from the entrance of Sieglinde to the moment when the spring night floods into the room. Dramatic significance is of the highest, the musical structure is complex and, therefore, examination of both is in greater detail than usual. As so often, the Scene is in three parts.

A   The first introductory part establishes the situation with the appearance of Sieglinde and is brief (27 bars out of the total of 160). We can sense that Wagner needed to move swiftly into the meat of the action.

B   Sieglinde, in a narration of 77 bars, which complements that from Siegmund in Scene 3, recounts her recent history from her marriage to Hunding, including the planting of Nothung in the tree. Throughout the episode, which lasts four minutes, her vocal line is a perfection of verse-melody as it melds with *leitmotiven* (easily recognised extended *valhalla* and *wotan's sword*). Nevertheless, this vocal line is quite detached from both motifs, save for one very subtle echo of the latter. First comes the voice floating above a full rendition of all parts of *valhalla*, after which the melody blossoms the more as the motif comes to an end. A descending phrase comes to a pause on 'Harm' (grief) in the passage 'Mir allein weckte des Auge suss sehnen den Harm, Thränen und Trost zugleich.' (Only in me did this eye awaken sweetly longing grief, tears and solace at once.) At that point the orchestra swells and changes key before expanding on 'Thränen' and 'Trost'. *valhalla* returns when Sieglinde says she realised the old man to be her father after he thrust the sword into the tree, and here is exemplary attention to *stabriem* in 'Da *wusst'* ich *wer* der *war*, der mich gramvolle *gegrüsst*; ich *weiss* auch wem allein in *Stamm* des *Schwert* er *bestimmt*.' (Then I knew who had greeted me, this woman laden with sorrow; I also know to whom alone he destined the sword in the tree.) Syllables in italics are emphasised in the melody: those starting with W in the first part and those giving weight to S and SCH in the second. And once again Sieglinde's melody is in rich counterpoint to *valhalla*.

C Finally, her excitement breaks bounds and pulls the vocal line entirely away from motifs. Narration of the past is over and present passion surrounds the lovers. As token of this, the emotion in the music is galvanized as the motifs change. The bars in question total 65 and a compositional motif *sieglinde comes alive* (CM10) fills 25 of these bars and holds the Scene together. On occasion this links up to *volsung battle cry* (CM11), yet another compositional motif which occupies twelve bars. These motifs, pulse across a total of 37 bars or 50% of the total. As Siegmund takes up the thrust, it is easy to overlook the single robust *fated volsungs* that forms his entry. The motif is transformed from lassitude to resurgent energy by a key change from the initial C minor into B♭ major - the forthright key of Brahms's *Haydn Variations*.

19.9 *sieglinde comes alive* **CM10**
This figure, unique to this scene, dominates 25 of the 65 bars and represents Sieglinde as she comes to sexual and emotional life.

19.10 *volsung bttle cry*

From the moment when Sieglinde acknowledges Siegmund as he who will claim the sword and herself with it (O fänd ich ihn heut' und hier, den Freund!) the music becomes symphonic in the following sense. When the vocal line soars and sustains long, loud notes, often above the stave, the orchestra supports the voice with motifs that conjoin: *wotan's sword* and the compositional *battle cry* plus what one might call bars of agitated excitement. Elsewhere the freely lyrical vocal lines that fulfil Wagner's intention as set down in *Opera and Drama* - verse-melody that self-generates the tune – are carried forward on the wings of *sieglinde comes alive*. She does so both sexually and emotionally.

This is the second love scene, the first being brought short by the arrival of Hunding. This second moves from a prosaic start, through a personal history to an explosion of emotion that swamps the two lovers. All this lies in the musical structure. The whole lasts only six minutes (half the length of Scene 1) but the audience feels no sense of haste. This may be because it realises that the story is but half told, and that this is so is made clear by the next Scene.

Scene 7: Sexual passion grows
[Schirmer: 52/1/2 to 64/2/4. Text: from 'Keiner ging, doch einer kam' to 'Mir zagt es vor der Wonne die mich entzükt!']
This Scene is different from all others in the *Ring* bar one. The other episode is that we will meet in the next chapter, as part of the final love scene between Siegfried and Brünnhilde – specifically when the music written for the *Siegfried Idyll* is introduced. Both of these Scenes introduce music that is different from the rest but the effect in this one might be thought the greater. In both episodes the lovers are taken out of this world and for a short period inhabit a magical realm where only they exist. In this Scene it is Siegmund's *Wintersturme* song, which is essentially a romance during which time is halted as in an operatic aria. Such fragments of motif that exist are absorbed into the compelling lyricism.

We can note that sexual arousal is seen in the woman rather than in the man. Siegmund's song enchants Sieglinde but, once over, she takes the lead and nowhere else, not even Act II of *Tristan und Isolde,* do we come across such sexually graphic music.

19.11 *sieglinde's passion (1)* **CM12**
The two bars are consecutive. The motif is in the second bar. The first bar is the accompaniment to Siegmund's *Wintersturme*. The motif has the same structure as the first save for the rests. This makes a very big difference: in this single bar, lyricism is replaced by urgency.

There are no less than four compositional motifs - CM10 in the previous Scene, CM12 and CM13 in this, and CM15 in the next - which depict her rising excitement. The Act as a whole is more about the emotional and physical freedom found by Sieglinde than it is about anything else. And once again, substantive motifs are few. In Siegmund's love song *love's bond* makes its mark. Sieglinde takes this up but then *sieglinde's passion (1)* (CM12) takes over and dominates many of the following bars. This develops from the accompaniment to 'Wintersturme' but becomes more urgent and more decisive. The love music returns but is then pushed aside by *sieglinde's passion (2)* (CM13) representing an extremity of passion as she sings 'was im Busen ich barg, was ich bin, hell wie der Tag taucht' es mir auf, wie tönender Schall schlug's an mein Ohr' (what I hid in my heart, what I am, bright as day, came to me). Siegmund's response introduces another motif,

19.12 *sieglinde's passion (2)* **CM13**

but one that only occurs in this Scene: *siegmund's passion* (CM14). Representative of sexual desire as it is, there is nevertheless a calmness, a realisation that consummation is inevitable and with it they will be made whole. This phrase dominates 48 bars and never reappears.

O sus-ses-te Won-ne!

20.13 *siegmund's passion* **CM14**

This eruption of compositional motifs is significant. The substantive motifs, as first expounded by Wolzogen, are designed to be instantly and easily recognisable; otherwise they would be of no use at all. A typical compositional motif is different: intended to merge into the background of the musical texture. So a listener should not think it odd that s/he cannot always discern when such a motif is doing its job, which is to help underline the drama and act as a glue that better positions a substantive motif.

Scene 8: Sieglinde works out who they are
[Schirmner: 64/2/3 to 70/1/1. Text: from 'Ein wunder will mich gemahnen' to 'Siegmund, so nenn' ich dich!']
In most cases the change of direction of the drama, the turning point into the next episode is obvious, such as when Sieglinde arouses the drowsy Siegmund in Scene 6. But sometimes the switch is only made clear by modification or transformation in the musical structure. This is what happens now and the herald is *valhalla* as Sieglinde sings 'Ein Wunder will mich gemahnen' (A marvel stirs in my memory).

The focus remains with Sieglinde. In three stages she is to uncover the truth and in order to do this Wagner now amasses motifs in a manner not seen before in this Act. Hitherto the deployment of motifs has been straightforward: the composer has knitted together two and never more than three motifs as he constructs discrete musico-dramatic episodes. But here, as passion gives way to memory, no fewer than six motifs are necessarily combined, plus three compositional motifs, to hold the structure together. The motifs are *valhalla, sexual desire, love's bond, fated volsungs, wotan's sword* and *will-to-power*. The two compositional motifs are *sieglinde's passion (1) & (2)*. The final seven bars, when the stage direction describes her as 'beside herself' and which lead up to the great cry 'Siegmund, so nenn' ich dich!' (Siegmund – that is your name!) are taken over by another 'riff' – *naming of siegmund* (CM14). We surely should not consciously be thinking about any of this as we see/listen: suffice it that we sense the change in direction and are absorbed into the accelerated final action up to the moment when Sieglinde names her lover as Siegmund, the man who will claim Nothung.

19.14 *naming of siegmund* **CM15**
Short term, violent excitement rising through the staves. This does not occur again. The passage was picked out in the first rehearsals: it 'must have a cutting edge.' (HP/WR,51)

Now undoubtedly this Scene can be called 'symphonic' but note that it extends only over 107 bars and lasts for about four minutes: an example as proposed on p.236.

Scene 9: Siegmund claims the sword
[Schirmer: 70/1/1 to the end. Text: from 'Siegmund heiss ich!' to 'So blühe den Wälsungen Blut!']

This Scene is an archetype of heroic achievement. Siegmund's action is representative of those symbolic feats by one man who performs a deed beyond the powers of others. We see this, writ small, in innumerable TV dramas and films: the man who wins through against superior odds, who comes up trumps when all others fail. The relevance of the motifs at this point are so clear that the audience just accepts them: the octave chord of *wotan's sword* spelled out again and again, a soaring return of *love* and *love's bond,* and the profound impact of *life choice*. The relevance of the last as Siegmund announces that 'supreme ecstasy's direst extremity, yearning love's aching need' is the moment when Alberich's own drastic choice is given the right perspective, namely a choice someone makes for his or her life. Note that Woglinde and Siegmund sing the motif in the key same key.

We do not immediately see that the music is also pushed through by a three-part dramatic structure; we may know the outcome but the power of the stage action never fails to grab the emotions.

A   Siegmund asserts his right to Nothung, as promised to him by Wälse. He commits himself irrevocably to the destiny that follows from possession of the sword.
B   Nothung now in his hand, he claims the woman that goes with its possession and presents it to her as a wedding gift.
C   Sieglinde completes their unity by giving out her name and declaring that she will be both sister and bride to her brother.

Wagner's approach to incest can be found on p.142. Included is reference to the 'divine' Antigone, born of the incestuous but true union of Oedipus and Jocasta, whose intervention is needed to bring down the corrupt State as embodied by Laius and Creon. It is hard not to think that the untainted blood of Wotan, via his children, is needed to conceive such a man as Siegfried. Moreover, at the risk of being thought too pseudo-psychological, Siegmund's last words 'So blühe den Wälsungen Blut!' suggest that at least Siegmund speculated on the prospect of having children.

The music builds relentlessly to that point. The melodic peak is as Siegmund claims Sieglinde as his own (19.15). This is the climactic mid-point of the tiny drama and Wagner knew he had to get this melody right. The composition draft shows that the quoted phrase - as found in the final score - is his fourth effort. The tune presents him to us: the sword in his hand is the supreme gift, a token of the new knowledge that - he believes - will carry them forward into a new existence.

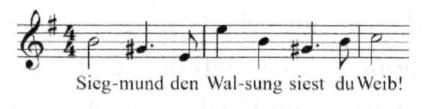

19.15 Simple as it sounds, this is Wagner's fourth attempt at it.

Sieg-mund den Wal-sung siest du Weib!

And the failure of the two lovers to realise this is a measure of the betrayal they suffer. (The background to the lives of the Volsung twins, as rooted in the sources, is to be found on p.139.)

# # # # # #

Readers can note that the only fully-fledged new motifs that are used in this Act are six in number: *siegmund, sieglinde, loves's bond, fated volsung, hunding* and *volsung empathy*. From *Das Rheingold* there are *wotan's sword, valhalla, sexual desire, love* and *will-to-power*. This makes a total of eleven in all. Siegmund's *Wintersturme* is a love song and cannot be called a motif. From the moment that Sieglinde joins her brother after she has drugged Hunding, the musical tapestry is held together not by acknowledged motifs but by those described as compositional, of which there are seven. These are largely designed to portray Sieglinde as she awakens to life, to hope and to love. The contrast between the music in this Act compared to that for *Das Rheingold* is prodigious: only a few months separate the composition of each and yet the sound worlds are entirely different. Melody in the vocal lines of the two lovers binds these two humans together in a manner foreign to the gods, dwarfs and giants. This verse-melody is vibrant within the precepts of *Opera and Drama* but runs independently of *leitmotiven*. Such could never have been planned, and what one must call the eruption within the composer's creative powers had a strong affect upon him (p.207).

◇ ◇ ◇ ◇ ◇ ◇

DIE WALKÜRE

ACT TWO

This Act is in nine Scenes.

1	Wotan instructs Brünnhilde to shield Siegmund.	100 bars	Set up and Rising action	Part 1 935 bars
2	Fricka trounces Wotan in argument.	427 bars		
3	Brünnhilde persuades Wotan to confide in her.	107 bars		
4	Wotan tells her the entire story to date.	301 bars		
5	Brünnhilde tries to rebel when Wotan commands her to abandon Siegmund.	167 bars	Mid-point	
6	Siegmund and Sieglinde enter in desperate flight.	303 bars	Falling action leading to tragedy	Part 3 899 bars
7	Brünnhilde tells Siegmund of his imminent death and entry into Valhalla. Siegmund refuses and his love for Sieglinde 'turns' Brünnhilde.	377 bars		
8	Siegmund in hope of victory watches over Sieglinde.	70 bars		
9	Sieglinde awakes to see the fight and the fall of Siegmund.	149 bars		
		Total 2001 bars		

This opera is about Brünnhilde because she undertakes the crucial journey within it, as seen in this Act. Despite the discursive content, the nine scenes can be broken into three parts. 1 to 4 lead up to 5, which stands alone and is the turning point in her life, when the principles which have governed it to date part company with those of her father. The bar in which Brünnhilde, for the first time in her life, defies her father is bar 984. This mid-point is only 16 bars adrift from the middle bar of the action. Part 3 sees the consequences of this implicit defiance, culminating in the tragedy of Siegmund's death. The total of 2001 bars includes the concluding orchestral postlude as Wotan storms off and the final 21 bars of the prelude. The former is a reflection of Wotan's anger and the latter encompasses that part of the prelude which anticipates the entrance of Brünnhilde.

Prelude
[Schirmer: 78/1/1 to 80/2/8]
The prelude is in two parts. The first part - an agitated combination of *wotan's sword* and *love* - represents the flight of the two lovers from Hunding's hut, and is a postscript to the first Act. These 54 bars do not connect with the opening Scene.

DIE WALKÜRE

Scene 1: Wotan instructs Brünnhilde

[Schirmer: 80/3/1 to 85/4/5. Text: from 'Nun zäume dien Ross, reissiger Maid' to 'Brünnhilde's final war cry.']

Within the prelude, the sound picture switches from the lovers and anticipates the oncoming Scene between Wotan and Brünnhilde. At full volume, we hear a version of the dotted triplets which signify *fierce action*. In this instance it can represent the excitement of riding through the air, for after 13 bars the celebrated *valkyr* motif (M37) enters as the curtain rises with Wotan facing his ebullient daughter. The stage action is a short and simple scene setter. The rhythm of *war cry* (M38) after Brünnhilde first bounds onto the stage is not precisely the same as in *fierce action* - the dotted triplet being differently positioned – as is to be found associated with Siegfried.

19.16 *valkyr* M37

19.17 *war cry* M38

Scene 2: Wotan and Fricka are in dispute

[Schirmer: 86/1/1 to 107/4/7. Text: 'Der alte Sturm, der alte Müh!' to 'lass ihn dir künden, wie das loos er gekiesst.']

The drama starts here, with the longest Scene in the Act. This is Fricka's biggest Scene when, in line with her powerful character, she engages with the plot to maximum effect. The action is a dispute, comprising a sequence of six dialectics. The classic dialectic (thesis, antithesis, synthesis) corresponds to each argument put forward. Thus if Wotan opens with a proposition, Fricka will make a counter proposition and Wotan will close the sequence with some sort of synthesis of the two. This will launch the next tripartite sequence but this time Fricka will open and close it. The sequence has a clear trajectory, and the dispute is played out. The six altercations are as follows.

A Wotan and Fricka confront each other.
B Fricka attacks via the breaking of marriage vows and the incest involved.
C Wotan says that love is all that matters, that incest is necessary to achieve a bigger goal, namely to come to the aid of the gods.
D Fricka cannot counter this so she switches attack. It may be necessary that mankind help the gods but this is only possible because Wotan has also shaped them to be able to do so. Siegmund is Wotan's tool and Nothung is the epitome of this.
E Wotan is in retreat and Fricka drives her argument through in three stages. First, Wotan thrust Nothung into the tree; second, the gods cannot turn a slave into an ally; third Wotan is putting this slave ahead of and above his own wife.
F Wotan acknowledges defeat. Fricka insists that Brünnhilde must not help; Wotan must also remove the magic power of the sword; Wotan must give her his word.

A The confrontation

One most significant motif appears, called *conflict* in this study (M39). This motif, and its variations, has a long reach into Wagner's works as Cooke explains in *Wagner's Musical Language*. (*The Wagner Companion,* Faber & Faber, 1978) He argues that both the interval of a falling fifth and the contour of the phrase indicate something - which can be anything - that stands in the way of a hope or intention or achievement. [B] At this point, it stands for Fricka's specific objections.

19.18 *conflict* **M39**

B Fricka attacks

No motifs are introduced but one phrase encapsulates both the best of verse-melody and Fricka's control of the action at this point. This is also a fine example of how Wagner uses the orchestra (the bass line with horns and bassoons in unison) first to mirror and, in the second line, to counterpoint the vocal line, with the expression marks, as indicated, against every instrument. The memorable phrase in which Hunding claimed ownership of Sieglinde on p.303 is brought forward as part of Fricka's case, and is the content of the bass line. (The phrase will now lie dormant until G1.2.)

19.19 Fricka's powerful presence
Note that the bass melody in the lower system is a that seen in 19.6.

Elsewhere, the motifs are *hunding, love, love's bond* (as Wotan argues for the incestuous twins) and *conflict,* as Fricka supports Hunding.

C Wotan defends love and incest

No new motifs here either. It opens with *love's bond* as Wotan makes the case for the twins. This brings in *conflict* as she launches into a 92 bar *scena* - almost a quarter of the entire scene. 49 bars of this are an aria which starts 'O was klag'ich um Ehe und Eid' (O, why do I mourn over marriage and vow). Disguised within it we can discern a distorted chromatic version of *love*, the absence of which between her and Wotan is the theme. *conflict,* thrice in a descending sequence, allows Wotan back in to state the cosmic case for what has happened.

[B] Cooke's paradigm example is the music announcing the prohibition on Elsa, forbidding her to ask anything about Lohengrin.

The dialectic is now pronounced. First, Wotan calmly argues for a blessing by Fricka on the young couple. This is countered by the anguish and turmoil of Fricka's aria: the fear of all that may happen. She ends it with 'So führ'es den aus! Fülle das Maass! Die Betrog'ne lass' auch zertreten! (Just finish it off; fill the mug to the brim! Let her you cheated be crushed too!) The music of Wotan that follows takes on authority and confidence, in contrast to Fricka's agitation. He is calm in his certainty and he concludes the sequence. 'Eines höre! Noth thut ein Held, der ledig göttlichen Schutzes, sich lose vom Göttergesetz.' (This impasse requires a hero, who, freed from the gods' protection, is independent of their laws.) Single utterances of *wotan's sword, will-to-power, ring* accompany his speech. These are the three artefacts or symbols of power in the *Ring* and we can marvel at the surety with which the composer summons and melds them, one after another, at this crucial statement. All in all, there are few motifs in this episode. Wagner wants us to hear the argument clearly and directly.

Fricka immediately sees she has lost that round. She is not able to maintain the moral high ground. Indeed, she seems unable, and certainly makes no effort, to turn her mind to Wotan's big picture, to the extent that one can wonder if she is aware of what her husband is about. Note that the high musical point in her Scene was the aria and this was about herself and not about Hunding's honour. One result is that her attitude actually elevates Wotan's moral viewpoint. For in (C), where he here argues his case, Wotan also acknowledges that the form of law he has imposed on society is not enough.

D *Fricka argues that Siegmund is not independent*

Despite (or perhaps because of) the truth that the earlier argument has diminished her morality, she now comes up with a mode of argument that is not based on any morality at all. This lack of a moral base and reliance on rigid custom may be the reason for an almost complete absence of motifs. *wotan's sword* and *will-to-power* are mentioned, as expected, when Wotan says he is not protecting Siegmund and as Fricka raises Nothung as an issue. The sword is the symbol of Siegmund's dependence on Wotan; he therefore cannot be the hoped-for free agent. This is the one truth, and it is a very obvious truth, that Fricka alone perceives. and she does so because her vision is unclouded by hope or by moral empathy. The argument is in taut recitative and much is unaccompanied - the words are important. The episode ends as Wotan violently sings 'Siegmund gewann es sich selbst in der Noth!' (Siegmund won it himself in his need!)

E *Fricka drives home her advantage*

In this dialectic, Fricka holds the stage throughout and Wotan can only respond with gestures of distress. This episode opens with the first statement of the motif best described as *wotan's balked will* (M40). (It is a distorted version of *will-to-power*.) To emphasise importance, the motif is

19.20 *wotan's balked will* **M40**

repeated three times in immediate sequence, rising by a third and then a further third. A break follows, filled by *conflict* in counterpoint with *will-to-power* before a fourth repetition of *wotan's balked will*. Then Fricka launches into her second *scena* in this Scene - an arioso recitative followed by an aria - of full melodic amplitude and self-confidence. The music is motif-free, save for *conflict*, and the verse-melody tells the story.

F   *Wotan admits defeat*
In the final stage Wotan is defeated. First, Fricka drives home her demands whilst *wotan's balked will* keeps pace with his muffled replies. Seven times it comes, the last three in rising thirds and quick succession until Wotan bursts forth in protest - 'I can't strike him down; he found my sword!' To avoid repetitious argument within the drama, Wagner now skilfully brings Brünnhilde onstage, her music as rumbustious as ever, and this enables Fricka to conclude the dialectic with a hymn to her victory. This is a full-blown aria and thereupon Wotan gives his oath and Fricka makes her final exit, having entirely misunderstood the situation.

This Scene is an immaculately structured mini-drama, lasting in the region of seventeen minutes. The dynamic is the fall of the protagonist Wotan counterbalanced by the rise of the antagonist Fricka. The Scene has six stages and the turning point – the issue with Nothung – comes in the middle, at stage D. The music conveys this subtly and without display. In the first half Wotan's music is self-confident and Fricka's is fretful. This changes once Nothung comes into the picture; thereafter it is Fricka's music that has the confident stride, ending in the rich amplitude of her 'aria'. But the triumph is muddied because it is almost entirely about her personal honour.

Scene 3: Brünnhilde persuades Wotan to confide in her
[Schirmer: 108/1/1 to 112/2/6. Text: from Schlimm, fürcht ich, schloss der Streit' to 'Mit mir nur rath'ich, red'ich zu dir']
This short Scene has eight speeches between Brünnhilde (B) and Wotan (W), plus an orchestral postlude. These nine exchanges break down into three dialectics, each one acting as a thesis (T), antithesis (A) or synthesis (S). Each synthesis pushes the action along into the next dialectic. Each dialectic is identified by a different musical character.

Dialectic 1
B asks what is wrong (T); W gives her a hint (A); B presses for more (S).
   The music consists entirely of five repetitions of *wotan's balked will*.

Dialectic 2
W gives violent voice to his distress (T); B says he can trust her (A); W fears that she may break free of his will (S).
   In the example on the facing page, the immense problem he faces is brought home.

DIE WALKÜRE

19.21 Wotan in despair
Line 1: bars 1-4 *wotan in revolt*, bars 5-6 *conflict*.
Line 2: bar 1 *despair*, bars 3-5 *wotan in revolt*.
Line 3: bars 1-2 *despair*, bar 3-6 *core life value*

As Wotan violently reacts in this Dialect, a melding of no less than four major motifs – *curse, conflict, love, core life value* – bursts in, plus one substantive and one compositional motif. The new substantive motif *wotan in revolt* (M41) is a distorted, rising inversion of *will-to-power* and accompanies Wotan when he is acutely distressed.

19.22 *wotan in revolt* **M41**

Such a name gains support from comments about the first 1876 production. Wotan's words 'Endloser Grimm! Ewiger Gram!' (Endless rage! Eternal grief) are sung to the self-same tune that brings the descent to Nibelheim in *Das Rheingold* to its climax, when Porges records Wagner's words: '[Wotan] rails against his compulsion to dominate the world.' (HP/WR,28)

The compositional motif CM16, a downward swoop from *ff*, is coupled with despair throughout the cycle. The impression is that the whole passage just flowed from his pen, with one motif merging into the next.

19.23 *despair* **CM16**

Dialectic 3
B says she *is* his will (T); W submits: 'I think aloud when speaking with you' (A); the orchestral postlude is the synthesis of their accord. B has calmed W. (S) The next Scene is prepared for.

> This has only one vestige of *love* and concludes with a wonderfully gentle descent over almost two octaves of *wotan's balked will*.

Scene 4: Wotan tells Brünnhilde the whole story
[Schirmer: 112/2/6 to 130/3/3 Text from 'Als junge Liebe Lust mir verblich' to 'Zernage ihn gierig dein Neid!']
This monologue lasts about 12 minutes and is a mini-drama in both words and the way that the music develops. The drama advances in six stages, which break down into two groups.

> The first group retells the history from the beginning to the present time. Motifs are few and there to underline the main narrative events within the story; the music is restrained in expression.

Stage 1
The history is told from the start of Wotan's rise to power to the point where he grabs the Ring from Alberich. (26 bars) The emotional temperature is low and the emphasis is on clear telling of a complex story.

Stage 2
The history lesson continues. At this critical point Erda intervenes; Wotan gives up the Ring; Brünnhilde and her sisters are conceived so that Valhalla is protected. (62 bars) Even fewer motifs here. The exposition is longer because there is a lot of information for the audience to take in. The emotional temperature remains subdued.

Stage 3
The threat that Alberich is preparing: the Ring may be with Fafner but woe betide if Alberich recovers it; Wotan is impotent before this. (40 bars) The tempo increases as the story moves toward the present. Motifs now put musical flesh on the emerging problem: *erda, ring, giants*. The motifs are carefully detached from each other, to emphasise key elements in the plot. They do not merge or overlap in order to increase tension.

> The past history covered, from Stage 4 onwards Wotan talks about current problems. The emotional temperature rises, aided by the use of motifs. But they are differently used in each Stage: Stage 4 is based around one motif alone; Stage 5 has many central motifs which finally combine in a full symphonic manner; Stage 6 has just two dominant motifs, both of which are redolent of hatred and stress. By this method the composer 'paragraphs' the closing stages of the Scene. This paragraphing is mirrored as each of these three stages conclude with an outburst to convey Wotan's explosive anguish.

Stage 4

A hero who is entirely independent (Siegmund) was needed to compensate for Wotan's impotence, but he has failed for he 'can only make slaves!', and can do nothing. (55 bars)

Now there arrives a new motif that embodies the way in which motifs in the *Ring* of different import can conjoin as if designed for each other. The conjunction here is between *erda* and *wotan's balked will*. Between them, in bar 2, is a fragment of *downfall*. Variously named in the past, it is here called *wotan's struggle* (M42). This becomes an important motif in this particular opera and is to find its apotheosis in the final Immolation in G3.2 as Brünnhilde bids her father to rest. Of the current 55 bars it occupies no less than 40, either spelled out or broken into repetitive bits. In terms of Wagner as a symphonic composer, this long passage is a poem on this motif, with Wotan's anguish made clear in the text. It lasts about two minutes and increases in intensity to build the first big musical climax. It is self-contained. Nietzsche wrote that 'Wagner is really . . . our greatest musical miniaturist who compresses an infinity of meaning and sweetness into the smallest space.' Here he does just that.

19.24 *wotan's stuggle* **M42**
Bar 1 is *erda;* bar 3 is *wotan's balked will* and bar 2 effects the juncture between them.

Stage 5

Brünnhilde intervenes: Surely Siegmund is not dependant on you? This brings Wotan to a critical admission: Fricka is right - Siegmund cannot go forward if this depends on Nothung and he must therefore be abandoned. Wotan's attempt to keep the Ring is the cause. All hope is now lost. (80 bars)

Motifs now pile in: *ring, love* (desperately presented as it is threatened), *core life value, wotan's sword, siegmund, wotan in revolt, curse* and, most powerfully, the compositional motif *despair*. The music grows in intensity. From the moment when Wotan admits his guilt ('Ich berührte Alberichs Ring') through to *'Das Ende!'* (54 bars - 1/6th of the entire monologue) it is fully symphonic and ends with the second huge climax. Wotan faces catastrophe.

Stage 6

Alberich now anticipates victory. For a 'free' son has just been born to him, in contrast to Wotan whose son is not free. Let Alberich, therefore, now take over. (42 bars)

As Erda foretold that this would happen, her motif heralds this final stage. Then 19 bars are given over to *malice* as Wotan contemplates the implications and this distends into a grossly distorted *valhalla* and *rhinegold* (21.25), as the god aban-

21.25 *valhalla* and *rhinegold* distorted

dons his vanished hopes to Alberich and the horrors he will bring. This is the third and most violent and most complex of the musical climaxes in this Scene, written down in the composition score without emendation.

#

Two powerful dramaturgic features emerge in this Scene. Firstly, if it is true that Wotan was always well-intentioned, this intent to bring benefit is nowhere explicit. He goes no further than to argue *in the abstract* for the strength that Valhalla brings, for the goodness inherent in the love of Siegmund and Sieglinde and for the need of a good man to do what he cannot. His moral nobility must therefore find expression in the music. It is only in the three mighty episodes of unassuaged grief (to which can be added his outburst in the previous Scene) that the god's agony in the face of his failure makes explicit the extent of his hopes: the music makes the drama. The second feature is that the whole Scene is a progression from gloomy recollection to a full realisation of the current state, and that this progression conveys 'thought in action'. The crisis with Fricka requires Wotan to take full stock of everything and the audience is privy to the emotional substance of each thought as it develops - in real time. The music gives this substance and the drama is instantly absorbed, with minimal thought on how it is done.

#

Scene 5: Brünnhilde rebels against Wotan's wish
[Schirmer: 130/3/3 to 138/3/9. Text from 'O sag, künde, was soll nun dein Kind' to 'Im höchsten Leid muss ich dich treulos verlassen!']
This is the central Scene in this Act, a forerunner to that which is shortly to follow, which is the central Scene in the whole opera which leads to the central Scene in the whole tetralogy - at the end of Act III. Its importance cannot be understated. As in Scene 2, also between father and daughter, this is in three dialectics made up by nine exchanges; these comprise seven 'speeches' and two orchestral passages. The three disputations are as follows, and the dialectic is indicated by T, A and S.

Dialectic 1
Brünnhilde pushes back against Wotan's decree. She asks what she must do (T); he tells her to 'fight for Fricka' and abandon Siegmund (A); she reminds Wotan that he loves Siegmund and pleads on his behalf (S).

Dialectic 2
Wotan reiterates his command even though it is hard (T); his daughter now refuses (A); he becomes very angry indeed (S).

Dialectic 3
Brünnhilde submits but establishes her enhanced understanding. Wotan's rage continues to be expressed in the orchestra as he storms away (T); she reflects sadly on the situation (A); her sadness is given expression in the concluding orchestral passage (S).

But a border has been crossed: whereas Wotan remains locked within the ordinances he has created, Brünnhilde has moved morally beyond and above them. This is the transitional scene within the middle of the Act.

19.26 *brünnhilde pleads for siegmund* **CM17**

19.27 *wotan's rage* **M43**

Motifs in the first two dialectics are few although they do play off each other. *wotan in revolt* (or often just the first part of it) bumps up against a compositional motif *brünnhilde pleads for siegmund* (CM17). Wotan's wrath rises steadily throughout *Dialectic* 2 and into the orchestral passage, the synthesis. All has been leading to 3(A), the moment when Brünnhilde is alone - for the first time in the Act.

In 3(T) we hear *wotan's rage* (M43) for the first time. This leads back to *wotan's balked will (ff)*. This last quietens during the final postlude: the music changes from distress to compassion as Brünnhilde moulds it to her new-found understanding.

The mythic Brynhild was endowed with surpassing wisdom but Wagner removes this from her, perhaps with the confidence that the music would supply this. That it did so is exemplified by the 14 bars that conclude the present Scene (illustrated on p.172). Here and in Scene 7 which is to follow we glimpse the perfection of womanhood as described by Campbell (p.170) and perhaps envisaged by Wagner

Scene 6: Siegmund and Sieglinde
[Schirmer: 138/4/1 to 152/1/1. Text from 'Raste nur hier' to 'Schweste! Geliebter!']
This is a depiction of the progressive descent by Sieglinde from terror into a delusional madness. It has a dual purpose: to give context both to Siegmund's response to the summons to death which is to follow and to the crucial impact this has on Brünnhilde. The progression is in five stages; it starts badly for Sieglinde and ends worse.

A Sieglinde is violently disturbed; the music is a symphonic extemporisation on a compositional motif *sieglinde's anguish* -

19.28 *sieglinde's anguish* **CM18**

a fragment of *love* repeatedly played fast and with distress (CM18) over 67 bars of the 171 that make up episodes A and B. This is a variation of the turbulent music heard in the prelude to this Act, which is based on *love*.

B She is filled with shame because Hunding had previously possessed her. Now there is a mental 'switchback' as she oscillates between desperate love for her brother and horror at the degradation of all previous sex. Wagner's skill in adapting a musical germ to a new purpose is shown in the first of these oscillations, to do with the love

DIE WALKÜRE

that Sieglinde has just found. The passage from 'Da er sie liebend um fing' (when in your loving embrace) to 'und seele durchdrang' (when my senses were won) - a total of 31 bars - is constructed around a softened *sieglinde's anguish*, which merges at the end with three rising repetitions of *siegmund's passion*. The music which follows is free composition and reflects the horror of the forced sex she endured with Hunding; without motif it must properly be, for nothing can convey the abominable effect of forced sex. c

C Siegmund asserts that Nothung will avenge her. This short section is clearly presented, opening a virile variation on *fated volsung* and ending with *wotan's sword*.

D But the hope offered is swept aside by Sieglinde's now violent and illusory imagination. To surging sextuplets she sees Hunding's dogs and kinsmen in pursuit and, as madness comes close, this changes to an insist remorseless falling phrase [19.29] that grinds through the bars. 'Never has the sound of terror been better captured . . . using bassoons, bass clarinet and violas in unison – an unforgettable torture that presses the knife to the bone.' (RS/RT,147)

19.29 Hunding's dogs in pursuit

E As Sieglinde nears collapse, *sieglinde's anguish* reverses itself and rises from a low F# in a similar rhythm to *erda*. Her vision extends to the end of all things and prophetically touches on the cosmic, as it ends with the fall of the World Ash Tree.

Save for brief appearance, this entire Scene is free of substantive motifs. The orchestra gives us some eight minutes of tight development of compositional motifs over which Sieglinde pours forth her terror. This music resists categorisation: it is what it is.

<u>Scene 7: Siegmund, for love of Sieglinde, declines the offer to go to Valhalla, and Brünnhilde is overwhelmed when she understands the nature of this love.</u>
[Schirmer: 152/1/2 to 172/4/1. Text from 'Siegmund! Sieh auf mich!' to 'auf der Walstatt she'ich.']
There can be few for whom this Scene is not amongst the most compelling: instinctive comprehension of dramatic structure expressed by music of immense beauty and immediacy. The Scene lasts about 24 minutes and is a mini-drama between two people. Brünnhilde is the protagonist, on a journey toward understanding, and Siegmund is her antagonist whose resistance wins her allegiance. Brünnhilde's surrender was foreshadowed in Scene 5 - the dramatic hinge around which the Act turns. Now we see the triumph of human compassion over the rigidity of law and - as a result - the irrevocable

---

c Paul Dawson-Bowling, a family doctor, writes thus: 'How on earth did Wagner know? He has here described minutely and exactly the desecration, the befouling of inner citadels, the misery and self-loathing that women who have been raped and abused often describe, and until the last fifty years the magnitude of the psychological damage was seldom recognized as does Wagner.' (PDB/WE,480)

choice of two people in favour of steadfast courage over expediency. The valkyr had lost her moral bearings when Wotan forced her submission in Scene 5 and here she is to rediscover them. The mini-drama is in five parts, in line with Freytag.

1 Set Up

This is orchestral, lasts a full three minutes and – in contrast to the previous Scene – is fully motific. An atmosphere is established – one completely unknown before the *Ring* – as we witness for the first time a dramatic interchange that is intended to chart the meeting of mortal and immortal in the context of imminent death; 'sacred' is not too strong a word. [D] After Sieglinde 'sinks senseless into Siegmund's arms', the compositional *sieglinde's anguish* reverts to its origins. The fragment of *love* from which it is made – just four notes – is played very slowly four times, virtually unaccompanied. Then the score reads 'A long silence, during which Siegmund bends over Sieglinde with tender care'. Whilst he does so *love's bond* enters and quickly the violas, cellos and double basses enter and swell to give almost the same harmonic grounding as in that first iteration. The audience is taken back to the moment when two fractured lives became aware of a mutual wholeness. The expressive power of the harmony moves on to two new and rich substantive motifs. As the drama unfolds, these are generally associated with cosmic matters and here they clearly relate to Brünnhilde and contrasted as to substance with the human lovers. Nevertheless, the orchestration works to unify – at this early stage – the fate of the lovers with that of the valkyr. It is a moment of high drama that goes beyond beauty. (51 bars lasting about 3½ minutes)

19.30 *destiny* **M44**

The audience knows it is in new territory firstly with the introduction of the motif which is here called *destiny* (M44). This is followed by *lament of death* (M45) – a motif that always hovers around mortal and fateful matters. Clearly M45 is a sequential augmentation of M44 and they can be linked together with ease.

19.31 *lament of death* **M45**

2 Rising Action

This is in two parts. Firstly, a sequence of six questions by Siegmund, duly answered by Brünnhilde; then the questions change to a sequence of five statements, with

---

[D] Great music sanctifies high points in opera. The closing ensemble in *Figaro*, after Countess Almaviva discloses herself, is one such and another is the final scene in *Fidelio* as Leonora prepares to loosen the shackles binding her husband with the words 'Welch ein Augenblick!'. In both cases cast and audience can be raised to a higher level of awareness.

DIE WALKÜRE

corresponding responses. Both people hereby learn to understand each other. (192 bars lasting about 12 minutes)

Motifs *destiny* and *lament of death* are to be the basis of the five questions and answers in the first part of this section. Valhalla is the subject so parts of *valhalla* occur six times; *valkyr* occurs twice and *sexual desire* twice. These latter three motifs are each able to conjoin effortlessly with the repetitions of *destiny* and *lament of death*. The questions are asked by Siegmund to the latter motif and the answers from Brünnhilde are weighted with *valhalla* and *valkyr*. Bearing in mind Wagner's assertion that the music was present in some way in his mind when he wrote the texts, it is difficult not also to think he made advance assumptions on how the musical fabric would knit together. The two motifs which drive this mighty episode were surely held back for this moment - perhaps the key encounter in the entire cycle. This Scene lifts the whole drama to new heights.

After Siegmund learns that Sieglinde is not to die with him, the dialogue changes: he *states* what he thinks and/or what he will do and forces a *counter-reply* from Brünnhilde. The 52 bars that follow, which include four of the exchanges between the two, are dominated by a compositional motif representing *siegmund's defiance* (CM19). This motif knits together *destiny, lament of death* and *wotan's sword*.

19.32 *siegmund's defiance* **CM19**

The proportions are significant. This section is almost 2/3^{rds} of the whole, in which the build-up of weighty dialogue steadily raises the emotional level so that the remaining sections carry the *action* forward at a hectic rate and a higher level of intensity

3   Mid-point

When Siegmund learns that Sieglinde must live on alone he declines to go to Valhalla. The reality of compassionate love is made clear to Brünnhilde. She moves into unknown territory where all is changed. (42 bars lasting about 3 minutes)

The crucial moment is upon Brünnhilde when Siegmund finally learns that the sword will no longer protect him. This short episode starts with an interlude of reflection, *sieglinde's anguish* accompanies his own concern for his sister-bride. He

So we - nig ach - test du   e - wi - ge Won - ne?   Al - les war' dir das
So you would sac - ri - fice joy ev - er - last - ing? Is she all in the

ar - me Weib, das mued' und harm-voll matt von dem Schos-se dirhaengt?
world to you, that girl who lies there, limp and af - raid in your arms?

19.33 Brünnhilde starts the journey from immortality to mortality.

cries shame on his father for betraying him; now he will certainly not go to Valhalla. This pushes Brünnhilde towards her deepest thoughts. To a melodic line of great beauty and simplicity (a tune worthy of Schubert) she asks why the woman is all-important to him (19.33). The stillness of this moment brings home to the audience how important it has become for Brünnhilde.

4 Falling Action

The Scene develops into a tussle between the valkyr and the Volsung as the former tries to find a compromise. She wishes to reconcile Siegmund to his fate by saving Sieglinde. She is, in fact, trying to get back to the 'safe home' she has hitherto inhabited. (60 bars lasting about 2 minutes)

Brünnhilde's puzzlement arouses only contempt in Siegmund. Another compositional motif - *siegmund's scorn* - surges up from the bass and slides into *sieglinde's anguish*. Composition is now in free flow and there is a flawless concordance between stage action, text and sound. We see and hear perfection. The stress of *sieglinde's anguish* (which occurs 14 times, in whole or in part) combines quasi-symphonically with the newly introduced *siegmund's scorn* (CM20) and, with an augmentation of *lament of death* (six times repeated), in ever-increasing dramatic tension. The climax is heralded by *wotan's sword*.

19.34 *siegmund's scorn* **CM20**
At the high C♭ it melds with *sieglinde's anguish* (CM18).

(5) Triumph

Siegmund holds firm and prepares to kill his sister and then turn the sword on himself. Brünnhilde yields before the threat of murder followed by suicide. [E] This is the crisis point: she is unable to accept this outcome, and rediscovers the morality she first found in Scene 5. Her previous safe home is now insufficient. (68 bars lasting about 2 minutes)

The crisis for the valkyr is passed and the conclusion is a paean to the freedom both she and Siegmund experience. There are no discernible motifs in this glorification of the human spirit as it decides for itself what is right.

Scene 8: Siegmund watches over Sieglinde

[Schirmer: 173/4/1 to 175/3/5. Text from 'Zauberfest bezähmt ein Schlaf' to 'Nothung zahlt' ihm den Zoll.']

Wagner judges the pace of this interlude perfectly and we can note that the slow and gentle passage as Siegmund prays over his sister is to be mirrored in small part by Sieglinde's first passage in the final Scene which follows. There are two parts only in this

---

[E] This episode would seem to be directly inspired by Wagner's plot for a work about *Achilleus* in 1848. Achilles refuses the immortality offered by his mother Thetis, and immortal water nymph. She bows before him, in acknowledgement that mankind is greater than the gods (p.450/1). This theme is based on the philosophy of Feuerbach (p.8).

short Scene: after Siegmund's prayer, all is action as he prepares for battle. The prayer has so much emotion that Wagner seems positively to *avoid* motifs: just the merest touch of *love's bond*, *destiny* and *sieglinde's anguish*, and a recollection of the *Wintersturme* song. Then a rush of *wotan's sword, hunding* and *sieglinde's anguish* as the fight approaches.

Scene 9: Sieglinde wakes to see the fight, and the fall of Siegmund
[Schirmer: 175/4/1 to the end. Text from 'Kehrte der Vater nun heim' to 'erreicht mein Ross ihre Flucht']
This Scene clearly partakes of a basic element within Greek tragedy, as derived from Homer (p.212). There, the gods intimately and decisively engage in the struggles of man against man: one supports a protegé who battles against a man shielded by another god. This feature is also to be found in the eddas. But there is a big difference: Greek and Nordic gods are emotionally detached from the outcome as it affects the warrior each supports, but Wagner presents us with two immortals who are deeply involved in different ways with one of them: Siegmund. We note that Hunding's fate, by contrast, is observed with indifference by both Wotan and Brünnhilde.

After Sieglinde's soft but sad arousal from sleep, all is action. The obvious motifs accompany the matching events. Wagner is more successful here in showing action than he is, for example, in the Siegfried/Fafner fight. It is powerful drama which does not much depend on the motifs to make its effect. The scene is a Freytag mini-drama in five parts: protagonist is Brünnhilde and antagonist Wotan; Siegmund, Sieglinde and Hunding are the avenues used to resolve the conflict.

1 *Set Up*: Sieglinde as she awakes and sees she is alone.
2 *Rising Action*: Siegmund and Hunding approaching each other with *hunding* and *wotan's sword* as intermittent motifs.
3 *Mid-Point*: Brünnhilde and Wotan confront each other - the moment of extreme violence in which Siegmund is killed. Very clear are *valkyr, wotan's sword, will-to-power, fated volsung, destiny*. Also, as Siegmund falls, for the first time in this opera, and with fearsome impact, we hear *woe* - four times repeated, alone and detached from all other motifs. Six key motifs within 15 bars. Up to this point in the Scene the motifs clashed and bounced off each other in welter: here they are stark.
4 *Falling Action*: Brünnhilde rescues Sieglinde; Wotan kills Hunding with a sweep of his hand. This is a slow and quieter episode between two of noise and violence.
5 *Conclusion*: Wotan begins the pursuit of his daughter to the sound of *wotan's rage*.

Once Sieglinde is awake, the action in this Scene takes over and moves apace. The audience is invariably shocked by Siegmund's death and Wotan's part in that death, and this is because the audience feels that the Volsung has been betrayed (p.195).

◇ ◇ ◇ ◇ ◇ ◇

DIE WALKÜRE

ACT THREE

Whereas the structure of Act II was unusually episodic for Wagner, the five Scene structure for Act III is the classic Freytag Pyramid, distorted in balance in order, perhaps, to provide the final triumph with a size and weight commensurate with its importance.

1	The famous prelude which represents the nature and tasks of the valkyrs.	215 bars	Set up	
2	Brünnhilde arrives and explains what has happened. She is being pursued by Wotan.	165 bars	Rising Action	
3	Before he arrives, Brünnhilde takes her second decisive action, as she hustles a recovered and newly inspired Sieglinde off stage and into safety	181 bars	Mid-point	Part 1 812 bars
4	Wotan announces her doom: to be deprived of divinity and to end up the wife of the man who wakes her from sleep	251 bars	Falling Action	
5	The central action of the *Ring* as a whole is played out. Brünnhilde persuades Wotan that she has done the right thing and wins for herself a reprieve from a bad fate, and Wotan now understands what is needed.	763 bars	Final Triumph	Part 2 763 bars
		Total =	1675 bars	

Scene 5 is the dramatic kernel of the entire cycle. The 763 bars take between 35 and 40 minutes to play - the longest dramatic sequence in the *Ring* and several minutes longer than the four previous Scenes put together. Save for some slow music for the grieving Sieglinde in Scene 3, the preliminary episodes move at a fast pace.

<u>Scene 1: The ride of the valkyrs</u>
[Schirmer: 184/1/1 to 193/ave1/1]
What some have called 'the blatant vulgarity' of this, the most well-known chunk of Wagner's music, entails that this is seldom the most favoured passage with those who know the *Ring*. But the whole of it does stick in the mind - *valkyr* motif, *war-cry* motif, manic laughter and all. Primarily, of course, it is the stupendous and unremitting energy that makes it work. So what is this episode about? The three aspects of Odin taken over by Wagner are his desire for knowledge, his sexuality - and his role as a war lord. The *Ride* makes sense as a representation of Wotan in this last capacity (pp.134/5) and as a reflection of the untrammelled energy of Odin. In this passage, Wotan is the director

only of his valkyr acolytes but this might be extended to embrace the warriors already assembled in Valhalla.

Note that *fierce action*, first heard in Loge's narration, drives the episode forward and that the *valkyr* motif emerges from within it.

Scene 2: Brünnhilde in flight from Wotan
[Schirmer: 193/1/1 to 218/3/2. Text from 'Nach dem Tann lenkt'sie das taumeinde Ross' to 'Retter dies traurige Weib!']

This new Scene starts before she actually appears on stage. The music switches from the previous manic excitement to the expression of personal stress. The motif *wotan's struggle* is now used to represent the turmoil of his daughter. This is, as Cooke described, a psychological development by means of *leitmotiven*: Wotan's problems affect everybody. This rolling motif is supported by the generic dotted rhythm associated with riding and other violent physical activity - to be found also in Siegfried's forging song. This relentless dual rhythm - duple in the bass and triple in the treble - surrounds the valkyrs' agitated dialogue. Brünnhilde's actual entrance is to the music associated only with her, which first burst forth when she undertook to save Siegmund and now repeated as she announces that she wants to save his sister from the death sought for her by the enraged Wotan. Fear of Wotan is shared by all, represented by fragments of the rising, dotted motif of *wotan's struggle*. Wagner's skill in pacing music is shown when the relentless rhythm breaks for 22 bars, and Brünnhilde gives detail of her defiance, Siegmund's death and Wotan's rage - all in swift recitative.

Scene 3: Brünnhilde comforts and inspires Sieglinde, who flees alone
[Schirmer: 218/3/1 to 229/2/5. Text from 'Nicht sehre dich Sorge um mich, to 'dich signet Sieglindes Weh!]

This Scene is about the two women, one immortal and one mortal, who act to change the world. The structure suggests it to be the central matter around which the Act turns. In it is the culminating action by which Brünnhilde breaks away from Wotan and sets the world on to the path of some sort of recovery. The music reflects this: it opens in the darkness of C# minor and closes in the light of G major, and this charts the dramatic movement from extreme misery to defiant resolution. If within the Scene Brünnhilde burns her bridges with Wotan, the immediate dramatic impact centres around what might be called (in the Biblical sense) Sieglinde's 'passion'. There are three parts to this: the start sees Sieglinde in prostrate misery; this is reversed, from misery to ecstasy, with the announcement of Siegfried's conception; from ecstasy is then born resolution, as the valkyr decides to divert Wotan's wrath on to her and thereby delay his pursuit, and Sieglinde is transfigured with hope and wisdom.

The change of tone at the start is dramatic as Sieglinde's opening words give us (after 380 bars to date) the first quiet, reflective music in this Act. No motifs, but 28 bars of poignant arioso. Then a sudden jerk into life for the second part with the news of Siegfried. Fragments of *wotan's struggle* remind all that he is dangerously near now

DIE WALKÜRE

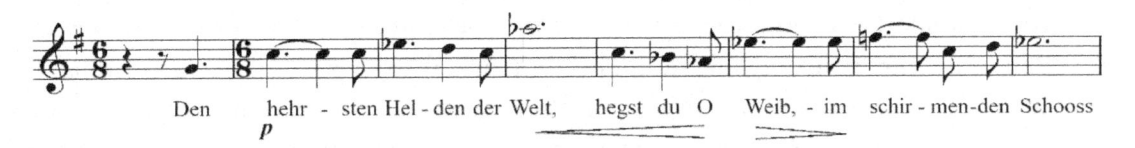

Den hehr-sten Hel-den der Welt, hegst du O Weib, - im schir-men-den Schooss

19.35 *siegfried* **M46**
The similarity to *curse* is like that between *valhalla* and *ring*.
The melody presents us with a bright alternative to the shadow of Alberich.
The English reads 'It's the world's noblest hero that you're bearing
in the refuge of your womb.'

and this prompts Brünnhilde's decision to stay and face him. The Scene moves toward its musical and dramatic climax. Old motifs in fresh guise now abound: *ring, dragon, love, wotan's struggle* clarify the remote forest where Sieglinde must hide. The culmination is the first appearance of the *siegfried* motif. Seemingly straightforward, the notes that finally appear in the score are Wagner's third effort. A second new motif is heard as Brünnhilde hands the shards of Nothung to Sieglinde, when *wotan's sword* climbs up to exultantly introduce Sieglinde's paean to the valkyr in the motif that Wagner called *glorification of brünnhilde* (M47).

19.36 *glorification of brünnhilde* **M47**

This Scene marks the last appearance of Sieglinde. Hitherto, she may have been little mentioned, but the life of Siegmund would have been meaningless without that of his sister. As with Siegfried and Brünnhilde, it is the woman Sieglinde who has the vision and knowledge that inspires the man. Firstly, and despite the gentleness of her temperament, she has a driving initiative. She it is who makes the first overture to her brother; she it is who holds him back when he intends to leave; she it is who plots that they will have time alone together. She understands the implication of Nothung and leads Siegmund to it. The visionary within her drags her toward madness and when this is still roiling within her, she sees the old man, whom she knows to be her father and who offered comfort at her wedding, cause the death of her brother and the old man's son. From this pit she is pulled by the news of her unborn son, she has a moment of glorious forward vision and gladly leaves to fulfil and lose her life in giving birth to him.

Scene 4: Wotan pronounces the punishment of Brünnhilde
[Schirmer: 229/2/5 to 264/5/2. Text from 'Steh, Brünnhild' to 'sonst erharrt Jammer euch hier!']
The three stage structure is simple and progressive. First the audience is prepared for Wotan's arrival as the valkyrs comment distractedly on his approach. Second, he draws Brünnhilde out from behind her sheltering sisters. Third, he becomes more specific as he expands on her doom.

The short first section builds to a climax toward the close of a choral wail by the eight valkyrs to Brünnhilde that she should hide. Rising semi-tones from a low F introduce the closing bars from Act 2 as Wotan enters.

Another short valkyr chorus moves us to the second section, where Wotan shames his daughter into revealing herself. This is marked by a switch to unaccompanied heightened recitative-cum-arioso which alternates with short clearly defined interpolations of *wotan's balked will*. This episode is really a conversation between the god and his daughter; one can envisage the hidden Brünnhilde cowering at the brutal sounds of octaves-in-unison as they convey Wotan's demeanour.

The third section resembles a traditional operatic *scena* for Wotan, prompted by Brünnhilde's quiet acceptance that she will be punished. The totality of this *scena* is 100 bars and the first two parts are almost entirely free of motifs. The first 17 bars are as an *arioso* introduction which builds to the opening of the second part - the 'aria'. This starts with 'Wunschmaid wars't du mir' and these words are the first of six expectations held by Wotan with regard to Brünnhilde's role and behaviour, linked to the current dereliction. The episode is held together by a fleeting compositional motif – *brünnhilde's punishment* (CM21) as

19.37 *brünnhilde's punishment* **CM21**

prelude to each stage of her sentence. The third part of the *scena* is another 'aria' constructed around the *lament of death* motif. There is logic to this. As Brünnhilde announces death to Siegmund, so is Wotan preparing to announce a manner of death to his daughter. The melody blossoms as Wagner extends and expands upon *lament of death* as the specifics of Brünnhilde's fate become clearer.

After further outbursts from the valkyrs, Wotan finally and brutally spells out Brünnhilde's fate, punctuated by short, coarse and crashing interjections of *will-to-power*: she is to stay on this rock and become slave to the man who first finds her. It can be no coincidence that Wotan's gross depiction of her fate - to 'sit by the hearth and spin, the butt and plaything of all who despise her' - echoes Siegfried's words to the cowering valkyr in ST1.3: 'To all the world will I show how tame at home in my hall a woman spins and weaves'. Those words were toned down in *Götterdämmerung* but Wagner still held in mind the total degradation originally envisaged for Wotan's daughter. The composer is also being true to life: excessive rage by a father to an errant daughter is not uncommon. Witness King Lear toward Cordelia in Act 1: 'Better thou hadst not been born than not t'have pleased me better.'

To tumultuous and understandably agonised repetitions of *valkyr*, Brünnhilde's sisters flee, clearing the stage for the two principles.

Scene 5: Brünnhilde conquers Wotan
[Schirmer: 264/2/3 to end. Text from 'War es so schmählich' to the end.]
This Scene is different to all others in the opera and is best seen as a unity during which the dispute between the two principals is finally resolved. The drama is clear when the exchanges between Brünnhilde and Wotan are paired off - statement or question on one side; response or answer on the other. There are sixteen such exchanges in total - long

or short. In the two last it is the orchestra that gives us the relevant response, first for Brünnhilde and then for Wotan. This exercise reveals consummate presentation of the issues to be resolved. Short exchanges are preparation for those that are longer; where short the musical temperature is low but the musical (and thereby dramatic) ferment expands in the longer passages. Such important dramatic moments are 'boxed', and the musical and dramatic analysis that follows studies these key stages in the conversation.

	Question/Statement	Answer/Response
	Brünnhilde	**Wotan**
1	What have I done that is so shameful? So dishonourable that my honour should be lost? Do not continue to remain silent. Look at me and tell why the penalty is so cruel.	Examine what you have done to find the answer.
2	I did what you wanted.	What? To defend Siegmund?
3	Yes, that is what you wanted.	But I countermanded that order!
4	You were persuaded by Fricka, and were false to yourself.	You thought yourself strong and me weak - so you could disregard me.
5	I am not wise but I knew you loved Siegmund and that you forced yourself to ignore this in spite of your pain.	Yes! You knew and ignored me.
6	Yes, because I saw Siegmund and you did not. I saw the love he had for Sieglinde. I felt something new in me and was ashamed of what was being done. I had no choice but to save him, for you planted within me the love I felt.	Exactly! You saw the truth of their love and thought this was the truth for the whole world. Whilst I - trying to manage that world - was forced to abandon him. And as my world collapsed in ruin to my most bitter pain, you revelled in the hopes that love offers. You must now take the consequences: you have made yourself free from me and we must be parted.
7	Yes, I did not understand you and so I followed my heart, to love him whom you loved. But if we are to part do not forget who I have been: for you also will suffer if I become a figure of scorn.	You chose love instead of obedience to me. You must now obey the man who chooses to love you.
8	If so, can you not make sure that the man who finds me is worthy of me?	But you have turned from me and I cannot choose for you!
9	You fathered the Volsung race. That must produce a hero!	Do not mention them! My rage will destroy all the Volsungs.
10	Sieglinde has escaped - she is pregnant.	Then I shall not help her - nor her child.
11	She has Siegmund's sword!	Which I smashed!

331[1]

DIE WALKÜRE

There is a long pause and the dialogue starts afresh, Wotan now taking the lead. This is obviously a watershed in the Scene. Up till now the two have come to terms with the issues and each understands the other. What follows is the consequence of that mutual understanding.

	Wotan	**Brünnhilde**
12	I must leave you; the sentence must be carried out.	What will happen to me?
13	You will be put to sleep and the man who wakes you will make you his wife.	If so, let me not become the property of a coward. Shield me so that only a hero finds me.
14	You ask too much!	You *must* grant me this! Crush and destroy me rather than abandon me. Surround me with fire!
15	Yes, then! If I must part from you, let a bridal fire surround you. Flames will scare away cowards - and one man alone shall win you. A new, free man - more free than I shall ever be.	[The orchestra speaks for Brünnhilde in the mighty crescendo as she rushes into Wotan's arms.]
16	The great farewell wherein Wotan bids goodbye to his daughter - in words and with the final kiss.	[The attention again switches to the orchestra as the valkyr submits to Wotan's embrace and sinks into sleep.]

<u>The message within each of the boxed exchanges</u>

1   The tone of this exchange is presaged by a melody of great beauty which enters as the last echoes of the valkyrs' flight die away. This is derived from the theme of their

19.38 Twilight falls as father and daughter are alone.

chorus of flight and readers will see that the melodic contours of *lament of death* are shadowed. Porges said this: 'An effect of inexpressible tragic sadness was created by the mood of the moment, the anxiety, the expectancy.' (HP/WR,72) This melody never comes again.

There follows a memorable remoulding of *wotan's balked will*. This bears its full emotional weight only in this episode as it accompanies Brünnhilde's efforts to understand and to pacify Wotan – *brünnhilde pacifies wotan* (CM22). Into this mix soon comes the motif that Scruton

19.39 *brünnhilde pacificies wotan*
CM22

332

[musical notation]
War es so schmae-lich, was ich ver-brach, das mein Ver-brech-chen so schmae-lich du be-strafst?
Was it so shame-ful, that I have done, that such de-grad-ing an end should be my fate?

19.40 *brünnhilde's purity* **M47**

calls *brünnhilde's purity* (M47). His reason is easy to see: her patently straightforward honesty, conveyed by supremely beautiful music, is the thing that jolts her father into a new way of looking at the world. As with CM22, this is a remoulding of a Wotan motif, *will-to-power*: it turns Wotan's will against himself. After Brünnhilde's two poignant - and unaccompanied - questions to her father, there enters the compositional motif *siegmund's defiance,* heard in his crucial episode with the valkyr. His steel now lurks within her. These three motifs lock closely into each other.

This exchange gives the daughter an immediate advantage over the father, whose gloomy silence and averted gaze allow the music to convey her bewilderment and pain which *must* impact on the god, as it does on the audience. The purity of the music spreads over 86 bars whilst the god's gruff response takes but three!

6   This major episode extends for 155 bars and encompasses both Brünnhilde's most urgent pleas and also Wotan's bitterest resistance to them. Within it are 77 bars (50%) comprised of two related compositional motifs which represent *brünnhilde pleading for herself*. The first (CM23) is present as the episode starts and the second (CM24) shortly after. Both have roots in *wotan's balked will* and that motif, along with *brünnhilde's purity* are the only two ongoing motifs that feature in the first 30 bars. They express the valkyr's desperate need to compel her father to do the right thing. Brünnhilde's vocal line throughout is freely lyrical without motifs, save for at the very end when a sequence of seven *brünnhilde's purity* motif provides a halo to her last plea: 'You who put this love into my heart, whose will it was that drove me to meet the Wälsung, to confide in him, it was your command I defied.'

19.41 *brünnhilde pleads for herself (1)* **CM23**

19.42 *brünnhilde pleads for herself (2)* **CM24**

The summary of Wotan's reply and the music demonstrate how deeply the daughter's character and motive penetrated. Traces of *brünnhilde's purity* are followed by eleven bars of *brünnhilde pleads for herself (2)*. Thus a feature of the valkyr's pleading is carried over into the music as Wotan sings 'When I turned against myself, wounding myself, foaming as I shot up out of the pains of powerlessness'. Then, as Wotan contemplates the collapse of his world, the music moves on to *wotan's rage, core life value* and *curse*. The climax lies toward the end – after the detached but marked repeat of *curse*. The words convey envy at his daughter's rapture, so different from his own unhappiness, but the music goes beyond envy and rage as it sinks down to profound despair - the dynamic starting and ending *pp*. So intense is this music that the vocal line throughout has no motifs. (See illustration on p.193.)

The most telling feature is that Wotan adopts the music of his daughter's anguish in order to express his own. The music derives from the drama and not the other way round. This long section is both all of a piece as drama and is as 'through composed' as can be imagined. In that sense it must be thought of as symphonic and also as a clear and straightforward representation of what the composer intends within the drama. It is also a prime example of how Brünnhilde's musical eloquence is a substitute for the wisdom possessed by Brynhild in the sagas. That feature had to be skipped in the making of stage drama (p.172).

7 'Truth to life' - the dramatic touchstone seen in Shakespeare - is here exemplified. Brünnhilde's spirit is bare and plain to see, and Wagner concentrates on this by avoiding all motifs. Undoubtedly the music could only be constructed from *Ring* material but whatever is used is subsumed into Verdi's *tinta* - a uniformity of 'colour' present in each of his middle and late operas. Only in the switch from daughter to father is one clear echo of *love* heard in the bass.

8 This small exchange is given its own unity: there are no motifs but the briefest of compositional fragments invests the short conversation. The purpose of the dialogue is to prepare us for the climax that looms and is to close the first part of the conversation. The effect of the compositional fragment is to give contrast, by musical structure, to the concentration of central motifs that follows in the three exchanges that follow.

9-11 The table shows the controlled progress of the conversation between daughter and father but these three exchanges are a unity in musico-dramatic terms. With a clarity that appositely adorns the words we hear *fated volsung* (twice), *siegfried* (thrice) and *wotan's sword* as Brünnhilde presses home her excitement, and *will-to-power* and as Wotan struggles against her. The position of daughter and father as protagonist and antagonist could not be more clear.

13 Two major motifs enter now, as the Scene enters the second stage. First is *magic sleep* (M49), as Wotan gives detail of the spell he will cast. The second motif is always to refer to the actual state into which the valkyr is cast, and is here called *brünnhilde's sleep* (M50). Her hope now is that this sleep will be broken by Siegfried. So the

19.43 *magic sleep* **M49**

19.44 *brünnhilde's sleep* **M50**

DIE WALKÜRE

20.44 *loge as fire* **M15F**

sequence of 10 almost continuous bars of this motif (a mini-symphonic development) ends with *siegfried*. In the build up to this we can also note the clearest and most graphic expression of *loge as fire*. This is M15F and whereas the other five Loge motifs often indicate cunning or cleverness, this one does not. It is peculiarly suggestive of a flickering and very hot fire.

15   It would be otiose even to try to distinguish what is key at this point. Wotan's vocal line rings free and the music that surrounds it is in full flood. Even the first time spectator is likely to make out *valkyr, magic sleep, loge as fire* and *siegfried*. But the drama is synonymous with the music.

The orchestral passage which follows Wotan's song of farewell focusses on Brünnhilde as she first perceives the victory that is hers and then rushes into her father's arms. *brünnhilde's purity*, haloed by string configurations, climbs up and up over seventeen bars to reach a mighty climax which launches (*ff*) eight bars of *brünnhilde's sleep*: a total of 24 bars where two motifs pile sequentially on top of each other. Such a concentration rarely happens. (See p.235 for the observations of Bryan Magee and Roger Scruton on this passage.)

This is a peerless moment in the lives of both Wotan and his daughter. Simultaneously it brings a personal development beyond parallel to both, and this lifting of the drama to the highest plane is instinctively recognized by the audience.

16   In Westernhagen's *The forging of the Ring* is found a facsimile of the composer's composition sketch for the whole of Wotan's song to his daughter. As Westernhagen puts the matter 'it is written straight out in sketch in one flow without alteration. The handwriting responds expressively to the sound of the music' (CvW/FR,123) This is distinct from the many occasions when what seems spontaneous and inevitable was achieved only by much amendment and emendation. Of this music one can quote what Wagner wrote about Weber: '[his music] speaks directly to the hearts of men no matter what their national peculiarity, simply because in it the purely human is preserved untarnished.' The only other comment worth making is that the whole stretch of melody is accompanied by manipulations and variations of *brünnhilde's sleep*.

The orchestral 'response' on behalf of Brünnhilde starts with *magic sleep* set forth in the most tender manner and this is followed by the first two refrains of Wotan's melody (also accompanied by *brünnhilde's sleep*) which shifts into *destiny*.

It would be impertinent to go beyond the comments of Magee and Scruton on the orchestral epilogue to the above, which closes the opera. It is the summation of the whole story to date and the central moment in the cycle - that when Wotan changes. The musical symbols are there: *will-to-power* to summon Loge, perhaps for the last time, *loge as fire* in its richest charge of emotion, *magic sleep, brünnhilde's sleep, siegfried* and *destiny*. No motif exists that signifies the resignation which permeates the god, but the close that follows on from the great scene between father and daughter unmistakeably tells us that nothing can be the same again.

One structural aspect in respect of dramatic symmetry is worthy of note. The Act starts with an orchestral depiction of the valkyrs, and this can also be seen as an aspect of Wotan as warlord. This orchestral postlude gives us the defining picture of Wotan as a father. Prelude and postlude are matching opposites.

◇ ◇ ◇ ◇ ◇ ◇

Siegfried

The remarkable structure of *Siegfried* is outlined on p.37. Wagner sets himself the formidable task of incorporating Siegfried's confrontation with and victory over each of his three antagonists (Fafner, Mime and Wotan) into one opera. These three tasks were the prelude to the fourth: winning the prize of Brünnhilde's love. Additionally, and in order to bind Siegfried into the wider story inside which his own sits, the plot expands the motivations of the three antagonists, each of whom has a continuing interest in Siegfried's actions and fate. This requires a two-track structure: Siegfried's personal journey from ignorant adolescence to manhood is played against the journeys of these three who – in one way or another – oppose his advancement.

Cogent as is the structure, the execution is flawed in one matter, namely that of Siegfried's lack of fear. Wagner makes Siegfried fearless but the Sigurd within the eddas is never described as fearless. Brynhild welcomes him as her lover because she maintains that he is and must be so. Problem solved: she is prosecutor, judge and jury in one. Wagner takes this fearlessness as a mandated quality (p.81) but it impedes rather than assists the drama, as we shall see.

ACT 1

1. Siegfried needs a strong sword that will equip and enable him to leave Mime, whom he loathes. Deep but unfocussed frustration leads him to think hard: he realises that he only returns to stay with Mime for two reasons. The first is that he has no weapon with which to protect himself. (Mime knows that only Nothung will serve but, for all his skills, he cannot join the two shards together, and Siegfried shatters everything that Mime *can* forge.) The second reason is that only Mime can give him the beginnings of an identity. Accordingly, he forces the dwarf to divulge his parent-hood. When, in the process, he doubts the truth of this, Mime is finally obliged to show him the shattered remains of Nothung. He tells Mime to repair it and rushes off. — 1238 bars; 31 mins

2. Wotan, as the Wanderer arrives. With his head at stake he engages Mime in a question and answer contest. Mime loses because he cannot say who will successfully re-forge Nothung. The Wanderer tells him that it will be he who knows no fear. — 698 bars; 25 mins

3. Siegfried returns. Mime evades questions about Nothung; he tries but fails to explain the nature of fear to Siegfried. — 315 bars; 12 mins

4	Realising that the dwarf has not the skill to re-forge Nothung, he takes over and does the job himself, thereby attaining the weapon he needs.	724 bars; 14 mins
	Total	2975 bars 82 minutes

This Act shows Siegfried on the first stage of his growth from adolescence towards manhood. He has no contact with Wotan and is not in any way personally engaged with the nature of fear. Of the four Scenes, therefore, only 1 and 4 are about Siegfried, and these comprise just short of $^2/_3$ of the score. A clear narrative lies through Scenes 1 & 4. Scene 4, in which Siegfried uses the knowledge he has gained and forges the sword he needs, is the continuation of Scene 1. This is to be his first emancipation.

Scene 2 - between Wotan and Mime - and Scene 3 - between Mime and Siegfried, are self-contained, and diversions from the main narrative. They have a different logic within the drama

Scene 1: Siegfried finds the information that enables him to leave home
[Schirmer: 1/1/1 to 48/3/4. Text from 'Zvangvolle Plage' to 'Hey, Siegfried! Hey!']
This Scene is a continuous progression on Siegfried's part from ignorance to the knowledge he needs to move on. For all its length - about 30 minutes - the Scene is only in three parts. Rather than the Scene descriptions following those of Freytag, it is better to think in terms of knowledge.

1 Ignorance	Nothung is the central preoccupation of both Mime and Siegfried. The former knows he cannot re-forge the two splinters; the latter makes two references to it in the short passage as he first enters. Siegfried loses patience when the sword offered by Mime shatters when struck against the anvil and the dwarf tries to pacify him with arguments that have obviously been used by him frequently in the past. Whether or not they worked before, now they fail. (14 minutes)
2 Realisation	Mime flinches before Siegfried's calm, steady gaze and as he asks questions which we presume have never been asked before. Why, Siegfried asks, do I loathe you despite the care you have offered all my life? Why do I not have a mother around as do all the animals in the forest? Mime procrastinates and Siegfried's consequent fierce anger leads to the critical moment of the Scene. He realises that he repeatedly returns to the cave because only the dwarf can answer questions about his mother and father. This realisation is the start of Siegfried's journey in the cycle as a whole, as well as within this Act. Continuing evasion from Mime requires physical force to extract the truth: he is neither father and mother of the lad. This gives Siegfried the first clues toward an identity, commonly seen as a necessary pathway in life. (9 minutes)
3 Necessary knowledge	The truth about Sieglinde is only believed by Siegfried when Mime shows him the broken shards of Nothung. Instinctively he knows that this is the weapon he needs in order to make a successful break. He instructs that the sword must

now be made for him and rushes off-stage in excitement: with that in his hand he will find his future elsewhere. (7½ minutes)

Stage 1 - Ignorance

Composition began in about September 1856, some two years after reading Schopenhauer for the first time. This music, therefore, is the first to be composed in accordance with the emphasis, additional to that of all the other arts, proposed by the philosopher (p.232). The impact is immediately perceived in the orchestral prelude, an integral part of this first episode, and a psychological study of Mime, visible as the curtain rises. This state of mind is permanent with the dwarf: he ponders perpetually on Fafner's hoard, of the need to repair Nothung, of the woeful life he has brought upon himself, on the Ring in the possession of the dragon Fafner, on Nothung itself should he manage to repair it. He does not know what to do. Porges reports of the rehearsal in 1876 that the prelude is a 'depiction of a being whose will is impelled by forces of irresistible power and yet confounded by weakness and irresolution.' (HP/WR,79) Given the topsy-turvy growth of the poems, one can only marvel both at the surety of psychological penetration and also that Wagner's composition sketch was 'written out in one continuous flow without alteration.' (CvW/FR,149)

The prelude leads straight into Mime's soliloquy and the music remains the same: a tapestry of *hoard, nibelung slavery, woe, ring, wotan's sword*. These move in and out of each other for over 8 minutes. The only additional motif is that for *scheming* (M51) - the first defined sound heard in the prelude. (In point of fact, the motif was unobtrusively introduced in R2 but here it dominates.) The motifs collectively tell the course of Mime's obsessive but fruitless calculations. Two further points: (1) the

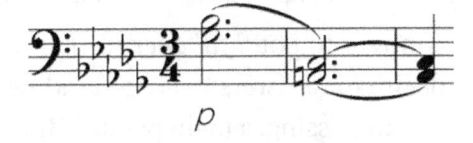

21.1 *scheming* **M51**

two widely spaced chords that constitute *scheming* are the top and bottom chords of *ring* (p.292); (2) the horror that lurks behind everything bursts forth at the *ff* climax of the prelude, when *woe* expands into *servitude to the ring*.

This entire opening episode extends for 249 bars – 130 or so prelude and 120 with Mime centre stage - and the orchestra supplies combinations of the aforesaid seven motifs as forefront in the prelude and as backdrop to Mime. A prolonged psychological portrait such as this does not occur in the first two operas and bears witness to the changes in compositional technique and, perhaps, of Schopenhauer lurking in the background. All the motifs, save for *scheming* come from *Das Rheingold*. The bars of *nibelung slavery* are 90 and Mime's voice never echoes a motif. It must have been the achievement of *Die Walküre* and the confirmatory support of the philosopher that gave Wagner the confidence to relax into this music.

Something similar is repeated when Siegfried bursts in: 46 of the first 80 bars give us *horn call* (M52); the following 125 bars are dominated by 78 of the next new motif - *youthful energy* (M53). These contiguous passages form the core of Siegfried's nature in this Act: the desire for freedom that is felt by young people when circumstances cramp action. Both passages are simple in objective: the first establishes Siegfried's character - essentially buoyant - and the second his main characteristic - impetuous energy. Both of these impel Siegfried toward a course of action which cannot be discerned because he lacks both the knowledge of what to do and also the means to do almost anything. At this juncture *youthful energy* represents his rage that Mime has failed to produce a decent sword for him. In slightly different formations, it represents other traits, all of which require energy and purpose. Mime can only react to this torrent of furious energy. Wagner makes effective use of this: slowing the tempo in the same 2/4 to a smoothed-out version of *nibelung life*, first heard when Mime described his early happy life to Loge in R3. The more thoughtful *mime as nibelung* music (CM25) now runs as a compositional contrast to *youthful energy*. This reflective moment infects Siegfried and awakens the desire for answers to long-standing questions.

21.2 *horn call* **M52**

21.3 *youthful energy* **M53**

21.4 *mime as nibelung* **CM25**

In passing, a main plank in the defence Mime sets before Siegfried is to recite all the things he has done for him over the years. He presents this in the form of a folk-song ditty, which Siegfried is to deride as a 'Starenlied'. This ditty has an important function that will soon become clear.

Extended as this episode has been, and replete with motific development, the music has been dominated by the compositional *mime as nibelung*. The text of Siegfried is more loquacious than the first two operas: perhaps the compositional expansion was encouraged by Schopenhauer's vision of music.

Stage 2 - Realisation
The music slows and stills as, for the first time, Siegfried looks steadily into Mime's eyes. The certainty at this point is that a discussion of this type between the two has not happened before. The musical substance for the first 135 bars remains the same: a gentler *youthful energy* and the compositional *mime as nibelung* switch in and out of each other. Indeed, *youthful energy* is now clearly compositional - a means of making music rather than an adjunct of character. This passage underlines Siegfried's earnest need to establish the truth about himself and the tension increases a notch when he asks

the critical question: 'Why do I return to this cave if I so dislike it here?' At which point enters the exquisite *longing for love* (M54). Wagner in rehearsals in 1876 said it should sound 'as though out of a dream . . . as though coming from a distance.' (HP/WR,83)

Mottologists, to use Forman's caustic description, seek to link this to other motifs but Cooke, whom Bryan Magee suspected knew the *Ring* music better than Wagner himself, thinks it to be 'independent'. Some connection with nature is obvious by the context, for Siegfried has just been reciting how much more he likes the birds in the trees and the fish in the stream than be does Mime. But it is also to do with sexuality, representing the natural pulse of creation as the basis of all life; at times in the coming Scene it verges on the tumescent. Wholly representative of the good, it is Siegfried's particular motif in this opera and is surely a mark of grace. (The motif never appears in *Götterdämmerung*.)

21.5 *longing for love* **M54**

Siegfried's interrogation of Mime, which the latter visibly finds most uncomfortable, tightens focus. The music symphonically develops *longing for love* and includes a notable motif of premonition (p.226). A small variation on *youthful energy* results - over a period of only eleven bars - in delicate figurations in the woodwind that accompanies Siegfried's description of birds as they care for their fledgling chicks. This returns in the Forest Murmurs in Act II as Siegfried listens to the birds in the trees. But it is not mentioned now, so far in advance, as an adjunct or aid to the immediate drama. It may be there because this particular bird song is - as it happens - a relative of *youthful energy*. Such a perfect musical adornment that is also in accord with the drama brings a smile of delight and admiration to all who hear and comprehend the background. A musical dramatist who is at home with all the tools he needs.

Soon after this we reach the crucial question that Siegfried has for Mime, and which the latter must have dreaded: 'I see each animal has a mother and father - who and where is my mother?' He calls the dwarf a liar as he procrastinates. Since Siegfried looks nothing like Mime, who and where is the person he does resemble? And now it is clear why he returns - it is to learn the truth from Mime. But to get at it he must fiercely manhandle the dwarf, perhaps for the first time: 'thus have I to force things out of you!'. Mime collapses and yields the truth.

Stage 3 - Necessary knowledge
The change from one stage to the next is obvious in the music: a switch from the compositional *mime as nibelung* to a merging of *volsung empathy* with *sieglinde* heard so poignantly in Scene 1 of *Die Walküre*. The sadness of these sounds impact Mime's delivery of the story showing that the dwarf, for all his scheming, is not just an immoral monster. (Wagner always seeks for reality.) His vocal line counterpoints the crucial

love's bond as he recalls Sieglinde's death.[A] *siegfried* (marked *dolcissimo*) precedes his 'Doch Siegfried, der genas.' Siegfried's response 'So starb meine Mutter an mir?' is but part of a passage that is perfect 'voice-melody' as per *Opera and Drama*. From the start of Mime's narrative, the voice is fully expressive of the meaning but does not follow the orchestra. Siegfried's poignancy leads to three repetitions of *volsung empathy* as the orchestra gives us his thoughts, despite the attempted interruptions from Mime.

Then the dialogue gathers pace with *siegfried* as he asks about his name, forces an answer about his mother's name but fails to learn that of his father. *volsung empathy* is never far away. Mime's interruptions once again turn around the 'folk-song' 'Starenlied'. Listeners by this time will be familiar with this as it is the basis of all Mime's wheedling but doomed desire to find favour.

21.6 Mime's 'starenlied' song.

The narrative is heard to move on again after Siegfried asks for proof. This jolts Mime. We hear two sharp renditions of *scheming* followed by two *wotan's sword* as he brings forward the broken shards of Nothung. As soon as Siegfried learns what they are he knows that, along with his emerging identity, they are the final key to his freedom. *wotan's sword* joins to *horn call*[B] and the orchestra takes up *youthful energy* as he hails this knowledge. To Mime's question about what he will do with the sword, he asserts simply that it will enable him to leave forthwith.

21.7 *siegfried's mission* **M55**
The simplicity of genius transforms Mime's 'starenlied' ditty into something where the link between the two can elude the ear.

We hear new and memorable music at this point, and the joy with which Siegfried anticipates his freedom finds final expression in a motif *siegfried's mission* (M55). The motif occurs in this form here, in the duet with Brünnhilde in G1.1 and in the Rhine Journey. Nonetheless, a link within this Scene gives a further clue to compositional method: *siegfried's mission* has a direct connection to Mime's 'Starenlied' (21.6). Mime's ditty is an attempt to keep Siegfried 'at home' and its development into *siegfried's mission* shows him breaking free.

Having told Mime to weld together the shards by the time he returns, Siegfried takes off to dying echoes of *siegfried's joy*. He leaves Mime with a problem.

[A] Compare Gollum in Tolkien's *Lord of the Rings*. On his long journey with Frodo to Mordor, the latter is notably kind to him. In response Gollum has a long conversation with his *alter ego*; Gollum now wants to help but his other half holds him back.

[B] This brilliant fanfare is obvious and the two motifs are clear in the jointure. But it only makes impact in this opera and is easily seen as an extension of *wotan's mission*. It is not separately listed in this study.

Scene 2: Wotan arrives, as the Wanderer, and offers to help Mime

[Schirmer: 48/3/5 to 81/1/4. Text from 'Da stürmt er hin!' to 'Fafner! Fafner!']

The Scene is in five parts. Wotan is clearly the protagonist in a struggle with Mime as the antagonist; Mime is to take a journey which ends in failure.

1. Mime is alone and ponders once again on his inability to forge Nothung. (39 bars; 1½ minutes)

2. The Wanderer arrives and offers to help Mime, who reluctantly accepts the offer. (102 bars; 4½ minutes) c

3. The procedure is the Question and Answer trial as found in the sagas. Wotan is the first to be put to the test and does so successfully. (195 bars; 8 minutes)

4. In response, Mime fails when asked who is able to re-forge Nothung. Wotan asks why Mime put questions to which he already knows the answer rather than for the knowledge that is so critical for him. He tells him the answer: Siegfried, who knows not fear, is the one who will succeed. (316 bars; 7½ minutes)

5. Wotan leaves and Mime is alone again, as at the beginning, and in sore mental distress. (46 bars; 1½ minutes)

The music at the start of this Scene recalls the problem that Mime has with the forging of Nothung at the opening of the opera and at the end the dwarf is vastly perturbed after Wotan leaves. The music is an affirmation that Mime is the real subject of the Scene.

# # # # # #

These bare bones, of course, give us only half the story. Wotan enters and dominates the stage for 20 minutes. Why is he there? He does not impact on Siegfried, about whom the action turns, and he seems not to advance the drama - Mime ends as he began. What lies behind this?

To start with the obvious: Wotan does bring up Siegfried's lack of fear for the first time. The assertion that fearlessness is the necessary condition for the repair of Nothung is Wagner's invention: no such requirement lies in the sagas. It is probably a dramatic device for pushing the plot along; as such a device it is appropriate that the information surfaces only at the conclusion of the actual dialogue between god and dwarf - ready for the next Scene.

The real function of Wotan's presence in this Scene is to be found in the previous 18 minutes or so: the purpose is to show Wotan in the round. There are six aspects.

- Firstly, one can discern a comprehensive wish to sink the roots of this opera into the soil of the dialogues that make up so much of the *Poetic Edda*. Wotan is different from Odin but as the latter participates in so many one-to-one debates in the eddas

---

c   It can be something of a jolt to realise that the time elapsed between the end of *Die Walküre* and the opening of *Siegfried* cannot be less that 18 years.

so does Wagner wish to characterise his Wotan. The episode with Mime in this Scene was obviously inspired by that in the *Poetic Edda* in which Odin engages with the giant Valthruthmir in a question and answer debate, the loser of which is to forfeit his life. (PE, 68) [D]

- Secondly, up and until now almost all has been turmoil, from the first altercation with Fricka in *Das Rheingold* through to the end of *Die Walküre*. The audience now surely sees Wotan as he would have been before the stress caused by the building of Valhalla. The music with which he is associated presents him as both obviously in command and also happy within his own skin. This Scene seeks to saturate Wotan with something of the mightiness of Odin. The magisterial *wanderer* motif is to give us the Wotan outlined in the *Myth* - redolent with good intent, and with the god's power to be used without coercion. The same might be said about the closing pages of *Die Walküre,* but now Wotan's attitude is quite different. His imperious *Will* is pacified (p.200) and he becomes the archetype of a great ruler before the stress and contradictions inherent in any effort to govern grow into the conflict seen in *Das Rheingold* and *Die Walküre*.
- Thirdly, Wagner is at pains to show that Wotan, as the Wanderer, gives no aid to Siegfried. On the contrary, he actively tries to help Mime in his wickedness (as he is to attempt with Alberich in Act II). This is not only the direct opposite to his position with Siegmund; more importantly he is addressing the critical problem of the nature of his own power (p.196).
- Fourthly, the Scene is also the first in which we see Wotan as he 'orchestrates' Siegfried's progress from childhood to maturity. Without intervention, the god nevertheless 'oversees' the growth of his grandson throughout the opera (*pace* Campbell).
- Fifthly, the music will also remind us of another and less amiable aspect of Wotan's character: his imperious and dangerous attachment to the wielding of power. We are to be shown this in the abstract and in a quite different manner than that illustrated in *Das Rheingold* and *Die Walküre*.
- Sixthly, he is prepared to put his own life in jeopardy - as does Odin in fact. Now we may think that there is nothing that Mime can ask that Wotan cannot answer but that misses the point: the proposal can be seen as an attempt to make clear to the dwarf that this is no ordinary visit and that he needs to pay attention. On that same basis, after Mime fails, he advises what must be done to save his life.

# # # # # #

[D] Odin is a multifarious personage but Wagner constructed his Wotan out of three features: one of which was as a seeker after knowledge. To establish this, in addition to this interchange with Mime, he also has a 'debate' with Alberich, Erda and finally with Siegfried himself.

Stage 1 - Mime alone
Short as it may be, this episode has direction and power. Extending no further than the limitations of Mime's world it encapsulates the sorrow that lies behind events. Motif laps slowly but relentlessly into motif: *ring* into *nibelung slavery*; *nibelung slavery* into *scheming*; *scheming* into *woe* and *nibelung toil*; and these two last motifs lift the last seven bars into *core life value,* plangently repeated three times - the interval a third higher each time. We are reminded of the happy life he lived before Alberich took over. Now Mime is at a loss, his mind 'plagued by uncontrollable forces, and the degraded lust for power.' (HP/WR,86) There has been irrecoverable loss and Wagner needs only seven bars to convey it.

Stage 2 - Wotan arrives as The Wanderer. He offers to give advice and, in the face of Mime's reluctance, ups the stakes by making the contest a matter of life and death.
The high emotion of those previous seven bars leads to and contrasts with the benignly authoritative *wanderer* (M56) that accompanies the god's entrance. The opening bars resemble the *magic sleep* motif, first heard as Wotan prepares Brünnhilde for her long sleep. It therefore has the same aura of peace, carried forward into the next stage of the drama. There are similarities to no other motif, and to try to find such does little to enhance the drama. The tranquil melody, with subtle variations in the follow up to this entrance, build this into a symphonic tapestry. This is interspersed with Mime's agitated resistance to his presence, within which *hoard* can be heard within the bass. This may be, regardless of circumstance, because Mime cannot shift this from his mind, or it may be because he fears Wotan might lay his hands on it. Either way, Cooke's view of the motifs as essentially psychological is endorsed.

21.8 *wanderer* **M56**

Wagner does not complicate the musical exposition. This episode is largely monothematic - the longest in the *Ring* thus far. Whether it be due to Schopenhauer or to the composer's confidence in his new musical style, he just lets the music flow: the new Wotan, liberated from the stress of life as universal arbiter, is set firmly before us.

Stage 3 - Wotan answers Mime's three questions
This episode is not to do with Mime. He is not trying to defeat Wotan and neither is he trying to uncover information that is new to him. Moreover, if he knows the answers, he also knows that his guest will know them. Three aspects of the drama are evident: (1) Mime's obvious questions indicate that he does not understand what is happening. (2) the cosmological questions nevertheless link them to the social conventions to be found in the eddas. (3) They give Wagner additional opportunity to present Wotan as one who - in spite of appearance and demeanour - remains in control: answering the questions

SIEGFRIED

about dwarfs, giants and gods in the manner chosen confirms a sense of ubiquitous authority.

Progression from the moment of Wotan's arrival is conveyed in the music: where it was mono-thematic before, now the motifs are many and frequent. Presentation and purpose continue to be straightforward. Mime's music finds it way with hesitation as it mirrors Mime's uncertain purpose. As he formulates his questions, we hear an erratic, jerky tapestry of *nibelung slavery* (ie: problem with Nothung) and *scheming*. The task of formulating complex questions where we are ignorant is a big one, and we therefore focus on what we know. So, for all that the answers to his questions serve Mime in no practical manner, they are psychologically accurate and true to the drama. [E]

The motifs, however, that accompany Wotan's answers are uncluttered and distinct: they assist in the telling of the narrative and also convey the authority of Wotan's knowledge. As orchestral platform to this response to the dwarf's question there is prolonged *nibelung slavery, woe, ring, will-to-power*; to the question about the giants: *giants, ring, woe, dragon*; to the question about the gods: *valhalla, nature, wanderer, woe, ring, will-to-power*.

The conclusion to this last is the mighty climax illustrated in 21.9. The first two bars are a foretaste of *power of the gods* – a motif that is only to be really established by Waltraute and the Norns in *Götterdämmerung* Act I. It relates to part of *wotan's struggle* but fits perfectly here as the quiet start to Wotan's assertion of power. Then, in bar 3, *wanderer*, blazoned by the full orchestra with immense emphasis, moves into the loudest occurrence to date of *will-to-power*. Wagner reinforces this climax with a stage direction: Wotan 'strikes the spear as

21.9 The power of the gods – in music.
The English: 'All will submit for all time to the spear's strong master.'

[E] In *The Hobbit* Gollum will be entitled to eat Bilbo if he finds the answer to one last riddle. In his panic to think of anything at all, the hobbit's mind goes blank: 'Bilbo pinched himself and slapped himself, he gripped on his little sword; he even felt in his pocket with his other hand. There he found the ring he had picked up in the passage and forgotten about. "What have I got in my pocket?" he said out loud.'

SIEGFRIED

if by accident on the ground. A low sound of thunder is heard at which Mime is violently startled'. This cumulative symphonic crescendo and climax may be designed to impress the audience as well as Mime. The composer needs to *show* the audience, by means of music, what the text and overall impression of this Scene does not *tell*, namely that Wotan, for all his newly awakened wisdom, continues to relish the continuation of his power over his cosmos (p.201). This episode extends over 64 bars and lasts in excess of 2½ minutes, and stands out amongst all manifestations of Wotan's power.

Stage 4 – Mime signally fails to answer Wotan's three questions and also takes no note of the implications behind them.

In Stage 3 Wotan placed his life in the scales and, regardless of his omniscience, the wager was nevertheless genuine. Now, the questions from the Wanderer are actually designed to help the dwarf save his life. They address both what Mime knows and intends with regard to Siegfried and, where they do not, they warn him of danger. The music for the god throughout this stage links the older, primal Wotan to the reformed Wanderer; that for Mime demonstrates his failings.

The music is rich with motifs. Before the questions, to full-fledged and expanded *wanderer*, Wotan reminds Mime of his mistake with respect to those *he* asked: he wanted to show off rather than to learn. But Mime does not understand: as a continuation of *nibelung slavery* we hear a new motif - one that is only to be associated with the dwarf from now until his death in Act II. The name *clever mime* (M57) tells us that the dwarf thinks he is doing OK, and this before the first question is even put!

21.10 *clever mime* **M57**

The first question (Which race does Wotan both love and treat harshly?) comes easily on the ear with *volsung empathy*). Mime knows the answer and uses the same motif but staccato and with 'etwas belebter' (somewhat more lively) expression: he knows but does not understand. Nevertheless, *clever mime* rounds off his answer.

Question 2 presumes that Siegfried is predestined to kill Fafner and, in doing so, alerts the dwarf that this interrogation is serious. *scheming* and *nibelung slavery* - as heard in the prelude - should concentrate his thoughts anew in preparation for the question as to the weapon that is also predestined to be used. Mime does not get the point: *nibelung slavery, clever mime, wotan's sword* dance along to record his excessive self-satisfaction.

With great skill Wagner increases the pace of the music that leads up to question 3: Who is to forge Nothung? The music does not change: *nibelung slavery, clever mime, scheming*. By every standard this is a tremendous passage as Wotan takes up Mime's jollity and pushes along this short, 32 bar symphonic passage which brings about the dwarf's collapse. Music, story-telling and structure are in swift and perfect harmony. Mime panics and Wagner leads the music back to a recapitulation of the powerful distress which was the theme of Stage 1 of the Scene. But Mime is not now alone, as he was at the beginning, and *wanderer, core life value* and *wotan's sword* lead to words from Wotan that both give Mime crucial information and confirms that he does not help Siegfried. Wotan's last words, 'Only he who's never felt fear, shall forge Nothung anew' – put forth with majestic emphasis - virtually tell the dwarf that it will be Siegfried who is to refashion Nothung and kill Mime. ᶠ This sets the theme for the next Scene.

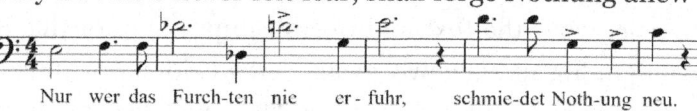

21.11 Mime must guess that this refers to Siegfried. Wotan is thus detaching himself from his grandson and also giving guidance to Mime – if he pays attention.

Stage 5 - Mime is alone and in great fear
The Scene ends with Mime in greater trouble than when it began. Based on *dragon* and *loge as fire* the music represents Mime in a waking nightmare.

Scene 3 – Siegfried returns. Mime evades questions about Nothung; he tries and fails to explain the nature of fear
[Schirmer: 81/1/5 to 91/1/3; Text: 'Heda, du Fauler!' to '. . . nun lügt er sich listig heraus!']
About half of this Scene is about fear – a description of what it is and how to learn about it. The other half is about Siegfried's obsession with the sword, which he now realises can be used to kill Fafner. Taking note of the unusual structure of the Act, this portion concerned with the sword is a necessary bridge between Scene 1 – the end of which sees Siegfried leaving in expectation that Mime will re-forge Nothung – and Scene 4, when he sets about repairing it himself.

The matter to do with fear is not. The eddas offer little evidence that unmatched courage particularly applies to Sigurd. The only reference to his lack of fear is in Brynhild's assertion that she will only marry a man with such an attribute. In the *Nibelungenlied* Hagen states that killing the dragon is the feat for which Sigurd is famous; lack of fear does not feature. Relying therefore on the eddas, the condition Brynhild imposes is best seen as a device for bringing the two together, thereby moving the plot along. We can accept (*pace* Cooke) that Wagner wanted to keep faith with his sources, but he also wanted to bolster the case for an heroic Siegfried when compared to Sigurd: he defeats Fafner in fair fight; he confronts the lord of lords and sees him off; he climbs up toward and penetrates a monstrous wall of fire. Moreover, Wagner takes pains that we both see and hear him do these three things. We do not have to be told that Siegfried is brave: we can see and hear his courage in action. Of the three feats, surmounting the wall of fire is the one that counts the most, for this matchless resolution is immediately preceded by the symbolic destruction of Wotan's spear - and hence his power.

ᶠ This most important statement by Wotan is a further example of Wagner's penchant for a succession of huge intervals in the vocal line when important things are to be said.

Wotan refers to Siegfried's lack of fear only at the very end of the previous Scene. This reference is not needed to further Wagner's plot, although it was needed in the sagas. In the opera, Wotan could just as easily have warned Mime that his death would be brought about by the blade of Nothung, after it is forged anew and in the hand of him whom they both knew to be the only one able to do the job. This would be quite sufficient motive for Mime to prepare the poisoned drink and would also be in accord with all the sagas (#VS18&19).

The plot limps and this affects the music which has a lower level of invention. This applies throughout the Scene but particularly during the 50% where fear is the subject. Wagner struggles to find motifs that give life to the words or the plot. There is *loge as fire* and *brünnhilde's sleep*. What case can be made for these? *loge as fire* will of course relate to Siegfried's ultimate feat of breaching the fire wall. But understandably the musical tone and spirit of that triumph to come will be quite different when associated with the craven Mime. The present appearance takes colour from its use as the background to Mime's nightmare at the end of the previous Scene; it may be reintroduced as a reminiscence of the nightmare but not of fear in general. Loge's six motifs already function as fire and as (generally malicious) cunning, so to pull them into service specifically to represent fear may be considered a step too far. It can also be argued that Wagner managed to portray Mime's beggarly nature as and when needed by other musical means in the previous Scenes with Siegfried and Wotan. But not now, and many who know the *Ring* want this Scene over and done with, anticipating the driving energy of the forthcoming Scene of the forging. The audience now wants Wagner to get on with what matters.

The use of *brünnhilde's sleep* is a bigger problem and will be better examined in the next Act.

Scene 4 - Siegfried re-forges Nothung
[Schirmer: 98/1/4 to 135/5/8. Text from 'Her mit den Stüken, fort mit dem Stümer!' to 'So schneidet Siegrieds Schwert!']
The transition towards this Scene is Mime's assertion that, if nothing else serves, a confrontation with Fafner will certainly be fearful. So Siegfried calls again for his father's sword and, when it is clear that Mime is impotent, the son sees that be must step in.

This long Scene last eighteen minutes and is quite different from all those that have come before. It is a musical *scena* that celebrates the strength, practical intelligence, energy and sense of hope that Wagner invests in his vision of heroism. There is a structure but, rather than one shaped by turns within the drama, it is the five different stages of the forging process and the different music that accompanies each that engage the mind. This sequence is preceded by a short episode in which Siegfried takes over.

SIEGFRIED

A	Siegfried takes over	1½ mins
B	He files down the sword into shavings. These are tipped into a crucible which he places in the forge fire.	3 mins
C	He drives the bellows to fan the fire and so melt the filings. (At the close Mime counterpoints Siegfried's energy with his plans for murder - 2 mins.)	5 mins
D	The molten metal is tipped into the mould for a sword and this is thrust into water to cool. The mould is withdrawn and the glowing sword is laid on the anvil.	2 mins
E	Siegfried hammers the sword into shape and hardens the metal. (Mime again counterpoints with his plotting whilst the finishing touches are made. 1½ mins.)	4½ mins
F	The rivets fasten the sword on to the hilt, Siegfried holds aloft the finished item and smashes the anvil with it. All the time now Mime is plotting alongside.	2 mins
	Total time:	18 mins

The Scene is Siegfried's but Mime is now deciding how to bring about his death and the music is something of a duet for about 5½ minutes.

In the original outline for the *Ring* Wotan seizes hold of a sword from the treasure brought up by the Nibelungs and brandishes it. The idea that this might be Nothung was soon dropped for the notion has no dramatic force. We are not told how Wotan came by the sword that he thrust into Hunding's tree but the assumption has to be that he either forged it himself or arranged for it to be made. When Siegmund wrested it from the tree he was accepting a personal gift from god to man. The significance of this Scene is that Siegfried remakes it without any assistance from Wotan. The skills used are considerable, instinctive and not those which Mime may have attempted to instil. In every sense Nothung comes into the hands of Siegmund and Siegfried by totally different means.

21.12 *filing* **CM26**

21.13 *at the bellows* **CM 27**

21.14 *cooling steel* **CM 28**

During each of the five stages B through F, from filing down the broken sword fragments to the drastic use of the finished article, a fresh compositional motif is introduced. They come and go as the music progresses, join and merge or counterpoint one with another so that the eighteen minutes of the actual forging present a unified but everchanging musical tapestry. The motifs, never to appear again other than mere reminiscence of the action illustrated, dominate the substantive motifs, which join as appropriate. What these are will not surprise: *wotan's sword, horn call, loge as fire, clever mime, dragon, ring, nibelung slavery, hoard*. The music extends over 37 pages of vocal score and the substantive motifs listed above occur on no more than sixteen of them – and then fleetingly.

21.15 *mime and siegfried thinking* **CM 29**
(This is as as the cooled steel is crafted.)

21.16 *hammering the iron* **CM 30**

In this Scene, the words take second place and Wagner uses the development of the five compositional motifs to portray the young hero as a whole and without any psychological overtones. The episode is self-contained but the music is not symphonic.

◇ ◇ ◇ ◇ ◇

SIEGFRIED

ACT II

This Act is in six Scenes which divide, as in Act 1, into those that trace Siegfried's journey (2, 3, 5,6) and those that look outward and beyond that journey (1, 4).

1	Wotan meets up with Alberich as he now waits upon the fateful day when Fafner is to be challenged.	529 bars	24 minutes
2	Siegfried and Mime arrive after a night-long trek through the forest. Fafner and fear continue to be the subject. Siegfried hustles Mime away	137 bars	5½ minutes
3	Left alone, the magical tones of nature – deep in the forest – enchant Siegfried and his attention finally settles on the singing of the wood bird. The blasts of his horn as he tries to communicate with the wood bird arouse Fafner. Siegfried kills him in the fight that follows. The dragon's blood touches his hand and when he puts finger to mouth he understands the wood bird, who tells him to get hold of the Ring and Tarnhelm.	507 bars	20 minutes
4	Whilst Siegfried is inside the cave, Alberich and Mime meet at its entrance and engage in a ludicrous dispute about which of them has greater right to the Ring.	113 bars	3 minutes
5	The wood bird warns Siegfried against Mime. As he understood birdsong so does he divine Mime's murderous intent, and Siegfried kills him.	350 bars	13 minutes
6	Finally, the wood bird tells Siegfried about Brünnhilde and undertakes to lead him to her.	209 bars	7½ minutes
	Total	1855 bars	71 minutes

Scene 1: Wotan engages with Alberich in close proximity to Fafner's cave
[Schirmer: 136/1/1 to 160/5/1. Text from 'In Wald und Nacht' to 'trügen wird euch sein Trotz']

The above table shows that over one quarter of the bars in the Act and about one third of stage time are occupied by this opening Scene which can itself be divided into six parts, of which B, C and D comprise the bulk.

- A Alberich is alone.
- B Wotan arrives and Alberich mounts a tirade about past history and the current conflict.
- C Wotan attempts to disabuse Alberich about his current attitude and intentions.
- D To reinforce matters, Wotan wakes Fafner and encourages Alberich to negotiate with the dragon.
- E In a short coda, Wotan reinforces yet again his present situation before he leaves.

A Alberich is alone

The detailed content of this Scene between Wotan and Alberich may be different from that with Mime in the previous Act but the underlying purpose is the same. In both, the dwarf is alone at the beginning, the god arrives with the express intention of discussing the current concern of each, and each dwarf is alone again when the god leaves. All initiatives stem from Wotan and serve to reinforce the larger purpose, which is to speak and act in in a manner that shows that the god has changed.

The opposition from Alberich is greater than that from Mime and this is established in the prelude, which is five minutes long. This expression of hate, envy and all manner of ill will has few equals in music and conveys the terrible reality of the tyranny promised by Alberich. That this goes beyond words reflects the change in Wagner's view of the balance between text and music. In modern productions the curtain can rise with the opening notes to reveal Alberich on stage and this emphasises the function of the prelude: to illustrate the bleak stage picture and also to portray the dwarf's equally bleak state of mind. Evidence of this is the closing music of the prelude that merges into the opening bars of Alberich's soliloquy. One new motif is introduced, namely that representing Fafner as the dragon (M58). This is remarkable: the motif is introduced by three bars of *dragon* – first heard in *Das Rheingold*. *fafner as dragon* is clearly derived from *giants* but, lying below and *underneath* the cellos and double basses and with the falling interval increased by a semi-tone from a fourth to an augmented fourth, the original motif is transformed in tone from aggression to wickedness. This tone reflects Alberich's malice as he waits outside the dragon's cave, rather than the more passive Fafner.

21.17 *fafner as dragon* **M58**
dragon extends over all four bars.
The distinctive *fafner as dragon* is in bar 4. The upward run at the end of bar 3 is taken from *malice*.

The orchestration of Act II was not fully completed until 1869 – when Wagner restarted composition after the 13 year break and so, in this Act, we can assess how compositional technique had developed. The *fafner as dragon* motif, stretching over two bars, occurs no less than seventeen times – extending, therefore, over 34 bars or 1/3rd of the 104 bars of this prelude. It mixes and merges with six substantive motifs: *dragon* (six times), *scheming* (twice), *ring* (three times), *curse* (twice), *malice* (twelve times) and *woe* (twice). The atmosphere of black malevolence is palpable. If 'symphonic' is interpreted as the melding of disparate themes, then this passes the test. Another remarkable feature is the transformation of *scheming* into a short, violent, presto descending sequence (*ff*) on clarinets, horns, bass clarinet and bassoons. However, the only obvious 'structure' is the repetition of *fafner as dragon*. The episode is a confirmation of Abbate: 'for Wagner the symphonic was a continuous spinning out of never-ceasing thematic webs.' (p.236)

B - Alberich berates Wotan

Alberich has time only to greet this 'fateful day' when *fierce action* and *wotan's struggle* announce Wotan's imminent arrival. Alberich's consequent long tirade of grievance and spite ends in a violently leaping melodic line of a type that Wagner uses to show

```
Dann zitt' - re der Hel - den e - wi-ger Hue - ter!    Wal-halls Hoeh-en
Now quail, you e - ter - nal guard-ians of her - roes!  Storm and ru - in

stuerm ich mit Hel-las Heer:  der Welt____  wal-te dann ich!
come with my fearsome host:   the world____  then shall be mine!
```

21.18 Alberich's venomous tirade comes to its climax.
Violent thoughts violently articulated.

ungovernable rage. At this point, and in contrast to the forceful orchestral sound as previously heard, this vocal line dominates and brings home to the listener that the climax of the episode is now reached. All emphasis in this episode is on Alberich: 58 lines of dialogue as opposed to 14 for Wotan.

C – Wotan responds to Alberich

```
Er steh' o-der fall', sein Herr ist er;  Hel - den nur   Koen-nen mir from-men.
He stands or he falls, he owns his life; help   for me   comes now from her - oes.
```

21.19 Wotan once again steps away from Siegfried.

The contrast is marked when Wotan explains that his position is quite other than that conceived by Alberich. Once again we can refer to the dialectic process that underlies drama. If Alberich's diatribe was the thesis, Wotan's response is the antithesis, defined by the change in musical style. A listener will be aware that many motifs have come to the aid of Alberich, though most are sensed rather than clearly defined. But now, as Wotan seeks to calm matters down, there are just two instances of *wotan's sword* and one of *wotan's balked will*. At the critical moment, Wotan makes a very clear statement about his position (21.19). This is sung to a solid noble tune in F major. So different is the tone and the purpose, and so conjoined with the evolution of Wotan's changed character, that it takes a while to realise that it derives from *siegfried's mission*. The rise of the heroic man is in parallel with the decline of the god: in line with Cooke's thesis that development of a motif depends upon psychology within people. A theme first appears as an appeal from Mime to Siegfried (the 'Starenlied'), becomes an assertion by Siegfried that he will break free, and ends as a reflection by Wotan of the effect this freedom has upon himself.

SIEGFRIED

Stage 4 – Wotan and Alberich waken Fafner

This is the synthesis. Alberich has listened and absorbed and takes part as Wotan now puts the new perspective of his persona into action. He attempts to help Alberich to his goal by immediate negotiation with Fafner. The somewhat throw-away, jovial nature of this three-way exchange belies the serious implication behind it. Wotan will lose all if the negotiation succeeds. Alberich, who is not foolish, takes the matter seriously. The episode is dominated by *fafner as dragon* and *dragon*.

D – Wotan takes leave of Alberich

Wotan's neutrality again. The brevity of the 24 bars cannot disguise their force. Within them we hear the primal motive *life energy* (M2, being the prime derivation of *nature* M1) for the first time in the opera. With it Wotan makes his second seminal pronouncement – this time to do with the ineluctable nature of fate, including his own. The combination of sentiment, situation and music results in a revelation of absolute sincerity.

21.20 Wotan's second confirmation of his detachment – based on *life energy*.

E – Alberich alone

The dwarf is alone again, as was Mime in Act I. This is another short episode. Alberich observes Wotan leaving to *wanderer* and *fierce action* – a masterly combination of serenity and determination to get things done. There also occurs perhaps the most eccentric musical reminiscence in the *Ring*. As Wotan exits, the great melody which closes his farewell to Brünnhilde in W3 sings gently out. The best explanation may be that Wotan is now making his way to the foot of the mountain upon which his daughter is sleeping, there to await Siegfried. It works very well musically but, once again, if it pushes the audience to *think* about the drama, then it can be considered an impediment. The episode continues with three increasingly massive renditions of *curse*, followed by *malice* and *fafner as dragon*, as Alberich leaves. The stage is now ready for Siegfried.

Scene 2 – Siegfried and Mime arrive

[Schirmer: 160/5/4 to 171/1/5. Text from 'Wir sind sur Stelle' to 'Oh, brächten Beide sich um!']

The opening of this Scene, as Siegfried and Mime enter, is outstanding. Including two bars of a growling reminder of *fafner as dragon* in the bars that see out the previous Scene, the illustration on the following page pulls together no less than seven motifs and one vocal refrain from the forging Scene. The themes relate to Siegfried, but they are transformed, by the chamber music orchestration, to represent the bearing and

21.21 Scene 2 opening

<u>Top system</u> Upper stave, bars 4-6 Siegfried's actual song from bellows episode. Lower stave (and upper), bars 1-3 *fafner as dragon;* bars 4-6 *at the bellows.*
<u>Middle system</u> Upper stave, bars 1-3 *youthful energy;* bars 4-6 Siegfried's bellows song with added triplets as in Act I. Lower stave, bars 4-6 *at the bellows.*
<u>Bottom system</u> Upper stave, bars 1-2 *loge as fire;* bars 3-4 variant of *nibelung life;* bars 5-6 *brünnhilde's sleep.* Lower stave, bars 1-2 *at the bellows.*
The chamber music orchestration with the persistent staccato in the bass depicts the quick and light-footed entrance of dwarf and Siegfried.

demeanour of Mime. He is animated and exhilarated by the adventure, bad though his motives are.

The substance of this Scene is a continuation of Scene 3 in Act I, in which Mime tries to teach Siegfried about fear; if it was otiose there, it is equally so here. Since the drama is weak, the music suffers once the lively entry music is over. One only has to compare this with the music of the Forest Murmurs which follows to sense the difference. Most mature listeners or spectators want Wagner to skip this and move on!

It is now appropriate to refer to the motif *brünnhilde's sleep* which, finds frequent voice here. It is now neither truly a motif of reminiscence nor of presentiment (p.226); it does not recall the end of W3, except by an elaborate extension of the concept; if premonition, it must be the fear that Siegfried is to feel when he sees the sleeping Brünnhilde. The problem with that idea is the almighty mismatch that exists between the first emergence of *brünnhilde's sleep* at the close of *Die Walküre* Act III and its development as the Act concludes, and its use here. The motif is introduced as Brünnhilde persuades Wotan to shelter her with a wall of fire. As Wotan is won over to her view – the major turning point in the *Ring* – the motif expands in scale and harmony and is therefore integral to the power of the closing pages of the opera (p.235). The splendour of that pedigree is squandered when it becomes an indication of the mere *possibility* of fear on the part of Siegfried. The musical presentation is mechanical: Siegfried does not want to hear about fear and the reference leads nowhere. It cannot be argued that this is an effective development, an example of change of use on account of changing psychology, and this is made clear when it is compared to the seemingly similar treatment of *siegfried's mission* as described in Stage C of the previous Scene between Wotan and Alberich. We recognise that development with delight, this with a yawn: the former gives meaningful connections and the latter a debilitating regression.

Patrick McCreless argues that this is a prime example of Wagner's flagging creative energy which he, along with other commentators, see at this point. He abandoned composition at the end of this Act. This for a variety of reasons but people think high amongst them would have been fatigue. (McCreless, *Siegfried: its Drama, History and Music*. UMI Research Press, 1982) Perhaps that is so but Wagner held on to the concept. In the sagas, fearlessness is a device introduced to justify Sigurd as a worthy mate to Brynhild (p.82). Wagner always wanted to be true to the mythic sources and this also seemed a good way to orchestrate his own plot. So Wotan, at the end of *Die Walküre*, sings 'He who fears my spearpoint shall never pass through the fire'. Now this statement does make clear that only an exceptional man, not within the current society, could do the job but it does not mandate that he must be *fearless*, and Wagner may also have seen it to be of limited value for, when Brünnhilde fully offers herself to Siegfried at the end of the opera, he says that he has now forgotten what it had been like when he had been fearful. So what sort of fearing was that?

The first structural analysis of the *Ring* in Chapter 3 (p.38) depends solely upon the theories of Freytag *et al* as introduced in that same chapter. Siegfried's triumph is signalled by the winning of Brünnhilde. The conclusion of Chapter 5 (The hero Siegfried) is a first listing of what is exceptional in the persona established by Wagner and the theme is taken up at the end of Chapter 15. The most far-reaching of these characteristics is Siegfried's proclaimed fearlessness. Perpetual and total lack of fear might be seen as a sufficient condition to win Brünnhilde, the point being that it is not a human characteristic at all. Only an insane person has no fear. So it could be, therefore, that this is the reason for the composer's emphasis: lack of fear is simply an easy way to *tell* the audience something he thinks (falsely, as it happens) cannot be *shown*. If so, can it not also be seen as something rather 'cheap'?

<u>Scene 3 – Siegfried becomes one with nature (Forest Murmurs) and this culminates with the understanding what the wood bird says.</u>
[Schirmer 171/1/5 to 198/3/3. Text from 'Das der meiner Vater nicht ist!' to 'Gern folg'ich dem Ruf!']
This Scene is of great moment. The length and variety might suggest – as has happened in previous Acts – that the content includes more than one action. But this is not so. Siegfried's life turns around this episode in which he first fails and then succeeds in

moving up a critical notch toward his particular type of heroism. Entry into this remote forest is the culmination of his absorption into the life of nature, as introduced in Act I, Scene 1. Properly staged and sung, Siegfried can be thought of as sanctified during this process - an indication that such a person is peculiarly marked out.

21.22 Siegfried finds himself.
longing for love enters on bar 4, bends into *love* in bar 7. The marking indicates that the melody is one continuous phrase from bar 4 through bar 12. In bar 13 we hear a return of *natural life*.
The music cannot meaningfully be matched with English words, which are: 'Ah, if I, my mother's son, could only see her! My mother – a man's wife!'

The Scene illustrates a three stage progression into the natural world.
A Siegfried becomes absorbed into nature and attempts to enter it by communing with the wood bird. (The music above is the heart of this, as discussed on the facing page.)
B This does not work but he does waken the moribund Fafner who, as dragon, has almost been subsumed into the natural world.
C They fight and Fafner's blood gives him access to something decidedly beyond the bounds of the normal.

A – Forest Murmurs

The forest in which Siegfried now finds himself and the river Rhine are the two overt descriptions of nature in the *Ring*. Accordingly, the shimmering of the sunlight on the forest leaves and the penetration of its beams through the water as the Rhine Gold is revealed have the same simplicity of lucid innocence, and the primary song of *wood bird* (M59) resembles that of the Rhinedaughters (M3).

21.23 *wood bird* **M59**
The motif is closely related to that of the Rhinedaughters.

The intention is that we should be transported. The dramatic purpose of this episode is to depict the crucial arrival of full self-awareness as to who he, Siegfried, might be. This is when he deliberates firstly on his father, and then with deeper passion in 21.22, on his dead mother. In this long musical stretch, he considers the course of his life as never before. It is one of the most beautiful in the entire opera and perhaps in the tetralogy. Additionally, it is embraced, fore and aft, by contrasting episodes which are both of striking beauty: the shimmering sound of the forest before and the wood bird's song afterwards. The passage in 21.22 is preceded by *longing for love*. Love and the longing for it come together in Siegfried's perception of nature; for him, love is about nature and he has no concept of sex. It is worth recalling that the important *natural life* motif – as introduced by Loge in *Das Rheingold* – acted as the harbinger of *core life value*. Nature is the core of human life. [G] It is this growing awareness of the complexity of life that brings him to the stage that he can understand the song of the wood bird. The claim that Siegfried is something of an oaf must be qualified by the exquisite music in this Scene, which turns around Siegfried's reaction to what he hears and sees, and not simple nature. Of the major players in the four operas, only Siegfried is deeply attuned to the natural world.

B – Siegfried fails to connect with the wood bird but does so with Fafner

After the horn call rouses Fafner there is much *dragon* and *fafner as dragon* as the two prepare to and then engage in combat. Now music can effectively convey conflict in general terms but it is not so easy to match it to stage action, where the reality of theatrical contrivance makes it difficult to deliver. Generally, it is better to keep it short: good examples are those from *Lohengrin* (between Telramund and Lohengrin) and between Cassio and Montano in Verdi's *Otello*. The former extends over 16 bars and is enclosed with a formal, ritualistic setting; the latter extends over 36 bars and is accompanied by much general hullaballoo by on-stage chorus and onlooking characters. The fight between Siegfried and Fafner at his point spreads over 41 bars and is

---

[G] We do not need to be reminded of this in the 21st century. By common consent, mankind has pillaged the earth in which we live and we are now paying for the privilege.

concentrated solely on the two opponents. The music is fully competent but still routine. In no way does it live up to the fame associated with Siegfried's iconic victory: the music and action do not really work as drama. It is, however, followed by a moving threnody to the dying giant

21.24 *fafner's obsequy* **CM31**
A version of *malice* is in the top line; a fragment of *horn call* and *giants,* twice repeated, in the lower lines.

that lasts for 70 bars. Reminiscent of a funeral march that can be placed alongside that for Siegfried, Wagner honours Fafner (*fafner's obsequy* CM31) with a striking dignity in his last moments. In the bass we hear a version of *horn call* and *giants*.

Why and what for? Perhaps no more than that Fafner was always true to his nature. In the myths (p.128) the giants are primordial; Fafner is now in a primitive environment again – and evidently feels at home there. He is not aware that his death is part of a bigger story. The music is ritualistic and repetitive. The threnody is set going with a triplet on the first beat in the lower stave. This continues for nine bars and is then superseded by *siegfried, ring, dragon, curse* – all clearly and sequentially presented.

Siegfried is instructed in much: it is Fafner who obliquely puts him on his guard against Mime, who tells him both about the golden treasure and also something about the wider world. In truth, Siegfried may be well instructed but he learns little. This is the second tranche of knowledge that comes his way but he does not much take it in, unlike that about his mother and father. Wagner is deliberate and it may be that he does not see it as part of Siegfried's function to know much (p.219). The important information is to come with the gift of tongues that Fafner's blood is to give him.

C – Fafner's blood leads to knowledge of bird song.
As the music marked the change from *A* to *B*, so does the music take us in an instant from thoughts of Fafner to the third stage in which Siegfried is elevated to a higher symbolic plane. The elevation of Fafner, the giver of the gift, in his dying moments is matched by that of Siegfried, the receiver. The episode is brief but the brilliance of the (ideally light and airy) soprano voice adds to the break-through from darkness to light.

Scene 4 -Alberich squabbles with Mime whilst Siegfried is in Fafner's cave
[Schirmer 198/4/1 to 206/1/4. Test from 'Wohin schleichst di eilig und schau, schlimmer Gesell?' to 'und doch, seinem Heern soll'er allein noch gehören.']
This little Scene undeniably works for following reasons.
- Continuity from Scene 1. Almost the last words from Wotan before he leaves Alberich alone are 'I leave the field to you: stand firm! Try your luck with your brother Mime.' Here you see the fruits of this advice.

SIEGFRIED

- The bounce of hope offered by the wood bird's advice now opens up aspects of the ridiculous that lie in the two dwarfs. The energy and determination of each is there, but the malignity and mutual antipathy expose them as losers.
- The very fast tempo contrasts with all that comes before and after.
- Despite brevity, the music builds in force until it explodes under its own vituperance. Traces of motif scuttle past: *woe, nibelung slavery, scheming* and the ungainly jerking associated with both dwarfs in *Das Rheingold*, but all are gone as soon as they arise. The audience is vastly amused and barely notices the reasoning behind the Scene, nor the necessity for the interlude which allows Siegfried to take possession of Ring and Tarnhelm. It thus prepares us for the penultimate stage of the conquering progress, the hallmark of this opera.

Scene 5 – Mime betrays himself and is killed by Siegfried.
[Schirmer: 206/1/4 to 222/1/4. Text from 'Was ihr mir nützt, weissen nicht' to 'Neides Zoll zahlt Nothung.']
A regular routine from the comic duo Laurel and Hardy was for the former repeatedly to make the same mistake despite being hit around the head by the latter. Wagner treats us to a version of this here. After the wood bird has warned Siegfried to guard against Mime - a classic example, of course, of the supernatural helping the hero, as defined by Campbell, Mime exposes his hatred of Siegfried no less than five times. On the fifth, the latter strikes him dead. As with the previous Scene with Alberich and Mime, we are in comic territory. Not even in *Die Meistersinger* did Wagner surpass the clarity with which he displays the various fixed and compositional motifs as they dance along.

21.25 *wheedling mime (1)* **CM 32**

21.26 *wheedlling mime (2)* **CM 33**

21.27 *wheedling mime (3)* **CM 34**

The dramatic shape of this Scene invites scrutiny of Wagner's symphonic style. In the strict sense it might be thought that variations on a motif would be developed within each of the five sequences when Mime declares his hatred unwittingly and is then pulled up short by Siegfried. This expectation is partially confirmed. *wood bird* occurs near the beginning of the first four sequences and in the middle of the fifth; there are three *wheedling mime* compositional motifs. The first (CM32) is prominent near the beginning of sequence 1; the second (CM33) dominates sequence 2 and the third (CM34) powerfully influences sequences 4 and 5. Sequence 3 is extensively filled by the *starenlied*: (21.6, p.342) - as derisively named by Siegfried in Act I. The motifs, whether substantive or compositional, join up with each other in accordance with their different melodic contours. Therefore, as each constituent of the music differs (there are a total of nine when *scheming, nibelung slavery, clever mime* and *longing for love* are dropped in as appropriate) so does the actual *sound* differ, regardless of any *structural* similarity within the five episodes. There is little sense of a musical unity that would justify the word 'symphonic'.

One deft refinement must be mentioned. *clever mime* was introduced when the dwarf was being too clever by half with Wotan in Act I, Scene 2. In this Scene, when the dwarf really thinks he has the measure of Siegfried, the motif is given a tail as illustrated in 21.28. This comprises two fragments of *loge as cleverness* – much slowed down.

21.28 An extension to *clever mime* by the addition of *clever loge,* much slowed down, in the third bar. The dwarf is killed shortly afterwards – too clever by half!

At the moment of Mime's death, the final significant rendition of *scheming* appears four times, falling *(ff)* through four octaves (woodwind > upper strings > horns > lower strings): a comment on a wasted life.

Scene 6: The wood bird leads Siegfried towards Brünnhilde
[Schirmer: 222/2/2 to 238/6/5. Text from 'Neides Zoll zahlt Nothung' to 'Wohin du flatterst folg'ich dir nach!']
The Act has progressed from the dark before dawn to midday, from dark to light and – most decidedly – this and the two preceding Scenes offer joyous and positive progress. Alberich and Mime have been diminished by their mutual self-centred vituperation and then Mime's uncomprehending over-confidence leads him to disaster. In this final Scene, the way to fulfilment is clear when the wood bird tells Siegfried of Brünnhilde: the coda to his growth.

The Scene is clearly in three parts and forms a large-scale dialectic.

A Siegfried wraps up the situation, and does the best he can to make a clean ending for his two defeated foes. (Thesis)

B He suffers a depressive reaction after his physical and emotional struggle with the two of them. (Wagner is subtly perceptive when Siegfried says that he is tired after all the effort. When can one imagine him being 'tired'?!) He does the only thing he can and asks help from the wood bird. (Antithesis)

C The two of them find the answer to his need. (Synthesis)

By far the longest episode is that in the middle. Of the 260 bars in the Scene, more than one third give voice to 23 lines of verse in which Siegfried, as he lies in the dappled shade of the forest, expresses the loneliness that has afflicted his whole life. Wagner gives us sentiment without sentimentality and this may give reason to doubt Michael

Buckley's observation in an otherwise excellent article from 2004 that 'Siegfried exhibits little more than enormous energy, disregard for conventional wisdom, a determination to get what he wants without regard for either persons or principles.' (MB/FM) This is not an uncommon view but the music here and in the earlier Forest Murmurs tells us differently. The music in this episode largely leaves behind recitation of motifs. An extended sequence of *longing for love,* each repetition higher by the interval of a third, is prompted by the sight of the wood bird with its companions in the trees; *scheming* and *nibelung slavery* reflect his thoughts on Mime. And then occurs a compositional motif redolent of what one might call *joyous agitation* (CM35) as he asks his only friend for help. The period from the moment when the motif appears to the end of the Act extends over 151 bars and *joyous agitation* fills 43 of them: it is the musical glue that holds together *longing for love,* the wood bird motifs and three repetitions of *brünnhilde's sleep* – a mini symphony.

21.29 *joyous agitation* **CM 35**

Prior to this and his colloquy with the wood bird comes the putting to rest of Fafner and Mime, and this is heavily laden with motifs as the stage action is illustrated. Laborious *horn call* as the bodies are carried, *nibelung slavery, fafner as dragon* and *ring* as Siegfried bids the dead to guard the remains of the hoard with their bodies.

The break at the end of Act II heralds, as is well attested, the break of 13 years in composition and the subsequent further elaboration of musical style we are to see in Act III. Only nine new motifs are introduced in this opera up to this point. However, no fewer than twelve compositional motifs can be found. These serve to carry bigger musical structures forward, merging with the general musical fabric and the main motifs.

◇ ◇ ◇ ◇ ◇

SIEGFRIED

Act III

The more examined, the more remarkable does *Siegfried* appear, emerging as it does from *Der junge Siegfried*. Act III is the most striking of the three. Within it lie crucial events in the existence of all the players who enter – Wotan, Erda, Siegfried and Brünnhilde. The action presents the coming together of the mortal with the immortal at its most intense, and this is increased by the decision to make Wotan and Erda the parents of Brünnhilde, as invented by Wagner in *Der junge Siegfried*.

Such unparalleled opening up of the story may have been one of the reasons for the thirteen years break in composition between Acts II and III: the weight of back story behind each event in the Act demanded greater musical resource. This impacts immediately with the prelude: not only the sound but also the mere sight of the vocal – let alone the orchestral – score speaks of the change. The weight of sound and the complex exploitation of the motifs show us that big things are afoot. This is not to say that the music is better from now on than it was before but it is different and certainly the scale of the score matches the stretch of the plot. In this Act are to be found the first examples of the music taking over at the expense of the poem (p.236).

The structure within the Act is also different. Long as it is, there are only five Scenes, one of which is short. The reason for this is that each of the four longer Scenes integrates several layers of plot, which can now be carried forward by Wagner's changing use of the motifs and by broad-backed sequences within the quasi-symphonic musical tapestry. The structure is as follows.

A	Wotan and Erda wrap up the current situation as far as they are able. Their paths diverge and that for the god becomes clear to him. The prelude is included since it depicts Wotan's state of mind as he advances upon Erda.	418 bars; 19 minutes
B	Wotan confronts Siegfried. The destinies of both are confirmed: Wotan loses power and Siegfried is the necessary agent.	313 bars; 13 minutes
C	Siegfried broaches the wall of fire that encircles Brünnhilde.	69 bars; 3 minutes
D	Siegfried discovers the sleeping Brünnhilde and awakens her with a kiss.	221 bars; 14 minutes
E	Brünnhilde is wooed by Siegfried. At first she resists but then joyfully accepts him as lover.	739 bars; 34 minutes

Total = 1760 bars; 84 minutes

The Act has three groupings. Scenes A & B are about Wotan, Scenes C & D are about Siegfried and Scene E is about Brünnhilde. Wotan and Siegfried meet in B; Wotan is the protagonist who loses out and Siegfried is the antagonist who wins through. The encounter matters deeply to the god but not to the man. As the remaining Scenes demonstrate, he is only interested in meeting the woman singled out by the wood bird. This is why the last Scene is focussed on Brünnhilde.

Scene 1: Wotan connects with world ethical problems, of which Erda is the symbol.
[Schirmer: 239/1/1 to 261/2/1. Text: from 'Wache, Wala!' to '. . zu Ewigen Schlafe!']
The Scene is in five parts and refers to deep matters. The evidence that Wagner perceived this to be the case lies in the gestation of *Der junge Siegfried*. The main events for Wotan in that draft are held back to this Act: the encounters in Act III with Erda and with Siegfried. That with Siegfried is not fully developed due to the absence of Nothung breaking Wotan's spear. But the composer invested no less intensity of plot and dramatic force in the Wotan/Erda Scene as found in that first draft than as is now found in the finished score. The pairing of Wotan with Erda is the key link back to the mythology: of the four conversations he has in this opera – with Mime, Alberich, Siegfried and Erda - this is the only one that directly derives from that between Odin and the Wala, being identical in tone and setting with *Balder's Dream* in the *Poetic Edda*. In addition to the denial of the other's identity, as there described, Erda persistently wants to be free of Odin in seven of the fourteen verses. These find cogent expression in the texts of both *Der junge Siegfried* and *Siegfried*.

The structure is best matched with the Freytag Pyramid. Wotan is the protagonist and Erda the antagonist.

1	Set-up	The prelude sets the tone for the entire Scene as it depicts Wotan's state of mind as he makes his way to see Erda.
2	Rising Action	Wotan rouses Erda from her primeval sleep. As the crisis mounts and comes closer to him, there is the need to talk to someone who understands and, hopefully, will agree with him. His time in charge is to end. But Erda cannot help. For whether or not her time also draws to an end, she has lost interest. In sequence she tells Wotan to ask first the Norns and then Brünnhilde for guidance.
3	Mid-point	Wotan rejects both suggestions and this opens a rift at the cosmic level, which foretells the crisis to come. Erda becomes hostile and confirms what we, the audience, feels: that, whatever the circumstances, Brünnhilde was right and Wotan wrong.
4	Falling action	Wotan pushes back and, quite simply, the two row together. The climax is when Wotan asserts that, for the first time perhaps, he has knowledge beyond that of Erda.
5	Resolution	Wotan moves on alone and with advice and help from no one; Erda returns to the earth.

SIEGFRIED

1 – Set up

The celebrated prelude depicts Wotan as he advances toward his confrontation with Erda. The music tells us he is agitated and anxious, with his thoughts turning round the large-scale issues that date back 50 years. Motifs abound. From *Das Rheingold* there is *will-to-power, woe, erda, downfall;* from *Die Walküre* we hear *wotan's struggle, destiny, magic sleep,* and from earlier in this opera there is *wanderer*. Whether or not a reader readily recalls these to mind or not, it is easy to see that the names point to the major crises during those years. Additionally, in 45 of the 65 bars, there is heard the rhythmic pulse of the compositional *fierce action*, first heard in *Das Rheingold,* and which is the base rhythm of *valkyr* (this most powerful occurrence has prompted Roger Scruton and others to call the motif *riding*) and some of Siegfried's forging. All this musical activity is crammed into two minutes of music, written out in the composition sketch in one continuous flow. Those eight substantive motifs permeate the entire prelude.

2 – Rising action

Almost immediately, to the words 'Wala! Erwach!' we hear *wotan summons erda* (M60). The melodic profile is that of *love*, although it is difficult to make a con-

21.30 *wotan summons erda* **M 60**

nection to the passion between Siegmund and Sieglinde when this clarion call is first heard. The sexual conjunction between the Volsung twins is far removed from whatever might have occurred between Wotan and Erda. Be that as it may, this memorable fanfare-like motif crops up frequently in this *rising action* part which extends over 201 bars (almost 50% of the whole Scene). No fewer than 101 bars give space to *wotan summons erda* (11 times), *magic sleep* (28), *will-to-power* (18), *erda/downfall* combined (40). These four delve toward fateful matters: the looming danger to the gods and the whole existing order, the emerging centrality of Brünnhilde, and the importance to Wotan of this particular encounter with Erda. The remainder also have moral import: *natural life* (8 times), *life energy* (10), *valhalla* (11), *ring* (6), *core life value* (4), *destiny* (5). The music is telling the story and the motifs used tells us that the roots are deep. This is an occasion where knowledge of the text helps toward a complete understanding of the drama. For this is the first of a sequence of serious discussions , and therefore of a different nature, for example, from the emotional outburst from Sieglinde in W1.

The enhanced melding of motifs is exemplified in the example at the top of the facing page. *erda* breaks five notes in on the upward sweep, at which point the notes reached becomes the top notes, and form therefore the start of the downward course of *ring*; after a repeat of the latter, the fundamental goal of *erda*, namely *downfall*, returns. Wotan is saying that the Norns (related in some way to Erda) can no longer foretell events but are compelled to take note of the machinations which swirl around the Ring.

21.31 The melding of motifs.
Bars 1 & 4: versions of *erda* & *downfall* enclose bars 2 & 3, two renditions of *ring*

3 – Mid-point

The change of mood is brought about by a repetition of the great melody with which Wotan bids farewell to Brünnhilde. This tune (see notation on p.235) reminds us that it was her purity of intent that gained victory over Wotan and it now launches Erda into a heartfelt attack on the god. With a realisation that this Scene is a crux in the tetralogy as a whole, the expectation is that the dramatic objective is supported by powerful music. We are not disappointed. This Part is no more than 34 bars in length but its intensity is clear. Erda's sentiments, which cannot be made to fit the music, are as follows:

> You would teach defiance, yet it's defiance you punish?
> You incite an act, yet against that act you rage?
> You preserve rights, you protect vows,
>   yet rights you oppose, and through perjury you rule?

21.32 Erda rejects Wotan.
The increasingly wide intervals in the voice are characteristic. The intervals increase steadily until that on *Meineid* is an octave and a half.
The first ten bars of the bass line comprise *brünnhilde's purity* and from then onwards we hear *destiny*.

The vocal line is Wagner at his most highly charged (in line also with *Opera and Drama* voice melody tenets) and the bass line powerfully brings Brünnhilde before us. After that final high A flat (the utmost top of the contralto range) Erda wearily asks to be released again to sleep. 'Let me return to the deep, let sleep lock my wisdom away'. She wants to be rid of Wotan, as the Wala did with Odin in *Balder's Dream*.

4 – Falling action

The answer from Wotan is a characteristic 'Not yet!'. He still must dominate. This push-back is characterised by *wotan summons erda* and *wanderer*. Each asserts a claim to

SIEGFRIED

precedence ('You are not what you say you are.') and the Part ends with his own assertion of independence from Erda: 'Weisst du was Wotan will?' The rift between the two is final.

5 – Resolution

Wotan bids Erda depart into primeval sleep and her part in the drama is done. With that there comes an uncommon period when Wotan is at peace with himself. Different in tone and content to the question and answer debate with Mime, we nevertheless again glimpse the god as he was in the past plenitude of his power. A 'long silence' introduces

21.33 Wotan's farewell to Erda. *Bars 1-3 erda; bars 4-6 downfall.*

a fine vocal line, accompanied in the bass by the rise and fall of *erda* and *downfall*: Erda may now rest in peace. With sharp focus, text and motifs combine to tell the story. Wotan continues to this effect:- Times have changed. I mistakenly had fear for the future but now I confidently release myself from care. Siegfried, without my help, has gained the Ring; free from all greed, Alberich's curse will not taint him. He will waken and claim Brünnhilde ('wisdom's child') and set the world free. So sleep, Erda, and in your dreams observe my downfall. To Brünnhilde and Siegfried, the eternally young, I now gladly yield place.

Erda does descend into her primal sleep, and to the same *magic sleep* that cast Brünnhilde into her long repose. Along with the similarities of the motif to *wanderer*, this confirms that this summons is a power unique to Wotan. Its reappearance here fits both the drama and the re-emergence of a god who is now calm and imperial.

One new motif now arrives. Grandiloquently previously labelled 'The World's Inheritance', it is here more prudently called *future hope*. The varied, but emphatic and purposeful rising scale may also be thought to gainsay the rationale for a pessimistic *Ring*. A hope for a regeneration can quickly and simply arise as the motif is heard, and might also remind us of the regeneration of the earth and the re-emergence of Balder after the great flood (p.87).

21.34 *future hope* **M 61**

<u>Scene 2: Wotan confronts Siegfried, thereby making the last contact with his cosmos.</u>
[Schirmer: 261/2/1 to 280/1/3. Text from 'Dort seh' ich Siegfried nah'n' to 'Ich kann dich nicht halten.']
This Scene complements Scene 1. Then Wotan broke ties with the eternal; now he is to say goodbye to his grandson – the exemplar of humanity. The critical journey lies with

the god, being a continuation of the previous encounter. Although Siegfried is also on his own journey, the coming encounter is not important to him and, if Wotan had not been in his path, the wood bird would presumably have led his way to the fire, explained what he must do and then have left. What matters to Siegfried is the whereabouts of Brünnhilde. We have seen that it *must* be Siegfried who overcomes the power of the Ring (p.218). So here, because of Wotan's last words in *Die Walküre*, it is necessary that Wotan's spear be demolished by a man who does not fear it. (Not to fear something is not the same as being fearless.) For Siegfried, Wotan is just a man who bars his way. For Wotan, the confrontation brings his two faces (before and after of his epiphany with Brünnhilde at the end of *Die Walküre*) into confrontation with each other. This is the hinterland of the drama within this Scene and it can be imagined that when *My Life* reports that reading Schopenhauer helped Wagner to understand Wotan, and confirmed and comforted him in his huge task, as proposed by Thomas Mann (p.18), this was an important part of what he meant.

The structure of this Scene has five parts, set out below as a Freytag Pyramid.

1 Set-up		Calm and at and at ease with himself as he leaves Erda, Wotan starts on his last journey.
2 Rising action		The conversation between man and boy is the sort that a king or a great tycoon (to take up Cooke's description) might have with a young relative: cheerful, but pointed and self-centred.
3 Mid-point		Wotan's kindly but masterful laughter upsets Siegfried and Wotan is now nonplussed.
4 Falling action		Mounting withering contempt and indifference by Siegfried, and the insistence that his only interest is Brünnhilde, knock Wotan off balance. The ingrained compulsion to have his way combines with the universal desire of a father to protect a daughter.
5 Defeat		Wotan reveals his identity and Siegfried sees him, as would have been obligatory in Nordic times, as his enemy. Inevitably the spear opposes the sword and is shattered. Wotan leaves.

A symmetry can be seen between these two final episodes in Wotan's active life. Each has a classic five stage structure; in each Wotan is opposed by a hitherto unimagined antagonist. Wotan overcomes Erda but is then overcome in the second contest. Together they trace the route to his demise.

1 – Set-up
Wotan's contentment is conveyed by the stage direction: as Siegfried approaches, he 'leans with his back against the rocks' – those into which Erda has just disappeared. Sprightly reminiscence of *wood bird* and *longing for love* pronounce that all is well. Wotan is happy because matters with Erda are concluded, his mind is made up and the path ahead is clear. The drastic action to come is necessary if he is to leave the world in

a better place. Moreover, he is to meet his grandson for the first time. Variations of *wood bird* accompany the opening exchanges, during which Siegfried tells Wotan of his journey to find Brünnhilde. The root keys throughout are G and C major – forthright and open.

2 – Rising action

These 52 jaunty bars are another question and answer engagement. The questions elicit Siegfried's recent history, from the wood bird's help, through the deaths of Fafner and Mime. Nothung's part in all this brings forth how Siegfried forged the sword himself, at which Wotan breaks 'into a laugh of joyous good humour'. Many of the questions are posed to the strains of a cheerful compositional motif: *wotan's questions* (CM36). This exchange came to an end when Wotan could not resist a forthright laugh.

21.35 *wotan's questions* **CM 36**

3 – Mid-point

21.36 *volsung bond (1)* **CM 37**

When, in Act 1 Scene 1, Siegfried learnt how his mother Sieglinde died, *volsung empathy* (M34) mutated into *volsung bond (1)* (CM37). A tail, in the form of a triplet was added. Since then it has lain dormant but now, when Siegfried is disturbed by Wotan's laughter, this mutation reappears and comes into its own. It serves to indicate Siegfried's growing opposition to Wotan. To name it is difficult, and the only dramatic logic I can see is the indication it might give of the integrity, the sense of identity inherent in being part of the Volsung race. The triplet tail is seen at the end of bar three in 21.36. The continuing appearance of the triplets first rising and then falling in the succeeding five bars contribute to the musical shape of the episode. Triplets characterise Siegfried's dismissal of Wotan's attempt at friendship across a total of 37 bars.

Wotan's music is quite different. There are three runs of *volsung bond (1),* and then we can compare his response, as given in 21.37, to the brutality of his opening

21.37 Wotan reasons with Siegfried; *wotan's questions* moved from E♭ major to C minor.

contentions with Brünnhilde in W2. (See *brünnhilde's punishment*.) Here there is calmness toward the rude youth. The music is a softening of *wotan's questions* from a bold E♭ major to its relative C minor.

Half-way through the episode, Siegfried asks why Wotan wears such a strange floppy hat. Wotan sees this as an opportunity to take control with the imposing *wanderer*. When Siegfried, with pronounced rudeness, asks how the god lost his eye, Wagner puts forth Wotan's majesty with a full exposition of all four *valhalla* motifs, with extensions and spread over 16 bars, as an accompaniment to his answer: we know this is important to the god. The stage direction then reads: 'Siegfried, who has listened thoughtfully, now involuntarily bursts out laughing'. His sentiment?: My, you are at least good for a laugh. But if you can't tell me the way, then be off with you!

4 – Falling action
The music now tells us that Wotan is pushed out of his depth by such treatment. *wotan's balked will* returns five times in sequence. The god sings softly as he tries to keep control of himself. His message? Hold off, or I will destroy you and in consequence my hopes will also be destroyed. The words are of no avail. Out of my way, says Siegfried - the wood bird will lead me. Then Wotan reverts, in the manner suggested by Schopenhauer to his pre-Brünnhilde persona (p.201): *will-to-power* descends the full two octaves *ff*. But Siegfried is indifferent.

5 – Conclusion
The die is cast. Fifteen bars of a speeded-up *wotan's balked will* see Siegfried throw Wotan's aggression back at him. This sequence is only broken by four most distinctive bars which, as with the *volsung empathy* mutation, offer what might be thought a stretched interpretation of an earlier motif *domestic life*. Discussion of this, however, is best delayed to Scene 4 (after Siegfried has breached the fire and is on the mountain top) where yet a further mutation of the original motif happens. As it is, after these opening bars, the Scene rushes to a conclusion. *valkyr, loge as fire* and *brünnhilde's sleep* accompany Wotan's description of the dangers; *siegfried, force of the gold, wood bird* convey Siegfried's response. Thereafter follows a crush of motifs: *force of the gold, wood bird, will-to-power, wotan's balked will* and *volsung empathy* (this time in its original format) repeated four times. Then *wotan's sword* rises up and, as the spear disintegrates, *will-to-power* also breaks into pieces and Wotan disappears from the stage to the sounds of *downfall*.

Readers will note the listing of *force of the gold* in the previous paragraph. Were there to be a fall in the motif of a semi-tone, we could think of it as an expression of woe and stress. But this is not so and the full tone drop unambiguously indicates the emotions first evinced by the appearance of the Gold within the river. This is an oddity. The imagination is stretched to see a connection between the Rhine Gold and Siegfried's terminal struggle with Wotan. If there be none it means that there is no reason for it *in the drama* and this entails that the cause lies in the music. In the score it sounds very well as a counterpoint to a portion of *siegfried* – an example of the capacity for motifs to meld with each other as and when they will. Each listener/spectator must make what they will of this.

Scene 3: Siegfried climbs the mountainside and breaches the wall of fire.
[Schirmer: 280/1/1 to 285/1/1. Text (only in opening bars) from 'Mit zerfocht'ner Waffe floh mir der Feige?' to 'Jetzt lock'ich ein liebes Gesell!']
These bars glorify Siegfried. The first 20 bars set out his hopes that, once through the flames, he will find a companion to love and we hear *bird song,* which cleverly tells us that Siegfried takes up his journey again after the interruption by Wotan, whom he saw as irrelevant. So *siegfried* is accompanied by *bird song* until *horn call* takes over as he starts the climb. There follow seventeen bars of *horn call* almost alternating with *siegfried,* whilst around them *loge as fire* is increasingly prominent: a short poem of joy. *loge as fire* then counterpoints the compositional *fierce action* as the interlude reaches its climax. With the sound volume declining, the ubiquitous *brünnhilde's sleep* sings with *loge as fire* and eventually we hear *siegfried* again, accompanied now by soft echoes of *bird song* as the fire totally recedes.

The glorification of Siegfried that Wagner surely intended this passage to show is that the climb through the fire wall is mythically heroic even if it be improbable. All is splendour and conveys the culminating victory which follows the forging of Nothung, and the defeats of Fafner, Mime and Wotan. Indubitably the music *shows* us Siegfried's fearlessness. Of the feats that precede this, only the forging has musical grandeur. The killing of Fafner is musical bombast; that of Mime is amusing but never heroic; finally, the defeat of Wotan was conveyed with musical turbulence and without opulence.

This is a burnished and golden Siegfried – the best of his attributes encased in the vivid heat of the fire, and a halo of triumph that is to return again just once, and *in exactly* this fashion, in the Immolation as fire and flood destroy the Gibich palace. [H] The Scene is obviously the mid-point of the Act, both because it breaks the Act in two and also because it takes Siegfried into a totally new world.

Scene 4 – Siegfried discovers and awakens Brünnhilde with a kiss
[Schirmer: 285/1/1to 295/4/2. Text from 'Selige Öde auf wonniger Höh!' to 'Sollt'ich auch sterbend vergeh'n.']
It can surprise that this Scene, with Siegfried alone on the mountain top from the moment the fire dies down behind him to when he bends down to kiss Brünnhilde, lasts only about fourteen minutes. So little action on stage but much on the development of the man. The Scene is in two stages.

[H]   Nevertheless, the fire here is a puzzle. Siegfried does not know that the encircling fire is 'magic'. Moreover, what does this mean? Surely it is not unreal – Loge is the god of fire and not of 'pretend' fire. It would burn anyone whether feared or not but Siegfried comes through without a scorch. The only rational explanation might be to liken it to the ritual of walking on live coals: a practice still to be seen in Northern Greece. Perhaps it is best not to examine this too much!

A   Siegfried enters a new world, quite unknown to him until that time. He sees a sleeping figure under a shield.
B   He discovers the figure is a woman and not a man and to see a woman for the first time is a big step into the unknown. But he regains equilibrium and makes the classic folklore decision to wake the woman with a kiss.

Stage A – A new world
The stage direction is for the clouds to part to reveal 'the bright blue sky of daylight . . . with a veil of reddish morning mist . . . [Siegfried] mounts to the top of the height and, standing on a rock at the edge of a precipice . . . gazes with surprise at the scene.' The music gives us a high and isolated landscape, pure on that account alone but also washed clean of the venality and turmoil as witnessed in the previous 2½ Acts. *destiny* and fragments of *brünnhilde's sleep* are heard as *all* the first violins (always *pp*) soar ever higher until at the highest reach *destiny* underpins them. The melodic line continuously traces *brünnhilde's sleep* as it sinks down. For 23 bars (10% of the Scene) this magical silence remains. Wagner rarely 'scene paints', so Siegfried's purity is the subject matter.

After Siegfried's first salutation to this marvel, 'Selige Öde auf wonniger Höh!', there occurs a second mutation of *domestic life*. The first occurred at the end of Scene 2, at the point when Wotan tells Siegfried that if his child is to be wakened from her sleep then he, Wotan, will lose his power. The second, in this Scene, is to appear again as Siegfried contemplates the pellucid landscape before him. *domestic life* refers to the moment when Fricka bewails her inability to keep Wotan both at home and faithful. This brings up an issue that is discussed below.

When Siegfried notices the sleeping human form there wells up the great tune of Wotan's farewell to her. No problem of relevance exists here, as it refers not to Brünnhilde herself but to the decisive acknowledgement by the god of his submission to his daughter's superior understanding. As Siegfried continues to observe his surroundings, the theme given languorously in 21.38 (on the next page) returns and is developed twice – then to disappear. Except for the occasional surge, the music is *p* and *pp* throughout. The only other motifs are fragments of *valkyr* and *wotan's sword*.

# # # # # #

This therefore is the opportunity to trace the development of *domestic life* (M9) first heard in *Das Rheingold*, earlier by some 8 hours of music. JK Holman lists the first appearance of this mutation as a new motif and names it 'Resistance'. At that moment, when Wotan is squaring up to Siegfried, Holman suggests that the god is also both hanging on to power and protecting his daughter against a suitor. The name given by Holman, and also by Ernest Newman, at its *first* appearance in *Das Rheingold* is 'Love's enchantment', and Holman now says that 'Siegfried is about to discover [such enchantment] in Brünnhilde'. But this cannot be sustained: the motif is called *domestic life* in this study because that is what it sounds like; for Cooke it is 'Domestic Bliss' which has something of the same meaning. If Holman and Newman are using this moment of recall to suggest that there was also an enchanted and obsessive love between Wotan and Fricka, then the counter suggestion is that it is not possible for anyone in the audience to believe this. As humans, we are aware of the delirium that can be felt as part of sexual love. Such is the passion that Siegmund and Sieglinde had and that Siegfried and Brünnhilde will experience. The audience cannot, just *cannot* think of Wotan and Fricka being 'in love' in the same fashion. Wagner also tells us that Wotan risked going blind in order to win Fricka as wife (for by then he only had one eye) but this, too, is mighty hard to believe (*telling* and not *showing*). The motif of their past love speaks not of passion. Furthermore, Wotan is not interested in protecting Brünnhilde but simply wants to assert power over Siegfried.

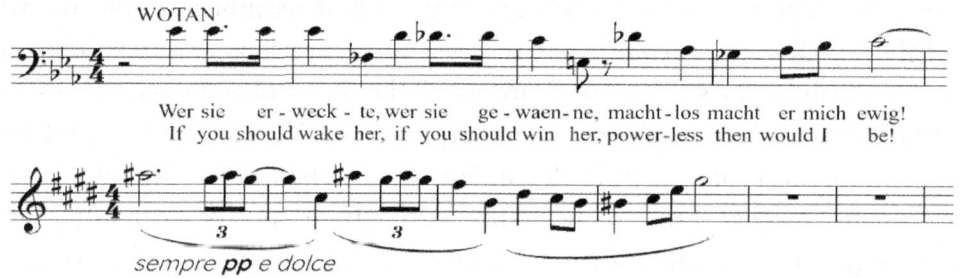

21.38 Two mutations of *domestic life*.
The upper is from Scene 2 and bars 3 & 4 follow the contour of the original melody.
This has no motif number.

The lower is from this present Scene. Here bars 3 & 4
follow the melody exactly. This also is not designated as a motif.

What implications can be drawn from such recycling of an earlier motif in a manner that questions its relevance? Firstly, if the motifs as seen by the composer are psychological, whose psychology are we thinking of? In the first appearance of the *domestic life* mutation it could be that of Wotan as he thinks back to his first overwhelming love, though the audience won't buy that! At the second appearance, with Siegfried on the mountain top, it could be a premonition of the peaceful 'domestic bliss' (Cooke) he may hope for. If so, this runs in opposition to the extreme excitement he felt at the end of Act II and also in this and the following Scenes. Secondly, perhaps Wagner summoned music up that could certainly be thought relevant in some vague way to the stage picture and situation and used it as part of his musical tapestry. It could indeed be that Wagner now did think more in terms of music, following on from the expansion of his musical powers and the composition of *Die Meistersinger* and *Tristan und Isolde*. This study relies on adherence to Wagner's principles as regard to good drama and that he meant what he said. He distrusted any act of reflection in order to appreciate a drama, so it does not make for good drama if we stop and think about what we hear. It must be for the reader to decide.

# # # # # #

Stage B – Brünnhilde is revealed as a woman

This episode reveals much about the mode of composition after the thirteen-year break. The duration is 118 bars and more than half of these involve the deployment of four motifs, which switch in and out of each other at such speed that the listener is not expected to keep up.

21.39 *anxious agitation* **CM38**
This is very like *despair*, but fear and joy can be seen as different sides of the same coin.

- First up is *anxious agitation* (CM38). Siegfried's disquiet is beyond his power of understanding. The motif is in all parts of the episode.
- Wagner's stage direction has that Siegfried 'is seized with terror' and calls on his mother. This makes it clearer that when Wotan's laughter got under his skin at the end of Scene 2 and the mutation of *volsung empathy* into *volsung bond (1)* came to the fore, the underlying reason was that Siegfried was disturbed by something he could not grasp. At this point, that earlier mutation is once more changed into *volsung bond (2)* (CM39) - *agitato* and at speed.

21.40 *volsung bond (2)* **CM39**
Develops from CM38 and thus is also a variation of M34.

- Later on within these 118 bars we hear a modification of *anxious agitation* by means of rhythmic variation. It can be assumed that by now what Newman called 'tics' in composition will, to some degree, be embedded somewhere in the listener's mind. This can be likened to a vocabulary of sounds that is but semi-conscious. In this episode, the listener has a familiarity with these 'tics' and this produces a comfortable feeling of being at one with the emotions. It is as though the motifs, compositional motifs and general musical texture combine to create sub-conscious echoes with which the listener is at home.

21.41 A variation on CM38.
The agitation is increased by the insertion of triplets, ties across the beat and the occasional staccato.

We do not *reflect* as the music flies past us but we still know where we are. *brünnhilde's sleep, destiny* and *wotan's sword* are other motifs that figure throughout the Scene and they bring it to an end. They are premonitions of the coming together of the man and the woman.

<u>Scene 5 – At first Brünnhilde resists Siegfried as a lover but finally accepts and exults with him</u>
[Schirmer: 295/4/2 to the end. Text from 'Heil dir, Sonne!' to '. . . lachender Tod!']
Wagner's achievement here is magnified by association with the previous Scene, where the purity of atmosphere within the opening music transferred Siegfried into a new

world, free of the dross below. The composer needed to step up to a yet higher level with the awakening of Brünnhilde.

Hitherto in this opera, the emphasis has been on Siegfried's journey from boyhood to manhood. Wotan, Fafner and Mime were, in different ways, adjuncts to that journey. With Brünnhilde, however, matters are different. Finding and winning her is actually the only chosen purpose in Siegfried's life. Things are different with the woman, whose journey is to stretch over three operas, and for whom what is now to occur is, second only to her understanding with Wotan, the cardinal moment in her life.

The Scene, long as it is – 739 bars and lasting over 30 minutes – is one long sequence of discovery by Brünnhilde. She is changed by the momentous journey she travels from awakening to new life to the acceptance of Siegfried as a lover. As she wakes up, she is reborn first to life and then to the reality of sex (p.177). Wagner's feat is to make us believe in both these experiences in half-an-hour. The Scene is in four stages.

A *Instantaneous love* The predestined lovers fall instantly in love with each other (p.111). All is untrammelled joy. (186 bars)
B *Siegfried's sexuality is quickly aroused.* (116 bars)
C *A fearful Brünnhilde rejects him and tries to retreat back into her previous valkyr persona.* For the first time in her life she is in an unknown place and is scared: this is because she is not in control. (256 bars)
D *Siegfried presses – ardently but tenderly – and she yields.* Her long passages in part C give back to Brünnhilde some control over matters. Fear is dissolved by her own aroused sexuality and she welcomes Siegfried as lover. (113 bars)

A – The lovers follow their destiny
The first 39 bars are orchestral and the first twelve of Brünnhilde's greeting to her new world stay with that music. These 51 bars evoke the dawn of promise without limit. In course, therefore, the opening call is – and must be – seldom heard. It is for this event alone. The staging almost always represents a sunrise in some way so this motif, in its dual capacity is best called *the dawn* (M62). In this Act to date, there have been only two new substantive motifs: *wotan summons erda* and *future hope*. But this Scene represents a new start and welcomes new motifs. *the dawn* is quickly followed by two more: *heroic love* (M63) and *love's ecstasy* (M64), which now take control. Before these Siegfried announces himself in counterpoint to his motif and accompanied by a clarion fanfare in the bass – Wagner aiming for maximum masculine heroism.

21.42 *the dawn* (lower clef) **M 62**

21.43 *heroic love* **M 63**

21.44 *love's ecstasy* **M 64**
Two motifs in counterpoint. *love's ecstasy* in the treble and *siegfried* in the bass clef.

SIEGFRIED

Fleeting but clear appearances of past motifs *brünnhilde's purity, destiny* and variations of *volsung empathy* attach themselves and, as described at the close of the previous Scene, bits and pieces of motifs fasten themselves as chemical molecules adhere to a biological cell that has receptors designed for such attachments. This sort of thing is the bedrock of Wagner's symphonic style and is not easily susceptible to examples but careful listening makes the notion plain.

Just one distinct and powerful compositional motif emerges, at the moment when Brünnhilde says how long she has looked over him. This is *brünnhilde's love for Siegfried* (CM40). Prominent for ten bars, it then breaks up and its fragments attach themselves to the melodic cells which make up the remainder of the music – and then disappears.

21.45 *brünnhilde's love for siegfried*
CM 40

Stage B – Siegfried is sexually aroused
After the opening passage, when the two lovers exult at their mutual discovery, the previous Stage concludes with a long solo by Brünnhilde (broken once by a puzzled Siegfried who wonders for a moment whether she might not be his mother) which extends for 87 bars and in which she explains why and how she has always loved the man destined to wake her up. The purity of this beautiful panegyric is lost on Siegfried. Whilst she sings, he does not move as he takes note solely of her physical beauty. When she is finished, he says as much: I was not using my ears but only my eyes. This response starts with repetitions of a gentle and softened version of *heroic love* and the moves on to the speeded up *volsung bond (2)*. This now becomes entirely a compositional motif in its own right. Brünnhilde's resistance to his gentle but persistent ardour is unforgettable and is shown in 21.46. This punctuates the dialogue between them. Prominent in Siegfried's ardour are *anxious agitation* and *heroic love* until his restraint breaks: he grabs at the woman he wants and she flies from him.

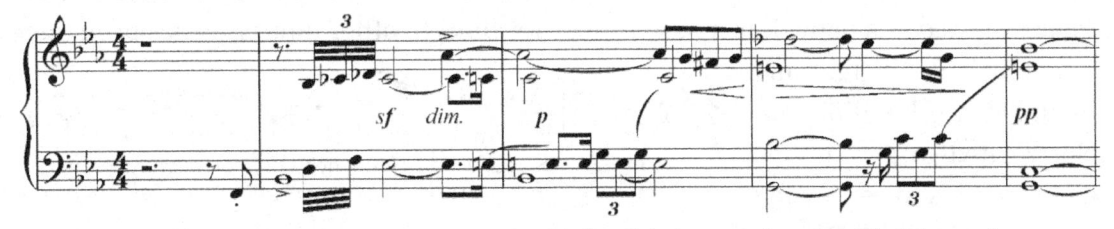

21.46 Brünnhilde's resistance to Siegfried. This is a mini-tutorial in Wagner's 'symphonic' style.

This passage is full of what have been described as thematic molecules.
At the start are the first two notes of *wotan's sword;* these are now instantly recognisable. Then in the treble is the triplet 'tic' that came to prominence in *volsung bond*, and continues in *heroic love* and *brünnhilde's love for siegfried*. Bar 3 sees a fragment of *valkyr* in the bass and, with the last three notes in the treble clef, the note configuration which sustains *volsung bond (2)* – CM39. Finally, in bar 4 is a molecule of *love*. The example ends with a repeat of *valkyr* in the bass.

Stage C – Brünnhilde recoils and withdraws on to safer ground.
The episode lasts 256 bars – longer than most Scenes to date – and therefore analysis must be confined. The opening 61 bars comprise music familiar from the earlier Stages, but then Brünnhilde's distress throws the music back to earlier times. She has already sensed that the wisdom which guided the struggle with Wotan is weakened. Now she bewails that her inner vision has dimmed and she is in the dark. At this point, the orchestra takes us back to Wotan's moment of acute suffering in *Die Walküre* Act II (See 19.21, p.317) – and with great subtlety. To *wotan in revolt* and *conflict* are added two iterations of *curse*. The music is not loud but, over 23 bars, Brünnhilde is assailed by fear. The narrative message must be that Wotan has left the stage but his mission, as gloriously shown at the close of the previous opera and exemplified by Nothung, has been passed to his daughter.

Siegfried, too, has recovered his balance and, to *future hope* he 'gently takes her hands away from her eyes.' The music for the woman takes her back to unsolved problems, for the man forward into a positive future. She is not yet ready for that. She is similar to those who, in times of uncertainty, turn back to a period when they felt safe, however bad it might have been in reality.

Wagner's genius was to see that something new was needed, something that expressed Brünnhilde's retreat into another world and which would depict her underlying serenity before the first encounter with the Volsung twins. So, as the *Wintersturme* episode in W2 conveyed the dreamlike world into which Siegmund and Sieglinde moved in their hour of

21.47 *happiness* **M65**

joy, the composer now sought for something similarly new for the woman. Thus it is that we hear the *Siegfried Idyll* music in M65 and M66. No doubt it does refer to the domestic happiness felt by Wagner at Christmas 1869, with Cosima in residence and their Siegfried as a baby. It is no use to seek for links to other motifs, as has been done. This music is different and intended to be different. Not related to any motifs, its purpose is to convey the new world in which Brünnhilde finds herself. The two

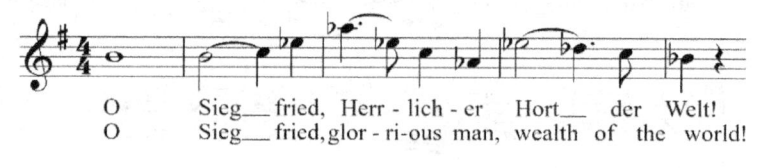

O Sieg___ fried, Herr - lich - er Hort___ der Welt!
O Sieg___ fried, glor - ri - ous man, wealth of the world!

21.48 *how brünnhilde saw siegfried* **M66**

motifs are played out over 81 bars. Into this mix come – but briefly – *brünnhilde's sleep* and *future hope*. The effect of this is to restore her equilibrium so that she accepts what has happened and is yet to happen. It would be ruinous for a listener to make effort to identify compositional motifs and molecular fragments of such. It goes without saying that the musical ingredients are mixed consummately. We hear *brünnhilde's sleep*, *volsung empathy, future hope, heroic love, ecstasy* come and go until the emotional dam breaks.

Stage D – Brünnhilde accepts Siegfried

21.49 *tumult in the blood* **CM41**

Tumultuous joy to the end of the score. The melodies comprise compositional motifs which are designed to latch on here and latch on there. As the woman yields with words such as 'Keuschestes Licht loddart in gluthen' (Chastest light reddens with passion) there enters one that is new and is, in fact, a blending of *joyous agitation* and *volsung bond (2)*. This is *tumult in the blood* (CM41) and it quickly blends back into *volsung bond (2)* and *heroic love* (M63). In due course the extensive triplets of *volsung bond (1)* enter, and when Siegfried is 'embraced passionately' by Brünnhilde, *siegfried* repeatedly storms in - *ff*. Finally, *ecstasy* leads to the climax with the entry of *laughing at death* (M67). This frequently runs in counterpoint with *heroic love* as the opera rushes to its end.

21.50 *laughing at death* **M67**

◇ ◇ ◇ ◇ ◇ ◇

Götterdämmerung

ACT I

The action of *Götterdämmerung* is identical with that for *Siegfrieds Tod* and the roots of the plot may well resemble the scenario as developed on p.56/7. Wagner constructed the original plot and poem with deliberation and with the intent to make something new (p.114). Although the subsequent expansion into three more operas produced dramas of a very different nature from the first, these differences did not impact on the content and style of *Siegfrieds Tod/Götterdämmerung*.

Assuming a continuity between the Prologue and the Scenes in the Gibichung palace, this Act lasts for a full two hours – almost as long as the entirety of Verdi's *Otello*. The drama can be broken into seven Scenes.

1	The Norns provide a history lesson from the earliest times to the present.	304 bars 17 minutes
2	Siegfried and Brünnhilde rejoice in each other and the former anticipates making his way in the world.	364 bars 21 minutes
3	Siegfried leaves the Ring with Brünnhilde and journeys to and down the Rhine.	222 bars 5 minutes
4	In the Gibich palace, Hagen induces Gunther and Gutrune into a plot that will wed Brünnhilde to Gunther.	370 bars 14 minutes
5	Siegfried arrives, forgets Brünnhilde, falls for Gutrune and agrees to help Gunther wed Brünnhilde. Hagen, left alone, anticipates victory	646 bars 32 minutes
6	Back in the hills, Brünnhilde is visited by Waltraute, whose plea that she should relinquish the Ring for the common good is violently rejected.	562 bars 25 minutes
7	Siegfried, in the guise of Gunther, overwhelms Brünnhilde's resistance to his assault.	298 bars 13 minutes

Total 2766 bars; 124 minutes

Scene 1: The Norns augment the past history that now permeates the present.
[Schott: 1/1/1 to 19/2/1. Text from 'Welch Licht leuchtet dort?' to 'Hinab! Zur Mutter! Hinab!']

In the first (long lost) draft of *Siegfrieds Tod,* as read to Eduard Devrient in October 1848 the opera started in the Gibich palace. This Scene (and the one which follows) were added by Wagner in the following month on the advice of Devrient.

The *Götterdämmerung* Scene is much longer than that in *Siegfrieds Tod* but the purpose of both is the same: to provide a potted pre-history. In *Siegfrieds Tod,* 50 lines offer little more than a summary of the *Myth*, from Alberich acquiring the Ring to Siegfried winning Brünnhilde. A criticism of what we now hear about this Scene and indeed of the other similar augmentations such as Waltraute's long description of the gods awaiting their doom in Valhalla, in Scene 6, and Alberich's Scene with Hagen in Act II) is that it but clumsily brings cosmic matters into what is a melodrama at heart. Taking the criticism seriously, the accusation is that the 'form' does not match the 'meaning'. But that is not how it can seem in performance. We find ourselves in the same place where we left the very human lovers, but the music returns us to a deeper history, and the audience does not find this to be eccentric. Now the Norns take 154 lines to tell us of Wotan tearing his spear from the World Ash Tree to craft his spear of power, through the Tree's decline and up to the moment that it is chopped down to provide the wood for the fire that will destroy Valhalla.

A complex and eccentric structure
The configuration, however, is different from other Scenes. There is a short prelude A, that sets the scene and an even shorter postlude E as the Norns leave, such power as they had now removed from them. Together, these two episodes occupy only 59 bars.

The remaining 243 bars cover the history of Wotan's epoch from its beginning to the present moment. The narration is organised into three Stages, B, C and D, and each Norn, First, Second, Third, take it in turn to tell the story. So there are a total of nine interjections from the first mention of the World Ash Tree to the sundering of the rope of fate. Diminishing performance time features in two separate dimensions. Each of the three Stages is progressively shorter. This tightening is repeated in the total time allotted to each Norn: taking account of the three narrative stages, 101 bars are sung by the First, 73 by the Second and 64 by the Third. Tension and anxiety rise as each group runs its course, so in each it is the Third Norn who sings the least but who also voices the greatest fear. With this combination of shorter stages and differing proportions between the singers, Wagner subtly increases the stress felt, and this leads to the mounting hysteria of the Third Norn.

This process is enhanced by a further pattern within each group. The First and Second Norn conclude each of their contributions either by singing to or being accompanied by *lament of death* or *destiny*. The fateful implication is clear: these two are progressively handing over to she who concludes each cycle in ever-increasing distress. This gives structure and symmetry to the Scene.

If the whole Scene be such an elaborate narration of events, one might expect it to lack drama: this is the only appearance of the Norns and, unlike Erda (their mother, as they imply?) they have no practical role. Wagner's grasp of dramatic structure ensures this is not so. The emphasis falls on the music. James Holman says of it 'that at no other point in the *Ring* does Wagner so effectively engage in reminiscence ... Motives are not merely restated ... they are piled atop one another, swept along like leaves in the wind ... It is a huge musical achievement, perhaps the most purely musical scene in the *Ring*.' (JKH/CR,156)

A - 46 bars

The opera opens before dawn with *the dawn* motif, first heard as Brünnhilde awakens, but this time darkened into E♭ minor. This leads straight into *life energy* also in the same key. Over and above this is *river movement (basic)* (M2A). It is still night and no river is anywhere in sight but these oddities are overborne in the mind of a spectator by the awareness and acceptance of a new beginning. The music tells us this will not be all joy. Wagner's musical mastery is the prerequisite for his overall dramatic goal, namely to bring before our minds the numberless years of Wotan's rule, now approaching dissolution at breakneck speed.

The opening 26 bars of music moves on to *destiny* which promptly introduces the compositional *norns' rope of fate* (CM42), the motif that is to dominate this whole Scene, binding together the other motifs which fill the Scene with reminiscence. This dominance is similar to the manner in which the two *river movement* motifs dominated the opening Scenes of *Das Rheingold*. It relates to *valhalla*,

21.1 *norns' rope of fate* **CM42**
This relates to *world ash tree* (and thereby to *valhalla* and *ring*) and also to *river movement (basic)* - M2A.

ring and the soon to be heard *world ash tree*. *erda* is twice cut short by *destiny*; *loge as fire* switches into *norns' rope of fate*. This is before any exposition of the back-plot is started.

B - 147 bars

This is the first and by far the longest part of the narration. It is about the World Ash Tree, from the beginning of Wotan's time in power, as a result of his despoliation of the Tree (p.191) down to the recent past with the god's order that it be cut down. Anxiety rises until the Third Norn pronounces, to an appropriate musical climax, the alarming and imminent end of the gods, and the destruction of Valhalla.

Before the introduction of new motifs, the opposite page has an extended passage that explores the very particular nature of the music in this Scene (21.2). This comes as

[Musical notation with text:]

An der Welt-esch-e wob ich einst, da gross und stark den Stamm ent-grue-te
At the World Ash Tree long I spun, when fine and strong the trunk bore forth a

weih-li-cher Ae-ste Wald. Im kueh-len Schat-ten
mass of wond-rous green. In cool-ing shad-ow a

rauscht' ein Quell: Weis-heit rau-nend ann sein Ge-well da sang ich heil-ger Sinn.
fount-ain stood: wis-dom whisp-ered forth on its swell: I sang there a hol-ly song

21.2

Only the much simpler passage in *Das Rheingold,* when Loge describes the wholesome world in which he could find no one prepared to give up love, attempts to match the verdant world before the stress caused by the seeking of power changed things for ever.

world ash tree is in bars 1-3 and returns in bars 2&3 of the last line. Readers will instinctively sense the presence of *norns' rope of fate* throughout and that *sexual desire* crops up in the first and fourth bars of line two. *Sex* as currently perceived would not have been around in that primal time but then neither was Valhalla. But M8D – the final topping out of the *valhalla* motif – can be heard in bar 3 of the second and bar 4 in the third line.

---

early in the opera as bar 49 – the opening statement of the First Norn. The listener is quickly absorbed into a quite different sort of music. The caption gives some detail but the whole has the subliminal effect of blending the long distant primal past with the events which have been the subject of the whole drama. We glimpse a long-gone period of peace, lost when the inevitable wish to control matters arrived on the scene, in the form of Wotan's encroaching will.

One new substantive motif is prominent: *world ash tree* (M68). The few appearances it makes have impact, because it is related to both *valhalla* and *ring*. There is also a powerful motif, heard briefly before in *Siegfried*, Act I, Scene 2 (p.346) as Wotan put forth all his majesty in order to impress

21.3 *world ash tree* **M 68**

21.4 *power of the gods* **M 69**

GÖTTERDÄMMERUNG

Mime. This is *power of the gods* (M69). Once heard, the musical tread of this motif is never forgotten. We are to hear this music in Parts B and C of this Scene, in Waltraute's narration later in this Act and in the Immolation finale. Such passages as this lie outside the melodrama and act as a counterweight. This is the only direct reference in the cycle to how Wotan came by his spear. All who hear this passage will think it nobly majestic.

The other motifs are as one would expect: *norns' rope of fate, world ash tree,* a fragment of *wotan's sword, will-to-power, valhalla, downfall, ring*. At this point the Second Norn describes how Wotan formalised his power by carving the laws (runes) on to the spear's shaft.

21.5 The impact of *power of the gods*

<u>Bar 1</u> has the rhythm of the first four notes of *power of the gods* and this rhythm continues into the two that follow. But the intervals are different: they are those of the latter part of *wotan's sword*.

In <u>bar 2</u>, the texture thickens, whereas the first was played by the solo bass trumpet, the sound was passed to four horns in harmony.

<u>Bar 3</u> is played by three trombones and, as the bar is filled out, what we hear is a variation of a part of *valhalla*. This is a moment of high tension.

The orchestral score is marked as *marcato* and this is why the vocal score has added emphasis on the shortest notes. It ensures equal emphasis throughout and avoids 'rumpty-tump'.

Any effort to explain how the music works in detail must have benefit ffor readers. The 'molecular' nature of Wagner's technique is basic and one tiny example must do (21.5). Before the climax, the Third Norn is about to describe the huge faggots of the World Ash Tree. They are piled up around Valhalla and voracious to bring about the oncoming ruin of the fortress. We hear these three consecutive bars; the sounds have never been heard before but they seem to be familiar. The caption tells us why.

C - 66 bars

In the second group, the narration moves on to the manner of that destruction: Loge's fire as summoned for the purpose by Wotan. This is vividly described by the Third Norn. The comparative shortness, reflects the growth in tension due to the increased violence of the events being reported. The music is dominated by *loge as fire* – sometimes fast, sometimes slow. *will-to-power* is nudged by *power of the gods* into the adoption of the dotted format to be seen in 21.5. As the Third Norn imagines Wotan commanding Loge to do his job, *loge as fire* is in counterpoint with *power of the gods*.

D - 32 bars

The narrative breaks down in the third group. First Norn reports that she cannot now make out whether and where the rope is sound. They flounder until the Third cries that the rope is broken for good. Swift exchanges now: 12 bars for the First, 9 for the Second and 8 for the Third, ending with 'Es riss!' (It breaks!) Everything changes in this short conclusion. The imminent collapse is heralded by *woe* and *magic sleep,* and followed by *woe* and *ring* (both repeatedly) and *rhinegold*. As the Third Norn approaches the fateful climax, we have *wotan's mission, horn call* and *curse*.

E - 13 bars
The Norns depart; their powers have gone Very short and in sequence there is *curse, downfall, curse, magic sleep* and *destiny*. ᴬ

Scene 2: Siegfried and Brünnhilde rejoice in each other
[Schirmer: 19/2/2 to 39/2/2. Text from 'Zu neuen Taten' to 'Heil, Brünnhilde! Heil!']
This has little of the complexity of Scene 1. The 364 bars contain no more than thirteen motifs and four of these, important as they may be in the cycle as a whole, are but fleeting presences here. The structure also is simple and in two parts: *recollection* of the immediate past, followed by *anticipation* of the immediate future. There are no compositional motifs but the three that are new seem designed to be fragmented into smaller parts, thereby forging a continuous but ever-changing fabric.

Recollection
The Scene starts with a brief depiction of the dawn and this is another of those few occasions when Wagner unwinds a single melody across fourteen bars accompanied by a low F in the double basses.

21.6 *womanly brünnhilde* **M70**

One bar has a fragment of *love* that comes and goes almost as soon as it is heard. After hints of a 'new' Siegfried motif comes a rich and continuous exposition of *womanly brünnhilde* (M70). The four bars of 21.6 show three but there are twelve in all, one after the other. The repetition in the four bars is an indication of how Wagner keeps a new motif in play. There follows *manly siegfried* (M71). The choice of these names indicates both the epic range of the cycle as a whole and also the painfully realistic and human portrayal of the people within it. Then quickly comes *victorious love* (M72). Both Newman and Cooke call M72 'Heroic

21.7 *manly siegfried* **M71**

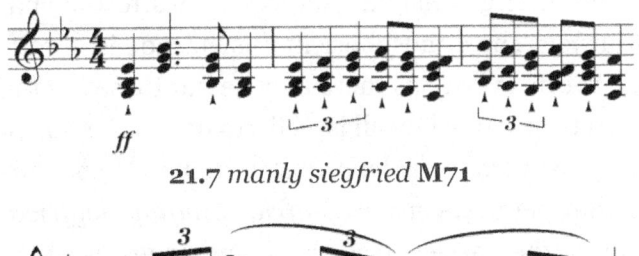

21.8 *victorious love* **M72**

ᴬ So compelling is the music in this Scene, that everyone is likely to forget that everything to do with Wotan and the World Ash tree happened after Siegfried's encounter with the god in S3.1.

GÖTTERDÄMMERUNG

Love', but this Scene moves toward an exultation that speaks of hubristic invincibility, which might be thought to move beyond heroism. From the moment that Brünnhilde starts to sing until the end of this first part, the score runs for 141 bars and no less than 50% include the whole or part of one of the three motifs.

On occasion a portion of *manly siegfried* takes off on its own to form *siegfried's energy* (CM43). Elsewhere each of the three motifs will extemporise or extend itself by a bar or two. A few other important motifs make fleeting appearances but the totality of these does not occupy more than eight bars. They are: *heroic love, valkyr, siegfried, destiny* and *horn call*. This episode is a symphonic development of motifs which exemplify fulfilment and hope, and glory in new found sexual delight.

dolce e stacatto

21.9 *siegfried's energy* **CM43**

Brünnhilde acknowledges her surrender of both body and wisdom; Siegfried cannot remember the lessons he has been taught, but only that Brünnhilde loves him. They recall the breaching of the fire and the kiss which awakened the woman from her long sleep; finally they re-pledge themselves to the vows already taken. A listener may note the truncation of all to do with wisdom (p.100/1).

Anticipation

The break from past to future is indicated by the only appearance in this Scene of *future hope*, one of the dominant motifs of Wotan's last Scene with Erda. Prior to their parting, each now offers the other the most valuable object they possess: the Ring from Siegfried to Brünnhilde; Grane from Brünnhilde to Siegfried. The horse is her main link with the past, so this is no light gift.

At this point, the excitement in the music grows and gallops forward to the end, when Siegfried leaves on his Rhine Journey. The atmosphere in this episode is of self-adulatory, almost godlike invincibility. Erotic overtones there may be but these are the consequence of the anticipated all-round triumph: when all is well, sexual joy cannot be far behind. Motifs now pile in and combine: *victorious love, valkyr, womanly brünnhilde, siegfried's mission* (last heard in the opening Scene in *Siegfried*), *manly siegfried, siegfried's energy*. The best illustration is the passage (see the facing page) in which Siegfried sets this all going. Since the beginning of the cycle, some ten hours of music have passed before we hear music that is so forthright and uncomplicated, energetic and heroic in the best sense, the ideal moral and uncomplicated man as Wagner perceived him. It occurs at this point because it shows Siegfried at the peak of his life, the moment when no task would have seemed impossible. This is the moment in the lives of both when they are on an equal footing as they move forward together in joint experience.

GÖTTERDÄMMERUNG

21.10 The hero Siegfried.

The motifs heard are as follows.

<u>Bass clef</u> *valkyr:* virtually throughout the passage; the energy of the woman drives the man.

<u>Treble clef</u> *victorious love:* bars 13-14 / *womanly brünnhilde:* bar 16 / *manly siegfried:* bars 22-24 / *siegfried's mission:* bars 25-27 / The heroic Siegfried awakens Brünnhilde (not a motif but the unforgettable syncopated bars in S3.2): bars 17-21

Scene 3: Siegfried's journey to and down the Rhine
[Schirmer 39/2/3 to 44/7/8]

Well before composition was even thought of or the poems completed, Wagner wrote that the start of this interlude was to be the sound of Siegfried's horn being taken up by the orchestra. The finished score suggests this to be when 'the curtain closes quickly' and this stage direction prompts a search for structure which is in three parts.

A   Before the curtain falls, with Brünnhilde still on stage. (54 bars)
B   The climb down to the Rhine and the journey along it. (134 bars)
C   Reminiscence of past conflict, as the journey nears the Gibich court. (24 bars)

A listing of the motifs in each part tells us how Wagner manages this dramatic and musical tapestry

A – Before the curtain falls
At intervals, the score gives stage directions which the music echoes. 'Siegfried leads Grane quickly to the edge of the rocky slope, followed by Brünnhilde.' – *siegfried's energy, siegfried's mission.* // 'Siegfried disappears behind the rocks with Grane whilst Brünnhilde looks down at Siegfried as he descends.' – *womanly brünnhilde, heroic love,* merging into each other. // 'Siegfried's horn is heard from below.' – *horn call.* // 'Brünnhilde listens.' – *womanly brünnhilde, horn call.* // 'She steps further out on the slope, catches sight of Siegfried again and waves rapturously.' – *love* at its utmost power and with big spread and *laughing at death,* similarly broad. This stage action almost never happens now but the changing music exactly conveys the relevant emotions.

B – The journey to and down the Rhine
horn call, at its richest and most buoyant, switches to a remote variant of *love*. When the crescendo tops out *laughing at death* sweeps on to and down the Rhine itself in its basic manifestation of *life energy*. This once again builds and breaks into a massively broad *downfall,* before returning to memory of the Rhine. A prime river motif is *force of the gold,* and this turned progressively to the bad, concluding with *servitude to the ring*. The music then returns to the most touching mutation - *rhinedaughter's lament* - heard as part of the cries of despair at the loss of the gold and sung to the indifferent backs of the gods as they climbed to Valhalla. Starting *ff*, it fades over nineteen bars and then touches the melodic contour of *ring*. Imperceptibly, from the appearance of *downfall,* the music turns sour over the remaining bars – 25% of the interlude.

C – The river enters the territory of the Gibichungs
When the *ring* motif is established, musical sourness turns into foreboding. A sequence of three takes us into a sequence of two *core life value* – the second an octave lower. Both renditions are plangently mournful – the first in the woodwind, with trombones and horns hold the underlying harmony, and the second with woodwind alone. This second descent of the motif ends in *rhinegold* and this is repeated twice with increasingly gloomy harmony. The moral turpitude that approaches is heralded by *servitude to the ring*. The agent is to be Hagen and a fragment of that motif is recycled

GÖTTERDÄMMERUNG

21.11 *treachery* **CM44**

as *treachery* (CM44) and is to reappear within the music of Gutrune as she enters into the plot. The scene is set for the treacherous world of the Gibichungs. Wagner does not write just for effect – always the drama must be served. The journey is not physical, but from safety into danger.

Scene 4: Hagen gets to work on Gunther and Gutrune

[Schirmer 45/1/1 to 52/3/3. Test from 'Nun, hör, Hagen!' to 'Heil, Siegfried, theurer Held!']

The relationship between Hagen and Gunther in this Scene is similar to that between Iago and Othello. The former guilefully leads the latter, who goes on a journey.

- A – At the start, Gunther is satisfied with his lot but wants more.
- B - Hagen makes a proposal which seriously disrupts Gunther's self-complacency: he wants something that is unattainable.
- C - Hagen then suggests a way out of Gunther's dilemma.

This little journey is classic Freytag: from security to insecurity and back, with the promise of better things to come. Hagen tricks and betrays Gunther (and Gutrune) in three stages. The movement from one stage to the next is conveyed in the music by two moments when it changes tone, falters briefly and then takes off in another direction.

A – Gunther's certainty

The poem confirms Hagen's forceful influence. The music shows both his ambiguous relationship with his half-brother and also something of an inherent nobility in Gunther that is now to be suborned. First to be heard, however, is *the gibich hagen* (M73) that is to be developed into a very sinister motif but one that also links easily to *gibichung* (M74) that follows. The falling intervals are a precursor to the definitive motif for Hagen - to emerge in *B*. The impression from the poem in this section, unchanged over 26 years of thought and creation, is the hold Hagen had on Wagner's imagination. Gunther is complacent, as seen in the several repetitions of *gibichung*. But this is periodically undercut by the falling interval of the seventh in *the gibich hagen*. All this comes to a stop

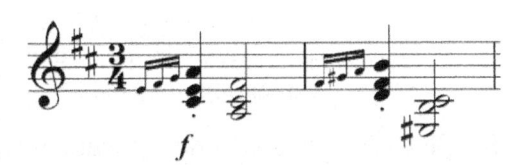

21.12 *the gibich hagen* **M73**
The fall of a seventh to the last chord undercuts the forthright nature of *gibichungs*.

21.13 *gibichungs* **M74**
This is often called 'Gunther'. Looked at dispassionately, it has nobility, but Gunther is a weak man. By widening reference to the tribe which he leads, a dignity can be restored that matches the sound.

with Hagen's cleverly delayed comment that neither brother or sister are married, at which point the music slows and loses lustre.

GÖTTERDÄMMERUNG

Stage B – Gunther's discomposure
Now old motifs reappear. *valkyr* and *loge as fire* as Hagen proposes the solution: that there is a bride worthy of the lord of the Gibichungs. That Hagen knows the truth of the situation with regard to Siegfried and Brünnhilde is shown by the fleeting appearance of *birdsong*. And then, as he tells Gunther that he is not up to the task of winning her, there

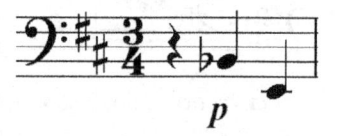

22.14 *hagen* **M75**

comes the first clumping, if quietly announced, *hagen* (M75). Siegfried is the only man who can succeed, at which point there is *fated volsungs* and *wotan's mission*.

Now it is that we first hear from Gutrune as she 'hesitatingly' asks what's so special about Siegfried. This motif *wholesome gutrune* (CM45) appears in this Scene alone and only thrice here. Prolonged over ten bars in the orchestra and heard in the voice in counterpoint, the music has both charm and sexuality. In *Das Rheingold* (p.270) this question was raised about *seductive allure*: If this is seen as an appropriate depiction of the Rhine-daughters, why was it not to be used with Gutrune? The answer is that in the next Scene a second Gutrune motif is to appear, one that has a touch of the malign. This present has a sweetness that is to be lost and which seems personal to her; this gentleness would not suit the Rhinedaughters, nor Sieglinde, nor Brünnhilde. Gutrune may be weak and malleable but this music suggests she is a 'good girl', soon to be corrupted and betrayed along with her brother.

21.15 *wholesome gutrune* **CM45**
The lyricism is evident in the extended expression marks.

Gutrune asks and Hagen explains: he killed the hitherto invincible dragon and took possession of his hoard. *dragon, fafner as dragon, wotan's sword, horn call*. The episode moves toward its climax – the information that Gunther is not the man for the job - and a novel combination of motifs and text is heard. This is the immediate juxtaposition of *ring, core life value* and *rhinegold* (21.16). These make a powerful musical impact. The motifs may not seem to have much to do with each other, but a rationale can be discerned. Hagen is manipulating, leading Gunther by the nose. Three motifs, all central to the story, accompany the words: 'Whoever knows how to use [the Ring] is indeed on their way to win the world'. The conjunction of such music with his encouraging but deceitful words make clear that

21.16 Hagen in control
ring (bars 1-2); *core life value* (bars 3-6); *rhinegold* (bars 4-6)

Hagen is in control. This might offer both a psychological insight into Hagen and a

390

coded pointer to a subliminal effect on the audience, but the question then arises as to whether this pushes beyond the boundary of what actually strikes home in the drama. Wagner and his distrust of the 'reflective intellect' suggests we should not be *thinking* about this sort of thing. However that may be, the passage quoted is also the point when Hagen has succeeded in pushing his half-brother into a corner of extreme frustration. Much has been speedily communicated. The stage directions read 'Gunther rises angrily from his seat and paces the hall with agitation' and 'Hagen, without leaving his seat, stops him with a commanding gesture.

C – Gunther's way forward

The action, on stage and supported by energetic music, comes to a halt as Hagen stops Gunther in his tracks. For seven bars the pulse changes from 4/4 to 3/4, the music slows and the key moves from B♭ major to E minor (after which it reverts to the previous configuration). The first notes in E minor relate to *tarnhelm*, a motif which has lain dormant throughout *Die Walküre* and *Siegfried*. The *tarnhelm* reference stops short of its full extent to allow *the gibich hagen* to insinuate itself within the texture. All is *p* and *pp* as the nature of the coming deceit is established by Hagen's words: 'What if Siegfried brought the bride home, wouldn't Brünnhilde then be yours?' All this in seven bars, before *gibichung* brings the tempo up to speed again. When Hagen puts the other side of the deal, that Gutrune can be the bride of Siegfried, she scoffs at the possibility and this to a new motif *deception* (M76). This remains present through to the end of the Scene, during which the plot to deceive Siegfried is developed. Gutrune is not yet corrupted, for *wholesome gutrune* supports

21.17 *deception* **M76**
Note that the first interval of a seventh is the last falling interval of M73 and that bar 2 is almost identical with bar 4 of *gibichungs*. Thematic molecules of one motif become part of another.

her modest disclaimer of such a distinction. But then *deception* takes over for ten bars as Hagen reminds his relatives of the potion of forgetfulness. These ten bars are broken into two groups and, in the middle, are six that have the same character as that identified in 21.16: they offer a glimpse of deep implication. The first three bars offer *core life value* in counterpoint with primal *sexual desire* and the last two have *wotan's sword*. The message must be that Hagen has the big picture; Gunther and Gutrune look no further than themselves. *tarnhelm* and *sexual desire* then return and this time continue into a new motif: *potion* (M77). This leads into *the gibich hagen* and the definitive *hagen* as he explains the effect the

21.18 *potion* **M77**

potion will have. The game is now afoot and the Scene ends in a maelstrom with the nearest thing in modern drama to the mythological 'Wild Hunt', with Siegfried as the game to be hunted even before he arrives at the palace. In the maelstrom of motifs *horn call, hagen, gibichungs* and *rhinedaughter's lament* are always to be heard. The climax is heralded by two demonic renditions of *ring* and, as Siegfried enters, an unprecedentedly massive *curse*. This is followed by *deception* on the solo oboe, hanging quietly in the air above.

Scene 5: Siegfried falls
[Schirmer: 61/4/1 to 84/1/7. Text from 'Wer ist Gunthers Sohn?' to 'Siegfried, mein!']
Carried through virtually unchanged from *Siegfrieds Tod*, this Scene is crucial to the tetralogy: within it lies the great conundrum of Siegfried's fall. Whatever view taken about it, the dramatic form could not be bettered, and is in line with the Freytag Pyramid. Hagen is the protagonist, as in the previous Scene, and Siegfried the antagonist. The former wins the contest in a classic five-part structure. Now Hagen has dominance over the other two men.

1 Set up	Siegfried and Gunther establish a friendship.	125 bars
2 Rising action	Gutrune gives him the potion and Siegfried falls.	96 bars
3 Mid-point	Siegfried agrees to bring back Brünnhilde if he can have Gutrune in return.	74 bars
4 Falling action	The fatal contact of blood-brotherhood between Siegfried and Gunther is made.	234 bars
5 Resolution	Hagen is triumphant.	104 bars

This Scene brings into prominence the full development of Wagner as a 'symphonic' composer. If *Siegfried* Act III and onward saw the flowering of the composer's compositional mastery, it is now that we hear the culmination of that style for the first time: a continuity of motifs over almost every bar. In the 125 bars of the first stage only 14 are not variations upon a motif. Moreover, within these bars, twelve are a short song from Gunther which *deliberately* breaks free of all motifs. This rarely happens in this opera from this point onwards. There are two reasons for this. The first is the now-established Beethovenian break down of motifs into molecular fragments (pp.375-7). The second is that the new motifs are longer but no less plastic: portions can be detached and used independently. Many believe that *Götterdämmerung* and *Die Meistersinger* show Wagner at the peak of his compositional powers, and no one can underestimate the spectacular manner by which sheer musical skill manipulates the mass of material. From this follows no conclusion that this music is better than that which came before: it can be thought that the mixture in *Die Walküre* of music with and of that without motifs has added force by virtue of that contrast.

Readers will now perceive that analysis is different. Discussion of earlier operas often turns around the switch between motif-based music and recitative, and between highly wrought voice-melody (to use Wagner's term) and either motif or recitative. Now this has gone: motifs surround the voice for much of the time.

GÖTTERDÄMMERUNG

1 Set-up – Siegfried and Gunther establish friendship

The music follows the narrative and fluently and tells the straightforward story. The sequence is as follows.

- The two men introduce themselves: *siegfried, gibichungs*.
- Siegfried asks how Hagen knew who he was: *deception, curse, siegfried*. The similarity of the last two motifs is shown with sinister power when *curse* leads immediately into *siegfried*. So similar are they that it can come as a shock when Siegfried's words 'You called me Siegfried: have you seen me before?' are sung over *curse* and Hagen's reply that it was his strength that identified him are accompanied by *siegfried*. (The mismatch is unnerving.) These introductory passages conclude with *womanly brünnhilde*.

  12.19 Note *curse* in bars 1-4, the last bar also serving as the first for *siegfried*

- Hagen leaves with Grane; Gutrune quietly departs. Gunther and Siegfried pledge themselves in friendship. The *friendship* motif (M78) is now introduced by a warm and suave Gunther. (He would be a good politician!) Gunther offers 'title, land and people' and Siegfried offers Nothung to compositional forging motif *bellows* and Siegfried's bellows song.

  21.20 *friendship* **M78**

- Hagen returns and turns the discussion to the Nibelung treasure: *nibelung slavery, hoard*. When Siegfried shows the Tarnhelm, *tarnhelm* is heard and the news that the Ring is with Brünnhilde brings in *ring, heroic love*.
- Finally, as Gunther reaffirms their bond to *friendship*, Gutrune returns.

2 Rising action – Siegfried drinks the potion

- Gutrune reenters, bearing the poisoned drink and, at the same time, we hear her second motif: *gutrune seductress* (M79). The long melody twines its way through 37 of the 96 bars in this episode.

  21.21 *gutrune seductress* **M79**

- As Siegfried remembers Brünnhilde: *heroic love, future hope, potion*.
- As the potion takes effect: a perfect merging of *gutrune seductress* and *deception*. Then, as Gutrune raises her eyes to look Siegfried straight in the face, he becomes

entranced to the point of delirium, and this brings with it eight bars with no recognisable reference to any motif whatsoever. What we hear is a man outside of the plot in which he is immersed: Shakespeare's 'unaccommodated man', the 'purely human', now riven with passion. Not only might this be seen as similar to Gunther's noble welcome but also it may be a hint that the potion is not the only cause of his downfall. *gutrune seductress* surrounds the nine bars in which Siegfried addresses his memory of Brünnhilde.

- Siegfried negotiates with Gunther: *deception, gutrune seductress, friendship* as Siegfried asks Gutrune whether she agrees with her brother. *hagen* and *gutrune seductress* as the woman leaves.

3 Mid-point – Siegfried agrees to fetch Brünnhilde

- Siegfried asks whether Gunther has a wife: *curse, friendship, treachery, the gibich hagen.*
- Gunther describes Brünnhilde and her situation: *gibichung, ecstasy, loge as fire.*
- This means nothing to Siegfried: *potion.*
- He says that he fears no fire and will fetch her. At this point *loge as fire* clearly turns into a compositional motif. The score has the expression *strepitoso* which indicates overexcitement and this figure (*loge as energy*, CM46) runs through 20 of the remaining bars in this episode, as Gunther gladly offers Gutrune to

21.22 *loge as energy* **CM46**

Siegfried, and Siegfried says that he will use the Tarnhelm to change shape with him (p.73). Siegfried it is who chooses blood-brotherhood as the oath they shall swear, to the first of the relevant new motifs. Thereby he willingly moves into danger.

Siegfried is not fooled by Hagen, as is sometimes suggested. But undoubtedly he is not the same man who, with the help of the wood bird, saw through Mime's lies. He has lost that power of perception. At the end of *Siegfried* Brünnhilde happily replaced her wisdom with sexual love. Similarly, perhaps here Gutrune's sexual pull obliterates all else.

4 Falling Action – blood brotherhood

This episode is by far the longest and comprises three distinct sections.

- The first section includes the actual swearing of the oath and is made up in its entirety of *curse, will-to-power, loge as energy, wotan's sword, gibichungs, hagen, siegfried's mission* (more of this later), or melodic continuations of each, and the various new *blood brotherhood* motifs (M80). This is melodrama very near its violent peak and can put one in mind of the *Swearing of the Swords* in Act IV of

GÖTTERDÄMMERUNG

Meyerber's *Les Huguenots*. If readers think that to be an inappropriate comparison, a hearing of that comparison will be instructive. In neither case is this complicated music.

21.23 *blood-brotherhood* **M80A**
Others are listed in Chapter 17, and there are significant dramatic echoes which stretch backwards into the drama

- The second section is brief and is actually a contrasting interlude, for the third section is to return in large part to the thematic content of the first. Here there is *deceit* and *treachery* as Siegfried asks why Hagen did not also take the oath; he replies that he is not high-born and that his blood is not suited to that sort of thing.
- Section three has the two men bonding again, continuing section one but to music associated with Hagen: many bars of *loge as energy* encompass *valkyr* (she being the point of the chase), *deception, tarnhelm, hagen* and molecules of *gutrune seductress,* thrice repeated, float overhead as she sings 'Siegfried mein!'. The Scene moves quietly toward its end where, to reinforce what is happening, the same element of *gutrune seductress,* slowly now, accompanies an equally slow *horn call*.

5 Resolution – Hagen in triumph
The celebrated 'Hagen's Watch' is both the conclusion of this mini-drama and also the interlude that removes us from the Gibich palace. There is nothing else in opera like it. Nothing exceeds, from first to last, the grip of brooding wickedness that surrounds all the motifs. By harmony, orchestration and shape they are transformed. In 21.24, the ebullient *horn call* is slowed, and played on the lower horns and bassoons in a minor key. The tempo can be translated as 'very moderate speed, which drags'. Above this runs a pulsing throb derived from *malice*. Ostensibly, this passage is to represent Siegfried as he powerfully drives the boat forward, but it is also a louring cloud that depresses hope.

21.24 The rise of Hagen.

Upper stave is a heavy, slow version of *malice* which spreads across bars. The whole is underpinned by what one can call a 'tolled' *hagen*, which stretches across the whole bar. The sluggish *horn call* is distorted by an initial rising interval of a seventh instead of a fifth. This robs the sound of any vitality it might have had.

Equally discomforting are two repetitions of *core life value* (M16), the first with oboes and clarinets and the second, an octave lower, with bass trumpet and trombones – virtue being thereby scorned. *will-to-power*, now applying to Hagen rather than Wotan, is transmuted into something that is clearly very bad. The motif has featured twice before in this opera: in Scene 1, as the Norns refer to Wotan's actions, and earlier in this Scene as part of the blood-brotherhood oath. But it has been used descriptively

GÖTTERDÄMMERUNG

or ritualistically and the orchestration has been moderate. In the former it is descriptive and ritualistic in the latter. All is transformed when Hagen's obsessive wish to dominate is now the subject. Twice the motif is heard at maximum volume but now almost the entire orchestra is involved. The motif is in trombones and lower strings but all the woodwind, four tubas, and the higher strings, sustain a prolonged minor chord above and below the motif. Such harmonic insistence has not previously been attached like this. Additionally, there is the lead-in, the octave leap up to the first motif note that launches the downward descent, never heard before or ever again. Seldom has one short leading note been of such force.

Slow syncopations reminiscent of *hate* (as visible in 21.24), are often present. Otherwise, and in addition to *will-to-power* and *horn call*, it is the motifs we would expect: *hagen, treachery, siegfried, nibelung slavery, ring, woe*. Capping all is the

21.25 Hagen anticipates his triumph.

magnificently baleful tune, never to be repeated again in full, with which Hagen gives voice to the poison he has inherited from Alberich. This is perhaps the premier example of Wagner abandoning the use of *leitmotiven* when in pursuit of optimum dramatic impact. It is also the culmination of the issue of long melodies, first raised in respect of *Das Rheingold* (p.272). Wagner's melodic powers are at a peak, to be used when needed.

It were as otiose to give further details here as it was at the end of *Die Walküre*. The second descent of *will-to-power* concluded, the composer brings in one of his magical transitions from one mood to another as the setting transforms to the mountainside where Brünnhilde awaits.

The switch may signal an end to this black interlude but not, however, to an end of uncomfortable sounds as the *mis-en-scène* changes. We know where we are heading when we hear *womanly brünnhilde*. But why is it first on a solo clarinet and then via the rancid sound of the bass clarinet? Then, as accompaniment to a melody associated with the valkyr's beauty, we hear the unsettling off-beat throb as illustrated in 21.24. As has been described to me, 'it's as if some prescient hobgoblin is above her gloating at the imminent destruction of all she holds dear.' (David Stannard, in a letter.)

One final observation. At the beginning of the next Act, Hagen complains to his father that he has never been happy. 'Hagen's Watch' surely bears this out. The barren nature of wickedness is seen in the pall of almost inexpressible sadness that invests it.

GÖTTERDÄMMERUNG

Scene 6; Brünnhilde rejects Waltraute's plea to return the Ring to the Rhinedaughters and thereby save Valhalla

[Schirmer 89/5/1 to 114/3/1. Text: 'Altgewohntes Gerausch' to Wallhals Götter! Weh!]
The purpose of the episode with all the valkyrs in *Siegfrieds Tod* was that they could learn from Brünnhilde why she had been punished by Wotan and about the 'escape clause' of the magic fire which enables Siegfried to win her. They leave when this was done – on their way to choose more warriors for Valhalla. In short, it was no more than a means by which the audience could be told what had happened before.

# # # # # #

To every intent and purpose, therefore, this Scene with Waltraute is a totally new invention: new drama for new circumstances. It is, in truth, one of the most important episodes in the entire cycle. The changes to the Immolation texts have exercised many minds over the years but these do not amount to much in the final analysis. This Scene, on the other hand, makes a real difference. Text and music bring front of stage the immense reach of the drama, in the midst of which Brünnhilde now sits: her harsh disregard of the painful and immediate reality brings the story down to the human level and is a fitting preparation for her actions in Act II. These will be *exactly* as set down in the *Myth,* written 26 years before the music for Waltraute was written.

The first difference to note between the earlier and the later texts is that Waltraute knows all that has happened to her sister and now it is Brünnhilde who is to be enlightened. She knows nothing whatsoever about the world she left 20 years ago. The second thing is that, from first to last, she is not interested in what she does learn. Her response when she finally becomes aware of Waltraute's intense distress is certainly one of alarmed surprise but is nevertheless best paraphrased by: 'What's up with the eternal gods, then?' She is as any young person who has just experienced very good sex for the first time and can barely bring thought to bear on anything else. [B] She is of a naturally serious disposition, however, and listens carefully to the story. The news is stark and unnerving. From the time when Wotan summoned the magic fire to surround Brünnhilde and up to the moment when he returned with the remnants of his broken spear, he had barely been in Valhalla and had neglected even the most pressing matters. But when he did return, the situation for the gods (and the valkyrs) became worse. Wotan ordered that the World Ash Tree should be cut down and its logs piled up to make a funeral pyre for the fortress. This first part of the narration is followed by a report on the exceedingly gloomy state of everyone as they await the great conflagration.

The entirety is presented in music of such majesty that the audience feels empathy with Wotan. Stagings of this long episode invariably present Brünnhilde as immobile

---

[B] 'Sexual desire . . . is the daily thought and desire of the young and the constantly recurring reverie of the chaste . . .' (Schopenhauer, see p.177)

and expressing little emotion. Accordingly, it can come as a shock at the end when she flatly declares her indifference to the news. But since Wagner moves us in favour of Wotan with the music of Waltraute's narration, he obviously intends that the audience *should* be shocked when Brünnhilde does not feel the same, for the spectator bears in mind that she heard of the same dangers from Wotan himself in *Die Walküre* Act II.

The deepest meaning of the story is carried by the music and, for all the vigour and resource within Brünnhilde's music, it is that for Waltraute that the listener remembers. And with good reason. Parts of her narration are delivered over sounds that give voice to Wotan's vision of the world he wanted to create and which we cannot fail to perceive as noble. It is music that is to recur in the Immolation. The only music prior to this that has resonance as deep is at the very end of *Die Walküre*. At this point the strength of the music is due to the drama: by the contrast between the music of the two sisters, Wagner imbues significance into the melodrama of the remainder of the opera.

So important is the perspective on the *Ring* that is revealed within this Scene, that it is placed here, before the detail that supports this observation. (Background to this matter can be found on p.177/8.) The Scene is to end with Brünnhilde breaking free not only from Waltraute but also from the last vestiges of her previous valkyr existence. Where does that leave the drama? When Waltraute is to press home that she should relinquish the Ring, Brünnhilde's aroused sexuality is to engulf her reason. In her person and emotions at this moment she is to move the main conflict within the plot away from its default position – that between love and power. It now becomes human desire for satisfaction versus the greater good for humanity as a whole. This is a momentous development. Not everyone lusts for power; few people want to be a Dictator or a Prime Minister or a President or an obsessed CEO of a vast commercial empire. For almost everybody the conflict between love and power is not a conflict at all: to use a cliché, 'it's love that makes the world go round'. But everyone can be and is tempted to place a strong personal desire before the interests of others. The great story now touches the mundane roots of everyday life, and brings humanity into contact with what Shaw would call allegory.

Two separate issues come together at this point: form and viewpoint. By looking at the *form* which Wagner uses, as formulated by Kitto (p.2), the *meaning* becomes clear. The contrast between the music of the two sisters tells us, on one hand, what had been Wotan's hopes for the world and, on the other, how ineffective such plans can be when pitted against personal emotion. That is certainly a major part of the meaning of the *Ring*. The second point follows from this, namely that such a conflict has nothing to do with pessimism or optimism. This Scene points us to the conclusion that neither view is correct. The conflict between the benefit of the few and the benefit of the many may be seen as a moral issue but it can also be seen as a description of how things are. 'Everything is what it is and not any other thing', and the same applies as much to human nature as it does to a hammer.

# # # # # #

GÖTTERDÄMMERUNG

If in every drama there is a journey, this Scene must trace part of that which Brünnhilde travels. The structure here is openly in three parts.

A   She is filled with real, even manic, joy when she realises that it is Waltraute who now visits.

B   Waltraute cogently explains why such joy is misplaced.

C   Brünnhilde can be in no doubt of the serious situation which surrounds Wotan's cosmos but she is unable to connect with it.

The music is almost always so synonymous with the drama that one can do little in what follows except match the one with the other.

A – Brünnhilde's anticipation

- After expression of her initial excitement, conveyed by *valkyr* and *war cry*, there follows a long passage of 47 bars that borders on delirium and is void of motifs. Her deepest hopes find expression here, that Wotan will have relented because he had always sympathised with her desire to save Siegmund. The intention was that Siegfried, in whose love she now exults, would awaken her. The music represents unmediated emotion.
- The text then turns to the protection she was offered: *brünnhilde's purity, sexual desire, heroic love, siegfried*.
- As Waltraute gives voice to distress: *wotan's balked will*, four times repeated. Now her sister is ready to listen.

B – Waltraute's narration

- For the last 20 years, since Brünnhilde was put to sleep, Wotan has seldom been in Valhalla. He has roamed the world, only returning after his spear was shattered: *wotan's struggle, valhalla*. He orders that the World Ash Tree be cut down. The music is mightily impressive and extends over seventeen bars. One has to think the purpose was to convey what the world needed, rather than what he, Wotan, thought was good for it.
- The trunk and branches have been fashioned into the great logs that surround Valhalla in preparation for its destruction: *valhalla* and *power of the gods*. The combination of these two motifs over 16 bars is the strongest foretaste of the oncoming Immolation, and an affirmation of the high principle of Wotan's original project. It is hard to think of music that better expresses elevated moral endeavour.

21.26 *valhalla* is underpinned by *power of the gods*. Both are now doomed in the final conflagration.

GÖTTERDÄMMERUNG

- Now Wotan sits immobile, says nothing. None of the gods eat of the Golden Apples: *destiny*; they are as paralysed: *valhalla*. The valkyrs have no aim: *wotan's balked will, core life value, ring, curse*.
- Waltraute understood that Wotan wants the Ring to be returned to the Rhinedaughters and left Valhalla to find Brünnhilde: *wotan's balked will, fierce action*.

C *Brünnhilde's rejection of Waltraute*

This episode, of course, is the locus of the valkyr's fall from grace, as previously described.

- The valkyr's reply is calm but reserved. The voice-melody is exquisite. But the return of *wotan's balked will*, as it now surrounds this critical statement, is unexpected. This is, in fact, to be the motif's last appearance. Wotan now has no power that can be 'balked' and that lust has now passed to Hagen. The result of this is soon revealed.

21.27 Brünnhilde's measured but cold response to Waltraute

- For *wotan's balked will* mutates unnervingly when Brünnhilde's tone changes. This motif made fleeting appearances as Waltraute sang; in line with Cooke's principle

21.28 *vengeance* **M81**

This motif applies to the actions and motives of the valkyr, Hagen and Gunther alike. *wotan's balked will* is interrupted by the insertion of the rising and falling interval of a seventh, which is the main feature of *deception* (M76).

that the development of motifs was psychological, one can assume that this tentative introduction relates not to Wotan, nor to Waltraute but to Brünnhilde. Now it quickly and insistently occurs seven times. It is to return with great impact over a large part of Act II and in the great vengeance trio and so is here called *vengeance* (M81). The implications of this are deep. The original block to his will, imposed by Fricka in W2 so as to frustrate Wotan's initiative to rescue the situation, might here be seen to spawn malevolence where it is least expected: in his beloved daughter. If she is to be fatally corrupted, then Wotan's collapse will be total. The unsettling rise and fall in the middle is a reflection of the interval of a seventh in *deception* which introduces the corruption to be found in society.

GÖTTERDÄMMERUNG

At this moment the motif is heard as the valkyr gives voice to her indifference to what she has heard:

> Sad woman: what bad dreams / and tales you're telling me! / I'm just a foolish girl, who's emerged from the mists / of the gods' sacred sky; / I see nothing in what I'm learning. / To me your point seems / tangled and desolate; / in your eyes, / deprived of sleep, / flickers a quivering flame. You pale sister, / with ashen cheeks, / wild woman: what do you want of me?

- The selfishness that now emerges in the valkyr, exemplified in the motif *vengeance*, emerges when Waltraute's answer to her last question, as given above, is that the Ring should be returned to the Rhinedaughters. Derivative variations of *ring* explosively erupt and are joined by a compositional motif *brünnhilde's woe* (CM48), related to *woe*. Twelve times these two motifs jostle each other as the two sisters fail to connect.

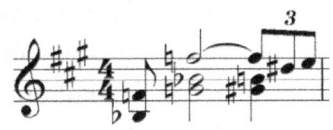

  21.29 *brünnhilde's woe* **CM47**

- Brünnhilde breaks free of this argument and, to *future hope* and *heroic love*, declares that *only* the love Siegfried has for her matters. Slow renditions of *vengeance* introduce a rare appearance of *core life value* as she declares that she will never stop loving and that love cannot be taken from her – even if it means that Valhalla should crash down. *wotan in revolt* storms up and launches *curse*. (This sounds great but is hard to justify within the drama, unless we accede to the idea that the revolt has passed from god to daughter.) Waltraute leaves to repetitions of *conflict* and *woe*. Brünnhilde is now not the person seen in *Die Walküre*.

Scene 7: Brünnhilde succumbs to Siegfried
[Schirmer: 114/3/2 to end of Act. Text from 'Blitzend Gewölk' to '. . . trene mich von seiner Braut!']

This Scene is simple in comparison to that previous Scene, and turns again around Brünnhilde. She may not have seen it like that, but breaking away from her past and cleaving to Siegfried was in itself a trauma. In this Scene she suffers another and greater – in her consciousness at least – to a degree that is difficult to envisage. There are no stages in this catastrophe: the route from ecstasy to despair is one sequence of increasing terror. This is traceable in the music, starting at the moment when Waltraute leaves and the approach of Siegfried is evident. Setting the drama out like this entails no suggestion that readers attempt to trace these motifs, some of which occur with frequency. The only useful thing that might be done is to think through how they cohere to create the ambience of the plot.

- Joyful anticipation: *valkyr, loge as fire, horn call*.
- Incomprehension as the figure of Gunther emerges: *tarnhelm, potion, gibichungs, woe*. The first three merge continuously into each other.

GÖTTERDÄMMERUNG

- The terrible belief that this is Wotan's final punishment: *despair, brünnhilde's woe, woe.*
- Siegfried states what he will do: *hagen, tarnhelm, potion, woe, ring, treachery, servitude to the ring.*
- Siegfried and Brünnhilde struggle, and Siegfried wrests the Ring away from her: *curse, valkyr, womanly brünnhilde, tarnhelm, potion, the gibich hagen.*
- Brünnhilde reflects on the disaster: *malice, womanly brünnhilde, brünnhilde's woe, woe.* The return of *malice* in association with the valkyr has been much noted. It represents the culmination of her descent into self-centred isolation from which she will not emerge until the end of the opera.
- Siegfried drives her into the cave; 'trembling and with tottering steps she goes into the chamber': *hagen, wotan's sword, will-to-power, friendship, blood-brotherhood, potion, womanly brünnhilde.*

# # # # # #

No greater contrast could there be between the Brünnhilde who enters this Act and the Brünnhilde who leaves it. Immense musical and dramatic knowledge and resource are to be found within it so that the violent events to follow would be believable.

◊ ◊ ◊ ◊ ◊ ◊

GÖTTERDÄMMERUNG

Act II

Wagner broke this Act into five Scenes and so does this study. The structural changes between *Siegfrieds Tod* and *Götterdämmerung* are minimal. The original force of Wagner's invention finds its clearest expression in this Act.

1	Hagen, still on his 'Watch', is visited by Alberich.	164 bars; 15 minutes
2	Siegfried returns and is greeted by Hagen and Gutrune.	198 bars; 6 minutes
3	Hagen summons the vassals, who welcome back Gunther – with Brünnhilde in train.	354 bars; 7 minutes
4	Brünnhilde discovers the deception and confronts Siegfried, who swears his honour on Hagen's spear.	528 bars; 21 minutes
5	Brünnhilde, Gunther and Hagen agree that Siegfried must die.	381 bars; 16 minutes

Total: 1625 bars; 65 minutes

Scene 1: Alberich comes to Hagen
[Schirmer 129/1/1 to 141/1/1. Text from 'Schläfst du, Hagen, mein Sohn?' to '... sei true!']

The changes between the *Siegfrieds Tod* text and what we now read are not comparable with those in the Waltraute Scene. The text is updated and recapitulates Alberich's history in some detail but, surprisingly repetitive, it tells Hagen nothing that he does not already know. The abiding effect of the repetitions is to convey Alberich's crippling fixation on what he has lost. One significant change lies in the response of son to father. In the earlier exchange Hagen explicitly declares that he will offer the recovered Ring to Alberich, the 'first of the Nibelungs'. Now the implication is that it will be Hagen's. When Alberich asks him to swear, he pushes that aside: he only needs to swear to himself and not to Alberich. An added disturbing touch is that Wagner deliberately leaves it unclear whether or not Hagen is asleep and dreaming. He remains immobile and disregards his father; the stage direction reads 'he still seems to be asleep, even though his eyes remain permanently open'. This adds an unearthly aura to the whole Scene.

The musical atmosphere is of inveterate malevolence. The opening is in B♭ minor with a syncopation, based on *malice,* that is intensified beyond that in the 'Watch'. After a harshly fierce *woe,* the music offers up a vivid tune (21.30). First heard in this short

21.30 The sadness of Hagen, to be inflicted upon all, epitomised in this tune. The words used later in the Scene: 'If my mother gave me spirit, I'm not minded to thank her... old too soon, sickly and pale, I loathe the lively; never rejoice.'

GÖTTERDÄMMERUNG

prelude it is later sung by Hagen; and reinforces the joylessness of the 'Watch' music and the gnawing rage of Alberich's music in this Scene. In the prelude, this tune pulls us forward into three immense octave falls in the bass, each a tone higher. The music is hammered out by three bassoons, bass tuba, cellos and double basses and leads into the last refrain from Hagen's song in his 'Watch' (p.396).

As to be expected, the music of the dialogue between father and son is a tissue of *ring, malice, woe, curse* that rotate and return again and again. When the narrative demands it, there is *horn call, brünnhilde's purity, fafner the dragon, wotan's sword*. As Alberich fades from view: *curse, malice, woe* close the Scene.

Scene 2: Siegfried returns and is greeted by Gutrune and Hagen
[Schirmer 141/1/2 to 150/1/4. Text from 'Hoi-oh, Hagen! Müder Mann!' to 'Dir zu helfen ruh'ich aus!']

Hagen is the centre of most Scenes in which he appears. Not this one: all the focus is upon Siegfried and Gutrune, and the structure of the Act deliberately contrasts this Scene with those that come before and after. Nothing in good drama happens by chance and the purpose of this short episode is better appreciated if we try to see and hear it out of context. Firstly, Siegfried is clearly happy, and happy in the everyday, prosaic sense. He is a normal man who has got his girl. Secondly, Gutrune revels in her role as seductress but is understandably bowled over: a good girl led astray. It is clear also that she must have great beauty and sexual allure. Even if one were to accept the central role of the potion, we would think it odd were she to be ugly.

The most interesting exchange occurs in the middle. This is when Gutrune questions Siegfried about the night he spent with Brünnhilde. Wagner is deliberately ambiguous. Although we know that Siegfried did not approach Brünnhilde sexually during that time, he gives evasive answers to the four questions Gutrune puts to him, and we are uncertain at the end whether she believes him. The only *personal* comment she subsequently makes about him is that he scares her.

The triple internal structure is obvious.

A   Siegfried arrives, announces what he has done and is greeted first by Hagen and then by Gutrune.
B   Question and Answer between Gutrune and Siegfried. The questions are not really answered.
C   The cloud, if there has been one, passes. Siegfried tells the others what Gunther and Brünnhilde are now doing; Hagen sees their boat in the distance; the two would-be lovers depart.

A *Arrival*

Before Siegfried appears, a bold rising melody in B♭ major evokes the approaching dawn. Although it seems associated with Hagen, it comes into its own only in the next Scene when Hagen summons the vassals. That fits very well, for Hagen is the instigator

GÖTTERDÄMMERUNG

of all the events that are about to unfold. When *horn call* enters it is here to stay and it proceeds to bustle along with a new motif.

21.31 *siegfried & gutrune* **CM48**

siegfried & gutrune (CM48). The first four chords replicate *treachery* (CM46) which is a portion of *servitude to the ring*. But in this form, with a new continuation and a bounce at the end, it is undeniably jolly, and shows Seigfried as straightforwardly happy. The fourth bar is to become an invitation to a party.

B *Gutrune questions Siegfried*

Soon into this stage, a new compositional motif *siegfried's evasion* (CM49) holds sway for 20 bars; it is most insistent but disappears when questions move on to the current activity of Gunther and Brünnhilde. Surely it is descriptive of unease within both people.

21.32 *siegfried's evasion* **CM49**
The edgy and slippery motif is in the lower line. Above it runs that for *tarnhelm*. Although we know that Siegfried is telling the truth, we also know that he may sense it's not the whole truth.

C *Siegfried and Gutrune depart*

For the concluding 40 bars it is Wagner giving us party-time music as the Scene ends in jollity. The music associated with Loge returns so often throughout the cycle, in one form or another, that repeatedly to illustrate it serves no purpose. But a listener will pick up a smooth and calm adaptation of M14B lying behind Siegfried's description of how he accompanied Brünnhilde down to meet up with Gunther. Cooke adds to the attributes normally associated with Loge, that of being the source of demonic mental activity. This is a very difficult concept to convey on stage but, at this particular moment, it readily speaks of energy, even though it is not easy to particularise it as demonic.

Scene 3: Hagen summons the Gibichung vassals

[Schirmer: 150/2/1 to 177/1/1. Text from 'Ho-ho! Hoi-ho-ho!' to 'Willkommen!']

In many ways *Siegfrieds Tod* has the structure and panoply of a Grand Opera. The chorus is an essential part of that genre but, although a good director can instil actions that bring it to life, its main function is to comment on and react to the motions and words of the principals. This choral interlude is magnificent and its dramatic function is to give the appropriate stage setting for the mighty Scene that is to follow. Another reason for a chorus at this stage is to show that this is now a drama fully within the human sphere. Energy, suppressed violence, and good cheer infuse and combine at a sound volume never less than *f* and up to *ff* – the loudest marking Wagner used.

GÖTTERDÄMMERUNG

21.33 *vassals #1* **CM50**    **21.34** *vassals #2* **CM51**

The score introduces two persistent compositional motifs that bear the weight of what resembles a vocal symphonic poem. The first is a fragment of the dawn music as Hagen waits for Siegfried to arrive. As this builds to a climax a three note figure emerges and leads up to the moment when the music juddered to a halt as Hagen awakes. The motif *vassals#1* (CM50) is used by both voice and orchestra and is never far away; *vassals#2* (CM51) is purely orchestral.

These two motifs are around all the time. They mix into *treachery*, variations of *ring, gibichungs, siegfried & gutrune*. It is difficult, however, to make a case for the appearance of *core life value*, first heard when, in *Das Rheingold*, Loge points to the centrality of love to everyone except Alberich. Readers may think of some good reason but the truth may again be that Wagner occasionally makes music for its own sake which sounds magnificent but is tangential to the drama.

The Scene ends with the ceremonial greeting on the entrance of Gunther as he leads in Brünnhilde. This resembles no motif or anything similar in the opera but it certainly crowns the Scene. And there is something of grandeur in it: the respect shown to Gunther by his vassals is genuine. It might be best to see him as an averagely good leader, but one caught up in abnormality.

Scene 4: The confrontation between Brünnhilde and Siegfried
[Schirmer: 177/1/2 to 208/3/3. Text from 'Brünnhild, die hehrest Frau' to '. . . thu'es der Glückliche gleich.']

This Scene of mighty melodrama is in four stages comprising a mini-drama in its own right. Brünnhilde is the protagonist, the one who continues on her journey.

A *Confusion* What has happened is both traumatic in the extreme and also incomprehensible to her. The sight of the Ring on Siegfried's hand adds another trauma with which to cope.
B *Realisation* The mists clear when she realises it was he and not Gunther who took it from her.
C *Confrontation* Siegfried's denials launch the altercation between them that can be seen as the episode toward which the plot of the original *Siegfrieds Tod* had been moving. Tension rises until Siegfried reaches a point of no return.
D *Resolution* Oaths are sworn on Hagen's spear and Siegfried leaves, seemingly untouched by what has happened.

A – *Confusion*
- As Gunther leads in Brünnhilde, the music he sings would be seen to have nobility in any other context. We know, and he knows, that he is a fraud but, by taking up

the previous splendour of the choral tribute - the final phrase of which is repeated when he has finished – he retains in his own mind an image of the man he would like to be.

- Introduction to the Gibichungs over, enter Siegfried and Gutrune: motifs *siegfried & gutrune, friendship* – urbane and stately.
- All changes when Brünnhilde sees the Ring on Siegfried's finger. After the initial explosion: *vengeance, destiny, tarnhelm, potion, the gibich hagen* follow each other. These motifs have both a close dramatic relationship with each other (witness their names) that is matched by the ease with which they interconnect. The words uttered by the chorus are few.

B – *Realisation*

- This has two phases. The trauma of recent events breaks down Brünnhilde's composure and grasp of events, and the music drifts in and out of motifs until she sees the Ring on Siegfried's finger.
- At this point, violently descending segments of *ring* over four octaves are followed by *curse,* and then by 29 repetitions of *malice* or rhythmic variations upon it. Desire for revenge is now uppermost as she questions first Siegfried and then Gunther about why the Ring is with the former and not the latter. Alberich's poison has taken her over. Gunther is rightly puzzled when he is asked the whereabouts of the ring 'that you stole from my hand'. (To avoid exonerating him from at least part of the trick played, *treachery* joins up with *potion* as she puts the question.) His inability to answer introduces six bars during which Brünnhilde divines the truth. The motif *potion* (the first two notes, as heard here, being part of *treachery*), a dim throb in the bass of *malice, rhinegold* and *tarnhelm* are played as the tempo slows from 'piu moderato' to something that in performance is near to stationary. She is in the process of understanding that something grossly base has happened to her.

21.35 Brünnhilde gets to the truth.
At the top, *potion*, three times repeated. The three final bars are *tarnhelm*. In the middle, across the first three bars is *rhinegold*. At the bottom, a slowed down variation of *malice* throbs across three bars.

C – *Confrontation*

- Her realisation that Siegfried ('the treacherous thief') is the culprit and Siegfried's robust denial brings Hagen into the fray: *ring, vengeance, dragon, rhinemaidens' lament, rhinegold, malice, hagen.*

GÖTTERDÄMMERUNG

- The appallingly wicked sound of Hagen's insinuation that Siegfried is the 'betrayer who must pay the price' (the German: ". . . den der Treulose büssen soll't" is particularly chilling on '*büssen*') brings on a ferocity of accusation by Brünnhilde that dominates all. To put it simply, no passage by any composer in any opera exceeds the expression of a woman's howl of fear-filled rage against abuse from men and, in her case, also by Wotan. The vocal score cannot convey the weight of the orchestra. The sustained chord over her great cry is produced by all the woodwind and horns. The bassoon and double basses hold the low E♭ at the bottom. The motifs heard are *potion* in support of Hagen's accusation in the first bar, *hagen* (trombones) at the beginning of the second and the newly emerged *brünnhilde's woe* in flutes and clarinets as they top out the immense chord. The rising chromatic run over two octaves is by violins and violas; the illustration shows it an octave lower than played to avoid clutter in the score. Brünnhilde's cry is repeated: twice 'Betrug!' (Betrayed!) and twice 'Verrat!' (betrayal!) over the ten bars.

Brünnhilde is no termagant. She had put her faith in Siegfried because Wotan

21.36 Hagen's accusation accelerates the drama

had endorsed him. His frailty must, therefore be placed at the feet of the god. She is now so human. She forgets that she rejected Valhalla and the gods the previous day. Nevertheless, Wotan was her beloved and wise father and he has unaccountably turned against her. The great cry opens floodgates into a drama that must end in death. They lead to two *ff* descents over two octaves of the first four notes of *ring*, followed by *vengeance, malice, woe,* and a derivation of *despair* first heard as Wotan bewailed his own fate in *Die Walküre*. Her words are as follows:

> Trickery! Trickery! Violent Trickery!
> Treason! Treason! To be avenged as never before!
> Sacred gods, arbiters of the skies!
> Is this what you muttered to yourself in council?
> Teach her sorrows as none have suffered?
> Design her disgrace to give unimagined pain?
> *[She appears to be utterly unglued from her surroundings . . . after an inner, hugely painful struggle, she then erupts.]* §
> Then tell me of vengeance, such as it has never raged!
> Fire in me a fury never before restrained!

GÖTTERDÄMMERUNG

> Instruct Brünnhilde to shatter her heart,
> that she may rip apart the man who cheated her!
> § *The stage direction score added by the composer at the 1876 Bayreuth rehearsals, and included by John Deathridge in his translation.*

Brünnhilde is her human self, outside of any story. No remnant remains of the wise valkyr. Much of the above is largely without motifs: only fragmentary *malice*, *vengeance* and a very slow *woe*.

- Tumult ensues: *vengeance* again and again as Gunther and the chorus engage.
- Brünnhilde lies: 'He forced pleasure and love from me.' These words are sung to *core life value*, played without irony on the violins. This practice of the vocal line carrying the motif in unison with the orchestra is rare. The combination suggests that truth is being told. The audience is nudged to believe her, or at least to perceive that all should be forgiven her, on account of the abuse she has suffered.
- Siegfried knows that a foul trick has been played on the woman but also that this accusation is a lie. He fights back with *blood-brotherhood, wotan's sword, will-to-power* (soon to be brought back when the oath is sworn). Immense tension now as the Gibichungs fully engage: motifs are splintered and merged until Siegfried shouts 'If I refute the charge by swearing an oath, who among you will wager their weapon upon it?' Hagen steps forward to *vengeance*.

D – *Fatal Resolution*

- The motifs *vengeance, blood-brotherhood* set the scene in the mode of an established tribal ritual. As Siegfried and Brünnhilde each swear in turn on Hagen's spear, and to the

  21.37 The oath

  same music we hear *vengeance* and *hagen*. The oath itself is a fine tune (21.37). At the mid-point Siegfried says 'If a sharp point is to pierce me, let it be you.' This is sung to the *death oath* motif (M82). This motif accompanied (rather than being sung) Hagen's assurance to Alberich earlier in the Act that Siegfried was already, if

  21.38 *death oath* **M82**

  inadvertently, working for him and toward his own death. It had little impact there but now is to feature to the end of the Act.
- From here to the end of the Scene, there is no point in trying to disentangle motifs. The people call upon the gods to stop the quarrel amongst their rulers. Siegfried tries to calm both Gunther and the people. He apologises to Gunther that the Tarnhelm failed properly to work and finally, by his energetic cheerfulness, persuades the crowd to leave with him. The music is a patchwork of motifs already heard.

  21.39 *siegfried soothes gunther* **CM52**

GÖTTERDÄMMERUNG

When there is such profusion, Wagner introduces a compositional motif to hold things together; in this case thirteen bars carry *siegfried soothes gunther* (CM52).

The Scene ends with *heroic love* and *siegfried & gutrune* as Siegfried bustles the people off the stage. He remains an enigma.

Scene 5: Brünnhilde, Gunther and Hagen agree that Siegfried must die
[Schirmer: 208/3/4 to end of Act. Text from 'Welches unhold's List' to 'nieher zu horchen dem Racheswur!']
The structure tells us that this Scene continues to trace Brünnhilde's journey, the trajectory of which is a progression from dumbfounded sorrow to participation in an unholy conspiracy.
A   Brünnhilde communes with herself about what she has lost. (78 bars)
B   Vengeful rage takes over and Hagen joins her. He prompts toward the obligatory solution. (95 bars)
C   Brünnhilde and Hagen pull a reluctant Gunther into their plot (147 bars)
D   The three join together in the great revenge trio. (53 bars)

A – *Brünnhilde alone*
As Brünnhilde reflects on recent events, the music moves calmly between reminiscence of past love and the rage that has just engulfed her. For the first there is *victorious love, core life value, future hope, destiny*. For the latter *treachery, siegfried & gutrune, vengeance*. Wagner is now able, by a musical commentary alone, to convey a great deal. Brünnhilde cannot initially understand what has happened but then moves from incomprehension to master one incontrovertible fact: the man who loved her has now cheerfully cast her aside.

Reference to one key motif which bridges both sides of the conflict has been left out. The motif *woe* is the substance of the cry that wells up and signifies the full realisation of her loss. It is left out because the outburst is so painfully lyrical that it just does not *sound* like a motif; it sounds like human pain. From that moment,

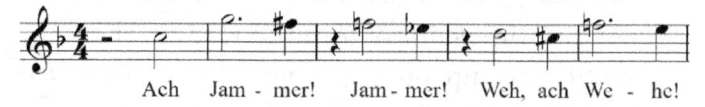

Ach   Jam - mer!   Jam - mer!   Weh, ach We - he!

21.40 Brünnhilde's sorrow strikes home. *woe* is the vehicle.

matters speed up (*poco a poco più animato*) until rage takes over.

B – *Brünnhilde is joined by Hagen*
Three violent *ff* repetitions of *death oath*, the third with notes doubled in length as it becomes a descent over 1½ octaves, down to a low F#, are rasped out by all the woodwind, eight horns, two trumpets, four trombones – 23 instruments in total. There it joins to *vengeance* and *woe*. Five repetitions of *vengeance* bring Hagen forward to offer help. Loudly in the bass, as the offer is made, is heard the fine opening phrase of

the oath (21.37). *death oath, cunning loge* accompany Hagen's tactic with Brünnhilde as he probes for Siegfried's weakness (cf Loki in the sagas and Hagen in *Nibelungenlied*.) As she tells him that his back was not protected by her magic there enters *brünnhilde's lament* (CM53). The sweetness of her memories – fragments of *love's ecstasy* – are juxtaposed with *malice* (and this time *exactly* following Alberich's music as Wotan took the Ring from him in *Das Rheingold*). Most poignantly, as she tells Hagen to strike at Siegfried's back, *brünnhilde's lament* overlaps with *siegfried*, pp on the horns, and *wotan's sword* on the trumpet. The sound now is as from a chamber orchestra and the frequent entry of overlapping motifs was described by David Stannard, in a 2017 workshop, as reminiscent of Bach. After 38 bars, *brünnhilde's lament* fades away at the moment when Hagen is told that Siegfried's back is unprotected.

22.41 *brünnhilde's lament*
CM53

C – Brünnhilde, Hagen, and now Gunther

'That is where my spear will strike' says Hagen and, as *vengeance* rises five times in the bass, he calls on Gunther to join with his wife to the melody *core life value*. This may seem odd but the motif has resemblance to M79C – *blood-brotherhood* – and it is that loss that Gunther bewails, for he believes himself to be honourable.

The motif *despair* leads to a repetition of *core life value* and the words which Gunther now sings to that motif refer to himself as 'the most pitiable of men'. Twice before has it been similarly used: by Alberich after the Ring has been wrested from his hand by Wotan, when he describes himself as 'the most desolate of desolate slaves'; and by Wotan when he calls himself 'the unhappiest of beings'. Each of them recognize that they had lost what had been most valuable to them: Gunther – his honour, Alberich – the Ring, Wotan – the means to improve his cosmos.

Brünnhilde rubs this in as *vengeance* (with *malice* low in the double basses) supports the accusation that Gunther is a coward. Gunther sees himself as betrayed and Wagner cleverly makes it he, rather than the truly-wronged woman or the half-brother who instigates the plot, who drives the music toward the assertion that Siegfried must die. He cannot bring himself to pronounce sentence himself but asks Hagen for help. The symphonic texture is made from *vengeance, core life value, woe, blood-brotherhood*. Tension is high now. Brünnhilde affirms that Siegfried betrayed Gunther (thereby thrusting him toward revenge for loss of honour) and then goes on violently to say that *everyone* has betrayed her.

At this point a remarkable transformation of the last three notes of M80B (*blood-brotherhood*) bursts in every other bar, five times in ten bars. Each time it is with all the brass, followed by the tremolo on the strings. Then CM54 disappears but this eruption abnormally accelerates the drama towards its intended end – the trio of the three

21.42 *fragment of M80B*
CM54

conspirators. Now revenge is all Brünnhilde thinks of: *vengeance* followed immediately by *death oath* is the music as she says that *all* are guilty but the death of Siegfried will be sufficient. With this she takes prime ownership of the forthcoming assassination.

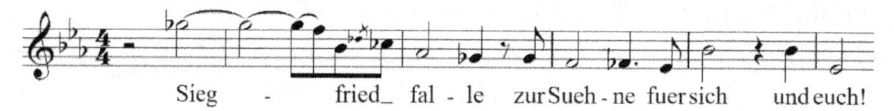

Sieg - fried_ fal - le zur Such - ne fuer sich und euch!

22.43 Brünnhilde takes ownership of the assassination. To emphasise this, she sings the critical words to the *death oath* motif.
The words matter: he is to die for all: 'Siegfried shall die, as atonement for himself and for you.'

The remaining 47 bars until the trio starts is a condensation of motifs that turn and return. *hagen, malice, woe, the gibich hagen, ring, treachery, siegfried & gutrune, vengeance, gutrune seductress, core life value, victorious love, horn call*: they are all heard. The presence of the last three is worthy of comment. What are they doing here? *core life value* is sung by Hagen to the sentiment that death will deprive Siegfried of the Ring's power; *victorious love* accompanies comments as to whom the Ring actually belongs; *horn call* supports the notion that Siegfried's death could be hidden from Gutrune by organising a hunting party which Siegfried will gladly join. It is nigh impossible to find any justification for the first two motifs, and the third reminds us of Debussy's jibe that Siegfried is 'presenting his calling card'. But it surely sounds fabulous!

D – *The 'revenge' trio*
This does not last long (3 minutes) but is, by common consent, one of the great dramatic trios in opera – put alongside that for Manrico, Leonora and di Luna in *Il Trovatore* Act I, and that between Iphigénie, Orestes and Pilades in Gluck's *Iphigénie en Tauride*. Each is a touchstone within its respective genre.

One thing merits discussion: why does the Scene not end when the singing ends? Compare it with the great duet between Otello and Iago at the end of Act II of Verdi's *Otello* – 'Sì, per ciel marmoreo giuro!' At the end of the singing there are just a handful of harsh cords and then the curtain descends. What we hear and see now was there in *Siegfrieds Tod*. Wagner was then out to show a full story of Siegfried and he did not budge from this. The end of the Act shows Siegfried and his bride-to-be taking over the stage in celebration. His insouciance at this moment, after the strong events that have just passed, has a dramatic purpose. He is a guilty man with regard to Brünnhilde and Wagner rubs this in.

◇ ◇ ◇ ◇ ◇ ◇

GÖTTERDÄMMERUNG

Act III

The structure now is encompassed in five big Scenes, as first envisaged in 1848.

1	Siegfried meets with the Rhinedaughters and rejects their advice.	489 bars; 19 minutes
2	Siegfried is brought down by Hagen	346 bars; 15 minutes
3	Siegfried's death and his Funeral Music	127 bars; 12 minutes
4	The Gibichungs react to Siegfried's death	343 bars; 12 minutes
5	The Immolation	354 bars; 19 minutes
	Totals	1559 bars; 77 minutes

In this Act the drama runs its necessary course. An air of ritual surrounds Siegfried: his fateful behaviour with the Rhinemaidens, the passage of his body back to the palace and the final immolation. All is ritual. Dramatic development is over.

The previous Act saw Siegfried vigorously deny Brünnhilde's accusations and swear the most solemn of oaths to support this denial. At the same time, and in contrast to the valkyr, Gutrune, Gunther and the Gibichungs, he was remarkably unaffected by the storming drama in which he participated. He advises Gunther to calm down, thereby inferring that Brünnhilde had momentarily lost her wits. He sallied back on stage with gaiety as the vengeance trio comes to its end, and the stage direction has him lifted up on shoulders along with Gutrune as they lead the procession off to the wedding. In the opening Scenes of the upcoming Act, Siegfried is back to something of his earlier nature, before he met Gutrune. Furthermore, until Hagen strikes him down, he is to retain the insouciance revealed in the previous Act. In short, and taking into account the revelatory narration of his previous history and the action of his dead hand as it repulses Hagen, Siegfried is to live his last hours on a high note.

Scene 1: Siegfried meets with the Rhinedaughters and rejects their advice
[Schirmer 231/1/1 to 273/1/2. Text from 'Frau Sonne sendet lichte Strahlen' to '. . . der zieren Frauen eine hätt'ich mir frischgezähmt.']
Wagner has a considered story to tell here and the structure is a classic Freytag Pyramid.

1 – Set up	The Rhinedaughters wait for Siegfried, fully aware that he is on his way.	149 bars 6 minutes
2 – Rising action	He duly arrives, is accosted by the Rhinedaughters, is not in the least surprised - and flirts with them.	56 bars 2 minutes
3 – Mid-point	They ask that the Ring be returned and, after a cheerful discussion, he offers it to them. Suddenly they refuse to accept it.	75 bars 3 minutes

GÖTTERDÄMMERUNG

4 – Falling action	The refusal is conditional. By implication, it is not the Ring itself but rather the attached curse that matters. The issue is explained thoroughly: he will be killed if he does not now give them the Ring. When so threatened, he refuses.	123 bars 5 minutes
5 – Conclusion	The Rhinedaughters leave, with another warning about his forthcoming death. Siegfried retains the blithe unconcern as at the end of the previous Act, and at the start of the Scene	92 bars 3 minutes

495 bars : 19 minutes

It appears as a whim that he offers up the Ring and a further whim when he withdraws it. This is the Scene to which Wagner refers in the *Myth* - as some sort of explanation to himself – that Siegfried is guiltless but is doomed to take upon himself the guilt of the gods (p.431). This Scene was undoubtedly necessary as part of *Siegfrieds Tod*. Along with the Norns, the valkyrs and Alberich, they connect the story to the sources. Now the necessity is different: it takes Siegfried back to the person he was before he met Brünnhilde or the Gibichungs – and even before he got hold of the Ring and Tarnhelm. (The 'woodland boy' as described by Thomas Mann).

1 Set up - The Rhinedaughters await Siegfried

A very short prelude where solo *horn call* is answered by *woe* establishes the menace that now threatens Siegfried. Then softly played *nature, rhine gold* and *rhinedaughters' lament* introduce the three water sprites as they swim to the surface and the Scene takes shape. This is established by 90 bars of new music that is to return frequently but is barely repeated after the Scene is finished (CM55 & CM56). These two motifs are both sung by the Rhinedaughters and played by the orchestra and immediately amount to five minutes of music – and this is undoubtedly symphonic. For this purpose, the music is and probably has to be new. The world has moved on and the sprites are not as they were.

21.44 *mature rhinedaughters (1)* **CM55**

There is also one notable aspect of CM56, which this extended example shows: not one note with # or ♭ is to be seen. This is pure, open music without stress in which each

21.45 *mature rhinedaughters (2)* **CM56**
The three vocal lines are given.

voice totally accords with the other two. This may reflect the detachment now apparent between the Rhinedaughters and their loss, when compared to that at the end of *Das*

Rheingold. But it also chimes with Siegfried's open lack of concern about anything other than the present moment – a central feature of his character.

2   *Rising action - Siegfried duly arrives and flirts with the Rhinedaughters*
He has been lost in the woods. A compositional motif (*siegfried's imp:* CM57) much heard in this episode brilliantly exemplifies the imp he thinks has both led him astray and hidden the game he was after. This now mixes with the main motifs as he flirts with the Rhinedaughters.

21.46 *siegfried's imp* **CM57**

3   *Mid-point - The Ring is bargained for and finally refused*
The Rhinedaughters ask for the Ring as payment for telling him where the hunted animal is to be found. For just a few moments the music is darkened by *ring* and *dragon*. Then the previous music of flirtatious banter returns as they laugh and circle him in the water, and suggest he is scared of Gutrune. The imp music is prominent until Siegfried says that the sprites can have the Ring. It is a shock when, to a doleful rendering of *rhinegold,* Flosshilde declines.

4   *Falling action - The Rhinedaughters try to make Siegfried self-aware*
The music darkens ominously and with concentration. For five minutes the Rhinedaughters try to pass the moral weight of the story on to Siegfried's shoulders. The music is a deft assemblage of fateful motifs: *rhinegold* in a minor key, *core life value, woe, curse, dragon, nibelung slavery, life energy, downfall, destiny, norns' rope of fate, will-to-power.* The urgency of this music from the hitherto detached Rhinedaughters conveys a dangerous crisis in the offing beyond any music so far – 45 bars in which Siegfried is given a comprehensive history lesson. His response is as though they had never spoken. To the final threat that his fate has been inexorably recorded by the Norns he responds by repudiating such threats. Siegfried's defining rejection of all this advice is the act of picking up a clod of earth and throwing it behind himself with the words 'As for body and soul, look: I just toss them from me!'

5   *The Rhinedaughters leave*
That is the end of the dialogue but the warnings continue – addressed in the third person - as the sprites exit to very near the same music as at the beginning. 'Oaths he has sworn, and does not keep! Runes he knows and can't unlock! A generous gift was given him: (*womanly brünnhilde*); he doesn't know that he's squandered it; only the Ring, which will be his death, it's only the Ring he wants to keep!' As their voices fade, Siegfried thinks he would have tried to win one for himself if he had not been married to Gutrune.

# # # # # #

That this remarkable Scene has remained intact in the plot for 24 years indicates that Wagner thought long about it and perhaps bore in mind the *aide memoire* within the

Myth about Siegfried bearing guilt that was not his own. Two aspects impress in the 21st century: the beauty and symmetry of the Rhinedaughters' music, and the power of the message passed to Siegfried, which message he ignored.

This and the Scenes in the Forest in Act II have the most beautiful music (used in the sense derisively directed by some at such as Rachmaninov) in the whole tetralogy. This beauty also embraces the glory of the physical world, the world that the mistakes of Wotan and the malice of Alberich have endangered. This beauty is a reflection of something within Siegfried that is not found in any other character. Two features spring to mind. In this Scene, Wagner emphasises the beauty by musical symmetry, as he does in the initial revelation of the Rhine Gold, luminous at the bottom of the river. The Rhinedaughters sing ensemble in every one of the stages within this Scene and one aspect is the similarity of their song in the first and last episode. The second feature is the anguish that invests the warnings imparted. These build upon and augment the true emotion heard in *rhinedaughter's lament* at the close of *Das Rheingold*. At this point Wagner presents the naked truth of Siegfried's situation in sounds that strike home to the audience. This is similar to Waltraute's narration to Brünnhilde in Act I and, in both cases, the person addressed ignored it.

This brings us naturally to the power of the message passed to Siegfried. Given what we know about Siegfried, what did Wagner intend? The words have barely changed in the 26 years between the *Siegfrieds Tod* poem and the music that carries them, but the music is given immense emphasis by the composer. Explanations that Siegfried is unconcerned about the sort of matters conveyed to him or that he *had* to behave like this in order to be free of Wotan's power are insufficient. The first is true but underperforms as an argument and the second overlooks that the Rhinedaughters have nothing to do with Wotan.

But there are pointers. Firstly, in the summing up at the end of Part 2 (p.219) is the thesis that a hero must serve the community, but does so unwittingly. Secondly, within this study the concept that a hero is defined by what he is rather than by what he does is cited more than once. Thirdly, as with Brünnhilde in her discourse with Waltraute, any attempt to shackle Siegfried to the current reality is bound to fail. Whatever the answer to this might be, it behoves us to think of Kitto's maxim: clearly Wagner is making no careless slip. This Scene tells us something crucial about his character.

# # # # # #

Scene 2: Siegfried is brought down by Hagen
[Schirmer 275/2/1 to 297/2/1. Text from 'Hoi Ho!' to 'Meineid rächt'ich!']
If there is a simplicity to this Scene, it results from Siegfried's good cheer – concrete evidence that his fate, made 'visible' by the music that carries the warnings from the Rhinedaughters, does not get through to him as it does to the audience. The Scene is in two parts:

GÖTTERDÄMMERUNG

A   Hagen sets Siegfried on course to 'betray' himself. 151 bars; 11 minutes
B   Siegfried finds himself. 195 bars; 5 minutes.

A – Hagen goes to work
No difficulty in identifying the change of atmosphere as Hagen's voice is heard off-stage: *curse, treachery, woe* in immediate succession and all exposed with minimum orchestral accompaniment. Then these alternate with *horn call* as Siegfried invites the Gibichungs down, and then all is *horn call (sempre più forte)* as, under Hagen's directions, the Gibichungs settle down for some liquid refreshment. As Hagen starts to bring Siegfried out: *deception*. Siegfried's first information is the forecast of his imminent death: fresh, open music: *mature rhinedaughters (1) & (2), horn call*. But *vengeance, deception* take over again as Hagen passes this off. At the question whether Siegfried does indeed understand bird song we hear *birdsong* and then, as he offers to share his drink with Gunther, there is a further example of the uncanny capacity of a part of one motif to join seamlessly with another. The first bar of 21.47 is the opening of *siegfried & gutrune* and bar two is identical as makes no difference to the middle bar of *gibichungs*. Both motifs convey Siegfried's good cheer. Thereafter, as Hagen pushes Siegfried on, despite Gunther's trepidation about the whole business, the music is threaded through, with a variety to be wondered at, by *vengeance, loge as energy, blood-brotherhood*. When Siegfried prepares to tell his life story, prompted by Hagen, we hear *birdsong, deception, nibelung life*.

21.47 The merging of part of *siegfried & gutrune* with part of *gibichungs*.

B – Siegfried eventually finds himself
This episode of recollection, even detached from its continuation after the death blow takes the audience straight back to the 'woodland boy' (in Thomas Mann's words) who moved from obscurity and followed his destiny as he saw it. Everything in this narration is in keeping with a man who is a hero because of what he is rather than what he did.

- Mime looked after him as a boy in the hope that he would kill Fafner the dragon. He learnt by himself how to work metal and made the sword Nothung. He killed the dragon: *nibelung life, wotan's sword, scheming, dragon*.
- When Fafner's blood touched his mouth, with wonder he realised he could understand the meaning of the bird's song: *volsung bond (1), birdsong* and the Forest Murmurs music.
- The bird told him about the Ring and Tarnhelm and he took them both: *birdsong,* Forest Murmurs music.
- That done, he listened again and the bird told him that Mime was treacherous. When the dwarf approached him with a poisoned drink, Siegfried could understand his

GÖTTERDÄMMERUNG

hidden thoughts of hate, so Siegfried killed him: *volsung bond (1), nibelung life,* Forest Murmurs music.
- Then Hagen offers Siegfried the drink with the antidote to the drug of forgetfulness: *deception, tarnhelm, potion.*
- Siegfried remembers that the bird told him about Brünnhilde asleep on the mountain and guarded by fire: *heroic love, womanly brünnhilde, birdsong, loge as fire.*
- He climbs and surmounts the fire, found the woman asleep as promised, removed armour and helmet, kissed her awake and 'Oh, how fervently the lovely arms of Brünnhilde embraced me!' : *loge as fire, brünnhilde's sleep, sexual desire, victorious love.*
- Hagen strikes him down: *curse, siegfried* and the new compositional *death* motif (CM58). After a few horror-struck bars in which *destiny* is joined to *blood-brotherhood,* Hagen leaves the stage. His last words to the aghast Gibichungs: 'I've avenged perjury!'

21.48 *death* **CM58**

Scene 3: The death and apotheosis of Siegfried
[Schirmer 297/2/1 to 305/1/2]

These bars encompass Siegfried's reconciliation with Brünnhilde before he dies, and the Funeral Music which accompanies the cortège as his body is born off-stage. Musically the two parts are different but both are a memorial that can be used to bring together some questions that circle this enigmatic hero.

Musical commentary and the *leitmotiven* used are not much to the purpose. The ear is aware that Siegfried's greeting to Brünnhilde as he sinks to death is identical in tone and almost so in notes to the welcome he gives her at she awakes at the end of *Siegfried*. In the Funeral Music, the chain of mighty motifs that rise up in defiance of the seven crashing repetitions of *death* are instantly identifiable after fourteen hours of music. When joined together, the two contrasting episodes (that last about 12 minutes in total) offer a potted history of Siegfried and his parents, and of Wotan's hopes.

The full recapitulation of his life starts at the end with what the audience recognises as a musical replay of its supreme moment – the winning of Brünnhilde. The mythic Brynhild, as seen by Joseph Campbell and within the sources, is the perfection of womanhood. When Siegfried's story is then reviewed from the beginning, within the Funeral Music, the opening four motifs that emerge from the *death* motif apply to his parents. And how appropriate the audience finds this, for it bears in mind the heroic (used in the modern, non-epic sense) lives and attitudes of Siegmund and Sieglinde. Of the 70 bars in this episode, 31 feature *death* or associated fragments of it, 21 recall the Volsung twins, to be followed by 13 associated with Siegfried himself. The last four remind us that Brünnhilde is still around.

GÖTTERDÄMMERUNG

Clearly, therefore, the Funeral Music is not a straightforward requiem for Siegfried, but also encompasses Wotan's hopes for the world, namely that it should be rescued by mankind from the disastrous grip of gods, dwarfs and giants (as suggested by Shaw). For Wotan at this moment all is uncertain: Hagen is clear and confident, Gunther is broken and Waltraute must have told him of Brünnhilde's defection. [C] What must have been clear to him was that there seemed no safe place for the emerging world.

# # # # # #

Two final observations on Siegfried

The link with Brünnhilde
Shaw likened Siegfried's dying utterance to the death-bed aria of any Donizetti tenor, thereby reducing *Götterdämmerung* to the level of what was then regarded as routine Italian melodrama, but surely he misses the dramatic point. The words Siegfried sings are:

> 'Brünnhilde! Sacred bride! Awaken! Open your eyes! . . . Who embalmed you in such restless slumber? Your awakener has come: - he wakes you with a kiss . . . he rends the bride's shackles asunder! . . . Ah, these sweet stirrings of breath! Sweet sinking! [D] . . . Brünnhilde offers me greeting!'

These are strange words. They are completely different from those in *Siegfrieds Tod*, which anticipate meeting Brünnhilde (presumably when she also dies) prior to their joint ascent to Valhalla. What do they mean as a whole? He sees himself, who is dying, as awakening she whom is 'embalmed' in 'restless slumber' and, at one and the same time, he is aware that he is falling away into some form of oblivion. The words cannot be said to be beyond understanding but, once again, where there seems little necessity for it, Wagner creates an obscurity. Obscurity or no, however, the music is the same at the end of their active relationship as it was at the beginning: it joins them together again. This may be an admission that over the last couple of days, Brünnhilde had been as dead to him. Or they may be some form of call that they are truly as one in what matters. Perhaps one of the reasons the audience is not too puzzled by the change in the valkyr between the end of Act II and her reappearance at the end of Act III is that these words and this music create a psychological bridge between the man and the woman.

Nevertheless, we can add this obscurity to that associated with Siegfried's indifference to the warnings of the Rhinedaughters. Questions remain to the very end.

[C] For those who see the *Ring* as pessimistic at core, this purple/black musical interlude may be the true musical epitaph.

[D] The word 'sinking' is a translation of 'vergehen' which can mean: fade, die away, die, decay. This translation is by John Deathridge.

GÖTTERDÄMMERUNG

The link with Wotan

One action remains for Siegfried in the drama: to repulse Hagen with his lifeless hand. This action exemplifies that he is exceptional, the word being used in its most extreme sense. He is framed by Wagner in terms that apply to no other being. This can be seen in the differences between the mythic Sigurd and the hero of the *Ring* (p.92).

One feature of the man stands out as the bench mark for his exceptional nature. This is his dominance over Wotan, from which follows the intrinsic understanding we all have that the higher being must sacrifice him or her self for the lower. In Wagner's theory within myth and also as set down in his own *Myth*, Wotan saw the *Ring* gods go into decline with the rise of mankind. The point of the remaking of Nothung by Siegfried from the shards broken by Wotan is that, by this action, authority passed from god to man. This is presented to us on stage as the destruction of Wotan's spear. Without this cast-iron link between man and god, the fall of the latter is arbitrary.

# # # # # #

Scene 4: The Gibichungs react to Siegfried's death and the reappearance of Brünnhilde
[Schirmer 303/1/3 to 318/1/1. Text from 'War das sein Horn?' to 'Brünnhilde war die Traute, die durch den Trank er vergass!']
There is unfinished business between the Gibichungs. With Siegfried dead and in possession of the Ring, any person in Hagen's position would expect opposition from one such as Gunther. In this Scene he handles that but is dumbfounded by the hidden powers of Siegfried and Brünnhilde. The Scene has three distinct parts.

A   The Set-up, with Gutrune fearful of Brünnhilde and for Siegfried's safety.
B   The conflict between Hagen and Gunther over Siegfried's Ring, which is resolved by the lifeless hand rising to repulse Hagen.
C   The arrival of Brünnhilde, who ties up and concludes the involvement of the Gibich tribe.

Much happens in only twelve minutes of stage time. Critics write of the *longuers* in Wagner's operas but never of this Scene. Speed and violence reminiscent of Jacobean drama are central.

A   Gutrune alone
This episode is *p* or *pp* throughout and the music follows Gutrune's thoughts with masterly economy.
- The mists clear to reveal the Gibich palace: *woe, treachery, manly siegfried*.
- Bad dreams have woken her: *woe, treachery; horn call* as she wonders where Siegfried is.
- She heard Grane neigh loudly and saw a woman go down to the river: *valkyr*.
- She fears Brünnhilde: *womanly Brünnhilde, destiny, woe*.
- The valkyr's room is empty and Gutrune is alone: *seigfried & gutrune, treachery*.

GÖTTERDÄMMERUNG

B The Gibichungs react to Siegfried's death

All now is fast-moving action, meticulously mirrored in the music.

- Hagen's off-stage 'Hoi-ho': *woe*. As he enters, eleven grinding repetitions of *deception* in bassoons and horns, with *woe* in trombones, ironic *siegfried & gutrune* in the horns and Hagen himself singing to *core life value* that Siegfried will no longer 'ask sweet women for love' to a viola accompaniment.
- Two bars of *fierce action,* four of *despair:* Gutrune collapses on Siegfried's corpse.
- Gutrune rejects her brother who in turn accuses Hagen: *death oath*. Magnificently defiant, to *blood-brotherhood* Hagen owns the murder and thereby asserts his right to the Ring. The two men fight: *ring, curse, woe* – and Gunther is struck down. Hagen advances on Siegfried but, to *wotan's sword,* the dead hand with the Ring rises to confront Alberich's son. The reaction is universal horror.

    The lifeless arm rising to repulse Hagen is without point if it is thought of as some hocus-pocus to get Wagner out of a hole. It has point if seen as indication that the Ring is Siegfried's as of right, and that ownership gives him authority.

The music over this period is often without motif and those that appear, other than those specifically identified, come and go. The compositional *despair* returns regularly in the last bars.

C Brünnhilde arrives

- As *wotan's sword* rises to its peak, *downfall* starts an immense descent over 3½ octaves in the violins and flutes. *erda* on the rise and *downfall* on the drop proclaim Brünnhilde's ascendency over the company. Her final comment is that they are as children who 'whine to their mothers: but a grave lament, fit for the most noble of heroes, has yet to reach my ear' is sung over *lament of death*.
- As she disabuses Gutrune of her claim to Siegfried, we hear *despair, gutrune seductress;* when Gutrune turns on Hagen: *potion, deception*. Her last action is to bend in grief over her brother's body, where she remains until the end.

Scene 5: The Immolation

[Schirmer 318/1/1 to the end. Test from 'Starke Scheite schoichnet mir dort' to 'Zurück vom Ring!']

No one who is sitting through or listening to the *Ring* actually *needs* any listing of the motifs. This might have been found useful to a reader in earlier Scenes, as an end to understand the drama in full. That is not the purpose now. Each of the six sections as detailed on p.183 is part of a ritual. In each section, a final delineation of the ritual can be heard in Brünnhilde's words, as they are

> The motifs used in this Scene.
>
> *power of the gods / loge as fire / siegfried / valkyr / valhalla / heroic love / destiny / wotan's sword / lament of death / woe / brünnhilde's purity / curse / downfall / glorification of brünnhilde / life energy / ring / rhinegold / will-to-power / erda / rhinedaughters* (3 motifs) */ war cry*

GÖTTERDÄMMERUNG

clothed with one of 24 motifs selected by the composer to end this story of restitution and future hope. To go into more detail about such a closing ritual would do nothing but bore the reader. The motifs listed in the box may now be recognized as those that best accompany the *action* as well as the *emotion* of the conclusion.

A summary of the poem is here simplified and with it is a brief explanation of structure.

A   The stage is set in which the ritual is to take place.
B   Brünnhilde's first address is to the dead Siegfried in the form of a eulogy.
C   The second address is to Wotan, whom she absolves and bids him be at rest.
D   She prepares to return the Ring to the Rhine
E   Brünnhilde has authority and now pronounces that the rule of the gods is over.
F   The Immolation itself. She greets Siegfried in their mutual sacrifice.

A – Setting
Words and music combine to establish Brünnhilde's complete authority over men and gods.

B – The Siegfried eulogy
The emergence of *heroic love* is the start of this oration in praise of Siegfried. In CM59, part of this motif is deftly joined to part of *love*. This compositional motif is prominent. The eulogy cannot easily be rationalised: if it ties up with reality, it does so obscurely, thereby sustaining the enigma that surrounds Siegfried. Brünnhilde even closes the eulogy with the unanswerable question as to why Siegfried's behaviour was as it was!

21.49 *recollection of love* **CM59**
Bar 1 is part of *love* and bar 2 is part of *heroic love*.

C – The address to Wotan
The necessity that Siegfried should die is laid at the feet of the gods. She claims that it is her great suffering (linked to Wotan's errors and to the pain brought to her by Siegfried) that now gives her the authority to absolve Wotan. She does so in the unforgettable passage 'Ruhe, ruhe, du Gott.' In this, bars 1 & 2 are part of the now melancholy *force of the gold,* bar 3 and bars 6 & 7 are *Valhalla,* and in between (bars 4 & 5) is *wotan's struggle* – now ended.

21.50 Brünnhilde exonerates the gods and the word that is passing.

D – The action is set in train
The music changes to repetitions of *valhalla* and *power of the gods*. Brünnhilde directs that Siegfried's body be placed on the pyre, removes the Ring from his finger and calls on the Rhinedaughters to be ready, at which their music and that to do with the Rhine takes over.

E – The power of the gods is at an end
A *ff* statement of *will-to-power* signifies that authority has passed from Wotan, via Siegfried, to Brünnhilde. She instructs Loge to set Valhalla ablaze. All that is necessary on earth is fulfilled: funeral pyre and the Rhinedaughters are ready, and the end of the gods is at hand. At the conclusion, she flings a torch into the pyre.

F – The Immolation
As the flames take hold, she calls Grane to her. To *glorification of brünnhilde* and *war cry* she urges the horse forward into the great and final leap. The glory of the music at this point obscures for the audience the horrible nature of being burned to death. This is something religious martyrs in the 15th and 16th centuries seemingly accepted with some equanimity, and we have to think that Brünnhilde was of their kind.

The fire takes hold, the Rhine floods up, carrying the Rhinedaughters with it. Hagen plunges after them in pursuit and is pulled down. Valhalla is seen burning as its motif rises in full splendour, and the straightforward interpretation must be that it is a justification of Wotan's initial mission to improve the world. *valhalla* and *rhine-daughters* run in counterpoint to *glorification of brünnhilde*.

# # # # # #

At this conclusion of fourteen hours of music, each listener will have his or her own thoughts. Many, many moral and dramatic aspects have been set winding forward in the preceding pages: some will have found a secure place in a reader's mind, some may have withered in that same mind as soon as the page has been turned. So it should be: the *Ring* is the property of those who see/listen to it and not those who write about it.

# # # # # #

A personal note on 'love versus power'

For me, the author, consequent upon a prolonged period of intense thought, the mighty work is confirmed as amongst the greatest but also the most mysterious products of the human mind. At times it exposes the moral and emotional essence of what it means to be a human being. Nevertheless, despite the previous paragraph, such a long period of immersion has concentrated my mind on the love versus power aspect, and I give my thoughts here for what they are worth.

For decades, this conflict within the cycle has been seen by commentators as central – a view that gained much traction with the publication of *I saw the world end* by Deryck Cooke in 1976. Problems, however, follow from the weight of such a pivotal influence. Wagner wanted his characters to be as 'flesh and blood' to his audience and – the other side of the coin – not to to be allegorical (p.15/16). Talk of 'the struggle between love and power' diverts thought toward the allegorical and away from the onstage characters as we see and hear them. Alberich and Hagen (and Mime, in his fatuous fashion) desire power to distraction but both, and Alberich in particular, are not too far removed from the prototype of a 'pantomine' villain. By this is meant that their lust is one dimensional, almost being self-gratification for its own sake. The horror that would emerge were either to be successful would be untold and without hope. So in that sense at least, it is difficult to find something in either of them that touches a dramatic chord in the spectator's mind. Their situation can be contrasted to that of Macbeth: Shakespeare makes clear that his reign had turned into bloody tyranny for his subjects, but the audience sees that the mayhem in the kingdom also weighed down on Macbeth and his demented wife with appalling effect. The drama continued within them.

Wotan and Fricka want power. But both are fully recognizable as richly human. Fricka's motives are mean but understandable: to keep Wotan under control and to maintain her high status and reputation. Wotan has recognisably major aims and stresses. He is, of course, a protagonist who is also his own antagonist. The end game of *his* drama is a draw between the two warring sides of his personality, and this is a compelling if unusual outcome.

So it is left to Brünnhilde to take the story of love versus power to its conclusion. She is made fully aware of the potential in human life by Siegmund and Sieglinde. And in her new-born humanity, she alone experiences a conflict which might be thought to connect to our own lives. This is brought to life in *Götterdämmerung* Acts I & II. Her sum of knowledge as she enters in Act III can be found on p.181. *Alles, alles weiss ich* she sings before she bids Wotan to find rest, and the clear implication of this is that she fully understands the conflict between personal desire and the call of the common good (p.398). It seems to me that this is the 'cash value', the reality of the love/power conflict. All of us are subject in our own small lives, to Brünnhilde's conflict, and thus her understanding is a beacon of future hope for humanity. The Immolation music tells us that this is so.

◇ ◇ ◇ ◇ ◇ ◇

APPENDICES

APPENDIX A

THE NIBELUNGEN MYTH
as a sketch for a drama

The text below is as Wagner wrote it and as translated by Ashton Ellis. Only the format is different. In the original there were no breaks, no subheadings and obviously no indication of the final work as composed. The *Myth* is a sketch for *Siegfrieds Tod* alone. For the sake of clarity subheadings are added, to indicate the final destination, as staged, of each part of the story. Additionally, tenses have been standardised into the present tense, and the names used are those which were finally carried forward into the *Ring*. In one instance, indicated by a footnote, the order of paragraphs has been changed.

The text can be divided into two parts: by far the larger and latter proportion relates to what became *Siegfrieds Tod* and the smaller part is the prehistory, which was later expanded to make *Das Rheingold, Die Walküre* and *Siegfried*. In detail, the *Das Rheingold* part of the story makes up 15% of the total *Myth*, 13% makes up the *Die Walküre* part and a bare 7% is devoted to what became *Siegfried*. Thus, in all, 35% is prehistory to the proposed stage action. Of the *Siegfrieds Tod* section, 12% of the total *Myth* refers to Act 1 events, 17% to Act 2 and no less than 36% to Act 3. In this 65%, which eventually became *Götterdämmerung*, we can recognize every detail of plot and emotion. These percentages are not simple statistics, for they provide significant indication of the earliest part of the creative process.

The text is italicised in the *Götterdämmerung* sections where extended passages of dialogue are given, some of which is carried forward into *Siegfrieds Tod*.

# # # # # #

<u>Das Rheingold – background</u>   In the womb of night and death the Nibelung race was engendered. It lives in Nibelheim - a place of dark underground clefts and caverns. With restless energy they burrow through the bowels of the earth, like worms in a dead body; they heat, refine and forge metal.

<u>Das Rheingold – Scene 1</u>   Alberich seizes the pure and noble gold of the Rhine, wresting it from the water's depth.

<u>Das Rheingold – Scene 2</u>   The race of giants - boastful, violent, primevally born - is worried in its primitive way of life. For their immense strength and basic mother-wit are no longer a match for Alberich's crafty plans of conquest. With alarm they see the Nibelungs forging new weapons that one day - in the hands of human heroes - will bring about their downfall.

THE NIBELUNGEN MYTH

This strife is taken advantage of by the race of gods, now waxing toward their supremacy. Wotan bargains with the giants to build a castle from whence the gods will be able to rule the world in peace and good order. When the building is finished, the giants ask for the Nibelung Hoard in payment.

<u>Das Rheingold – Scene 3</u>   With magic art Alberich fashions a Ring from the gold and this gives him the power to rule over all the other Nibelungs. He becomes their master, forcing them to work for him so that he can accumulate the immense Nibelung Hoard.

Alberich also forces his brother Mime to make for him the Tarnhelm, the greatest treasure in the Hoard, which gives the wearer the power to take on any shape at will. Thus equipped, Alberich sets out to gain dominion over the world and all that it contains.

By using their superior intelligence, the gods succeed in capturing Alberich. [A]

<u>Das Rheingold – Scene 4</u>   The gods force Alberich to ransom his life with the Hoard. He tries to keep the Ring but the gods, knowing very well that in it lies the secret of all Alberich's power, extort this also from him. Alberich then curses it: the Ring shall be the ruin of all who possess it. Wotan hands over the Hoard to the giants, but means to keep the Ring, which he will use to ensure his overall dominion. The giants resist this and Wotan hands the Ring over on the advice of the three Norns, who warn him of the downfall of the Gods themselves.

<u>General Background</u>   Now the giants have the Hoard and Ring, which is kept safe by a huge dragon. Alberich and the Nibelungs remain subjugated to the Ring. The giants, however, do not understand how to use the power of the Ring; their dull minds are satisfied with having control over the Nibelungs. So the dragon simply lies on the hoard for untold ages, in inert dreadfulness.

Confronted by the emerged splendour of the gods, the giants' race fades away and ossifies into impotence. Wretched and deceitful, the Nibelungs continue their life of fruitless labour. Alberich broods unceasingly on how he can get the Ring back.

With daring, moral enterprise the gods organise the world, bind all elements by prudent laws, and devote themselves to careful nurture of the human race. Their strength stands over all. Yet this power which enforces the existing peace is not legitimate for it was achieved by violence and cunning. Moral awareness by all is the objective behind the order the gods impose but the gods themselves are compromised by their own moral failings. Consciousness of their guilt rises up to them from the depths of Nibelheim. The slavery of the Nibelungs is not broken. The power has been wrested from Alberich but this was not for any noble end, and the soul, the freedom of the Nibelungen lies buried uselessly beneath the belly of an idle dragon. Therefore Alberich has justice on his side.

[A]   Wagner's original has the substance of Scene 3, before that of Scene 2.

Background to *Die Walküre* Wotan himself, however, cannot undo the wrong without committing yet another: only a free will, independent of the gods and able to assume and atone for this guilt, can resolve the situation. It is in mankind that the Gods see the hope for such free will. In Man the gods seek to plant their own divinity, to raise his strength so high that he may rid himself of the gods' protection. Thereby of his free will he can do what he sees for himself to be necessary.

So the gods bring up Man for this high destiny, to be the canceller of their own guilt. And they also accept that, should this happen, their own power would pass away; through the freedom of man's conscience the gods would lose all influence. Resolute human tribes, stemming from the gods themselves, already flourish: in strife and struggle they have become strong. Wotan's wish maidens shelter them with their shields and, as Valkyrs, lead those who die in battle to Valhalla. There heroes live a glorious life of jousts in Wotan's company.

Die Walküre – Act 1 But the destined hero has not yet been born. He it is who is both sufficiently strong and self-reliant, and also fully conscious of his destiny so that he can willingly embrace death should this be required. In the race of the Wälsungs shall this hero be born: a barren union is fertilised by Wotan, who gives the wedded couple one of Holda's apples to eat. Twins, Siegmund and Sieglinde (brother and sister) are born. Siegmund takes a wife and Sieglinde marries a man (Hunding) but both their marriages are infertile. To bring forth a genuine Wälsung, brother and sister then marry each other. Hunding, Sieglinde's husband, learns of the crime, casts off his wife, and goes out to fight with Siegmund.

Die Walküre – Act 2 Brünnhild, the Valkyr, shields Siegmund counter to Wotan's commands, who had sentenced him to death in expiation of the marital crime. Siegmund, under Brünnhilde's shield, draws his sword (that Wotan himself once had given him) for the death-blow at Hunding but the god receives the blow upon his spear, which breaks the weapon in two pieces. Siegmund is killed.

Die Walküre – Act 3 For her disobedience Brünnhilde is punished by Wotan: he expels her from the band of the Valkyries, and imprisons her on a mountainous rock, where she - the virgin goddess - shall become the wife of the first man to find and wake her from the sleep into which she is to sink at Wotan's command. She begs successfully for one favour, namely that Wotan will surround the rock with a terrifying fire, thereby ensuring that only the bravest of heroes will win her.

Siegfried – Backgound In due course the outcast Sieglinde gives birth in the forest to Siegfried (he who brings Peace through Victory). Mime, Alberich's brother, hears her cries and comes up from a cleft in the ground to help her. After giving birth, Sieglinde tells Mime of her fate and commits the baby to his care. She then dies.

THE NIBELUNGEN MYTH

<u>Siegfried – Act 1</u> Mime brings up Siegfried and teaches him how to smith and forge. He brings him the two pieces of the broken sword, from which, under Mime's directions, Siegfried forges the sword Balmung.

<u>Siegfried – Act 2</u> Immediately Mime suggests that the boy should kill the dragon, as proof of his gratitude for his upbringing. However, Siegfried's first act is to avenge his father's murder by killing Hunding. Only then does he do what Mime asks – he attacks and kills the dragon.

When his fingers burn from the dragon's hot blood, he puts them in his mouth to cool them; on tasting the blood he understands at once the language of all the birds singing in the forest around him. They praise Siegfried for his glorious deed, tell him about the Nibelung hoard lying in the dragon's cave and warn him against Mime, who now seeks to kill him - for he has merely used him as a means to gain possession of the Hoard.

Siegfried kills Mime, and takes the Ring and Tarnhelm from the Hoard. The birds then suggest he should woo and win Brünnhilde, the most perfect of women.

<u>Siegfried – Act 3</u> Siegfried sets forth, reaches Brünnhilde's mountain, penetrates the flames that rage around it and wakes her. In Siegfried she joyfully greets the highest hero of the Wälsung race, and gives herself to him.

<u>Background to *Götterdämmerung*</u> Siegfried marries Brünnhilde with Alberich's ring, which he places on her finger. After a while, he seeks adventure and Brünnhilde teaches him her secret wisdom. She also warns him of the dangers of deceit and treachery. They swear vows of fidelity to each other, and Siegfried sets out.

Another heroic race, descended like the Wälsungs from the Gods, is that of the Gibichungs. This race is located on the Rhine and is currently ruled by Gunther and Gutrune, his sister. Their mother, Grimhild, was once seduced by Alberich, and bore him an illegitimate son, Hagen. As the hopes and wishes of the Gods depend on Siegfried, so Alberich sets his hope of gaining back the Ring on Hagen.

Hagen is sallow of complexion, and saturnine and serious in behaviour; his features are prematurely hardened and he looks older than he is. Alberich has told him how he lost the Ring and brought him up with the purpose of regaining it. Hagen is of powerful personality and physically strong, but Alberich knows he is not strong enough to kill the dragon. Once Alberich lost his power, he could not prevent his brother Mime from trying to gain the Hoard through Siegfried. But now Hagen shall bring about Siegfried's ruin, and take the Ring from his dead body.

He is cagey and careful with Gunther and Gutrune; in their turn they fear him but prize his foresight and experience. Gunther knows there is something remarkable about his father and that he is illegitimate: he calls him once an Elf-son.

Götterdämmerung Act 1 Gunther has learned from Hagen that Brünnhilde is the most glorious of women and already desires her, when Siegfried speeds along the Rhine on a boat into Gibichung territory. Gutrune, thanks to the praises heaped on Siegfried by Hagen, falls in love with him and is persuaded to welcome him with a drugged drink. This is prepared by Hagen's magic art and is of such power that it makes Siegfried forget Brünnhilde and his marriage to her. Siegfried now wants to marry Gutrune and Gunther gives his consent on condition that he helps him win Brünnhilde. Siegfried agrees: they drink to blood brotherhood and swear oaths, in which Hagen takes no part.

Siegfried and Gunther set out, and arrive at Brünnhilde's mountainous rock. Gunther remains behind in the boat and Siegfried for the first and only time exerts his power as ruler of the Nibelungs. He puts on the Tarnhelm and uses it to take Gunther's appearance; thus transformed, he passes through the flames to Brünnhilde. In losing her virginity to Siegfried, she also lost her superhuman strength (and her wisdom, which she has bestowed on Siegfried but who has not used it) and she has only the strength of a mortal woman. Her resistance to this new, seemingly powerful lover is weak and he tears the Ring (by which she is now to be married to Gunther) from her and forces her into the cave. There he spends the night with her though, to her surprise, he places his sword between them.

Götterdämmerung Act 2 The next morning Siegfried brings Brünnhilde down to the boat and, unnoticed by her, he lets the real Gunther take his place by her side. He transports himself instantly to the Gibichung castle through the magic of the Tarnhelm.

Gunther sails back to his home on the Rhine a little later, with Brünnhilde following him in sullen silence. Siegfried, with Gutrune at his side, and Hagen are there to receive them. Brünnhilde is horrified when she sees Siegfried as Gutrune's husband and is amazed at his calm, if friendly indifference toward her. When he points her toward Gunther as her husband, she recognises the ring on his finger, suspects the deceit played upon her and demands the ring – on the grounds that it belongs not to him but to Gunther who had taken it from her. Siegfried refuses to hand it over, so she demands of Gunther that he claim it from Siegfried. Gunther is confused and hesitates.

Brünnhilde: So was it Siegfried who took the ring from her?
Siegfried: I did not take it from any woman - my right arm won it for me from the giant/dragon; through it I am the lord of the Nibelungs, and to no one will I give over that power.

Hagen steps between them, and asks Brünnhilde if she is certain about the Ring? If it is hers, then Siegfried gained it by deceit, and it can belong to no one but her husband Gunther. Brünnhilde loudly denounces the trick played on her and she is filled with an appalling thirst for vengeance against Siegfried.

She proclaims to Gunther that he has been fooled by Siegfried: "Not to you - to *this* man am I married – he it is to whom I gave myself."

Siegfried charges her with shamelessness: Faithful had he been to his blood-brotherhood and his sword lay between Brünnhilde and himself. He calls on her to say that this was so.

Deliberately, and thinking only of his ruin, she refuses to support him. All the Gibichungs and Gutrune entreat Siegfried to clear himself of the accusation and he solemnly swears that he is speaking the truth.

Brünnhilde accuses him of lying: he has broken all the oaths he swore to her and Gunther and now he forswears himself. Universal commotion follows. Siegfried demands that Gunther prevent his wife from slandering her own and her husband's honour and then he leaves with Gutrune.

Gunther sits down to one side with downcast face, in deep shame and dejection. Hagen approaches Brünnhilde, racked by the horrors of her inner storm, and offers to avenge her honour. She mocks him, as powerless to cope with Siegfried: one look from his glittering eye, which shone upon her even through that mask, would wither Hagen's courage.

Hagen: He well knows Siegfried's immense strength, but perhaps she will tell him how he may be defeated? So she who once had worshipped Siegfried and armed him by magic spells against all weapons, now advises Hagen to attack him from behind; knowing that such a hero would never turn his back upon the foe, she had not bothered to protect it.

Gunther must be brought into to the plot, so Brünnhilde and Hagen call on him to avenge his honour. Brünnhilde accuses him of cowardice and trickery. Gunther admits his fault and the necessity of ending his shame by Siegfried's death but he shrinks from betraying his blood-brotherhood oath.

Brünnhilde taunts him: What betrayals has she not had to endure?

Hagen also spurs him with the prospect of gaining the Nibelung's Ring, which Siegfried certainly will never part with until death. Gunther consents. Hagen proposes a hunt for the following day, when Siegfried shall be set upon. And perhaps his murder can be concealed from Gutrune, for Gunther is concerned for her. However, Brünnhilde's desire for revenge is sharpened by her jealousy of Gutrune. So Siegfried's murder is decided upon by the three.

Siegfried and Gutrune, brilliantly dressed, appear and invite everyone to the sacrificial rites and wedding ceremony. The conspirators make show of concord, and Siegfried and Gutrune rejoice that peace is restored.

<u>Götterdämmerung – Act 3, Scene 1</u> Next morning Siegfried strays into a lonely gully by the Rhine, in pursuit of quarry. Three mermaids, fortune telling daughters from the waters' depths, dart up from this same river from which Alberich had snatched the shining gold from which he had forged the fateful Ring. They know that the curse and power of the ring would be destroyed if it were returned to the waters, and thereby reformed into its pure original element. The daughters beg Siegfried to give it them but

he refuses. (He is guiltless but he takes upon himself the guilt of the gods and atones for their sin by means of his defiance and independence.)

The daughters prophesy evil, and tell him of the curse attaching to the ring. He must throw it back into the river or he will die that very day.

Siegfried: "You women are glib of tongue but you shall not cheat me of my power. The curse and your threats I do not count as worth a hair. As my spirit and courage bid, so do I act. And whether you call this curse or blessing, I will follow my instinct."

The three daughters: "So you think you can defy the Gods?"

Siegfried: "Show me the possibility of defeating the Gods and I will do my best to do so. I know three wiser women than you and they know where the gods struggle in fear. The gods had better beware should I choose to battle with them. So I laugh at your threats: the ring stays mine, and thus I cast my life behind me." (He lifts a clod of earth, and hurls it backwards over his head.)

The daughters taunt Siegfried, who believes himself as strong and wise whereas, in fact, he is blind and enslaved to his fate. "He has broken oaths and does not know it; he has lost a blessing far greater than the ring and does not know it; wisdom and magic were taught to him, and he has forgotten them. Goodbye, Siegfried! We know a noble woman and wife, who even today will possess the ring, when you have been slaughtered. To her! She will listen to us more carefully."

Siegfried, laughing, gazes after them as they move away singing. He shouts: "Were I not true to Gutrune, any one of you three could have seduced me!"

He hears his fellow hunting comrades drawing nearer, and blows his horn to attract them. The huntsmen - Gunther and Hagen at their head - gather around Siegfried. The midday meal is eaten. Siegfried, who is in high spirits, mocks his own lack of success at the hunt. But some 'water game' had come his way for whose capture, alas, he was not equipped! Otherwise he'd have brought his comrades three wild water-birds that told him he must die to-day.

Hagen takes up the joke, as they drink: Does he really know the song and speech of birds, then? Gunther is sad and silent and Siegfried tries to cheer him up. He sings songs about his youth: his adventure with Mime, the slaying of the dragon, and how he came to understand bird song. This train of reflection brings back memory of the birds telling him about Brünnhilde, who was destined to be his. His memory rises clearly now: how he surmounted the flame enshrouded rock and wakened Brünnhilde. Two ravens suddenly fly past his head.

Hagen interrupts him: "What do these ravens tell you?" Siegfried springs to his feet. Hagen: "*I* understand them well: they hurry to bring news of you to Wotan." He hurls his spear at Siegfried's back. Gunther, understanding now, from Siegfried's story, the background to the inexplicable scene with Brünnhilde, and realising that Siegfried is innocent, throws himself at Hagen but is unable to prevent the blow. Siegfried raises his shield, to crush Hagen with it but his strength fails and he falls to the ground. Hagen leaves. Gunther and the Gibichungs stand round Siegfried, in shock and sympathy.

He opens his eyes once more: "Brünnhilde, Brünnhilde! Wotan's radiant child! How dazzlingly bright you are as you come near to me! With a holy smile you saddle your horse and lead it toward me through the dewy air! Here am I waiting to be chosen and happy am I that you chose me for husband! Now lead me to Valhalla that, in honour of all heroes, I may drink All-father's mead, pledged to me by you, shining wish-maiden! Brünnhilde, Brünnhilde! Greeting!"

He dies. The men lift the corpse up onto his shield, and solemnly bear it over the rocky heights, lead by Gunther.

Götterdämmerung – Act 3, Scene 2   Siegfried's corpse is set down in the Hall of the Gibichungs. The forecourt extends at the back to the bank of the Rhine. Hagen calls stridently for Gutrune and tells her that a savage boar has gored her husband. Gutrune falls in horror on Siegfried's body and accuses her brother of the murder.

Gunther points to Hagen: He was the savage boar, the murderer of Siegfried.
Hagen: "So be it; if I killed him, which no one else would dare to do, then whatsoever was his is my lawful fair spoils. The ring is mine!"
Gunther confronts him: "Shameless son of an elf, the ring is mine, assigned to me by Brünnhilde: all of you heard her say it."

Hagen and Gunther fight and Gunther falls. Hagen tries to wrench the Ring from the body but it lifts its hand aloft in menace and Hagen staggers back in terror. Gutrune cries aloud in her sorrow.

Then Brünnhilde solemnly enters: "Cease your laments, your idle rage! Here stands his wife, whom you have all betrayed. My right I claim, for what must be done has been done!"
Gutrune: "Ah, wicked one! 'It is you who brought us to ruin."
Brünnhilde: "Poor soul, have peace! You were only his whore. I am his wife, to whom he swore vows before he ever saw you."
Gutrune: "Oh, I am undone! Cursed Hagen, why did you trick me into giving him the drink that drew her husband from her to me? For now I know that only through the drink did he forget Brünnhilde."
Brünnhilde: "Oh, he was pure! Never were oaths more loyally held than by him. But it is not Hagen that has killed him; for it is Wotan that marked him out and it is to Wotan that I now conduct him. And I also have atoned and I am both pure and free. For it is only he, the glorious one, who has ever possessed me."

She commands that logs be piled on the shore, on which Siegfried's body will be cremated. But neither horse, nor vassal shall be sacrificed with him: she alone will give her body in his honour to the gods. And first she takes possession of her heritage: the Tarnhelm shall be burnt with her and the Ring she puts upon her finger.

"You obstinate hero, how you constrained me! All my runic knowledge I divulged to you, a mortal man, and so deprived myself of it. But you did not use it and relied

only on your own powers. Now, however, since death has taken it from you, so does it return to me again and with it I can divine both the message on this Ring and also the oldest prophesies of the Norns!

"Hear then, you mighty gods: your guilt is atoned; thank the hero who took it upon himself! To me has he granted the power to end his work. The Nibelungs can go free - the Ring no longer binds them. Alberich will not regain it, so he will no longer enslave you. And Alberich himself shall be as free of the Ring as are you.

"Now I give this Ring to you, wise sisters of the waters' depths. May the fire that burns me cleanse and melt the evil toy and keep it forever harmless. One only shall rule: All-father in your glory! I bring this man to you as a token of your eternal power. Give him a good welcome, for he is worth it!"

To the sound of solemn chanting Brünnhilde mounts the pyre where lies Siegfried's body. Gutrune, broken with grief, remains bowed over the corpse of Gunther in the foreground. The flames meet across Brünnhilde and Siegfried. Suddenly a dazzling light is seen - above a pall of heavy cloud the light streams up and discloses Brünnhilde, armed and mounted on her horse as Valkyrie as she leads Siegfried upwards by the hand. Simultaneously the waters of the Rhine flood the Gibichung Hall, bearing the three water maidens on their waves. They seize and carry away the Ring and Tarnhelm. Hagen dashes dementedly after them, snatching for the treasure, and the Daughters seize and drag him down also into the depths.

◊ ◊ ◊ ◊ ◊ ◊

APPENDIX B

Das Nibelungenlied

The poem was written in about 1200AD by an unknown author for performance at a court somewhere between Passau and Vienna.

It tells a story of murder and revenge, the final outcome of which is the destruction of the first Burgundian Kingdom based at Worms on the Rhine. Historically this was spread over a period of 100 years but the critical event, from which the kingdom never recovered, was the catastrophic defeat suffered by King Gunnar in 436AD at the hands of the Romans. So, if an historical date for the legend has to be given, it runs from about 380AD to 436AD.

The two main characters are Kriemhilde, the sister of Gunther, and Hagen, the senior counsellor and warrior in the Kingdom. The violent deaths of Kriemhilde, Gunnar and Hagen bring the legend to a close.

The story is in two parts, this first dealing with the marriages of Sigurd and Brynhild to Kriemhilde (Gutrune in the Ring*) and Gunnar, and ending with the death of Sigurd. A critical aspect of this part is that Sigurd and Brynhild are different in kind from all the other characters: of almost superhuman strength and 'charisma' (almost to the point of caricature) they enter into and undermine Gunnar's royal court.*

* * * * *

The Kingdom of Burgundy has three princes, the eldest of whom was Gunnar, and a princess Kriemhilde – a woman of legendary beauty. Hagen was the kingdom's senior counsellor. The kingdom of the Netherlands had Sigurd as prince – of celebrated strength, virtue and courage. Hearing of Kriemhilde, he wished to marry her and set off south with his entourage.

When Sigurd was seen approaching, Hagen told the court about his legendary history and prowess. He has killed two Nibelungen princes in battle, thereby gaining great treasure, a celebrated sword Balmung and a cloak of invisibility. With the sword he killed a great dragon and, after bathing in his blood, his skin became impenetrable and he invincible.

Sigurd asks Gunnar for the hand of Kriemhilde but does not meet her. Thereafter he serves the Burgundian court and shields the country by fighting or negotiating with enemies. After a year, Sigurd and Kriemhilde meet and fall in love. Gunnar, as heir to the kingdom needs a queen and the most famous prospect was Brynhild – a princess in Iceland. A deal is done: if Gunnar weds Brynhild, then Sigurd can wed Kriemhilde. Gunnar, with entourage and accompanied by Sigurd, departs for the north in the hope

DAS NIBELUNGENLIED

of courting her. On arrival the princess notices Sigurd's magnificence first and he has to point out that it is his companion Gunnar who is the man in charge. This gives Brynhild the impression that he is but a liegeman.

Brynhild is beautiful but wild and of amazonian strength and will only marry a man who can outperform her athletically in prodigiously difficult contests. Gunnar has not the strength but Sigurd has and, in friendship to Gunnar, defeats Brynhild. He dons the cloak of invisibility, stands in for Gunnar in the several contests and thereby tricks her. She accepts Gunnar as suitor and returns to Burgundy with them.

There is a joint wedding at which Brynhild weeps – ostensibly at seeing a vassal marry a princess. On the wedding night, Brynhild wrestles and overcomes Gunther, binds him in her girdle and hangs him up on the wall. So the next night Sigurd has to step in again: in the dark he swaps with Gunnar and wrestles his bride into submission. He swaps places again with Gunnar but – ambiguously and fatally – takes from Brynhild her ring and the girdle from around her waist.

Sigurd and Kriemhilde, still in love, depart for the Netherlands. Ten years pass, during which Brynhild becomes increasingly resentful that the 'vassal' kingdom of the Netherlands has not sent tribute. She gets Gunnar to invite them back to Burgundy. Matters seem OK until the two queens quarrel outside the church as to who should precede the other inside; both claim their husbands as the greater. Tempers flare, Kriemhilde forgets herself and tells her rival that actually she is really only a concubine since it was Sigurd who first had sex with her. To prove it Kriemhilde parades the ring and the girdle which Sigurd had given to her after taking them from Brynhild.

Hagen, always resentful of Sigurd's influence over Gunnar, allies himself to Brynhild in a conspiracy against Sigurd. Gunnar also reluctantly agrees to join, after Hagen reminds him that – with Sigurd gone – he will have far greater power. Then Hagen tricks Kriemhilde into telling him that Sigurd is vulnerable to a blow on his back. (This is because it was known that he would never run from a foe, so no protection was offered.) Hagen's pretext was to know how to defend him in any upcoming battle, (similar to Loki's ruse with Balder's mother). The men go on a hunt together and Hagen murders Sigurd by striking him in the back. The story is that robbers killed him but Kriemhilde realises the truth when the wounds on Sigurd's corpse start to bleed afresh as Hagen approaches the bier at the funeral. She accuses Hagen and Gunnar and retreats into a long seclusion.

The murder occurs well before half way through the poem and then the second and longer part of the story starts. This is a chronicle of how Kriemhilde exacted vengeance on Gunnar and Hagen and is presented as a family feud which brings about the decline and destruction of the Burgundian kingdom. Brynhild virtually disappears from the story: she vanishes along with Sigurd.

This dynastic decline is condensed into a period of about 40 years up to 436AD - as reflected in the disasters and mayhem of this second part of the story. The summary is now very condensed since very little can be related to the Ring.

Kriemhilde lives in grief and pain for 13 years, brooding vengeance. After thirteen years she is approached by Attila the Hun who needs a wife. She moves to Hungary and marries him. After a further seven years she asks Attila to invite Gunnar and Hagen to Hungary. Once there, fearful mayhem and bloodshed cuts down many friends and allies alike over a period of weeks. Finally, Kriemhilde corners and captures Gunnar and Hagen. She has Gunnar beheaded and herself decapitates Hagen before she is killed by one of her enemies.

Two incidents in this second part are relevant to the *Ring*.

- The first is an encounter between Hagen and two non-human 'water sprites' as he journeys along the Danube. He is the advance guard of the Burgundian court as it makes its final, fateful trip to Hungary in which all were to die. This fate was foretold them by these sprites: Hagen and the others should turn back or face certain death.

- The second concerns the treasure won by Sigurd when he slew the two Nibelung princes. On his death ownership passed to Kriemhilde but, when she and her brothers were away on a visit, Hagen took the entire treasure and threw it into the Rhine. The purpose was to deprive Kriemhilde, and to make it available for future use by Gunnar. Because of the disaster which followed, the treasure was never found.

◇ ◇ ◇ ◇ ◇ ◇

APPENDIX C

THE VOLSUNG SAGA

The unknown Icelandic author, writing in the first half of the 13th century, intended to construct as continuous a narrative as was possible. Much material comes from what we find in The Poetic Edda *and in Sturluson's* Prose Edda; *verses from the former are quoted. We cannot be certain, however, that the author had these actual compilations to hand, since the dates of both are not known with any accuracy. However, if the compilations did not as yet exist that does not mean the author could not access the contents from the piecemeal manuscripts from which the two Eddas were themselves constructed. He also had sources of which Sturluson and the compiler of* The Poetic Edda *were unaware. For the* Volsung Saga *is the only source wherein Sigmund's full ancestry is indicated and from which Wagner derived his own version:- where brother and sister produce a son in incestuous union; where the complexity of the relationship between Sigurd and Brynhild is tackled; where a sword is thrust into and withdrawn from a tree, is broken on Odin's spear and where the shards of which are preserved and then reforged.*

In this summary, direct quotations are in italics.

The names are not changed and the correspondences with the names used by Wagner – where applicable - are in this table.

Andvari : Alberich	Brynhild : Brünnhilde	Fafnir : Fafner
Frigg : Fricka	Gjuki : Gibich	Gram : Nothung
Gudrun : Gutrune	Gunnar : Gunther	Hogni : Hagen
Loki : Loge	Odin : Wotan	Regin : Mime
Sigmund : Siegmund	Sigurd : Siegfried	Volsung : Wälsung

1 Volsung's forbears [A]

The Volsung line descends from Odin through three generations to Volsung himself. Volsung's parents were infertile so, on the prompting of his wife Frigg, Odin arranges for an apple of fertility to be sent to Volsung's father.

2 Volsung and his sons

Volsung has ten sons, of whom Sigmund is the eldest, and one daughter Signy. Sigmund and Signy are twins and acknowledged as the foremost and finest-looking of all the

---

[A] The chapter headings are my own.

siblings. The hall of his palace is built around a huge tree called Branstock, which stretches through the roof.

3 Sigmund draws the sword from the Branstock

A neighbouring king called Siggeir asks Volsung for Signy's hand. She is reluctant but defers to her father's wish that she marries him. Into the wedding celebration strides an old man: a stranger with only one eye. He thrusts a sword up to its hilt into the Branstock, saying that it was the strongest sword imaginable and would be his gift to the man who could withdraw it. [B] All try and fail, including Siggeir, until at the last Sigmund draws it forth without effort. Siggeir offers to buy it with treasure but Sigmund refuses: if the sword were intended for Siggeir it would have come to him. Siggeir is resentful at Sigmund's refusal.

4 Siggeir's malevolent invitation to Volsung

The marriage is consummated but Signy does not want to live with Siggeir, prophesying that the marriage will bring much misery. But Volsung says that honour now demands the marriage must go forward. As the couple leave, Siggeir invites Volsung and all his sons to visit him.

5 The death of Volsung and the survival of Sigmund

In due course the invitation was taken up and Volsung, his ten sons and entourage anchored in three ships off shore. Signy visits and warns that Siggier has gathered many warriors and intends to kill them all. Volsung refuses to leave, for he has never fled through fear and will not do so now. He also declines to take Signy back into protection. The next morning the company land in full armour; Siggeir and his army surround them, and in the battle Volsung and his entourage are killed. Siggeir claims the sword.

Sigmund and his nine brothers are captured. To give herself time to effect a rescue, Signy pleads that they be not immediately executed but imprisoned so that she can see them for a little more time. Siggeir maliciously agrees: a set of stocks is fashioned from a tree trunk, into which the ten brothers are locked. During each of the following nine nights, a wolf kills and eats one of the brothers until only Sigmund remains alive. During the tenth day, Signy sends a servant who smears honey over Sigmund's face and puts some in his mouth. The wolf takes the bait: first he licks the honey from the face and then pushes his tongue inside the mouth. Whereupon Sigmund bites into and grips it with desperate tenacity. In the ensuing struggle the wolf smashes the stocks, its tongue is torn out by the roots and it dies.

6 Signy and Sigmund kill her sons by Siggeir

Next morning Signy helps Sigmund to make a hideout in the forest and over the next two years Signy sends her two sons in turn to Sigmund for him to both try their courage

---

[B] This is the first of five appearances of a thinly disguised Odin.

and check whether they would help him against their father. Neither are up to it and Signy tells Sigmund to kill them.

7 Signy gives birth to Sinfjotli

To find the child who will exact revenge, Signy pays a good looking sorceress to change shape with her and, in this guise, visits and sleeps with Sigmund for three nights. She conceives, in due course is delivered of a son and rears him as the son of Siggeir. At age 10 – strong, brave and handsome – she sends him to Sigmund. Sinfjotli hates Siggeir and also passes the test of courage.

8 Sigmund and Sinfjotli kill Siggeir

From then until the boy is mature, he spends time with Sigmund in the summer. They harass, loot and kill Siggeir's people and are outlawed. On one of their expeditions they kill two men and put on the wolf skins hanging by them as they slept. They could wear them at will and for a period they roam separately as wolves, killing many who hunt them and coming to the assistance of each other when needed.

The time comes to seek vengeance against Siggeir but the attack they mount fails and they are captured. Siggeir designs a terrible end for them: to starve them to death in an enclosed tumulus, inside which they are separated by a great stone across the centre of the void, so that each would hear the suffering of the other. But Signy secretly passes the Branstock sword to them and with it they saw through the stone, escape and set fire to the hall in which Siggeir and his men sleep.

Signy comes out to tell them how it came about that Sinfjotli *'is the child of both a son and a daughter of King Volsung'*. She refuses to escape with them. She has fulfilled her destiny: to be revenged on Siggeir for the death of her father. She is content to go back into the fire to die with her husband. c

Sigmund, with Sinfjotli's help, regains his rightful kingdom which he rules well. He marries Borghild with whom he has two sons, Helgi and Hamund.

9 Helgi, son of Sigmund

Helgi appears in this chapter only and his adventures have no connection with his father Sigmund or Sigurd, his half-brother to come. That the author included him in this family saga was probably due to the prominence given to him in *The Poetic Edda* and the desire to offer comprehensive coverage of the Volsung clan. Helgi fights victorious battles with Sinfjotli as his right hand man.

His wife Sigrun is portrayed as a princess but there is also a hint that she might be more than that – namely a valkyr. In the edda this is presented as a fact: for Helgi meets and loves a valkyr, who provides him with a special sword and also protects him in battle. This tells us that there is overlap in the stories about Helgi and Sigurd. Another

---

c Text passages set in italics are direct quotations taken from the version used for this book: *The Saga of the Volsungs* translated and edited by Jesse L Byock.

THE VOLSUNG SAGA

such is that both are credited with avenging the death of Sigmund. There seems to have been two separate heroic traditions which were muddled together. (See #15 below)

The unknown author takes this incoherent matter no further. The reason is obvious: Brynhild is to be at least something of a valkyr in *this* story and Sigurd is to be the hero who is given a mighty sword. The last sentence of this quite long chapter is: *And he is out of the saga.* (So much for Helgi!)

10 The death of Sinfjotli

Sinfjotli kills a brother of Borghild (Sigmund's new wife) in a quarrel over a woman and, in revenge, she poisons him.

Sigmund takes his body to arrange his funeral. At a fjord he meets an old man who offers to take them across in a boat. Since the boat can only carry two people, Sigmund waits on the bank for his turn, from where he witnesses the disappearance in mid stream of boat, old man and Sinfjotli's corpse.

He returns home and casts out Borghild who soon dies.

11 Sigmund's last battle

Sigmund then courts Hjordis, the surpassingly beautiful and wise daughter of King Eylemi. She chooses him, old as he is, in preference to King Lyngvi, son of King Hunding.

Soon afterwards Lyngvi attacks Eylemi's kingdom. Sigmund wields his unbreakable sword to mighty effect in the ensuing battle, until an old man in wide hat and cloak appears and interposes his spear between Sigmund and his foe. Sigmund's sword breaks on the spear, Sigmund is wounded to death and the battle is lost – Eylemi also being killed.

12 The death of Sigmund

Hjordis hides in the nearby forest and watches the battle and, after Lyngvi and his army leave, having failed to find her, she comes out and finds the wounded Sigmund. She wants to succour and save him but he says:

> *Many a man lives where there is little hope, but my luck has forsaken me, so that I do not want to be healed. Odin does not want me to wield the sword since it is now broken. I have fought battles whilst it pleased him . . . You are carrying a son. Raise him well and carefully, for he will be an excellent boy, the foremost of our line. Guard well the broken pieces of the sword. From them can be made a good sword, which will be called Gram. Our son will bear it and with it accomplish many great deeds which will never be forgotten . . . My wounds tire me and I will now visit our kinsmen who have gone before me.*

On to the desolate scene comes King Alf, son of King Hjalprek. To protect herself Hjordis changes clothes with her servant: she was no longer to be the king's daughter. Natural distinction marked her out, however, so Alf tested this. He asked the same question of both women and by their answers knew who was the queen. He then married Hjordis.

13 The birth and upbringing of Sigurd

In a few months, Hjordis gives birth to Sigurd who she entrusts to the care of his grandfather Hjalprek. As tutor to the boy he appoints Regin, son of Hriedmar, who teaches him sport, chess, runes and languages. But not, however, how to choose a horse. When the time comes, Hjalprek gives him leave to choose as he wishes; on the way to the stables he meets and is accompanied by an old man who helps him choose a descendant from the great Sleipnir, Odin's horse. Sigurd names him Grani and the old man disappears.

Regin points out that Sigurd is not rich and adds that he, Regin, knows where great wealth is to be had. He knows because its whereabouts is part of his own life.

14 Regin's tale of his father and brothers

He, Regin, is one of three brothers, the sons of wealthy Hreidmar; the others being Fafnir and Otr. Regin became a smith, Otr a fisherman; Fafnir was fierce and dominant.

Otr would take the form of an otter and one day was eating fish by the river bank when the gods Odin, Loki and Heonir came by. Loki killed the otter with a stone; the gods skinned it and arrived by chance with it at Hreidmar's hall. They were captured and the price for freedom was to fill the skin and then cover it with gold. The dwarf Andvari had a great store of gold; Loki captured him in a net and took the gold and then a ring, which the dwarf tried to hide. Andvari said that the gold and the ring would be the death of whoever owned them.

The skin was duly filled and covered by the gold but Andvari's ring was needed to cover a whisker on the snout. The gods left. Fafnir killed Hreidmar and ignored Regin. To protect the treasure, he became a dragon. Regin fled and now serves Hjalprek.

15 The forging of the sword Gram

Sigurd is sympathetic to Regin but needs a sword to kill the dragon. Regin, the smith, makes two swords but Sigurd smashes them. His mother Hjordis gives him the shards of Gram and Regin reforges it. Sigurd splits the anvil to the base and the blade is unharmed. Regin wants him immediately to kill the dragon but Sigurd insisted that he first avenge the death of his father.

16 Gripir – the brother of Hjordis – foretells Sigurd's fate

This chapter is extremely short because no detail is given as to what Gripir actually says. In *The Poetic Edda* there is more detail, in which Siigurd learns of his future love for and betrayal of Brynhild, of his infatuation with Gudrun, The author may have included it because Sigurd poignantly refers to this prophecy as he dies (chapters 32/33).

17 Sigurd's vengeance for the death of Sigmund

Kings Hjalprek and Alf supply him with a fleet and men for the enterprise – a splendid dragon ship. After a few days at sea a great storm descends; as they sail by a craggy headland an old man calls from its height and is told that Sigurd, son of Sigmund, now

THE VOLSUNG SAGA

the most famous of men, is in command. He takes the old man aboard, the wind subsides and they sail to Hunding's lands, whereupon the old man vanishes.

In the ensuing battle, Lyngvi and his brother Hjorvard and all the other sons of Hunding are slain. Sigurd, with Gram in hand, wreaks the havoc.

18 Sigurd kills the dragon Fafnir

On his return, Sigurd agrees to fulfil his promise to Regin. They journey to the vicinity of Fafnir's dragon lair. Regin advises Sigurd to dig a ditch across the path along which the dragon regularly crawls to drink in the river and to lie in ambush there. Sigurd rides on to the heath and Regin runs off in fear.

As Sigurd is digging the ditch, an old bearded man appears and tells him that Regin's advice is inadequate and that he must dig several ditches. Sigmund can lie low as the dragon approaches.

The dragon comes and Sigurd thrusts upwards into his heart. As Fafnir lies dying he asks who Sigurd is and who were his parents and why he has come to kill him. He warns that the gold will bring about his death.

19 Sigurd understands bird song

Fafnir dies and Regin reappears. Sigurd cuts out Fafnir's heart and – at Regin's request - roasts it. He dips his finger in the juice to test whether it is cooked and when it touches his tongue he finds that he can understand the meaning of birdsong.

20 The advice of the wood birds

The birds give him advice which he follows. First he kills Regin when he learns that his tutor intends to betray him. Second he rides to Fafnir's den and takes the hoard (to be carried by Grani), the helm of terror and Andvari's ring. Thirdly, on being told of the wondrous Brynhild he rides to the hill where she sleeps.

21/22 Sigurd braves the fire and meets Brynhild

The hill is bright, as though a fire burns and reaches to heaven. Climbing up he comes to a rampart of shields; inside the rampart lies asleep a man in armour; cutting away helmet and armour with Gram he finds Brynhild.

On waking she asks *'is it that Sigurd son of Sigmund has come, the one who has the helmet of Fafnir and carries Fafnir's bane in his hand?'* She tells Sigurd that she had disobeyed Odin and protected the wrong man in battle and that Odin has *stabbed her with a sleeping thorn in revenge.* Odin also decreed that she must marry. *'And I made a counter-vow that I would marry no one who knew fear'.*
Sigurd: *'Teach me the way of mighty things.'*

Brynhild tells him all her knowledge – and at great length and in more detail than any other aspect of the story that the author gleaned from the Eddas. In conclusion, we have the following exchange between the two.

Sigurd: *'No one is wiser than you. And I swear that I shall marry you, for you are to my liking.'*

Brynhild: *'I would most prefer to marry you, even should I choose from among all men.'*

23 What Sigurd was like

Much is a eulogy: about his physique, colour of hair, shape of face and proportions; about physical prowess, wisdom, eloquence of speech and diplomatic skills. This is not found in the other Eddas and takes its tone from the Germanic sources: from *Thydriks Saga* in particular which, although Germanic in content, was written in old Norse.

Significant - and significantly ignored by Wagner - is the following: *He was a wise man, knowing events before they happened . . . Because of these abilities, little took him by surprise. He could speak at length, and with such eloquence, that when he took it upon himself to press a matter, everybody agreed even before he finishes speaking that no other course other than the one he advocated was possible.*

The aspect of most direct import, however, is the fame that attaches to him on account of the slaying of Fafnir. All his splendid armour and weapons were emblazoned with images of the dead monster. [D]

24 Sigurd goes to Brynhild's family home

Leaving Brynhild, Sigurd rides to an estate owned by Heimir who is married to Brynhild's sister, Bekkhild. He is told that Brynhild had chosen *to go to battle* in contrast to her sister who wanted a domestic life. Everyone marvelled at his victory over the dragon and his consequent wealth and he *remained there a long time in great honour.*

25 Sigurd and Brynhild meet for a second time and renew their love pledge with greater force

Brynhild returns home to Heimir's estate; he is described as her 'foster father'. She does not meet Sigurd but spends her time making a tapestry of his great deeds.

Returning from hunting one day, Sigurd sees her through a window and is struck by the beauty of her person and also of the tapestry. He enquires and is told that she is Brynhild, daughter of Budli. Note that Budli is also the father of Atli, the King of the Huns – not seen here as Oriental. This is clearly no ordinary household. Sigurd asks:

'When did she get here?'

'There was only a short time between your two arrivals.'

'This I learned just a few days ago. This woman seemed to me to be the best in the world'.

Sigurd then courts Brynhild in the presence of her handmaidens.

'Now it has happened as you promised me.'

'You will be welcomed here.'

[D] This feat is given great prominence by Hagen in the *Nibelungenlied* as he summarises Siegfried's achievements to Gunther before he arrives at court.

Then she rose up and the four maidens with her. She brought him a gold cup and invited him to drink. He reached toward the cup but took her hand, drawing her down beside him. He put his arms around her neck and kissed her saying: 'No fairer woman than you has ever been born ... The best day for us would be when we can enjoy each other.'

'It is not fated that we should live together. I am a shield maiden. I wear a helmet and ride with the warrior kings.'

'If we do not live together, the grief will be harder to endure than a sharp weapon'.

'I must review the troops of warriors and you will marry Gudrun, the daughter of Gjuki.

'No king's daughter shall entice me ... and I swear by the gods that I will marry you or no other woman'.

They swore their oaths anew.

26/27 Brynhild prophesies the future to Gudrun

Gjuki's kingdom lies to the south, on the Rhine. In addition to Gudrun he has three sons: Gunnar, Hogni and Guttorn. Gjuki's wife is Grimhild. Gudrun is unhappy and insecure and has bad dreams. When assured that she will marry happily she doubts it. *'It vexes me not to know who he is. I will visit Brynhild, she will know.'*

At the meeting they get round to discussing current great kings, prompting Gudrun:

'Why have you not mentioned my brothers, who are now considered the foremost of men'.

'They have not yet been sufficiently tried and I know of one who far exceeds them and that is Sigurd, the son of King Sigmund.'

Brynhild then briefly tells Gudrun of the death of Sigmund and his prophesy to Hjordis of her bearing a remarkable son and the rearing of Sigurd in the court of Hjalprek and Alf. Gudrun responds:

'You have learned about him because of love. But I have come here to tell you of my dreams for they have brought me grave concern ... I dreamt that many of us left my bower together and saw a huge stag. He far surpassed the other deer. His hair was of gold. We all wanted to catch the stag but I alone was able to do so. The stag seemed fairer to me than anything else. But then you shot down the stag right in front of me. That was such a deep sorrow to me that I could hardly stand it. Then you gave me a wolf cub. It spattered me with blood.'

Brynhild: *'I will tell you just what will happen. To you will come Sigurd, the man I have chosen for my husband. Grimhild will give him bewitched mead, which will bring you all to grief. You will marry him and quickly lose him. Then you will wed King Atli. You will lose your brothers and then you will kill Atli.'*

Gudrun: *'The grief of knowing such things overwhelms me.'*

Gudrun returns home.

28 Sigurd is slowly absorbed into Gjuki's family

Sigurd leaves Heimir in due course and comes to Gjuki's court on the Rhine and stays there. Grimhild knows that Sigurd loves Brynhild but wants him to marry Gudrun and thereby add great strength to the kingdom. A ceremonial feast is held where an oath of friendship is sworn between Gunnar, Hogni and Sigurd. Grimhild offers a drugged drink to Sigurd, and he forgets Brynhild. Over the next 30 months Sigurd is absorbed into the royal family and helps Gjuki strengthen his kingdom. Sigurd and Gudrun fall in love and marry. Sigurd and Gunnar *now swore a pact of brotherhood, as if they were brothers born of the same parents.* Gudrun bears a son Sigmund. Sigurd, Gunnar and Hogni fight and conquer together. Then Grimhild suggests to Gunnar that he marry Brynhild. Sigurd says he will ride with him.

29 Sigurd wins Brynhild for Gunnar

Sigurd, Gunnar and Hogni ride to Heimir's domain and Gunnar asks permission to marry Brynhild; Heimir said it is up to her. The three ride on to the fire-surrounded hall but Gunnar's horse will not approach it; Grani will but not with Gunnar on his back; so Sigurd and Gunnar change shapes (by a spell taught them by Grimhild) and, in friendship to Gunnar, he jumps through the fire on Grani and confronts Brynhild.

In a courtly but constrained conversation Brynhild reluctantly accepts 'Gunnar' as husband. 'Gunnar' stays three nights sharing a bed but with the sword Gram between them. On leaving, 'Gunnar' takes Andvari's ring from her, which Sigurd had previously given to her and gives her another ring from Fafnir's treasure. Then Sigurd rides back, he and Gunnar regain their proper forms and they ride home.

> *That same day, Brynhild journeyed home to her foster father. She told him in private that a king had come to her 'and rode through my wavering flames, declaring he had come to win me. He called himself Gunnar. Yet when I swore the oath on the mountain, I had said that Sigurd alone could do that and he is my first husband'. Heimir said that it would have to remain as it was. Brynhild said 'My daughter by Sigurd, Aslaug, shall be raised with you.'*

In due time Brynhild arrives at Gjuki's court and she is married to Gunnar. But *when the celebration ended, Sigurd remembered all his vows to Brynhild although he did not let this be known.*

30 Brynhild learns the truth

Some little time later Brynhild and Gudrun quarrel about whose husband is the greater and Gudrun loses her temper:

> *'It would be wiser for you to hold your tongue than to insult my husband. Everyone agrees that no one at all like him has come into the world. It is not fitting for you to insult him because he was your first man. He killed Fafnir and rode through the wavering flames when you thought it was King Gunnar. He lay with you and took*

from your hand Andvaranaut [Andvari's ring] which you can now see here for yourself.' Gudrun points to her finger and Brynhild turns pale.

31 The torment of Sigurd and Brynhild

Brynhild confronts Gunnar and tells him of her first meeting with Sigurd and their vows, and swears to bring about Gunnar's death. She destroys the tapestry of Sigurd's deeds and keeps her door open so that all can hear her lamentation and sorrow. She will speak to nobody so eventually Sigurd is persuaded to talk to her. Their conversation circles around the issues; the tension between them increases until we have:

'You surpass all men, yet no women has become more loathsome to you than I'

'Something else is closer to the truth. I love you more than myself, although I was the object of the deceit that cannot now be changed. Always when my mind was my own it pained me that you were not my wife.'

Sigurd offers to undo matters and live with Brynhild but she refuses. The conversation climaxes with this exchange.

Now she recalled their meeting on the mountain and sworn oaths – 'but now everything has changed and I do not want to live'

'I could not remember your name', said Sigurd. 'I did not recognize you until you were married. And that is my deepest sorrow.'

'I swore an oath to marry that man who would ride through the wavering flames and that oath I would rather hold to or else die.'

'Rather than have you die, I will forsake Gudrun and marry you.' And Sigurd's sides swelled so that the links of his mail burst.

'I do not want you or anyone else.'

32/33 The deaths of Sigurd and Brynhild

Brynhild then presses Gunnar to kill Sigurd but Gunnar and Hogni had sworn oaths of blood brotherhood so it was settled that the third brother Guttorn should kill him. He strikes at him when asleep and Gudrun awakes to see Sigurd soaked in blood. Sigurd and Gudrun are reconciled as he dies but among his last words to her are the following:

'And now it has come to pass as has long been foretold. I refused to believe it but no one can withstand his fate. Brynhild, who loved me more than she did any other man, caused this betrayal. I will swear this, that I never did a disservice to Gunnar. I respected our oaths and I was never over-friendly with his wife.'

Brynhild stabs herself. Then she prophesies the collapse of his kingdom and the death of each and every one of the royal family. She asks for one huge funeral pyre to be built – large enough to consume her own body and that of Sigurd. This is conceded as is her wish that a sword be laid between their bodies as on the night they resolved to marry.

# # # # # #

The remainder of the story, the last 20% of the text, is a shortened variant of the second half of the *Nibelungenlied*, moving toward the deaths of Gudrun, Gunnar and Hogni. To this is added the history of Gudrun's three children by Sigurd: sons Erp and Hamdir and daughter Swanhild. The concluding sentence records the death of Hamdir, the last of the three children to die, thereby bringing to an end the Volsung race.

◊ ◊ ◊ ◊ ◊

APPENDIX D

CHRONOLOGY – 1843-1856

A selective chronology from first stirrings to the completion of the final *Ring* text in 1856

Matters relating directly to the work itself are set out to full measure. Matters which may be thought to do no more than influence or which relate only tangentially to the work are indented.

1842, February

    He arrives in Dresden from Paris to rehearse the first performances of *Rienzi*, which take place in October.

1843, February

    He is appointed as conductor at the Court Opera in Dresden, following first *Der Fleigende Holländer* performances in January.

1843

The study of German folklore and history commences. We can be sure he read the 13th century *Nibelungenlied*. Here, Sigurd is a legendary Germanic hero with vague historical antecedents who finds himself embroiled with one Brynhild in the court of 5th Century Burgundy. By the 1840s this book, with several 19th century translations, had become the unofficial national epic and lay near the intellectual heart of the rising pan-Germanic nationalism – a search for national identity. (By the time Wagner left Dresden in 1849 four different editions were on his bookshelves.) We know also that on holiday he read Jacob Grimm's *Deutsche Mythologie* with excitement and benefit. Despite its complex content and construction, he was gripped 'by a strange enchantment: even the most fragmentary legends spoke to me in a profoundly familiar tongue . . . I saw them clearly and could hear their speech I could grasp the sources of the virtually tangible familiarity and certitude of their demeanour.' (RW/ML, 260)

1844, January

The first loan to Wagner concerning the Siegfried project from the Library is recorded. It is by the celebrated scholar von Hagen. (EM/WN, 40)

1845, October

    First performances of *Tannhäuser*.

1845, November

The *Lohengrin* poem, just completed, uses a critical scene from the *Nibelungenlied* as source for the confrontation before the cathedral between Elsa and Ortrud in Act 2. Wagner was well acquainted with this first of his *Ring* sources by this date.

1846, March

Between completing the *Lohengrin* poem and starting the composition, Wagner takes three months to write a substantial report for the Court: *Concerning the Royal Orchestra*. This is not to be found in the *Prose Works* but Newman offers a cogent summary which conveys its scope and good sense. (See EN/LRW1,463-471)

1846, May to 1847, July

This is the composition period of *Lohengrin*: first draft completed July 1846; orchestral elaboration completed July 1847. Wagner works slowly, often in the isolation of the large gardens attached to the apartment to which he moved in Spring 1847. He is now semi-detached from the practical musical life of the city. (The final orchestration was not completed until Spring 1848.)

This is the swansong and artistic apogee of the German Romantic tradition. Accordingly, on its completion Wagner found himself with a problem: what to do next? In this work he had sucked dry the potential of the genre. [A] His creative powers, in musical construction and in dramatic force, had reached new heights: witness the prelude, with its remarkable symphonic development based upon just one melody, and the musico-dramatic structure in the Ortrud/Telramund scene at the opening of Act 2. His subsequent endeavours show that he came to an artistic dead end, and there now followed a period of over three years before Wagner set down the *The Nibelungen Myth*.

1846, October

He sketches an historical drama on the subject of Friedrich Barbarossa.

1847, Spring

The report *Concerning the Royal Orchestra*, sent one year ago, is rejected by the Court. Newman believes this rejection to be a crucial element in Wagner's life. (See EN/LRW2, 473-475) After four years in the Kappelmeister saddle he reacted to the rejection by rejecting in turn the system of governance as applied to the arts by the Royal Court. He showed this by 'absenting himself wholly from meetings of the theatre committee at which the weekly affairs of the Opera were arranged, or, if he designed to put in an appearance by treating [the others who attended] with studied indifference.' (EN/WL2, 474)

Wagner was politically to the left in principle but perhaps this is the moment when he drifted toward revolution because he found good theatrical art to be

---

[A] A common theme runs through such operas, namely a sexual relationship between a mortal and an immortal. The genre started in 1816 with Louis Spohr's *Faust* and ETA Hoffman's *Undine*. There followed significant works such as *Der Freischütz* (Weber, 1817), and Heinrich Marschner's *Der Vampyr* (1828), *Hans Heiling* (1833) and Lortzing's *Undine*. Wagner carries both aspects of this supernatural engagement forward into *The Ring*.

trammelled and emasculated by established authorities. In the *Communication to my friends* he writes:

> 'While reflecting on the possibility of a thorough change in our theatrical system, I was insensibly driven to a full understanding of the worthlessness of social and political conditions which, of their very nature, could only produce the very same artistic conditions for the public which I was attacking.' (RW/PW1, 354)

From this moment, therefore, we can probably date Wagner's personal involvement in the growing social unrest, which was to influence the initial thrust of *Siegfrieds Tod*.

1847

Wagner, ensconced in the fine gardens of his apartment, reads *The Oresteia* of Aeschylus for the first time. This entrenches Wagner's fascination with both the format and purpose of Greek drama and probably plants in his mind the scope offered by a sequence of plays/operas. He also takes up again his study of the sources to be used for the Siegfried project. In 1843 he had found the *Nibelungenlied* to be too full of irrelevant incident. Much of the background to such German epics came from 10th century Nordic sources – the Icelandic eddas and the *Volsung Saga*, to which he now turns. In *My Life* he cites Grimm's mythological works, the *Nibelungenlied* again, other versions of German heroic legends and the *Volsung Saga*, from which he 'began to form this material to my own purposes. The consciousness of the close primeval kinship of these old myths, which had been shaping in me for some time, thus gradually gained the power to create dramatic forms which governed my subsequent works.' (RW/ML, 343)

1848, Spring

With the orchestration of *Lohengrin* now complete, Wagner turns his attention to political issues and working out his Siegfried project, now being seen as a political allegory.

1848, 1 April

The singer/actor/director Eduard Devrient (1801- 1877) notes in his diary that Wagner 'told me about a new plan for an opera based on the Siegfried legend'. This is the first contemporary notification we have of the project. (SS/WR, 59)

1848, May

> Despite the above, Wagner works out a plot for a drama *Achilleus*. Achilles is the son of Thetis, an immortal water-nymph. The outline plot is that she visits her son as he is mourning for Patroclus and offers him immortality if he foregoes vengeance for his friend. Achilles rejects divine immortality, choosing the stress and struggle of humanity. The goddess bows before him, recognizing that he is greater than the gods. 'Man is god perfected. The eternal gods are only the elements which create man. Creation finds its ultimate conclusion in man. Achilles is higher and more

perfect than the elemental Thetis.' The theme, as given in the last quotation, (CvW/RW,139) finds its ideal expression, three years later, in the figure of Brünnhilde, who finds fulfilment as a mortal woman. This may have yet been far from Wagner's mind but, in any case, as an expression of a Greek myth, it could never fully engage his imagination in the way that Siegfried was now doing. [B]

1848, June

He delivers a speech to the *Vaterslandverein*, a Dresden political club: a fiercely republican tirade, calling for the dissolution of the aristocracy but not the removal of the king, who would become the 'first person' of a new Republic. The speech (full text is in RW/PW7) is of value as a guide to Wagner's attitudes in the early development of the Siegfried story and is referred to in Chapter 8. This is the period when Wagner's writings changed direction. Up to then they had been almost entirely concerned either with matters of the theatre and drama. Now they were to be charged with revolutionary politics which involved searching, if dimly focussed, thoughts on history and the future nature of society. But Wagner was not a hot-headed revolutionary. The year as a whole saw him in the act of preparing himself for the expansion of his artistic horizon, by writing or thinking, and the development of new projects. It took another year before he became an active revolutionary.

Nevertheless, from the beginning, Wagner saw his Siegfried project as revolutionary in content and in style – the two aspects went hand in hand. James Treadwell describes this aspect exactly: 'As the *Rheingold* prelude quietly hints, *The Ring* . . . was born in dreams of a world wiped as clean as a blank slate, ready to receive the imprint of what Wagner's 1849 essay called "the artwork of the future"; one that the goddess Revolution had turned to "nothing", to "dead rock", so that "fresh life" could well from it as the watery scales of the prelude spring up from the utter silence.' (JT/IW, 68)

1848, October

The story outline: *The Nibelungen Myth, as a Sketch for a Drama* is completed.

1848, October

Wagner develops the outline he had made in 1846 on the subject of Friedrich Barbarossa. This enlarges his concept set out in his June *Vaterslandverien* speech. This expansion has a detailed speech in which Barbarossa reflects on the nature of kingship.

There is a puzzle here. Looked at with a clear eye, there was no likelihood that the project would ever come to fruition.

[B] Ernest Newman gives us a comprehensive view of the range of Wagner's activity during 1848 in Chapters 1 and 2 of Volume 2 of his *Life of Richard Wagner*.

1848, 12 October

Devrient's diary: 'He reads us his compilation on the Siegfried legends; it showed great talent. He wants to turn it into an opera, but nothing will come of it, I fear. Nordic myth finds little sympathy, not least because it is unknown; and these rough-hewn giants must be left to the imagination, theatrical reality belittles them and turns them into playthings.' (SS/WR, 60) The clear implication is that Wagner read the entire *Myth* to Devrient but what seems to stand out in his mind are the giants and the Nordic background which occupy the first third.

1848, 20 October

The prose draft of *Siegfrieds Tod* is completed. In the shaping of the dramatic action, he used the historico-legend mayhem and murder of the Gibichung (Burgundian) Court, which he had sketched out in the latter section of the *Myth*. This focussed on Siegfried's arrival at the Court and on his betrayal and foul murder. This draft opens in the hall of the Gibichungs and there is no prologue with the Norns, Brünnhilde and Siegfried. Wagner reads the draft to Eduard Devrient, who tells him that the audience will need to know some history of the lovers if the drama is to make sense.

1848, November?

Lohengrin had been accepted and money spent towards its staging by the theatre, but at about this time the production was cancelled. Wagner must now surely have wondered whether there was a future for him in the city.

1848, November

Wagner completes the poem of *Siegfrieds Tod,* which now includes the prologue – as advised by Devrient.

1848, very late

He finishes a 52 page sketch for a drama *Jesus of Nazareth*. This includes explanatory notes on its underlying meaning and interpretation. Jesus is depicted as a revolutionary hero fighting against almost all aspects of current society. The dominating influence is that of Pierre-Francois Proudhon (1809-1865) a French politician and social philosopher. In his 1840 book *What is property?* he coined the phrase 'La propriété – c'est le vol!' (Property is theft!): to store up more than you need is to rob your neighbour. The laws on property ownership must, therefore, be sinful: 'The more laws the more corrupt the world.' Property governs everything: marriage is about the protection of property. (Full English text available on-line in PDF format.)

Jesus is shown as planning and shaping his own death in order to destroy the law; as Wagner put it, 'The atonement of the world is therefore to be effected by nothing but the upheaval of the law'. This portrayal is derived from the philosophy of Ludwig Feuerbach, whose work much influenced Wagner in the 1840s. Jesus is presented as a man – and not divine - who 'redeems' Mankind by leading it to realise that it can protect itself from evil simply by overturning the law.

This whole text is Wagner's revolutionary fervour at its most raw and didactic, and it would not have made good drama. However, for all its faults, the work has drive and passion, which is more than can be said for his Barbarossa and Wieland projects (qv). Proudhon's philosophy finds but a vestigial corner in the text of the *Ring* but Feuerbach's influence is noticeable in more than one way.

In *A communication to my friends* the reason given for writing *Jesus of Nazareth* is that he saw little prospect of taking the Siegfried project forward and that he was 'burning to write something that would take up the message of my tortured brain and speak it in a fashion that would be understood in present day life.' (RW/PW1, 378) Creative energy and thought went into these pages – 'burning' seems an accurate word. To turn a cliché on its head, however, although his heart was in them his head must have known they would be still-born. (Full text is in RW/PW8)

1849, January?
The first revision to the Immolation text in *Siegfrieds Tod* removes the original concept of Siegfried's death as the means whereby the gods survive and stay in power, and replaces it with text that predicts their extinction.

1849, early
Die Wibelungen is written and published: a rambling mix of history and myth. Newman quotes William Ashton Ellis with approval: for Wagner, 'the Hoard was also the Grail, and Friedrich was Siegfried, and Siegfried was Baldur, and Baldur was Christ.' Topics include: the centrality of Siegfried and the hoard to German myth, the function of myth, the pre-eminence of the German race and the enfeebling of our awareness of myth which results in a society based on property. One third specifically covers Barbarossa – his lineage, heritage and expectations. It would be easy to think that the essay relates more to this aborted project than to the *Ring,* but it is worth noting Ernest Newman's observation that Wagner saw Friedrich as 'a historical rebirth of the old-pagan Siegfried'. (EN/LWR2,21) For, although the space devoted to Siegfried is not large, the references and their context are important. Unmistakeable clues as to Wagner's view of his hero are found in it though there is no reference at all to the actual plot as outlined in the *Myth*. (Full text is in RW/PW7)

1849, April
The Revolution: Wagner writes an explosive journal article anonymously: Europe is in ferment; there is a coming storm brought about by the 'goddess of revolution'. (Full text is in RW/PW8.)

1849, May

Wagner flees into exile from Dresden after the abortive rising and ends up in Zurich. This heralds the start of a period of intense creativity: a flood of essays on theatre, politics and mythology, plus a detailed sketch for one more drama.

1849, June

Art and Revolution published. This is the first of the treatises to appear after his flight to Zurich, though it was actually written in Paris. The message is that modern society should look to the Greek city state to see how it should be done. It is also a diatribe against bourgeois art. (Full text is in RW/PW1)

1849, September

The Artwork of the Future: This is the second Zurich treatise, elaborating and expanding the themes of the previous piece. (Full text is in RW/PW1)

1849, December

Completes a sketch for an opera – *Wieland der Schmied* – which he hopes will be suitable for Paris. (Full text in RW/PW1) He is urged on in this by Minna and Liszt. The story derived from Norse mythology about a lame smith who wreaks vengeance and forges wings that enable him to escape. Nothing comes of it and the drama is poorly articulated. This is the last of the 'competitors' to the Siegfried project to bite the dust, being preceded by *Achilleus, Friedrich Barbarossa* and *Jesus of Nazareth*.

1850, August

Composes some musical sketches for the opening prologue of *Siegfrieds Tod* – 150 bars in total. This activity is clear indication that Wagner's mind is now solely focussed on Siegfried. He was by then preparing to write *Opera and Drama*, which sets out his artistic stall and commitment to something entirely new; we can be confident that the die was now cast.

Why did it take so long for Wagner to make up his mind on the Siegfried project? The answer must be uncertainty of will. He never lacked courage in his work but he must have had questions in his mind from the start about the feasibility of bringing it off, which doubts prompted the comment about *Jesus of Nazareth* previously quoted.

1851, January

Wagner's major theoretical work, *Opera and Drama*, is written - in three parts. The first part – *Opera and the nature of music* – sets down how current operatic practice is all astray. The second part – *The play and the nature of dramatic poetry* – offers a history of theatre from the Renaissance to the present and sees the current state as in the doldrums. The need now is for a means of bringing together music and poetry in a new type of combination. The third part – *The arts of poetry and tone in the drama of the future* – attempts to show in detail how this integration might work. Essentially the whole is a theoretical 'thinking through' of the creative process slowly developing in Wagner's mind – a rationalisation of the *why* and the *how*. (This book makes up RW/PW2)

1851, June
Der junge Siegfried: the prose draft and poem are written.

1851, November
The prose sketches for *Die Walküre* and *Rheingold* are completed.
    A communication to my friends is written, though it is not published until 1853. This is a long essay in which Wagner sets down the pattern of his artistic career and progress up to that point and is a valuable source for Wagner's artistic life at this time. (Full text is in RW/PW1)

1852, June
The poem for *Die Walküre* is written.

1852, November
The poem for *Das Rheingold* is written.

1852, December
The final amendments are made to *Siegfrieds Tod* which now becomes the *Götterdämmerung* text that will be set to music.

1853, January
50 copies of the complete poem of the *Ring* are privately printed and circulated to intimate friends and well-wishers.

1854, November
The composition of *Das Rheingold* is started.

1856
From the year 1851 onwards, Wagner had worried at the words that Brünnhilde would sing at the end of *Götterdämmerung*. He changed or amended text two more times, the second of which occurred in this year 1856. The changes were not set to music.

◇ ◇ ◇ ◇ ◇ ◇

APPENDIX E

Sigurd der Schlangentödter

This work encapsulates the romantic view of the ancient tale - how the majority of scholars and writers interpreted the sagas - best exemplified in the *Volsung Saga*. It is examined in some detail to illustrate the different view taken by Wagner - from inception to conclusion. Elizabeth Magee (Footnote, p.55) suggests that it was a resource for the composer as he crafted the *Myth* and *Siegfrieds Tod*, and there is evidence for this. Be that as it may, in one sense it does not matter: comparison with the *Ring* throws light on the paths Wagner did not follow as well as those he did.

Friedrich de la Motte Fouqué - a German of French extraction - was a notable and popular author, and a leading proponent of the growing interest in the Nordic sagas underway in the early part of the 19th century. He is remembered now only as the author of the 1811 novella *Undine*, the first writer to reinterpret the ancient Greek myth of the water sprite who wanted to be human. The story was used by ETA Hoffman for his 1816 opera of the same name. This work is regarded as the first manifestation of what became a popular plot in German theatre and opera, namely the wish of an immortal man or woman to bond with and love a human. Commentators consider that Wagner's first opera *Die Féen* took colour from Hoffman's work. It is the basis of Dvořák's *Rusalka*.

Fouqué was widely read in his time; was a friend of Madame de Staël, of the celebrated poet and critic August Schlegel and of the theatrical authority Ludwig Tieck. He was also a friend of Wagner's scholarly uncle Adolph. When Wagner got to know Adolph well, he was in his 50s; their relationship was particularly strong during a prolonged visit in 1827 when the composer was 14, and he both lovedthe man, and was proud of his achievements as a scholar. It is possible that Wagner came across *Sigurd* when young and in his uncle's house. In all events, he knew and liked Fouqué's work. The night before he died he was reading *Undine* and comparing her with his own Rhinedaughters.

Sigurd der Schlangentödter was written in 1808, the first modern German dramatization of the Nordic sagas. It is based very closely on the *Volsung Saga* with the odd tiny touch from the *Nibelungenlied*. The text is not a play but a dramatised poem (ideal for a play-reading) which covers Sigurd's life from the time he owns his father's invincible sword to his death - encompassed by the two Wagner operas in which Siegfried appears. The poem consists of a prologue, followed by six 'adventures', every one of which features Sigurd.

Given Wagner's interest in the subject it is nigh impossible to avoid an image of him glancing at a copy of *Sigurd der Schlangentödter* from time to time during the period when he sorted and sifted the primary sources. This appendix examines and compares the text with the *Myth, Siegfrieds Tod* and *Der Junge Siegfried*. I shall start by lining up the *Sigurd* plot structure against that in *Der junge Siegfried* and *Siegfrieds Tod*, and summarising the main lines of the story.

Adventure = *Ring*	Action
Prologue = JS1	Regin reforges Sigmund's sword for Sigurd.
1 = JS 2	Sigurd kills the dragon Fafner, is warned about Regin by the woodbird and kills him too.
2 = JS 3	Sigurd woos and wins Brynhild in two encounters.
3 = ST 1.2	Sigurd arrives at Gunnar's court, forgets Brynhild and loves Gudrun.
4 = ST 1.3	Sigurd wins Brynhild for Gunnar.
5 = ST 2	Gudrun flaunts the ring in a quarrel with Brynhild, who resolves that Sigurd must die.
6 = ST 3	Sigurd is murdered and is cremated on a joint pyre with Brynhild.

Were it a case of plagiarism in a modern court, three prime pieces of evidence would first be presented. Firstly, as seen in the table, the Act structure of the two Wagner operas is very like that of the poem. Secondly, there is the *coup de theatre* of Sigurd's instant infatuation for Gudrun. Fouqué is not so sudden with this as is Wagner, who needs to speed things up for the stage; his poem, designed to be read rather than performed, can be relaxed about the time scale. Nevertheless, Sigurd is lost from the instant that he first sees Gudrun and the author's writing here has a potency that would appeal to the composer. Thirdly, the scene in which Sigurd, mounted on Grane, breaches the wall of fire is preceded by one in which the three Norns stand at the foot of the mountain and explain what has happened in the past and what is to happen next. There is no hint in the primary sources that the Norns had any particular interest in any of the valkyrs, nor in Sigurd. Fouqué's Norn's scene is powerful in its own right and he places it judiciously within his own plot. That positioning could not work for Wagner: he took the event and placed it elsewhere. Other indications of influence are mentioned under each section below.

In the summary of each section of the poem, direct quotations are italicised. Commentary and comparison between the poem and the different texts of the *Ring* follow each summary.

Prologue compared to *Der Junge Siegfried*, Act 1

Summary
Sigurd, his mother Hjordis and his 'mentor' Regin live in the great household of his grandfather King Hjalprek. The scene is in Regin's forge.

Regin tries and fails to make the sword with which Sigurd hopes to avenge the death of his father Sigmund. Sigurd smashes the sword to pieces on the anvil and is furious. He already has his horse, chosen by him from his grandfather's stable on the advice of an old one-eyed man who suddenly appeared and pointed out a horse that was descended from Odin's own horse. He waits only for the sword.

As he chases off Regin, his mother appears, attracted by the row. She exonerates Regin: the problem is with the materials he is using. She knew in advance that the sword made with such local materials could not survive in Sigurd's mighty hands. Therefore she brings him now the shards of his father Sigmund's sword, Gram, and tells him about it. Years ago an old one-eyed man had thrust it up to the hilt into the great tree that stood in the hall of Volsung, Sigmund's father. Only Sigmund was able to pull it from the tree. (Sigurd thinks immediately of the old man who had helped with his horse and senses that it is his ancestor.) Sigmund used it successfully in battle until the old man came again in the middle of a fight with King Lyngvi and interposed his spear. The sword broke and Sigmund was mortally wounded. His dying words to Hjordis were to guard the shards and give them to their as yet unborn son, who would be a great hero.

Sigurd vows to avenge his father.

Regin reappears, is persuaded to reforge Gram. With it Sigurd splits the anvil in two. Hjordis advises him to be less wild. Nevertheless, she knows that he is a Volsung and must leave home. He may never come back. As Sigurd rushes off with Regin, Hjordis returns to her room – a mother who suffers in silence.

Commentary

The content of this scene derives from the *Volsung Saga*. The relevant chapter summaries in the Appendix are: 2, 11, 12, 13 and 15. Fouqué changes little, other than to reorder to fit with his narrative.

When Wagner was constructing the *Myth* he had already chosen Sieglinde as Siegfried's mother, so all trace of Hjordis was erased. But Mime is retained as he who reforges Siegmund's sword. The plot in the *Myth* for this first scene in which Siegfried appears is a rerun of Fouqué, without Hjordis. By 1851 and *Der junge Siegfried* nothing of Fouqué remains other than that the sword is forged. All Siegfried's pre-history is derived from elsewhere.

Adventure 1 compared to *Der Junge Siegfried*, Act 2

Summary

Sigurd has killed King Lyngvi and avenged his father, and is now willing to fulfil an obligation to Regin and kill Fafnir. Then he will have his own money (for he does not want to depend on his mother's fortune) and with this he'll have a good life and beautiful women. He relies on his experience in defeating Lyngvi to question the advice now tendered by Regin as he advances on the dragon's lair: *Was I foolhardy when I fought*

Lyngvi? He had made my kingdom his own and knew it better than I did – the thief had been there a long time. But I found him there in the middle of my land. Did I not avoid all his treacherous doings? Didn't I discover the ambush in the valley? Didn't he finally succumb there to my shining blade? I struck him and the land was mine!

Regin brings Sigurd to the path along which the dragon Fafnir drags himself each day to drink from the river. The dragon approaches and Regin leaves. The old man appears again and tells him of a better place to hide. Sigurd recognizes him easily now. On his way to avenge his father the same man had come aboard the ship he commanded and helped him weather an immense approaching storm. He now tells Sigurd where to hide and leaves. Sigurd kills Fafnir by thrusting Gram into his heart. The dragon dies instantly without speaking.

Regin returns and takes centre stage. He turns on Sigurd: Fafnir was his brother and now Sigurd has slaughtered a member of Regin's family, and must absolve himself by getting the gold from Fafnir's house and handing it over to Regin. *It's my inheritance. Fafnir and I killed our father to get the gold, then Fafner threatened and forced me to flee - he took the form of a dragon and protected the gold. Now he is dead and I must inherit.*

Sigurd points out that if Regin was involved in his father's murder, then he also stole the gold. So now he, Sigurd, should have rightful possession. Regin must think of some other form of atonement and Sigurd will oblige him.

As alternative, Regin suggests that Sigurd roast Fafnir's heart and bring it back so that he, Regin, can eat it. Regin gloats as Sigurd goes off to do so: he has already drunk some of Fafnir's blood; to eat the heart will give him possession of Fafnir's magic powers and with these he will kill Sigurd. Then he, Regin, will be transformed by magic into a handsome, rich young man who looks like Sigurd (no mention of anything like a magic helm). He will win the hand of Brynhild – the nearby lord's daughter – who lies surrounded by flames in the fells. He can already feel power rising in him, and he falls asleep and dreams of his future conquests.

Sigurd returns but he is changed. Whilst cooking the heart, fat and blood splashed on him and he can now understand what the birds are singing. They have told him of Regin's falsity. With his sword he mortally wounds him as he sleeps. As Regin dies he tells Sigurd of cosmic matters that only he, of all men on earth, knows.

The form of Regin's narration suggests a song or chant: Odin and Loki came down to earth. Loki killed Otter, the third son of Hreidmir and therefore Regin's brother. The gods came to Hreidmir's house and were captured. The ransom was to be gold. Regin concludes his narration, which might have been in song, as follows:

> *Loki went swiftly away into the wide world -*
> *Caught Andvari the dwarf - forced from him the gold.*
> *Andvari cunningly pleaded: 'Let me keep this ring,*
> *For it will guide me on to fresh shining treasure!'*
> *But Loki would not:*

> *'No, nothing for you!' Wrenches the ring away.*
> *Andvari's curse has terrible force: 'Tear your master!*
> *Whoever he may be - pull him to ruin!'*
>
> *Hriedmer took ring and gold -*
> *Was battered by his children to death.*
> *Hreidmer's children - Fafnir and Regin -*
> *They are red!*
> *Red with the father's blood - and all for the gold.*
> *Beware, barbaric child, beware the ring and its power!*
> *Shun the fearful ring of Andvari! Curses come with it*
> *And as Regin and Fafnir fall,*
> *Now the curse passes to you!*

Sigurd nevertheless decides to keep both gold and ring.

<u>Commentary</u>
Relevant chapters within the Volsung Saga are: 14, 17, 18, 19, 20.

In the Prologue, various narrations tell us that Odin planted the sword and the other past involvement with Sigurd, and the god appears in this adventure. But his involvement is not followed through and this is a weakness: Odin is only there because he is in the *Volsung Saga*. Moreover, as the story developed and as we see in *Der junge Siegfried*, when the connection between god and hero has emerged, Wagner discarded all reference to Odin as ship's pilot, and as adviser on horse flesh and dragon slaying. Instead, he presents Wotan in four confrontations with major characters: the first in JS1, the second in JS2, and the third and fourth in JS3.1.

The critical matter here is Wagner's concision when compared to Fouqué's loose narrative. Let us first look at the *Myth*. We are not to think of this as in any way finished, and this is demonstrated by the inclusion, possibly influenced by Fouqué, of the reference to Siegfried killing Hunding as an act of vengeance for Siegmund's death. Even without Wotan's involvement, that is an irrelevance in the drama, and with that removed, all is terse and large scale: the fateful encounter with the dragon, the advice of the wood bird, the killing of Mime and the departure in pursuit of Brünnhilde. All the Fouqué material, which emanates from the sagas, is jettisoned: gone is Odin's advice to Sigurd, Regin's wish to eat Fafnir's heart after Sigurd has cooked it, with all the paraphernalia that would require. Moreover, Wagner's emphasis on the young Volsung persists right through *Der junge Siegfried* and the later *Siegfried*. In the finished story, as composed, Siegfried is on stage for 70% of the time and the other scenes for the dwarfs and the god occupy 30% of stage time. Fouqué efficiently crams in much myth and legend but it is too much for the staged drama.

Note that the wood bird tells Sigurd about Regin but not about the gold or about Brynhild.

Adventure 2 compared to *Der Junge Siegfried*, Act 3, Scene 2

<u>Summary</u>

In the castle on the mountain, Brynhild lies asleep and in armour. Three Norns circle round her. Their names: Wurdur, Werdandi and Skuld are as in the *Poetic Edda* and respectively they monitor the past, present and future – the happenings of all time until all will end. This end will include their own.

They record the circumstances which lead to Brynhild's punishment. Now she can only dream of battles, surrounded by the 'flickering flames'. *But somebody will dare, riding with sword through the threatening, flickering flames - to spur on the horse and enter in glory. Brynhild will awaken to thoughts of a wedding of splendour . . . He, the daring one, arrives quickly through the whirlwind of the fire - reflected back from the gleaming gate. What is he after now? A quick prize for a daring ride? He mounts the stone steps; his armour clatters inside the building.*

Their song ends in unison: *as we leave, fog will engulf us and our fate looms.*

Sigurd enters and sees the armoured youth lying in sleep. He cuts away the armour. 'Oh! That's not a man! Ah! A young woman – the perfect image of grace and of supreme love.'

Brynhild wakes but feels she is still in a magic dream. Sigurd accepts the magic: '*If it is thus, let it last forever, whether asleep or awake. I have never been happier. Do not sleep again even though you were even then so calm and beautiful – with your flower-like mouth.*'

Brynhild welcomes him '*as the daring one who knows not fear. It that were not so you would not have awakened me, to claim the flower of my beauty . . . I am yours given you by the gods . . . I know you – Sigurd son of Sigmund, grandson of Volsung, the killer of the dragon Fafnir.*' When Sigurd asks her how she knows him she replies: '*Oh Sigurd, are you surprised? Don't you know that the first flower of the world must always find its destined perfect home?*' She raises a goblet.

'Greetings to the daylight hours,
Greetings to the evening hours.
Daylight look at these lovers
And give them eloquence and wisdom!
Give them victory!
We salute the gods and goddesses.
We salute the richness of the earth!'

She gives him the goblet: '*I offer you this drink, consecrated to your strength and daring, and to the magic that protects you*'.

Sigurd: '*The drink honours our wedding. I swear faithfulness to you forever, and you are now mine in holy marriage.*' As they prepare to go to the marriage bed, she tells Sigurd that his adventurous spirit will take him to new adventures, lists the runes to help him and gives advice on behaviour.

Sigurd: *'Whatever happens I remain yours. Take this ring as proof. It is known as Andvari's ring.'*
Brynhild interrupts: *'Do you hear the Norns? They have been circling us and now are leaving. Our union is protected by them . . . When you leave me go to my brother-in-law King Heimir . . . Don't ever change.*

Then there is a short interlude with implicit change of scene, rather as we find in a film script, and in which we are introduced to Grimhilde, the mother of Gunnar and Gudrun. She has heard about Sigurd's victory and has plans to entice him into their kingdom. She is in a wood gathering the herbs that can be used for the drug of forgetfulness. This ominous scene of witchcraft is a prelude to the second love scene.

Sigurd has travelled to the family home of Brynhild, where he sees her making tapestry - now very much the princess and the valkyr aspect negligible. After discussion with a relative he meets with her again. There is a second love scene (a full 12 pages of text – 8% of the book – are love scenes between the two of them) which Fouqué manages to meld effectively with the earlier one: hints that this double meeting was fated and that Sigurd and Brynhild are inseparable.

They plight love anew but their future together is now clouded by Brynhild's power of prophesy. This trait within the sagas is heavily emphasised by Fouqué as Brynhild warns Sigurd of the problems before them. *'I warn you of a deluding net. You look only at the beauty of women and so believe them. But they break promises . . . No day will dawn when we two will be united . . . Your fate lies with Gudrun . . . Know that the love of we two women shines on you as you travel your short path on earth.'*

Sigurd protests: *'I call on you gods! I swear that Gudrun's charms will not lure me from this woman here whom I won in the heat on the mountain.'*

Brynhild rises to her feet. *'You are binding us together. Be it so unto death. The token of your faith is Andvari's ring on my left hand.'* The scene ends movingly with Brynhild's words: *'Wait! Stand before me just once more. Ah, that is what you look like. Look at me again and do not forget me. Who knows how and when we will see each other again. Now go! No human pleasure lasts for ever.'*

Commentary

Relevant chapters within the *Volsung Saga* are: 21, 22, 24, 25, 26 and 27. Chapter 23 is descriptive and not a narrative, so we see that Fouqué here follows the story closely.

A distinctive element is Brynhild's power of prophesy which so shadows the action. This has its roots in *Volsung Saga* 26 and 27, when Gudrun visits Brynhild and asks for her dreams to be decoded. These scenes are bypassed by Fouqué, for whom Gudrun is a minor character - as is Wagner's Gutrune. Fouqué cleverly uses this prophetic ability in Brynhild to fashion tension. The effect is to provide a unique context for Sigurd's betrayal of his lover. Wagner chose to ignore all this and to articulate this central issue by different means.

In the *Myth* the courtship of Brünnhilde by Siegfried and the consummation of their love is sketched in very briefly. Wagner uses about 80 words but they are nevertheless a succinct summary of this second adventure. The two encounters are specifically indicated. In the first (*Myth*, *Siegfried*, Act 3), Siegfried braves the fire, wakens Brünnhilde, and they become lovers. In the second (Background to Götterdämmerung) they marry and exchange rings (Alberich's ring being that given to the woman) and 'after a while' Siegfried leaves for adventure. Fouqué has Brynhild imparting her wisdom in the first encounter and, in the *Myth,* Wagner transfers this to the second, but there is good dramatic reason for this. The sagas show Sigurd and Brynhild as a pair destined for each other, which is followed by Siegfried's journey to her ancestral home where they marry (VS 25). Wagner simplifies this in his very first outline by combining courtship and consummation within the first encounter. When we move beyond the *Myth*, the two love scenes we see in Fouqué are replicated in JS3.2 and ST1.1.

In the first of these love scenes, the similarity of the words with which Brünnhilde greets Siegfried to those in the *Poetic Edda* has been noticed by many, notably by Deryck Cooke. It is surely possible, however, that the prompt came equally from Fouqué. And if not, Sigurd's first sight of Brynhild without her armour (Oh, that's not a man!) must be the only previous source for Siegfried's identical cry.

Now we come to the Norns, whose appearance is prime evidence that Wagner had *Sigurd der Schlangentödter* to hand. Fouqué was the first to introduce the Norns into drama as characters who speak. In the primary sources they are abstractions. It may be that Wagner was inspired suddenly to think of and introduce them in ST1.1 as a response to Devrient's suggestion that he should recount some prehistory, so that the audience could follow the story. To insist on that, however, is perverse if at the same time Fouqué's impressive invention is completely overlooked. The impact of the first meeting between Sigurd and Brynhild is in part brought about by the mysterious activity of these three representatives from another dimension.

Adventure 3 compared to *Siegfrieds Tod*, Act 1, Scene 2

Summary

King Guiki (Gibich) sits with his wife Grimhild; they worry that their sons Gunnar and Hogni will be killed by the enemies they are now fighting. Guiki also knows, however, that Grimhild brews potions that stir dangerous ambitions in their children. As they talk, Sigurd arrives - as Grimhild had anticipated. She hopes he will stay and help strengthen the kingdom. Sigurd is already uneasy that his vows to Brynhild will fade and is impressed with the rich life he sees in the court. His first request is that someone will tend his horse (of 'noble lineage') and the next that they will protect the treasure he brings. Almost immediately Gunnar and Hogni arrive; they aggressively challenge Sigurd: the contests are first a spear thrown against a protecting shield and second a wrestling match. Sigurd overwhelms Gunnar in the first and throws Gunnar and Hogni simultaneously to the ground in the second. Mutual friendship then ensues.

Grimhild offers him a drink that is to seal a union between her two sons and Sigurd. The effect is instantaneous: *'I have forgotten something that was very dear to my heart . . . as though it fell from my mind into a bottomless ocean . . . I saw a mountain and a great fire . . . Sigurd and - Hildis? - was it?'* Grimhild persuades him to finish the drink and Sigurd lets his fears go. *'I was a fool, like one who wakes from a sleep and vaguely remembers a fading dream.'*

He enters the alliance with Gunnar and Hogni - *faithful in adversity and death* - and the three immediately prepare to leave for another battle. Sigurd says that on returning he hopes he will see Gudrun – he has heard that she is very beautiful. Again, as might be in a film, the scene flits briefly to Brynhild by herself. The scene is short. She knows what is happening: *'To my sorrow, my darling's love for me is blown to the wind. I must forsake the world and embrace my grief. His marriage to someone else may perhaps bring me peace, rock me to sleep once again, from which no one now will ever awaken me.'*

Sigurd has returned victorious from the battle, and festivities are under way. He now expects to see Gudrun, and Grimhild brings her in. Sigurd falls instantly: *'What? Can the earth hold such beauty? Can the brightness of the sky find a match on earth?'*

An oath of blood brotherhood is sworn between Sigurd and the two brothers. Sigurd kisses Gudrun to seal the bond of marriage between them. He is to be the joint ruler of the kingdom. With his fame and his treasure and his wife, Sigurd feels that he could live a thousand years.

Commentary

There is but one relevant chapter in *Volsung Saga*, namely 28. For Fouqué, this episode, from the moment when Sigurd forgets Brynhild to when he marries Gudrun, is to be the heart of the Sigurd story.

However, he embroiders matters. The trials of strength with Gunnar and Hogni are not in the Nordic sources and are likely to have been lifted from *Nibelungenlied*, where Sigurd bests Brynhild in similar contests. The requests to look after his horse Grani and the treasure cannot be found in the sagas. I mention these, unimportant and irrelevant as they may be to the main story line of Siegfried's defection, because Wagner refers in passing to two of the three: the care of the horse and the trials of physical prowess. These find mention in *Siegfrieds Tod* when Siegfried arrives at the Gibich court. The challenge 'Fight with me or be my friend!' and Gunther's emollient reply are Wagner's somewhat slapdash way of shaping this first greeting.

Readers may be willing to put these incidental pieces of dialogue alongside the bigger issue of Siegfried's instant infatuation. Because *Sigurd der Schlangentödter* is a non-stageable poem, Fouqué was able to indicate a spread of time between Sigurd forgetting Brynhild and falling for Gudrun. He does this by interpolating the short vision of Brynhild in her worried loneliness. But the 'performance time' between imbibing the drug and seeing Gudrun is brief and the effect drastic - markedly urgent when compared to the leisurely pace of *Volsung Saga*, where over two years pass before Sigurd marries Gudrun. Wagner further telescopes this narrative in *Siegfrieds Tod*: Siegfried drinks the potion, is overcome by desire for Gutrune and then joins with Gunther in 'blood brotherhood' in double quick time because the staging demands it. But it is the explosive impact of Gudrun on the bewitched Sigurd that is the model and is prime indication that Fouqué's plot part shaped that of Wagner's.

Adventure 4 compared to *Siegfrieds Tod*, Act 1 Scene 3 and part of Act 2

Summary

Grimhild finally proposes that Gunnar court Brynhild. Gunnar is confident he can do it, but talk of the flames surrounding her mysteriously disturbs Sigurd. Nevertheless, he agrees to help his brother-in-law to win his bride, even though he must leave wife and toddler child. (As in *Volsung Saga*, some 30 months may have passed.)

Gunnar and Hogni muse on his kindness and Hogni concludes with: '*It gives me pleasure when I think there is a person who loves us more than he loves himself.*' To which Gunnar responds: '*Yes, it is good but also a bit foolish!*' Grimhild sums up with: '*We need people like this in this world; willing, guileless, cheerful like him. And if in addition he has broad shoulders and is daring – that brings fortune to us, the clever ones.*'

The warriors leave together. Guiki is dubious, now as always, about his wife's plans and motives. He forecasts disaster and retires from the narrative for good.

The scene changes to the foot of Brynhild's mountain castle. Sigurd feels himself to be in a dream. Gunnar rides at the flames but the horse refuses; Sigurd offers him Grane but the horse will not accept Gunnar as rider, so Sigurd offers to stand in for him. Hogni recalls Grimhild telling him of her magic to distract him from some painful war wound: '*Some of it I remember well: it enables two people to swap their bodies but they have to give up their own will.*' Gunnar protests that he will not marry a woman who has slept with another but Sigurd reassures him: '*I shall go with her into the marriage bed, but shall put Gram - my double sided sword - between us as a barrier . . . I will tell her that a prophesy has warned me to deny myself married bliss during these first nights.*' Hogni recites the spell and the two men are transformed into the other's body. Sigurd leaves and Hogni reassures Gunnar that this is the only way.

Sigurd stands before Brynhild in the form of Gunnar. They have a courtly but guarded conversation until Brynhild accepts the new suit for her hand.

Sigurd: *Give me your ring as a bridal gift.*

> Brynhild: *What, This one? My dear, this is Andvari's ring and has a dangerous magic.*
> Sigurd: *I once dreamt that I had Andvari's ring – but now the memory is dim. It is time for me to have the ring again. There! Take this one in exchange.*
> Brynhild: *It has to happen as you wish. So take it!*
> Sigurd: *Look! Look! The magic ring of Andvari - surely I should know it!*

The party of four returns to the palace and the wedding celebrations begin. Sigurd holds back and memories return as he surveys the scene.

> Sigurd: *I have done this already – raced through the fire - and found a sweet sorrow. What was it? I am so close! . . . Brynhild is coming! Brynhild? The one over there? It's her! It was Sigurdrisa! [The name she gave herself when she was mine!] And now? King Gunnar's wife? . . . Oh, my sweet love, Brynhild! Slowly the fog is clearing from my mind! Oh, and why so late? . . . I have pawned my love, broken my word. I am lost! I was tricked with a magic drink and won for another the one who was all my life! . . . Well, still son of a hero, let me bear now what can't be changed.*

Commentary

The narrative follows *Volsung Saga* 29, save that all reference to Brynhild's family is removed. This includes Brynhild discussing with Hermir, her foster father, what had happened. By these omissions, Fouqué concentrates the story on Sigurd.

The remaining plot is an expansion of matters referred to but briefly in the sagas. No detail, for example is given as to how Grimhild's spell works or the lead up to Sigurd riding through the fire. The verbatim text as given, tells us how Fouqué exonerates Sigurd: he is gullible and kind and is tricked. His final speech enlarges the sentiments of *Volsung Saga* with the intent of arousing maximum possible sympathy. The contrast with *Siegfrieds Tod* is obvious.

Adventure 5 compared to *Siegfrieds Tod*, Act 2

Summary

Brynhild and Gudrun sit amicably together on the banks of the Rhine. They decide to wash their hair in the river. Brynhild wants to go first to avoid using the water already used by Gudrun. A quarrel develops: Brynhild maintains her father Budli to be greater than Guiki and points out that her husband Gunnar is a king whereas Sigurd is in the service of Gunnar. And also Gunnar rode through the fire to win her.

> Gudrun destroys her: *'You really believe Gunnar rode through the fire to win you? Well, I know that the person who went to bed with me, who gave me this ring, Andvari's ring, which he took from your hand as a wedding gift, came to you in the shape of Gunnar, changed by magic runes.'*

But Fouqué's Gudrun has not the capacity to become the Medea-like creature we see in *Nibelungenlied* and in the sagas and she regrets her outburst.

'Why is she like that all of a sudden? Have I said too much? – Listen to me, Brynhild! Oh sister-in-law please listen. I am sorry I was so difficult – all for nothing. Ah! She is going to the castle with slow heavy steps, like a pale angry ghost, scarcely breathing and drained of blood . . . And I went against [Sigurd's] command, telling Brynhild what he lovingly confided during a blissful night. We sealed my promise never to divulge with a kiss. If only she were at peace! But she never will be - peace and grace will remain strangers to our house. I have done ill.'

The story jumps forward: Brynhild has returned to her room and has lain on her bed in a catatonic stupor: *dumb and still, as she were almost dead.* Gunnar cannot animate her but she responds to Sigurd and proclaims her knowledge of the deceit practised upon her.

Sigurd responds thus: *'Stay calm. The hour will come when your vow of vengeance will be fulfilled and a sharpened sword will pierce my heart. You are not wishing anything worse for me than for yourself. But you, Brynhild, won't be able to bear it - to survive me for any length of time. For both of us there are only a few days from now on. . . Listen to me now! A magic forgetfulness took hold of me so that I did not remember the pact, nor what else was happening. It was only when you stepped in front of me as Gunnar's wife, only then - and still not completely, only in fragments – the past came back. . . and I am become sick of all I stand for and I have done. I was silent in front of the king, your brother-in-law, overcome by the sight of you – your sweet image. Yes, Brynhild, I won't keep it from you any longer – death being so close loosens my tongue – you are more to me than my own life. Grimhild's deception, her evil magic spell has separated us in spite of love and what is right.'*

He offers to leave Gudrun and his child and to go with Brynhild but she refuses:

'Gunnar has my word of faithfulness. I will keep it. However, there is also the earlier oath to you which compels me to be the wife of the one who rode first through the fire. And it was Sigurd who did that, and not Gunnar; but I can never be Sigurd's wife and therefore neither that of any other man. I therefore pay for the guiltless mistake with voluntary death.' Sigurd now also foresees his own death and recalls that his *'uncle prophesied I would have a short life'*. (VS #16)

He leaves and Brynhild sums up the situation with Gunnar:

Sigurd deceived me as he deceived you; you have shared my bed with him. I have two husbands . . . and feel revulsion. One of us three has to die: you, I or Sigurd!

Her silence broken, she shouts her distress throughout the palace.

When the younger brother Guttorn returns in triumph from a battle, he is drawn into the plot for he did not swear blood brotherhood and so can attack Sigurd. He is very reluctant but Brynhild seduces him to her wishes.

Brynhild: *Come with me into my secret chamber so we can discuss the deed. Don't be frightened of me, young warrior – you have heard of the Valkyrs?*
Guttorm: *Yes. They pass sombrely through the 'place of choosing' and decide which warrior shall fall in battle. And the one they choose can see at once her radiant face. He breaks - full of joyful shock - through the night of death and into the halls of Valhalla.*
Brynhild: *See what astounds you in my face as the joyful message of the Valkyr. If you now die young, you will not live through many troubles.*
Guttorm: *You are not sending me out to a chosen place but to an undefended bed.*
Brynhild: *Just follow. You are still tired from the journey. There is a lovely meal in my room served in golden bowls, full of good strength. Follow and enjoy. Then join our council.*

Commentary

Fouqué exclusively uses *Volsung Saga* 30, 31 and 32; there are no additions from *Poetic Edda* or *Sturleson's Edda* and no trace whatsoever of *Nibelungenlied*. The reliance on *Volsung Saga* is exemplified by an apparent throw-away line *Why are the harness rings clattering like that against each other?* This is a direct quote and relates to Sigurd's distress as he leaves Brynhild. (It is out of place and an ineffective attempt to include as much as he can of the original material.)

Emphasised throughout is Sigurd's awareness that something is wrong in what on the surface is the normality of human life - as we see in Gudrun's remorseful reaction when Brynhild is psychologically ruined by the revelation of Sigurd's betrayal. Wagner chose differently: there is no suggestion of normal life in *Siegfrieds Tod*.

Finally, there is Brynhild. The poem shows us a woman traumatised and unhinged - one who veers from near coma to clarity of vision, to an unfocussed desire for death. The conclusion is the blatant seduction of Guttorm. She has decided: if one of the three principals has to die, it must be Sigurd - the most noble. This goes beyond *Volsung Saga*.

Adventure 6 compared to *Siegfrieds Tod*, Act 3

Summary

The poem opens in the bedroom of Gudrun and Sigurd, with Sigurd asleep in his wife's lap. The palace is full of tension and Gudrun praises Sigurd as she looks down: '*He has lived his life like an innocent child and therefore is allowed to sleep like a child - Oh you almost dutiful, friendly, mild hero!*' She is now remorseful about the whole transaction: '*But for him to be like this was a bad joke for me and for him. It took his love away and also . . . the dignity of life. Oh woe - to both of us! We can't lament it enough and the tears are caught in my burning eyes.*'

Gudrun falls asleep and Guttorn enters. He too has doubts when he sees Sigurd (*A noble face, a mighty body. I would have liked to go into battle at your side – but I am now seeing you for the last time.)* but he strikes as his victim sleeps. But Sigurd wakes, raises himself and throws Gram across the room, killing Guttorn as he tries to leave. Sigurd dies in Gudrun's arm with the words: *'I only half believed the prophecy, the warning song of the bird. Today comes the fulfilment . . . for me darkness has come.'*

All the family now engage in what becomes a dynastic family drama. Slowly they realise the terrible thing that has now befallen them all, for somehow in the mayhem Sigurd's three-year old son Sigmund has also perished. An 'off-stage' chorus lament contributes - the only such occasion in the poem. Brynhild interrupts with wild laughter. Gunnar, Hogni and Gudrun turn on each other as to who now owns the treasure brought by Sigurd from his victory over the dragon. The death of Guttorn is discovered, and this increases the tension.

The long episode ends with Gudrun leaving: *Farewell, you who were once friends but are now deadly enemies. May everything be left behind, may it fade away! A hermit now, in gentle mourning, I lower my despondent eyes. My grief is my food, my tears are my drink! Good night to you all. You are living here in splendour, but it is better to live outside. Air! Air! Air!*

Brynhild now takes over.

First a prophesy of doom to the dynasty: *'Regarding Attila, my brother, he takes as much notice of your threats as of the shine on burnished bowls. He will survive and be more powerful than all of you - because your tribe, the Nibelungs, have fashioned your disaster out of this shameful deed.'*

She orders Fafnir's gold to be distributed to all, stabs herself with Gram, and gives final instructions.

'Let them build a high pyre on the dark grounds outside, a bed for Sigurd and me. Surround and decorate it with rich carpet, freshly coloured by the blood of sixteen of my servants. Lay him . . . by my side and then those who fell with him; his three-year old child, the tender baby Sigmund, next to him; Guttorn, the murderer . . . Let Gram lie between us, just as it was on the high fell where the marriage bed first united and then separated us. Will you arrange this as I want it, Gunnar?

Gram, you honoured sword, you kept us apart before and you will now lead the bride, you will prepare the path of the bride with red blood. Flow blood of my heart but not too fast – I must see the pyre, then find my darling! Is it not yet burning - the bridal fire? The wound is streaming away - hot and away! Let my soul escape from this dark habitation – and why should I hesitate while my love's light is glittering brightly through the dark night?

Leave me, I am not weak. The flame is lighting the last path for me. [Sigurd's] noble courage was drawn to the fire surrounding me! The bridal walk is meant for both of us; through threatening heat to the sweeter heat of love. You first came to me, now I am coming to you – Are you smiling, dear bridegroom? How the sparks are flying, crowning your head! In we go! The flames do not hurt the glowing heart!

As the flames rise, the Norns reappear. They circle the pyre and sing a dirge. Skuld, she who prophesies the future, takes over and concludes thus:

Skuld: *Comfort yourselves, you two who have been degraded by deceit. The truth grows quietly, truth grows clearly; it will judge, will shine through me, shine like a distant column of fire.*

Deceit over the fraudsters, deceit and lies, / Dripping blood of those who ladled blood,

Cries of pain for those who spread pain! / Glorious song for the heroes,

Those who are free from desecrating guilt.

Wurdur and Werdandi:

Come revengeful queen, we now wait for you. / Proclaim the unity of revenge and guilt.

Skuld:

I will not hurry, I will not linger. / We advance with steady pace.

The court has sat and found judgement. / Run, Mankind - you will never escape us!

Commentary

This adventure is also based solely on VS 32/33, with one obvious and major exception. Fouqué brings on the Norns at the end; he suggests clearly that supernatural forces are engaged with the two lovers. In narrative or action Odin may be concerned with Sigurd but the encounter before the fight with Fafnir is brief and, all in all, the connection has little or no dramatic force. In contrast, the Norns first appear as a mini prologue to the main action, namely the relationship between Sigurd and Brynhild, and then re-appear at the end to round off the story. The message they give chimes with those of the romantic scholars (p.48), namely that the story of Sigurd and Brynhild - tryst, betrayal, murder and joint immolation - is a prelude to a wider collapse.

A distinctive feature is the final emergence of dynastic/family strife. This first surfaced in Adventure 5, in the treatment of the quarrel between the two high-born wives. They are arguing about family precedence and are not portrayed other than as sisters-in-law, women who cannot get on with each other. As the consequences of that quarrel unfold, the story becomes a straight tale of family discord which culminates in the departure of Gudrun. She is shown throughout as a simple, loving woman, duped by her own mother into a treachery that will destroy the family.

Sigurd's murder is the standard saga narrative. There is nothing epic about it, either in the sagas or as seen by Fouqué. Then comes the family discord and it is not fanciful to envisage Wagner holding this in his mind at the beginning of ST3.2, leading up to the death of Gunther and the collapse of Gutrune. Finally, Brynhild takes control and in a manner very similar to that used by Wagner: Fouqué says that *all is done according to Brynhild's words* and this might have served as a clue to Wagner. The prophecy of dynastic collapse derives from all the primary Nordic sources and is somewhat routine but the tone changes to the majestic from the moment when Brynhild ordains the nature of the funeral. Such is exactly reflected in Wagner's 'Immolation' text, although the detailed sentiments are not the same.

The poem as a whole

Fouqué was hampered by his wish to encapsulate as much of Sigurd's story as he could in these seven adventures, which are really seven mini-dramas. This particularly applies to the two opening episodes which deal with the forging of Gram and the killing of Fafnir and Regin. But from the moment when Sigurd and Brynhild first meet to the end of the tale, when Brynhild mounts the pyre to join her dead lover, the author makes the most of the sources available to create a particular view of the story. Sigurd and Brynhild are two good people who are drawn into an ordinary family. Sigurd is frequently described as kind, and more than once as gullible: no fault is to be found in him by any other character and Fouqué makes no attempt to hint at an underlying flaw. With Brynhild he follows the implied morality within the sagas, which has her turning against Sigurd rather than Gunnar. No one will think this to be perverse, for the former has always the same distinction as has Brynhild, which lifts him above Gunnar. However, her seduction of Guttorn is surely gratuitous and not in accord with the morality of the story.

Nevertheless, Fouqué then hallows the death of the two lovers by bringing on the Norns. In this way he elevates their relationship toward the supernatural, in a way not dissimilar to Wagner in *Siegfrieds Tod*. In this respect, even if the composer had not the wider canvas in mind, as implied in the *Myth*, the different ethical background of political change would be sufficient by itself to switch the cosmic focus from the Nordic equivalent of the three fates and toward Wotan.

All human characters are given as high a sense of morality as is possible. Gudrun's remorse is extreme and even Grimhild thinks better of her actions; Gunnar cannot be anything other than dishonourable in his acquisition of Brynhild but, other than that, he does his best. The great epic becomes a tragic romantic tale with only the presence of the Norns and the prophecies of dynastic disaster to hint at a wider perspective. As such it encapsulates the general view of the tale as seen in the first part of the 19th century.

◊ ◊ ◊ ◊ ◊ ◊

APPENDIX F

FIVE BOOKS ON THE SOURCES FOR *THE RING*

I SAW THE WORLD END by Derrick Cooke (1978)

This is by far the longest but even so is perhaps just one quarter of the massive all-encompassing volume envisaged by the author, work on which was cut short by his death in 1976. Even so, it is impressive: 275 pages are devoted to description of the sources and the roots of the drama as a whole, plus detailed surveys of *Das Rheingold* and *Die Walküre*. The most illuminating section is a 30 page 'summing up', which comes after the section on *Das Rheingold*.

What we have before us is, of course, a first draft of the first quarter and it is certain that what we have now would have been amended had the author lived to complete the work. At the stage reached, Cooke saw the work as symbolic: Wotan is 'the symbol of immemorial, historical and contemporary man-in-supreme-power . . . the sum of *political* intelligence of the time.' The drama is perceived as the conflict between love and power to the exclusion of other conflicts but – enigmatically and without explanation - Cooke suggests that the answer to what it is about is 'metaphysical'. Inevitably perhaps in this draft stage, the author forgets a central precept, namely that it is the music that tells the story. He analyses the text of an outburst from Fricka as though it were a complex psychological drama, as though it were by Shakespeare. Nevertheless, the ramifications of possibilities he sees in the sources is of abiding interest and value.

RICHARD WAGNER AND THE NIBELUNGS by Elizabeth Magee (1990)

The goal here is to trace the history of what source Wagner read and when he read it, and also the influence that the contemporary commentators and translators of these source might have had on him. The procedure is to probe the contents of his own library in Dresden, what and when he borrowed books from the Royal Library in Dresden, and those books neither in his own or the main public library but which he mentions.

The exposition is meticulous but leads to at least one significant conclusion, namely that Wagner did not read the *Volsung Saga* until October 1848. From this it follows that the *Myth* was written without knowledge of this source which, as Cooke and others say, is the main one. (The content of the first twelve chapters of the *saga* is found nowhere else.) Magee's argument is that Wagner could have found all he needed to complete the *Myth* from *Sigurd der Schlangentödter*.

The exegesis can be more detailed than Cooke on precise derivations of words and can roam into byways to find the clue to why Wagner used this or that. Magee makes little attempt to explain why the composer would use one option rather than another: she presents the incidents and people in the sources somewhat as pieces of a jigsaw that Wagner moved around in order to find the story that he wanted.

THE LEGENDS OF THE WAGNER DRAMA by Jessie L Weston (1896)

Almost half is devoted to *The Ring*. The analysis starts with summaries of *Thidriks Saga* (which the other books ignore to a degree), the *Volsung Saga*, and *Das Nibelungenlied*. H475er purpose is to identify the similarities and differences between the sources and the final outcome and her analysis spreads widely, to the myths of Egypt, the Celts and the Ayrians.

Miss Weston was writing with the benefit of the new studies of heroism by Tyler, von Hahn and Frazer. Alone amongst those listed here, she places Siegfried, for example, within the pantheon of archetypal heroes and discusses how he fits into mythic theory. (Her best known book is *From Ritual to Romance*, published in 1920, the starting point of which is the work of Frazer and the mythologist Jane Harrison.)

On the wider issue of the drama as a whole, the judgement is that the Brünnhilde of *Götterdämmerung* bears little resemblance to the valkyr seen in the earlier operas – the theme taken up by Shaw at about the same time. Nevertheless, she contends 'that the version [of the 'great legend of the North'] given by the drama, so far as it goes, does represent what was probably the original shape of the story more accurately than any one of the versions from which Wagner drew'. But there are qualifications: despite its power on the stage, *Götter-dämmerung* is not his greatest success as a drama because the material from which it is crafted is of such vast scope. Disregarding the involvement of the gods, four operas would have been required to 'deal adequately with the source of the Hoard, the Life and Death of Siegfried, the vengeance on his murderers and the final loss of the Treasure'.

The style is of its age but the content offers the most manageable conspectus of all four books and is highly readable. Her book remains available in modern reprints.

THE KINGDOM ON THE RHINE by Nancy Benvenga (1982)

Dr Benvanga traces the historical connections of characters in *Götterdämmerung* and how Wagner adapts these to the needs of his drama. The focus is on the turbulent 5th and 6th centuries. Chapters are devoted to Sigurd, Brynhild, Hagen (by far the longest), Gunnar and the Nibelungen Hoard. Some links are made to the Germanic and Nordic sagas and the musical force of Hagen is touched upon. The book complements all the others.

WAGNER AND THE VOLSUNGS by Ārni Björnsson (2000)

Björnsson's proclaimed remit is to restrict reference to the Icelandic/Nordic sources and examine the same six main sources used in this book. However, the extensive quotations are only from the Nordic and these are tied into the text of *The Ring* to show the exact textual connections. In essence, this is a catalogue of links between source and final outcome. From this detail, Björnsson tabulates 98 'themes', be they people, plot lines, artefacts or events. He then lists how many of the 98 occur in each of the six main sources. In summary there is the following table. The themes have been divided into those relating to Gods and those to Heroes.

	Gods	Heroes	Total
All sources	38	60	98
The Poetic Edda	26	43	69
Sturluson's Edda	27	34	61
Volsung Saga	15	49	64
Nibelungenlied	7	17	24
Thidriks Saga	5	23	28
Hurnen Seyfried	5	8	13

The six break into two groups. The two Eddas, when added together, have a gods:heroes ratio of roughly 2:3, which is the same as for all sources. The remaining four have a ratio of 1:3.

◊ ◊ ◊ ◊ ◊

APPENDIX G

RESOURCES CITED, WITH ABBREVIATIONS

AB/WV	Árni Björnsson, *Wagner and the Volsungs*, University College London, 2003. Translated by Anna Yates & Anthony Faulks
AH/NL	Arthur Hatto (translator), *The Nibelungenlied*, Penguin Books, 1965
AS/WWR (1-2)	Arthur Schopenhauer, *The World as Will and Representation* (Two volumes), Dover Publications, 1966. Translated by EFJ Payne
BC	Burrell Collection, Letters of Richard Wagner, Gollancz, 1951
BE/WCL	Barry Emslie, *Richard Wagner and the Centrality of Love*, Boydell Press, 2010
BM/S	Bryan Magee, *The Philosophy of Schopenhauer*, Oxford University Press, 1983 ; revised edition, 2009
BM/WP	Bryan Magee, *Wagner and Philosophy*, Allen Lane, 2000
CA/AO	Carolyn Abbate, *Analyzing Opera: Verdi and Wagner*, California University Press, 1989
CL/NM	Carolyne Larrington, *The Norse Myths, a guide to gods and heroes*, Thames & Hudson, 2017
CD/WMD	Carl Dahlhaus, *Wagner's Music Dramas*, Cambridge University Press, 1979. Translated by Mary Whittall.
CvW/FR	Curt von Westernhagen, *The Forging of the Ring*, Cambridge University Press, 1976. Translated by Mary Whittall
CvW/W (1-2)	Curt von Westernhagen, *Wagner, a biography* (Two volumes), Cambridge University Press, 1978. Translated by Mary Whittall
CW/D (1-2)	Cosima Wagner, *Diaries 1869-1882*, Collins, 1978. Translated by Geoffrey Skelton
DC/V	Deryck Cooke, *Vindications*, Faber & Faber, 1982
DC/WE	Deryck Cooke, *I saw the world end*, Oxford University Press, 1979
DF/GWG	Denis Forman, *The Good Wagner Opera Guide*, Weidenfeld & Nicholson, 2000
DH/C&S	Derek Hughes, *Culture and Sacrifice*, Cambridge University Press, 2007
EC/B	Edward Conze, *Buddhism: its Essence and Development*, Bruno Cassirer, 1951
EM/WN	Elizabeth Magee, *Richard Wagner and the Nibelungs*, Oxford University Press, 1990
EN/LRW(1-4)	Ernest Newman, *Life of Richard Wagner* (Four volumes), Alfred Knopf, 1937-1946
EN/WN	Ernest Newman, *Wagner Nights*, Putnam, 1949
FH/CWL (1-2)	*Correspondence of Wagner and Liszt,* Vienna House, 1973. (Two volumes) Translated by Francis Hüffer,
ES/RWAR	Eleanor Sellar, *Richard Wagner's letters to August Röckel*, JW Arrowsmith, 1897

RESOURCES CITED

GBS/PW	George Bernard Shaw, *The Perfect Wagnerite*, Constable, 2nd edition, 1912
GF/TD	Gustav Freitag, *Technique of the Drama*, 1863. Translated into English by Elias MacEwan. Scott, Foresman, 1894
GS/DT	George Steiner, *The death of tragedy*, Faber & Faber, 1961
GS/WTP	Geoffrey Skelton, *Wagner in thought and practice*, Lime Tree, 1991
HB/PE	*The Poetic Edda*, translated and edited by HA Bellows. American-Scandinavian Society 1923 Forgotten Books 2012
HK/FMD	Humphrey Kitto, *Form and Meaning in Drama*, University Paperbacks, Methuen, 1960
HP/WR	Heinrich Porges, *Wagner rehearsing the* Ring, Cambridge University Press, 1983. Translated by Robert Jacobs
HSW/W	Houston Stewart Chamberlain, W*agner*, Dent, 1897
JB/VS	Jesse Byock (translator), *The saga of the Volsungs*, Penguin Books, 1999
JC/HTF	Joseph Campbell, *The hero with a thousand faces*, New World Library, 2008
JD/R	John Deathridge, translation of The Ring of the Nibelung, Penguin, 2018
JD/WGE	John Deathridge, *Wagner beyond good and evil*, University of California Press, 2008
JG/DM	Jacob Grimm, *Deutsches Mythologie*, George Bell, 1892. Reprinted by Dover Publications,1966. Translated by James Stallybrass
JK/LT	Joachim Köhler, *The Last of the Titans*, Yale University Press, translated by Stewart Spencer 2004
JKH/CWR	JK Holman, *Companion to Wagner's Ring*, Amadeus Press, 1996
JN/WA	Jean-Jaques Nattiez, *Wagner Androgyne*, Princeton University Press, 1993. Translated from the French by Stuart Spencer
JP/NM	Joan Peyser, *The new music, the sense behind the sound*, Delacorte Press, 1971
JS/B	Jan Swafford, *Beethoven – anguish and triumph*, Faber & Faber, 2014
JS/LDF	J Shedlock, *Letters to his Dresden friends*, H Grevel, 1890. Translated by JS Shedlock
JS/RWSA	Jack Stein, *Richard Wagner and the synthesis of the arts*, Wayne State University Press, 1960
JT/IW	James Treadwell, *Interpreting Wagner*, Yale University Press, 2003
JW/LWD	Jessie Weston, *Legends of the Wagner Drama*, Scribners, 1896. Available in facsimile reprint.
K&S/FE	Kitcher, Philip & Schacht, Richard. *Finding an Ending*, Oxford University Press, 2004
LP/AP	*Aristotle's Poetics, the art of fiction*. Cambridge University Press, 1959. Translated by L J Potts
MB/FM	Michael Buckley, *Form and Meaning in the Ring*, Wagner Society, *Wagner,* Vol. 25/2
MB/TBLF	Mark Berry, *Treacherous Bonds and Laughing Fire*, Ashgate, 2006

RESOURCES CITED

ME/WA	Michael Ewans, *Wagner and Aeschylus*, Cambridge University Press, 1982
MT/W	Michael Tanner, *Wagner*, Harper Collins, 1996
MW/W	Mark Wiener, *Richard Wagner and the anti-Semitic imagination*, University of Nebraska Press, 1995
OL/WR	Owen Lee, *Wagner's Ring – turning the sky around*, Summit Books, 1990
PDB/WE	Paul Dawson Bowling, *The Wagner Experience, and its meaning to us now*, Old Street Press, 2013
RD/WRS	Robert Donington, *Wagner's 'Ring' and its symbols*, Faber & Faber, 1963
RR/WM	Robert Rayner, *Wagner and 'Die Meistersinger*, Oxford University Press, 1940
RS/QH	Robert Segal, *In quest of the hero*, Princeton University Press, 1990
RS/RT	Roger Scruton, *The Ring of Truth*, Penguin Books, 2016
RW/ML	Richard Wagner, *Mein Leben*, Cambridge University Press, 1983. Translated by Andrew Gray
RW/PW (1-8)	Wagner's Prose Works. Kegan Paul, Trench and Trübner, 1884-99. Reissued by Nebraska University Press, 1995. Eight volumes. Translated by William Ashton Ellis.
SS/E	Storri Sturluson, *Edda*, JM Dent, Everyman, 1987. Translated by Andrew Faulks
SS/SL	Stewart Spencer & Barry Millington, *Selected Letters of Richard Wagner*, Dent, 1987
SS/WR	Stewart Spencer, *Wagner Remembered*, Faber & Faber, 2000
SW/WRH	Simon Williams, *Wagner and the romantic hero*, Yale University Press, 2004
TM/PCW	Thomas Mann, *Pro and Contra* Wagner, Faber and Faber, 1985. Translated by Allan Blunden
WAE/FL	*Family Letters of Richard Wagner*, Macmillan, 1991. Translated by William Ashton Ellis
WAE/LMW (1-2)	*Letters to Minna Wagner* (Two volumes), H Grevel, 1909. Translated by William Ashton Ellis
WM/SV	William Morris, *The story of Sigurd the Volsung*, 1922. Reissued Bibliobazaar 2006

◊◊◊◊◊

INDEX
For people and themes

This index is circumscribed in scope. With one exception, no link is made to any page within the four chapters which discusss the operas in detail. This is because there is no sound way to control the number of references. The ex-ception is the reference to the symphonic element in the music: there are not that many and the subject is of importance

Abbate, Carolyne – 235/6
Achilleus - 8
Alberich - 146-157
Attila – 94, 129
Avenarius, Eduard - 206
Balder – 87/8
Beethoven - 30, 32, 232 -236
Brunechild, 93
Campbell, Joseph – 24-27, 28, 32, 170/1, 172, 173, 176, 194
Carnegy, Patrick - 113
common good, the - 66, 91, 114, 398, 424
Cooke, Deryck – 11/12, 36, 52, 91, 118, 135, 136, 137, 148, 159, 166, 168, 214, 215, 227-230
Darcy, Patrick - 208
Das Nibelungenlied - 50
death, the nature of - 20, 42, 64, 65, 67, 68, 69, 71, 78, 85, 91, 114, 179/80, 181/2, 187, 197, 212, 216
Deathridge, John - 209
Die Wibelungen - 47, 48, 68, 71, 85, 127, 150
Donington, Robert - 2, 67, 142, 227
Erda – 124/6, 134, 191
Feuerbach, Ludwig - 8, 17/8, 182, 185/6
Finding an Ending - 211
Freytag, Gustav – 24-28, 56, 171, 184
Freya – 165
Fricka - 164
Giants -128
Greece - 6, 8-16, 28, 41, 90, 212
Hagen - 103-107
Halevy, Frohmental - 107
Hegel, Georg - 22, 66, 191
historical drama – 7/9, 13-16
Hughes,Derek - 73

Jesus of Nazareth – 196, 452
Kerven, Rosemary - 119
Kitto, Humphrey – 2/3, 191
Leitmotiven – 224-7
Liszt, Franz - 18, 160, 203-208
Loge – 166/8
Magee, Bryan - 17, 180, 199, 200, 209-211, 227, 235
Magee, Elizabeth – 48, 55, 63, 164, 167
Mann, Thomas – 18, 86, 417
Morris, William - 84, 85, 91
Mozart, 6, 21, 24, 30, 31
My Life, 1, 8, 17, 53, 200
Mythology – 7-12
Newman, Ernest - 18, 59, 127/8, 143, 189-91, 206
Norns - 117
Odin – 132/3
Opera and Drama - 5, 7, 14, 15, 16, 21, 46/7, 142, 221-26, 232
Oresteia – 9-12, 30, 138
pessimism – 197-99, 203-211
Porges, Heinrich - 15, 113, 161, 215
Prose Edda - 51
proto-plot for *Siegfrieds Tod*, - 57, 65, 67, 77, 93, 103, 107, 190
Puccini - 21, 24, 289
Racine - 7, 12, 13, 25, 28, 30, 44, 212, 213
Ragnarök - 48
Röckel, August - 3, 40, 45, 49, 90, 115, 137, 160, 175, 178, 179, 181, 182, 185, 187, 190, 192, 194, 201, 217, 218
Romanticism – 47/8
Rossini - 7, 31, 214
Schiller – 13/4, 15/6, 28, 29, 30, 213
Schopenhauer, Arthur - 2, 5, 16-20, 176/7, 179-80, 182, 185, 186/7, 198-201, 209, 216-219, 231-33, 235, 236
Scruton, Roger - 59, 72, 161, 224, 235
Sex - 70, 78, 94, 99, 152/3, 171, 176-178, 185
Shakespeare - 4, 7, 12, 13-15, 16, 28, 40, 43/4, 53, 56, 59, 76, 80, 113, 140, 146
Shaw, G.B - 59, 109-10, 113/4, 162, 175, 208/9
Siegfried – 64-92
Sigurd der Schlangentödter – 4, 50, 55, 59, 63, 72, 77, 100, 117, 456
Sophocles – 10/11, 25, 47, 213
Stabriem – 221-224

Symphonic tendency in the *Ring* - 233-36, 273, 281, 288, 303, 307, 310 , 319, 321, 325, 334, 341, 347, 353, 386, 392, 411, 414
Tanner, Michael - 158
Teutonic Mythology - 52
The Poetic Edda - 51
Thelma and Louise - 20
Thidriks Saga of Bern - 50
Tolkein, J.R.R. - 160

Treadwell, James - 114, 181
Verdi - 24, 30, 31, 99, 208, 213/4, 225
Volsung Saga - 51
Wesendonck, Mathilde - 205
Wagner, Minna - 206
Weston, Jessie - 59, 71, 112
Yorke, John – 26/7, 29, 31, 35

CHAPTER AND SECTION INDEX TO CHAPTERS 1 TO 15

This is a guide to content. This time, in page order, selective sections within the chapters are highlighted. This gives indication of the structure of the first sixteen chapters which, in turn, suggests how the narrative develops. Major sections are full out; minor are indented.

1 INTRODUCTION
Describing musical drama 4
2 WAGNER & DRAMA
Two guiding principles 5
Myth and mythology in the new drama 8
    Wagner's theory of myth 8
    Eclipse of historical drama 8
    The Greek connection 9
    The nature of the action resulting from myth 11
Wagner and the theatre 12
    Shakespeare 13
    Schiller & history play 13
    Acting, Mime and Gesture 14
    A summary 15
Schopenhauer 16
To show or to tell 20
3 STRUCTURE OF PLAYS/OPERAS
The dialectic within drama 23
    Real time drama 24
Freytag and Campbell 24
    Four story structures 26
The mechanisms that drive drama 28
The operatic dimension 31

The structures within the Ring drama 32
    The ring as a whole 32
    Das Rheingold 34
    Die Walküre 36
    Siegfried 37
    Götterdämmerung 39
The Aristotelian Unities 41
The remarkable stretch of the *Ring* 42

4 BUILDING BLOCKS
The cast of Wagner's imagination 45
The sources of the *Ring* 49
How Wagner used the sources 52
Wagner's journey starts 53
A drama takes shape 55
Wagner makes plot choices 57
Wagner's originality 62
5 THE HERO SIEGFRIED
Nature of the mythic hero 65
A note about Hegel 66
Siegfried in the proto-drama 67
Siegfried in the *Myth* 69
Siegfried in *Siegfrieds Tod* 77
Interim summary on Siegfried 78
Siegfried in *Der junge Siegfried* 80
    Shaping Siegfried's character 81
Siegfried's fearlessness 81
Siegfried and Wotan 83
Siegfried, the sun god 85
Siegfried in *Siegfried* and *Götterdämmerung* 86
Siegfried and Balder 87
What is unique about Siegfried 88
What is Siegfried's flaw 90

Siegfried's death and the common good 91
From Sigurd to Siegfried 92
6 BRÜNNHILDE, THE TROPHY BRIDE
Brünnhilde in the proto-plot 93
Brünnhilde in the *Myth* 95
The love of Brünnhilde and Siegfried 97
Brünnhilde imparts her wisdom to Siegfried 100
7 HAGEN & THE GIBICHUNGS
Hagen and the sources used 103
Hagen in the *Myth* 105
Hagen in *Siegfrieds Tod* 106
Hagen in *Götterdämmerung* 107
Gunther and Gutrune 108
8 *SIEGFREDS TOD*
Shaw on *Siegfrieds Tod* 109
Choices made in *Siegfrieds Tod* 110
The early Immolation texts 114
The Norns and Wotan 117
Two salutary perspectives 119
9 *DER JUNGE SIEGFRIED*
Wotan and Siegfried 122
Wotan as embryonic parent 123
Erda 124
Mime 126
Alberich 127
The giants 128
The critical summer of 1851 130
10 HOW ODIN BECAME WOTAN
From Odin to Wotan 132
Wotan, the father 139
The power of love 142
11 THE INVENTION OF ALBERICH 146
The price paid to turn the Gold into the Ring 152
The Rhine Gold 153
Alberich as a slave driver 155

The power of the Ring 156
12 WOTAN'S COSMOS
Wotan in time and place 157
How Wotan's world is peopled 162
13 BRÜNNHILDE'S TRANSCENDENCE
Brünnhilde's journey 171
Brünnhilde dominates Wotan 174
From immortality to mortality 175
Schopenhauer and Brünnhilde's knowledge of love 177
Schopenhauer and the nature of death 179
The later Immolation texts 180
14 WOTAN'S JOURNEY
Ernest Newman's error 189
The history of Wotan's world 190
Wotan and Siegmund 195
Wotan, Schopenhauer's pessimism and the *Will* 197
The *Will* and Denial of the will-to-live 199
15 QUESTIONS ABOUT THE RING
Is the *Ring* pessimistic ? 203
Tragedy, pessimism and the *Ring* 212
Is Wotan tragic? 214
The nature of the Ring? 216
The nature of Siegfried? 217
16 *STABREIM, LEITMOTIVEN,* THE SYMPHONIC WAGNER
Stabreim 221
Leitmotiven 224
Deryck Cooke on the *Ring* motif problems 227
Convergence of Wagner and Schopenhauer on music 231
Wagner as a 'symphonic' composer 233

Made in the USA
Monee, IL
26 December 2023